Whole Line Inference Rules for SL

Premise (PR)   PR may be used only to enter premises at the beginning
p of a proof. Once other rules of inference have been used,
              PR may not be used again.

Conjunction Elimination (CE)

$$\frac{p \ \& \ q}{\therefore \ p \ (or \ q)}$$

Conjunction Introduction (CI)

$$p$$
$$\frac{q}{\therefore \ p \ \& \ q}$$

Modus Ponens (MP)

$$p \rightarrow q$$
$$\frac{p}{\therefore \ q}$$

Modus Tollens (MT)

$$p \rightarrow q$$
$$\frac{\sim q}{\therefore \ \sim p}$$

Conditional Proof (CP)

$m.$	p	PA-CP
.		
.		
.		
$n.$	q	

$n + 1. \quad p \rightarrow q \qquad m–n \quad$ CP

Reductio ad Absurdum (RAA)

$m.$	$\sim p$	PA-RAA
.		
.		
.		
$n.$	$q \ \& \sim q$	

$n + 1. \quad p \qquad\qquad m–n \quad$ RAA

Replacement Rules for SL

Any statement, whether appearing as a whole line in a proof or as part of a
statement in a proof, may be replaced by its logical equivalent according to
the following rules ('$\leftrightarrow$' means 'is logically equivalent to'):

De Morgan's Laws (DeM) $\sim(p \vee q) \quad \leftrightarrow \quad (\sim p \ \& \sim q)$
                                   $\sim(p \ \& \ q) \quad \leftrightarrow \quad (\sim p \vee \sim q)$

Material Implication (Impl) $(p \rightarrow q) \quad \leftrightarrow \quad (\sim p \vee q)$

Material Equivalence (Equiv) $(p \leftrightarrow q) \quad \leftrightarrow \quad [(p \rightarrow q) \ \& \ (q \rightarrow p)]$

Double Negation (DN) $\sim\sim p \qquad\quad \leftrightarrow \quad p$

www.wadsworth.com

wadsworth.com is the World Wide Web site for Wadsworth Publishing Company and is your direct source to dozens of online resources.

At *wadsworth.com* you can find out about supplements, demonstration software, and student resources. You can also send e-mail to many of our authors and preview new publications and exciting new technologies.

wadsworth.com
Changing the way the world learns®

ELEMENTS OF DEDUCTIVE INFERENCE

AN INTRODUCTION TO SYMBOLIC LOGIC

Joseph Bessie
UNIVERSITY OF CENTRAL OKLAHOMA

Stuart Glennan
BUTLER UNIVERSITY

Wadsworth Publishing Company

I⟨T⟩P ® An International Thomson Publishing Company

Belmont, CA • Albany, NY • Boston • Cincinnati • Johannesburg • London • Madrid • Melbourne
Mexico City • New York • Pacific Grove, CA • Scottsdale, AZ • Singapore • Tokyo • Toronto

Philosophy Editor: Peter Adams
Development Editor: Jake Ward
Assistant Editor: Kerri Abdinoor
Editorial Assistant: Mindy Newfarmer
Marketing Manager: Dave Garrison
Print Buyer: Stacey Weinberger

Production: Matrix Productions Inc.
Copy Editor: Betty Duncan
Cover Design: Bill Stanton
Compositor: Thompson Type
Printer: Phoenix Color Corp

For permission to use material from this text, contact us:
web *www.thomsonrights.com*
fax 1–800–730–2215
phone 1–800–730–2214

Printed in the United States of America
2 3 4 5 6 7 8 9 10

Wadsworth Publishing Company
10 Davis Drive
Belmont, CA 94002

International Thomson Editores
Seneca, 53
Colonia Polanco
11560 México D.F. México

International Thomson Publishing Europe
Berkshire House
168–173 High Holborn
London, WC1V 7AA, United Kingdom

International Thomson Publishing Asia
60 Albert Street #15–01
Albert Complex
Singapore 189969

Nelson ITP, Australia
102 Dodds Street
South Melbourne
Victoria 3205 Australia

International Thomson Publishing Japan
Hirakawa-cho Kyowa Building, 3F
2–2–1 Hirakawa-cho, Chiyoda-ku
Tokyo 102, Japan

Nelson Canada
1120 Birchmount Road
Scarborough, Ontario
Canada M1K 5G4

International Thomson Publishing Southern Africa
Building 18, Constantia Square
138 Sixteenth Road, P.O. Box 2459
Halfway House, 1685 South Africa

Library of Congress Cataloging-in-Publication Data
Bessie, Joseph.
    Elements of deductive inference: an introduction to symbolic logic / Joseph Bessie, Stuart Glennan.
        p.   cm
    Includes index.
    ISBN 0–534–55121–1
    1. Predicate calculus.   I. Glennan, Stuart.   II. Title.
QA9.35.B48   1999
511.3—dc21   98-48446

 This book is printed on acid-free recycled paper.

Table of Contents

CHAPTER NINE
Some Applications, Limitations, and Extensions of $L*$ 383

Preface

Our principal aim in writing *Elements of Deductive Inference* has been to offer a logically and philosophically rigorous introduction to first-order predicate logic that presupposes neither in substance nor in style a background in mathematics or philosophy. It is our conviction that, suitably conveyed, a formally rigorous approach to logic can be appreciated by students with relatively little mathematical background or inclination. There are a number of fine introductory symbolic logic texts, but it has been our experience that they tend either to be so formally precise and philosophically rigorous that our students are intimidated or, in being accessible to a wide audience, their expositions tend to obscure important technical and philosophical issues associated with the study of logic. *Elements of Deductive Inference* seeks to claim a middle ground. It is unique in its suitability for a range of course levels, from a brief symbolic logic course for first-year undergraduates through a more detailed first course for seniors and first-year graduate students.

The formal approach has several benefits. First, we believe that a proper understanding of formal methods, especially symbolization and natural deduction, can greatly improve a student's critical thinking and informal reasoning skills. Second, symbolic logic provides students who are not pursuing college-level mathematics or logic with a fairly accessible glimpse of advanced mathematics. Third, for philosophy majors, the benefits of a formally rigorous course in logic are especially obvious. For better or for worse, philosophical methods in the twentieth century have been deeply informed by the theory and methods of symbolic logic. For a variety of topics in the philosophy of language, the philosophy of science, meta-physics, epistemology, and even ethics, many contemporary debates in philosophy simply cannot be understood without a reasonable grounding in first-order predi-cate logic. All philosophy majors, even those not interested in "technical" philoso-phy, will encounter these topics in the philosophical literature.

From a pedagogical standpoint, our text aims at accessibility for the student and flexibility for the instructor. To these ends, the book contains several distinc-tive features in both form and content. The first such feature is our treatment of metatheory. Whereas most texts either ignore metatheory altogether or else pre-sent finished proofs of the basic results, we have taken a middle course. Our text contains substantial discussions of metatheory, but the emphasis is primarily on clearly explaining the meaning and philosophical significance of the central metatheoretical results. We have eschewed formal proofs of these results but in most cases provide informal discussions in which we indicate why it is that our for-mal systems have the desirable properties they do and why, had we constructed them differently, they would lack these properties. A second feature of the text in-volves our treatment of the philosophy of logic. In many introductory texts it is typical to pass quickly over underlying philosophical issues when presenting formal semantics (e.g., problems of propositional identity). We don't pass judgment, but we do take time to discuss these issues as they arise. We endeavor to alert the reader when the choices we make in the formal approach reflect philosophically contro-versial commitments. The familiar Fregean scheme is employed periodically in our narrative as a tool for highlighting and discussing semantic and syntactic issues that arise in natural languages, in our formal languages, and in the relationship between these the two types of languages.

A third distinctive feature of our text appears in the material presented in Chapter 9. In this chapter we briefly introduce a number of historically important applications of symbolic logic, together with brief synopses of a number of predi-cate logic's alternatives and extensions. It has been our experience that, at the con-clusion of a logic course, students often wonder what can be done with the imposing apparatus that has been developed. The applications we discuss provide some answers to this question. In this chapter we also briefly discuss how certain more advanced logical systems (higher-order logic, modal logic, free logic, etc.) have been developed in an attempt to address the limitations of predicate logic. These discussions are deliberately brief and incomplete, but they should provide students with ideas about directions in which they can proceed in the further study of logic.

A fourth feature of our text is *modularity*. While some sections will of course naturally presuppose others, the presentation has been developed in such a way that the instructor may choose a course from among many different components of formal logic. The instructor may elect to present semantic methods (truth tables, and truth trees), syntactic methods, or both. Metatheoretical elements may be required of students or can be set aside in favor of a focus on practical techniques. Although the text develops predicate logic all the way through identity and function symbols, the instructor may restrict a course to certain sublanguages (monadic logic, monadic logic with identity, or relation logic *without* identity, etc.).

Fifth, *Elements of Deductive Inference* contains an abundance of exercises. The exercises have been integrated into each section of the text. They range in difficulty from basic through advanced, the latter typically involving theoretical or philosophical aspects of the material studied in the section. Approximately 20 percent of these problems have been answered in the back of the book, in Appendix 2.

Finally, our text is accompanied by a versatile and innovative software package, *Inference Engine*. Although the text itself may be used in complete independence of the software, the software is designed to be used in an integrated fashion with the text. Students may use Inference Engine for self-tutoring, as well as for the completion of homework assignments. A notable feature of Inference Engine is its ability to give immediate context-dependent feedback to students completing problems, as well as its ability to grade and record homework. The instructor's edition of Inference Engine is accompanied by a unique editing application, *Exercise Editor,* which enables the instructor to tailor problems and grading to suit her or his specific needs. (For further details concerning Inference Engine, see the documentation enclosed with the CD-ROM at the back of the text.)

In planning a course an instructor must first decide how much of first-order logic to cover. There is enough material in the first four chapters, in fact, to spend an entire quarter on statement logic alone, if desired. If predicate logic is to be included in the course, there are several options. Our basic system of predicate logic, called *L,* is relational predicate logic without identity. Although formally we introduce relational predicates from the start, we have divided our discussion of semantics and symbolization in such a way as to permit an instructor to restrict attention to monadic predicates. Section 5.7, which treats symbolization with polyadic predicates and nested quantifiers, can be omitted. Even in sections where there is no reason to separate the monadic from the polyadic case in the exposition, exercises are so arranged to allow an instructor to restrict problems to the monadic case. Chapter 8 contains two extensions to predicate logic, identity and functions, which can be included if time permits. It is possible to cover the material on identity without functions, but our discussion of functions presupposes identity.

Besides deciding how far to go into predicate logic, an instructor has a choice of proof methods. The alternatives are a truth tree method (Chapters 3 and 6) and a natural deduction system (Chapters 4 and 7). We presume that most instructors will cover only one of these, so the chapters devoted to these can be studied independently of each other. Our discussions of these methods both presume that students have worked through the material on truth tables at the beginning of Chapter 3. Chapter 3 also contains a section on brief truth tables. These provide a natural bridge from truth tables to truth trees, but they may be omitted without loss of continuity.

The instructor must also choose whether to include metatheory. Although there are occasional references to metatheory in the presentation of our semantics and proof methods, the main sections on metatheory (3.11, 4.7, 6.5, 6.6, and 7.4) may all be omitted. If one is not going to present the metatheory of truth trees in predicate logic, Section 6.4 (which discusses the problem of infinite trees) may be omitted as well.

Finally, the topics in Chapter 9 may be taken selectively and in whatever order is most convenient or desirable. In this case, of course, some of the sections presuppose having completed preceding material in the text. The discussion of definite descriptions, for example, requires identity, while our discussion of arithmetic and incompleteness requires functions. The sections on modal logic and conditionals require neither of these.

Acknowledgments

Elements of Deductive Inference was begun by Joseph Bessie and used in manuscript form for several years. It became a collaborative project when Bessie and Stuart Glennan chanced to meet while attending an NEH seminar directed by Paul Humphreys at the University of Virginia. Glennan had developed an early version of a software application, Inference Engine, for use with his own logic students. What began as an attempt to wed an existing manuscript to an existing program became a full-scale collaboration on both projects. Both have been revised, reorganized, and greatly expanded as we formulated and realized a joint vision of the text and software.

Neither the text nor the program could have been completed without the help of many friends, colleagues, and students. Our views on logic and pedagogy have been greatly influenced by our logic teachers, especially C. A. Anderson, William H. Hanson, Leonard Linksy, Ruth Barcan Marcus, and David Malament. We have also learned much from the outstanding texts by Jeffrey, Boolos and Jeffrey, Mates, and Mendelson.

Many improvements to the text were suggested in reviews by John Bickle, East Carolina University; Patricia Blanchette, University of Notre Dame; David Buller, Northern Illinois University; Robert Causey, University of Texas, Austin; Andrew Christie, University of New Hampshire; John E. Clifford, University of Missouri, St. Louis; Jeffrey Coombs, Our Lady of the Lake University; Erich Reck, University of California, Riverside; Alexander Rosenberg, University of Georgia; Howard Kahane; Scott Lehman, University of Connecticut; Robert McArthur, Colby College;

Randolph Mayes, California State University, Sacramento; and David Shier, Washington State University. Michael Degnan, Jim Hawthorne, and Ruth Ginzberg have used parts of the manuscript in their logic courses and have offered comments on its pedagogical effectiveness. Our students at Butler University, the University of Minnesota, Normandale Community College, and the University of Central Oklahoma used earlier versions of this book, endured its blemishes, and provided valuable feedback, and to all of them we are most thankful. Donald Everett, in particular, helped locate several typographical errors in the manuscript.

The Inference Engine project could not have been started without the financial support of the Holcomb Research Institute at Butler University. The program received helpful reviews from John Bickle, Drew Christie, Randy Mayes, and David Shier. We are thankful to our students at Butler University and the University of Central Oklahoma who weathered untested software and helped us find many bugs. They also offered valuable suggestions for improvements to the human–computer interface.

The editorial staff at Wadsworth has provided us with constant encouragement and support. We gratefully acknowledge the assistance of past philosophy editors Ken King and Tammy Goldfeld, and of the present philosophy editor, Peter Adams. We are indebted to Keri Abdinoor, Merrill Peterson, Jake Warde, and Betty Duncan for their valuable assistance.

Finally, we give our heartiest and most sincere thanks to our wives, Sylvia Stavig and Sally Glennan. They have been patient and supportive of us during a sometimes arduous process. They have offered commentary on and suggested rewording of many passages. During the final phase of revision, Sylvia proofread the entire manuscript, helping us correct technical and grammatical errors and providing us with valuable suggestions on style and exposition. She also suggested changes to help make the examples and exercises more gender neutral and gender inclusive. Without Sylvia and Sally's help, it is certain that this text would never have been completed.

CHAPTER ONE
Introduction

1.1 Logic and Argument

Logic may be broadly defined as the study of methods for determining whether or not a conclusion has been correctly drawn from a set of assumptions. The study of logic stretches back at least as far as the Greek philosopher Aristotle (384–322 BCE). Aristotle is one of the first writers of whom we are aware to recognize that correctly drawing a conclusion is itself a subject worthy of formal study. So significant were Aristotle's contributions that his pronouncements in logic, as well as in many other scholarly areas, have continued to exert a powerful influence throughout our intellectual history.

Logic has grown enormously in the years since it was first formally discussed by Aristotle. In fact, the science of logic has developed more rapidly over the past 150 years than throughout its previous history and contains much of what Aristotle discovered as a small part. The techniques developed by modern logicians are important not only for determining which conclusions may correctly be drawn from given assumptions, but also for having opened up fruitful lines of research in such fields as philosophy, mathematics, linguistics, and computer science.

Our focus in this text will be on that part of logic known as *deductive* logic. The specific nature of deductive logic will be taken up starting in Section 1.2. We begin our study here with the introduction of some standard logical vocabulary. Instead of using the somewhat vague term 'assumption', we will use the word 'premise'. A **premise** is a statement that is being used as a reason for accepting the truth of some other statement, which is called the **conclusion.** By the word 'statement' we will mean, roughly, 'sentence that is either true or false'. It will be convenient to think of the collection of all statements as approximately equivalent to the collection of all declarative sentences—that is, sentences ordinarily understood as making assertions (as opposed to giving commands, asking questions, etc.).[1] Some examples of statements are

> Two plus two equals four
>
> Most people believe that table salt is poisonous
>
> All events in the universe are predetermined
>
> Einstein's theories have been proved true.

Some typical examples of nonstatements are

> How many toes do you have?
>
> Go to your room!
>
> Oh, yeah?
>
> Hey, you!

A statement is said to have a **truth value.** The truth value of a true statement will be denoted by 'T', and the truth value of a false statement will be denoted by 'F'.

A collection of premises, taken together with a conclusion, is what logicians call an *argument*. When an argument is seriously advanced by someone, the premises are meant to provide reasons for taking the conclusion of the argument to be true, or probably true. Formally, however, we omit reference to the intention of the arguer and define an argument as follows:

> **Definition**   An **argument** is a collection of statements, one of which is the **conclusion** and the rest of which are **premises.**

Notice that the word 'argument', in the sense just defined, has a somewhat different meaning than it does in normal usage. Arguments in our sense are not disputes between persons but are simply sets of statements. There is of course a connection between the logician's usage and normal usage, for it is common when there is a dispute over some claim for someone to offer an argument, in the logician's sense, with that claim (or its denial) as a conclusion. Ordinarily, that is, an argument's premises are intended by its author to support the conclusion. *Formally,* however, nothing in the definition requires that an argument's premises must be true or even plausible, nor that the premises should provide reason to

---

[1]More details about statements will be given in Section 1.3.

believe the conclusion. There is not even the requirement that an argument ever be presented by anybody or be intended to persuade anybody. Thus, for instance, the following is an argument:

> **Premise:**   Elephants have wings
>
> **Conclusion:**   Porpoises write passionate poetry.

This is of course a very bad argument—an argument that nobody would be likely to make—but it *is* an argument by our definition, nonetheless. Much of our task in studying logic is to understand what exactly it is that distinguishes good arguments from bad.

Let's look at more ordinary examples of arguments:

(A) Since all astronomers are stargazers and Hypatia is an astronomer, it follows that Hypatia is a stargazer.

(B) Two is an even number. Two is also a prime number. From these facts it can be concluded that there is at least one even prime number.

(C) If Laplace is correct, then all actions are predetermined and we have no free will. If Laplace is not correct and quantum mechanics is the correct theory of physical reality, then some of our actions occur purely by chance. However, if some of our actions occur purely by chance, then again we do not have free will. Thus, whether or not Laplace is correct, we do not have free will.

(D) Concerning morality, we may rightly conclude that capital punishment is sometimes justified: An action is good only if it promotes good consequences. But 'good consequences' are simply consequences that satisfy the population at large. Similarly, 'bad consequences' are those that cause people dissatisfaction. It is obvious that in many cases the execution of a criminal will produce much more satisfaction than any other available punishment. Hence, capital punishment is justified in these circumstances.

Although the level of complexity in each of these arguments varies from one argument to another, it is clear that each *is* an argument; that is, each passage contains a conclusion, together with a number of premises. They also count as arguments in the more "ordinary" sense in that the premises are more-or-less obviously intended to support their respective conclusions. Indeed, without explicit indicators like the words 'premise' and 'conclusion', we must rely largely on the perceived "intention" of a passage's author, to identify a passage *as* an argument and to separate its premises and conclusion. We are aided in recognizing the presence of an argument by the inclusion of certain indicator words and phrases that announce the assertion of premises and the drawing of a conclusion. Some typical premise indicators are the following:

Since	Given that	As
Because	On the assumption that	From the fact that

The occurrence of any of these expressions in a passage typically informs the reader or listener that an argument is being presented and that premises follow. Similarly, arguments often contain conclusion indicators, some of which are

Thus	We may conclude that	We may infer	It follows that
Therefore	Entails that	Ergo	Implies that
Hence	We may deduce that	So	

Using these expressions, along with our intuitive grasp of the conventions of our language, it is easy to sort out the statements of passage (C), for example, neatly into premises and conclusion. Looking for the "main point" of the argument, we see that the conclusion is introduced by the word 'thus':[2]

(C)   Whether or not Laplace is correct, we do not have free will.

The remaining statements in the argument are premises. Taking them in the order in which they appear, we list them:

(P1)   If Laplace is correct, then all actions are predetermined and we have no free will

(P2)   If Laplace is not correct and quantum mechanics is the correct theory of physical reality, then some of our actions occur purely by chance

(P3)   If some of our actions occur purely by chance, then we do not have free will.

Notice that lines from the original expression of the argument have not been copied exactly. Instead, the original English has been paraphrased in order to focus just on the essentials of each premise asserted. In (P3), for example, we have omitted the words 'however' and 'again'. In the original argument, such words aid us in

---

[2]In this sentence, two different kinds of quotation mark are used: single quotes and double quotes. This usage is explained in Section 1.4.

recognizing the structure of the argument. However, once we have identified the argument's premises and its conclusion, such expressions can be eliminated.

In many cases, arguments are intended for an audience who shares a common body of beliefs or assumptions. For the sake of brevity or convenience, these assumptions, though necessary to the argument, are simply not stated. A simple example of such an argument is

Hypatia is a stargazer, since all astronomers are stargazers.

The conclusion 'Hypatia is a stargazer' depends upon more than just the single premise following the premise indicator 'since'. The unstated premise is 'Hypatia is an astronomer'. In cases like this one, where an obvious premise has been left unstated, the argument is called an **enthymeme.**

The examples we have discussed so far are quite evidently examples of arguments, and within these arguments it has been fairly easy to distinguish premises from conclusions. The relative isolation of these passages, together with their use of indicator words, makes it hard to interpret them other than as arguments. But when arguments occur in their "natural habitat"—for example, in newspaper editorials, political speeches, or scholarly books and journals—they are often harder to identify. Arguments generally occur interspersed with statements used for other purposes, including giving explanations and descriptions or simply presenting unsupported assertions of personal feeling or opinion. To isolate and analyze arguments and to distinguish them from other uses of language, we must rely on our understanding of meaning, the rules of language, and the context in which statements occur.

Although people possess quite remarkable abilities to recognize arguments and to distinguish premises from conclusions, the task can sometimes be formidable. Particularly challenging is the job of distinguishing arguments from *explanations*. This distinction does not really affect the logical concepts that we will be discussing in this text, but the distinction does arise in ordinary cases of reasoning in which one is called upon to determine whether a set of statements is intended to *prove* or, instead, to *explain*. For this reason we will briefly discuss the distinction between arguments and explanations.

Explanations are best understood as answers to a question of *why* something is the case. Consider, for example, this question: Why does Masha the cat have such short whiskers on one side? The answer to this question consists in giving a *reason*: Masha has such short whiskers on one side because of a specific type of infection she had at birth. We might formulate this explanation like this:

Masha was born with an infection, and most cats who are born with this type of infection grow very short whiskers on one side of the face. Thus, Masha has very short whiskers on one side.

This set of statements is not only an *explanation* of why Masha has short whiskers, but also *appears* to be an *argument* that Masha has short whiskers. Should we then say that this explanation is really an argument? Is it both an explanation *and* an argument?

From the point of view of our formal definition, these statements *do* form an argument. Still, if you were asked to classify this passage as an explanation or as an argument (as you will be in the exercises following this section), it would be better to call this an explanation. Why? The reason for this is that, though these statements have the logical structure of an argument, the premises are being offered not to prove *that* Masha has short whiskers, but rather to say *why* Masha has short whiskers. That Masha has short whiskers on one side of her face is not in doubt (it's in plain view, after all), so there is no need to provide evidence *that* she has. On the other hand, a person seeing Masha would naturally wonder how or why she came to have such short whiskers on one side of her face.

An alternative way to clarify the matter would be to define a collection of passages called, say, 'inferential passages'. An inferential passage could be defined just as we have defined 'argument'. Arguments would then be classified as those inferential passages intended to *prove that* a conclusion is true, whereas explanations would be classified as inferential passages intended to *explain why* an explanandum is true.[3] The essential point to grasp here is that the distinction between an explanation and an argument is a distinction between *how* inferential passages are used.[4]

For our purposes in this text, it will be more convenient to omit the notion of intention from our formal definition of argument and instead just say the following: When asked to determine whether a set of statements is an argument or an explanation, you must rely (1) on the context in which the statements appear and (2) on your understanding of which statements in the set are known or believed to be true by the intended audience. If a set of statements is put forward by someone as an argument, it is ordinarily the case that the conclusion is more in doubt than the premises—for, otherwise, there would seem little reason to present an argument in support of it. If, on the other hand, the truth of the conclusion is

---

[3]Corresponding to the premises and conclusion of an argument, an explanation is said to contain *explanans* (which do the explaining) and *explanandum* (which gets explained), respectively.

[4]Philosophers express this fact by saying that the distinction between explanation and argument is *pragmatic*. The question of whether all explanations are, formally speaking, arguments is a subject of debate among philosophers of science. For an excellent discussion of differing views on the nature of explanation and its relationship to argument, see Wesley Salmon, *Four Decades of Scientific Explanation* (Minneapolis: University of Minnesota Press, 1990).

not in doubt, the passage is being used as an explanation—that is, to show *why* the conclusion is true.[5]

In our study of logic, whether we are looking at arguments that can be used as explanations or at arguments aimed at proving a conclusion, we will confine ourselves to examples that clearly *are* arguments in our formal sense and in which there is an evident distinction between premises and conclusion. Although some exercises on argument identification have been included at the end of this section, we will not spend any more time on this subject. It's not that such study is unimportant; indeed, it is only if you can identify an argument, along with distinguishing its premises and conclusion, that the study of logic will be very useful to you. The reason that we will not spend time on this subject is that its proper place comes *after* one has mastered some of the skills that logic has to teach. Once you've spent some time looking at very clear examples of arguments and learning precisely what it is that makes them good or bad arguments, you will be in a much better position to determine whether or not some given passage contains an argument.[6]

Now let's adopt a convention about how to write out an argument. Given an argument, place all the premises, along with the conclusion, in a vertical list with the premises at the top and the conclusion at the bottom. Separate the premises from the conclusion with a horizontal line and use the triangular configuration of dots, '$\therefore$', to stand for the word 'therefore'. Applying this convention to arguments (A) and (B) produces

> All astronomers are stargazers
> Hypatia is an astronomer
> _____
>
> $\therefore$ Hypatia is a stargazer

> Two is an even number
> Two is a prime number
> _____
>
> $\therefore$ There is at least one even prime number.

---

[5]At least one more complication about the explanation/argument distinction is that explanations are sometimes *used* as arguments. Suppose, for instance, you notice that a steak you left on the kitchen counter is gone. When you look around, you find your dog guiltily skulking about the house. You infer that the dog ate the steak. The process of reasoning you likely employed goes something like this: *If* the dog had eaten the steak, then the steak would be gone; hence, the dog's hypothesized action is an explanation of why the steak is gone. Furthermore, it is (let us suppose) the best explanation of why the steak is gone, so you infer that the hypothesis is correct. This pattern of argument is called **inference to the best explanation.**

[6]This view is not endorsed by everybody. Some may think that we are sidestepping an issue that really ought to be studied right from the start. If you are interested in argument identification, we encourage you to consult the references listed in Appendix 1, for some good discussions of that subject.

In this way we can focus at a glance on an argument's essential components: its premises and conclusion. Notice that, in the "Hypatia" argument, the first statement of the original has been broken into two premises. This is because the word 'and' in the original functions to connect two whole, distinct statements that are both asserted to be true. In such a situation, separating the distinct assertions helps us even more to "see" the structure of the argument in order to evaluate it. As an exercise you may want to rewrite argument (D), using this standard format.

Occasionally we will use an alternative convention in which premises and conclusion are listed horizontally. For example, the argument about Hypatia can also be written this way:

> All astronomers are stargazers, Hypatia is an astronomer / ∴ Hypatia
> is a stargazer.

When written this way, each premise is separated by a comma.

To summarize, an argument is a collection (or *set*) of statements consisting of a conclusion and one or more premises. When an argument is seriously advanced by someone, the premises are given as reasons intended to support the conclusion. Every statement has a truth value: true (or T) if the statement is true and false (or F) if the statement is false. Our next step will be to describe the ways in which a set of premises can support a conclusion and to state some of the ways in which arguments are called "good" or "bad" by the logician.

Exercises for Section 1.1

Arguments Versus Nonarguments   For each of the following passages, indicate whether an argument is being presented. If you think that a passage does not present an argument, describe what kind of passage it is. For instance, it might be an explanation, a report, a description, or simply the assertion of an unsupported opinion. If the passage is an argument or an explanation whose logical form is that of an argument, clearly list its premises and conclusion, using the format introduced in this section. Those exercises marked with the diamond, '♦', are answered in the back of the book.

♦ 1. Earth and this bowling ball are both massive objects. According to the classical Newtonian law of gravity, there is a relation of attraction between any two massive objects. Thus, as Earth and the bowling ball exert attractive forces on one another, it follows that when the bowling ball is held suspended in the air and then released, it falls.

2. The new dormitory has been an expensive undertaking: new doors, new windows, fresh paint, and new furniture. The university has gone to great

lengths to refurbish these old, temporary student dwellings, and it is expected that when students return in the fall they will be both thrilled and delighted with their renewed residence.

3. Because rainwater becomes mixed with pollutants in the air, much of our drinking and recreational water has become polluted. It is thus likely that our health is endangered simply by drinking water.

4. If the square root of two were a rational number, it would be equal to some fraction m/n, where m and n are relatively prime. Yet it can be shown that this latter consequence leads to a contradiction. Therefore, the square root of two is not a rational number.

5. Democritus, the ancient Greek scientist, speculated that reality was composed solely of "atoms and the void." Democritus's views were severely criticized by Aristotle and, indeed, the whole Western scientific tradition up through the nineteenth century. Yet, as we all know, today the atomistic theory of matter is regarded as a proven fact about our universe.

6. Astrology and astronomy have both been studied for centuries. At one time both enjoyed widespread respect (indeed, it was thought that astronomy was important only because it was needed for astrology), but only one of the two has come to enjoy an elevated status. Astrology continues to be highly popular, but is hardly respected scientifically.

7. We can be quite sure that the universe was created by an all-knowing, all-powerful, all-good Being. This fact is evident from the simplest observations we can make: the beauty of the natural world, the impeccable machinery of nature, and our ability to experience human love. It is clear that, unless such a Being existed, none of this would even be possible.

8. The concept of probability is wholly antithetical to that of causality. If one event A causes another event $B,$ then there must exist a deterministic law that connects them together. If it should turn out that at root our world is physically indeterministic—if the quantum mechanical view is borne out—then it would follow that the physical world obeys purely probabilistic laws. This being the case, it would follow as well that "causes" do not really exist in this universe.

♦9. Course grades represent a specific level of mastery of the material covered during the semester. If grades were given on a curve, they would be relative to the achievement of students enrolled in a given semester—so that, for example, a student receiving an A one semester might have received only a B if she or he had been registered during a different semester. It is for this reason that grading for this course is not given on a curve, i.e., in order that a course grade should have the same meaning independently of the semester during which the course was taken.

10. Logical Positivism exerted great influence over American philosophy for the better part of this century; indeed, its influence is still felt today. One of the essential features of this school of thought was that the methods of formal logical analysis, along with the "scientific method," formed the only legitimate way to reason meaningfully about the world. While most of the elements of this approach have been either disproved or discarded, Positivism has provided us with invaluable analytical tools for the investigation of classic philosophical problems.

11. The idea of an "artificial heart" has today gained prominence and even a certain amount of acceptance. But this was not always so. Although in the eighteenth and nineteenth centuries (the dawning of the "machine age") the idea of "body-part-as-mechanical-device" seemed quite plausible, advances in biochemistry and physiology revealed the human body to be of such an order of organization and complexity that the simple "mechanical" view has been made to seem naive, or even ridiculous.

12. Technology is a wonderful thing, yet it also has its drawbacks. While working on my computer last week, I neared the end of a project. Then, the power went out! The next day at work, my colleague had her part of the project neatly typed and ready to go, because she had the foresight to own an old manual typewriter and some candles! It only goes to show that in bringing great strides and advances, technology also provides us with new stumbling blocks and problems as well.

♦13. Human intellectual history is filled with cases where an idea that had no application at the time of its discovery bore fruit later. Such is the case, for example, with the slow development of the mathematical theory of tensors. Stemming out of work in vector analysis and differential geometry over at least two centuries, it was really not until Einstein employed this mathematical idiom in his general theory of relativity that the full physical application of the theory was realized. Innumerable similar cases can be found.

14. The concept of "probability" is quite ambiguous. The idea that a die has a "one-sixth" probability of landing with the six on top involves a ratio of "favorable" outcomes to "all possible" outcomes. By contrast, when a weather forecaster says that there's a "20 percent" probability of rain, there is no set of "all possible outcomes" to refer to. Moreover, we often use the concept of probability in a very subjective sense—as when one says something like "He will probably be very surprised to see you"—when there are no numbers involved at all. Obviously, the great ambiguity in this use of probability concepts makes probability's utility enormously small.

15. While it may not be proper for a student to offer judgments to a professor on the professor's attire, neither would it be proper for the professor to publicly rebuke the student for doing so. For one thing, it only exposes the student to

the same potential humiliation that makes the student's remark improper to begin with. For another, the teacher's power to crush a student's spirit in the classroom is magnitudes greater than the student's ability to harm the teacher's self-concept or standing in the classroom.

16. Is ethics even possible? Some philosophers say not. According to these thinkers, in order for a sentence to be meaningful, there must exist a method for determining whether or not the sentence is true. If a sentence does not fall into this category, then it is neither true nor false. It would of course be very difficult to propose a method—a method that all people would agree is correct—for deciding the truth or falsity of a sentence like 'Killing is bad'. This illustrates the difficulty of the matter, thus inclining some thinkers to accept the proposal that sentences expressing ethical judgments simply lack truth values.

17. Once it was thought that burning produced a gas called 'phlogiston'. As a candle in an enclosed space burned, it was reasoned, phlogiston accumulated, thus suffocating the flame. Long since discredited by the discovery of oxygen and the modern understanding of combustion, the phlogiston theory remains to this day an example of incorrect but respectable scientific thinking.

18. Suppose that a person desires to walk from point A to point B. Now, as we all know, space is infinitely divisible: Between any two points there is always a third point halfway between them. Thus, between points A and B, there are infinitely many points, since for any point between them—say, C—there is another point between A and C (and also one between B and C). We see from this that a person *cannot* walk from point A to point B, for to do so that person would have to pass infinitely many points. This can't possibly be accomplished in any finite amount of time.

◆ 19. According to the eighteenth-century physician Mesmer, a subtle fluid or "animal magnetism" could be transferred to medical patients by, for example, holding iron rods immersed in dilute sulfuric acid. Today the "cures" he produced for physical ailments are understood to be merely symptomatic relief produced by hypnotic suggestion—although hypnosis has, in its own right, become a respectable approach to treating certain psychological conditions.

20. According to Immanuel Kant, an act is good only if it is warranted by the Categorical Imperative. The Categorical Imperative states that one must act according to that maxim that can be willed as a universal law. For example, on Kant's view, it would be immoral for someone to steal for a living instead of working for a living. This is because the maxim 'I will steal for a living and not work for a living' can't be willed as a universal law: If everyone stole for a living instead of working, there would be nothing to steal. This illustrates the fact that, for Kant, logical consistency is an essential element of morality.

21. Scientists have discovered a new method for determining the distance of galaxies observed through the Hubble space telescope. The usual method relies on spreading received light into its spectrum, then analyzing its colors to determine the age of the galaxy. Some galaxies are so distant, however, that their light is too dim for this method to work. Instead, photographs of the galaxies are made through four different-colored lenses. The more colors the different lenses filter, the more distant, and hence the more ancient, is the galaxy being observed.

1.2 Deduction and Induction

As stated at the outset, logic has as its business the production of techniques for determining whether or not a conclusion has been correctly drawn from assumptions. To put it in the language introduced in Section 1.1, we would say that logic has as its business the evaluation of arguments. For the logician, argument evaluation consists, in essence, of inspecting the logical relationship between an argument's premises and its conclusion.

There are two basic ways in which the premises of an argument may be intended to support the conclusion. In the first case the premises are supposed to be so related to the conclusion that the truth of the premises would be an absolute guarantee of the conclusion's truth. Arguments of this type are called **deductive arguments.** In the second case the premises are supposed to be so related to the conclusion that the truth of the premises would render the conclusion probable, without being a guarantee of the conclusion's truth. Arguments of this kind are called **inductive arguments.**

When an argument's premises, if true, *would* provide an absolute guarantee of the conclusion's truth, we say that the argument is *deductively valid*. To put it precisely:

> *Definition*   An argument is said to be **deductively valid** when it is impossible for all of its premises to be true and its conclusion false. An argument that is not deductively valid is **invalid.**

We will usually use simply the word 'valid' in place of 'deductively valid'. When an argument is valid, we say that the premises *entail,* or *imply* (or *logically entail* or *logically imply*) the conclusion, that the conclusion is a *valid consequence* of the premises, or that the conclusion *follows* deductively from the premises.

A fairly clear and obvious example of a deductively valid argument is argument (A) from Section 1.1, concerning the ancient Alexandrian astronomer Hypatia:

All astronomers are stargazers
Hypatia is an astronomer
∴ Hypatia is a stargazer.

What makes this a valid argument is the fact that it would be logically impossible for both of the premises to be true while the conclusion is false. Notice that this is quite different from saying that the premises and the conclusion *are* true. Although truth is important, it takes something rather different than simply having true premises and a true conclusion to make an argument deductively valid. What is meant is that *if* the premises were both true, *then it would not be possible* for the conclusion to be false. Asking whether an argument is valid is equivalent to asking whether it is impossible for the premises to be true and the conclusion false. The notion of "impossible" that we have in mind here will be made clear by example and discussion. Actually deciding whether or not an argument is valid is what much of this text is about.

At this point, it is important for you to appreciate just what it means to say that an argument is deductively valid or invalid. Consider, then, another argument:

All persons with herpes are persons who were exposed to herpes
Jack was exposed to herpes
∴ Jack has herpes.

To determine whether or not this is a valid argument, we ask: Could the conclusion be false while the two premises were true? Let's imagine that the premises *are* true. (In fact, the first premise *is* true.) Given this supposition, is it still *possible* (i.e., logically compatible with the premises being true) that the conclusion is false? The answer is 'yes'. Jack was unfortunate in being exposed to herpes. However, the first premise does not say that everyone who is exposed to herpes has it—only that those who have it must have been exposed to it. Thus, even supposing that the premises are both true, it would still be *possible* that the conclusion is not true. That is, the truth of the premises would not provide an absolute guarantee that the conclusion is true. Therefore, the argument is invalid.

In the "Hypatia" argument, it was easy to see that the argument is valid. In the argument about herpes, a bit of thought was needed to determine whether or not the argument was valid. Thought was required only partly because we did not know the truth values of all the statements contained in the argument. But there is one kind of case in which knowing the truth values of all an argument's statements will help you decide whether or not it is valid. To be specific, if you *know* that an argument has true premises and a false conclusion, then you know at once that the argument is not valid. Such an argument is the following:

> Sodium is poisonous
> Chlorine is poisonous
> _____
> ∴ Sodium chloride is poisonous.

Sodium and chlorine are indeed poisonous. Sodium chloride, however, is ordinary table salt, which isn't poisonous. Since the premises are true and the conclusion is false, the argument certainly isn't valid.

It is extremely important for you to recognize that the question of whether an argument is valid is entirely separate from the question of whether the argument's premises and conclusion are in fact true. Logic is in general concerned with what *would* be the case if an argument's premises *were* true, not with whether the premises are in fact true. In applications, truth does of course come into play, and we have a useful piece of terminology for distinguishing valid arguments, without qualification, from valid arguments that have true premises:

> **Definition** An argument is said to be **sound** when it is a deductively valid argument with all premises true. An argument that is not sound is **unsound**.

An argument is unsound if either of the two conditions in the definition is not met. A sound argument is, logically speaking, the strongest kind of support that can be given for a conclusion. An argument can be valid and unsound, but an argument can't be sound and invalid. Some examples will help illustrate this point. First, here is a sound argument:

> Anyone who lives in Los Angeles lives in California
> Anyone who lives in California lives in the U.S.A
> _____
> ∴ Anyone who lives in Los Angeles lives in the U.S.A.

This argument is sound because it satisfies the two conditions of the definition. First, it is deductively valid—if the premises were true, then the conclusion could not be false. Second, the premises are in fact true. What can we say, then, of the truth value of the conclusion?

Now, consider an argument that is unsound but valid:

> Hydrogen and oxygen can't exist on the same planet
> Hydrogen does exist on planet Earth
> _____
> ∴ Oxygen does not exist on planet Earth.

This is unsound because the premises aren't both true. It is valid, however, because if the premises were both true, then the conclusion would have to be true. Contrast this with the following argument, which is also unsound:

> Some people are American
> Some people are accountants
> ───────────────
> ∴ Some people are American accountants.

Although this argument has both true premises and a true conclusion, it is not a valid argument. It's not valid because, even given the truth of the premises, it would still be possible that no Americans were accountants. That is, the premises would still both be true if, for example, all accountants were Danish. To see that an argument is invalid, it is sometimes helpful to ask yourself this question: Supposing you knew that the premises were true, would you also know that the conclusion is true? Or, perhaps, imagine that a Martian, whom we know to be a Perfect Logician, knew just that the premises were true. Would this individual then know that the conclusion is true? Although the validity of an argument does not depend on whether or not you could know the truth of the conclusion, given the premises, it is nevertheless a useful strategy to proceed by asking yourself this question when honing your own logical sensibilities.

Finally, here is an argument that is not valid and does not have true premises:

> There is at least one mouse who speaks English
> There is at least one mouse who writes poetry
> ───────────────
> ∴ There is at least one mouse who both speaks English and writes
> poetry.

The argument is invalid since, even if there were a mouse who spoke English and a mouse who wrote poetry, it would not have to be true that they were one and the same mouse.

Although it is deductive logic that will concern us in the rest of this book, we should pause before moving on in order to comment on the "other" kind of argument analysis. This will help paint a more complete picture of what argument evaluation, in its broadest sense, is all about and will also help to clarify, by contrast, the nature of deductive argument.

If an argument is not deductively valid, this does not necessarily mean that the argument's premises provide *no* support for the conclusion. The "other" kind of support that premises might give to a conclusion is to make the conclusion *probable*. The idea of "being probable" is rather hard to explain, especially at an elementary level. A rough, intuitive idea of probability that most of us share comes from flipping a coin. If we believe that the coin is just as likely to land heads as tails, we will say that the statement 'The coin lands heads up' has a ".5 probability" of being true.

It is more difficult to say in simple terms what makes an inductive argument good than it is to say what makes a deductive argument good. Intuitively, a good inductive argument should make its conclusion probable, but several problems arise in making this intuition precise. First of all, whether the premises of an inductive argument appear to you to make the conclusion probable typically depends on other things that you know or believe. If, for instance, you encounter a pile of charred pieces of wood along a hiking trail, you would infer that it is probable (indeed nearly certain) that a person had lit a fire there earlier. However, our Martian Perfect Logician, whom we mentioned earlier, might not make the same inference, due to unfamiliarity with human camping practices. You might attempt to remedy this disagreement by supplying the Martian with additional premises about what humans do when they go camping. As it turns out, however, even after one has added new premises, determining that the new premises in conjunction with the old make the conclusion probable may require still *more* background knowledge.

A related difficulty is that inductive arguments, unlike deductive arguments, can be weakened by additional premises. Suppose you are going to a political rally at which a senator with whom you are not familiar will be speaking. You might reasonably form the following argument:

> The speaker is a senator
> Most senators are male
> ∴ The speaker is male.

This is a strong inductive argument, in that the truth of the premises make the conclusion probable. Suppose, however, that upon arriving at the rally you discover that the senator's first name is 'Sylvia'. Adding this piece of information to your other premises, the argument suddenly looks rather weak. This fact—that the strength of an inductive argument can be reduced by adding additional premises—contrasts markedly with deductive arguments: If an argument is deductively valid, *no addition of premises to the argument can make it invalid.*

As a consequence of these and other difficulties, there is no widely agreed-on characterization of what constitutes a good inductive argument. Still, for the sake of comparison with inductive logic, we can offer the following definition:

> *Definition*   An argument is said to be **inductively strong** when it would be improbable that the conclusion is false, if all its premises were true.

Inductive strength is, to an extent, analogous to deductive validity; indeed, the expression 'inductive validity' is sometimes used for what we call inductive strength. A very important difference between inductive and deductive arguments is that, whereas deductive validity is an all-or-nothing affair, inductive strength is a matter of *degree*. Inductive arguments may be more or less strong. Although the previous definition stipulates that in an inductively strong argument the falsity of the conclusion given the premises is improbable, it is in fact extremely difficult—perhaps impossible—to specify just what the required degree of improbability should be.

Despite the difficulties that arise in giving a precise meaning to 'probability' and related inductive concepts, many ordinary cases of inductive reasoning exist that appear intuitively correct. Consider the following as an example:

> The downtown bus has always arrived at the corner of Main and Broadway at 10 AM on Thursdays
> The current bus schedule states that the downtown bus will stop at the corner of Main and Broadway at 10 AM Thursdays
> There have been no announcements to the effect that the current bus schedule has changed
> ─────────────────────
> ∴ The bus will arrive at the corner of Main and Broadway at 10am this Thursday.

Though the conclusion of this argument does not follow with the same logical necessity as the conclusion of a deductively valid argument (i.e., even if the premises were all true, it would still be possible for the conclusion to turn out false), we would ordinarily say that these premises, if true, give one *good reason* for thinking that the conclusion is very probably true. The above argument, then, constitutes an example of an inductively strong argument.

In deductive logic we distinguish questions about the relationship between the premises and conclusion from questions about the truth of the premises. By analogy to the concept of soundness, we define 'cogency':

> **Definition**   An argument is said to be **cogent** when it is an inductively strong argument with all of its premises true.

As an example of a cogent argument, take the following:

> There are at least hundreds of thousands of entrants to the Publisher's Clearinghouse Sweepstakes
> Joe has entered the Publisher's Clearinghouse Sweepstakes
> Only one person can win the Grand Prize of the Publisher's Clearinghouse Sweepstakes
> ─────────────────────
> ∴ Joe won't win the Publisher's Clearinghouse Sweepstakes Grand Prize.

The subject of inductive reasoning is large and rather difficult. The concept of "being probable" really must be spelled out in detail. If you are interested in learning more about induction, there are references to some excellent introductory texts in Appendix 1. Nothing more will be said about inductive reasoning in this text, and we now return to the subject of deductive logic.

Although our definition of 'valid argument' is useful, as it stands it is somewhat vague, because the notion of possibility invoked in the definition has not yet been made precise. We have to rely on "logical intuition" to tell us whether or not it is possible simultaneously for the premises of an argument to be true and the conclusion false. Beginning in the next chapter, we will try to remedy this by providing rigorous techniques for determining whether an argument is valid. Our method will be to translate arguments into a special logical language that will enable us to be completely precise about what it means for an argument to be valid. The methods to be introduced and developed are quite powerful, but we will not, unfortunately, be able to eliminate all imprecision from the business of argument evaluation. The success of our technique depends on translating arguments into our logical language, and because of the vagueness of our language, it is sometimes not clear exactly how to accomplish this translation.

Exercises for Section 1.2

Part I: Arguments   Consider the following brief arguments. Put each one into our standard format. As best you can, classify each one as deductively valid, inductively strong, or neither.

◆ 1. Since Harry likes to eat tofu and tofu is healthy, it follows that there is at least one healthy food that Harry likes to eat.

2. Louise has made her payments late every time they were due over the last two years. Therefore, she will not make her payments on time this year.

3. The car will start only if there is gas in the tank. Since the car started, there must be gas in the tank.

4. The car will start only if there is gas in the tank. Since there is gas in the tank, the car will start.

◆ 5. If ESP really occurred, it is highly probable that more people would know about it than presently say that they do. Therefore, ESP does not really occur.

6. Some people without brains do an awful a lot of talking. Therefore, it is possible to talk without a brain.

7. The results of a recent survey indicate that most men prefer to eat a large breakfast and have a light lunch. George will therefore not want to go out for a large lunch today.

8. Either Apple will win the election or Orange will. If Apple wins, then the Republicans will be unhappy; if Orange wins, the Democrats will be unhappy. As it turns out, the Republicans will not be unhappy. Therefore, if only one candidate can win the election, Apple will not.

♦9. Some fish have tails, and some fish have scales. Therefore, some fish have both tails and scales.

Pessamistic induction

10. Every supposed "law" of physics that has ever been produced has eventually been disproved. Thus, the longer Einstein's theory is around, the closer it is to being disproved.

11. Everyone who got an A in geography was allowed to move on to geophysics. Hal was not allowed to move on to geophysics, so he must not have received an A in geography.

12. Most domestic cats are shorthairs, and most domestic cats love catnip. Thus, it is certain that some animals that love catnip are shorthairs.

Part II: Soundness and Validity   It is important for you to master the distinction we have drawn between sound arguments and valid arguments. The following exercises are intended to help you see this distinction clearly.

♦13. Give an example of a valid argument with two premises and a conclusion, where each statement in the argument is true.

14. Give an example of a valid argument with two premises and a conclusion, where the premises are both false but the conclusion is true.

15. Give an example of a valid argument with two premises and a conclusion, where one of the premises is false, one of them is true, and the conclusion is true.

16. Give an example of a valid argument with two premises and a conclusion, where one of the premises is false, one of the premises is true, and the conclusion is false.

♦17. Give an example of an invalid argument with two premises and a conclusion, where the premises are both false but the conclusion is true.

18. Give an example of an invalid argument with two premises and a conclusion, where both premises are true but the conclusion is false.

19. Give an example of an invalid argument with two premises and a conclusion, where both premises and the conclusion are true.

20. Suppose you were presented with an argument that had more than one premise. If you knew that the argument is valid but that the conclusion is in fact false, what must be true of at least one of the premises? Why?

1.3   Statements, Propositions, and Context

We began this chapter by defining *statements* to be sentences that are either true or false. We will keep to this definition, but there are some difficulties with it that need to be addressed. We have said that statements are "sentences that have truth values." However, the question of whether or not a given sentence *has* a truth value is not always easy to answer. Furthermore, even if one thinks that a sentence *does* have a truth value, it is not always clear precisely which truth value it has. The reason for this is that one and the same sentence may express *different* things, depending on the *context* in which the sentence is expressed (i.e., written or uttered).

Consider the sentence 'I am a professor of philosophy at Butler University'. If Stuart Glennan utters this sentence, it will be true; if Joe Bessie utters it, it will be false. This is because, when Stuart Glennan utters the sentence, it expresses the thought that Stuart Glennan is a Butler philosophy professor, which is true, but when Joe Bessie utters it, it expresses the thought that Joe Bessie is a Butler philosophy professor, which is false. Thus, we must distinguish statements—which are a kind of sentence—from what those statements express in various contexts. Philosophers call the "things expressed by statements" *propositions.*

You might think that it is only certain types of sentences that express different propositions in different contexts. After all, the word 'I', like the words 'here' and 'now'—called *indexicals*—are unusual, in that their reference varies depending on where, when, and by whom they are used. But this fact about sentences is not confined to use of these special words. Consider, for example, the sentence 'Stuart Glennan is a professor of philosophy at Butler University on July 10, 1998'. Perhaps this sentences *looks* like one that would express the same proposition in all contexts; in fact, it does not. Suppose, say, that Stuart Glennan (the philosophy professor) had named his son 'Stuart Glennan'. Suppose furthermore that at Glennan the younger's preschool, Glennan the younger's teacher, while introducing Glennan the younger to the class uttered (as a philosophical joke perhaps) the sentence 'Stuart Glennan is a professor of philosophy at Butler University on July 10, 1998'. In this context, the proposition expressed would be that Glennan the younger was a philosophy professor, which would very likely be false. The problem here results from the ambiguity of the expression 'Stuart Glennan' in the given context. You can probably imagine ways to rephrase the problematic sentence so that this ambiguity is avoided, but we could with a little ingenuity describe yet another context that would reveal ambiguity in the rephrased sentence.

The problem of context can be illustrated even more dramatically: Suppose that you and another person are international spies. You arrange that, if you manage to obtain certain secret documents, you will call your partner at her hotel (her telephone line is monitored!) and utter the sentence, 'Can you meet me for lunch today?' In reality, this apparent question is your signal to your partner that you've got the documents! So, in effect, you would be using a sentence that is grammatically a question to make a statement. This shows that, to meaningfully say that a statement is 'a sentence that has a truth value', we must assume that there is some background context that "fixes" (i.e., anchors or "holds in place") some specific meaning of the sentence.

Besides understanding how the same sentence may express different propositions in different contexts, it is also important to understand that a *single* proposition can be expressed by several *different* sentences. For example, consider the sentences that say something about Joe Bessie's cat, Ratso:

> Ratso is on the mat
>
> Ratso está en la alfombrilla
>
> Ratso liegt auf dem Teppich
>
> Ratso est sur le tapis.

These are four different sentences in four different languages, but they all express the same proposition—namely, the proposition that Ratso is on the mat. One can also find examples of different sentences in the same language that express the same proposition. For instance,

> Stuart Glennan's cats are named 'Masha' and 'Nina'
>
> Stuart Glennan's cats are named 'Nina' and 'Masha'.

It would be odd to claim that merely switching the position of the words 'Masha' and 'Nina' from one sentence to the next causes the two sentences to express different propositions.

Despite the difficulties with taking sentences to be truth bearers, some philosophers have found the concept of a proposition to be problematic. There are at least two reasons for this. First, although it is clear what propositions are not, it is not clear what they are. They are not linguistic objects, since, as we have seen, propositions don't belong to any particular language. Neither can they be thought of as "mental entities" (such as thoughts or ideas), since presumably many propositions would be true or false even if there were no intelligent life in the universe to think about them. Propositions are one of a class of objects that philosophers call *abstract entities*. Because the notion of an abstract entity has proven very hard to pin down, many philosophers have doubted that such things exist.

A second difficulty—one that is of more practical importance for us—is this: It is not at all clear when two sentences express the same proposition. This problem is called the problem of *propositional identity*. Some of the examples offered above seem clearly to involve different sentences expressing the same proposition, but many cases are harder to decide. Consider the following pair:

> Sally went to the party, but John did not.
> Sally went to the party, and John did not.

It may plausibly be debated whether these two sentences express the same proposition. On the one hand, it seems that it would be impossible for one of them to be true while the other one were false, which suggests that they *do* express the same proposition. On the other hand, something different seems to be suggested by the use of the word 'and' as opposed to 'but'. Some of the exercises at the end of this section will explore the problem of propositional identity.

Many more examples compel us to make a distinction between propositions and sentences. Some of these will appear shortly, as we introduce logical symbolism. Although it is important for you to recognize this distinction, it would be unnecessarily difficult at the introductory level to integrate this idea into our presentation. It will be convenient for us to assume that all sentences we use appear in a fixed context and that a sentence expresses the same proposition whenever it is used. Also, we will work exclusively with declarative sentences, so for practical purposes we can ignore the distinction between sentences and statements. When it is important to do so, we will call attention to the difference between the two.

The distinctions discussed in this section involve an even broader distinction between *syntax* and *semantics*. The concept of a proposition introduces the concept of semantics. Semantics has to do with such things as meaning, interpretation, and truth conditions. Statements, at least as we understand them in this book, fall mainly under the heading of syntactic objects. Syntax has to do with such things as the order and arrangements of symbols and is generally not concerned with their meaning or interpretation. The distinction between syntax and semantics forms the basis of the better part of the material discussed in this book, and you will come to see its significance more clearly in the analysis of deductive inference.

Exercises for Section 1.3

Part I: Statements and Sentences   In this text we use the word 'statement' to mean 'sentence that is true or false'. Some difficulties with this definition were discussed in this section. To get a sense of the kinds of difficulties involved, it is instructive to try to decide particular cases for yourself. Below are several sentences. Some of these would ordinarily be understood to be statements, whereas others clearly would not. Which would you ordinarily take to be statements? Which not? Discuss any difficult cases that you find.

◆1. Snow is white.

2. Jack Sprat could eat no fat, his wife could eat no lean.

3. Go to your room!

4. Never before have I seen such beauty in so tragic a time.

5. Was not pity the cross to which was nailed he who loved men most? (Nietzsche, *Thus Spoke Zarathustra*)

6. Logic is hard.

◆7. Logic is hard!!

8. It was the best of times, it was the worst of times. (Dickens)

9. $2 + 2 = ((2 \times 3) + 4) - (3 + 1)$

10. $3 = 7 + 8$

11. The Crest group showed 53% fewer cavities than average.

12. The LEM landed on the moon in 1969.

◆13. Gary used to weigh considerably more than he does now.

14. Every positive integer greater than two can be expressed as the sum of two primes.

15. We have nothing to fear but fear itself.

16. Sexism is a social disease.

◆17. Beauty is only skin deep.

18. Who's on first?

19. Who's on first.

20. Exercise 20 in Section 1.3 of Bessie and Glennan's *Elements of Deductive Inference* is false.

Part II: Sentences and Propositions In this section we have distinguished between sentences and propositions. One difficulty with the notion of a proposition is that it can be difficult to decide when two sentences express the same proposition. In each of the following exercises, you will be presented with a pair of sentences. Indicate whether you think the sentences express the same or different propositions. Justify your answer.

21. (a) I love my mother [spoken by yourself]. (b) I love my mother [spoken by a sibling].

22. (a) I worked while I was in college. (b) Even though I was in college, I worked.

◆23. (a) Bill Clinton is president. (b) Bill Clinton is president of the United States.

24. (a) Bill Clinton threw out the first pitch at the Orioles game. (b) The president of the United States threw out the first pitch at the Orioles game. [Suppose both of these sentences are uttered at the time of an Orioles game during Clinton's presidency.]

25. (a) God exists [spoken by a devout Muslim]. (b) God exists [spoken by a devout Quaker].

26. (a) $2^2 + 2^2 = 8$ (b) $4 + 4 = 8$

27. (a) Just imagine what will happen to you if you don't study for the exam [spoken by your worried mother]. (b) You should study for the exam [spoken by your roommate].

1.4   Use and Mention

To complete this introductory chapter, let's examine one further distinction that will prove useful in subsequent chapters. This is the distinction between *use* and *mention*. Consider the following pair of statements:

(1) The postman has ten letters

(2) 'The postman' has ten letters.

The assertion of statement (1) would ordinarily entitle us to ask of the person asserting it such questions as, "Oh, really? Are all the letters for me? Or are some of them for you?" Statement (2), however, does not contain a reference to the postal carrier; instead, the expression 'The postman' is *itself* being referred to: It is stated that the expression consisting of the letters 'T', 'h', 'e', (etc.), in that order, are altogether ten in number. In statement (1) we say that the expression 'The postman' is being *used,* whereas in statement (2) the expression 'The postman' is being *mentioned.* In general, an expression is *used* in order to *mention:* In statement (1) the expression

The postman

is being used to mention (i.e., to *refer to*) the individual mail carrier. In (2) the expression

'The postman'

is used to mention (refer to) the *expression* that was itself used in statement (1). In this context it is our use of single quotation marks surrounding an expression that indicates that the quoted expression is itself the object of reference.

We should note at this point that there are differing approaches to the use of single and double quotes. In this text we will adopt the approach of always using *single* quotes to mention expressions. We say, for instance,

The word 'noun' is a noun

rather than

The word "noun" is a noun.

In addition, as you may have noticed already, there are several more ways to mention expressions. Besides placing them in single quotes, an expression can be mentioned by setting it off on an indented line. This is a method we have employed in this section. In the text above, for instance, we mention the expression 'The postman' by setting it off *without quotation marks* on its own line. We then mention the expression "The postman" by setting it off three lines below. In general, any expression that we would have to mention using quotes may be mentioned without quotes by setting it by itself on a separate line. Other methods of signaling that an expression is being mentioned are the use of italics or boldface type. Often, as in this text, use of italics serves the dual role of mentioning an expression (as when the word 'deductive' was introduced on the first page of this chapter) as well as emphasizing a point (as in the italicized '*without quotation marks*' in this paragraph). Italics are also used to indicate titles (such as book titles). The context of use will ordinarily make it quite clear for which purpose italics are being employed. Use of boldface type in our text is limited almost exclusively to the introduction of new words and expressions.

Although standard double quotes are sometimes used to mark the distinction between use and mention, we restrict the use of double quotes to three purposes: (a) Double quotes are used as so-called scare quotes. Scare quotes are used to suggest irony concerning the quoted expression—that is, there may be some question about the legitimacy or correct meaning of the quoted expression. An obvious example is 'That "dinner" you gave me was not fit for a dog'. (b) Double quotes are used to enclose the title of an article cited in a reference. (c) Double quotes are used for direct quotation of what someone has actually said or written. An example would be 'Paul announced, "I find Nietzsche's aesthetic sensibilities disturbing."'.

At least one thing that is interesting about the distinction between use and mention is that it helps us describe and discuss important logical features of statements and their components. Notice, for example, that when an expression is used in a statement, one can often replace that expression by another one that refers to (mentions) the same object without a change of truth value. So, for example, if the postman referred to in (1) is Sam Mitchell, we can rewrite (1) as

(3)   Sam Mitchell has ten letters.

Notice that if (1) is true, then so is (3); if (1) is false, then so is (3). In (2), however, this kind of substitution does not work: if we replace the expression 'The postman' in (2) by 'Sam Mitchell', we get the false statement

(4)   'Sam Mitchell' has ten letters.

If an expression occurs in a statement in such a way that substituting a different expression that refers to the same object fails to preserve the truth value of the original statement, then that expression is said to occur in an **opaque context.** Quotation marks create opaque contexts, since, when an expression is mentioned, the truth value of the statement depends upon the expression itself rather than the object to which the expression refers. In subsequent chapters we will discover other kinds of opaque contexts that pose difficulties for the analysis of certain kinds of arguments.

Exercises for Section 1.4

Part I   Insert single quotation marks as needed to properly mark the distinction between use and mention. Note that this may sometimes involve the use of quotation marks around quoted expressions, as in the following example:

"Sandra" itself refers to the name 'Sandra', which is itself the first name of a philosopher.

In this example, notice that the philosopher's name is 'Sandra', and the name *of the name* of this philosopher is "Sandra".

1. Rhonda is the name of my barber.
2. Rhonda's barber shop is called Rhonda's Barber Shop.
♦ 3. Not everybody is named Anna Livia Plurabelle.
4. The name of Maria is Maria.
5. The numeral 2 is the Arabic sign for the number two.
6. 2 + 3 and 1 + 4 both refer to the number referred to by (3 + 3) − 1.
♦ 7. In the United States the expression the United States stands for the United States.

8. The name of the name Harold is Sarah.

9. Barbara is a quotation name, because quotation names are expressions together with the single quotation marks around them.

10. If quotations names are expressions together with the single quotation marks around them, then the quotation name of the word 'Joel' is 'Joel'.

♦ 11. While the letter x is standardly used as a letter of the alphabet, x is also employed in mathematics, as when one writes an algebraic expression such as $x + 3 = 6$.

12. While the sentence I'm going to the store later is syntactically different from the sentence I am going to go to the store later, it would be plausible to say that they express the same semantic content.

Part II   Give examples satisfying the conditions indicated in each case.

13. Give an example of an English sentence in which the name 'Hillary Rodham Clinton' is *used* but not mentioned.

14. Give an example of an English sentence in which the name 'Hillary Rodham Clinton' is *mentioned* but not used.

♦ 15. Give an example of an English sentence in which Hillary Rodham Clinton is *mentioned,* but the expression 'Hillary Rodham Clinton' is *not* used.

16. Give an example of an English sentence in which both Hillary Rodham Clinton is *mentioned* and the expression 'Hillary Rodham Clinton' is *used*.

Part III   The following questions require a clear understanding of the distinction between use and mention.

17. The sign '=' from arithmetic indicates identity. Thus, for example, the sentence 'Two plus two is identical to four' can be expressed as '$2 + 2 = 4$'. In the equation '$2 + 2 = 4$', are the expressions '$2 + 2$' and '4' being used or being mentioned? Explain why your answer is correct.

18. The statement '$2 + 2 = 4$' has the truth value true. What is the truth value of the following?

$$`2 + 2` = `4`$$

Explain why your answer is correct. Under what conditions would an expression of the form

$$`p` = `q`$$

be true, where the symbols 'p' and 'q' are replaced by syntactic objects?

CHAPTER TWO

Statement Logic I: A New Language

2.1 Introduction

Consider the following two arguments:

(A1)   It is raining or it is snowing

        It is not the case that it is raining

    ∴ It is snowing

(A2)   Two is odd or two is even

        It is not the case that two is odd

    ∴ Two is even.

Each argument is valid. But beyond the fact that both are valid, notice that these two arguments have an interesting *structural* (i.e., syntactic) property in common. In each case, the first premise is a statement of the form '_____ or _____', where the blanks are filled by statements. The second premise of each argument is the denial of the left-hand component statement, of the form, 'It is not the case that _____'. And the conclusion of each argument is the right-hand component statement of the first premise. Using the lowercase letters 'p' and 'q', called **statement variables,** to stand as placeholders for statements, we can diagram the structure that the two arguments have in common:

(F1) p or q

It is not the case that p

∴ q

This argument pattern, in which statement places are held by statement variables, is called an **argument form.** The statement patterns from which the argument form is built are called **statement forms.** An argument form becomes an argument when its statement variables are replaced by statements, and a statement form becomes a statement similarly. An argument or statement that comes from a form by plugging in statements is called an **instance** of that form. Thus, arguments (A1) and (A2) are instances of the form (F1). When an argument or statement is an instance of a particular form, we will say that it *has* that form.

A fact of particular interest about form (F1) is that each and every instance of it is a valid argument. There are infinitely many instances of this argument form, hence there are infinitely many valid arguments having this form.

Now consider a third argument:

(A3)   It is raining or it is snowing

∴ It is snowing.

This argument, of course, isn't valid. As above, we can omit some of the content of the argument and look just at its form:

(F2) p or q

∴ q

As we have just seen, there is at least one instance of this form that is not valid (i.e., argument (A3)).[1]

Argument forms and statement forms are both aspects of the general category called **logical form.** These examples illustrate the fact that the validity of an argument generally depends on its logical form. One standard way to look at deductive validity is this: To say that an argument is deductively valid is to imply that it is an instance of a form *whose every instance is deductively valid.* Let's call such argument forms **valid argument forms.** Then, to say that an argument is invalid is to say that *there is no valid argument form of which it is an instance.* Many, perhaps even most, logicians will insist that the validity or invalidity of an argument depends *entirely* on the question of whether or not the argument is an instance of a valid argument form. There is room to debate this claim, but it is not necessary to take up this

---

[1]There are, however, many instances of this form that are valid arguments. See Exercises 12 and 13.

matter further at this point in your study of logic. It is the formal aspects of deductive validity and invalidity that will concern us in this text.[2]

Our goal in this chapter is to introduce a method for revealing the forms of given arguments. This amounts to showing how to uncover the form of the statements out of which an argument is built. At this stage of investigation, we will confine our attention to statements considered as whole units and to the ways in which whole statements can be connected together. This branch of logic is known as **statement logic** (also known as **sentential** or **propositional logic**). Starting in Chapter 5 the analysis of logical form is taken somewhat deeper into the 'interior" of statements.

Exercises for Section 2.1

Part I: Statement Forms   For each of the following statement forms, produce two English instances. One instance should be true, the other false.

> *Example 1:* Given the form *p*. Case (a): Let *p* be the statement 'Earth orbits the Sun'. Then, *p* is true. Case (b): Let *p* be the statement 'Earth is the center of the known universe'. Then, *p* is false.
>
> *Example 2:* Given the form 'If *p*, then *q*'. Case (a): Let *p* be the statement 'Today is Monday' and let *q* be the statement 'Tomorrow is Tuesday'. Then, the statement 'If *p*, then *q*' is true. Case (b): Let *p* be the statement 'Earth travels around the Sun' and let *q* be the statement 'The Moon is a tropical paradise'. Then, the statement 'If *p*, then *q*' is false.

In some cases (especially items 6, 8, and 10) this exercise might prove difficult. These difficulties are examined and resolved, beginning with Section 2.2.

1. *p*
2. It's not the case that *p*
♦3. *p* and *q*
4. *p* or *q*
5. *p* if, and only if, *q*

6. If *p*, then it's not the case that *q*
7. Either not *p* or not *q*
8. If it's not the case that *p*, then *q*
♦9. Neither *p* nor *q*
10. If *p*, then *q* and not *r*

---

[2]A standard debatable example is the following argument: 'Jim is a bachelor; therefore, Jim is not married.' It certainly seems right to say that this is a *valid* argument, since it would be impossible for 'Jim is a bachelor' to be true while 'Jim is not married' is false (assuming the word 'Jim' refers to the same individual in each case). However, there is no standard way of giving the form of this argument so that *all* instances of that form are deductively valid. A possible response is to suggest that this argument contains the implied premise 'All bachelors are unmarried'. As you can see, following this train of thought would take us into theoretical entanglements leading away from our main subject at this point.

Part II: Argument Forms

11. Using statement variables such as '*p*' and '*q*', give an example of a *valid* argument form that has not been discussed in the text.

12. Any argument form that is not valid is called an **invalid argument form.** Argument form (F2) is an example of an invalid argument form. Using statement variables such as '*p*' and '*q*', give another example of an invalid argument form.

13. There are some instances of *invalid* argument forms that are in fact *valid* arguments. Show that this is the case by finding a valid argument that is an instance of the invalid argument form (F2) discussed above.

2.2 Truth-Functionally Simple and Truth-Functionally Compound Statements

Consider the following two statements:

(1) Sue loves Brian and Brian loves Sue

(2) It's not the case that the Moon is made of green cheese.

Statement (1) is the result of taking two simpler statements, 'Sue loves Brian' and 'Brian loves Sue', and sticking the word 'and' between them. Statement (2) is also the result of adding something to a simpler statement. In this case, the expression 'It's not the case that' has been prefixed to the statement 'The Moon is made of green cheese'. When a word or expression is used to connect whole statements together (as in (1)), or attached to a statement as a whole to produce another statement (as in (2)), we say that the word or expression is being used as a **statement connective.** Some examples of statements containing statement connectives are

> Ratso is angry *because* Ratso wants his dinner
>
> People will be admitted *only if* room is available
>
> *It's logically possible that* the Moon is made of green cheese.

The statement connectives in these examples have been italicized. Many statements, like the following, contain several connectives:

If Ratso eats before Annie does, *then* Ratso will be happy *and* Annie will be unhappy; *however,* both cats will be fed at the same time.

Finally, some statements contain *no* connectives:

Hypatia is a woman

Marcia works for the University of Minnesota

Waldo really likes to read Bertrand Russell's philosophy.

In each case we can make a distinction between the connectives, on the one hand, and the component statements, on the other. In the above examples, it has been made clear whether or not a statement contains connectives. However, in a natural language such as English, there are many ways in which distinct statements can be combined into a larger whole. In many such cases it may require a little work to recover the simpler distinct statements from which the whole was built.

The point of distinguishing between statements and connectives is to help us identify the logical form of statements. In logic we focus on five connectives of special interest. These connectives are expressed in many different ways in English, but in logic they are standardly denoted by the following five expressions:

it's not the case that

and

or

if . . . , then

if, and only if.

These five expressions will be our standard idiom for expressing a specific set of logically interesting connections among statements. In the usage we adopt here, they are called the **truth-functional** (or **logical**) **connectives.** A statement that contains *none* of these, nor anything being used equivalently to one of these, is called **truth-functionally simple** (or, more tersely, just **simple**). A statement that has been built from simple statements using some combination of the above connectives is called **truth-functionally compound** (or, more tersely, just **compound**).[3] We associate each truth-functional compound with its own standardized statement form:

---

[3]Truth-functionally simple and truth-functionally compound statements are also often called 'atomic' and 'molecular' statements, respectively.

> It's not the case that *p*
>
> *p* and *q*
>
> *p* or *q*
>
> If *p*, then *q*
>
> *p* if, and only if, *q*.

Just like simple statements, all compound statements have a truth value. The truth value of a compound statement *depends entirely upon the truth values of the simple statements from which it has been built*. An illustration of what this means is in order.
Consider the following statement:

> It's not the case that two is even.

This is a compound statement since it contains the expression 'It's not the case that' prefixed to the whole statement 'two is even'. It is also obviously a false statement. It is false because (1) two *is* even, but (2) the statement asserts that two is *not* even. By similar reasoning, we know that the statement

> It's not the case that two is odd

is true: (1) Two is not odd, and (2) the statement asserts that two is not odd. These two cases illustrate the special logical feature of the connective 'It's not the case that' that interests us here. Using the word 'not' to abbreviate the expression 'It's not the case that', the general point can be put like this: The truth value of *any* statement of the form

> not *p*

is *completely established by the truth value of the component statement p*. That is, if *p* is true, then not *p* is false. If *p* is false, then not *p* is true. The truth value of the compound is a *unique function* (a *truth function*) of the truth value of the component.

Our use of the word 'function' in connection with the negation is just like the use of 'one-place function' in mathematics, where a unique value of a second variable *y*, is associated with the value of a first variable *x*. It is usual to say in this case that *y is a function of x* and to write $y = f(x)$. For example, the doubling function $2(x)$ gives an "output" value of twice *x* for every "input" value of *x*. Applied to the values 0 and 1, for example, we may write

$$2(0) = 0$$

$$2(1) = 2.$$

Analogously, the negation function ~p gives a unique "output value" for every "input value" of p. Using symbols in a very loose way, to say that the negation reverses the truth value of a statement can be represented like this:

$$n(\text{T}) = \text{F}$$

$$n(\text{F}) = \text{T}.$$

In this case, the letters 'T' and 'F' stand for the truth values true and false.

All truth-functional connectives have this feature—namely, that the truth values of compounds built from them depend entirely on the truth values of the simple statements from which they are constructed.[4] There do, however, exist connectives in English that are not truth-functional. For instance, the statement

Chicken Little believes that the sky is falling

is a compound statement consisting of the simple statement 'the sky is falling' to which is prefixed the one-place connective 'Chicken Little believes that'. This compound statement is not *truth-functionally* compound because the truth value of 'the sky is falling' does not determine the truth value of 'Chicken Little believes that the sky is falling'. In general, the truth value of statements of the form 'S believes that p' is not determined by the truth value of p.

Expressions like 'Chicken Little believes that' are one type of non-truth-functional connective, and there are many others as well. In fact, some of the expressions whose truth-functional meaning we have discussed in this section also have uses that are not truth-functional. For instance, as we will show in Secion 3.2, statements of the form 'if p, then q' are sometimes used to express *causal* relationships, and such relationships are not truth-functional.

In our text, compound statements like 'Chicken Little believes that the sky is falling' must be treated as truth-functionally simple. Thus, unless otherwise specified, the words 'simple' and 'compound' will be used to mean, respectively, 'truth-functionally simple' and 'truth-functionally compound'.

Exercises for Section 2.2

Simple Versus Compound Statements   For each of the following, indicate whether the statement is truth-functionally simple or truth-functionally compound. If a statement is compound, identify its simple components. Note that some of the

---

[4]This fact concerning how the truth value of a compound statement depends on the truth value of its components is an instance of a property called 'extensionality'. Extensionality, and its contrasting case known as 'intensionality', will be taken up in Chapter 3.

statements contain connectives that are not equivalent to any of the five truth-functional connectives introduced in this section and thus cannot be represented by a connective symbol.

    1. Mallory left for England last spring.

    2. If Melody teaches Marxism, she is happy.

 ◆3. All that glitters is not gold.

    4. Jack and Jill are a twosome.

    5. Only under extreme circumstances will Betty get up early.

    6. Although there is nobody in the shower, the water is on.

    7. The television isn't working.

    8. The television isn't working, but the radio is. ↰

 ◆9. Even with complete information, quantum mechanics says that predictions about the behavior of a physical system give only probabilities at best.

  10. Jackie grades tests with Merle under the oak tree in the back yard. ↰

  11. Unusual indeed are men who don't wear tweed.

  12. Where angels go, trouble follows. ↰

◆13. We have nothing to fear but fear itself.

  14. I deny that I have been involved in any wrongdoing.

  15. A bird in the hand is worth two in the bush.

  16. Unruffled, intact, the man walked slowly, steadily, and without fear up to the stand and ordered himself an ice cream cone.

  17. On his wise shoulders through the checkerwork of leaves the sun flung spangles, dancing coins. (James Joyce, *Ulysses*)

  18. Susan thought, "If Sam stayed out late, he must have found a really good party!"

◆19. "And what if I refuse?" Einar asked.

  20. Ellen's not known to avoid a good book on transformational grammar.

  21. Jack's father is unhappy.

  22. Jack's father is not unhappy.

  23. Jonathan was dismissed.

  24. The fire started because a match was lit.

  25. The fire started because a match was lit, but the fire was soon put out.

  26. I said to him, "Mind your own business!"

  27. Bob told me, "If you don't read or exercise, then you're missing out on some fine things that life has to offer."

2.3   Symbolizing Simple and Compound Statements

Our job in this section is twofold. First, we need to introduce the rudiments of a precise language for the unambiguous representation of truth-functional connections. This takes us into the study of **symbolic logic** (also known as **mathematical logic**). Second, we need to say something about how to translate statements of English into this new idiom. To do these two things, it will be useful to introduce some terms that will allow us to talk more clearly and efficiently about connectives and compound statements. Here is a list of sample compound statements:

> *It's not the case that* Andrea is a baby
>
> Roz is happy *and* Victor is emotionally drained
>
> Snow will fall *or* rain will pour
>
> *If* Joe finishes his book, *then* Sylvia will be happy
>
> Brian will marry Sue *if, and only if,* Sue loves Brian.

Each of these compound statements is an instance of one of the truth-functional statement forms on page 33. The first statement is the denial of another statement. It is an instance of 'It's not the case that p', where the statement variable 'p' has been replaced by the statement 'Andrea is a baby'. This type of statement is called a **negation.** When the word 'and' is used, as in the second statement, to produce an instance of the form 'p and q', we have a case of **conjunction.** A **disjunction** is a statement in which statements are connected by 'or'. The fourth statement is called a **conditional,** and the final statement is a **biconditional.**

Compound Statement Form	Name of Compound
It's not the case that p	Negation (p is the **scope** of the negation)
p and q	Conjunction (p and q are **conjuncts**)
p or q	Disjunction (p and q are **disjuncts**)
If p, then q	Conditional (p is the **antecedent,** q is the **consequent**)
p if, and only if, q	Biconditional (p and q are **conditions**)

We will be using this terminology in the rest of the book, so it is important that you understand its application well. We will often speak, for example, of the *antecedent* and *consequent* of a conditional. In the previous list of compound statements, 'Joe finishes his book' is the antecedent and 'Sylvia will be happy' is the consequent of the conditional statement. Similarly, we will often want to refer to the right- or left-hand disjunct, conjunct, or condition of a given statement.

The language we now present is, as we've noted, used to represent the logic of truth-functional statements. This language is called '*SL*', for 'statement logic'. In *SL*, there are three kinds of symbol:

1. **Statement letters:** We will use capital Roman letters 'A', 'B', 'C' (etc.) to stand for *simple statements.*
2. **Punctuation symbols:** We will use parentheses, '(' and ')', and brackets, '[' and ']', for logical punctuation.
3. **Connective Symbols:** We will use the symbols '~', '∨', '&', '→', and '↔' for the truth-functional connectives 'it's not the case that', 'or', 'and', 'if . . . , then . . .', and 'if, and only if', respectively.

Like any other language, *SL* has certain grammatical rules for the production of meaningful statements. Perhaps paradoxically, however, it will be easier for us if we first look at examples of how to translate statements of English into *SL,* and later (in Section 2.5) talk about its grammar. Going from English into *SL* we will call 'symbolization'. In symbolizing an English statement, we do basically four things: (1) Paraphrase the statement in standard logical form, (2) replace distinct simple statements by distinct statement letters, (3) replace all truth-functional connectives by appropriate symbols, and (4) add any appropriate punctuation.

The simplest case of symbolization concerns a simple statement, like 'Professor Kitcher wrote a new book'. When we symbolize a statement like this one, we merely associate with it a statement letter, say, 'A'. When we do this, we always include a "dictionary" or, as we will say, a **statement key** that tells us which statement letter stands for which statement. In the case of this single statement, the statement key is just

A: Professor Kitcher wrote a new book.

This is just short for 'The statement letter 'A' stands for the statement 'Professor Kitcher wrote a new book''.

Now take a slightly more complicated case—say, the statement 'Sue loves Brian and Brian loves Sue'. In this statement, we distinguish two simple statements and one truth-functional connective, 'and' (i.e., a word expressing conjunction). First, we replace the simple statements by distinct statement letters, being sure to indicate an appropriate statement key. It is convenient to choose statement letters that suggest the simple statements they represent:

S: Sue loves Brian

B: Brian loves Sue.

In the end, of course, the choice of statement letters is arbitrary, except that you can't use the *same* letter to stand for *different* statements in the same symbolization. Take note, too, that these letters stand for *whole simple statements,* not just single words or names. Putting these letters in the appropriate places gives us

S and B.

Next, we replace 'and' by the sign for conjunction:

S & B.

Except in the case of statement letters and negations, we also require that some punctuation be added. This is done by putting parentheses or brackets around the whole statement:

(S & B).

The parentheses should be understood as exhibiting the fact that the whole string of symbols constitutes *one* whole compound statement. We'll say more about punctuation later.

Consider now the statement, 'If Marcel gets his way, then his dissertation will be about the philosophy of caring'. To symbolize this statement, we proceed exactly as in the previous cases. We assign distinct statement letters to the distinct simple statements contained in the whole compound statement, and then we replace the truth-functional connective by its appropriate symbol. Notice, however, that when we provide the statement key, we have to add a piece of information that is implicit, not explicit, in the original English:

M: Marcel gets his way

D: Marcel's dissertation will be about the philosophy of caring.

The missing piece is the word 'Marcel's' in the consequent of the English statement. Although we have no difficulty in recognizing that the pronoun 'his' in the consequent refers to Marcel, whose name was used in the antecedent, we must make this information *explicit* in the statement key. Each statement letter must stand for a statement that can be clearly recognized as definite with respect to truth value; in the statement key, that is, we try to "de-contextualize" each simple statement. Next, replacing statements by statement letters, we get

> If M, then D.

The symbol '$\rightarrow$' stands for the conditional. Putting this in, along with punctuation, gives us

> $(M \rightarrow D)$.

Although in this chapter we focus on connections between symbols and English, we will soon see that what matters most in logical analysis has less to do with the specific English statements associated with statement letters than it has to do with the *truth values* of those associated statements. More will be said about this in Chapter 3. In the remainder of this section, we consider the five connectives in turn. We indicate some of the many ways in which these truth-functional connectives are expressed in English (known as **stylistic variants**), as well as cases in which expressions that we use truth-functionally in logic are not being used that way in English. We go on in Section 2.4 to consider more complicated symbolization, and in the final section (2.5) we take up some of the formal details of *SL*.

Negation ('Not')

As we have noted, the truth-functional character of a negation is that it reverses the truth value of the statement to which it is applied. When used in English, in place of the rather cumbersome and formal 'it's not the case that p', we often see

> That p is false
> That p is denied
> It is false that p
> That p is not true
> It is not true that p.

All are statement forms whose symbolic representative is $\sim p$. For example,

> That John ate the last piece of pie is false
> It isn't true that I am over 1000 feet tall.

The first can be symbolized as '~J', and the second can be rendered '~O'. Of course, the above two English statements are also rather cumbersome forms of expression. It is more usual to employ devices that allow the negation to be integrated among the other words in a statement. Such is the case, for example, when we employ contractions:

Jack isn't nimble

Jack wasn't on time

Jack doesn't have money

Jack won't get out of bed

Jack hasn't any new clothes

Jack can't abide a dirty house

and so on . . .

When you find a denial buried inside a statement like this, your job (as a logic student) is to rethink the statement so that the denial is made open to plain view. This is done by distinguishing the denial from what is denied. In each of the above cases, we can extract the denial and prefix it to what remains. The object is to produce a restatement that makes the same assertion as the original but that has the advantage of letting us see clearly what the different components of the statement are and how they are connected. In the case of the preceding statements, this gives us

It is not the case that Jack is nimble

It is not the case that Jack was on time

It is not the case that Jack does have money

It is not the case that Jack will get out of bed

It is not the case that Jack has some new clothes

It is not the case that Jack can abide a dirty house

and so on . . .

When you go on to symbolize, the logical connective 'it is not the case that' is replaced by the negation symbol (*tilde*), '~' , and the simple statement that is negated is replaced by a statement letter. Choosing distinct letters for the six distinct simple statements above produces

~A

~B

~C

~D

~E

~F

and so on . . .

In this list, 'A' replaces the simple statement 'Jack is nimble', and so on for each of the capital statement letters.

Another bit of natural language that requires care to analyze is exemplified by the following:

Jack is unhappy.

Should we take the prefix 'un' to represent a negation? Answering this question correctly requires some thought and care. There are two possibilities: (1) The statement is simple, or (2) the statement is compound. If compound, the most reasonable possible reading would seem to be

It's not the case that Jack is happy,

which we'd symbolize as '~H', where

H: Jack is happy.

If we've got it right, then (using this statement key) '~H' makes the same assertion as 'Jack is unhappy'. However, this is not so. Imagine that Jack is unconscious. It would be true to say 'It's not the case that Jack is happy', but it would not be right to say 'Jack is unhappy'. In such a state it is more plausible to say that Jack is *neither* happy *nor* unhappy. Thus, we would be incorrect if we interpreted 'un' in this context to be the expression of a negation. Instead, the statement must be counted as truth-functionally *simple* and symbolized by a single statement letter:

U: Jack is unhappy.

Some caution is also in order for the prefix 'a' (as in 'amoral'). Although such caution is less needed with prefixes like 'im', 'in', and 'non', it is still worthwhile to carefully consider each such case on its own.

By contrast, in many cases interpreting a prefix like 'un' as an expression of negation is proper. An example is 'The dark side of the Moon is unexplored'. Here, we do have a case where the same assertion is made by pulling out a negation, to obtain

It's not the case that the dark side of the Moon has been explored.

In this case, the component is the simple statement 'The dark side of the Moon has been explored'. The statement is correctly symbolized as '~E'.

You might at this point start to really appreciate the need for the distinction (made in Section 1.3) between statements and propositions. The question of whether or not the symbolization of an English statement should contain a connective cannot in general be decided solely on the basis of what words or phrases occur in that statement. To make this determination we must understand what the English statement means. In the strict sense this amounts to understanding what *proposition* is being expressed.

Conjunction ('And')

We have already looked at the way negation works truth-functionally. As for conjunction, we note that there is only one way for a conjunction to be true: *Both* of its conjuncts must be true at once. In any other case a conjunction is false. This information will help us in many cases of analysis.

When we want to say of two or more things that they have a certain property in common, it is typical in English to streamline our statement of this fact. For example, instead of writing

(1) Nancy Cartwright is an important contemporary philosopher, and Margaret Wilson is an important contemporary philosopher

we would say or write

(2) Nancy Cartwright and Margaret Wilson are important contemporary philosophers.

In logic we're going to UNstreamline our statements—we're not going to be very poetic or elegant at all. Thus, when a statement such as (2) is found, we will rewrite it as a standard conjunction.

To see how the truth-functional character of conjunction helps us recognize that a statement is a conjunction, notice the following about the preceding examples. The truth of both (1) and (2) depends completely on the joint truth of

(3) Nancy Cartwright is an important contemporary philosopher

and

(4) Margaret Wilson is an important contemporary philosopher.

That is, the truth of (1) implies the truth of (3) and (4), as does the truth of (2). Conversely, the joint truth of (3) and (4) implies the truth of both (1) and (2). We thus see that the truth or falsity of (2) turns precisely on the joint truth of the two distinct statements (3) and (4). This tells us that (2) expresses a conjunction. In particular, it expresses the conjunction of the two statements on whose joint truth it depends.

There are many uses of 'and' in English that are not truth-functional. Such is the case with

Two and two equals four

Jack and Jill are a pair.

It wouldn't make much sense to interpret these as conjunctions and rewrite them as

Two equals four and two equals four

Jack is a pair, and Jill is a pair.

In the first case the word 'and' is used as a synonym for 'plus' or 'added to'. In the second statement the context reveals that the word 'and' is used not to conjoin two distinct statements, but to indicate that both people belong to a single collection.

Here is a list of some other English expressions often used to express conjunction:

Both p and q

p, but q

p, although q

Although p, q

p, however, q

p, in spite of the fact that q.

Some instances of the above are the folowing:

My house is blue, in spite of the fact that I hate blue

Although Alice has a car, she bought a bicycle

I did not get a grant; however, I will stay in school.

In these conjunctions the particular English words used as connectives help emphasize a *contrast* between what is asserted by each conjunct. For example, one might have thought it peculiar that a person who has a car should buy a bicycle. Use of the word 'although' in the second statement suggests this belief. But in logic this is an aspect of the statement that we generally ignore. When we interpret such statements, we ask ourselves, "If this compound were true, what could we say about the truth of its components, and vice versa?" Working to answer such a question in a given case helps decide whether or not a particular statement expresses a truth–functional compound.

Disjunction ('Or')

The truth–functional character of a disjunction is this: A disjunction is true whenever *at least* one of its disjuncts is true. A disjunction is false *only* when both disjuncts are false. This is called the 'inclusive' sense of disjunction, upon which we'll comment in the next chapter. When an assertion of the form

p or q

is made, it is to be understood as the assertion that at least one of the two statements, p and q, is true and that possibly both are true.

Just as in the case of conjunctions, disjunctions can be expressed in more streamlined fashion than in our logical idiom. Thus, instead of

I will buy an Apple computer, or I will buy an IBM computer

a more likely statement would be

I will buy an Apple or IBM computer.

As with conjunction our job is to unpack such condensed talk. Thus, the symbolization of both of these is '$(A \lor I)$', where

    A: I will buy an Apple computer

    I: I will buy an IBM computer.

Some typical expressions for disjunction are the following:

Either p or q

p, alternatively, q

p unless q.

We say more about 'unless' in Section 2.4.

Conditional ('If . . . , Then . . .')

The only case in which a statement of the form 'If p, then q' is false is when p is true and q is false simultaneously; in any other case the conditional statement is true. The justification for this way of looking at this connective is somewhat more involved than the previous three. More will be said about the truth-functional status of the conditional in the next chapter. Here, let's focus on wording that is typically used to express the conditional in English. The following partial list contains expressions that are equivalents to 'If p, then q':

> p only if q
>
> q, if p ~~antecedent~~ $p \rightarrow q$
>
> If p, q
>
> On condition that p, q
>
> q, whenever p
>
> Only if q, p.

Symbolically, each of these would be represented as $(p \rightarrow q)$. Of these expressions, some typically cause initial confusion for beginning logic students. Three in particular are 'p only if q', 'only if q, p', and 'q, if p'.

We begin by emphasizing that the word 'if' can usually be relied on to introduce (i.e., come in front of) the *antecedent* of a conditional. This is the statement that, when symbolized, goes to the *left* of the arrow. Thus, the two expressions

> Abhi will be happy if he gets to sleep late

and

> If Abhi gets to sleep late, he will be happy

express the *same* proposition and are *both* symbolized by '(S $\rightarrow$ H)', where

> S: Abhi gets to sleep late
>
> H: Abhi will be happy.

However, there is a special case in which 'if' does not introduce the antecedent of the conditional. This is when 'if' appears as part of the phrase 'only if'.

In this case, 'only if', as a single unit, introduces the *consequent* of a conditional. That means, for example, that the statement

Abhi will be happy only if he gets to sleep late

must be symbolized as '(H → S)', using the statement key just given. To see that this really is how 'only if' is best understood, an example will help. Let's consider this statement:

(1) Francis has herpes only if Francis was exposed to herpes.

This statement is a conditional. Our question, however, is, Which of the two following more explicit conditionals is correct? In other words, which one has it right about antecedent and consequent?

(2) If Francis has herpes, then Francis was exposed to herpes
(3) If Francis was exposed to herpes, then Francis has herpes.

To decide, notice that, whoever Francis is, the statement 'Francis has herpes only if Francis was exposed to herpes' must be *true,* since it is a medical fact that no person can have herpes unless she or he were first exposed to it. Next, notice that (2) must also be true. However, (3) is *not* medically true: it is quite possible that Francis was *exposed* to herpes without actually *getting* herpes. Thus, the truth of (1) does not entail the truth of (3). Thus, these two statements do not express the same proposition. Since (2) is the only alternative, (2) must be the correct paraphrase. Letting 'H' stand for 'Francis has herpes' and 'E' stand for 'Francis was exposed to herpes', the symbolization is '(H → E)'.[5]

You may have wondered why we didn't use the double arrow, '↔', here. The double arrow, representing the biconditional, is read 'if, and only if'. Although 'only if' might sometimes be used by people who mean to assert the biconditional relationship, there are a couple of reasons for not treating 'only if' in this way. For one thing, 'if, and only if' should be recognized for what it is: a *combination* of 'if' and 'only if'. When a statement of the form '*p* if, and only if, *q*' is asserted, it should be understood as a conditional in 'two directions'. That is, it should be understood to mean the conjunction of 'if *q*, then *p*' with '*p* only if *q*':

---

[5]The discussion of statements (1), (2), and (3) in fact relies on some subtleties that are not in evidence. Notice that we speak of the fact that statement (1) *must* be true, not merely that it *is* true. Though detailed consideration of these and related issues would take us far afield, see also the brief comments on the differences between 'if *p,* then *q*' and '*p* implies *q*' in the following discussion.

Both *p, if q,* and *p only if q.*

Symbolically, that's [(*q* → *p*) & (*p* → *q*)], but we'll come to that later. A second argument for keeping the distinction between 'only if' and 'if, and only if' is this:

1. '*p* only if *q*' *always* means *at least* 'if *p*, then *q*'
2. '*p* only if *q*' *never* means *only* 'if *q*, then *p*'.

Thus,

3. By rendering '*p* only if *q*' as 'if *p*, then *q*', we will always get at least part of the meaning right, without including too much.

Another useful point connected with the conditional is that conditional statements are often used to assert necessary and sufficient conditions. A **necessary condition** is something that *must* be the case in order for something else to be the case; that is, the necessary condition is *presupposed* by the other. For example, since combustion can't occur unless oxygen is present, the presence of oxygen is a *necessary condition* for combustion. In logic this fact can be represented by putting the statement expressing the necessary condition in the consequent position of a conditional. In this case we would write

If there is combustion, then there is oxygen

(symbolically, '(C → O)'). Notice that this helps us recognize the consequent of the conditional considered on page 46. In the statement 'Francis has herpes only if Francis was exposed to herpes', our knowledge that being exposed to herpes is a necessary condition for getting it tells us that the conditional's consequent must be 'Francis was exposed to herpes'. On the other hand, having oxygen present is not *sufficient* for combustion.

A statement expresses a **sufficient condition** if its being true would be enough to make another statement true. For example, since receiving an A is a sufficient condition for passing a course, the statement 'Raymond got an A in Latin' expresses a sufficient condition for 'Raymond passed Latin'. In logic, sufficiency is represented by putting the statement expressing the sufficient condition in the *antecedent* position of a conditional. In this case we would write

If Raymond got an A in Latin, then Raymond passed Latin

or '(A → P)'. Notice the difference between necessity and sufficiency. Getting an A is sufficient, but not necessary, for passing a course. The presence of oxygen is a necessary, but not sufficient, condition for combustion.

The concepts of necessity and sufficiency can be used to help analyze statements recognized to be conditionals. This is because, as noted above, conditionals are often used to express just this relationship. Of course, it's not a foolproof guide. If someone actually asserted 'If there is oxygen, then there is combustion', she or he would have reversed the nature of the actual physical relationship between oxygen and combustion; we would be wrong in such an explicitly expressed case to rewrite the statement with antecedent and consequent in reverse order. On the other hand, when the language of sufficiency and necessity is used, this talk can be symbolized using the conditional. Thus, the statements

> For Ratso to be happy, it is necessary that he have dinner
>
> For Ratso to be happy, it is sufficient that he have dinner

should be interpreted, respectively, as

> If Ratso is happy, then he has dinner
>
> If Ratso has dinner, then he is happy.

Letting 'R' stand for 'Ratso is happy' and 'D' stand for 'Ratso has dinner', we get the symbolic versions, respectively:

> $(R \rightarrow D)$
>
> $(D \rightarrow R)$.

Finally, the words 'implies' and 'entails' are often used as expressions of the conditional relationship. In our text we will avoid these uses. Although this isn't the place for an extended discussion, it is worthwhile to make a few remarks concerning these words. We will refer to the word 'implies' in our brief remarks and note that similar remarks apply to the word 'entails'.

In our text, we use the word 'implies' only in connection with the validity relationship. Specifically, to say

> '(A & B)' implies 'A'

means

> '(A & B) / ∴ A' is a valid argument.

Or, to put it another way, implication is the relationship in which the premises of a valid argument stand to the conclusion. When statements are related in this way, it is sometimes said that the premises **strictly imply** (or **logically imply**) the conclusion.[6] Strict implication is contrasted with **material implication,** which is the name typically given to the connection between statements expressed by our arrow symbol. In fact, if one statement, *p*, strictly implies another, *q,* it follows that the statement $(p \rightarrow q)$ is *true.* However, if $(p \rightarrow q)$ is *true,* it does *not* necessarily follow that *p* strictly implies *q*. More will be said of this in Chapter 3.

The history of logic is filled with discussion and debate on this topic. Some philosophers have claimed that imprecise use of the word 'implication' has produced confusion and incorrect logical theory. They argue that the relation called 'material implication' is not an implication relation at all, since such an "implication" can be true even if the antecedent and consequent of the conditional bear no logical relationship to one another. Just as with the other statement connectives we have discussed, the relationship expressed by '→' is a truth-functional relation, and (as we discuss in Chapter 3) if two arbitrarily selected statements *p* and *q* are true, then the statement $(p \rightarrow q)$ is true as well. So, for instance, if 'B' symbolizes the (true) statement 'Joe Bessie is a philosopher' and 'G' symbolizes the (true) statement 'Stuart Glennan is a philosopher', then the conditional '(B → G)' is true, even though the fact that Joe Bessie is a philosopher in no way implies that Stuart Glennan is a philosopher.

In our text we use 'implication' only to refer to what was just called 'strict implication'—that is, the relation between the premises and conclusion of a valid argument. We refer to the relationship expressed by the arrow as the **material conditional.**

The question of which conditional statements in ordinary language are appropriately understood as material conditionals is a subject of considerable philosophical debate. For example, in some circumstances the terms 'necessary' and 'sufficient' are used to represent a relationship other than that of the material conditional, such as the relationship of strict implication.[7] Fortunately, we can generally ignore this problem and interpret most ordinary-language conditionals as material conditionals. As an example, the word 'implies' is often used in a sense

---

[6]Notice that there is also a grammatical difference between use of the word 'implies' and the conditional: To be properly formed, the statements that flank the word 'implies' must occur within quotation marks, whereas this is not the case when we use the conditional. A discussion of this point can be found in Quine's *Methods of Logic* (see Appendix 1). On the other hand, if one wants to express implication as a statement connective, the usual sign for strict implication is the fishhook, ' ⥽'. Statements of the form $(p \unlhd q)$ can be read '*p* strictly implies *q*'. A statement of the form $(p \unlhd q)$ is true just in case the argument '*p* / ∴ *q*' is deductively valid. It is also usual to equate $(p \unlhd q)$ with $\Box(p \rightarrow q)$, which is read 'It is necessarily true that if *p*, then *q*'.

[7]There are, besides strict conditionals and material conditionals, a number of other types of conditional statements. We discuss some of these briefly in Chapter 3, and again in Chapter 9.

that can safely be *interpreted* as the 'if . . . , then . . . ' of the material conditional. Thus, for example, the statement

(1) That Ratso has eaten implies that Ratso is happy

might, without any harm done, be taken as equivalent in meaning to the statement

(2) If Ratso has eaten, then Ratso is happy.

To be technically precise, however, we should note that statement (1) strictly implies statement (2), but statement (2) does not strictly imply statement (1). This is what is meant by saying that statement (1) is *logically stronger* than statement (2). It is for this reason that not too much harm is done in rendering (1) as (2). The main point is that, from our point of view, the two expressions have very different meanings. Discussion of the conditional's truth-functional meaning will be given more attention in the next chapter.

Biconditional ('If, and Only If')

One rarely sees the biconditional in any form other than that in which it is given in the section title, although a couple of other useful forms are the following:

p just in case *q*

p when, and only when, *q*.

It is also standard practice in logic and mathematics to abbreviate the English 'if, and only if' with the expression 'iff', as in '*p* iff *q*'.

Truth-functionally, a biconditional is true when both conditions have the same truth value. To make a statement of the form '*p* if, and only if, *q*' is to assert '*p* and *q* are either both true or both false'. So, for example, the statement

The frogs are happy if, and only if, the pond is above freezing

is to be understood as

Either the frogs are happy and the pond is above freezing, or the frogs are not happy and the pond is not above freezing.

It is also important to recognize, as was pointed out in the section on the conditional, that the biconditional is simply the conjunction of two conditionals. Thus, the biconditional above is also properly read as

If the frogs are happy, then the pond is above freezing; and if the pond is above freezing, then the frogs are happy.

Notice that this last point implies that the biconditional can be used to assert that one statement is *both* necessary *and* sufficient for another. Using the language of necessity and sufficiency, our biconditional can be put this way:

The frogs' happiness is both necessary and sufficient for the pond's being above freezing,

or, equivalently,

The pond's being above freezing is both necessary and sufficient for the frogs' being happy.

All these English statements can be symbolized by the symbolic statement '(C ↔ A)', where 'C' stands for 'The frogs are happy' and 'A' stands for 'The pond is above freezing'. It is important to note that the double arrow, '↔', does not represent bi-*implication*. The double arrow is usually referred to as the **material biconditional** (or **material equivalence**). Just as we do not take the arrow to stand for strict implication, neither do we take the double arrow to stand for strict bi-implication.[8]

Another important function of the biconditional is in giving a definition. In fact, starting with the next chapter, we will begin using this idiom to give definitions. Because we are developing a language of connectives with very precise meaning, it is especially useful to have available an unambiguous idiom for the introduction of new words or expressions. For example, the biconditional can be used to give the definition of validity:

> ***Definition*** An argument is **deductively valid** if, and only if, that argument could not possibly have all true premises but a false conclusion.

Although the biconditional used in this statement is truth-functional, we cannot adequately symbolize the definition in *SL*. This is because, despite appearances, the statement as a whole is not really a biconditional at all, even though it makes use of the biconditional connective. That is, the statement cannot be correctly represented as a biconditional of two separate statements: The two apparent conditions

---

[8]Strict bi-implication, or **strict equivalence,** is sometimes represented by the symbol '=', and the statement form '($p = q$)' ('p is strictly equivalent to q') can be equated with the statement form '□(p ↔ q)', where the '□' is the sign of necessity.

employ a kind of cross–reference whose formal representation requires a more so-
phisticated logical language than *SL*. Beginning in Chapter 5 we will introduce a
language, more powerful than *SL,* that will allow us to correctly analyze statements
like this one.

Exercises for Section 2.3

Symbolization   Below are listed a number of compound statements. Provide a
statement key for each one in which you assign statement letters to the simple
components and then symbolize the statement in *SL.*

1. I didn't go to the Moon yesterday.

2. It's false that I went to the Moon yesterday.

♦ 3. Arnold has not had a bath in the last ten years.

4. I deny that I have eaten the last banana.

5. It is impossible to travel backward in time.

6. Socrates' argument is invalid.

7. There is no computable utility function.

8. Inkyo won't wear socks.

♦ 9. Betsy and Alex have spouses.

10. Both Betty and Bob are macabre.

11. Betty and Bob are both macabre.

12. Tom is six foot two, eyes of blue.

13. Although smoking is permitted, no one is smoking.

14. We have free will, even though God knows everything we're going to do.

15. Women and men have both studied logic.

16. The first little piggy had roast beef, but the second little piggy had none.

17. Either the cat or the mice are away.

18. At least one of the two, Sylvia and Sally, is going to show up at the party.

♦ 19. The alternatives are these: You go to work, or you call in sick.

20. You have won either a million dollars or a faux diamond necklace.

21. My cat or my dog ate my shoes.

22. If smoking is allowed, then I'm leaving.

23. Creationism is a good theory only if all good theories are naively falsifiable.

24. Music is necessary for Bernice to really enjoy life. B $\rightarrow$ M

◆25. In order for Lenny to get into the show, it's necessary for him to produce a ticket. $T \rightarrow S$

26. For Ratso to solve the equation, it is sufficient that he understand Maxwell's equations for electromagnetism. $R \rightarrow E$

27. Annie will solve the problem before Ratso, if Ratso tries to use linear regression analysis.

28. A sufficient condition for the existence of miracles is the fact that Omnipotent Olivia has the power to change the laws of physics.

29. Only if Lovely promises undying passion will Candice reconsider the proposal of marriage.

30. Lovely's promise of undying passion is both necessary and sufficient for Candice to reconsider the proposal of marriage.

◆31. The mice will play just in case the cat's away.

32. Either tachyons exist and there are faster-than-light particles or neither are there tachyons nor faster-than-light particles. $(T \mathbin{\&} F) \lor (\sim T \mathbin{\&} \sim F)$

33. I will allow you to read the comics if, and only if, you give me the front page.

2.4 Symbolizing More Complex Statements and Arguments

In the previous section we considered symbolizing statements that contain at most one logical connective. We saw how to replace a simple statement by a statement letter, how to turn a negated simple statement into a tilde followed by a statement letter, and so on for the other truth-functional connectives. In general, however, statements are more complicated than this; often they involve more than two simple statements connected by more than one connective. Consider this statement, for example:

(1) If Norma and Robert wear ribbons, then Jason wears his yellow hat.

This statement expresses a connection among three simple statements:

Norma wears ribbons

Robert wears ribbons

Jason wears his yellow hat.

In particular this statement is a conditional of the form 'if p, then q'. But in this statement, the antecedent is

Norma and Robert wear ribbons

which is itself a compound statement. It expresses the conjunction of 'Norma wears ribbons' with 'Robert wears ribbons'. Rephrasing (1) in our standard form and replacing the three simple statements by the letters 'N', 'R', and 'J', respectively, we get

If N and R, then J.

Replacing the remaining English by symbols and adding parentheses gives us

(2) (N & R → J).

But this last statement is ambiguous: without the punctuation that is present in the English (i.e., the word 'both' and the comma), it is not clear whether this symbolic statement expresses (a) the *conjunction* of the statement 'N' with the statement '(R → J)' or (b) the *conditional* whose antecedent is the statement '(N & R)' and whose consequent is 'J'. To put this another way, if you were just given the string of symbols (2) along with the statement key, you could not determine whether it was a symbolization of (1) or a symbolization of

(3) Norma wears ribbons, and if Robert wears ribbons, then Jason wears his yellow hat.

This is why we insist that parentheses be used to indicate a whole compound statement. To indicate that the statement

Norma wears ribbons and Robert wears ribbons

as a *whole* is the antecedent of the conditional, we use parentheses like this:

((N & R) → J).

This allows us to show that the *form* (i.e., the "logical shape") of the statement is $(p → q)$, not $(p \& q)$.

The situation here is analogous to that in arithmetic. For example, the expression

$2 \times (3 + 6)$

has a different numerical value than the expression

$(2 \times 3) + 6.$

The first one is a product, and the second is a sum. To find the value of the first expression, we first add six to three and then multiply the result by two. This gives eighteen. In the second case we first multiply two times three and then add six. This gives twelve. Similarly, use of the parentheses in the symbolic statement '((N & R) → J)' makes a different assertion than the statement

$(N \& (R \to J)),$

which is the symbolization of statement (3) above. Whereas in arithmetic the placement of parentheses can affect the numerical value of the expression, in *SL* the placement of parentheses can affect the *truth* value.

Each symbolic statement must be completely unambiguous with respect to logical form. Notice that a negation is the denial of *a* statement (but not necessarily of a *simple* statement). A conjunction is a connection between exactly *two* statements (but, again, not necessarily between two *simple* statements). In the case of negation, the statement that is denied might be a compound statement—but it is *one* statement nevertheless. Similarly, although two compound statements might be in conjunction, it is still exactly *two* compound statements that are in conjunction. Negation is called a **one-place** (also 'unary' or 'monadic') connective, and the rest are called **two-place** (or 'binary' or 'diadic') connectives. In any symbolic expression it must always be evident whether a statement is a negation, a conjunction, a disjunction, a conditional, a biconditional, or simple.

Let's work through some examples. Consider the following statement:

(4) Neither Kant nor Mill was completely right about ethics.

It is apparent that this statement contains two simple components:

K: Kant was completely right about ethics
M: Mill was completely right about ethics.

An expression 'neither *p* nor *q*' can be understood in two equivalent ways. Perhaps the easiest is to understand 'neither' to mean 'it's not the case that' and to take 'nor' as 'and it's not the case that'—that is, as 'not *p* and not *q*'. Then,

Neither K nor M

becomes

It's not the case that K and it's not the case that M,

that is,

(~K & ~M).

Thus, 'neither *p* nor *q*' expresses the *conjunction* of two negations.

A second, equivalent way to understand 'neither *p* nor *q*' is to read it as 'it's not the case that either *p* or *q*' (remembered perhaps by thinking of the 'ne' in 'neither' as suggesting '*not either*'). In the case we are considering, this would give us

It's not the case that either K or M.

Notice that this statement is the denial (negation) of a disjunction; that is, the whole disjunction 'either K or M' is being negated. To show this symbolically the disjunction that is negated is surrounded by parentheses, and the tilde is prefixed to the result:

~(K ∨ M).

We have a general rule for understanding exactly what the symbolic negation covers:

> **Definition**   In any symbolic statement, a negation applies to *the short-est string of symbols immediately following it that is a statement.* This statement following the negation sign is called the **scope** of the negation.

Thus, we can tell that the scope of the negation in '~(K ∨ M)' must be the statement '(K ∨ M)', because none of '(', '(K', '(K ∨', nor '(K ∨ M' are statements. The shortest string of symbols immediately following '~' that is a statement is just the string '(K ∨ M)'. The statement '~(K ∨ M)' is a quite different statement than

(~K ∨ M).

In this latter case, the shortest string of symbols immediately following the tilde that is a statement is just the statement letter 'K'. Hence, in this statement, just 'K' is the scope of the negation. Read back in English, this statement is

(5) Either Kant was not completely right about ethics, or Mill was completely right about ethics.

This is certainly a different assertion than our original English statement (4). Statement (5) leaves open the possibility that Mill was completely right about ethics, but statement (4) rules out this possibility.

Another example is the following:

(6) Combustion isn't possible unless oxygen is present.

The two simple statements contained in this are

C: Combustion is possible

O: Oxygen is present.

Making the replacement and symbolizing the negation, we get

(7) ~C unless O.

It is clear in the English and explicit in *SL* that the scope of the negation is just the statement 'C'. But how should we understand 'unless'? This word, like the expressions 'only if' and 'or', has a weaker and a stronger connotation. In logic it is usual to take the weaker sense, because we are then assured of getting at least part of the logical content without going too far. 'Unless', in its weaker sense, is synonymous with 'if it is not the case that' or, more briefly, with 'if not'. This gives us

~C if not O,

that is,

~C if ~O.

Since 'if' introduces the antecedent of a conditional, this gives us the symbolization of (7) as

$(\sim O \rightarrow \sim C)$.

In general, a statement of the form 'p unless q' can be rendered '$(\sim q \rightarrow p)$'. That having been said, however, it can be shown by the methods to be introduced in Chapter 3 that *any* statement of the form '$(\sim q \rightarrow p)$' is *equivalent* to a statement of the form '$(p \vee q)$'. This allows us to bypass the above and to use the much simpler route of merely putting the symbol '∨' in place of 'unless'. A perfectly acceptable alternative to '(~O → ~C)', therefore, is to change (7) into the somewhat easier to read and more economical

(8) (~C ∨ O).

Let's consider a longer statement, which was used at the start of this chapter:

If Ratso eats before Annie does, then Ratso will be happy and Annie will be unhappy; however, both cats will be fed at the same time.

There are four simple statements here, which we specify in the following statement key:

B: Ratso eats before Annie does
H: Ratso will be happy
U: Annie will be unhappy (Recall the remarks about 'un'!)
S: Both cats will be fed at the same time.

Replacing statements by statement letters in the original, we get

If B, then H and U; however, S.

In this case you need to recognize that the semicolon (';'), together with 'however', represents a strong logical break between components of the statement. The statement to the left is one component; the statement to the right of these is the other. The semicolon functions in English as a sign of conjunction. Thus, we put the conjunction into standard form (i.e., insert 'and' between the relevant statements) and add appropriate punctuation to show exactly what the two conjuncts are:

((If B, then H and U) and S).

The left-hand conjunct is '(If B, then H and U)', and the right-hand conjunct is 'S'. The comma in the left-hand conjunct is also used, though of course not exclusively, to indicate logical grouping—in this case between 'B' and 'H and U'. As usual, 'if' introduces an antecedent—in this case 'B'. Thus, putting in the rest of the symbols and parentheses,

(9) ((B → (H & U)) & S).

Finally, after all our discussion about the importance of parentheses, we can adopt a convention of convenience. If a statement is a conjunction, disjunction, conditional, or biconditional, the outermost parentheses may be removed. They will be understood to be present implicitly. For instance, we may rewrite statement (9) as

(10) (B → (H & U)) & S.

The statement is still a conjunction, with the same left- and right-hand conjuncts as when the parentheses were present. We can adopt this convention because, as long as we confine ourself to the outermost parentheses, no ambiguity can result from removing them.

The reason that we can drop parentheses only for conjunctions, disjunctions, conditionals, or biconditionals is illustrated by the following example. The statement '~(A & B)' is the denial of a conjunction, and it is true just in case 'A' and 'B' are not both true. If we took the parentheses away, we'd be left with '~A & B', which makes an entirely different statement than the original. *Now* we have a conjunction whose left-hand conjunct is denied.

Another interesting case for symbolization has to do with the expressions 'at least' and 'at most'. Recall that in the brief remarks about the disjunction's truth conditions, it was stated that a disjunction is true whenever at least one of its disjuncts is true. What this means is that a statement like the following

(11) At least one of the pair, Bill and Tracy, will come to the party

can be symbolized as

(12) (B ∨ T),

where 'B' stands for 'Bill will come to the party' and 'T' stands for 'Tracy will come to the party'. Notice that the phrase 'at least one of the pair' in (11) would be incompatible with a reading of the word 'and' as a conjunction. The only sensible way to read 'and' in this context is as a device for referring collectively to the couple who form the pair in question, not as a word that connects whole statements.

Now notice what happens when we add '~(B & T)':

(13) (B ∨ T) & ~(B & T).

This symbolic statement, translated into English, is

> At least one of the pair, Bill and Tracy, will come to the party, but they won't both come to the party.

The left-hand conjunct of (13) may be understood roughly as "at least one of the statements 'B' and 'T' is true," while the right-hand conjunct may loosely be understood as "at most one of the two statements 'B' and 'T' is true." Thus, by conjoining 'at least one' to 'at most one', we obtain the result 'exactly one'; that is, the assertion of statement (13) is the assertion that exactly one of the two people, Bill and Tracy, will come to the party.[9]

This idea can be multiplied. For example, the following statement is true just in case exactly *two* of the three statements, 'A', 'B', and 'C', are true:

$$[(A \& B) \lor ((A \& C) \lor (B \& C))] \& \sim[A \& (B \& C)].$$

The left-hand conjunct "says" that at least one pair of statements is true, whereas the right-hand conjunct "says" that they're not all true. (Notice how the use of brackets helps make a statement containing many punctuation symbols easier to read. Notice also that the binary (two-place) nature of the connectives is always made explicit by the use of logical punctuation.)

Probably the most difficult part of symbolizing English involves the identification of the logical form of the statement. If a statement is ambiguous in English, then you should go ahead and put it into the various forms it could take. This is in fact one of the virtues of the symbolization process. Statements that are ambiguous in English can have their ambiguity clearly demonstrated in *SL*. For example, the statement

It's not true that I have ten cents and you have two cents

is potentially ambiguous. This statement can be used to make *two* distinct assertions, depending on how, when, and where it is uttered. Notice that this could either be a *conjunction* with a negated left-hand conjunct or a *negated* conjunction:

$$(\sim A \& B) \qquad \sim(A \& B),$$

where 'A' is 'I have ten cents' and 'B' is 'you have two cents'. Using *SL*, the ambiguity can be seen at a glance by comparing the two symbolizations. As the technique

---

[9]Yet another perfectly acceptable symbolization is this: $(B \& \sim T) \lor (T \& \sim B)$. As the symbolic language becomes more familiar to you, many syntactically different but semantically equivalent symbolizations can be discerned just by thinking about the case in question.

becomes familiar to you, you will acquire some ease in going from English into symbols and back.

We will finish this section by saying something about how to symbolize arguments. The real trick has already been discussed: Symbolizing an argument amounts basically to symbolizing the statements from which it has been built. To complete the task we then arrange the statements in our standard argument format. A simple example is the following:

> Hydrogen and oxygen don't both exist on Earth. Since oxygen does exist on Earth, it follows that hydrogen does not.

In standard format

> Hydrogen and oxygen don't both exist on Earth
> Oxygen does exist on Earth
> _____
> ∴ Hydrogen does not exist on Earth.

The conclusion indicator, 'it follows that', is symbolized in the usual way by the three dots. Our next move is to symbolize the statements remaining in the argument:

> H: Hydrogen exists on Earth
> O: Oxygen exists on Earth.

This allows us to write:

> ~(H & O)
> O
> _____
> ∴ ~H

As a final example, let's use argument (C) from Section 1.1:

> If Laplace is correct, then all actions are predetermined and we have no free will. If Laplace is not correct, and quantum mechanics is the correct theory of physical reality, then some of our actions occur purely by chance. However, if some of our actions occur purely by chance, then again we do not have free will. Thus, whether or not Laplace is correct, we do not have free will.

In standard format, we obtain

If Laplace is correct, then all actions are predetermined and we have no free will

If Laplace is not correct, and quantum mechanics is the correct theory of physical reality, then some actions occur purely by chance

If some of our actions occur purely by chance, then we do not have free will

∴ Whether or not Laplace is correct, we do not have free will.

The relevant statement key is

L: Laplace is correct

P: All actions are predetermined

F: We have free will

Q: Quantum mechanics is the correct theory of physical reality

C: Some of our actions occur purely by chance.

Although a partial symbolization is never a requirement, it is often helpful to construct one. This can help you see how the complete symbolization should go:

If L, then P and not F
If not L and Q, then C
If C, then not F

∴ Whether L or not L, not F.

Now we simply insert logical connectives and appropriate punctuation:

$L \rightarrow (P \& \sim F)$
$(\sim L \& Q) \rightarrow C$
$C \rightarrow \sim F$

∴ $(L \vee \sim L) \rightarrow \sim F$.

The conclusion could also have been written this way:

$(L \rightarrow \sim F) \& (\sim L \rightarrow \sim F),$

that is, 'If Laplace is right, we don't have free will; and if Laplace isn't right, we don't have free will'. Notice that, intuitively, this is equivalent to just '$\sim F$' by itself.

Exercises for Section 2.4

Part I: Symbolizing Statements   Below are statements whose symbolizations are somewhat more complex than those in Section 2.3. Provide a statement key for each and symbolize in *SL*.

$(\sim(A+L) + \star \vee (J)$

◆1. Andy and Luc will not both stay at the party, but at least one of them will.

2. Exactly one of the two, Luc and Andy, will stay at the party. $(\sim(A+L)$

3. Exactly two of the three, Luc, Andy, and Sam, will stay at the party.

4. Some, but not all, laws of physics are deterministic. $S \& \sim A$

◆5. The concept of an electromagnetic field should be introduced in physics only if the problems of wave–particle duality cannot be satisfactorily resolved.

6. Special relativity, but not quantum mechanics, is generally thought to be compatible with complete physical determinism.

7. Light isn't both a wave phenomenon and a particle phenomenon. $(\sim(W \& P)$

8. Although some existentialists are theists, Sartre was not a theist; he did believe, however, that faith plays a fundamental role in all our beliefs.

9. Heidegger's *Sein und Zeit* was possible only if Heidegger had first read and understood the works of Husserl. $P \rightarrow (R \& U)$

10. A person's hidden motives are often revealed by slips of the tongue, <u>and</u>, if this is so, we have good reason to try to interpret slips of the tongue.

◆11. If these two people can stay together only if they constantly fight, then it appears that the relationship isn't a good one and they should split up.

12. If Larson does not either deal with his hurt feelings or completely suppress them, he will not be able to function at all.

13. Unless I am mistaken, you have a large, multilegged creature crawling on your shoulder.

14. If Kate and William each win a karate title, then if Kelly competes this summer he will have a tough pair of challengers to face. $\sim (W \leftrightarrow N)$

◆15. It is not the case that war will occur if, and only if, there are nuclear weapons.

16. That war will occur if, and only if, there are nuclear weapons is a false statement.

17. If world peace will be achieved only if every country has equal power, then if Russia has nuclear missiles but China does not, peace will not be achieved.

Part II: Symbolizing Arguments   Below are several arguments. Provide a statement key for each one and give its *SL* symbolization in our standard format.

18. Although Sam is still full of energy, Luc is tired. If Luc is tired, then Sam can't have a good time. Thus, Sam can't have a good time.

♦19. Luc does not want to stay at the party. Luc will stay only if Sam will. Thus, if Sylvia has a good time only if Luc stays, then if Sam leaves Sylvia won't have a good time.

20. Coke and Pepsi are carbonated drinks. Carbonated drinks upset Martin's stomach. Thus, Martin's stomach will be upset, if he drinks Coke or Pepsi.

21. If Martin drinks both Coke and Pepsi, he falls asleep; if he drinks only one of them, he burps a lot. If Martin burps a lot, Maurice is disgusted. Thus, Maurice is disgusted only if Martin does not drink both Coke and Pepsi.

22. If the mockingbird won't sing, then I'll buy you a diamond ring. If the diamond ring turns brass, then I'll buy you a looking glass. If that looking glass gets broke, then I'll by you a billy goat. If that billy goat takes logic, then it's a pretty smart goat. So, since the mockingbird won't sing, that goat is a pretty smart goat.

♦23. Either everyone will be allowed to go or someone will not be allowed to go. If everyone is allowed to go, then Lisa will go; but if someone is not allowed to go, Lisa will stay here. Since everyone is allowed to go, Lisa will go.

24. If William does his homework before ten o'clock, then he watches television. If William watches television, then he will see images of violence and advertising. Thus, if William finishes his homework by ten o'clock, he will see images of advertising.

25. If there is a nuclear war, then it will be started either by the United States or by Russia. But neither of these countries will start a nuclear war. Hence, there will be no nuclear war.

26. The game will be won if, and only if, Samson is allowed to play. But Samson is tied up for a while, and if he's tied up he won't be allowed to play. Thus, the game will not be won.

27. The concert will be given outside, unless there is rain. If there is rain, the concert will be held in the auditorium. Unless the concert is held in the auditorium, many people will stay home. If many people stay home, the concert won't be well attended. Thus, the concert will be well attended only if it rains.

28. If Einar opens his diner, called 'The Forty-Niner', there will be no finer food, and Del will have a real choice for dining out. If Einar does not open his diner, called 'The Forty-Niner', then Hoggy Diner will be the best buy for fast food. But Hoggy Diner fast food isn't very good and does not give Del a real choice for dining out. Del won't stay around if she has no real choice for dining out. Thus, unless Einar opens his diner, Del won't stay around.

♦29. When Annie swats Ratso, Ratso appears to cower. Sylvia worries that Ratso is being psychologically stunted only if he appears to cower. However, when Ratso realizes he's a third larger than Annie, he will neither cower nor appear to cower. At that time, Annie won't swat Ratso. Consequently, Sylvia will not worry that Ratso is being psychologically stunted.

30. Neither utilitarianism nor Kantianism is the best ethical theory. However, we can't live without an ethical theory. Thus, if we live with an ethical theory, it will not be the best ethical theory if it is utilitarianism or Kantianism.

31. If ethical relativism is true, then there are no objective moral values. If Kantianism is true, then there are objective moral values. Since these two theories are not both true at once, it follows that if there are objective moral values but Kantianism is false, then some other ethical theory must be true.

32. Exercise 32 is a valid argument if, and only if, it is not the case that its premises are simultaneously true while its conclusion is false. Unfortunately, this argument has a false conclusion and premises that are simultaneously true. Therefore, Exercise 32 is not a valid argument.

2.5   Spelling It Out Formally

The preceding discussions have been motivated by a desire to highlight the ways in which the symbolic language *SL* coincides with ordinary English. However, it is now time to spell out in more systematic detail the symbols and grammar of this artificial language. This section introduces you to the study of systems of symbolic logic as a theoretical enterprise in its own right.

First, *SL* contains an *infinite* list of symbols called **statement letters:**

A, B, C, . . . , Z, A_1, B_1, . . . , Z_1, A_2, B_2, . . .

The reason for having an infinitely long list is theoretical: There are an infinite number of distinct simple statements. Hence, from a theoretical standpoint we make available an infinite number of symbols to stand for as many statements as we would ever wish to represent.

Next, we have a collection of **logical symbols** used to represent the truth-functional connectives:

$\sim$ & $\vee$ $\rightarrow$ $\leftrightarrow$

As we have already seen, the standard way to read each of these symbols, from left to right, is 'not', 'and', 'or', 'if . . . , then . . .', and 'if, and only if'.

Finally, we add four **punctuation symbols:**

(   )   [   ]

As indicated in the previous section, these symbols are used to group other symbols in order to avoid ambiguity.[10]

Now that we have listed all the symbols of our language *SL,* we need to say exactly what its grammar is. We do this by stating precisely what it means for a string of symbols to be an **SL statement:**

Definition

1. All statement letters are **SL statements** (i.e., all capital Roman letters, with or without subscript, are *SL* statements).

2. Let *p* and *q* be any *SL* statements at all. Then, the following are also **SL statements**:

   a. ~*p*

   b. (*p* & *q*)

   c. (*p* ∨ *q*)

   d. (*p* → *q*)

   e. (*p* ↔ *q*)

3. Nothing except what follows from (1) and (2) is an *SL* statement, save that left and right brackets may be used in place of left and right parentheses, respectively.

This definition gives the grammar (or **syntax**) of *SL*—it tells you how to write syntactically correct statements of this language.[11] Just as the rules of grammar tell you, for example, that 'Jack is tall' is a statement of the English language but that 'is tall Jack' is not, this definition tells us that '(A → (B & C))' is an *SL* statement but that '~) & BA' is not. In this particular case it's because the first string of symbols can be constructed by following rules (1) and (2), but the second string of symbols cannot be so constructed. Since the second string cannot be constructed by following rules (1) and (2), we infer from clause (3) that the second string is not an

---

[10]If you are using the program Inference Engine that accompanies this text, note that it does not allow subscripts larger than 255 or the use of square brackets.

[11]In many systems of symbolic logic, a correctly formed statement is called a **well-formed formula,** usually abbreviated 'wff'. This type of definition—in which first the simplest objects satisfying the definition are given and then rules are included for generating more complex cases—is called a **recursive** definition. Clause (1) is the **basis** clause, (2) is the **recursion** clause, and (3) is the **closure** clause. Clauses (1) and (2) tell you what sorts of objects *are SL* statements, whereas clause (3) tells you what sorts of objects are *not SL* statements.

SL statement. Here is how we would move step by step to construct the first string, according to the rules:

1. By clause (1) of the definition, 'A', 'B', and 'C' are all *SL* statements.

2. By clause (2), any two *SL* statements with the sign '&' between them, with the whole thing surrounded by parentheses, is an *SL* statement. Since 'B' and 'C' are statements, it thus follows that '(B & C)' is a statement.

3. By clause (2), again, and the fact that 'A' and '(B & C)' are *SL* statements, it follows that '(A → (B & C))' is an *SL* statement.

Our general principle for symbolization is this: When you symbolize an English statement, except for our informal convention about outermost parentheses, the symbolic statement *must* be formed according to the rules in the previous definition. Doing so produces unambiguous symbolic statements. Let's look at this more closely.

Though we have a convention that allows outermost parentheses (or brackets) on a statement to be dropped, this convention cannot be used on a statement until the statement has been fully constructed. Notice that if we left the parentheses off of the symbolic statement forms in the definition (clauses 2a–2e), the definition would allow us to construct ambiguous statements. When a compound statement is constructed strictly according to the definition (i.e., without the convention that allows omission of parentheses), the resulting *SL* statement will be an instance of *exactly one* of the following five statement forms:

$\sim p$
$(p \mathbin{\&} q)$
$(p \lor q)$
$(p \to q)$
$(p \leftrightarrow q)$.

To say that a symbolic statement is an **instance** of one of these forms means that the symbolic statement can be obtained from one of these forms by substituting appropriate *SL* statements for p and q. When a statement is an instance of the first form, we say that the statement is a **negation,** and we say that the statement's **main connective** is the tilde. Similarly, any instance of the second form is referred to as a **conjunction,** and we say that its main connective is the ampersand. Instances of the other statement forms are described analogously.

As an example of this, consider that *all* of the following statements are examples of conjunctions, because each can be obtained from the form '$(p \mathbin{\&} q)$' by making the right substitutions:

((B → (U & A)) & S)

((B ∨ T) & ~(B & T))

([[(A & B) ∨ ((A & C) ∨ (B & C))] & ~[A & (B & C)]]).

If you replaced '*p*' by the statement '(B → (U & A))' and '*q*' by the statement 'S' in the form '(*p* & *q*)', you would get the first statement. Similarly, appropriately replacing '*p*' and '*q*' by statements in the form for conjunction will produce the other two statements. In each case we identify the sign for conjunction ('&') as the *main connective*. Observe that there is no possible way to replace '*p*' and '*q*' in the other statement forms that will produce these three *SL* statements. This fact is quite significant. Each and every compound *SL* statement has one, and only one, of the five truth-functional forms.

Here is a brief review of the procedure for symbolizing English. Given any statement of English,

1. *Identify the logical form of the statement.* This means you must decide whether the statement is simple, a negation, a conjunction, a disjunction, a conditional, or a biconditional. You will in general have to rethink the statement and paraphrase it using our standard idiom for the truth-functional connectives.

2. *Identify the simple components of the statement* and make a list in which you assign distinct statement letters to distinct simple statements. This list is called a **statement key.**

3. *Identify all the truth-functional connectives in the statement.* Sometimes it helps to produce an intermediate symbolization—that is, a partial symbolization in which simple statements have been replaced by statement letters and the truth-functional connectives are written in their standard idiom.

4. *Replace connectives by appropriate logical symbols.* Using appropriate symbols for the truth-functional connectives, combine these with the interpreted statement letters, adding punctuation so that, using the given statement key, the symbolic statement makes the same assertion as the original English.

This process can of course be reversed. Given an *SL* statement and a statement key, one can translate the symbols into English. For example, suppose you are given the *SL* statement

(F ∨ D) & ((D → ~S) → (S → F))

along with the following statement key:

F: We have free will

D: Determinism is true

S: The determinism/free will problem is solvable.

Replacing the logical symbols by their standard translations we get,

(F or D) and (if (if D then not S) then (if S then F)).

Replacing the statement letters by the simple statements provided in the statement key, we get

(We have free will, or determinism is true) and (if (if determinism is true, then the determinism/free will problem is not solvable) then (if the determinism/free will problem is solvable then we have free will)).

Finally, we rewrite this as a more easily understood statement of English:

Either we have free will, or determinism is true; however, if determinism is true only if the determinism/free will problem is unsolvable, then the determinism/free will problem is solvable only if we have free will.

When translating, the most important goal is to produce an English statement that preserves the same unambiguous logical structure as the original symbolic statement. This can be done by the careful use of such words as 'either' and 'both', the placement of commas and semicolons, and the choice of a particular idiom for a connective.

Exercises for Section 2.5

Part I: Statement Forms In each problem below, a symbolic statement form is followed by three statements. In each case, determine which of the statements, if any, could not be obtained from the given form.

Example: We are given the form $(p \rightarrow \sim q)$ and the three statements '$(A \rightarrow \sim B)$', '$((A \lor B) \rightarrow \sim(C \& D))$', and '$\sim(A \rightarrow \sim(C \lor D))$'. Notice that the third statement cannot be obtained from the given form, because there is no way to replace 'p' and 'q' by statements in the form in such a way that the result is the third statement.

1. p: (a) A (b) $(\sim(A \lor \sim(B \& \sim C)) \rightarrow D)$ (c) $\sim(A \rightarrow \sim(C \lor D))$

2. $\sim(p \& q)$: (a) $(\sim A \& B)$ (b) $\sim((\sim A \lor B) \& \sim C)$ (c) $\sim \sim(A \& B)$

♦ 3. $(\sim p \rightarrow q)$: (a) $\sim(A \rightarrow B)$ (b) $(\sim(A \rightarrow B) \rightarrow \sim(C \rightarrow D))$ (c) $((\sim A \rightarrow B) \& C)$

4. ((*p* & *q*) ∨ *r*):   (a) [(((A & B) ∨ C) & (A → D)) ∨ (L & M)]
   (b) (A & (B ∨ C))   (c) [~((P ∨ Q) & H) ∨ (L & M)]
5. (*p* & (~*p* → *q*)):   (a) [(A ∨ B) & (~M → (A ∨ C))]
   (b) (~M & (~ ~A → (K ∨ H))) (c) (~V & ((~ ~ ~D ∨ ~J) → S))

Part II: SL Statements   Several strings of symbols are listed below. Some of these strings are *SL* statements, and some are not. State which are not and say why in each case. If a string is an *SL* statement, identify its logical form and main connective. (In this exercise, we *will* adopt the convention that allows dropping outermost parentheses.)

6. A   14. A ↔ (B → C)

♦7. ~AC   15. ((A) & ~L) ↔ ~(~R)

8. A,B   16. (A ∨ B) → [C & (D ∨ A)]

9. [((M & R) → (Q ∨ O)) ↔ ~(~M ∨ (L & P))] 17. (A ~& B)

10. (A & B) ∨ ~C   18. → (A & B)

11. [S → (A → B → C)]   ♦19. A; (B ∨ C)

12. (A & (B))   20. (A ~ C)

♦13. (A ∨ M ↔ L)   21. ~(A & ~ ~(L ∨ M))

Part III: Some Philosophical Problems for Thought and Discussion   Now that you have had some experience thinking about statements and statement components, the question of statements versus propositions may be more interesting to consider. Here are some problems to think about.

22. What difficulties do you see connected with speaking of *the* proposition that a statement expresses? What kind of evidence can we use to show that two different statements express the same proposition?

23. From the point of view of empirical observation, it would seem that propositions, like numbers, do not really exist. At least, they don't exist in the same way that tables, chairs, and other physical objects exist. Can you think of any ways, not using the concept of a proposition, that we would be able to talk about the "meaning" of statements and to answer the question whether two statements of the same or different languages "mean the same thing"?

CHAPTER THREE
Statement Logic II: Semantic Methods

3.1 Introduction

The question of whether or not an argument is valid is just the question of whether or not it is impossible for the argument to have true premises and a false conclusion. In Chapter 1 we tested our logical insight against various examples. These examples were relatively simple. There are, however, plenty of arguments whose validity cannot readily be determined merely by using our innate logical sense. Consider, for example, the following:

> Either quantum mechanics doesn't hold true or we have free will. Furthermore, either Newtonian physics holds true or quantum mechanics does not. Thus, if we do not have free will, then Newtonian physics holds true.

This example is rather artificial—but it exhibits a kind of complexity that can be easily handled by the tools of this chapter. Such tools are building blocks to the formal analysis of much more interesting arguments, such as the following:

> It is necessarily true that, if God exists, then God's existence is necessary and not contingent. But it is certainly *possible* that God exists. Hence, it follows necessarily that God exists.

This is a version of a classic argument, first presented centuries ago, in an attempt to prove the existence of God. The argument continues to be an object of philosophical analysis and discussion, and its analysis has been facilitated by developments in symbolic logic. Full analysis of this argument using symbolic logic requires tools that we consider only briefly in the final chapter of this text. But, in order to employ such tools, all the material leading up to them must first be mastered. Between the first argument, above, and the next exists a range of arguments of varying degrees of size and complexity to which the tools and techniques of this text are eminently applicable.

In this chapter we use the symbolic language *SL* as an aid to argument evaluation. In particular, we develop some mechanical tests that can be used to evaluate arguments for validity and to investigate certain interesting logical properties of statements. Although the mechanical tests we develop in this chapter have certain rather dramatic limitations, they also constitute a very powerful method of logical analysis. Furthermore, the methods introduced here are prerequisite to the development of even more powerful logical techniques to be presented in later chapters.

Our focus here is on *semantic* methods of analysis. As noted briefly in Section 1.3, *semantics* is the study of those properties of statements related to their *meaning* and *truth conditions.* Semantics is contrasted with *syntax,* which is the study of those properties of statements related to their grammatical or logical form. The aspect of meaning that is of particular importance for our semantic methods is truth value. The methods we study in this chapter depend on the connection between the truth or falsity of a statement and its logical form. We are going to look specifically at how the truth or falsity of a truth-functional compound statement is connected with the truth or falsity of the simple statements from which it is built. When we speak of a *semantic test for validity,* we mean a test that runs through all the situations in which an argument's premises would come out true and checks to see whether or not, in those cases, the argument's conclusion is true. Semantic methods are contrasted with *syntactic* methods, which deal with how statements of one logical form may be legitimately transformed into others, without explicitly talking about truth or falsity. Syntactic methods for *SL* will be taken up in Chapter 4.

3.2   Truth Tables

All simple statements have a truth value. If a statement is true, its truth value is *true,* or T. A false statement has the truth value *false,* or F. In statement logic we remain at the level of simple statements considered as whole units; we do not look deeper into their grammatical structure. That is why we use single capital letters to stand for simple statements. The "inner structure" of the statement is sealed off, and we're left with only the statement as a whole. From the point of view of statement logic alone, the most we can say about the truth or falsity of any simple statement is *that* it is either true or false. Consider, for example, the statement

'Sarah went on a safari'. From the point of view of statement logic, this is a truth-functionally simple statement. It might be true, and it might be false, but there is nothing about its logical structure that indicates *which* truth value it has. To know whether or not the statement is actually true, we would have to have further information—say, a postcard from Sarah. Because it is truth-functionally simple, we represent this statement in *SL* by assigning a letter to it, say, 'S'. While we don't know the truth value of this statement, we can at least spell out clearly what we *do* know—namely, that there are two possible truth values that it could have:

S
T
F

This table, called a **truth table,** displays the two possible truth values that the simple statement 'S' can have. It's just a way of concisely showing that 'S' might be true and that 'S' might be false.

Suppose, in addition to the statement 'S', we have a second statement—say, 'Ralph wore diamonds', represented by 'R'. As with 'S', 'R' might be true or false:

R
T
F

As far as the *pair* of statements, 'S' and 'R', is concerned, there are *four* possibilities concerning their joint truth and falsity. Both statements could be true, 'S' could be true while 'R' is false, 'S' could be false while 'R' is true, or both statements could be false. These four possibilities can be represented on a single truth table:

S	R
T	T
T	F
F	T
F	F

If we had three statements in which we were interested, 'S', 'R', and, say, 'Marvin ate fish on Friday' ('M'), we would have eight possible combinations of truth values:

S	R	M
T	T	T
T	T	F
T	F	T
T	F	F
F	T	T
F	T	F
F	F	T
F	F	F

Each row on the table represents a possible state of affairs, a "possible reality." Reality could be such that, for example, Sarah went on a safari, Ralph wore diamonds, and Marvin ate fish on Friday; this is a possibility represented by the first row of the above table. Or perhaps Sarah went on a safari, Ralph wore diamonds, but Marvin did *not* eat fish on Friday; this case is represented by the second row of the table. *Every* possible arrangement of truth and falsity for the three statements is represented in the table.[1]

Notice that each time we add a statement letter, the number of combinations doubles. In general, if we have *n* distinct statement letters, there are 2^n possible combinations of truth and falsity to write down. Thus, if we had four statements, there would be $2^4 = 16$ rows on the truth table, representing the sixteen possible combinations of T and F for the four statements.

The above tables can be used to tell us whether certain arguments are valid or not. For example, consider this symbolic argument:

$$\frac{S}{\therefore R}$$

Obviously, the argument 'Sarah went on a safari; therefore, Ralph wore diamonds' is not valid. But instead of relying on our logical insight, notice that we can use a truth table to decide *mechanically* whether or not the argument is valid. Let's repeat the truth table from page 73 that contains 'S' and 'R', but this time label it so that its columns correspond to the premise and conclusion of the preceding argument:

Row	S	R
1	T	T
2	T	F
3	F	T
4	F	F
	Pr	C

Recall that an argument is valid if it is *not possible* for it to have true premises and a false conclusion. The above table exhibits *all* possibilities that exist for statements 'S' and 'R' taken together. Now observe that in the second row, 'S' has the value T while 'R' has the value F. Thus, the truth table above *displays* the fact that the argument is not valid, by *showing* in row 2 that it is possible for the given

---

[1]A subtlety should be noted. Under certain circumstances some of the "possibilities" listed on the table might not be genuinely possible. Suppose, for instance, that 'A' symbolized the statement 'Masha is entirely white' and 'B' symbolized the statement 'Masha is entirely black'. Given what these statements mean, it would be impossible for them both to be true at the same time. However, when we represent an English statement by a capital letter, we are in effect "sealing off" its internal semantic content from further analysis and assuming that each statement letter may have either the value T or the value F, regardless of the value of the other statement letters. When this assumption is not warranted, more powerful logical tools (some of which we will develop in subsequent chapters) must be applied.

argument to have a true premise but a false conclusion. Since the construction of the table is a completely mechanical procedure, and since it is equally mechanical to simply run through the combinations of T and F to see whether or not the premise ever takes the value T while the conclusion takes the value F, it is apparent that here we have the rudiments of a completely mechanical test for validity. Our next step is to show how to build truth tables for truth-functionally compound statements so that arguments built from compound statements can be evaluated. Let's consider the truth-functional compounds in the order in which they were first introduced.

Recall our discussion of the truth-functional nature of negation in Chapter 2. There we noted that negation reverses the truth value of the statement to which it is applied. That is, given any statement of the form ~p, we know that the statement has the truth value F if p has the value T and that it has the value T if p has the value F. This fact about negation can be represented on a truth table:

p	~p
T	F
F	T

This table is called the **basic truth table** for negation. It is a *basic* truth table because it is being introduced here for the purpose of defining how truth-functional negation works. Because the table contains a statement variable, it tells us about *all* negations—whether negations of single statement letters or negations of whole complicated compounds. Reading from left to right, this table shows exactly how a negation is a truth function of what is negated. To say that ~p is a **truth function** of p means that the truth value of ~p is *determined by* the truth value of p.

Consider next conjunction—that is, the truth-functional 'and' whose symbolic form is (p & q). As we noted in Chapter 2, a conjunction takes the value T in just one case: when *both* of its conjuncts are true. In any other case the value of a conjunction is F. The basic truth table for conjunction is

p	q	(p & q)
T	T	T
T	F	F
F	T	F
F	F	F

As the table shows, any statement of the form (p & q) gets assigned the value T when, and only when, both p and q have the value T. Any conjunction has just two conjuncts. To determine whether or not a conjunction is true, you must first determine whether or not its conjuncts are true. Then, using the above basic table, you will have the truth value of the conjunction.

There are two ways in which disjunction can be defined truth-functionally. One, called **inclusive disjunction,** is weaker than the other. Inclusive disjunction is what is standardly represented by the symbol 'v'. As noted in Chapter 2, inclusive disjunction takes the value true when at least one of its disjuncts is true and is false when both of its disjuncts are false. The basic truth table for inclusive disjunction, therefore, is

p	q	$(p \lor q)$
T	T	T
T	F	T
F	T	T
F	F	F

The stronger truth-functional disjunction is called **exclusive disjunction.** Exclusive disjunction has the sense of the English 'or' when we use it to mean 'either one or the other, but not both'. When dining out, for example, the menu might announce that, with your entrée, 'you may choose either ice cream or pie for dessert'. An exclusive disjunction is true when, and only when, exactly one disjunct is true. There is no standard logical symbol for exclusive disjunction, although of course we could invent one. Using, say, '$\veebar$' as a symbol for this connection, the basic truth table for exclusive disjunction is

p	q	$(p \veebar q)$
T	T	F
T	F	T
F	T	T
F	F	F

In this text, as is usual in most logic texts, we will avoid the use of a special logical symbol for exclusive disjunction. However, whenever exclusive disjunction is needed, we can always express it *without* bothering to add a special symbol to the language. We will see presently how to do this.

The truth tables for negation, conjunction, and disjunction are relatively unobjectionable as explications of the truth-functional uses of the English 'not', 'and', and 'or'. This is basically because these truth functions correspond almost exactly to how we use 'not', 'and', and 'or' in English when we are using them as statement connectives. When we come to the conditional, however, our logical intuitions hit a stumbling block. This is because the 'if, then' construction has many different senses as used in English—even when being used as a statement connective of some kind. Sometimes it is used to express a *causal connection:*

(1) If you hit the dynamite, then it will explode.

In this case the assertion of this conditional would mean that the event referred to in the antecedent (you hitting the dynamite) would *cause* the event referred to in the consequent (the explosion of the dynamite).

We also typically use the *counterfactual* form:

(2) If you had hit the dynamite, then it would have exploded

(3) If you had not hit the dynamite, then we would be in no danger now.

Philosophers and logicians refer to such grammatically subjunctive statements as 'counterfactuals' because, as the name implies, they arise in connection with alternative possibilities in contrast to what is actually the case.

Finally, as discussed in Chapter 2, the 'if, then' construction is often used in a sense called 'strict implication'—that is, to assert that a logically necessary connection exists between the conditional's antecedent and its consequent. An example would be 'If all ancient astronomers were stargazers and Hypatia was an ancient astronomer, then she was a stargazer'. In this case, it would not even be possible for the antecedent to be true but the consequent false.

The difficulty produced by these uses of the conditional is that *none* of them can be defined truth-functionally. When we say that a statement connective is truth-functional, we are saying that the truth value of the statement formed with the connective is uniquely fixed by the truth value of its constituent statements. In the case of the conditional, this means that the truth value of the antecedent and consequent fix the truth value of the whole statement. Consideration of a few examples will show that many types of conditional statements do not have this property.

If a connective is truth-functional, it has a truth table. So, if the conditional is truth-functional, we should be able to fill in the following table:

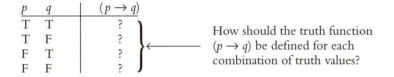

p	q	$(p \rightarrow q)$
T	T	?
T	F	?
F	T	?
F	F	?

How should the truth function $(p \rightarrow q)$ be defined for each combination of truth values?

What should be the truth value in the first row of the table? Let's begin with the causal use of the conditional. It seems plausible that the first row of the table should be T, and in many cases this answer is correct. Suppose you hit the dynamite mentioned in statement (1) and the dynamite then explodes. Both the antecedent and consequent of the statement are true, and we would likely say that the statement (1) as whole is true as well. Here, however, is another causal conditional:

(4) If Judith asks the tooth fairy for rain, then it will rain.

Suppose Judith asks the tooth fairy for rain and subsequently it does rain. Would we say that statement (4) is true? We would more likely say that this statement is *false*, because we would regard the fact that the rain came after Judith made her request to the tooth fairy as a coincidence. The point here is that we have described circumstances in which the causal statements (1) and (4) both have true antecedents and true consequents, yet we took (1) to be true and (4) false under the circumstances described; the truth value of a causal conditional depends on *more* than merely the truth values of antecedent and consequent. Thus, for causal conditionals at least, there is no definite value for the first row of the truth table, and this shows that *causal conditionals aren't truth functional.*

For similar reasons we can see that counterfactual conditionals aren't truth-functional. Consider the following statements:

(5) If Clinton hadn't won the 1992 presidential election, George Bush would have won

(6) If Clinton hadn't won the 1992 presidential election, George Washington would have won.

Both are conditionals with the common false antecedent 'Clinton did not win the election'. Both have a false consequent as well. However, the first statement is almost certainly true, while the second is clearly false. This shows us that, for counterfactual conditionals, knowing that both the antecedent and consequent are false is not enough to tell us the truth value of the whole statement. Thus, *counterfactual conditionals are not truth-functional.*[2]

Although many uses of the conditional are not truth-functional, there are also many uses of conditionals in English that are. So, the question remains: When the use of 'if, then' *is* truth-functional, what is its truth table? The answer is this: If we simply *assume* that the 'if, then' construction *is* truth-functional, it turns out that there are excellent reasons for accepting the following as its basic truth table:

p	q	$(p \rightarrow q)$
T	T	T
T	F	F
F	T	T
F	F	T

The conditional defined by this truth table is called the **material conditional.** It is also called the **Philonian conditional,** because it assigns a truth function to the conditional that was endorsed by the ancient Megarian philosopher Philo. According to this interpretation the truth-functional conditional is false in *only* one situation: when it has a true antecedent but a false consequent. This case is represented on the second row of the basic truth table. In every other case the conditional takes the value T. Thus, in *SL,* any statement of the form $(p \rightarrow q)$ is equivalent to both $\sim(p \And \sim q)$ and $(\sim p \lor q)$, in

---

[2]In Section 9.8 we discuss how modal logic can provide an analysis of both strict and counterfactual conditionals.

the sense that all statements of these three forms will have the same truth value for any given values of p and q. Another consequence of this interpretation of the conditional is that conditionals may be true even if the antecedent and consequent have nothing to do with each other. Thus, for instance, the material conditional 'If pigs can fly, Michael Jordan is the worst basketball player in the NBA' is true, just because the antecedent and the consequent are both false, and our truth table assigns T to this circumstance.

Although the truth table for the material conditional may strike you as unintuitive, it is the best that can be done *if* the conditional is assumed to be truthfunctional. And we are indeed making this assumption here. We will provide a justification for our choice of the Philonian interpretation of the conditional later on, but for the moment we suggest committing its truth table to memory.

We come finally to the biconditional. To discover its basic truth table, recall the discussion of the biconditional in Chapter 2. There we noted that the biconditional is equivalent to a conditional in two directions: 'p if, and only if, q' can be rephrased as 'both p, if q, and p only if q'. Symbolically, this means that statements of the form $(p \leftrightarrow q)$ are equivalent to statements of the form $(q \rightarrow p) \mathbin{\&} (p \rightarrow q)$. Since we already know the basic truth tables for all the connectives in the latter statement form, we can use this information to find the biconditional's basic truth table.

First, notice that $(q \rightarrow p) \mathbin{\&} (p \rightarrow q)$ is a conjunction. It is true when both conjuncts are true and false when either conjunct is false. But when are the conjuncts jointly true? Since each conjunct is a conditional and since a conditional is true whenever it does not have a true antecedent and false consequent, we know that the two conjuncts are true whenever they don't both have a true antecedent and a false consequent. This chain of reasoning is quite easy to follow once you've mastered the method of displaying it in the step-by-step construction of an appropriate truth table.

Begin by noting that any given biconditional will have exactly *two* conditions. Call these p and q. These two statements will have at most four possible combinations of truth and falsity:

p	q
T	T
T	F
F	T
F	F

Given these possibilities, let's add the statement $(q \rightarrow p)$ to the table and calculate its column of truth values:

p	q	$(q \rightarrow p)$
T	T	T
T	F	T
F	T	F
F	F	T

Notice that in this conditional q is the *antecedent* and p is the *consequent*. Referring to the basic truth table for the conditional, we see that—when the antecedent has the value T but the consequent takes the value F—the conditional takes the value F. For the conditional on the above table, this occurs just in the third row. Each truth value in the column beneath the compound is completely determined by the truth values of the component statements from which the compound is built. The procedure "moves" from left to right as you construct the table. Consider, for example, the top row. First, observe that in this row both p and q have the value T. Second, note that the basic truth table for the conditional tells us that whenever a conditional has a true antecedent and true consequent, the conditional takes the value T. For these two reasons, we put the value T beneath the conditional in the first row. In each row the truth values of the components in that row determine the truth value of the compound.

Next, add the statement $(p \rightarrow q)$ to the table and calculate its column of values in just the same way that the first conditional's column was constructed:

p	q	$(q \rightarrow p)$	$(p \rightarrow q)$
T	T	T	T
T	F	T	F
F	T	F	T
F	F	T	T

Once again, the values of p and q in each row determine the value of the conditional in that row.

Finally, we can add the statement $(q \rightarrow p)$ & $(p \rightarrow q)$ to the table:

p	q	$(q \rightarrow p)$	$(p \rightarrow q)$	$(q \rightarrow p)$ & $(p \rightarrow q)$
T	T	T	T	T
T	F	T	F	F
F	T	F	T	F
F	F	T	T	T

The statement we've just added is a conjunction, and a conjunction takes the value T when, and only when, both of its conjuncts are true. This conjunction's conjuncts are $(q \rightarrow p)$ and $(p \rightarrow q)$, and these are jointly true in the first and fourth rows. Hence, the conjunction takes the value T in the first and fourth rows. Now, since the form '$(q \rightarrow p)$ & $(p \rightarrow q)$' is *equivalent* to the form '$(p \leftrightarrow q)$', we have arrived at the desired basic truth table:

p	q	$(p \leftrightarrow q)$
T	T	T
T	F	F
F	T	F
F	F	T

This completes the presentation of the basic truth tables for the truth-functional connectives. We summarize them as follows:

p	$\sim p$
T	F
F	T

p	q	$(p \mathbin{\&} q)$	$(p \vee q)$	$(p \rightarrow q)$	$(p \leftrightarrow q)$
T	T	T	T	T	T
T	F	F	T	F	F
F	T	F	T	T	F
F	F	F	F	T	T

Basic truth tables: These tables are to be used as instructions for calculating the truth tables of any compound *SL* statements.

This abbreviated definition of the truth functions can also be stated completely in English:

1. A **negation** is assigned the value T when, and only when, the negated statement has the value F.

2. A **conjunction** is assigned the value T when, and only when, its conjuncts both have the value T.

3. A **disjunction** is assigned the value F when, and only when, its disjuncts both have the value F.

4. A **conditional** is assigned the value F when, and only when, it has simultaneously a true antecedent and false consequent.

5. A **biconditional** is assigned the value T when, and only when, both of its conditions have the same truth value.

The truth tables we have been discussing so far have been used to define the meaning of our statement connectives. As such, we have used statement variables ('p' and 'q') rather than particular statement letters in our tables. In this chapter you will learn to use truth tables to investigate the conditions under which a particular statement is true. To make truth tables for these statements, you need to substitute particular statements for statement variables in the basic truth tables. In some cases this substitution process is easy. For instance, the truth table for the statement '(A $\vee$ B)' is

A	B	(A ∨ B)
T	T	T
T	F	T
F	T	T
F	F	F

Since 'A' and 'B' are the only statement letters, we have listed them on the left-hand side of the truth table. Next we use the basic truth table for disjunction, substituting 'A' for p and 'B' for q. Because '(A ∨ B)' is a relatively uncomplicated statement, you could probably recognize the conditions in which it is true without building a truth table. The real usefulness of truth tables becomes apparent only when we consider more complex statements.

Let's consider how to construct a truth table for the statement '(~(A & B) → (D ∨ A))'. We start by listing all possible combinations of truth values for the statement letters 'A', 'B', and 'D':

A	B	D
T	T	T
T	T	F
T	F	T
T	F	F
F	T	T
F	T	F
F	F	T
F	F	F

Let's also make explicit the technique we are using to list the possible combinations of truth values. First, list all statement letters at the top of the table in alphabetical order. We need to make sure to list *every* possible combination of truth values beneath these letters. There is more than one way to do this, but we always use the following technique. As we said earlier, a table with n statement letters has 2^n lines. In this case, n is three, so the number of rows is eight. In the right-most column, begin by alternating values of T and F until you have the required number of rows. In the next column to the left, alternate two rows of T, followed by two rows of F. In the next column, alternate four rows of T, followed by four rows of F, and so on, until you have filled in all columns. In general, as you move one column to the left, you double the number of contiguous Ts and Fs in the pattern of alternation.[3]

To fill in our truth table, we must use the basic truth tables we have defined for the statement connectives. For a complex statement like '(~(A & B) → (D ∨ A))' we have to proceed in steps. We have already seen how this can be done

---

[3]If you know how to count in base 2, notice that this is simply counting from zero to $2^n - 1$ in base 2, where '0' stands for T and '1' stands for F and n is the number of statement letters.

in our discussion of the truth table for the biconditional. There we constructed a truth table for the statement form '$(q \to p)$ & $(p \to q)$'. We first did truth tables for the forms '$(q \to p)$' and '$(p \to q)$', and then used these tables to produce our truth table for the whole statement form. The example we're working on here is a bit more complex, but we use the same approach. The statement '$(\sim(A \ \& \ B) \to (D \lor A))$' is a conditional statement with antecedent '$\sim(A \ \& \ B)$' and consequent '$(D \lor A)$'.[4] To construct the truth table for our statement, we must first construct truth tables for the antecedent and consequent, but to construct the truth table for the antecedent we must first construct a truth table for its constituent '$(A \ \& \ B)$':

A	B	D	(A & B)
T	T	T	T
T	T	F	T
T	F	T	F
T	F	F	F
F	T	T	F
F	T	F	F
F	F	T	F
F	F	F	F

We built this table using the basic truth table for conjunction. For instance, in the first and second rows, the conjuncts 'A' and 'B' have the value T, and the basic truth table tells us that if both conjuncts are true, then the conjunction is true; so we write 'T' in the first two rows of our table. Similarly, in the third and fourth rows, 'A' has the value T while 'B' has the value F, and the basic truth table indicates that if the first conjunct is true and the second conjunct false, then the conjunction is false; so, we write 'F' in the third and fourth rows of our truth table.

Using the truth table for '$(A \ \& \ B)$' and the basic truth table for negation, we can now add a column of values for '$\sim(A \ \& \ B)$':

A	B	D	(A & B)	~(A & B)
T	T	T	T	F
T	T	F	T	F
T	F	T	F	T
T	F	F	F	T
F	T	T	F	T
F	T	F	F	T
F	F	T	F	T
F	F	F	F	T

---

[4] It is crucial here that you be able to recognize the main connective of the statement. If you are having trouble doing so, you may wish to review Section 2.5 where this issue was discussed.

Now that we have completed a column of values for the antecedent, we need one for the consequent. We create this using the truth table for disjunction:

A B D	(A & B)	~ (A & B)	(D ∨ A)
T T T	T	F	T
T T F	T	F	T
T F T	F	T	T
T F F	F	T	T
F T T	F	T	T
F T F	F	T	F
F F T	F	T	T
F F F	F	T	F

Finally, we are in a position to finish the truth table for our whole conditional, using the truth table columns we have completed for the antecedent and consequent and the basic truth table for the conditional:

A B D	(A & B)	~ (A & B)	(D ∨ A)	~ (A & B) → (D ∨ A)
T T T	T	F	T	T
T T F	T	F	T	T
T F T	F	T	T	T
T F F	F	T	T	T
F T T	F	T	T	T
F T F	F	T	F	F
F F T	F	T	T	T
F F F	F	T	F	F

The method we have just used to build a truth table allows us to build a truth table for a statement of any degree of complexity. However, for complex statements the technique involves a lot of copying over of parts of the statement. We will henceforth use a more compact form of the truth table. We will be using the same techniques as before, but rather than writing each substatement of the complex statement at the top of the table, we will write the truth value of a substatement under the main connective of the substatement.

The key to successfully constructing these truth tables is to fill in the columns in the correct order. You must always begin with the statement letters and work outward, filling in the column for the main connective last.

Let's build a compact truth table for the statement we were just working on. We start by copying the truth values of each statement letter under the statement letters as they appear in the statement whose truth table we are constructing:

A	B	D		~	(A	&	B)	→	(D	∨	A))
T	T	T			T		T		T		T
T	T	F			T		T		F		T
T	F	T			T		F		T		T
T	F	F			T		F		F		T
F	T	T			F		T		T		F
F	T	F			F		T		F		F
F	F	T			F		F		T		F
F	F	F			F		F		F		F

Next we fill in the columns for the two statements that depend only on statement letters:

A	B	D		~	(A	&	B)	→	(D	∨	A))
T	T	T			T	T	T		T	T	T
T	T	F			T	T	T		F	T	T
T	F	T			T	F	F		T	T	T
T	F	F			T	F	F		F	T	T
F	T	T			F	F	T		T	T	F
F	T	F			F	F	T		F	F	F
F	F	T			F	F	F		T	T	F
F	F	F			F	F	F		F	F	F

Now we can calculate the truth values for '~(A & B)', negating the values in the '&' column:

A	B	D		~	(A	&	B)	→	(D	∨	A))
T	T	T		F	T	T	T		T	T	T
T	T	F		F	T	T	T		F	T	T
T	F	T		T	T	F	F		T	T	T
T	F	F		T	T	F	F		F	T	T
F	T	T		T	F	F	T		T	T	F
F	T	F		T	F	F	T		F	F	F
F	F	T		T	F	F	F		T	T	F
F	F	F		T	F	F	F		F	F	F

Finally, fill in the column under the main connective for the statement, using the negation column as the antecedent and the disjunction column as the consequent:

A	B	D		~	(A	&	B)	→	(D	∨	A))
T	T	T		F	T	T	T	T	T	T	T
T	T	F		F	T	T	T	T	F	T	T
T	F	T		T	T	F	F	T	T	T	T
T	F	F		T	T	F	F	T	F	T	T
F	T	T		T	F	F	T	T	T	T	F
F	T	F		T	F	F	T	F	F	F	F
F	F	T		T	F	F	F	T	T	T	F
F	F	F		T	F	F	F	F	F	F	F

Notice that the boxed column under the main connective matches the values of the expanded version of the truth table for this statement.

Exercises for Section 3.2

Part I: Truth Tables   Construct truth tables for each of the following *SL* statements.

1. $P \rightarrow Q$	6. A & B	11. F ∨ G	16. R ↔ S
2. ~P → Q	♦7. ~A & B	12. ~F ∨ G	♦17. ~R ↔ S
♦3. P → ~Q	8. A & ~B	13. F ∨ ~G	18. R ↔ ~S
4. ~P → ~Q	9. ~A & ~B	14. ~F ∨ ~G	19. ~R ↔ ~S
5. ~(P → Q)	10. ~(A & B)	♦15. ~(F ∨ G)	20. ~(R ↔ S)

Part II: Truth–Functional Connectives

21. Give English statements that are examples of each of the following kinds of conditionals: truth-functional, causal, counterfactual, and strict.

22. Explain why the phrase 'I hope that . . .' is not a truth-functional connective; that is, show that the truth value of 'I hope that *p*' can't be discovered solely by knowing what the truth value of *p* is.

3.3   Formalized Semantics for *SL*

In Section 3.2 we described techniques for constructing truth tables. The reason that truth tables are of interest is that they will provide us with a procedure for determining whether arguments in *SL* are valid and for investigating other interesting properties of *SL* statements. Before we can show how this is done, we must take a little time to describe the semantics of *SL* more formally. As we said at the beginning of this chapter, semantic properties of languages are properties having to do with meaning, so when we specify the semantics of *SL,* we are specifying the nature of meaning for the statements of the language.

In certain respects the way in which we will specify the semantics for *SL* is similar to the way in which we might describe the semantics of a natural language, say, German. In both cases, we use English to describe the meanings of the various words of the language.[5] To do this with German, we might accomplish this by a kind of dictionary with entries like

---

[5]Logicians often refer to the language whose properties are being described or specified as the 'object language' and the language that one is using to specify or describe the object language as the 'meta-language'. Thus, *SL* is our object language, and English is the metalanguage.

The German word 'Katz' means 'cat'

The German word 'Hund' means 'dog'

The German word 'laufen' means 'to run'.

There are, however, some obvious differences between *SL* and German. First, whereas the words of natural languages like German or English include nouns, verbs, adverbs, adjectives (etc.) that refer to persons, places, actions, concepts (etc.), the "words" of *SL* (other than the connectives) are statement letters. Second, unlike German or English, the words of *SL*—the statement letters—do not have any fixed meaning (except that their "meanings" are restricted to simple statements). Each time we use *SL* for some purpose, we assign to some of the statement letters a meaning. On one occasion we might associate the statement letter 'A' with the statement 'Frege was the world's greatest logician', whereas on another occasion we could use the same letter to stand for 'God exists'. For this reason, *SL,* as well as all of the other logical languages we discuss in this book, are called **uninterpreted languages.** A symbolic language like that of ordinary arithmetic, on the other hand, constitutes, more or less, an interpreted language since its symbols—that is, the numerals, operation symbols ('+', '-', etc.), and relation symbols ('=', '>', etc.)—have specified meanings that don't change.

In Chapter 2 we spoke of a 'statement key', by which we meant an association of English statements with statement letters of *SL*. Statement keys are thus a kind of dictionary that provides a translation between statements of English and statement letters of *SL*. For instance,

A: The prime minister of Great Britain is directly elected

B: The prime minister of Israel is directly elected.

It was noted in Section 2.3, however, that what would turn out to be of special interest to us was not so much the specific English statements associated with *SL* statement letters but the *truth values* of the statements with which the statement letters are associated. We now introduce a new term, **interpretation,** which will supplement our more informal notion of a statement key. In particular we define what it means to give an interpretation for a *set* of *SL* statements.

To begin, a **set** is a collection of objects. These objects might be physical objects (e.g., chairs, people, cats, or flowers), or they might be collections of imaginary objects (e.g., gremlins, unicorns) or abstract objects (e.g., numbers, sets). The sets that interest us are those containing statements. We represent a set by putting braces around representatives of the objects in question. We place commas between each representative. For example, the set that contains the *SL* statements 'A', 'B', and 'A ∨ B' is represented thus:

{A, B, A ∨ B}.

Objects contained in the set are **elements** (or **members**) of the set. Thus, the above set contains three elements: 'A', 'B', and 'A ∨ B'. When we refer to an element of a set, we emphatically do *not* refer to a *part* of an element. Thus, consider the following set:

{A → (B & C), B ∨ (L & C), D}.

This set contains three elements: 'A → (B & C)', 'B ∨ (L & C)', and 'D'. The statements 'A', '(B & C)', 'B', and '(L & C)' are *not* elements of the set, although they occur as *parts* of elements in the set. Similarly, the set of trees contains all trees as elements, but trees' branches, though parts of trees, are not said to be elements of this set.

Here is how we define an interpretation of a set of *SL* statements:

> **Definition**   An **interpretation,** $\mathcal{I}$, of a set of *SL* statements is an assignment of truth values to each statement letter that occurs within a member of the set.

By an 'assignment' of a truth value to a statement letter, we simply mean the supposition that the statement letter in question *has* that truth value. Consider, for example, the set of statements {A, (A → B)}. There are exactly *four* possible interpretations of this set:

$\mathcal{I}_1$ 'A' is assigned the value T, and 'B' is assigned the value T

$\mathcal{I}_2$ 'A' is assigned the value T, and 'B' is assigned the value F

$\mathcal{I}_3$ 'A' is assigned the value F, and 'B' is assigned the value T

$\mathcal{I}_4$ 'A' is assigned the value F, and 'B' is assigned the value F.

Notice that the four assignments correspond exactly to the four rows of a truth table beneath the statement letters 'A' and 'B'. If we use the notation 'p:T' to mean 'The statement letter p is assigned the value T' and 'p:F' to mean 'The statement letter p is assigned the value F', we may abbreviate the above four possibilities as

$\mathcal{I}_1$ ⟨A:T, B:T⟩

$\mathcal{I}_2$ ⟨A:T, B:F⟩

$\mathcal{I}_3$ ⟨A:F, B:T⟩

$\mathcal{I}_4$ ⟨A:F, B:F⟩

Our definition of interpretation may strike you as a bit odd. Assigning a truth value to a statement does not seem to be the same as assigning a meaning to it; associating a statement letter with a statement of English seems more natural for this role. Nonetheless, interpretations so defined will prove useful in understanding a number of important properties of statements, sets of statements, and arguments.

Most logicians believe that what we call 'the meaning' of a statement can be divided into at least two parts, which are called its *intension* and its *extension*. When we begin to analyze simple statements into their parts in Chapter 5, we will find that the parts of statements have intensions and extensions as well, but for the moment we concentrate on the intension and extension of whole statements. Roughly, the **intension** of a statement is the proposition it expresses, and the **extension** of the statement is its truth value. Although we have said that the extension is one part of the meaning, truth value is not really part of what, in ordinary language, we think of as a statement's meaning. This is apparent when we consider that one can often completely understand a statement without having any idea of whether or not it is true. For instance, most of us have no idea of whether or not the following statement is true:

> Tiger Woods has a direct ancestor who, 3000 years ago, lived somewhere in what is now the Ukraine.

Nonetheless, we would have no hesitation in saying that we understand what this statement *means*. This example suggests that when we speak of meaning in the ordinary sense, we have in mind what logicians call intension.[6]

In light of the distinction between intensions and extensions, we can see that the statement keys we discussed informally in Chapter 2 are a kind of intensional interpretation, but the kind of interpretation we have just defined is an extensional interpretation. Because this latter is the primary kind of interpretation used in *SL*, logicians describe *SL* as a type of *extensional logic*.

Because all statement connectives in *SL* are truth-functional, all that is needed to determine whether or not an *SL* statement of any complexity is true is an interpretation of the statement letters contained within that statement. In fact, given what we have said about interpretations and the statement connectives, we can define precisely what it means to say that a statement of *SL* is true under some interpretation:

Definition A statement p of *SL* is **true under interpretation** $\mathcal{I}$ if, and only if, either

1. p is a statement letter, and $\mathcal{I}$ assigns T to p, or

2. p is of the form $\sim q$, and q is not true under $\mathcal{I}$, or

3. p is of the form $(q \ \& \ r)$, and both q and r are true under $\mathcal{I}$, or

---

[6]Notice that 'intension' is spelled with an 's'. The meaning of this word is not really connected with the more familiar word 'intention', even though the latter is also used by philosophers in discussions of logic, language, and meaning, as well as in other areas of philosophy.

> 4. *p* is of the form $(q \lor r)$, and either *q* is true under $\mathcal{I}$ or *r* is true under $\mathcal{I}$, or both, or
>
> 5. *p* is of the form $(q \to r)$, and either *q* is not true under $\mathcal{I}$ or *r* is true under $\mathcal{I}$, or both, or
>
> 6. *p* is of the form $(q \leftrightarrow r)$, and either both *q* and *r* are true under $\mathcal{I}$ or neither *q* nor *r* is true under $\mathcal{I}$.
>
> *Closure clause:*   A statement *p* is **false under interpretation** $\mathcal{I}$ if, and only if, *p* is not true under $\mathcal{I}$.

The above definition, like the definition of *SL* statements we gave in Chapter 2, proceeds in steps. We begin by stating the truth conditions for the simplest statements—the statement letters. Then we show how to obtain more complex true statements from simpler true statements using statement connectives. Clauses (2)–(6) describe the truth-functional meaning of the statement connectives that we originally set out in the basic truth tables of Section 3.2. Notice that, according to this definition, we cannot say whether a statement is true, except given a particular interpretation of the statement letters contained in that statement. It makes no sense to ask whether, for instance, the statement 'A' is true in *SL,* since 'A' has no definite meaning or truth value. The final sentence of the definition, the 'closure clause', tells us what to call an *SL* statement that is *not* true according to the definition.

Let's use this definition in a specific case. Consider whether the statement '~(A → D)' is true under the interpretation $\mathcal{I} = \langle$A:T, D:F$\rangle$. According to our definition, since 'A' is true under $\mathcal{I}$ and 'D' is false in $\mathcal{I}$, '(A → D)' is false in $\mathcal{I}$ (by clause (5) and the closure clause), so '~(A → D)' is true under $\mathcal{I}$ (by clause (2) and the closure clause). In practice we will not use this definition directly to determine whether a statement is true under an interpretation but will rely on other techniques like truth tables.

If we think of a set of statements as providing a description of some aspect of the world, each interpretation describes one of the possible ways that that aspect of the world could be. Consider, for instance, these two statements:

A: The prime minister of Great Britain is directly elected
B: The prime minister of Israel is directly elected.

The four possible interpretations correspond to the four possible ways our world might be. Either both Great Britain and Israel have directly elected prime ministers ($\langle$A:T, B:T$\rangle$), Britain does but Israel doesn't ($\langle$A:T, B:F$\rangle$), Israel does and Britain doesn't ($\langle$A:F, B:T$\rangle$), or neither do ($\langle$A:F, B:F$\rangle$). One of these possibilities, $\langle$A:F, B:T$\rangle$, represents the way the world actually is. For this reason, philosophers often think of interpretations as specifications of *possible worlds,* with the one interpretation that represents the way things actually are as the *actual world.*[7]

We close our remarks on interpretations with some notes about the limitations of extensional logic. When a complex statement is formed from simple statements by the use of truth-functional connectives, we can determine whether or not that statement is true whenever we know the truth values of the simple statements. For instance, for any statement of the form 'It's not the case that both *p* and *q*', if we know the truth values of *p* and *q,* then we can compute the truth value of the whole statement. The extensional interpretations of *SL* provide all the information required to determine the truth values of such statements. There are, however, a number of important *non-truth-functional connectives,* for which knowing the truth values of the constituent statements is insufficient to determine the truth of the compound statement in which they occur. We have already seen two examples of non-truth-functional connectives in causal and counterfactual conditionals. Two more examples of these connectives are illustrated in the following statements:

Aristotle believed that Earth was at the center of the universe

It is possible that gremlins really exist.

The first sentence has the form 'Aristotle believed that *p*', and we can think of the phrase 'Aristotle believed that . . .' as a statement connective. This connective is not truth-functional, for there is no logical connection between the truth or falsity of *p* and Aristotle's belief that *p.* Aristotle no doubt believed many statements that were true and many others that were false. Whether or not Aristotle believed that *p* depends not on the truth of *p* but on the *intensional* meaning of *p.* Consequently, we could never use an extensional language to analyze the truth conditions of statements like this.

Our second example is similar. We have a statement of the form 'It is possible that *p*', where 'It is possible that . . .' is a non-truth-functional connective. Consider this particular case. From the mere fact that the statement 'Gremlins really exist' is false, we cannot infer anything about whether or not it is *possible* for them actually to exist.[8]

---

[7]The idea of understanding possible assignments of truth values as describing possible worlds was first developed by the twentieth-century philosopher Ludwig Wittgenstein in his book *Tractatus Logico-Philosophicus.* Wittgenstein was also one of the first to develop the use of truth tables. We should remark that the kind of possibility we are discussing here is called 'logical possibility'. There may well be other more restricted kinds of possibility as well. For instance, if we are to believe Einstein's theory of relativity, it is *physically* impossible to travel faster than the speed of light, but it at least seems that it is *logically* possible to do so.

[8]Notice, however, that 'it is possible that' is partly truth functional: If a statement *p* is true, then it logically follows that what *p* asserts is possible, so 'It is possible that *p*' would thus be true. The connective 'believed that', however—as in 'Aristotle believed that Earth was at the center of the universe'—is not even partially truth functional.

Philosophers are of course interested in understanding the logical form of statements like these, and to analyze them they have developed special kinds of logical systems. *Intensional logic* is used to analyze statements like the first, and *modal logic* is used to analyze statements like the second. Both of these kinds of logic are philosophically controversial, and both require complex nonextensional semantics. We give a brief description of these alternative logics in Chapter 9.

Exercises for Section 3.3

Interpretations   For each of the following statements, give at least one interpretation under which the statement is true and one under which it is false.

♦1. A ∨ B	14. ~(A ↔ B)
2. A & B	♦15. ~(~A → B)
3. ~ ~A	16. A → ~B
4. ~A ∨ B	17. A ∨ (B & C)
5. ~A ∨ ~ ~B	18. (A ∨ B) & C
6. ~(A ∨ B)	19. ~A ∨ ~(B & C)
♦7. ~(A & B)	20. B → (~C ∨ A)
8. ~(A &~~B)	21. ~(C & B) → D
9. A → B	22. ~[D → (B ∨ ~A)]
10. ~(A → B)	♦23. A → (B → C)
11. ~A → B	24. (B → C) → A
12. A → ~B	25. (A & B) ∨ ~(C ∨ ~D)
13. A ↔ B	26. ~(A → ~B) & (~C ∨ ~ ~D)

3.4   Truth-Functional Validity and Tautologousness

In Chapter 1 we defined the notion of a valid argument. We said that an argument is valid just in case it is not possible for all the argument's premises to be true while its conclusion is false. To decide whether or not an argument is valid, we had to appeal to our "logical intuitions" about what is possible. Now, however, we see that possibility can to a large extent be understood in terms of "all interpretations" of a collection of statement letters. The concept of an interpretation can in turn be used to give a precise definition of validity for arguments in *SL:*

> ***Definition***   An argument in *SL* is said to be **truth-functionally valid** if, and only if, there is no interpretation under which all its premises are true and its conclusion false.

This definition is of *truth-functional* validity rather than of validity in general. Truth-functional validity is the kind of validity that we can study using *SL*. Truth-functional validity is *narrower* than the concept of validity introduced in Chapter 1. Although all truth-functionally valid arguments are deductively valid, not all deductively valid arguments are *truth-functionally* valid.

We will shortly see how to use truth tables to determine mechanically whether an argument is truth-functionally valid. First, we define another important truth-functional concept:

> ***Definition***   A statement of *SL* is said to be a **tautology** if, and only if, it is true under every interpretation.[9]

Truth tables provide a straightforward way to test for tautologousness because each row of a truth table corresponds to one of the possible interpretations of a set of statements having the statement letters listed on the left side of the table.

To determine whether a statement is a tautology, all we need to do is to discover whether it is true under every interpretation. To do this, we simply complete a truth table for the statement and scan the column containing the main connective. If that column has T in every position, the statement is a tautology; otherwise, it is not. Look, for example, at the truth table we completed for '(~(A & B) → (D ∨ A))' in Section 3.2 (p. 85). The main connective has F in rows 6 and 8. Consequently, this statement is not a tautology. Now consider a truth table for a statement that *is* a tautology:

A B		B	→	(A	→	B)
T T		T	T	T	T	T
T F		F	T	T	F	F
F T		T	T	F	T	T
F F		F	T	F	T	F

The second column, beneath the statement's main connective, contains T in every position, indicating that the statement 'B → (A → B)' is true under every interpretation.

The method we have used to test for tautologousness can be extended to test whether an argument is truth-functionally valid. To test whether an *SL* argument is truth-functionally valid, you must construct a *single* table that lists each of the premises and the conclusion along the top of the table. After completing the table,

---

[9]Some authors call tautologies 'truth-functionally valid statements'.

inspect each row to see whether or not there is a case in which the main connectives of the premises are all assigned T while the main connective of the conclusion is assigned F. If there is such a row, the argument is *not* truth-functionally valid. If there is no such row, then the argument *is* truth-functionally valid.

Let's begin with a simple argument in English:

> Congress will adjourn or Congress will vote on the new bill
> It is not the case that Congress will adjourn
> ―――――――――――――――――――――――――――――――――――
> ∴ Congress will vote on the new bill.

Notice that this argument is an instance of argument form given on the first page of Chapter 2. Hence, this is an example of a valid argument: It is impossible for the premises to be true while the conclusion is false. We can use the method of truth tables to *demonstrate* (i.e., prove) that this is a truth-functionally valid argument. Symbolizing the argument in *SL,* we get

> A ∨ B
> ~A
> ――――
> ∴ B

Whatever else is the case, there are two 'facts' or statements at issue, represented by statement letters 'A' and 'B'. There are four possible states of affairs (i.e., four possible interpretations), which we will represent by four rows on the truth table. As we have done before, we list these combinations on the left-hand side of the truth table. Along the top of the truth table, we list each of the premises, followed by the conclusion:

A	B	(A ∨ B)	~A	B
T	T			
T	F			
F	T			
F	F			
		Pr	Pr	C

Now we fill in the truth table:

A	B	(A ∨ B)	~A	B
T	T	T T T	F T	T
T	F	T T F	F T	F
F	T	F T T	T F	T
F	F	F F F	T F	F
		Pr	Pr	C

We put boxes around the columns containing the main connectives of the premises and the conclusion in order to highlight what now needs to be inspected. According to our procedure the argument is truth-functionally valid unless we can find a row on the table where all the premises are true and the conclusion false. There is only one row in the table where all the premises are true—row 3. But in this row the conclusion is true as well, so the argument is valid.

Let's consider another simple argument. This time we start with an argument already symbolized in *SL:*

$(A \rightarrow C)$
C
_____
∴ A

Since you are familiar by now with how we construct truth tables, we simply present the completed truth table needed for this example:

A	C		(A	$\rightarrow$	C)	C	A
T	T		T	T	T	T	T
T	F		T	F	F	F	T
F	T		F	T	T	T	F
F	F		F	T	F	F	F

We have again boxed the column containing the main connective for the compound statement. Now let's see whether the argument is truth-functionally valid. In row 1, both the premises and the conclusion are true. In rows 2 and 4, at least one of the premises is false. However, in row 3, which we have boxed, all premises are true while the conclusion is false. Thus, we have an interpretation ⟨A:F, C:T⟩, where the premises are all true and the conclusion is false, so the argument in question is *not* truth-functionally valid. For any argument, an interpretation in which all of the premises are true but the conclusion is false is called a **counterexample** to that argument.

When you are attempting to decide whether or not an argument is valid, pay attention to the following feature of our definition of validity: For an argument to be truth-functionally valid, *all that is required* is that, when the argument is symbolized in *SL* and evaluated on a truth table, there is no row where the argument's premises are all true while its conclusion is false. This does *not* mean that there must be a row in which all the premises are true! For instance, the following argument is valid, even though the conclusion has no relation to the premises:

A
~A
_____
∴ P

The two premises obviously cannot be true simultaneously. If it's not possible for all the premises to be true, then it's certainly not possible for the premises to be true while the conclusion is false. Consequently, *any* argument with contradictory premises is valid—certainly a good reason to avoid contradictory premises in ordinary argumentation!

The notion of 'truth-functional validity' is a semantic notion; its definition concerns truth and falsity among the premises and conclusion of an argument. When an argument is truth-functionally valid, we will, as noted earlier, say that the premises **truth-functionally imply** the conclusion or that the conclusion is a **truth-functional consequence** of the premises. To represent semantic consequence in general, it is convenient at this point to introduce the symbol '$\vDash$' (the "double turnstile"). Whenever a conclusion c is a semantic consequence of a set of premises $\{p_1, \ldots, p_n\}$, we will write $p_1, \ldots, p_n \vDash c$. This may be read as 'the set $\{p_1, \ldots, p_n\}$ semantically implies c'. In this chapter the only concept of semantic consequence we are concerned with is truth-functional consequence. Thus, for example, it would be appropriate to read

$$A, \sim\!A \vDash P$$

as 'the set $\{A, \sim\!A\}$ truth-functionally implies P', or, more simply as 'A, $\sim\!$A imply P'.[10] Furthermore, since a statement p is a tautology if it is true "no matter what," we will write $\vDash p$ to assert that p is semantically necessarily true. In the context of *SL,* it would be appropriate to read $\vDash p$ as 'p is true under every interpretation' or, more tersely, as 'p is a tautology'.

An interesting relationship holds between valid arguments and tautologies. Suppose you have an argument with premises $p_1, \ldots, p_n$ and with conclusion c:

$$p_1$$
$$\cdot$$
$$\cdot$$
$$\cdot$$
$$\cdot$$
$$\underline{p_n}$$
$$\therefore c$$

Take all the argument's premises and form a conjunction, which we abbreviate here as

---

[10]The clever reader may have noticed a violation here of our distinction between use and mention. To be strictly correct, we *ought* to have written that the expression in question can be read as follows:

'A', '$\sim$A' imply 'P'.

Strictly speaking, the occurrences of *SL* statements are being mentioned here, not used. Paying *too* much attention to the use–mention dichotomy, however, can sometimes be more confusing than enlightening!

$$p_1 \, \& \, \ldots \, \& \, p_n.$$

Now, make these the antecedent of a conditional statement with c as consequent:

$$(p_1 \, \& \, \ldots \, \& \, p_n) \to c.$$

This statement is called the **associated conditional** for the given argument (also called the **corresponding conditional**). For example, the associated conditional for the following argument

> F & ~G
> ~(F ∨ G)
> ∴ ~F

is the statement '[(F & ~G) & ~(F ∨ G)] → ~F'. To put it formally,

> *Definition*   **The associated conditional** for an argument is the conditional statement that takes the conjunction of the argument's premises as its antecedent and that takes the argument's conclusion as its consequent.

The question of whether or not an argument's associated conditional is a tautology is intimately connected with the question of the argument's validity:

> *Proposition 1*   An argument is truth-functionally valid if, and only if, its associated conditional is a tautology.

An argument is truth-functionally valid if there is no interpretation under which all of its premises are true and its conclusion is false. But these are exactly the same conditions under which the associated conditional turns out to be a tautology. Using the double turnstyle notation Proposition 1 may also be expressed this way: For any *SL* statements $p_1, \ldots, p_n, c,$

$$p_1, \ldots, p_n \vDash c \text{ if, and only if, } \vDash (p_1 \, \& \, \ldots \, \& \, p_n) \to c.$$

Thus, consider a truth table for the associated conditional for the argument just given:

F	G	[(F & ~ G) & ~(F ∨ G)]	→	~F
T	T	T F F T F F T T T	T	F T
T	F	T T T F F F T T F	T	F T
F	T	F F F T F F F T T	T	T F
F	F	F F T F F T F F F	T	T F

Since this statement is a tautology, we may infer (from this fact, along with Proposition 1) that the argument in question is truth-functionally valid. Using our notation, since

$$\vDash [(F \; \& \sim G) \; \& \sim(F \lor G)] \to \sim F$$

it follows that

$$(F \; \& \sim G), \sim(F \lor G) \vDash \sim F.$$

Proposition 1 helps elucidate the difference between the material conditional and what we've called 'strict implication'. Strict implication is the relation that obtains between the premises and conclusions of valid arguments. If an argument's premises truth-functionally imply the conclusion, then the argument's associated conditional is a tautology; hence, it is true under *every interpretation*. It follows that if some interpretation represents the way the world actually is, the associated conditional will be true under that interpretation as well. But the converse does not hold: If an argument's associated conditional is (merely) *true* (in the interpretation that represents the way the world actually is), it does not follow that the argument's premises truth-functionally imply the conclusion. This is what is meant when it is said that implication is a *logically stronger* connection than that between the antecedent and consequent of a material conditional that has the value T. Only when a conditional is *necessarily* true, not merely ("materially") true, does the antecedent strictly imply the consequent.

In closing this section we would like to emphasize an important point about the relationship between tautologousness and truth tables. Notice that tautologousness is defined using the concept of an interpretation rather than that of a truth table. What *makes* a statement tautologous is not that it has a certain truth table but that it is true *under all interpretations*. We can make the same point about truth-functional validity: What makes an argument truth-functionally valid is not that it has a certain truth table but that there is no interpretation in which its premises are all true and its conclusion is false. Truth tables provide us with *tests* for tautologousness and truth-functional validity, but these concepts are not defined in terms of truth tables. Truth tables are only one of a number of possible techniques for determining whether a statement is a tautology or an argument is truth-functionally valid. Two more techniques are introduced in this chapter: brief truth tables and truth trees.

Exercises for Section 3.4

Part I: Tautologies   Construct truth tables to determine whether or not each of the following is a tautology.

1. A ∨ B
2. A ∨ ~B
♦3. ~(A & ~A)
4. ~(A ∨ ~A)
5. (F ∨ ~F) & ~(G & ~G)
6. ~(~(H & ~G) & G) ∨ G
7. (P & Q) → Q
8. (X → Y) ∨ (Y → X)
9. ~(Q → R) → (~Q → R)
10. ((A & B) ∨ ((~A & B) ∨ (A & ~B))) ∨ (~A & ~B)

♦11. (P → Q) ∨ (P → ~Q)
12. ~(H → J) → ~(J → H)
13. ~[~(K ∨ ~L) & (~K → ~L)]
14. [(G & ~H) & (H & ~G)] ∨ (P → P)
15. [~W & (M → W)] → ~M
16. ~(Q & E) → ~(Q ∨ E)
17. (H → J) → ((H → ~J) → ~H)
18. [J → (H & K)] → [(J → H) & (J → K)]
♦19. [~A & (~B & ~C)] ∨(A & B)
20. [(X & Y) → Z] → [(X → Z) ∨ (Y → Z)]

Part II: Validity   Construct truth tables to determine whether each of the following arguments is truth-functionally valid.

21. A & B / ∴ A
22. A ∨ B / ∴ ~A ∨ ~B
♦23. ~(E & G) / ∴ E ∨ F
24. ~(P & Q) / ∴ ~P & ~Q
25. ~H, ~J / ∴ ~(H & J)
26. Z ∨ W, W → Z / ∴ Z
27. C ∨ ~D / ∴ D → C
28. E ∨ F, ~ ~E / ∴ F
29. ~G → H, ~H / ∴ G
30. ~(A → B) / ∴ ~B
♦31. F → G, ~F → G / ∴ G
32. F → G, ~F → ~G / ∴ ~(F & G)
33. J & K, ~K ∨ J / ∴ ~K ∨ J

34. H → J / ∴ ~J → (H → J)
35. ~(K & ~L), ~K / ∴ L
36. ~(~ ~K & ~ ~L), ~ ~K / ∴ ~L
37. J → K, ~(K ∨ L) / ∴ ~J
38. M → N, N → O, ~M / ∴ ~O
♦39. ~P ∨ Q, ~Q ∨ R, ~R / ∴ P
40. ~A, (C ∨ D) → ~A / ∴ A → ~D
41. X & ~Y, ~Y ∨ ~Z / ∴ X & ~Z
42. H → J, J → ~(L & M), ~M / ∴ H & J
43. H & (G ∨ F), ~(G → F) / ∴ ~H → G
44. ~[K ∨ (K → M)] / ∴ P & ~P
45. ~(S & ~L) / ∴ (L & S) ∨ (~L & ~S)
46. R ∨ (S → T), ~T & ~R / ∴ ~(S & U)

♦47. ~[H → (K → M)], K & ~M / ∴ H → (K → M)
48. ~[M ∨ (N ∨ O)], (~M → P) & (~O → P), P → ~N / ∴ ~N → P
49. (E ∨ G) → F, (G ∨ H) → F, (G & E) ∨ (G & H) / ∴ F & G
50. (A & B) → (C → (D & E)), ~(D → E) & C / ∴ ~(A & B)

Part III: Symbolization   Symbolize the following arguments in *SL*. Then build truth tables for each in order to determine whether the argument is truth-functionally valid or invalid.

51. If James enjoys everything written by Joyce, he likes *Ulysses.* Since he does not like *Ulysses,* James does not enjoy everything written by Joyce.

52. It's either true or false that there will be a sea battle tomorrow. If it is true, then the future is fixed. If it is false, the future is fixed. Thus, the future is fixed.

♦53. If animals speak English, then they think. But speaking English is not a necessary condition for animals to think. Thus, animals think.

54. If Rene really wants to appreciate Marcel Proust, she'll read all seven volumes of *À la recherche du temps perdu.* If she does this, then she will learn French. Thus, Rene does not really want to appreciate Marcel Proust unless she will learn French.

55. If set theory is logically consistent, then the foundations of mathematics are secure. If set theory is not logically consistent, then we will have to find other foundations for mathematics. Thus, either the foundations of mathematics are not secure or we will have to find other foundations for mathematics.

56. The "Socrates" argument is valid just in case it does not have both true premises and a false conclusion. However, it has a false conclusion and is therefore invalid.

57. Unless Jay pays his VISA bill, his creditors will be knocking at the door. But Jay does not pay his VISA bill unless Margo earns a steady income through her computer deals. This, however, Margo does not do. Thus, the creditors will be knocking at Jay's door.

58. My computer does not make mistakes unless either it has been incorrectly programmed or there is a power failure. Since there is no power failure but my computer does make mistakes, we must conclude that it has been incorrectly programmed.

♦59. Of Alice, Bob, and Cal, exactly two have received a passing grade. Cal received a passing grade. Thus, Alice received a passing grade only if Bob did not.

60. At least one of our children, Maria and Sally, will go to the university next year. If only one goes, we will not take out a student loan. But if they both go, we will take out a student loan. Thus, if we take out a student loan, Maria will go to the university just in case Sally does.

61. Either ethical standards are relative or they are absolute. If they are relative, then they depend on cultural norms. If they are absolute, then they don't depend on cultural norms. But ethical standards do depend on cultural norms. Therefore, ethical standards are relative and depend on cultural norms.

62. If the positivists are right, then neither statements nor propositions exist. If neither of these exist, then sentences are the conveyors of meaning. But if sentences are the conveyors of meaning, synonymy can't be reasonably explained. However, synonymy can be reasonably explained. It follows that either statements or propositions exist and that the positivists are not right.

♦63. If interstellar space travel is possible, it will take years to get from one solar system to another unless light speed is attained. Light speed won't be attained, if modern physics is right (and it is). Thus, it will take years to get from one solar system to another, if interstellar space travel is possible.

64. The doctrines of determinism and freedom are not both true. While Blanshard's view is correct only if the doctrine of determinism holds, Sartre is not right unless the doctrine of freedom is true. Thus, neither of these thinkers is correct.

65. If advertising proves effective, the number of ads on television will increase. The number of ads will remain the same, if advertising is simply ineffective. Finally, only if advertising proves detrimental will the number of ads on television decrease. Since the rate of advertising on television has neither increased nor decreased but has remained the same, we can conclude that advertising is simply ineffective.

Part IV: Truth-Functional Theory and Concepts

66. Explain why any truth-functionally valid argument that takes the statement 'A ∨ ~A' as its only premise *must* have a tautology for its conclusion.

♦67. Explain why any argument that has a statement of the form 'p & $\sim p$' among its premises is truth-functionally valid.

68. Give an example of an argument that is truth-functionally invalid but that is nevertheless deductively valid.

69. Give an example of a necessarily true statement that is *not* a tautology.

70. Explain clearly, and in detail, why it would be incorrect to read the statement 'A → B' as 'A implies B'.

71. Complete the following proposition and clearly show that your answer is correct:

> An argument $p_1, \ldots, p_n / \therefore c$ in *SL* is truth-functionally valid if, and only if, the following *SL biconditional statement* is a tautology:

72. Complete the following proposition and clearly show that your answer is correct:

> An *SL* statement p is a tautology if, and only if, the following *SL argument* is truth-functionally valid:

3.5 Further Semantic Properties and Relationships

In this section we consider several important semantic concepts. These are described in the following definitions:

Definition   A statement of *SL* is said to be **truth-functionally self-contradictory** if, and only if, there is no interpretation under which it is true.

Definition   A statement of *SL* is said to be **truth-functionally contingent** if, and only if, there is at least one interpretation under which it is true and at least one interpretation under which it is false.

Definition   Two statements *p* and *q* of *SL* are said to be **truth-functionally equivalent** if, and only if, *p* and *q* have the same truth value under every interpretation.

Definition   Two statements *p* and *q* of *SL* are said to be **truth-functionally mutually contradictory** if, and only if, *p* and *q* have opposite truth values under every interpretation.

Each of these expressions includes the qualification 'truth-functionally' to indicate that these concepts apply to *SL* statements in virtue of their truth-functional structure. Because these expressions are somewhat cumbersome, we will occasionally omit the qualifications, but you should always remember that these are truth-functional properties and relationships.

By inspecting these definitions, you will see that every *SL* statement is either a tautology, truth-functionally contingent, or a truth-functional self-contradiction. Tautologies are true under all interpretations, contingent statements are true under some but not all interpretations, and contradictions are true under no interpretations. To put it another way, a tautology is logically necessary, a contingent statement is logically possible but not necessary, and a self-contradiction is logically impossible.

Truth tables provide a simple method for determining whether statements of *SL* are contingent or contradictory. Here are three examples:

A	A	(A ∨ ~ A)	(A & ~ A)
T	T	T T F T	T F F T
F	F	F T T F	F F T F

Inspecting this truth table you can see that the first statement is contingent since it is true under one interpretation and false under another; the second statement is a tautology since it is true under every interpretation; and the third is a truth-functional self-contradiction, since it is false under every interpretation.

For the sake of clarity, we have given three very simple examples. However, tautologies and self-contradictions (as well as contingent statements) come in all lengths and degrees of complexity. Sometimes it is not obvious into which category a statement falls. For example, the statement

$$\sim((P \leftrightarrow Q) \leftrightarrow ((P \,\&\, \sim Q) \lor (\sim P \,\&\, Q)))$$

is a tautology, and the statement

$$(((A \,\&\, Q) \,\&\, (P \rightarrow \sim A)) \,\&\, (Q \rightarrow P))$$

is a self-contradiction. You may want to confirm this claim by building truth tables for each. If you do, you will find that in the first truth table the column containing the main connective will have T in every row and in the second table the column containing the main connective will have F in every row.

The final two semantic concepts we discuss in this section are *truth-functional equivalence* and *truth-functional mutual contradictoriness*. These two expressions refer to relations that hold between some pairs of statements and are not properties of single statements. Two *SL* statements are truth-functionally equivalent just in case they have the same truth value under every interpretation; they are truth-functionally mutually contradictory just in case they have opposite values under every interpretation. To determine whether two statements are equivalent or contradictory, you can complete a single truth table containing the two statements in question. If they are equivalent, the truth values beneath their main connectives will be the same in every row. If they are mutually contradictory, the truth values beneath their main connectives will be opposites in every row. As an example, we use this technique to show that the statements '$\sim(A \lor B)$' and '$\sim A \,\&\, \sim B$' are truth-functionally equivalent:

A	B	$\sim$ (A $\lor$ B)	$\sim$ A & $\sim$ B
T	T	F T T T	F T F F T
T	F	F T T F	F T F T F
F	T	F F T T	T F F F T
F	F	T F F F	T F T T F

Note that the two boxed columns are identical in every row, thus demonstrating the truth-functional equivalence of the two statements. Notice, too, that the statements '$A \lor B$' and '$\sim(A \,\&\, B)$' are mutually contradictory: Wherever under its main connective one has the value T, the other has the value F and vice versa. Of course, not all contradictories are this obvious. As you should verify by building a truth table, the two statements 'P → (R & S)' and '(~R & P) ∨ (~S & P)' are also mutually contradictory.[11]

The relation of truth-functional equivalence is of particular interest because it gives us a way to understand *synonymy* for statements in *SL*. Two statements are synonymous if they "mean the same thing." In *SL* we will take two statements to be synonymous just in case they are truth-functionally equivalent. The existence of synonymy relations explains to some extent why it is that, in going from English into *SL,* we can find more than one appropriate symbolization. Consider the statement 'Neither Masha nor Nina likes liver'. Using 'M' for 'Masha likes liver' and 'N' for 'Nina likes liver', we can symbolize this in either of the following two ways:

~(M ∨ N)

~M & ~N.

The fact that both of these symbolizations are intuitively acceptable is corroborated by the fact that the two statements are truth-functionally equivalent.

There is, however, more to synonymy in general than truth-functional equivalence. It is possible to find statements that intuitively mean quite different things but that nonetheless are truth-functionally equivalent. For instance, the statements we were just discussing are *also* equivalent to

(R → ~~R) → ~(~M → N)

where 'R' could stand for any English statement at all. So, for instance, taking 'R' to mean 'Ratso likes blueberry muffins', the statement

> If Ratso likes blueberry muffins only if it's false that he doesn't like blueberry muffins, then it's not the case that if Masha doesn't like liver then Nina likes liver

is truth-functionally equivalent to the statement that neither Masha nor Nina like liver. Nonetheless, it would be implausible to claim that these two English statements *mean* the same thing, at least as we ordinarily think of meaning in everyday conversation.

Similarly, notice that *every* tautology is true under all interpretations, so every tautology is truth-functionally equivalent to every other. Nonetheless, there seem to be important differences of meaning between various tautologies.

---

[11]Notice that we occasionally omit the prefix 'mutually' in our use of the term 'mutually contradictory'. Logicians often use the word 'contradictory' to mean either 'mutually contradictory' or 'self-contradictory', relying on the context to fix the meaning of the term. It is simple enough to recognize which concept is being used: Self-contradictoriness is a *property of statements,* whereas mutual contradictoriness is a *relationship between pairs of statements.*

The difference between the "ordinary" and the logical meaning of 'synonymy' has to do with the fact that here the synonymy relation, defined in terms of truth-functional equivalence, relies on *extensional* interpretations. As discussed earlier, the meaning of a statement can be divided into its intension (the proposition expressed) and its extension (its truth value). It is likely that many pairs of statements have the same truth value under all interpretations but are nonetheless different in intensional meaning. To understand the concept of intensional synonymy, we would have to solve the problem of propositional identity, which, as we mentioned in Chapter 1, is very difficult. Until this problem is solved, the extensional synonymy represented by the relation of truth-functional equivalence will have to do for *SL*.

Using the relation of truth-functional equivalence, let's fulfill a promise that was made earlier—namely, to show how *exclusive disjunction* can be expressed without relying on a special symbol for that truth function. We do this by showing that whenever we want to express exclusive disjunction, this can always be accomplished using a truth-functionally equivalent statement. Recall the basic truth table for exclusive disjunction:

p	q	$(p$	$\veebar$	$q)$
T	T	T	F	T
T	F	T	T	F
F	T	F	T	T
F	F	F	F	F

Exclusive disjunction has the sense of the English 'one or the other, but not both'. To express exclusive disjunction using the symbols already at our disposal, all we have to do is produce a symbolic version of this English phrase. Since '$(p \vee q)$' has the sense of 'at least one or the other' and '$\sim(p \mathbin{\&} q)$' has the sense of 'at most one or the other', we can represent exclusive disjunction by conjoining these two forms: $(p \vee q) \mathbin{\&} \sim(p \mathbin{\&} q)$. To show that this is correct, we show that this statement form is truth-functionally equivalent to the form for exclusive disjunction:

p	q	$(p$	$\vee$	$q)$	$\&$	$\sim$	$(p$	$\&$	$q)$
T	T	T	T	T	F	F	T	T	T
T	F	T	T	F	T	T	T	F	F
F	T	F	T	T	T	T	F	F	T
F	F	F	F	F	F	T	F	F	F

As the tables show, the column main connective in this statement (the '&' near the middle) has the pattern of the basic truth table for exclusive disjunction (note that p and q have the same columns of values beneath them on each table). Consequently, we can use this statement form to express exclusive truth-functional disjunction between any statements p and q.

We could actually use the technique just employed to define many other truth functions, eliminating the need for some of our basic truth functions. For example, we could define the conditional as '∼*p* ∨ *q*', since the forms '∼*p* ∨ *q*' and '*p* → *q*' are truth-functionally equivalent. In fact, it turns out that using just two connectives, '∼' and '∨', we can define *all* other connectives.[12]

We have so far defined a number of semantic concepts: truth-functional validity, tautologousness, truth-functional self-contradictoriness, truth-functional contingency, truth-functional mutual contradictoriness, and truth-functional equivalence. If you look carefully at our definitions, however, you will see that we have restricted them to statements and arguments in the language *SL*. We have, for instance, a definition of what counts as a tautology in *SL*, but we have not said what counts as a tautology in any other languages (such as English). Our goal in defining these concepts in an artificial language like *SL* is to help us understand how to apply them to statements and arguments in our own language. How do we do this?

With regard to arguments you have probably noticed our technique already. To find out whether an argument in English is valid, we identify its premises and conclusion, translate them into *SL*, and then determine whether the corresponding *SL* argument is truth-functionally valid. If it is we pronounce the original English argument to be valid as well. We can apply the same technique to investigate whether English statements are tautologous, contingent, or self-contradictory and to see whether pairs of statements are equivalent or mutually contradictory.

The semantic concepts we have defined in the last two sections all describe aspects of the *truth-functional structure* of the statements and arguments to which they apply. It is for this reason that we have prefixed the expression 'truth-functional' to our terms. The truth-functional structure of a statement is one aspect of its logical form, but the logical form of a statement may be richer than is suggested by its truth-functional structure. As we enrich our logical language in subsequent chapters, we will define a set of analogous semantic concepts that depend on other aspects of logical form. We can illustrate what we mean by an 'analogous semantic concept' by considering the truth-functional concept of a tautology. A tautology is a kind of **necessary truth**—that is, a statement that *could not possibly be false*, no matter what the world were like. Although there are several types of necessary truths, not all of them are tautologies.

Consider the statements '2 = 2', 'All people are people', and 'All bachelors are unmarried'. Although none of these could possibly be false, truth table analysis won't reveal this fact, for when each is symbolized in *SL* the result is a statement letter—say, 'E', 'F', and 'G', respectively. When you build a truth table for any of these, each will be shown to be *truth-functionally* contingent. Using concentric circles, Figure 3.1 shows the relationships among types of true statements.

Figure 3.1 illustrates the fact that every tautology is a logical truth, a necessary truth, and a truth without qualification but that not all logical, necessary, or

---

[12]In fact, all truth functions can be defined in terms of '∼' and '&', '∼' and '∨', or '∼' and '→'. However, *not* all truth functions can be expressed using just '∼' and '↔'. See the exercises in Part III at the end of this section.

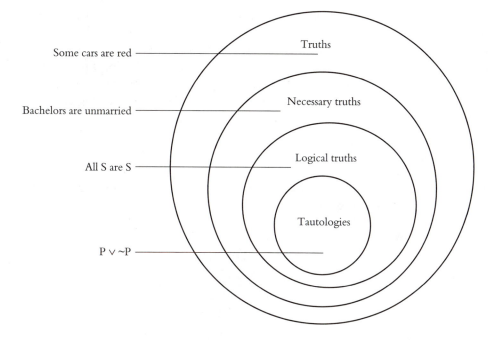

Figure 3.1

other truths are tautologies—and so on for each of the other types of truth indicated. The idea of a 'necessary truth' is yet one more concept that has drawn the attention of philosophers and logicians since the start of philosophy.[13]

Just as not all necessary truths are tautologous (i.e., truth-functionally necessary), not all valid arguments are truth-functionally valid. The following argument is valid (though, alas, not sound, since the first premise is false):

> All philosophers are charming and witty
> Joseph Bessie is a philosopher
> ∴ Joseph Bessie is charming and witty.

Though valid, its validity cannot be shown in *SL,* because we would have to symbolize it in *SL* using three distinct statement letters:

> A
> B
> ∴ C

---

[13]For more information on necessary truth, see D. W. Hamlyn, "Contingent and Necessary Statements," *Encyclopedia of Philosophy, Vol. 2* (New York: MacMillan Publishing Co., 1967).

A truth table for this argument would show, in its second row, the possibility of true premises but false conclusion. *SL* is simply not a rich enough language to represent the logical structure of the original English statements. In subsequent chapters we will extend our logical language in order to develop formal techniques for establishing the validity of many arguments that are not amenable to truth-functional analysis. In these more powerful languages, we will need to use techniques other than truth tables to test for validity.

Exercises for Section 3.5

Part I: Truth-Functional Properties   Use truth tables to determine which of the following are tautologies, which are truth-functional self-contradictions, and which are truth-functionally contingent.

♦1. G → ~G	10. G ∨ (H & ~G)
2. ~G → G	11. J → (K → J)
3. ~(G → G)	12. M → (~M → O)
4. ~G ↔ G	13. H ∨ (~I → ~H)
5. G ↔ G	14. [M & (L → P)] ∨ ~M
6. ~(A & A)	15. (G ∨ ~G) → ~(H → H)
7. ~A & A	16. (~O → M) ∨ (~M → O)
8. H → (H ∨ ~H)	♦17. (L & ~M) → ~(L → M)
♦9. F & ~(G → F)	18. ~[(A → ~B) → ~(A → B)]

Part II: Truth-Functional Relationships   Build truth tables and use them to determine which of the following pairs of statements are truth-functionally equivalent, which are truth-functionally contradictory, and which are neither.

♦19. ~(M ∨ L), ~M ∨ ~L	30. R ↔ R, R ↔ ~R
20. ~(M ∨ L), ~M & ~L	31. B → D, (B & D) ∨ (~B & ~D)
21. ~(M & L), ~M ∨ ~L	32. (G & G) & G, G
22. ~(M & L), ~M & ~L	33. S ∨ T, ~S ∨ ~T
23. ~R ∨ S, R & ~S	34. A → (B → C), (A→ B) → C
24. ~ ~M, M	♦35. G ↔ H, ~H ↔ ~G
25. R → S, S → R	36. ~(A & B), ~(~A & ~B)
26. ~(R → S), R → ~S	37. A, (G ∨ ~G) → A
♦27. P → (Q → R), (P & Q) → R	38. ~(A ↔ A), B ↔ ~B
28. ~(R → S), R & ~S	39. A → A, A
29. K ∨ K, K	40. (L → L) & M, M

Part III: Theoretical Problems

41. Give statements that are truth-functionally equivalent to 'A & B' and to 'A ∨ B', but that contain '~' and '→' as their only connectives.

42. Give statements that are truth-functionally equivalent to 'A → B' and to 'A ∨ B', but that contain '~' and '&' as their only connectives.

♦43. Give statements that are truth-functionally equivalent to 'A & B' and to 'A → B', but that contain '~' and '∨' as their only connectives.

44. For any statement *p*, *p* and ~*p* are mutually contradictory. Give an example of a pair of mutually contradictory *SL* statements that are *not* of this form.

45. In Aristotelian logic a pair of statements are defined as *contraries* when there is no interpretation under which they are both true. Find a pair of *SL* statements that are contrary but not mutually contradictory.

46. Suppose the associated conditional for an argument is truth-functionally contingent. Is the argument with which the conditional is associated truth-functionally valid or truth-functionally invalid? Show clearly that your answer is correct.

♦47. Suppose a statement of the form *p & q* is truth-functionally equivalent to a second statement of the form *r & s*. Suppose further that the statement *p* is truth-functionally equivalent to the statement *r*. Must it be the case that *q* is truth-functionally equivalent to the statement *s?* Show clearly that your answer is correct.

3.6 Truth-Functional Consistency

To say that a set of statements is *consistent* is to say that it is logically possible for all elements of the set to be true at once. In the context of *SL*, we must restrict our discussion to consistency insofar as it depends on the truth-functional structure of statements. We consequently offer a definition of *truth-functional consistency:*

> **Definition**   A set of statements in *SL* is said to be **truth-functionally consistent** if, and only if, there is at least one interpretation under which all the elements of the set are true. A set that is not truth-functionally consistent is said to be **truth-functionally inconsistent.**

You can probably see immediately how we can use truth tables to decide whether a set of *SL* statements is consistent. Simply construct a single truth table with each member of the set listed along the top row. Then fill in the truth table for each of the statements. If there is at least one row of the table that has T beneath the main connectives of *each* of the statements in the set, then the set is consistent; otherwise, it is inconsistent. Let's consider a simple set, {A, B, (A ∨ B)} :

A	B	A	B	(A	∨	B)
T	T	T	T	T	T	T
T	F	T	F	T	T	F
F	T	F	T	F	T	T
F	F	F	F	F	F	F

In the first row of the table, each statement in the set takes the value T, so the set is shown to be truth-functionally consistent.

An example of a truth-functionally inconsistent set is the following:

{~(A & B) → C, A → ~B, ~C}.

We demonstrate that this set is not truth-functionally consistent by building a truth table:

A	B	C	~	(A	&	B)	→	C	(A	→	~	B)	~	C
T	T	T	F	T	T	T	T	T	T	F	F	T	F	T
T	T	F	F	T	T	T	T	F	T	F	F	T	T	F
T	F	T	T	T	F	F	T	T	T	T	T	F	F	T
T	F	F	T	T	F	F	F	F	T	T	T	F	T	F
F	T	T	T	F	F	T	T	T	F	T	F	T	F	T
F	T	F	T	F	F	T	F	F	F	T	F	T	T	F
F	F	T	T	F	F	F	T	T	F	T	T	F	F	T
F	F	F	T	F	F	F	F	F	F	T	T	F	T	F

Examination of the table shows that there is no row where all the statements of the set are true at the same time. Thus, this set is not truth-functionally consistent.

There is an important relationship between consistency and validity:

> **Proposition 2**   An argument is truth-functionally valid if, and only if, the set composed of the argument's premises and the negation of its conclusion is truth-functionally inconsistent.

To put this another way, let $p_1, \ldots, p_n$ be the premises of some argument and let c be the argument's conclusion. Proposition 2 asserts that this argument is truth-functionally valid if, and only if, the *set* $\{p_1, \ldots, p_n, \sim c\}$ is truth-functionally inconsistent.

Although somewhat technical sounding at first, the idea is really quite straightforward. To see why the proposition is true, reflect carefully on the definition of truth-functional validity. To say that a given argument is truth-functionally valid just *means* that there is no interpretation under which the premises are all true and the conclusion false. But this is *equivalent* to saying that there is no interpretation under which all of the premises and the *negation* of the conclusion are true—and *this* is equivalent to saying that the argument's premises and the negation of its conclusion form an inconsistent set. To put it tersely we can say that an argument is truth-functionally valid if, and only if, the argument's premises are inconsistent with the denial of its conclusion.

This connection between validity and consistency has important practical consequences. As will be shown in Section 3.9, this relationship gives rise to a remarkably efficient mechanical test for truth-functional validity in terms of truth-functional consistency.

We have just shown that an argument is truth-functionally valid if, and only if, a related set of statements is truth-functionally inconsistent. In Section 3.4 we saw that an argument is truth-functionally valid if, and only if, its associated conditional is a tautology. What, do you suppose, is an interesting conclusion to be drawn from these two facts that will show a logical relationship between tautologousness and truth-functional consistency? Consider these facts:

(1) A statement is a tautology if, and only if, it is true under every interpretation

(2) A set of statements is truth-functionally inconsistent if, and only if, there is no interpretation where the elements of the set are simultaneously true.

A "logical bridge" that connects tautologousness with truth-functional consistency is thus provided by the following:

> **Proposition 3**   A statement p is a tautology if, and only if, the set $\{\sim p\}$ is truth-functionally inconsistent.

What this of course implies is that a statement is a tautology just in case its negation contains the value F in every row beneath it on a truth table.

Let's consider one last important proposition, this time connecting tautologousness and truth-functional equivalence. Truth-functional equivalence is a relation between two statements p and q that holds just in case p and q have the same truth value under every interpretation. Notice, however, that the basic truth table for the biconditional assigns T to a biconditional just in case its two conditions have the same truth value. So, if p and q are truth-functionally equivalent, the biconditional $(p \leftrightarrow q)$ will be true under every interpretation. In other words,

> **Proposition 4**   Two statements p and q are truth-functionally equivalent if, and only if, $(p \leftrightarrow q)$ is a tautology.

Proposition 4 suggests a second way to test for equivalence using truth tables. You can test whether two statements are truth-functionally equivalent by forming a biconditional with them and testing it for tautologousness. More important, in Section 3.10 we combine Propositions 3 and 4 to build an efficient test for equivalence in terms of consistency.

With Propositions 1–4 we have drawn a kind of "logical circle" that connects some of the semantic concepts discussed so far. This is significant. This not only brings some depth to our understanding of semantic concepts but also some practical utility can be derived from these connections. They provide us with some alternative methods of demonstration, and this is important because in some situations one method of demonstration is easier or more efficient to apply than others, even though the methods are theoretically equivalent. We consider two such methods in Sections 3.8 and 3.9.

Exercises for 3.6

Part I: Testing for Consistency   Construct truth tables for the following sets in order to determine whether each is consistent or inconsistent.

1. $\{P \rightarrow Q, P, \sim Q\}$
2. $\{Q \rightarrow \sim P, P, Q\}$
◆3. $\{A \vee B, A \vee \sim B, \sim A\}$
4. $\{\sim(P \& Q), P \& \sim Q\}$
5. $\{A \leftrightarrow B, A \leftrightarrow \sim B\}$
6. $\{A \& (\sim A \rightarrow A), B \rightarrow \sim A\}$
7. $\{A \vee \sim B, B \vee \sim C, \sim(A \rightarrow C)\}$

8. $\{\sim A, \sim B, (A \& B) \vee (C \vee D), \sim D\}$
9. $\{H \rightarrow K, \sim L \rightarrow (H \rightarrow \sim K), H \rightarrow L\}$
10. $\{\sim(A \rightarrow B), C \leftrightarrow B, \sim(C \rightarrow D)\}$
11. $\{A \vee \sim(A \rightarrow B), \sim A\}$
12. $\{M \rightarrow (P \& \sim P), M \rightarrow (R \vee L), \sim L\}$
◆13. $\{M \rightarrow (N \& O), O \& \sim N, M \leftrightarrow N\}$
14. $\{(J \vee K) \& H, \sim J \vee H, H \rightarrow \sim H\}$

15. $\{\sim \sim F \vee \sim \sim(G \vee H), \sim H, \sim(F \rightarrow H)\}$
16. $\{\sim X \vee (\sim Y \vee (Z \& W)), \sim(\sim X \vee \sim Y) \& \sim W\}$
17. $\{A \rightarrow B, A \rightarrow C, A \rightarrow D, \sim(A \vee (B \vee C))\}$
18. $\{A \rightarrow (B \& C), (C \vee D) \rightarrow A, \sim B, A \rightarrow C\}$

Part II: Theoretical Problems

19. Give an example of a set containing exactly three *SL* statements p, q, and r such that each of the sets $\{p, q\}$, $\{q, r\}$ and $\{r, p\}$ is truth-functionally *consistent*, but such that the whole set $\{p, q, r\}$ is truth-functionally *inconsistent*.

20. Give an example of an inconsistent set of English statements that is, nevertheless, *truth-functionally* consistent.

21. Suppose that a set of statements $\{s_1, \ldots, s_n\}$ is truth-functionally consistent. Must all elements of the set be truth-functionally contingent? Show that your answer is correct.

22. Suppose that all elements of a set of statements $\{s_1, \ldots, s_n\}$ are truth-functionally contingent. Must the set be truth-functionally consistent? Show that your answer is correct.

23. Suppose you are presented with an argument: $p_1, \ldots, p_n$ /∴ c & $\sim c$. Assume that this is a truth-functionally valid argument. Show that, given this assumption, the set $\{p_1, \ldots, p_n\}$ must be truth-functionally inconsistent.

24. Complete the following proposition and clearly show that your answer is correct:

> A set $\{p_1, \ldots, p_n\}$ of *SL* statements is truth-functionally consistent if, and only if, the following *SL argument* is truth-functionally invalid:

3.7 The Material Conditional Revisited

When we introduced the truth table for the material conditional earlier in this chapter, we showed that there are many kinds of conditionals (including causal conditionals, counterfactual conditionals, and strict conditionals) that are not truth-functional. In this section we present an argument for the following claim: *If a conditional is truth-functional, then* there is only one plausible option for its truth table. Our argument basically rests upon observations about how we ordinarily use sentences of the form 'if, then' in English.

We start by assuming that the conditional, like the conjunction, the disjunction, and the biconditional, *is* a truth-functional two-place connective. This means that it takes two truth-valued statements and assigns to the pair a unique truth-value. Our problem, then, is to discover just *what* this function consists in. There are only a small number of possible two-place truth functions. If p and q are statements, then they can take on only four possible combinations of truth values. A truth function of p and q must assign true or false to each of these possible combinations, and there are $2^4 = 16$ possible ways to do so. We list them here in the following truth tables. Above each column of the table is a statement form whose truth-functional meaning is described by that column:

p	q	$p \vee \sim p$	$p \vee q$	$p \vee \sim q$	p	$\sim p \vee q$	q	$p \leftrightarrow q$	p & q
T	T	T	T	T	T	T	T	T	T
T	F	T	T	T	T	F	F	F	F
F	T	T	T	F	F	T	T	F	F
F	F	T	F	T	F	T	F	T	F
		1	2	3	4	5	6	7	8

p	q	$\sim(p \ \& \ q)$	$p \leftrightarrow \sim q$	$\sim q$	$p \ \& \sim q$	$\sim p$	$\sim p \ \& \ q$	$\sim(p \lor q)$	$p \ \& \sim p$
T	T	F	F	F	F	F	F	F	F
T	F	T	T	T	T	F	F	F	F
F	T	T	T	F	F	T	T	F	F
F	F	T	F	T	F	T	F	T	F
		9	10	11	12	13	14	15	16

Our proposed truth table for the material conditional is the one listed in the fifth column of the first table. To show that this is correct, we proceed by a process of elimination. If we can show that *none* of the other possibilities is a plausible candidate, this will leave us with the Philonian conditional as the only candidate.

We can eliminate most of the possibilities quickly. What should be the value of a truth-functional conditional when a conditional has a true antecedent and true consequent? The only plausible answer is that it must be true. Suppose that you say to yourself, 'If I am offered the job in Chicago, then I will accept it'. Assume that subsequently you are offered the job and you do accept it. Would you say that the conditional statement you made was *false?* Definitely not. Since we assume that a statement is true if, and only if, it is not false, we thus must conclude that a conditional having both a true antecedent and a true consequent is true. Since the top row of the truth table—the row where antecedent and consequent are both true—must thus be T, we have eliminated possibilities 9 through 16.

Next, what if the antecedent is true and the consequent is false? Could the value of the conditional be anything but false? Suppose again that you say to yourself, 'If I am offered a job in Chicago, then I will accept it', and that you are subsequently offered a job in Chicago but decide *not* to accept it. If you do this, we would undoubtedly say that your original conditional claim was false: *It's not the case* that if you're offered a job in Chicago, then you will accept it. This implies that we can rule out the possibilities 1 through 4 because they have T in their second row (the row where the antecedent is true and the consequent false).

We are left with columns 5 through 8. Whatever else we say about the conditional, we think it expresses some relation between the antecedent and the consequent, so asserting it must not be the same as merely asserting *q*. This eliminates column 6. We can also say that it goes against the intuitive meaning of the conditional to demand that the antecedent be true for the conditional to be true, so it cannot be equivalent to *p* & *q* in column 8. This leaves us with columns 5 and 7. Column 7 is the truth table for the biconditional. An important feature of the biconditional is that it is *symmetric: p ↔ q* is truth-functionally equivalent to *q ↔ p*. Consideration of examples shows that the conditional is *not* symmetric. The statement 'If it is raining, then there's water on my driveway' certainly does not mean the same as 'If there's water on my driveway, then it is raining'. These considerations rule out column 7, leaving column 5 as the only possible truth table for the conditional.

Further justifications can be given for the truth table, but these are based on somewhat more intricate principles of logic than can be given at this stage. We will be able to say more, however, in Section 4.9.

Exercises for Section 3.7

1. A classic problem in the history of logic has been to give a proper solution to the following problems, known as 'paradoxes of material implication':

   a. If p is any false statement, then $p \rightarrow q$ is true no matter what statement q is. It thus appears that a false statement implies *every* statement. How can this be? Intuitively at least, a false statement should not imply *every* statement!

   b. Given any two statements p and q, it turns out that $(p \rightarrow q) \vee (q \rightarrow p)$ is a tautology. Thus, for *any two statements at all*, it is necessarily the case that one of them implies the other. How can this be? Intuitively at least, it shouldn't turn out that the relation of implication always holds between an arbitrarily selected pair of statements.

   For each of these, analyzing the formulation of the problem is part of providing a proper solution. In particular, use of the word 'implies' is misleading. Offer solutions to these two problems.

2. Consider the following: Ronnie's boyfriend said 'You will marry me if, and only if, I love you'. Ronnie responded, 'No way! That's a false biconditional if I've ever heard one! It's not the case that I will marry you if, and only if, you love me!' Now, the statement asserted by Ronnie's boyfriend can be symbolized 'M $\leftrightarrow$ L'. Ronnie denied this claim and asserted its negation: $\sim$(M $\leftrightarrow$ L). However, this latter statement *is truth-functionally equivalent* to 'M $\leftrightarrow$ $\sim$L', or, "I will marry you if, and only if, you do not love me"! Ronnie seems to be in a strange position, to say the least! Has something gone wrong in the symbolization of Ronnie's statement? If you think so, explain clearly where we went wrong. If you think that the statement is symbolized correctly, explain why there really is no problem here.

3.8   Brief Truth Tables

In this section we consider a technique that can be used to shorten a truth table. The method of brief truth tables allows us to make a quick search through a table, without always adding the unnecessary detail of a full-blown table. This technique anticipates the method of truth trees, which is taken up in Section 3.9.

We know that an argument is truth-functionally invalid just in case its truth table contains a counterexample—that is, a row in which the argument's premises all take the value true but its conclusion comes out false. The method of brief truth tables (also known as **indirect** or **abbreviated** truth tables) is a way of making a rapid search through a table just to discover whether or not an argument has a counterexample.

The method proceeds like this. Given some argument, we *assume* that the argument is invalid and write truth values beneath the premises and conclusion of the argument that show the premises true but the conclusion false. We then work "backward," assigning truth values to the components of each statement *based on the assumption* that the argument is invalid. *If* we can complete this process without being forced to make contradictory assignments of truth values, then the argument in question is indeed invalid. If, on the other hand, the assumption that the argument is invalid *forces* us logically to make contradictory assignments of values, this shows that the argument must be truth-functionally valid. To see how this works, consider the following simple argument:

$$R \rightarrow {\sim}S$$
$$\underline{S \qquad\qquad}$$
$$\therefore {\sim}R$$

To test this for validity using the brief truth table method, we start by listing the premises and conclusion in a row. The premises are put on the left, separated from each other by a single slash ('/'). The conclusion is put on the right, signaled by a double slash ('//'):

R → ~S / S // ~R

Next, we *assume* that the argument is invalid, by writing T under the main connectives of the premises and F under the main connective of the conclusion:

R → ~S / S // ~R
 T   T   F

If the argument has a counterexample, then, in that row on the truth table, this is what the truth values under these statements must look like. Now we use the definitions of the truth-functional connectives to infer the values of the simpler components from which the argument is built. First, since '~R' is supposed to be false, this implies that 'R' must be true:

R → ~S / S // ~R
 T   T   FT

Repeat this fact wherever the statement letter 'R' appears:

R → ~S / S // ~R
T T   T   FT

Next, repeat the value T under every occurrence of 'S':

R → ~S / S // ~R
T T   T T   FT

Finally, since 'S' is supposed to be true, this means that '~S' must be false:

R → ~S / S // ~R
T T FT T   FT

Now consider these facts: (1) We *assumed* that the argument is invalid, by assuming there is a row in which the premises are both true while the conclusion is false. (2) This assumption logically implies that the conditional's antecedent takes the value T but that its consequent takes the value F. But this implies, contrary to assumption (1), that the conditional is *false,* not true! This shows that it is impossible for the argument's premises to be true while the conclusion is false. Making the assumption that we can assign T to the premises but F to the conclusion leads to the contradiction that one of the premises (the first one) must be simultaneously true and false! Since it is thus impossible that the premises should be true while the conclusion is false, the argument has been shown to be truth-functionally valid.[14]

Here is another example. Consider that a complete truth table for the following argument requires sixteen rows and nine columns:

(A ∨ B) → (C & D)
A
∴ D

Here, we begin by listing the premises and conclusion and assuming that a counterexample exists:

(1)   (A ∨ B) → (C & D) / A // D
               T   T   F

We repeat the values for 'A' and 'D' wherever these appear:

---

[14]Observe that we are implicitly relying on Proposition 2. By showing that we can't make 'R → ~S' and 'S' true while '~R' is false, we have shown that we can't make all elements of the *set* {R → ~S, S, ~~R} true at once. Since this set is truth-functionally inconsistent, the argument in question must be truth-functionally valid.

(2)   (A ∨ B) → (C & D) / A // D
        T   T   F   T   F

Since the antecedent of the conditional is a disjunction with a true disjunct, the antecedent must be true:

(3)   (A ∨ B) → (C & D) / A // D
        T T   T   F   T   F

Similarly, since the consequent of the conditional is a conjunction with a false conjunct, the consequent must be false:

(4)   (A ∨ B) → (C & D) / A // D
        T T   T   F F   T   F
        Impossible!

Once again, we have a true antecedent but a false consequent. Once again, therefore, we have shown that it would be impossible for the premises to be true while the conclusion is false. Thus, this argument is truth-functionally valid. To illuminate the procedure, numbers can be placed under the truth value assignments to show the order in which they were made (corresponding to the numbered steps above):

(A ∨ B) → (C & D) / A // D
T T   T   F F   T   F
2 3   1   4 2   1   1

Now consider this argument:

~(A & ~B)
~(B & ~C)
∴ ~C → ~A

A complete truth table would require eight rows and eleven columns. Here, we first list the statements and assume that a counterexample exists:

~(A & ~B) / ~(B & ~C) // ~C → ~A
T   T   F

Now we look for cases in which we must make specific truth value assignments. Such is the case with the conclusion; the assumption that this conditional is false implies that it must have a true antecedent and a false consequent:

~(A & ~B) / ~(B & ~C) // ~C → ~A
T   T   T F F

The fact that the antecedent '~C' must be assigned T implies that 'C' must take the value F. By similar reasoning, the statement 'A' must take the value T:

~(A & ~B) / ~(B & ~C) // ~C → ~A
T   T   TF F FT

Repeat the assignments to these statement letters wherever they appear:

~(A & ~B) / ~(B & ~C) // ~C → ~A
T T   T   F   TF F FT

Next, observe that for the premises to be true, the negated components must be false:

~(A & ~B) / ~(B & ~C) // ~C → ~A
T T F   T F   F   TF F FT

Since the negated component of this first premise is a conjunction, it will be false just in case at least one of its conjuncts is false. Since the conjunct 'A' must be true, the conjunct '~B' must be false; hence, 'B' must be true:

~(A & ~B) / ~(B & ~C) // ~C → ~A
T TF FT   T TF   F   TF F FT

Finally, since the second premise is a negated conjunction and since the conjuncts are both true, the conjunction must be true:

~(A & ~B) / ~(B & ~C) // ~C → ~A
T T F FT   T TF TF   TF F FT

But this last step is *impossible,* for since the second premise is assumed to be true the conjunction itself *should* be false. Thus, it is not possible for this argument to have true premises and a false conclusion.

Here is another argument:

~A ∨ ~B
~A ⎯⎯⎯⎯
∴ ~B

Assume it has a counterexample:

~A ∨ ~B / ~A // ~B
      T   T   F

Since '~A' is assumed true, 'A' must be false; and since '~B' is assumed false, 'B' must be true. This gives the following completed brief table:

~ A ∨ ~ B / ~ A // ~ B
TF TF T   TF   F T

Notice that *no contradictions* were encountered. This means that it *is* possible to make the premises of this argument true while its conclusion is false—namely, by assigning F to 'A' and T to 'B'. Thus, this argument is not truth-functionally valid.

When using the brief table method, the object is to first work with statements that force you to make particular truth-value assignments. In each of the cases so far considered, this was possible from the start. However, many arguments provide you with more than one option about how to proceed. Such is the case with the following:

G ∨ J / H ∨ J // G & J

Assume that a counterexample exists:

G ∨ J / H ∨ J // G & J
  T   T   F

Notice, however, that there are *three ways* that the conclusion could be false and, similarly, three ways each that the premises could be true. To use the brief table method here, you have to go through some alternative assignments. If you find even one way to make the premises true and the conclusion false, the argument will have been shown truth-functionally invalid. However, if one assignment turns out to be impossible, you must continue until all possible ways to make the conclusion false or premises true have been exhausted. In this case, let's see what happens if we assume that the conclusion is false because both its conjuncts are false:

G ∨ J / H ∨ J // G & J
  T   T   F F F

Repeating the values under the appropriate statement letters,

G ∨ J / H ∨ J // G & J
F T F   T F   F F F

Notice that the assignment to the first premise is impossible: The disjunction could not be true if both disjuncts were false. This, however, does *not* show that the argument is invalid because there are at least two more possible ways to make the conclusion false. Put an 'X' next to this row to show that it is an impossible value assignment and consider next making 'G' true but 'J' false:

G ∨ J / H ∨ J // G & J
X F T F   T F   F F F
  T   T   T F F

Repeating the values appropriately gives

G ∨ J / H ∨ J // G & J
×F T F   T F   F F F
 T T F   T F   T F F

So far, no problems have been encountered. Assigning T to 'H' produces a counterexample:

G ∨ J / H ∨ J // G & J
×F T F   T F   F F F
 T T F T T F   T F F

Thus, this argument is *not* truth-functionally valid.

    In a case like the one just considered, in which you must run through several possibilities, an argument is not shown valid unless you can put an '✕' next to every row—that is, unless every possible way to make the conclusion false or premises true implies a contradictory assignment of values. (If there is no way to make the conclusion false, then the argument is certainly valid.) An example of a valid argument that requires us to consider cases is the following:

~(A → B) // A ↔ ~B
T   F

There are *two ways* in which the conclusion could be false. First

~(A → B) // A ↔ ~B
T   T F F

This implies that 'B' is true. Repeat these assignments appropriately:

~(A → B) // A ↔ ~B
TT   T   T F FT

This assignment would make the premise both true *and* false at the same time:

~(A → B) // A ↔ ~B
TT T T   T F FT

Impossible!

Thus, we put an '✕' next to this row and go on to the next possibility:

~(A → B) // A ↔ ~B
×T T T T   T F FT
 T   F F T

This implies that 'B' takes the value F:

```
  ~(A → B) // A ↔ ~B
×TT T  T    T F FT
  T F    F    F F TF
```

Again, however, this is impossible:

```
  ~(A → B) // A ↔ ~B
×TT T  T    T F FT
×TF T  F    F F TF
```

There are no possible ways remaining in which to make the conclusion false. Since each one implies a contradictory assignment of values, the argument is truth-functionally valid.

The method of brief truth tables can be used to test statements for tautologousness, truth-functional self-contradictoriness, truth-functional contingency, truth-functional equivalence, and truth-functional mutual contradictoriness. The method can also be used to test sets of statements for truth-functional consistency.

To determine whether or not a statement is a tautology, use the brief truth table method to answer this question: Could the statement be false? If the answer is 'yes', then it's not a tautology. If the answer is 'no', then it is a tautology. As an example, let's determine whether or not the statement 'A → (B → A)' is a tautology. We begin by supposing that the statement is false:

```
A → (B → A)
   F
```

Since this conditional is assumed to be false, we infer that it must have a true antecedent and a false consequent:

```
A → (B → A)
T F    F
```

As usual, whenever we have a truth value assigned to a single statement letter, we repeat that value wherever the letter occurs:

```
A → (B → A)
T F    F T
```

We see at once that this assignment of values is impossible. Since 'A' must be assigned the value T, it follows that the consequent of the conditional, 'B → A', must also take the value T, and this contradicts our knowledge that the consequent would have to take the value F if the whole statement were false. That means it is impossible for the original statement to be assigned the value F without contradiction. Thus, the statement is a tautology.

Here is a final, completed example. Each step has been numbered:

$$[A \to (B \to C)] \to [(A \to B) \to (A \to C)]$$

T T	F T F	F	T T F	F T F F
5 2	7 6 5	1	5 3 8	2 4 3 4

Impossible!

Since this statement can't possibly be false, it is a tautology.

It is left for you to discover on your own how the method of brief truth tables may be applied in each of the remaining cases.

Exercises for Section 3.8

Part I: Tautologies   In Section 3.4 (Part I), you were asked to use truth tables to determine whether the following statements were tautologies. Work these problems again, this time using brief truth tables.

1. A ∨ B
2. A ∨ ~B
3. ~(A & ~A)
4. ~(A ∨ ~A)
♦5. (F ∨ ~F) & ~(G & ~G)
6. ~(~(H & ~G) & G) ∨ G
7. (P & Q) → Q
8. (X → Y) ∨ (Y → X)
9. ~(Q → R) → (~Q → R)
10. ((A & B) ∨ ((~A & B) ∨ (A & ~B))) ∨ (~A & ~B)

11. (P → Q) ∨ (P → ~Q)
12. ~(H → J) → ~(J → H)
♦13. ~[~(K ∨ ~L) & (~K → ~L)]
14. [(G & ~H) & (H & ~G)] ∨ (P → P)
15. [~W & (M → W)] → ~M
16. ~(Q & E) → ~(Q ∨ E)
17. (H → J) → ((H → ~J) → ~H)
18. [J → (H & K)] → [(J → H) & (J → K)]
19. [~A & (~B & ~C)] ∨ (A & B)
20. [(X & Y) → Z] → [(X → Z) ∨ (Y → Z)]

Part II: Validity   In Section 3.4 (Part II), you were asked to use truth tables to determine whether the following arguments were truth-functionally valid. Work these problems again, this time using brief truth tables.

21. A & B / ∴ A
22. A ∨ B / ∴ ~A ∨ ~B
♦23. ~(E & G) / ∴ E ∨ F
24. ~(P & Q) / ∴ ~P & ~Q
25. ~H, ~J / ∴ ~(H & J)
26. Z ∨ W, W → Z / ∴ Z

27. C ∨ ~D / ∴ D → C
28. E ∨ F, ~ ~E / ∴ F
29. ~G → H, ~H / ∴ G
30. ~(A → B) / ∴ ~B
♦31. F → G, ~F → G / ∴ G
32. F → G, ~F → ~G / ∴ ~(F & G)

33. (J & K), ~K ∨ J /∴ ~K ∨ J   40. ~A, (C ∨ D) → ~A /∴ A → ~D
34. H → J /∴ ~J → (H → J)   ♦41. X & ~Y, ~Y ∨ ~Z /∴ X & ~Z
35. ~(K & ~L), ~K /∴ L   42. H → J, J → ~(L & M), ~M /∴ H & J
36. ~(~ ~K & ~ ~L), ~ ~K /∴ ~L   43. H & (G ∨ F), ~(G → F) /∴ ~H → G
37. J → K, ~(K ∨ L) /∴ ~J   44. ~[K ∨ (K → M)] /∴ P & ~P
38. M → N, N → O, ~M /∴ ~O   45. ~(S & ~L) /∴ (L & S) ∨ (~L & ~S)
39. ~P ∨ Q, ~Q ∨ R, ~R /∴ P   46. R ∨ (S → T), ~T & ~R /∴ ~(S & U)
47. ~[H → (K → M)], K & ~M /∴ H → (K → M)
48. ~[M ∨ (N ∨ O)], (~M → P) & (~O → P), P → ~N /∴ ~N → P
49. (E ∨ G) → F, (G ∨ H) → F, (G & E) ∨ (G & H) /∴ F & G
50. (A & B) → (C → (D & E)), ~(D → E) & C /∴ ~(A & B)

Part III: Further Development

♦51. Explain how to use brief truth tables in order to determine whether or not a statement is a truth-functional self-contradiction.

52. Explain how to use brief truth tables in order to determine whether or not a pair of statements are truth-functionally equivalent.

53. Explain how to use brief truth tables in order to determine whether or not a set of statements is truth-functionally consistent.

(A)   Using the procedure you found in Exercise 51, test each of the following for self-contradiction.

54. A → ~A   56. ~(A ∨ (B → ~A))   58. ~F ↔ (F & G)
55. ~(A ∨ ~A) ♦57. F & (F ↔ ~G)   59. (G ∨ F) ↔ (~F → G)

(B)   Using the procedure you found in Exercise 52, test each of the following pairs of statements for equivalence.

60. A → ~B, ~A → B   63. ~(H ∨ (J & I)), ~J & (~H ∨ ~I)
61. A ↔ B, ~A ↔ ~B   64. (A & ~B) ∨ C, (~C → A) & (B → C)
62. ~(A ↔ B), ~A ↔ B   65. A → (B ↔ C), (A → B) ↔ C

(C)   Using the procedure you found in Exercise 53, test each of the following sets of statements for consistency.

66. {A, A → B, ~B}   68. {M ∨ N, ~M ∨ N, ~N}
67. {~A, A → B, B}   69. {F ∨ ~G, F → H, H & ~G, F}
70. {A & B, B ↔ C, A & ~C}
71. {(A & ~B) → C, (C ∨ D) ↔ A, (C ∨ B) ↔ D, ~D ∨ ~A}

3.9 Truth Trees

The method of truth trees, like the method of truth tables, is a mechanical technique for testing statements for certain semantic properties. A truth tree can be used to determine whether or not a statement is tautologous, truth-functionally self-contradictory, or truth-functionally contingent. The method can also be used to test arguments for truth-functional validity and sets of statements for truth-functional consistency, as well as to test for equivalence and contradictories. The method is at once more efficient and potentially more powerful than the method of truth tables, because, unlike tables, truth trees can easily be extended to handle statements and arguments that are not amenable to truth-functional analysis.[15]

A truth tree "draws a picture" of the truth conditions for statements, yet without the unnecessary detail of truth tables. A truth tree tells us in particular two things. First, it tells us whether or not a set of statements is truth-functionally consistent. Second, if a set is truth-functionally consistent, the truth tree provides us with an interpretation under which all elements of the set are true. Because of the logical relationships that hold between consistency and other logical properties (e.g., as expressed in Propositions 2–4), we can use truth trees to test for these properties in terms of consistency.

Our plan now is to explain just what a *truth tree* is and to introduce specific rules for how to construct one. The first step in this program is to consider a statement letter, say, 'A'. On a truth *table* we represent the possibility that 'A' is true by the row beneath 'A' that contains the value T:

$$\frac{\text{A}}{\begin{array}{c}\text{T}\\\text{F}\end{array}}$$

A is true under this row $\longrightarrow$

On a truth *tree* we are concerned only with the top row—that is, with the possibility that 'A' is true. On a truth tree we represent this possibility thus:

A

That is, we simply write down the *SL* statement. Writing down 'A' can be thought of as meaning that 'A' is assigned the value T.

Next consider a disjunction, 'A ∨ ~B'. We are interested in cases where this statement is true, so we begin, as above, by simply writing down the statement.

---

[15]The method of truth trees presented here is essentially that developed by Richard Jeffrey. A more theoretically detailed account than the one presented here can be found in his book *Formal Logic* (see Appendix 1).

We know that on a truth table we can take two paths to make a disjunction true. On the one hand, we can assign true to 'A':

On the other hand, the statement 'A ∨ ~B' takes the value true if we assign true to '~B':

Assigning value true to '~B' of course just means assigning false to 'B'. If we combine these two pictures, we get a diagram that illustrates the paths that can be taken to make 'A ∨ ~B' true:

This diagram is a truth tree for the statement 'A ∨ ~B'.

Two new terms help us to describe trees. First, we define a **node** as any *whole statement* on a tree—that is, a statement that is *not* contained within another statement. Second, we define a **branch** to be any sequence of nodes that can be traced from a node at the bottom of the tree up to the top of the tree. The tree above has three nodes ('A', 'A ∨ ~B', and '~B') and two branches (the sequence 'A', 'A ∨ ~B', and the sequence '~B', 'A ∨ ~B'). Branches are also sometimes called **paths,** since following a branch from bottom to top yields a path through the tree.

In constructing the above tree for the statement 'A ∨ ~B' we applied a *basic truth tree rule*. Let *p* and *q* be any *SL* statements at all. We know that the statement *p* ∨ *q* takes the value T just in case *p* or *q* takes the value T. In other words, given *any* disjunction at all, there are two paths you can take to make the disjunction true:

This diagram (containing the variables '*p*' and '*q*') is to be read as a *rule*. It tells you that, given any particular disjunction, you must draw two branches beneath it. At the end of the left-hand branch is written the left-hand disjunct, and at the end of the right-hand branch is written the right-hand disjunct. Thus, applying the rule to the statement '(A → B) ∨ [Q & ~(R ∨ S)]' produces

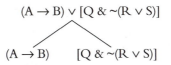

The disjunction rule states, in effect, that to make a disjunction true you must assign true to at least one of its disjuncts. Thus, to succeed in making the statement

(A → B) ∨ [Q & ~(R ∨ S)]

take the value T, you must *either* follow the left-hand branch

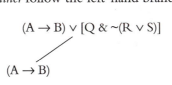

or you must follow the right-hand branch

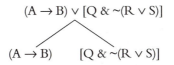

Because the rule for disjunction creates two branches from one, it is called a **branching rule.**

Consider now conjunction. A conjunction comes out true only on those lines of a truth table where both conjuncts have the value T. The truth tree rule thus requires us to enter both conjuncts on the *same branch:*

p & q
p
q

This instruction tells you that, given any conjunction, you simply list the two conjuncts vertically. Doing this indicates that the conjunction is true just in case both conjuncts are true. As an example, suppose you are given this statement:

K & (L ∨ M).

To apply the rule for conjunction, you are required to *list both conjuncts vertically:*

$$K \ \& \ (L \lor M)$$
$$K$$
$$L \lor M$$

This truth tree states, in effect, that the statement 'K & (L ∨ M)' is true just in case both 'K' and 'L ∨ M' are true. Because the rule for conjunction does not create any additional branches, it is called a **nonbranching rule.**

Let's pause for a moment to collect the material so far presented:

1. A statement letter, standing alone as a single node on a truth tree, means 'assign the value T to this letter'.

2. A negated statement letter, standing alone as a single node on a tree means 'assign the value F to this letter'.

3. A disjunction standing as a node on a tree is to be "broken down" into two branches, each containing one disjunct. This is taken to mean 'at least one of these disjuncts is true'.

4. A conjunction standing as a node on a tree is to be "broken down" into a list of both conjuncts. This is taken to mean 'both of these conjuncts are true'.

These four principles for "breaking down" statements and "reading off" assignments of truth values can be combined into a systematic procedure for testing sets of statements for truth-functional consistency. A full truth tree begins with a **trunk**—that is, a list of statements whose consistency is in question. Ordinarily, the tree is then extended by "growing" one or more branches below this initial trunk. The complete tree that results constitutes a kind of diagram of the conditions under which all members on the initial list take the value T together (if there are such conditions).

To demonstrate how this procedure works, using only the two rules so far presented, consider the following set of *SL* statements: {A & B, B ∨ ~D}. Is this set truth-functionally consistent? It is if there is at least one interpretation of the statement letters that makes both statements in the set true. This question is equivalent to asking whether or not there is at least one row on the truth table for the set where both statements take the value T at once. To use a truth tree to answer this question, we begin by simply listing the elements of the set as the first two nodes of the tree:

$$A \ \& \ B$$
$$B \lor \sim D$$

We can read this "trunk" of the truth tree as the assumption that both statements take the value T together. We want to know if this assumption is legitimate: *Can* these two statements be true at the same time? To answer this question we must discover whether or not there is an assignment of truth values to the statement letters in the two statements that makes both compound statements true at once. We make this discovery by applying the truth tree rules described above. First, applying the rule for conjunction, we know that the top statement is true just in case both conjuncts are true:

A & B ✓
B ∨ ~D
A
B

We indicate that a rule has been applied to a statement by placing a check next to it. Next we apply the rule for disjunction to the second statement:

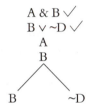

A & B ✓
B ∨ ~D ✓
A
B

B   ~D

Again, we put a check next to the statement to which a rule was applied. There now remain on the tree no statements to which a rule has not been applied (no rules apply to single statement letters or their negations). Thus, this tree is finished. But what does it tell us?

This tree tells us that the set {A & B, B ∨ ~D} is truth-functionally *consistent.* The tree tells us this by showing us an interpretation under which all statements in the trunk of the tree are true. Recall that a statement letter, standing alone as a node on the tree, is to be interpreted as an instruction to assign the value T to that letter and that a negated statement letter, standing alone as a node on the tree, is to be interpreted as an instruction to assign the value F to that letter. Let's read up along the left-hand branch. The first statement letter we come to is 'B'. Assign T to that letter. Continue reading up along the branch, until you come to the next statement letter (other than 'B'). The next one is 'A'. Assign T to that letter. We have now assigned T to both 'A' and 'B'. Under this interpretation, both elements of the set ('A & B' and 'B ∨ ~D') take the value T. Since there thus exists at least one interpretation under which all elements of the set are true, the set is consistent; *this* is how consistency is demonstrated using a truth tree.

So far, so good. But how would a tree tell us whether a set of statements is *inconsistent?* To find out, let's look at an inconsistent set that employs '∨' and '~' as its elements' only connectives: {A ∨ B, ~A, ~B}. Clearly, there's no row on a truth table where the set's elements are true simultaneously. Let's see what happens when we build a tree for this set. We begin by listing the elements of the set:

A ∨ B
~A
~B

The tree now offers the assumption that the set is consistent; the finished tree will tell us whether or not this assumption is correct. Starting with the first statement, we apply the rule for disjunction:

Our problem here is that, reading up along either branch of the tree, we get conflicting instructions on how to construct an interpretation under which all elements of the original set of statements are true. On the left branch we are told to assign both T *and* F to 'A', and on the right branch we are told to assign both T *and* F to 'B'. Clearly, neither pair of assignments is possible, so there is no possible interpretation that makes the original set of statements true. When a single branch contains a statement and its negation like this (i.e., as *two nodes* on the *same branch*), we say that the branch **closes,** and we put an '✕' at the bottom of the branch that contains the inconsistency:

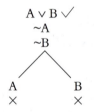

Since all branches close on this tree, we know that no assignment of truth values would make the elements of the set simultaneously true. The set is therefore truth–functionally inconsistent. On the other hand, not all branches closed on the tree for the set containing 'A & B' and 'B ∨ ~D'. A branch that is not closed is called an **open** branch. Because the finished tree for this former set contains at least one open branch, we conclude that the set is truth-functionally consistent.

We have seen that we can "read off" an interpretation from a branch through a truth tree by assigning T to all statement letters that occur as nodes on that branch and F to all negated statement letters that appear as nodes on that branch. This technique only works as long as we have broken down all complex statements on the branch to the point where there are no unchecked statements other than statement letters and their negations. Consider the following tree, consisting of a single statement:

A & ~A

This statement is of course a truth-functional self-contradiction, but the tree method does not reveal this fact until we have applied our rule to break down the conjunction:

A & ~A ✓
A
~A
×

To ensure that we have found all possible inconsistencies, we thus need rules to break down *any* statement that is not a statement letter or negated statement letter. If one considers our syntactical rules, there are a limited number of kinds of complex statements. We have statements that are formed by putting two statements together with one of the four binary connectives: conjunction, disjunction, conditional, and biconditional. We need one rule for each of these types of statements. We also have statements that are formed by negating statements. There is no single rule for negation. Instead, we have a rule for each of the five possible kinds of complex statements that could be negated: negated negation (double negation), negated conjunction, negated disjunction, negated conditional, and negated biconditional. Altogether that makes nine rules. We have examined two so far; the rest work in basically the same way. One extends the tree using the rule and then checks off the statement to which the rule was applied. Here are the nine rules:

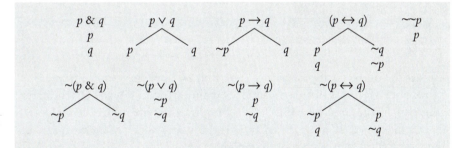

Let's look at the rule for conditionals. What it says is that there are two possible ways to make a conditional true. Either the antecedent p must be false or the consequent q must be true. (This follows from our basic truth table for the conditional.) Here is how we would apply the rule in a specific case:

The fact that the rule looks as it does can be explained in another way. Recall that the conditional form '$p \rightarrow q$' is truth-functionally equivalent to the disjunction

'~p ∨ q'. If we apply the disjunction rule to this latter statement form, we get exactly the same result that is given by the rule for the conditional.

Next let's look at the rule for a negated conditional. There is only *one* way for a conditional to be false: Its antecedent must be true and its consequent false. This is also the only way for a *negated* conditional to be true. Consequently, our rule for negated conditionals is nonbranching. Here is an example of how to apply it:

$$\sim(A \rightarrow B) \checkmark$$
$$A$$
$$\sim B$$

We can also explain our rule in the following way: A negated conditional form '~(p → q)' is truth-functionally equivalent to 'p & ~q'. Applying the conjunction rule to this second statement form yields the same result as applying the rule for the negated conditional.

We'll consider one more of the rules—the rule for the biconditional. The rule for the biconditional looks different than any of the rules we have discussed, since it is a branching rule with two statements under each branch. The justification of the branching rule is this. There are two ways for a biconditional to be true: Either both conditions are true or both are false. Consequently we have one branch in which we list both conditions and another where we list the negation of both conditions. Here, once again, is a concrete application:

$$(A \rightarrow B) \checkmark$$

| A | ~A |
| B | ~B |

We leave it to you to justify for yourself the four rules we have not discussed.

Probably the most difficult part of learning how to construct truth trees is learning which rule should be used to decompose a statement. In the case of short statements like 'A → B' or '~(B ∨ D)', it is fairly easy to see which rule to apply, but the task gets trickier with long statements like

$$(\sim(P \leftrightarrow Q) \rightarrow C) \vee P$$

or

$$\sim(A \rightarrow ((B \leftrightarrow \sim C) \, \& \, C)).$$

The problem here is the same problem we ran into in trying to decide which column of a truth table to fill in first. You need to recognize the overall form of the statement, which means that you have to recognize its main connective. (If you do not remember how to do this, review our discussion in Section 2.5!) If the main connective is one of the four binary connectives, simply apply the rule for that connective. If the main connective is a negation, determine the form of the whole statement in the scope of that negation and then apply the appropriate negation rule (unless, of course, the scope of the negation is a single statement letter). For example, the main connective of the statement '(~(P ↔ Q) → C) ∨ P' is the disjunction. Applying the disjunction rule produces

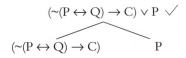

In the next statement, '~(A → ((B ↔ ~C) & C))', the main connective is the negation at the front of the statement; the main connective of the negated statement is a conditional; thus, we apply the rule for a negated conditional:

$$\sim(A \rightarrow ((B \leftrightarrow \sim C) \ \& \ C)) \ \checkmark$$
$$A$$
$$\sim((B \leftrightarrow \sim C) \ \& \ C)$$

Note that in each case, there is only *one* possible rule to apply to a node, since you must always apply the rule appropriate to the whole statement occuring at a node. You could not, for instance, choose to decompose the conjunction '((B ↔ ~C) & C)' first, since this conjunction does not occur as a whole statement at any node of the tree.

Let's now complete a tree that has a number of branches. We'll start the tree with the following statements:

$$A \rightarrow (C \vee D)$$
$$(B \vee A)$$

It does not matter which statement we decompose first, except that the order in which statements are decomposed can have an effect on how *long* the tree is. In this case we'll work in "reverse" order: The second statement will be decomposed first, and the first statement will be decomposed second:

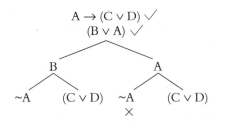

Notice how we've applied the rule for the conditional: The two branches created when we applied the disjunction rule to the second statement put the statement 'A → (C ∨ D)' on *two* open branches. Thus, when the first statement was decomposed using the rule for a conditional, the result was placed at the bottom of *every open branch containing the conditional*. As you can see, we could also close one of the branches. To finish the tree, apply the rule for the disjunction to 'C ∨ D', which is at the bottom of two open branches:

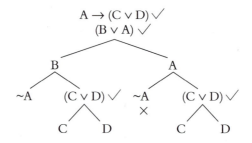

Inspecting all the open branches reveals that there is no further inconsistency. Because the completed tree has open branches, the original set of statements is consistent. Notice that the interpretation ⟨A:F, B:T⟩, read off the left-most branch, makes both statements true at once.

We'll now build a tree for a more complex set of statements than we have so far. We'll test the following set of statements for consistency: {C ∨ D, ~D, C ↔ (A & B), A → D, ~(D & B)}. Observe first of all how difficult it would be to construct a truth table to determine whether this set is consistent. The table would have sixteen rows and seventeen columns. Our truth tree will be much easier. We begin by listing the statements on the trunk of the tree:

$$C \lor D$$
$$\sim D$$
$$C \leftrightarrow (A \mathbin{\&} B)$$
$$A \to D$$
$$\sim(C \mathbin{\&} B)$$

Begin work on the tree by selecting any unchecked statement you please. Regardless of the order in which you select statements on the tree, you will always get the same answer in the end. Nonetheless, some choices are better than others because, by choosing certain statements to work on before others, you can minimize the number of nodes on your tree. The fewer the number of nodes, the less work there is for you. Here are two principles that you can use:

1. Whenever possible, choose a statement that can be decomposed by a nonbranching rule before choosing statements that are decomposed by branching rules.

2. Whenever possible, choose statements that when decomposed will allow you to close branches.

In our present example all four of the decomposable statements require branching rules, so we can't use Principle 1. However, decomposing the first statement will allow us to close a branch, so we'll start with it:

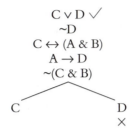

As you can see, the right-hand branch closes since it contains 'D' and '~D'. We also get closure of one branch if we work next on the fourth statement:

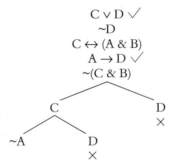

At this point we have two choices. We'll choose 'C ↔ (A & B)'. One of the resulting branches will close immediately, and the other will close after we decompose 'A & B':

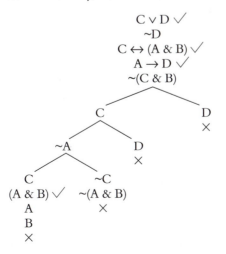

Since all branches have closed, the original set is inconsistent, even though the fifth statement was never used! When a branch closes it is not required that one of the statements in the contradictory pair be the last statement on the branch. Note, too, that in a tree this large there are many choices regarding the order in which one can decompose the statements. Try completing it in some other order; you should still get all branches to close.

Now that you have seen a more lengthy example of a truth tree, let's concisely state our procedure for tree construction:

> *Definition*   A branch is said to be a **closed branch** if, and only if, it contains a node p together with a node $\sim p$.
>
> *Definition*   A branch is said to be a **finished open branch** if, and only if, the branch is not closed and it contains no unchecked nodes except those consisting simply of statement letters or negations of statement letters.
>
> *Definition*   A tree is said to be **finished** if, and only if, either (1) all branches on the tree are closed (a **finished closed tree**) or (2) there is at least one finished open branch on the tree (a **finished open tree**).

Note particularly that, according to the third definition, a tree counts as finished even if there is only a *single* finished open branch. If you have one finished open branch, you need not finish the other branches. The reason you can stop is clear: Once a tree contains a finished open branch, you have found an interpretation under which all statements in the trunk are true, so you know the initial set of statements is consistent. Regardless of what happens on other branches of the tree (i.e., they all close, some close and some remain open, or they all remain open), the finished open branch in question remains unchanged. Of course, it does not hurt to finish other branches in the tree, and in some of our preceding examples, we have done just that.[16]

Finishing a tree involves repeatedly applying tree rules to statements until either we have closed all branches or found a finished open branch. We represent the procedure succinctly in Figure 3.2. Furthermore, as we've seen we can use a finished open branch to find an interpretation under which statements we started with are all true. The box on the next page gives the procedure in step-by-step fashion.

---

[16]The fact that we can treat a tree as finished as long as it has at least one finished open branch will be important when we extend the tree method to predicate logic in Chapter 6. There we will find that some trees have finished branches that remain open, as well as trees with branches that cannot be finished because they are infinitely long.

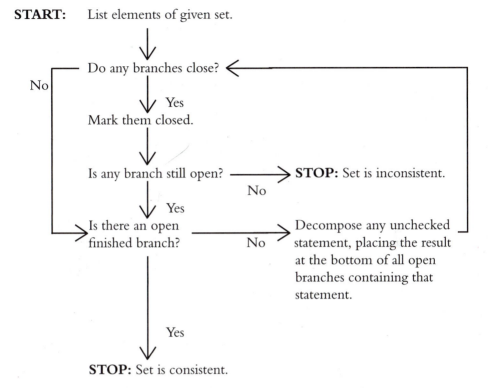

START: List elements of given set.

Figure 3.2 A flowchart showing the procedure for tree construction

> ***To use a finished open tree to find an interpretation under which all original statements are true:***
>
> 1. Start at the bottom of a finished open branch. Going up the branch, each time you encounter a statement letter p as a node on the branch, add the assignment $p{:}T$ to your interpretation. Each time you find a negated statement letter, $\sim q$, as a node on the branch, add the assignment $q{:}$ F to your interpretation.
> 2. Find any statement letters that occur in the statements in the trunk of the tree to which you have not assigned truth values. To these you may assign either T or F.

One thing this procedure makes clear is that more than one interpretation can be read off of a single branch of a tree. Consider the following example:

Using the instructions stated above, we can read two interpretations off the left-hand branch: ⟨A:T, B:T⟩ and ⟨A:T, B:F⟩. Similarly, we can read two interpretations off the right-hand branch: ⟨A:T, B:T⟩ and ⟨A:F, B:T⟩. Notice that the interpretation ⟨A:T, B:T⟩ can be read off either branch. These observations show us that *we can't infer anything about the number of interpretations under which a set of statements is true from the number of open branches in the tree.*

Exercises for Section 3.9

Consistency   In Section 3.6 (Part I), we asked you to use the truth table method to determine whether the following sets of statements were consistent. Rework these exercises using the truth tree method. If a set is truth-functionally consistent, read an interpretation off a finished open branch under which all elements in the set are true.

1. {P → Q, P, ~Q}
2. {Q → ~P, P, Q}
♦3. {A ∨ B, A ∨ ~B, ~A}
4. {~(P & Q), P & ~Q}
5. {A ↔ B, A ↔ ~B}
6. {A & (~A → A), B → ~A}
7. {A ∨ ~B, B ∨ ~C, ~(A → C)}

8. {~A, ~B, (A & B) ∨ (C ∨ D), ~D}
♦9. {H → K, ~L → (H → ~K), H → L}
10. {~(A → B), C ↔ B, ~(C → D)}
11. {A ∨ ~(A → B), ~A}
12. {M → (P & ~P), M → (R ∨ L), ~L}
♦13. {M → (N & O), O & ~N, M ↔ N}
14. {(J ∨ K) & H, ~J ∨ H, H → ~H}

15. {~ ~F ∨ ~ ~(G ∨ H), ~H, ~(F → H)}
16. {~X ∨ (~Y ∨ (Z & W)), ~(~X ∨ ~Y) & ~W}
♦17. {A → B, A → C, A → D, ~(A ∨ (B ∨ C))}
18. {A → (B & C), (C ∨ D) → A, ~B, A → C}

3.10   Using Truth Trees to Test for Other Semantic Properties

We can use truth trees to determine whether statements and arguments have the various semantic properties defined in Sections 3.4 and 3.5. We have already seen that trees provide a direct test for consistency: One simply finishes a tree with the members of the set in the trunk. If the finished tree is open, the set is consistent; otherwise, it is inconsistent.

Let's turn now to arguments. According to Proposition 2 (presented in Section 3.6), an argument is truth-functionally valid if, and only if, the set composed of the argument's premises and the negation of its conclusion is truth-functionally inconsistent. This means that the truth tree method can also be used to decide whether or not an argument is truth-functionally valid:

To determine whether or not an argument is truth-functionally valid, using the method of truth trees:

1. List the argument's premises and the negation of its conclusion as the trunk of a truth tree.
2. Build a finished truth tree.
3. If all branches close, the given argument is truth-functionally valid. If even one branch remains open, the argument is invalid.

As a first application of this technique, consider the following argument:

$$\sim H \rightarrow \sim G$$
$$\underline{G}$$
$$\therefore H$$

By Proposition 2 we know that this argument is truth-functionally valid if, and only if, the set $\{\sim H \rightarrow \sim G, G, \sim H\}$ is truth-functionally inconsistent. Thus, following step 1 of the instructions for testing an argument, we list the elements of this set:

Premises $\longrightarrow$ $\begin{cases} \sim H \rightarrow \sim G \checkmark \\ G \end{cases}$

Negation of Conclusion $\longrightarrow$ $\sim H$

The next step is to build a finished truth tree. In this case, only the first statement on the trunk can be decomposed:

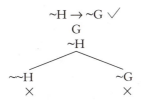

All branches are closed. (Note that the double-negation rule was not required on the left-hand branch!) Thus, the initial list of statements (the statements we listed as the trunk) form a truth-functionally inconsistent set. Therefore, the argument in question is truth-functionally valid.

Here's another argument as an example:

$$H \rightarrow J$$
$$\underline{J \rightarrow K}$$
$$\therefore \ {\sim}H \rightarrow {\sim}K$$

We begin the test for validity by listing the premises and negation of the conclusion:

$$H \rightarrow J$$
$$J \rightarrow K$$
$${\sim}({\sim}H \rightarrow {\sim}K)$$

Remember the importance of parentheses! In the bottom statement it is the *whole conditional* that is being negated. To start the tree we have a choice of three statements. Starting with the negated conditional will make the tree shorter, since if we start with a branching statement we'd have to repeat the next expansion at the bottom of two branches.

$$H \rightarrow J$$
$$J \rightarrow K$$
$${\sim}({\sim}H \rightarrow {\sim}K) \ \checkmark$$
$${\sim}H$$
$${\sim}{\sim}K$$

Notice that we have *not* tacitly applied the rule for doubly negated statements to '~ ~K'. Rules must be applied one at a time. Let's apply the rule for doubly negated statements next, since it is a nonbranching rule:

$$H \rightarrow J$$
$$J \rightarrow K$$
$${\sim}({\sim}H \rightarrow {\sim}K) \ \checkmark$$
$${\sim}H$$
$${\sim}{\sim}K \ \checkmark$$
$$K$$

Now take the first statement:

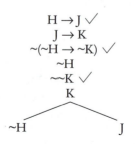

Still no closure. We apply the rule for the conditional to the one remaining unchecked compound statement, being sure to place the result at the bottom of every branch that goes through that statement:

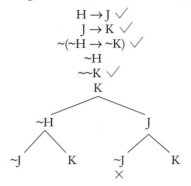

Since there are no more statements to which a tree rule can be applied, the tree is finished. Since there are open branches through the tree, we conclude that the set with which we started is consistent and, consequently, that the argument we were testing is not valid. Reading up along the left-most path, we find that the interpretation ⟨J:F, K:T, H:F⟩ provides a counterexample.

Here is one more example of an argument and its truth tree:

~A → (B & C)
~(D → A)
~(~D ∨ ~C)
∴ M → B

The completed tree is

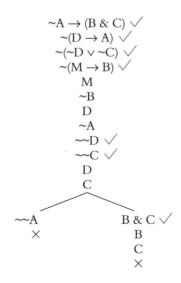

Carefully study this tree. You should be able to explain the presence of each node on the tree. What does the tree tell us about the truth-functional validity of the argument? How does it tell us this?

We come next to tautologies. Let's first point out a common mistake students often make in testing for tautologousness. If *every* branch of a tree beginning with a single statement is closed, there is no interpretation under which that statement is true. Hence, such a statement is self-contradictory. You might thus be tempted to think that if a tree for a single statement ends with *all branches open,* then the statement must be a tautology. To see that this is *not* the case, consider the simplest possible tree:

A

This is a finished open tree. It has only one branch. Obviously, however, 'A' is not a tautology. This shows us that, just because every path in a finished tree might be open, we cannot infer from this that the statements at the top of the tree are true under every interpretation.

To test for tautologousness, we must instead rely on Proposition 3 (Section 3.6). Proposition 3 tells us that a statement p is a tautology if, and only if, the *set* $\{\sim p\}$ is truth-functionally inconsistent. Thus, if a truth tree for a statement $\sim p$ finishes with all branches closed, the statement p is a tautology. If the tree finishes with even one branch open, the statement p is not a tautology.

> **To determine whether or not a statement is a tautology, using the method of truth trees:**
>
> 1. List the negation of the given statement to be tested.
> 2. Build a finished truth tree.
> 3. If all branches close, then the given statement is a tautology. If even one branch remains open, then the given statement is not a tautology.

As an example, consider the statement 'H → (G → H)'. An easily constructed truth table shows that this statement is indeed a tautology. We test it on a truth tree by listing its negation as the trunk:

$$\sim[H \to (G \to H)]$$

Now we construct a finished truth tree:

$\sim[H \to (G \to H)]$ ✓

H

$\sim(G \to H)$ ✓

G

$\sim$H

✗

Since there is no open branch, we now know that the statement '~[H → (G→ H)]' can't possibly be true; hence, 'H → (G → H)' can't possibly be false, hence it is a tautology.

Contrast the above example with '(A → B) → B'. To decide whether or not this is a tautology, we build a tree for the statement's negation:

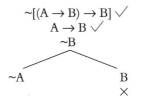

Since at least one open branch remains on the finished tree, it is possible for the statement '~[(A → B) → B]' to be true, hence possible for '(A → B) → B' to be false; thus this last statement is not a tautology. Reading up along the open branch, we see that assigning F to both 'A' and 'B' makes the statement false.

Finally, we'll consider how to use the tree method to determine whether two statements are truth-functionally equivalent. We combine Proposition 3, which tells us that a statement p is tautologous if, and only if, the set {~p} is inconsistent, with Proposition 4, which tells us that two statements q and r are truth-functionally equivalent if, and only if, the biconditional $q \leftrightarrow r$ is a tautology. The result is the following:

To determine whether or not two statements p and q are truth-functionally equivalent, using the method of truth trees:

1. List the negated biconditional, ~($p \leftrightarrow q$).
2. Build a finished truth tree.
3. If all branches close, then the statements are equivalent. If even one path remains open, the statements p and q are not truth-functionally equivalent.

Let's illustrate this by proving that the statements '(A → B)' and '(~B → ~A)' are truth-functionally equivalent. We start by forming the negated biconditional:

$$\sim[(A \rightarrow B) \leftrightarrow (\sim B \rightarrow \sim A)]$$

Here is the completed tree. Note the order in which rules have been applied so as to minimize the tree's length:

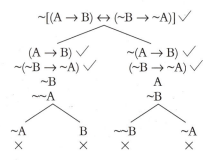

The fact that the tree closes tells us that the statements are equivalent.

We have not told you how to use the truth tree method to test statements for truth-functional self-contradictoriness and truth-functional contingency, nor how to determine whether pairs of statements are mutually truth-functionally contradictory. It is left to you as an exercise to discover the precise methods for these three cases.

Exercises for Section 3.10

Part I: Tautologies   In Section 3.4 (Part I), you were asked to use truth tables to determine whether the following statements were tautologies. Work these problems again, this time using truth trees. If a statement is not a tautology, read an incriminating interpretation off of a finished open branch.

   1. A ∨ B

   2. A ∨ ~B

♦3. ~(A & ~A)

   4. ~(A ∨ ~A)

   5. (F ∨ ~F) & ~(G & ~G)

   6. ~(~(H & ~G) & G) ∨ G

   7. (P & Q) → Q

   8. (X → Y) ∨ (Y → X)

   9. ~(Q → R) → (~Q → R)

  10. ((A & B) ∨ ((~A & B) ∨ (A & ~B))) ∨ (~A & ~B)

♦11. (P → Q) ∨ (P → ~Q)

  12. ~(H → J) → ~(J → H)

  13. ~[~(K ∨ ~L) & (~K → ~L)]

  14. [(G & ~H) & (H & ~G)] ∨ (P → P)

  15. [~W & (M → W)] → ~M

  16. ~(Q & E) → ~(Q ∨ E)

♦17. (H → J) → ((H → ~J) → ~H)

  18. [J → (H & K)] → [(J → H) & (J → K)]

  19. [~A & (~B & ~C)] ∨ (A & B)

  20. [(X & Y) → Z] → [(X → Z) ∨ (Y → Z)]

Part II: Validity.   In Section 3.4 (Part II), you were asked to use truth tables to determine whether the following arguments were valid. Work these problems again, this time using truth trees. If an argument is not truth-functionally valid, read a counterexample off of a finished open branch.

♦21. A & B /∴ A

22. A ∨ B /∴ ~A ∨ ~B

23. ~(E & G) /∴ E ∨ F

24. ~(P & Q) /∴ ~P & ~Q

25. ~H, ~J /∴ ~(H & J)

26. Z ∨ W, W → Z /∴ Z

27. C ∨ ~D /∴ D → C

28. E ∨ F, ~ ~E /∴ F

♦29. ~G → H, ~H /∴ G

30. ~(A → B) /∴ ~B

31. F → G, ~F → G /∴ G

32. F → G, ~F → ~G /∴ ~(F & G)

33. (J & K), ~K ∨ J /∴ ~K ∨ J

34. H → J /∴ ~J → (H → J)

35. ~(K & ~L), ~K /∴ L

36. ~(~ ~K & ~ ~L), ~ ~K /∴ ~L

37. J → K, ~(K ∨ L) /∴ ~J

38. M → N, N → O, ~M /∴ ~O

♦39. ~P ∨ Q, ~Q ∨ R, ~R /∴ P

40. ~A, (C ∨ D) → ~A /∴ A → ~D

41. X & ~Y, ~Y ∨ ~Z /∴ X & ~Z

42. H → J, J → ~(L & M), ~M /∴ H & J

43. H & (G ∨ F), ~(G → F) /∴ ~H → G

44. ~[K ∨ (K → M)] /∴ P & ~P

45. ~(S & ~L) /∴ (L & S) ∨ (~L & ~S)

46. R ∨ (S → T), ~T & ~R /∴ ~(S & U)

♦47. ~[H → (K → M)], K & ~M /∴ H → (K → M)

48. ~[M ∨ (N ∨ O)], (~M → P) & (~O → P), P → ~N /∴ ~N → P

49. (E ∨ G) → F, (G ∨ H) → F, (G & E) ∨ (G & H) /∴ F & G

50. (A & B) → (C → (D & E)), ~(D → E) & C /∴ ~(A & B)

Part III: Equivalence In Section 3.5 (Part II), you were asked to use truth tables to determine whether the following statements were truth-functionally equivalent. This time, use truth trees to answer the same question. If a pair of statements are not truth-functionally equivalent, read an incriminating interpretation off of a finished open branch.

51. ~(M ∨ L), ~M ∨ ~L

52. ~(M ∨ L), ~M & ~L

53. ~(M & L), ~M ∨ ~L

54. ~(M & L), ~M & ~L

♦55. ~R ∨ S, R & ~S

56. ~ ~M, M

57. R → S, S → R

58. ~(R → S), R → ~S

59. P → (Q → R), (P & Q) → R

60. ~(R → S), R & ~S

61. K ∨ K, K

62. R ↔ P, P ↔ ~R

♦63. B → D, (B & D) ∨ (~B & ~D)

64. (G & G) & G, G

65. S ∨ T, ~S ∨ ~T

66. A → (B → C), (A→ B) → C

67. G ↔ H, ~H ↔ ~G

68. ~(A & B), ~(~A & ~B)

69. A, (G ∨ ~G) → A

70. ~(A ↔ A), B ↔ ~B

♦71. A → A, A

72. (L → L) & M, M

Part IV: Theoretical Problems

◆73. The connectives of this exercise '/' and the next '↓' are known as 'Sheffer strokes'. Consider the following two truth tree rules for the first one:

Given this information, construct the basic truth table for the connective '/'.

74. Follow the instructions for Exercise 73, only this time with respect to to the connective '↓', whose tree rules are

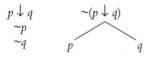

◆75. Give the truth tree rules for $(p \veebar q)$ and $\sim(p \veebar q)$, where '$\veebar$' is the sign of exclusive disjunction.

76. Follow the instructions for Exercise 75, only this time for the connective '∇', whose basic truth table is

p	q	$p \nabla q$
T	T	T
T	F	T
F	T	F
F	F	T

◆77. Using '/' of Exercise 73 as the only connective, write statements that are truth-functionally equivalent to '~A', 'A ∨ B', 'A & B', and 'A → B'.

78. Using '↓' of Exercise 74 as the only connective, write statements that are truth-functionally equivalent to '~A', 'A ∨ B', 'A & B', and 'A → B'.

◆79. True or false: If a finished tree has n open branches, then the statements in its trunk are true under *at least* n interpretations. Justify your answer.

80. True or false: If a finished tree has n open branches, then the statements in its trunk are true under *at most* n interpretations. Justify your answer.

81. Explain how to use truth trees to determine whether or not a statement is a truth-functional self-contradiction. Then give examples of the use of your method, by showing that one statement is a self-contradiction and that another is not.

82. Explain how to use truth trees to determine whether or not a statement is truth-functionally contingent. Then give examples of the use of your method, by showing that one statement is truth-functionally contingent and that another isn't.

83. Explain how to use truth trees to determine whether or not a pair of statements are truth-functional contradictories. Then give examples of the use of your method, by showing that one pair of statements are contradictories and that another pair are not.

3.11 The Adequacy of the Tree Method

In our discussion of tautologousness and the other semantic properties, we have been careful to distinguish our *definitions* of these properties from our *methods* for determining whether or not statements or sets of statements have these properties. All our definitions rely on the definition of 'truth under an interpretation', whereas the methods we use to determine whether statements or sets of statements have these properties do not (directly at least) refer to interpretations or the concept of truth. Rather, they specify certain syntactically definable rules that allow us to construct patterns of symbols, and it is these patterns of symbols that we take to demonstrate (or "prove") that the statements or sets of statements have certain semantic properties. These patterns may be called *proofs*. Consequently, we refer to these methods as *proof systems* or *deduction systems*.

We have so far considered three basic methods for examining the semantic properties of *SL* statements: truth tables, brief truth tables, and truth trees. The questions we discuss in this section can be asked about any of these methods, but we confine our discussion to truth trees. Truth trees are the most theoretically interesting of these methods because, as we will see in Chapter 6, they can be extended with relative ease to provide proof systems for more powerful logical languages. In the discussion of this section, as well as in later parts of this book, it will be convenient to give the tree method a name. We call the tree method for *SL* T_{SL}.

We have assumed without much argument that the methods we have given you are adequate to determine correctly whether a given *SL* statement or set of statements has the various semantic properties we have discussed. You need not fear; this assumption *is* in fact justified. In this section our goal is to make clear just what we have assumed. This will be accomplished by describing three important properties of our tree method. We will not actually prove that the tree method has these properties, but we will say enough to give you some confidence that it does.

We begin by asking a crucial question: Is T_{SL} adequate for determining whether or not a statement p of *SL* is a tautology? We could ask analogous questions about the adequacy of the tree method to determine whether (1) arguments are truth-functionally valid, (2) pairs of statements are truth-functionally equivalent, or (3) sets of statements are truth-functionally consistent. However, in light of the relationships that hold among these various concepts, expressed in Propositions 1–4, it follows that if we can show that the tree method provides an adequate test of tautologousness, then it is also adequate to these other tasks.

We begin by recalling how to use the tree method to show that a statement is a tautology. To show that a statement p is a tautology, construct a tree with the single statement $\sim p$ as its trunk. If the finished tree is closed, conclude that p is a tautology. We introduce now the following definition:

> **Definition**   A T_{SL} **proof** of an SL statement p is a finished closed tree with a single initial statement $\sim p$.

We call these trees 'T_{SL} proofs' rather than simply 'proofs' because truth trees provide only one of a number of possible proof procedures. In Chapter 4 we will examine an alternative procedure that provides a different sort of proof.

Next we define a T_{SL} *theorem:*

> **Definition**   An SL statement p is a T_{SL} **theorem** if, and only if, there exists a T_{SL} proof of p.

Let's elucidate what we mean by 'there exists' in this definition. The kind of existence we are concerned with is called 'mathematical existence'. When we say that a proof exists in this sense, we do not require that anyone has ever actually discovered it or written it down. Indeed, many (*infinitely* many) T_{SL} proofs are so long that there isn't enough paper in the universe to write them down. All that matters is that it is *logically possible* that someone could write the proof in a finite amount of time, even if that finite amount of time is longer than any person's lifetime.

When a statement p is a truth tree theorem, we write '$\vdash_{T_{SL}} p$'. The symbol '$\vdash$' is a standard symbol indicating syntactic consequence. In general terms, a **syntactic consequence** is a statement arrived at by manipulation of symbols according to the rules of a deduction system, without explicit reference to the meaning or interpretation of those symbols. The subscript 'T_{SL}' names the particular deduction system we have used. As you progress through this book, you will encounter the concept of syntactic consequence in connection with other deduction systems. The concept of a syntactic consequence is to be contrasted with that of semantic consequence, which we have denoted by the symbol '$\vDash$'.[17]

---

[17]Do not be confused by the fact that we have called the truth tree method a 'semantic' method. It is called 'semantic' because of the close parallels between the syntactic rules for constructing truth trees and the semantic properties of statements. Although there is a close parallel here, the rules for constructing truth trees refer only to the syntactic form of the statements involved.

For our truth tree deduction system to be adequate to the task of determining whether any given statement is a tautology, two conditions must be met:

Soundness   For any *SL* statement *p*, if $\vdash_{T_{SL}} p$, then $\vDash p$.

Put less formally: all truth tree theorems are tautologies.

Completeness   For any *SL* statement *p*, if $\vDash p$, then $\vdash_{T_{SL}} p$.

Put less formally: all tautologies are truth tree theorems. It turns out that both preceding conditions are met. Putting them together, we have the desired result that a statement of *SL* is a tautology if, and only if, it is a T_{SL} theorem.

Let's consider more closely what these conditions mean, starting with soundness. First, we need to be careful not to confuse the claim that the *truth tree method* is sound with the claim that an *argument* is sound. Sound arguments, as we defined them in Chapter 1, are valid arguments with true premises. 'Soundness', as used here, has nothing to do with the soundness of arguments. Soundness in the present sense is a property not of arguments but of deduction systems. We call a deduction system for *SL* 'sound' if, whenever we have a correct proof in that system, the statement proved is tautologous. In other words, if we have followed the rules of the system, it cannot mislead us into thinking that a statement is a tautology when actually it is not. Fortunately, the tree method is sound.

When we say that a deduction system for *SL* is sound, we mean that *only* tautologies have proofs in that system. When we say that a deduction system for *SL* is *complete*, we mean that *all* tautologies have proofs in that system. If a deduction system is incomplete, then some tautologies will be unprovable in that system. If we had a sound but incomplete deduction system, we would know that any statement for which we had a proof is in fact a tautology, but we wouldn't be able to infer from the fact that there was no proof of a certain statement that it is not a tautology.

Before saying more about soundness and completeness, we need to mention some other important properties of the tree method. It is useful to divide the method into two parts. First, there are the *definitions and tree rules,* that, together, provide us with the tools to decide whether a tree has been properly constructed and whether a given tree does or does not constitute a proof of a given *SL* statement. These definitions and rules together comprise what we have called the deduction system. The deduction system, by itself, does not tell us how we should apply these rules in order to construct a T_{SL} proof. The deduction system is like the rules of chess. Although the rules tell us what moves are legal, they don't tell us which moves to make to play a winning game. So, besides the rules and definitions for what constitutes a proof, we have also described a *procedure* for building trees that will allow us to decide whether or not a statement is a tautology. This procedure, which we have summarized in Figure 3.2, is called a **decision proce-dure.** Let us call this procedure 'TD_{SL}' (for 'tree decision procedure for SL').

In general, a decision procedure is a *step-by-step mechanical procedure* for an-swering some question. The steps must be spelled out in enough detail so that at no point is any thought or ingenuity required to decide how to proceed.[18] A deci-sion procedure for tautologousness in SL is a mechanical procedure that, for any SL statement p, can answer this question: Is p a tautology? If we have a decision procedure for tautologousness in SL, we can actually build a machine (in the form of a computer program, say) for determining whether or not any statement of SL is a tautology. Such a program would prompt you for an SL statement and would, after you had typed it in, tell you either that the statement is a tautology, or that it is not. A session with this program might look like this:

Enter a statement >> $(P \rightarrow Q) \vee (P \rightarrow {\sim}Q)$
That statement is a tautology.
Enter a statement >> $(P \vee {\sim}P) \rightarrow Q$
That statement is not a tautology.
Enter a statement >>

There are many ways to build decision procedures. They need not use truth trees at all, and even for a truth tree-based decision procedure, there are actually lots of choices about how to construct trees. For a decision procedure to be adequate for SL, it needs to have three properties: soundness, completeness, and effectiveness. Soundness and completeness for a decision procedure mean the same things as soundness and completeness for deduction systems. Sound and complete decision procedures for tautologousness give the right answers to questions about tautolo-gousness. To say that a decision procedure is *effective* is to say something more—namely, that the decision procedure gives its answer within a finite amount of time. Our tree-based decision procedure TD_{SL} has all of these properties:

---

[18]Our flowchart (Figure 3.2) does not actually offer instructions that are explicit enough to make it into a decision procedure. The instructions for a decision procedure must be sufficiently detailed to specify, at every step, what should be done next, until we have built a tree that tells us whether a statement is tautolo-gous. At each step there can be no choice about what to do. The procedure we have given in our flow-chart doesn't quite do this. If you look back at that chart, you will see at one point that there is an instruction to choose a statement to decompose. There may be several possible choices, and the flowchart doesn't specify which one we should take. To convert our procedure to a decision procedure, we would need to add some instructions for picking out a statement to decompose. One possibility is this: Choose the node closest to the top of the tree, or, if two or more of the closest nodes are the same distance from the top of the tree, choose the node farthest to the left. You can probably think of some others.

Soundness	For any *SL* statement *p*, if $\vdash_{TD_{SL}} p$, then $\vDash p$. In other words, whenever the procedure indicates a statement is a tautology, it is in fact a tautology.
Completeness	For any *SL* statement *p*, if $\vDash p$, then $\vdash_{TD_{SL}} p$. In other words, whenever a statement is a tautology, the procedure indicates that it is a tautology.
Effectiveness	For any *SL* statement *p*, TD_{SL} determines within a finite amount of time whether or not *p* is tautologous.

The soundness and completeness of the truth tree *decision procedure* TD_{SL} are consequences of the soundness and completeness of the truth tree *deduction system* T_{SL}. The underlying deduction system guarantees that the procedure correctly classifies statements as tautologous if they are and as not tautologous if they are not.

When we say that a decision procedure is *effective,* we are saying that it always terminates at some point with an answer. If we have written a program using an effective decision procedure, then, regardless of what statement is entered at the start, the program will eventually (i.e., in a finite amount of time) indicate either that the statement is a tautology or that it is not.

It is fairly straightforward to see that our truth tree decision procedure is effective. Look again at the flowchart (Figure 3.2) for tree construction. Our procedure is effective just in case we are guaranteed that, whatever statement we start with, we will always finish a tree, ending up at one of the two places on the flowchart marked 'STOP'. Our only worry is that somehow we might get stuck going around in circles, finding one statement after another to decompose and never getting out of the loop. Fortunately, this will never happen for *SL* statements. Our tree starts with a single unchecked statement. Using the tree rules we can break this statement into one, two, or four shorter unchecked statements. We can then apply the tree rules to each of these statements, producing one, two, or four statements, all of which are shorter than the previous ones. As long as each application of our rules produces a finite number of shorter statements, we will eventually reach a point where all the unchecked statements are so short that no further rules can be applied to them — they will either be statement letters or negations of statement letters. We will then have a complete tree.[19]

Now let's look briefly at how we know that the method of truth trees provides a sound and complete decision procedure. If a decision procedure is sound, then whenever it says a statement *p* is a tautology, it is in fact a tautology. But when

---

[19]For a detailed proof of the effectiveness of the truth tree method as a decision procedure for tautologousness in *SL,* see Jeffrey's *Formal Logic* or Bergmann, Moor, and Nelson's *The Logic Book* (see Appendix 1).

does our decision procedure say that a statement is a tautology? To determine whether a statement p is a tautology, the procedure constructs a tree beginning with ~p and looks to see whether all branches in the tree close. If they do, then the procedure indicates that {~p} is inconsistent and that p is tautologous. Consequently, to ensure that our procedure is sound, we need rules that make it impossible to close a tree unless that tree begins with a set of statements that is inconsistent.

Although a detailed proof of soundness is beyond the scope of our text,[20] we can give you a good idea of how we know that it is sound by looking at one of our tree rules and contrasting it with an alternate rule that would produce an unsound procedure. Suppose that, instead of our branching rule for negated conjunctions, our negated conjunction rule were this:

$$\sim(p \ \& \ q)$$
$$\sim p$$
$$\sim q$$

Let's use this rule on the statement '(A & ~A)', as if we were testing the statement to decide whether or not it is a tautology. We negate the statement and complete the tree:

$$\sim(A \ \& \ \sim A) \ \checkmark$$
$$\sim A$$
$$\sim \sim A$$
$$\times$$

The tree closes, incorrectly indicating that the statement '(A & ~A)' is a tautology. We started with a statement that is not self-contradictory, '~(A & ~A)', but applying the rule creates an inconsistency in our branch. Thus, even though we start with a consistent statement, we get a closed tree. If we used this rule, our method would therefore be unsound. The soundness of our tree method is ensured by employing only rules that correctly indicate the truth conditions for the statements to which they apply. To put the matter informally, what makes our decision procedure sound is that trees don't close unless they "should close."

Completeness is the converse of soundness: what makes our decision procedure complete is that whenever a tree "should close," it really does close. Let's look at why completeness comes down to this. To test for the tautologousness of a statement p, our procedure constructs a finished tree beginning with ~p. We know the tree can be finished since the procedure is effective. Our procedure is complete as

---

[20]For proofs of the soundness and completeness of the tree method, see again either Jeffrey's *Formal Logic* or Bergmann et al.'s *The Logic Book*.

long as it doesn't miss any of the tautologies—that is, as long as every finished tree beginning with the negation of a tautology is closed. To ensure this is the case, we need to ensure that, if a branch in a tree contains inconsistent statements, the branch eventually closes.

As an example of an incomplete decision procedure, imagine replacing our current rule for negated disjunction with the following:

$$\sim(p \lor q)$$
$$\sim p$$

If this rule replaced the correct disjunction rule in our system, the system would be sound but incomplete. To see this, note that the statement '(A ∨ ∼A)' is a tautology. Let's test this statement with our modified disjunction rule. Negating the tautology, we build a tree:

$$\sim(A \lor \sim A) \checkmark$$
$$\sim A$$

This is a finished open tree, so we would conclude, incorrectly, that the statement at the top of the tree is consistent and that '(A ∨ ∼A)' is not a tautology. Completeness is ensured by selecting tree rules that guarantee the eventual appearance of a pair of contradictory statements on every branch that stems from an inconsistent initial set.

To recapitulate what we've learned about the truth tree test for validity: Our tree rules are constructed in such a way as to guarantee that trees close if, and only if, the statements in their trunk are inconsistent. This in turn guarantees that our truth tree procedure is sound and complete. We have also found that the truth tree procedure is an effective decision procedure. From a theoretical point of view, the truth tree test thus provides an entirely adequate procedure for determining whether statements of *SL* are tautologous. From this fact we can immediately infer that our procedures for testing whether arguments are valid, whether statements are equivalent, and so on for the other truth-functional properties and relations are also adequate.

One final terminological point. Although we have discussed soundness, completeness, and decidability in the context of a particular decision procedure, logicians often say that *SL itself* (not just a particular procedure for determining tautologousness in *SL*) is sound, complete, and effective. What they mean by this is that there exist sound, complete and effective decision procedures for tautologousness in *SL*. TD_{SL} is one procedure, but there are others as well.

As we examine more powerful logical languages, we will find that our decision procedures lose some of the three properties described in this section. The language *L,* which we introduce in Chapter 5, is sound, complete, but not effective. Other languages that we will mention, but not study in this text, are both noneffective (or 'undecidable') and incomplete.

Exercises for Section 3.11

1. Every SL tree can be completed in a finite number of steps. Does this fact imply that TD_{SL} is sound, complete, effective, or none of these?

2. Every tree beginning with a set of statements that is inconsistent closes. Does this fact imply that TD_{SL} is sound, complete, effective, or none of these?

♦ 3. Every finished tree beginning with a set of statements that is consistent has at least one open branch. Does this fact imply that TD_{SL} is sound, complete, effective, or none of these?

4. Suppose that we replace all our truth tree rules by the following single rule:

$$p$$
$$A$$
$$\sim A$$

Is the resulting system (a) sound but not complete, (b) complete but not sound, or (c) neither sound nor complete? Justify your answer.

CHAPTER FOUR

Statement Logic III:
Syntactic Methods

4.1 Introduction

In Chapter 3 we introduced the methods of truth tables, brief truth tables, and truth trees.[1] These methods help us to determine whether or not an argument is truth-functionally valid, as well as to test *SL* statements for other semantic properties. These methods are called 'semantic' methods because they generally involve explicit reference to possible truth values of *SL* statements. In this chapter we consider an alternative method, the method of *natural deduction,* which also helps us investigate the validity of arguments and establish answers to related questions. The method of natural deduction is called a **syntactic method,** because the rules used

---

[1]We assume that you are familiar with the material through Section 3.6, which includes discussion of the semantics of *SL* and of the truth table method. We will sometimes refer to an alternative to truth tables called the truth tree method, which we introduced at the end of Chapter 3. Truth trees are like truth tables in that they provide a mechanical procedure for determining whether arguments are valid, statements are tautologies, etc. The major differences between truth trees and truth tables are that truth trees are more efficient than truth tables and that truth trees can be used with the language *L,* which is introduced in the second half of this book. You do not need to have studied truth trees to understand the material in this chapter.

do not explicitly refer to truth values of the statements under consideration but only consider their syntactic form.[2]

The expression 'natural deduction' is used because it refers to a method that in many ways resembles the "natural" process of deductive reasoning in which we engage when we are being especially careful and explicit in our thought or conversation, such as when we are trying to convince somebody that a conclusion really does follow from some premises. When you hear a political debate, for example, you don't expect the candidates to produce arguments that they then test with a truth table or truth tree at the front of the auditorium! What we ordinarily expect, and what we ordinarily do ourselves, is something more like playing a game of chess. There are certain "moves" of correct reasoning that everyone recognizes as legitimate and other "moves" that are recognized as incorrect. These logical "moves" correspond to specific argument forms that are intuitively recognized to be valid forms. The method of natural deduction amounts to using a relatively small collection of correct argument forms to show that a conclusion follows from a set of premises. Besides providing us with yet another method of logical demonstration and elucidating some of what goes on in ordinary deductive reasoning, practice using a system of natural deduction can help you organize and strengthen the presentation of your own arguments in English.

The comparison between the rules of natural deduction and the rules of chess is instructive, because it helps illustrate the most important difference between natural deduction and the methods of truth tables and truth trees. In a chess game the rules indicate which moves are *allowable,* but at any point in the game there are many possible moves. To win at chess you must be skillful in choosing which moves to make. The situation is similar in natural deduction. At each stage in the process, you can make any of a number of different moves. It takes ingenuity to decide which moves will advance you toward the conclusion you are trying to reach. The situation is markedly different from the one we faced with truth tables and truth trees. It takes no ingenuity to complete a truth table or truth tree. Once one understands the rules of these methods, the construction of a table or tree demonstrating the validity of an argument is straightforward. There is only one way to construct a truth table for a set of statements; there is more than one way to construct a truth tree for a set of statements, but no matter which way you choose, you will complete the tree in a finite number of steps. It is consequently easy to construct a machine that uses truth tables or truth trees to decide whether or not *SL* arguments are valid, *SL* statements are tautologies, and so forth. For this reason, truth trees and truth tables are said to provide **effective decision procedures** for

---

[2]It should be noted that both the truth tree and natural deduction methods are syntactic in the sense that the correctness of a proof using either method can be determined simply by examining the syntax of the statements in the proof. See Section 3.11 for related discussion.

truth-functional validity and tautologousness in *SL*. Our system of natural deduction will not provide such a procedure.[3]

To begin, consider that each and every instance of the following argument form is truth-functionally valid:

$$p \rightarrow q$$
$$\underline{p}$$
$$\therefore q$$

To see that every instance is valid, consider that, no matter *what* statements replace '*p*' and '*q*' , we know that if the two premises were true, then the conclusion would have to be true. Using '/' to separate the premises and '//' to indicate the conclusion, consider the case in which the premises both take the value T:

$$p \rightarrow q \: / \: p \: // \: q$$
$$ \text{T} \quad \text{T} \quad \text{?}$$

If the conditional *and* its antecedent both take the value T, the basic truth table for the conditional tells us that *q* must take the value T as well. Hence, any argument at all that has this form is truth-functionally valid. Therefore, if you recognize that an argument does have this form, you needn't bother to construct a full truth table to decide whether it is valid; once you see that it has this form, you will know that it *is* valid. In fact, this argument form is so standard and clearly correct that it has acquired a name: **Modus Ponens,** abbreviated 'MP'.

Each of the following arguments is an instance of MP:[4]

$$A \rightarrow B$$
$$\underline{A}$$
$$\therefore B$$

$$(E \vee {\sim}F) \rightarrow [G \rightarrow {\sim}(H \vee F)]$$
$$\underline{E \vee {\sim}F}$$
$$\therefore G \rightarrow {\sim}(H \vee F)$$

---

[3]When a question can be answered by some effective decision procedure, we say that the question is **effectively decidable.** A major research project of logicians in the twentieth century has been to determine what kinds of questions in logic are effectively decidable. Although the truth-functional validity of arguments of *SL* is effectively decidable (see Section 3.11), as we expand our system of logic to include non–truth-functional arguments of certain kinds, questions about validity become undecidable. This problem is discussed in Section 6.5.

[4]See Section 2.1 if you need a refresher about the meaning of the word 'instance' in this context.

In each instance one premise is a conditional, one premise is identical to the conditional's antecedent, and the conclusion is identical to the conditional's consequent. Since any argument having this form is truth-functionally valid, we can use MP as a **rule of inference**—that is, a principle for correctly drawing a conclusion:

> ***Modus Ponens***   Whenever a conditional is asserted and the antecedent of the conditional is also asserted, the consequent of the conditional may be drawn as a conclusion.

Another correct argument form is the following:

$$\frac{p \ \& \ q}{\therefore p}$$

It would be equally correct to draw the right-hand conjunct from the same premise:

$$\frac{p \ \& \ q}{\therefore q}$$

No matter what statements replace 'p' and 'q' , we know that if a conjunction is true, then both conjuncts are true. Hence, any argument in which a conjunct has been drawn as a conclusion from a conjunction is valid. We can thus also use this pattern as a rule for correctly drawing a conclusion:

> ***Conjunction Elimination***   Whenever a conjunction is asserted, the left-hand or right-hand conjunct may be drawn as a conclusion.

'Conjunction Elimination' is abbreviated 'CE'. When a conclusion is drawn by the rule MP or CE, we say that it has been *derived from* the statements that serve as its premises.

We can use these rules of inference in succession. For example, we can show that the following argument is truth-functionally valid by applying the rules MP and CE in succession until we get from the premises to the conclusion:

$$\frac{\begin{array}{l} A \rightarrow (B \ \& \ C) \\ A \end{array}}{\therefore B}$$

Let's list the two premises, with a notation indicating *that* they are premises:

1.	$A \rightarrow (B \ \& \ C)$	PR
2.	A	PR

Observe that line 1 contains a conditional and line 2 contains the antecedent of the conditional. By the rule MP, we know that if a conditional and its antecedent are true, then the conditional's consequent must also be true. Thus, we may extend the above list by adding the conditional's consequent with an appropriate justification:

$$
\begin{array}{llll}
1. & A \rightarrow (B \ \& \ C) & & PR \\
2. & A & & PR \\
3. & B \ \& \ C & 1, 2 & MP \\
\end{array}
$$

'1, 2 MP' indicates that the addition of line 3 is warranted by the rule MP and that the relevant conditional and antecedent appear on lines 1 and 2. (Following our convention regarding parentheses, the outermost parentheses have been suppressed in line 3.) Next, we can apply rule CE:

$$
\begin{array}{llll}
1. & A \rightarrow (B \ \& \ C) & & PR \\
2. & A & & PR \\
3. & B \ \& \ C & 1, 2 & MP \\
4. & B & 3 & CE \\
\end{array}
$$

The notation to the right of the new line again indicates both the rule that has been applied and the line from which the new statement has been derived. Notice that we have now demonstrated the validity of the given argument. We have shown that *if* the premises were true (lines 1 and 2), *then* the statement on line 3 would have to be true. Next we showed that if the statement on line 3 were true, then the statement on line 4 would have to be true. Thus, if the premises were both true, then 'B' , the argument's conclusion, would also have to be true.

A system of natural deduction is a set of inference rules that enables us to build proofs like the one we just constructed. The natural deduction system for *SL* that we present here is called 'D_{SL}'. A proof in D_{SL} is just a list of statements beginning with initial premises and proceeding in accordance with Modus Ponens, Conjunction Elimination, and other rules of inference to be presented shortly. Formally, we define a proof as follows:

> **Definition**   A D_{SL} **proof** is a finite, numbered list of *SL* statements, each statement of which either is a premise or else is warranted by a rule of inference of D_{SL}. Each statement is accompanied by a justification that gives the reason for the presence of that statement on the list.

A D_{SL} proof is a kind of *formal* proof. This means that it is possible to determine whether a list of statements is or is not a D_{SL} proof simply by examining the syntactic form of those statements together with the justifications that accompany them. We have defined a 'D_{SL} proof' rather than simply a 'proof' to emphasize the fact that what counts as a proof is determined by the rules of the deduction system. Some systems of natural deduction use rules other than those we provide here, and there are, besides natural deduction systems, other kinds of deduction systems with quite different rules of proof.[5] Since the proofs we discuss in the rest of this chapter are D_{SL} proofs, we often use the word 'proof' to mean 'D_{SL} proof'.

When we ask for 'a proof of a conclusion from a set of premises', or a 'proof for an argument', we are asking for a finite list of statements, the first of which are premises and the last of which is the argument's conclusion. A proof is also called a **derivation,** and when a line is added to a proof by a rule of inference, we say that the new statement has been *derived from* a line (or lines) *by* that rule. If it is possible to derive conclusion c from a set of premises $\{p_1, \ldots, p_n\}$, we say that c is **derivable** from those premises. We use the sign '$\vdash_{D_{SL}}$' (called the 'single turnstile') to abbreviate this. That is, the expression

$$p_1, \ldots, p_n \vdash_{D_{SL}} c$$

means 'there is a D_{SL} proof of c from $\{p_1, \ldots, p_n\}$'; that is, there is a proof of the statement c from premises $\{p_1, \ldots, p_n\}$ in the natural deduction system D_{SL}.

4.2   Whole–Line Inference Rules for D_{SL}

The system D_{SL} of natural deduction is given by simply listing a number of rules of inference. D_{SL} contains eleven rules. The first rule is not a rule of inference in the ordinary sense, but a rule that allows us to introduce premises:

---

[5]As noted in Section 3.11, we can define a kind of formal proof that can be constructed mechanically using the truth tree method. These proofs we called 'T_{SL} proofs'. T_{SL} proofs and D_{SL} proofs are both examples of formal proofs, and in each case it is an effectively decidable question (see note 3) whether or not a given proof has been correctly constructed. As noted at the beginning of this chapter, the biggest difference between natural deduction and the truth tree method is that we do not offer a mechanical procedure for constructing natural deduction proofs, whereas we do for truth tree proofs. Moreover, whereas in a truth tree the application of tree rules must eventually come to a halt, there is really no point in a natural deduction proof at which you are *required* by the rules of the system to quit extending the list of statements. There are only finitely many ways to correctly construct a truth tree for a set of *SL* statements, but there are in general *infinitely* many ways to correctly construct a natural deduction proof for *SL*.

> **Premise Rule (PR)**   Any statement *p* of *SL* may be entered as a premise on a line *n*, provided that there are no lines prior to *n* that are justified by any rule other than the Premise Rule. As a justification for the line, put 'PR'.

This means that if you wish to demonstrate the validity of an argument, you must begin by listing each of the premises using PR. Notice that PR is stated in such a way as to prohibit the addition of premises once other rules of inference have been applied. Derivations may begin with any finite number of premises, and all subsequent statements in the proof are said to be **derived from** those premises.[6]

The next four rules of our system are called **whole-line inference rules:**

Conjunction Elimination (CE)
$$\frac{p \mathbin{\&} q}{\therefore p} \quad \text{and} \quad \frac{p \mathbin{\&} q}{\therefore q}$$

Conjunction Introduction (CI)
$$\frac{\begin{array}{c} p \\ q \end{array}}{\therefore p \mathbin{\&} q}$$

Modus Ponens (MP)
$$\frac{\begin{array}{c} p \to q \\ p \end{array}}{\therefore q}$$

Modus Tollens (MT)
$$\frac{\begin{array}{c} p \to q \\ \sim q \end{array}}{\therefore \sim p}$$

Each of the four forms is a shorthand way of specifying instructions for adding new statements to a formal proof. If a statement (or statements) of the form above the three dots appears as the whole contents of a line (or lines) in a proof, then the statement to the right of the three dots may be added as a new line of the proof. For example, the way to understand the first two rules of inference, CE and CI, is as follows:

> **Conjunction Elimination (CE)**   If the statement *p* & *q* occurs as a whole line in a proof—say, line *m*—then the statement *p* or the statement *q* may be added as a new line of the proof. As justification for the new line, put '*m* CE'.

---

[6]As we discuss in Section 4.6, however, tautologies can be derived without any premises at all.

> ***Conjunction Introduction (CI)***   If the statements *p* and *q* each occur as whole lines of a proof—say on lines *m* and *n*—then the statement *p* & *q* may be entered as a new line of the proof. As justification for the new line, put '*m, n* CI'.

CI tells us that if we have two statements on separate lines of a proof, we are allowed to make a conjunction of them:

    m.   *p*
               .
               .
               .
    n.   *q*
               .
               .
               .
    o.   *p* & *q*   *m, n*   CI

It does not matter which of the two statements appears first in the proof: If *q* had been the statement on line *m* and *p* the statement on line *n*, the statement *p* & *q* may still be entered with the justification '*m, n* CI'. CE looks like the same thing, only in reverse:

    m.   *p* & *q*   *m.*   *p* & *q*
               .   .
               .   or   .
               .   .
    n.   *p*   *m*   CE   *n.*   *q*   *m*   CE

The justification informs anyone examining the proof that a correct principle of inference has been used. As long as the rules are applied correctly, we are assured that *if* the statements we start with are true, *then* so is each statement added to the proof.

As an example of how these four rules can be used together, consider a proof for the following argument:

    A → (B & ~C)
    A
    D → C
    ∴ B & ~D

The proof begins by listing all the argument's premises:

> 1.   A → (B & ~C)   PR
> 2.   A   PR
> 3.   D → C   PR

We now have to find some way to get the conclusion, 'B & ~D', as the last line of
the proof, using only our four rules of inference. Notice that 'B' occurs in the first
line. If we could somehow get 'B' on a line by itself, we'd have half of our conclusion. Be sure to see that we *cannot* use CE to get 'B' from line 1. CE applies only
to conjunctions, and the statement on line 1 is *not* a conjunction. That's why these
four rules are called 'whole-line' inference rules: To say that a statement is the
'whole statement' on a line means that the statement is not *contained in* another
statement on that line. For example, '(B & ~C)' is not the whole statement on line
1, because it occurs as *part* of a larger statement on that line. Since 'A → (B & ~C)'
on line 1 is not contained in a larger statement on that line, we see that it is the
'whole statement' on line 1. If the whole statement appearing on a line is a conjunction, then CE can be applied to it. So what can we do? Well, line 1 is a conditional, and on the very next line its antecedent appears as a whole-line statement.
Thus, we may apply MP to derive 'B & ~C' from lines 1 and 2:

> 1. A → (B & ~C)   PR
> 2. A   PR
> 3. D → C   PR
> 4. B & ~C   1, 2   MP

Take care to note that in order to apply MP, we must have *both* the conditional as
the whole statement on one line and the conditional's antecedent as the whole
statement on another line. Now we can apply CE to get 'B':

> 1. A → (B & ~C)   PR
> 2. A   PR
> 3. D → C   PR
> 4. B & ~C   1, 2   MP
> 5. B   4   CE

Half our work is done. If we can somehow get the right-hand conjunct of the conclusion, '~D', then we can put this together with 'B', using the rule CI. Observe
that 'D' occurs on line 3. If we had '~C' on a separate line, then we could use the
rule MT to add '~D' as a new line. And, in fact, we *can* derive '~C' from line 4,
again by using CE:

```
1. A → (B & ~C)              PR
2. A                         PR
3. D → C                     PR
4. B & ~C          1, 2      MP
5. B               4         CE
6. ~C              4         CE
```

(Line 4 has not been "used up" by the previous application of CE. In fact, either 'B' or '~C' could be derived again and again by CE if we found it useful, or even if we merely wished to be redundant.) Now we can apply MT:

```
1. A → (B & ~C)              PR
2. A                         PR
3. D → C                     PR
4. B & ~C          1, 2      MP
5. B               4         CE
6. ~C              4         CE
7. ~D              3, 6      MT
```

Finally, we can put the statements on lines 5 and 7 together by CI to get our conclusion:

```
1. A → (B & ~C)              PR
2. A                         PR
3. D → C                     PR
4. B & ~C          1, 2      MP
5. B               4         CE
6. ~C              4         CE
7. ~D              3, 6      MT
8. B & ~D          5, 7      CI
```

Thus, we have shown that the given argument is valid by producing a formal proof of its conclusion from its premises. Using the notation introduced at the end of Section 4.1, we may write

$$A → (B \& {\sim}C), A, D → C \vdash_{D_{SL}} B \& {\sim}D.$$

A final note. Technically, nothing prevents us from continuing on indefinitely with the proof above. That is, we *could* continue deriving statements by MP, CI, CE, and so on. However, because we have already succeeded, on line 8, in deriving the desired conclusion from the given premises, there is evidently no reason to continue. When a desired conclusion is reached as the last line of a D_{SL} proof, we call the derivation a 'finished D_{SL} proof' for the conclusion from the given premises.

Exercises for Section 4.2

Part I: Inspecting Proofs Carefully inspect each of the following derivations. Indicate any lines that have been added by the incorrect application of a rule presented in this section.

♦1. 1. A ∨ B   PR
    2. A   1   CE
    3. ~A   1, 2   MT

2. 1. A → ~B   PR
    2. B   PR
    3. ~A   1, 2   MT

3. 1. P ∨ Q   PR
    2. H → J   PR
    3. (H → J) & (P ∨ Q)   1, 2   CI

4. 1. J → K   PR
    2. J   PR
    3. K   1, 2   MP

5. 1. H → J   PR
    2. ~H   PR
    3. ~J   1, 2   MT

6. 1. (J ∨ K) → (L & M)   PR
    2. J ∨ K   PR
    3. L & M   1, 2   MP

♦7. 1. A & (B & C)   PR
    2. B   1   CE

8. 1. A & (B → C)   PR
    2. A   PR
    3. B → C   1, 2   MP

9. 1. F & G   PR
    2. ~G   PR
    3. ~F   1, 2   MT

10. 1. A ∨ B   PR
    2. C   PR
    3. A ∨ (B & C)   1, 2   CI

♦11. 1. P → Q   PR
    2. ~P   1   MT

12. 1. (H & I) ∨ (J & K)   PR
    2. ~(J & K)   PR
    3. ~(H & I)   1, 2   MT

Part II: Constructing Proofs Using only the rules PR, MP, MT, CE, and CI, give finished D$_{SL}$ proofs for each of the following arguments.

♦13. A & B, A → C /∴ C & B

14. A → B, B → C, ~C /∴ ~A

15. (G & F) → H, F & G /∴ H

16. H & (J & K) /∴ K & (J & H)

♦17. A → B, ~A → C, ~B & D /∴ C & D

18. (A → B) & (A → C), A /∴ B & C

19. (A ∨ B) & ~(C & D), (B & C) → (C & D)
   /∴ [(A ∨ B) & ~(B & C)] & ~(C & D)

20. [A & ~(P → Q)] & Q, Q → (P → Q) /∴ Q & ~Q

♦21. (A → B) → ~(C & ~D), E → (A → B), ~~(C & ~D) /∴ ~E

22. (A & (B & C)) → (J & ~D), (E & F) → D, B & (A & C)
    /∴ (A & J) & ~(E & F)

23. S & ~S, (S → G) & (~S → ~G) /∴ (~S & G) & (~G & S)

4.3   Replacement Rules for D_{SL}

The next four rules of D_{SL} are not whole-line inference rules. Furthermore, they are not "one-way" rules. With the first four rules, you are allowed to derive a specific whole from others, but you're not allowed to go "back the other way." For example, CE allows you to derive a statement *p* or a statement *q* from a statement *p* & *q,* but you are not allowed to go from *p* to *p* & *q*. Matters are somewhat different in the case of the following, which are called **replacement rules:**

Replacement   Any statement, whether appearing as a whole line in a proof or as part of a statement in a proof, may be replaced by its logical equivalent according to the following rules ('⇔' means 'is logically equivalent to'):

De Morgan's Law (DeM) $\sim(p \vee q)$ ⇔ $(\sim p \mathbin{\&} \sim q)$

   $\sim(p \mathbin{\&} q)$ ⇔ $(\sim p \vee \sim q)$

Material Implication (Impl) $(p \to q)$ ⇔ $(\sim p \vee q)$

Material Equivalence (Equiv) $(p \leftrightarrow q)$ ⇔ $[(p \to q) \mathbin{\&} (q \to p)]$

Double Negation (DN) $\sim\sim p$ ⇔ p

To see how the replacement rules may be used differently than the whole line inference rules, consider the following line:

   1. ~(A ∨ B) & ~(C → D)   PR

Notice that the left-hand conjunct is a negated disjunction. Using the replacement rule De Morgan's Law for a negated disjunction, this left-hand conjunct may literally be *replaced* by the statement to which it is equivalent according to the rule:

1. ~(A ∨ B) & ~(C → D)   PR
2. (~A & ~B) & ~(C → D)   1   DeM

Thus, the replacement rule allows us to change just part of a statement. Replacement rules are rather like "cut-and-paste" rules as one finds in modern word-processing programs. In saying that we can also go "back the other way," we mean that De Morgan's Law may be applied to the left-hand conjunct again to recover the original:

1. ~(A ∨ B) & ~(C → D)   PR
2. (~A & ~B) & ~(C → D)   1   DeM
3. ~(A ∨ B) & ~(C → D)   2   DeM

Of course, the replacement rules do not have to be applied only to parts of lines. Notice that the *whole statement* on line 3 is of the form (~p & ~q); that is, it is a conjunction of negations. Using the appropriate form of De Morgan's Law, we can derive from it a statement of the form ~(p ∨ q):

1. ~(A ∨ B) & ~(C → D)   PR
2. (~A & ~B) & ~(C → D)   1   DeM
3. ~(A ∨ B) & ~(C → D)   2   DeM
4. ~((A ∨ B) ∨ (C → D))   3   DeM

Be sure to note how parentheses (or brackets) must be introduced ("unsuppressed") to show that a negated disjunction has been added as a new line.

Let's go through a few more examples. Let us derive 'C' from the following two premises:

1. ~(~A & B)   PR
2. (A ∨ ~B) → C   PR

Notice that if we had the statement '(A ∨ ~B)' on a line of its own, we could use it together with line 2 and MP to get our conclusion. In such a situation a useful strategy is to try to somehow get the antecedent of the conditional. We can't derive the conditional's antecedent from the conditional itself. This suggests that we should look to the other premise. Let's see what happens if we apply De Morgan's law for a negated conjunction:

1. ~(~A & B)   PR
2. (A ∨ ~B) → C   PR
3. ~~A ∨ ~B   1   DeM

It is now clear that we almost have the antecedent of the conditional on line 2. There are two ways we could go, each of which would allow us to apply MP.

One way would be to use Double Negation (DN) to get the following from line 3:

1. ~(~A & B)		PR	
2. (A ∨ ~B) → C		PR	·
3. ~ ~A ∨ ~B	1	DeM	
4. A ∨ ~B	3	DN	

This now allows us to apply MP to lines 2 and 4:

1. ~(~A & B)		PR	
2. (A ∨ ~B) → C		PR	
3. ~ ~A ∨ ~B	1	DeM	
4. A ∨ ~B	3	DN	
5. C	2, 4	MP	

This gives us our conclusion. On the other hand, we could have applied DN to line 2 rather than line 3:

1. ~(~A & B)		PR	
2. (A ∨ ~B) → C		PR	
3. ~ ~A ∨ ~B	1	DeM	
4. (~ ~A ∨ ~B) → C	2	DN	
5. C	3, 4	MP	

Either way we have the desired conclusion. This illustrates the fact that there are many ways (in fact, *infinitely* many ways) to correctly complete a formal proof. Although some proofs are more economical than others, this does not make them "more correct." A proof is correct as long as every line has been added to the proof correctly.

Let's look at another example in which we must derive the antecedent of a conditional in order to use MP, so that we can ultimately derive '~A' from the following premises:

1. F ↔ G		PR
2. (~F ∨ G) → ~(H ∨ (J ∨ A))		PR

In this case the consequent of the conditional contains 'A', and it is apparent that some application of DeM to the consequent will enable us to derive '~A' from it, eventually. Our problem is thus how to obtain '~F ∨ G' on a line of its own so that MP can be used to get the consequent of the conditional on line 2. As in the previous case, let's see what we can do with the other premise. Only one rule applies to a biconditional, namely, Material Equivalence:

1. F ↔ G		PR
2. (~F ∨ G) → ~(H ∨ (J ∨ A))		PR
3. (F → G) & (G → F)	1	Equiv

Now let's use CE:

1. F ↔ G		PR
2. (~F ∨ G) → ~(H ∨ (J ∨ A))		PR
3. (F → G) & (G → F)	1	Equiv
4. F → G	3	CE

By Material Implication, we now derive

1. F ↔ G		PR
2. (~F ∨ G) → ~(H ∨ (J ∨ A))		PR
3. (F → G) & (G → F)	1	Equiv
4. F → G	3	CE
5. ~F ∨ G	4	Impl

This in turn allows us to use MP:

1. F ↔ G		PR
2. (~F ∨ G) → ~(H ∨ (J ∨ A))		PR
3. (F → G) & (G → F)	1	Equiv
4. F → G	3	CE
5. ~F ∨ G	4	Impl
6. ~(H ∨ (J ∨ A))	2, 5	MP

Using DeM,

1. F ↔ G		PR
2. (~F ∨ G) → ~(H ∨ (J ∨ A))		PR
3. (F → G) & (G → F)	1	Equiv
4. F → G	3	CE
5. ~F ∨ G	4	Impl
6. ~(H ∨ (J ∨ A))	2, 5	MP
7. ~H & ~(J ∨ A)	6	DeM

Now, we can finish the proof by applying CE, DeM, and CE once again:

1.	F ↔ G		PR
2.	(~F ∨ G) → ~(H ∨ (J ∨ A))		PR
3.	(F → G) & (G → F)	1	Equiv
4.	F → G	3	CE
5.	~F ∨ G	4	Impl
6.	~(H ∨ (J ∨ A))	2, 5	MP
7.	~H & ~(J ∨ A)	6	DeM
8.	~(J ∨ A)	7	CE
9.	~J & ~A	8	DeM
10.	~A	9	CE

In Section 4.4 the final rules of our full system D_{SL} are presented. In Section 4.5 several hints are given for constructing formal proofs.

Exercises for Section 4.3

Part I: Inspecting Proofs   Carefully inspect each of the following derivations. Indicate any lines that have been added by the incorrect application of a rule presented in this section.

♦1. 1. ~(A ∨ B)   PR
      2. ~A ∨ ~B   1   DeM

  2. 1. ~(~A & ~B)   PR
      2. ~~A ∨ ~~B   1   DeM

  3. 1. ~(A → C)   PR
      2. ~(A ∨ C)   1   Impl
      3. ~(A ∨ ~ ~C)   2   DN
      4. ~A & ~ ~ ~C   3   DeM
      5. A & ~ ~C   4   DN

  4. 1. (P → Q) → ~(R & ~S)   PR
      2. ~(P → Q) ∨ ~(R & ~S)   1   Impl
      3. ~(~P ∨ Q) ∨ ~(R & ~S)   2   Impl
      4. (P & ~Q) ∨ ~(R & ~S)   3   DeM
      5. (P & ~Q) ∨ (~R ∨ ~ ~S)   4   DeM

♦5. 1. J → ~K   PR
      2. (J → ~K) & (~K → J)   1   Equiv
      3. (~J ∨ ~K) & (~K → J)   2   Impl

    4. ~(J & K) & (~K → J)   3   DeM

    5. ~(J & K) & (K ∨ J)   4   Impl

    6. ~((J & K) ∨ ~(K ∨ J))   5   DeM

6. 1. P & ~Q   PR

    2. ~ ~P & ~Q   1   DN

    3. ~ ~ ~ ~P & ~Q   2   DN

    4. ~ ~ ~ ~ ~ ~P & ~Q   4   DN

    5. ~(~ ~ ~ ~ ~P ∨ ~Q)   4   DeM

    6. ~(~ ~ ~P ∨ ~Q)   5   DN

7. 1. A ∨ (B & C)   PR

    2. ~ ~(A ∨ (B & C))   2   DN

    3. ~ ~A & ~ ~(B & C)   2   DeM

    4. ~ ~A & ~(~B ∨ ~C)   3   DeM

    5. ~(~A ∨ (~B ∨ ~C))   4   DeM

    6. ~(A → (~B ∨ ~C))   5   Impl

    7. ~(A → (~ ~B → ~C)) 6   Impl

8. 1. ~[(A & ~B) → ~(J → K)] ∨ A   PR

    2. ~[(A & ~B) → ~(J → K)] ∨ ~ ~A   1   DN

    3. ~([(A & ~B) → ~(J → K)] & ~A)   2   DeM

    4. ~((A & ~B) → ~[(J → K) ∨ A])   3   DeM

    5. ~(~(A & ~B) ∨ ~[(J → K) ∨ A])   4   Impl

    6. ~ ~((A & ~B) & [(J → K) ∨ A])   5   DeM

    7. (A & ~B) & [(J → K) ∨ A]   6   DN

Part II: Constructing Proofs   Using only the rules PR, DeM, Impl, Equiv, and DN, give finished D_{SL} proofs for each of the following arguments.

  9. ~(~A ∨ ~B) /∴ A & B

 10. A & B /∴ ~(~A ∨ ~B)

♦11. F → G /∴ ~F ∨ ~ ~G

 12. G → H /∴ ~(G & ~H)

 13. ~(G & ~H) /∴ G → H

 14. ~(J ∨ K) /∴ ~ ~(~J & ~K)

♦15. ~[A & (B & C)] /∴ A → (B → ~C)

 16. (A → B) → C /∴ (A & ~B) ∨ C

17. P ↔ Q /∴ (~P ∨ Q) & (~Q ∨ P)

18. P ↔ Q /∴ ~[(P & ~Q) ∨ (Q & ~P)]

♦19. ~(P ↔ Q) /∴ (P & ~Q) ∨ (Q & ~P)

20. ~[~(~P ∨ Q) ∨ ~(~Q ∨ P)] /∴ P ↔ Q

21. ~[(H ∨ J) ∨ (J → K)] /∴ (~H & ~J) & (J & ~K)

22. A ↔ (B ↔ C)
    /∴ [A → ((B → C) & (C → B))] & [((B → C) & (C → B)) → A]

♦23. A ↔ (B ↔ C)
    /∴ [~A ∨ ~((B & ~C) ∨ (C & ~B))] & [(~(B → C) ∨ ~(C → B)) ∨ A]

Part III: Constructing Proofs   Selecting from all the rules presented in Sections 4.2 and 4.3, give finished D_{SL} proofs for each of the following arguments.

24. A → B, A & C /∴ B

25. A → B, A → ~B, A /∴ ~A

26. ~A ∨ B, ~C ∨ ~B, A /∴ ~C

♦27. ~(P & ~Q), P /∴ Q

28. ~(P & Q), P /∴ ~Q

29. ~(P & Q), Q /∴ ~P

30. ~H ↔ ~J, H /∴ J

31. H, J, K → (~H ∨ ~J) /∴ ~K

32. ~(~A ∨ ~B), (~ ~A & B) → C /∴ B & C

♦33. (P ∨ H) → (J & K), J → ~K /∴ ~P & ~H

34. (O ∨ P) → Q, ~(Q ∨ R) /∴ ~O

35. ~[(P & ~Q) ∨ (Q & ~R)], P /∴ R

36. ~[F & ~(~ G ∨ H)], (G → H) → F /∴ F ↔ (G → H)

37. ~(F → G), ~F ↔ ~H /∴ ~(F → ~H)

38. ~ ~A, A → (B & C), R ↔ ~B /∴ ~R

♦39. ~[A ∨ (B → C)], (~A → D) & (~C → E) /∴ B & E

40. ~[(W → X) ∨ (X → W)] /∴ (W & ~W) & (X & ~X)

41. ~(~M ∨ ~L), M → ~(P → ~Q), K → ~(P & Q) /∴ ~(L → K)

42. (P ∨ Q) → S, ~Q & R, ~(R → Q) → ~(L → S) /∴ ~P

43. (J → K) → (L → M), L & ~M, N → K /∴ ~(N ∨ K)

44. (A & ~B) ∨ (C & ~D), A → B /∴ ~(~D → ~C)

♦45. (A & B) → C, (C & D) → E, ~E & D /∴ A → ~B

4.4 Conditional Proof
and Reductio ad Absurdum

In this section we discuss two methods of proof, conditional proof and re-ductio ad absurdum. These are proof methods rather than rules, because they allow the derivation of statements not from prior *statements* in a proof but from prior *proofs* in a proof. To employ these methods, however, we will have to add a few new rules. Let's see how this works, beginning with conditional proof.

Conditional proof is a method for deriving conditional statements. The pattern of argument in conditional proof resembles informal methods of argu-mentation, so we begin with an informal example. One of the most venerable problems of philosophy concerns the relationship between determinism (which is roughly the view that every event in the world is caused by some set of prior events) and freedom of the will. Some philosophers believe that if determinism is true, then human beings do not have free will. This thesis, known as 'incompati-bilism', is a conditional statement. The incompatibilist does not argue either that determinism is true or that human beings do not have free will, but only that *if* determinism is true, *then* human beings do not have free will. How does the in-compatibilist argue for incompatibilism? Usually, she or he proceeds something like this: "Assume, for the sake of argument, that determinism is true. Now from this (and my other premises), we can infer [fill in some chain of reasoning] that human beings do not have free will. Since we can infer that humans do not have free will from this assumption, it follows that *if* determinism is true, human be-ings do not have free will."[7]

This method can be used to prove any conditional. To prove a statement of the form $p \rightarrow q$, *assume* that p is true. Derive q from p and any other prior lines. If p plus the statements from earlier lines entail q(as the derivation shows), the prior statements alone entail the statement $p \rightarrow q$.

The truth-functional justification for this rule is really quite straightforward. Recall from Chapter 3 our use of the symbol '⊨': When we write '$p_1, \ldots, p_n \vDash c$', we mean the argument '$p_1, \ldots, p_n$, therefore, c' is truth-functionally valid. With this in mind, note that the method of conditional proof amounts to devising a nat-ural deduction rule to accommodate the following logical fact about *SL*:

For any *SL* statements $s_1, \ldots, s_n, a, c,$ if $s_1, \ldots, s_n, a \vDash c$, then $s_1, \ldots, s_n \vDash a \rightarrow c$.

---

[7]For another example of an informal conditional proof, look at the argument presented in Section 3.7 justifying the truth table for the material conditional. There, we argued for the conditional, "If a conditional is truth-functional, then there is only one plausible option for its truth table."

To put it more simply: Suppose that some argument $p, q, / \therefore r$ is truth-functionally valid. Then, it *must* turn out that $p / \therefore q \to r$ is truth-functionally valid as well. The statement above is merely a generalization of this three-statement case.

We now spell out how to use this method in connection with our formal system D_{SL}:

Method of Conditional Proof   To derive a conditional statement $p \to q$, one may proceed by completing the following steps:

1. Add the statement p to the proof—say, on line m—with the notation 'PA-CP' for 'Provisional Assumption for Conditional Proof'. Indent line m to the right to indicate the beginning of a *subproof*.

2. Proceed with the indented subproof, employing any rules of inference, until the statement q occurs—say, on line n.

3. Enter the statement $p \to q$ on line $n + 1$, with the notation 'm–n, CP', meaning 'from lines m through n by Conditional Proof'. Move this line back to the left, so that it is indented to the same degree as the line immediately preceding line m. The provisional assumption is said to be **discharged** at line $n + 1$.

4. Place a partial box around lines m through n, indicating that these lines are sealed off and may not be used to justify subsequent inferences in the proof.

Here is a schematic picture of what this looks like:

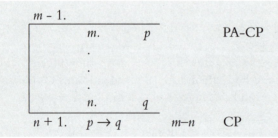

As indicated in the method outlined above, the indented portion of a proof is referred to as a **subproof.** With the introduction of subproofs, we must add to our definition of a finished D_{SL} proof the stipulation that a proof is not finished unless all subproofs are finished—that is, unless all provisional assumptions have been discharged. Here, then, is our formal definition of a finished D_{SL} proof:

> **Definition** A D_{SL} proof is a **finished D_{SL} proof of c from a set of premises** P if, and only if, (1) the statement c occurs as the last line of a proof that begins with all and only members of P listed as premises and (2) the proof contains no undischarged provisional assumptions.

Although you might not have thought otherwise, it is assumed here that P contains only finitely many statements. (If P were infinite in size, then a derivation from P would consist of a derivation from some finite subcollection of elements of P. This is a matter of theoretical interest that will not concern us in this text.)

As an example, we will use conditional proof to give a proof for the following argument:

$$E \rightarrow F$$
$$\underline{(E \ \& \ F) \rightarrow G}$$
$$\therefore E \rightarrow G$$

First, we list the premises:

1.	$E \rightarrow F$	PR
2.	$(E \ \& \ F) \rightarrow G$	PR

Now observe carefully: The statement we wish to derive is a conditional, '$E \rightarrow G$'. To use the method of conditional proof, we *provisionally* (i.e., *temporarily*) *assume* this conditional's antecedent, and then we proceed to derive its consequent:

1.	$E \rightarrow F$	PR
2.	$(E \ \& \ F) \rightarrow G$	PR
3.	E	PA-CP

Now we proceed until we get 'G':

1.	$E \rightarrow F$		PR
2.	$(E \ \& \ F) \rightarrow G$		PR
3.	E		PA-CP
4.	F	1, 3	MP
5.	E & F	3, 4	CI
6.	G	2, 5	MP

Now that we have the consequent, 'G', of the conditional we're after, the method of conditional proof states that we may *discharge* the provisional assumption and add the conditional as a new line of the proof:

1.	E → F		PR
2.	(E & F) → G		PR
	3. E		PA-CP
	4. F	1, 3	MP
	5. E & F	3, 4	CI
	6. G	2, 5	MP
7.	E → G	3–6	CP

Thus, the above constitutes a finished D_{SL} proof of 'E → G' from 'E → F' and '(E & F) → G'. When using CP, the provisional assumption is *always* the antecedent of the conditional you are trying to derive. When you derive the consequent of the conditional, the desired conditional is *immediately* entered on the next line.

Let's consider the significance of clause (4) in our description of the conditional proof method. The point of this clause is to prevent one from using as a justification for an inference a statement that has been inferred from a discharged assumption. The discharged assumption is *not* one of the given premises of the argument you are trying to prove, so it cannot be used to establish the conclusion. To see how failing to obey this rule would cause trouble, consider the following incorrect proof.

1.	A		PR	
	2. ~A		PA-CP	
3.	~A → ~A	2–2	CP	
4.	A & ~A	1, 2	CI	***Incorrect!***

The trouble here is that a truth-functional self-contradiction, 'A & ~A', has been derived from a truth-functionally contingent statement, 'A'. In general, failing to obey the restriction (clause (4)) would allow one to derive false statements from true ones. Thus, after a provisional assumption has been discharged, no statement enclosed within a box may be used to justify an inference outside the box. This underscores the importance of satisfying all requirements for a 'finished D_{SL} proof'.

CP can also be used in a **nested** proof—that is, a proof in which one conditional proof is contained within another. Begin, for example, with the following:

| 1. | P → (Q → R) | PR |

We will derive the conclusion '(P → Q) → (P → R)' from this premise. We begin by observing that the desired conclusion is a conditional. Therefore, we proceed by using the method of conditional proof, which starts with the assumption of the conditional's antecedent:

| 1. | P → (Q → R) | | PR |
| 2. | P → Q | | PA-CP |

Now that we've made this assumption, our goal is to derive the consequent of the conditional. The consequent is the statement 'P → R'. Notice that this, too, is a conditional. Thus, we may *again* make a provisional assumption in order to use CP:

1.	P → (Q → R)		PR
2.	P → Q		PA-CP
3.	P		PA-CP

Our task now is to derive the consequent of this second conditional:

1.	P → (Q → R)		PR
2.	P → Q		PA-CP
3.	P		PA-CP
4.	Q → R	1, 3	MP
5.	Q	2, 3	MP
6.	R	4, 5	MP

Now that we have the consequent of the conditional, we can discharge the provisional assumption from line 3 at line 7:

1.	P → (Q → R)		PR
2.	P → Q		PA-CP
3.	P		PA-CP
4.	Q → R	1, 3	MP
5.	Q	2, 3	MP
6.	R	4, 5	MP
7.	P → R	3–6	CP

Observe now that line 7 is just the consequent of the conclusion we're after, whose antecedent was provisionally assumed on line 2. Thus, we may discharge that provisional assumption at line 8, and the proof is finished:

1.	P → (Q → R)		PR
2.	P → Q		PA-CP
3.	P		PA-CP
4.	Q → R	1, 3	MP
5.	Q	2, 3	MP
6.	R	4, 5	MP
7.	P → R	3–6	CP
8.	(P → Q) → (P → R)	2–7	CP

Let's now be more precise in our statement of the rules for the method of conditional proof. Formally, the method requires the use of two rules, one (PA-CP) to make the provisional assumption and another (CP) to discharge it. Here is the first rule:

> ***Provisional Assumption for Conditional Proof (PA-CP)***   Any statement *p* of *SL* may be entered as a provisional assumption on a line *m* of a formal proof. Line *m* and the lines following it are shifted to the right, until the assumption has been discharged. As justification for line *m*, put 'PA-CP'.

This rule is similar to our premise rule, except that (1) we may apply PA-CP anywhere rather than just at the beginning of the proof and (2) it changes the indentation of its own and subsequent lines.

In the statement of rule CP, which we give below, we make reference to *provisional assumptions.* Provisional assumptions start subproofs, and you can always find them by looking for lines where the indentation to the right increases. So far, the only rule that introduces a provisional assumption is PA-CP, but we will soon meet another such rule, PA-RAA (and, in Chapter 7, a third rule). The references to provisional assumptions in the statement of rule CP below are to *any* provisional assumptions, not just those introduced by PA-CP.

> ***Conditional Proof (CP)***   A statement of the form $p \rightarrow q$ may be entered on line $n + 1$ of a proof if all of the following conditions are met: (1) A statement *p* occurs on a line m ($\leq n$) with the justification 'PA-CP', (2) a statement *q* occurs on line *n*, and (3) no further undischarged provisional assumptions have been introduced between *m* and *n*. Line $n + 1$ and subsequent lines are shifted to the left, and lines *m* through *n* are enclosed in a partial box. As a justification for line $n + 1$ put '*m–n* CP'. Line $n + 1$ discharges the assumption on line *m*.

Clause (3) stipulates that we *cannot* use CP on any but the most recent undischarged provisional assumption. This means that if we are working toward some goal and introduce a further provisional assumption, we must change directions and work to discharge the new assumption before returning to the original goal. For example, in the previous proof, the introduction of the provisional assumption 'P → Q' on line 2 made it our immediate goal to derive the statement 'P → R'. We then made the provisional assumption 'P' on line 3, and a *new* immediate goal was established— namely, to derive 'R'. Once this second goal was reached and the provisional assumption on line 3 was discharged, we returned to the initial goal introduced by the first provisional assumption.

Now let's turn to the one remaining proof method for D_{SL}, **Reductio ad absurdum (RAA),** which means 'reduction to absurdity'. This method also goes by the names 'indirect proof' and 'proof by contradiction'. Informally, the method goes something like this: To prove that a statement p follows from a set of premises, it is sufficient to show that it is logically impossible for p to be false given those premises. Consequently, if we can, by assuming that p is false, derive a logical impossibility (i.e., a self-contradiction), we can then infer that p must be true. Here is how the method is applied in our system of natural deduction:

Method of Reductio ad Absurdum To derive a statement p, one may proceed by completing the following steps:

1. Add $\sim p$ to the proof—say, on line m—with the notation 'PA-RAA' for 'Provisional Assumption for Reductio ad Absurdum'. Indent line m to the right to indicate the beginning of a subproof.

2. Proceed with the proof, employing any rules of inference, until any statement of the form q & $\sim q$ occurs—say, on line n. The lines should be indented to the same degree as line m.

3. Enter the statement p on line $n + 1$, with the notation 'm–n, RAA' meaning 'from lines m through n by Reductio ad Absurdum'. Move this line back to the left so that it is indented to the same degree as the line immediately preceding line m. The provisional assumption is said to be **discharged** at line $n + 1$.

4. Place a partial box around lines m through n, indicating that these lines are sealed off and may not be used to justify subsequent inferences in the proof.

Here is a schematic view of what this looks like:

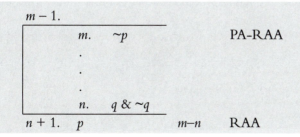

The intuitive appeal of this form of argument is that it amounts to showing that the provisional assumption that the conclusion is false leads to an *impossible* situation. Since we can't possibly have an impossible situation, it must be the case that the assumption is in error and that the conclusion is true. In terms of validity the underlying truth-functional principle is the following:

For any *SL* statements $p_1, \ldots, p_n$, *c*, and *q*, if $p_1, \ldots, p_n$, ~c ⊨ q & ~q, then $p_1, \ldots, p_n$ ⊨ c.

To put it more simply: Suppose that some argument *p*, ~q / ∴ r & ~r is truth-functionally valid. Then, it *must* turn out that *p* / ∴ q is truth-functionally valid as well. The statement above is merely a generalization of this three-statement case.[8]

As with conditional proof, the Reductio method requires the introduction of two new rules:

> ***Provisional Assumption for Reductio ad Absurdum (PA-RAA)*** Any *SL* statement of the form ~p may be entered as a provisional assumption on a line *m*. Line *m* and the lines following are shifted to the right, until the provisional assumption has been discharged. As a justification for line *m*, put 'PA-RAA'.
>
> ***Reductio ad Absurdum (RAA)*** A statement of the form *p* may be entered on line *n* + 1 of a proof if (1) a statement ~p occurs on a line *m* (≤ *n*) with the justification 'PA-RAA', (2) a statement *q* & ~q occurs on line *n*, and (3) no further undischarged provisional assumptions have been introduced between *m* and *n*. Line *n* + 1 and subsequent lines are shifted to the left, and lines *m* through *n* are enclosed in a partial box. As a justification for line *n* + 1 put '*m–n* RAA'. Line *n* + 1 discharges the assumption on line *m*.

Just as with the CP rule, the third clause of the RAA rule stipulates that one must always discharge the most recent provisional assumption—whether that assumption was introduced by PA-CP or by PA-RAA—before discharging earlier provisional assumptions.

As a simple example of the RAA method, consider a proof for the following argument:

A ∨ B
~A
∴ B

---

[8]Notice that RAA is the *syntactic* analogue of the method of argument analysis by the method of truth trees and brief truth tables. See the discussion on brief truth tables in Section 3.8. Notice, too, that the RAA method is justified by Proposition 2 of Section 3.6.

As usual, we start by listing the argument's premises:

1.	A ∨ B	PR
2.	~A	PR

To use the RAA method, we begin by provisionally assuming the *negation* of the desired statement. Since 'B' is the conclusion we wish to derive, we begin by assuming its negation:

1.	A ∨ B	PR
2.	~A	PR
3.	~B	PA-RAA

Now our goal becomes the derivation of any self-contradiction of the form p & $\sim p$. This can be accomplished in the present case by first conjoining the statements on lines 2 and 3:

1.	A ∨ B		PR
2.	~A		PR
3.	~B		PA-RAA
4.	~A & ~B	2, 3	CI

Now apply De Morgan's Law for a conjunction of negations:

1.	A ∨ B		PR
2.	~A		PR
3.	~B		PA-RAA
4.	~A & ~B	2, 3	CI
5.	~(A ∨ B)	4	DeM

Since the statement on line 5 is the negation of the statement on line 1, we can use CI to get our self-contradiction:

1.	A ∨ B		PR
2.	~A		PR
3.	~B		PA-RAA
4.	~A & ~B	2, 3	CI
5.	~(A ∨ B)	4	DeM
6.	(A ∨ B) & ~(A ∨ B)	1, 5	CI

Thus, we may discharge the provisional assumption and enter the conclusion, whose negation is the provisional assumption:

1.	A ∨ B		PR
2.	~A		PR
3.	~B		PA-RAA
4.	~A & ~B	2, 3	CI
5.	~(A ∨ B)	4	DeM
6.	(A ∨ B) & ~(A ∨ B)	1, 5	CI
7.	B	3–6	RAA

As a final example, CP and RAA are used together in a nested proof for the following argument:

A → (B & C)
A ∨ L
~L
∴ M → C

We start the proof by listing the argument's premises. Since the conclusion we're after is a conditional, we list its antecedent as a provisional assumption:

1.	A → (B & C)	PR
2.	A ∨ L	PR
3.	~L	PR
4.	M	PA-CP

What we want to do now is derive 'C', the conditional's consequent. Clearly, if we could somehow get 'B & C' out of line 1, we would have 'C' by CE. Is there a way to get 'B & C'? Well, if there were a way to get 'A' out of line 2, then 'A' to-gether with 'A → (B & C)' would imply 'B & C' by MP. Now, lines 2 and 3 clearly imply 'A', as proved on lines 5 through 9 by RAA:

1.	A → (B & C)		PR
2.	A ∨ L		PR
3.	~L		PR
4.	M		PA-CP
5.	~A		PA-RAA
6.	~A & ~L	3, 5	CI
7.	~(A ∨ L)	6	DeM
8.	(A ∨ L) & ~(A ∨ L)	2, 7	CI
9.	A	5–8	RAA

Now, using MP and CE:

1.	A → (B & C)		PR
2.	A ∨ L		PR
3.	~L		PR
4.	M		PA-CP
5.	~A		PA-RAA
6.	~A & ~L	3, 5	CI
7.	~(A ∨ L)	6	DeM
8.	(A ∨ L) & ~(A ∨ L)	2, 7	CI
9.	A	5–8	RAA
10.	B & C	1, 9	MP
11.	C	10	CE

Since we now have the consequent of the conditional we're after, our proof is done:

1.	A → (B & C)		PR
2.	A ∨ L		PR
3.	~L		PR
4.	M		PA-CP
5.	~A		PA-RAA
6.	~A & ~L	3, 5	CI
7.	~(A ∨ L)	6	DeM
8.	(A ∨ L) & ~(A ∨ L)	2, 7	CI
9.	A	5–8	RAA
10.	B & C	1, 9	MP
11.	C	10	CE
12.	M → C	4–11	CP

Exercises for Section 4.4

Constructing Proofs   Selecting from all the rules presented in Sections 4.2–4.4, give finished D_{SL} proofs for each of the following arguments.

♦1. A ∨ ~B /∴ B → A

2. (A ∨ B) → C /∴ (A → C) & (B → C)

3. ~A → B, A → B /∴ B

4. A → (B ∨ C) /∴ (A → B) ∨ (A → C)

5. A → B, A → ~B /∴ ~A

6. (A & B) → C /∴ (A → C) ∨ (B → C)

♦7. A /∴ B → B

8. A → (B & C) /∴ (A → B) & (A → C)

9. A & B /∴ A → B

10. ~T ∨ (S & U) /∴ (~T ∨ S) & (~T ∨ U)

11. K → K /∴ (A → A)

12. A → B, C → D, A ∨ C /∴ B ∨ D

13. P & ~P /∴ H

14. A → (B → C), (A → B) & ~C /∴ ~A

15. (A → B) → C /∴ B → C

16. O ↔ P, O ∨ ~P /∴ P ∨ ~O

♦17. T ∨ T, T → S /∴ S   20. ~(J & ~J) → (P → Q) /∴ P → Q

18. (L ∨ M) → P, M /∴ P   21. K → L /∴ K → (L ∨ M)

19. H ↔ K, ~(H & K) /∴ ~K   22. P → Q, P ∨ R, ~Q /∴ R & ~P

23. A → ~B, C → B /∴ A → ~C

24. ~(A → B), C ↔ B /∴ C → D

♦25. R → S, R → T /∴ R → (S & T)

26. H → K, (H & K) → L /∴ H → L

27. H → O, ~K → ~O /∴ (O & K) ∨ ~H

28. (A ∨ B) → (C & D), (C ∨ D) → E, A /∴ E

♦29. ~(J → K) → (G & F), G → (F → ~F), (J → J) → J /∴ K

30. ~(A ↔ B) /∴ ~A ↔ B

4.5   Proof Strategy

As noted at the start of the chapter, the method of natural deduction is not a decision procedure; that is, it is not a mechanical method for cranking out proofs. You have to be creative. In this section we offer some hints and suggestions on how to discover proofs.

A fundamental component of becoming proficient at proof construction is familiarity with the system of rules with which you are working. Different systems of natural deduction often use different sets of rules (although these sets usually overlap to some extent). Thus, a very helpful first step in gaining proficiency is to *memorize* the rules of inference. If half of your energy is spent reviewing a page of rules, you'll have less energy to devote to working out how a proof might go.

A second general pointer is that you should start thinking ahead. Ask yourself, "If I were to use rule *X* here, would I then be in a position to use any other rules?" Look for obvious possibilities first: For example, can any of the first eight rules of inference be applied to give the conclusion right away? Or perhaps an obvious application of one of these rules will indicate another obvious move that will produce the conclusion. Look especially for cases where applying MP, MT, CE, DeM, and Impl might be useful.

Try to identify the conclusion among the premises and "work backward", that is, imagine that you've succeeded in deriving the conclusion and ask yourself from which previous lines it could have been derived. You can then make it a goal to derive those lines from which it seems reasonable to believe the conclusion came.

Keep alert. Keep in mind the conclusion you're after and stay in touch with the location of statements in the proof. As you complete more and more proofs, be sure to make a mental note of steps or patterns that occur again and again so that the next time a similar situation arises the same pattern will suggest itself "automatically."

Finally, here are several specific pointers:

1. If you want to derive a conjunction, p & q: Try to derive both conjuncts. Then, CI may be used to get the conjunction.

2. If you want to derive a disjunction: (a) Try to derive either disjunct and then use a standard pattern to get the other one. That is, suppose you want to derive $p \vee q$. First, derive either p or q. If you've derived p, proceed like this:

$m + 1.$	$\sim(p \vee q)$		PA-RAA
$m + 2.$	$\sim p$ & $\sim q$	$m + 1$	DeM
$m + 3.$	$\sim p$	$m + 2$	CE
$m + 4.$	$p \sim p$	$m, m + 3$	CI
$m + 5.$	$p \vee q$	$(m + 1)-(m + 4)$	RAA

A similar pattern is used if you've been able to derive the other disjunct. (b) Use RAA. As soon as you've assumed the negation of the disjunction, De Morgan's law can be applied. This will give you a conjunction of negations to which CE can be applied. This will often suggest several possible moves. (c) Use CP to derive $\sim p \rightarrow q$, then use Impl and DN to infer $p \vee q$.

3. If you want to derive a conditional: CP is the most obvious choice. In fact, CP can be used in combination with RAA in the following way: Assume the antecedent of the desired conditional and then immediately assume the negation of the desired consequent as an RAA assumption:

$m.$	p	PA-CP
$m+1.$	$\sim q$	PA-RAA

Such moves typically prove fruitful. The finished proof will then have the following form:

$m.$	p		PA-CP
$m + 1.$	$\sim q$		PA-RAA
.			
.			
.			
$n.$	r & $\sim r$		
$n + 1.$	q	$(m + 1)-n$	RAA
$n + 2.$	$p \rightarrow q$	$m-(n + 1)$	CP

4. If you want to derive a biconditional, $p \leftrightarrow q$: Derive two conditionals, $p \rightarrow q$ and $q \rightarrow p$. Then conjoin these, using CI. The resulting statement is equivalent to the desired biconditional by Equiv. Sometimes, it will be necessary to perform two CP proofs in order to obtain the two conditionals.

Exercises for Section 4.5

Using the rules presented and discussed in Sections 4.2–4.4, give finished D_{SL} proofs for each of the following arguments.

1. P → ~P, M → P /∴ ~M
2. ~M ∨ L, ~M → L /∴ L
♦3. M ∨ L, ~M ∨ ~L /∴ ~(M ↔ L)
4. ~(H & K), P → H, ~K → ~L /∴ ~(P & L)
5. A ↔ (B ↔ C) /∴ (A ↔ B) ↔ C
6. (H & K) ∨ (H & L), (~K → L) → (H ↔ ~(R & S)) /∴ R → ~S
♦7. P → (R → S), [(P → R) → (P → S)] → (R & ~S) /∴ ~P
8. J ∨ K, K → L, J ↔ (M ∨ N), ~M & S, ~(S ↔ N) /∴ ~L → H

4.6 Proving Tautologousness and Other Semantic Properties

Natural deduction is most obviously suited to proving the validity of arguments, but as with the truth table and truth tree methods, it is possible to use natural deduction to establish that statements or sets of statements have the other semantic properties and relationships discussed in Sections 3.4–3.6.

Let's consider first how to prove that an *SL* statement is tautologous. When you derive a conclusion from a set of premises, you are demonstrating that in every interpretation under which all of the premises are true, the conclusion is true as well. The premises of the argument thus restrict the set of interpretations in which the conclusion must be true. But a tautology is, by definition, a statement that is true under every interpretation, so a tautology ought to be derivable from *no premises at all!* In other words, tautologies are true *independently* of any premises; they are true "no matter what."

To derive a tautology in D_{SL} without premises (from the "empty set"), we start the proof with provisional assumptions alone. Every proof of a tautology will begin with a provisional assumption for either CP or RAA. As a first example, let's prove that the tautology 'S ∨ ~S' is derivable from the empty set of premises. We begin by assuming that the statement is false:

1.	~(S ∨ ~S)		PA-RAA
2.	~S & ~ ~S	1	DeM

But this second statement is of the form p & $\sim p$, so the proof can be finished:

	1.	$\sim$(S $\vee$ $\sim$S)		PA-RAA
	2.	$\sim$S & $\sim$ $\sim$S	1	DeM
3.		S $\vee$ $\sim$S	1–2	RAA

From a semantic point of view, we've shown that the statement 'S $\vee$ $\sim$S' can't possibly be false, because the assumption that it is false implies a contradiction.

When a statement of *SL* can be derived as the last line of a finished D_{SL} proof containing no premises, like 'S $\vee$ $\sim$S' above, we say that the statement is a **theorem.** Specifically,

> **Definition** An *SL* statement p is a $\boldsymbol{D_{SL}}$ **theorem** if, and only if, there exists a finished D_{SL} proof of p from the empty set of premises.

If a statement p is a D_{SL} theorem, we write '$\vdash_{D_{SL}} p$'. As we discuss in the next section, tautologousness and theoremhood are directly related: An *SL* statement p is a theorem if, and only if, it is a tautology.

As a final example, we prove that $\vdash_{D_{SL}}$ A $\rightarrow$ (B $\rightarrow$ A). Since the statement to be proved is a conditional, we use the method of conditional proof:

	1.	A		PA-CP

The consequent is also a conditional. Thus, we write

	1.	A		PA-CP
	2.	B		PA-CP

We now need a logical "trick" to get 'A' from line 1 as the last line of the subproof with assumption 'B'. Such a trick is

	1.	A		PA-CP
	2.	B		PA-CP
	3.	A & B	1, 2	CI
	4.	A	3	CE

Closing the two subproofs finishes the proof of the theorem:

	1.	A		PA-CP
	2.	B		PA-CP
	3.	A & B	1, 2	CI
	4.	A	3	CE
	5.	B $\rightarrow$ A	2–4	CP
6.		A $\rightarrow$ (B $\rightarrow$ A)	1–5	CP

We have shown how to construct proofs demonstrating that a statement is a tautology. Using Propositions 1–4 from Sections 3.4 and 3.6, it is also possible to devise ways to construct proofs demonstrating that a statement is truth-functionally self-contradictory, that a pair of statements are truth-functionally equivalent, and that a set of statements is truth functionally inconsistent. For instance, Proposition 4 states that statements p and q are truth-functionally equivalent if, and only if, the biconditional $p \leftrightarrow q$ is a tautology. To demonstrate that two statements are truth-functionally equivalent, it is thus sufficient to form a biconditional with the two statements as conditions and then construct a proof that this new statement is a theorem. We leave it as an exercise for you to discover techniques for establishing that statements or sets of statements have the other properties mentioned here.

Exercises for Section 4.6

Part I: Theorems   Give finished D_{SL} proofs for the following theorems, using the rules given in Sections 4.2–4.4.

1. $B \rightarrow B$

2. $(A \rightarrow A) \rightarrow (B \vee {\sim}B)$

♦3. $G \rightarrow {\sim}{\sim}G$

4. $[(A \vee B) \vee {\sim}C] \vee ({\sim}C \rightarrow C)$

5. $G \leftrightarrow {\sim}{\sim}G$

6. $[(P \ \& \ Q) \rightarrow R]$
   $\rightarrow [P \rightarrow (Q \rightarrow R)]$

7. $(H \rightarrow {\sim}H) \rightarrow {\sim}H$

8. $[F \rightarrow (G \rightarrow H)]$
   $\rightarrow [(F \rightarrow G) \rightarrow (F \rightarrow H)]$

9. $({\sim}H \rightarrow H) \rightarrow H$

10. $(A \rightarrow B) \rightarrow (A \rightarrow (A \ \& \ B))$

♦11. $H \vee (G \rightarrow {\sim}H)$

12. $J \rightarrow ((J \ \& \ K) \rightarrow K)$

13. $(A \rightarrow B) \vee (B \rightarrow A)$

14. ${\sim}J \rightarrow [(J \vee K) \rightarrow K]$

15. ${\sim}(F \ \& \ G) \vee ({\sim}F \rightarrow K)$

16. $(J \leftrightarrow K) \rightarrow [(J \ \& \ L) \rightarrow (K \ \& \ L)]$

17. $(J \rightarrow K) \rightarrow ({\sim}K \rightarrow {\sim}J)$

18. $(J \leftrightarrow K) \rightarrow [(K \rightarrow J) \rightarrow (J \rightarrow K)]$

♦19. $(A \vee B) \vee ({\sim}A \vee {\sim}B)$

20. $(J \leftrightarrow K) \rightarrow [(J \rightarrow L) \rightarrow (K \rightarrow L)]$

21. $P \rightarrow (Q \vee P)$

22. $(P \leftrightarrow Q) \leftrightarrow [({\sim}P \vee Q) \ \& \ ({\sim}Q \vee P)]$

23. $(M \vee N) \rightarrow [({\sim}M \vee N) \rightarrow N]$

24. $[(R \rightarrow S) \ \& \ (R \rightarrow T)] \rightarrow [R \rightarrow (S \ \& \ T)]$

♦25. $[(R \rightarrow S) \ \& \ (R \rightarrow T)] \rightarrow [R \rightarrow (S \leftrightarrow T)]$

26. $[(S \rightarrow R) \vee (T \rightarrow R)] \rightarrow [(S \ \& \ T) \rightarrow R]$

27. ${\sim}[K \ \& \ (L \ \& \ {\sim}L)] \ \& \ [H \leftrightarrow ((H \rightarrow H) \rightarrow H)]$

28. $[(S \rightarrow S) \rightarrow A] \vee [A \rightarrow {\sim}(S \rightarrow S)]$

Part II: Theoretical Questions

29. Suppose that some statement, p, is a truth-functional self-contradiction. Explain how we could use our system of natural deduction to demonstrate that

it is a contradiction. Then, use your method to show that the following statement is a truth-functional self-contradiction: A & ((B → B) → ~A).

30. Suppose that a finite set of statements is truth-functionally inconsistent. Explain how we could use our system of natural deduction to demonstrate that the set is inconsistent. Then, use your method to show that the following set of statements is truth-functionally inconsistent: {~(A & (B → C)), A & (~B ∨ C)}.

4.7   The Adequacy of the Natural Deduction System D_{SL}

The main purpose of a natural deduction system is to provide a system of rules for constructing proofs demonstrating that valid arguments *are* valid and that tautologous statements *are* tautologies. We have assumed that our system is adequate to this task, but it is not obvious that this assumption is justified. In this section we say precisely what is meant by claiming that the system is 'adequate to the task' and indicate how this claim is justified.

For the sake of simplicity, we restrict ourselves initially to the question of whether the natural deduction system D_{SL} provides an adequate system for demonstrating that all tautologous statements are tautologies. For a natural deduction system—whether D_{SL} or any other—to be adequate for demonstrating that all tautologous statements are tautologies, it should have the following two properties. The first is *soundness:*

> **Soundness**   A system of natural deduction is **sound** if, and only if, every theorem of the natural deduction system is a tautology.

Note that soundness in the case of a natural deduction system is not the same as soundness in the case of an argument (Chapter 1). With respect to our specific system D_{SL}, the soundness condition may be expressed with the help of our notation for semantic and syntactic consequence:

The system D_{SL} is **sound** if, and only if, for any SL statement p, if $\vdash_{D_{SL}} p$, then $\vDash p$.

The second required property is *completeness:*

> **Completeness**   A system of natural deduction is **complete** if, and only if, every tautology is a theorem.

Stated with respect to our system D_{SL}:

The system D_{SL} is **complete** if, and only if, for any SL statement p, if $\vDash p$, then $\vdash_{D_{SL}} p$.

If our system were unsound, we would not be justified in saying that, by constructing a proof, we had demonstrated that a theorem is a tautology. If our system were incomplete, there would be tautologies that we could not *demonstrate* to be tautologies by the construction of proofs. Let's consider each property in turn.

Soundness guarantees that, if a statement is proved as a theorem, then that statement *really is* a tautology. More generally, it guarantees that if a conclusion has been drawn from a set of premises, then that conclusion *really does logically follow* from those premises. The soundness of our system is ensured by the way that its rules of inference have been chosen. In particular, the soundness of D_{SL} follows almost immediately from the fact that all the inference rules of D_{SL} have the following property, also called 'soundness':

> ***Definition***   A rule of inference is **sound** if, and only if, any statement added to a proof by the correct application of that rule is a deductively valid consequence of the statements from which it was inferred by that rule—that is, from the statements referred to in its justification.

If we think of rules of inference as allowable argument forms, then we may say that a rule of inference is sound just in case it is a valid argument form. Take Modus Ponens as an example: For any statements p and q, there is no interpretation under which both p and $p \to q$ are true but q is false. Thus, Modus Ponens is a valid argument form and, hence, a sound rule.

Contrast the case of Modus Ponens with the following: Imagine that, instead of Modus Ponens, we had included the following among our inference rules:

$$p \to q$$
$$\underline{q}$$
$$\therefore p$$

You can no doubt easily think of statements to put in place of 'p' and 'q' that would result in an argument of the above form having simultaneously true premises and false

---

[9]Notice that the rules associated with Conditional Proof and Reductio ad Absurdum work somewhat differently than the others, because the justification of the rules CP and RAA refer not to statements but to proofs. Assuming that the rules used in the subproof are sound, however, it can be shown that the use of CP and RAA does not permit the derivation from a set of premises of anything that is not a truth-functional consequence of those premises.

conclusion. This rule is thus unsound, and if it were included in D_{SL}, there would be theorems of D_{SL} that were not tautologies. Consequently, we avoid such rules.[9]

Although the fact that all rules of our system are sound gives strong intuitive support to the claim that the system as a whole is sound, this intuitive support does not amount to a rigorous demonstration. To give a rigorous proof that D_{SL} is sound, we would have to prove the following: No matter how long a proof is, every statement in the proof that results from the complete application of a rule is a logical consequence of the given premises. Showing that this is so for D_{SL}, however, requires use of a technique called 'mathematical induction', which is beyond the scope of this text.

That our natural deduction system is sound is not that surprising. It is much less obvious that the system is complete, however. If D_{SL} is complete, then there must be a finished D_{SL} proof for every tautology. Now, it is certainly clear that if certain rules were *removed* from D_{SL}, the resulting system would be incomplete. Suppose, for example, we were to remove the Material Equivalence rule from D_{SL}. Since there are biconditional statements in *SL*, we would have a system of formal proof for *SL* with no way to make inferences involving biconditional statements. Even the most straightforward biconditional tautology, like 'A ↔ A', would not be a theorem. Or, more obviously, note that if CP, RAA, and their associated PA rules were removed from D_{SL} the resulting system would not allow the derivation of *any* theorems at all. By definition, a theorem must be derived from no premises, and without rules for making and then discharging provisional assumptions, no such proofs could even begin.

Though it is apparent that D_{SL} would certainly be incomplete if various rules were removed, it must still be asked how we can be sure that the system D_{SL} as it stands *is* complete. It may seem entirely possible that we do not have sufficient inference rules to construct proofs for *all* tautologies. It is, however, possible to demonstrate that the set of rules we have given is sufficient. One way to give this demonstration would be to establish the truth of the following proposition:

> For any *SL* statement *s*, if the set $\{s\}$ is truth-functionally inconsistent,
> then $s \vdash_{D_{SL}} A \,\&\, {\sim}A$.

In other words, *if* there is no interpretation under which the statement *s* is true, *then* it must be the case that, using only rules of inference from D_{SL}, the statement 'A & ~A' can be derived from *s*. Once this has been established, we can reason as follows: Suppose that some statement *p* is a tautology. It then follows that the set $\{{\sim}p\}$ is truth-functionally inconsistent. This, together with the proposition above, implies that 'A & ~A' can be derived from the statement ~*p* in the system D_{SL}. But from this it follows that the statement *p* must itself be a theorem of D_{SL}. For, suppose that ~*p* is entered on the first line of a proof with the justification 'PA-RAA'. Since 'A & ~A' can be derived from ~*p*, we may use RAA to infer *p* as the last line of the proof from the empty set of premises. The proof of the proposition above, like the rigorous proof of soundness, is beyond the scope of this text, and so it is omitted here.[10]

In consideration of these facts, an interesting theoretical question is whether it would be possible to remove one or more inference rules *without* making the system incomplete. If a deduction system's set of rules is such that the deletion of any one of them would make the system incomplete, the set of inferences rules is said to be a **primitive set.** Our set of inference rules is not primitive in this sense (see Exercise 2 at the end of this section).[11]

On the other hand, a system of inference rules could contain any number of rules. It would be easy to add rules to our system. When a rule is added, however, it should be a sound rule; we would not want any invalid arguments to become provable by the addition of a rule. When a rule is added that allows nothing new to be proved, the rule is said to be a **derived rule.** Although a derived rule adds no new consequences, it may make many proofs easier to do. For example, instead of going through all the steps in the proof of a disjunction $p \vee q$ from a statement p, outlined in Section 4.5, we could simply add a new rule, 'Disjunctive Addition':

$$\frac{p}{\therefore p \vee q}$$

We know that adding this rule adds nothing new because, as the pattern of derivation given earlier shows, anything that you can derive with the new rule can already be obtained without it.

The type of completeness we have discussed here (i.e., that every tautology is a theorem) is what logicians call **weak completeness.** It is closely related to another concept called *strong completeness:*

> ***Strong Completeness***   A system of natural deduction is strongly complete if, and only if, every valid argument has a formal proof in that system.

Stated with respect to D_{SL},

> The system D_{SL} is **strongly complete** if, and only if, for any set P of *SL* statements and any *SL* statement c, if $P \vDash c$, then $P \vdash_{D_{SL}} c$.

---

[10]For proofs of the soundness and completeness of a system of natural deduction, see, for example, Benson Mates's *Elementary Logic* or Bergmann, Moor and Nelson's *The Logic Book* (see Appendix 1).

[11]For a nice example of a system of primitive inference rules, see Howard Pospesel and William Lycan's *Introduction to Logic: Propositional Logic* (Englewood Cliffs, NJ: Prentice Hall, 1997).

We use the symbol 'P' instead of the expression '$\{p_1, \ldots, p_n\}$' because, for theoretical reasons, the set of premises may be allowed to be infinitely large. Only finitely many elements of P could actually be used in the derivation of c, of course. The system D_{SL} is both strongly and weakly complete, though it is possible to construct systems that are weakly but not strongly complete, and vice versa.

Notice that a system of natural deduction for statement logic could be sound without being complete and a system could be complete without being sound. For example, if the only rules of inference in some system were PR and MP, it would be true that the only thing you could prove in the system would be truth-functionally valid arguments. However, there would be many truth-functionally valid arguments without proofs in the system. Thus, the system would be sound but not complete. On the other hand, a system that contained the rule 'write down any statement of *SL* you please as a new line' would certainly be a complete system: Since all arguments would have proofs, all truth-functionally valid arguments would have proofs too. But since invalid arguments could be proved, the system would not be sound.

In closing our discussion of the adequacy of our system of natural deduction, let's recall the principal difference between natural deduction and the truth table and truth tree methods. The completeness of our natural deduction system implies that there is a proof for every tautology, but nothing in our specification of the rules tells us how to construct a proof for a specific tautology. Unlike the truth table and truth tree methods, our natural deduction system does not provide us with a mechanical procedure for demonstrating that a statement is, or is not, a tautology.

Though our system does not provide an effective decision procedure for tautologousness, it is an effectively decidable question whether or not a rule of inference has been correctly applied and, consequently, whether or not a proof is correct. A system of natural deduction serves as a kind of guarantee that a conclusion really does follow from some premises. As we start to look more deeply into logic, we will find classes of arguments for which it is generally believed that *no* effective decision procedure exists. It thus becomes quite important to have available a way to *show* that a conclusion follows from some premises, if it does. If you believe something on the basis of a deductive inference, it is important at least to be certain that the steps in your reasoning are correct, for imagine a system with a rule of inference like this:

> **Rule W** Add as a new line to a proof any statement that logically follows from earlier lines.

Because there are arguments for which no decision procedure exists, it would be very difficult to apply Rule W (for 'worthless') in such cases, for you might never know whether a statement followed or not! And if someone claimed to have correctly applied Rule W, we would have a very difficult job in trying to determine whether or not the person was right. The question of whether or not a rule of inference in our system has been correctly applied *is* effectively decidable. (This is why it is possible for a computer to check the correctness of a proof.)

Exercises for Section 4.7

1. Show that the optional whole-line inference rules in Section 4.8 are all derived rules, by showing patterns of proof that could always be used in place of each additional rule.

2. Show that Modus Ponens could be eliminated from our system of natural deduction without causing a loss of completeness (i.e., show that there is a series of steps that can always be used to derive q from $p \rightarrow q$ and p that does not use MP).

3.   a. Construct a system of natural deduction that is sound but not complete.

       b. Construct a natural deduction system that is complete but not sound.

4. D_{SL} is both strongly and weakly complete. Modify D_{SL} (by eliminating rules) in such a way that:

       a. It is strongly but not weakly complete.

       b. It is weakly but not strongly complete.

5. Suppose you had a natural deduction system whose only two rules were these:

   R1:   Write down the premises of your argument.

   R2:   From any previous lines, derive as a new line any statement at all.

   Such a system of logic is complete—that is, there is a proof for every valid argument. Nonetheless, such a system isn't very useful. Why not?

6. The connectives '/' of this exercise and '↓' of the next are known as 'Sheffer strokes' (these were introduced in the exercises for Section 3.10). The basic truth table for '/' is the following:

p	q	$(p \,/\, q)$
T	T	F
T	F	T
F	T	T
F	F	T

   Invent at least one whole-line rule and one replacement rule applying to statements containing this connective that could be added to D_{SL} if we added this connective to our symbolic language. Make sure that with the addition of your rules the resulting system remains sound.

♦7. Consider the connective '↓' whose basic truth table is as follows:

p	q	$(p \downarrow q)$
T	T	F
T	F	F
F	T	F
F	F	T

Invent at least one whole-line rule and one replacement rule applying to statements containing this connective that could be added to D_{SL} if we added this connective to our symbolic language. Make sure that with the addition of your rules the resulting system remains sound.

8. Suppose you had a natural deduction system whose only two rules were these:

   R1:   Write down the premises of your argument.

   R2:   Write down any statement at all, as long as it is a logical consequence of the premises.

   Notice that R2 is significantly different than R2 in Exercise 5. However, like the system of Exercise 5, this system of logic is complete; that is, every tautology is a theorem. What problems can you see arising from the use of this system? Explain.

9. We have emphasized that it would be incorrect to read 'A → B' as "A' implies 'B". In this chapter we have seen that Conditional Proof can be intuitively explained this way: We show that a conditional statement must be true, given some premises, by showing that these premises together with the assumption of the conditional's antecedent imply the conditional's consequent. Does this in any way contradict the assertion that the conditional is not an implication? Even in the case where we use Conditional Proof to prove a theorem, say, 'P → (Q → P)'?

4.8   Additional Inference Rules

At the discretion of your instructor, the following inference rules may be used in addition to those presented in the chapter.

Whole-Line Inference Rules

Disjunctive Syllogism (DS)   **Hypothetical Syllogism (HS)**

$$\begin{array}{c} p \vee q \\ \sim p \\ \hline \therefore q \end{array} \quad \text{and} \quad \begin{array}{c} p \vee q \\ \sim q \\ \hline \therefore p \end{array} \qquad \begin{array}{c} p \rightarrow q \\ q \rightarrow r \\ \hline \therefore p \rightarrow r \end{array}$$

Simple Destructive Dilemma (SDD)

$$p \rightarrow q$$
$$p \rightarrow s$$
$$\sim s \vee \sim q$$
$$\therefore \sim p$$

Simple Constructive Dilemma (SCD)

$$p \rightarrow q$$
$$r \rightarrow q$$
$$p \vee r$$
$$\therefore q$$

Complex Destructive Dilemma (CDD)

$$p \rightarrow q$$
$$r \rightarrow s$$
$$\overline{\sim s \vee \sim q}$$
$$\therefore \sim p \vee \sim r$$

Complex Constructive Dilemma (CCD)

$$p \rightarrow q$$
$$r \rightarrow s$$
$$\overline{p \vee r}$$
$$\therefore q \vee s$$

Disjunctive Addition (DA)

$$\frac{p}{\therefore p \vee q} \quad \text{and} \quad \frac{p}{\therefore q \vee p}$$

Conjunctive Argument (CA)

$$\frac{\sim(p \,\&\, q)}{p} \qquad \frac{\sim(p \,\&\, q)}{q}$$
$$\therefore \sim q \qquad \text{and} \qquad \therefore \sim p$$

Replacement Rules

Material Equivalence (Equiv)	$(p \leftrightarrow q)$	$\Leftrightarrow ((p \,\&\, q) \vee (\sim p \,\&\, \sim q))$
Exportation (Exp)	$(p \rightarrow (q \rightarrow r))$	$\Leftrightarrow ((p \,\&\, q) \rightarrow r)$
Negated Conditional (NC)	$\sim(p \rightarrow q)$	$\Leftrightarrow (p \,\&\, \sim q)$
Absorption (Abs)	$(p \rightarrow q)$	$\Leftrightarrow (p \rightarrow (p \,\&\, q))$
Transposition (Trans)	$(p \rightarrow q)$	$\Leftrightarrow (\sim q \rightarrow \sim p)$
Commutation (Comm)	$(p \,\&\, q)$	$\Leftrightarrow (q \,\&\, p)$
	$(p \vee q)$	$\Leftrightarrow (q \vee p)$
Association (Assoc)	$((p \,\&\, q) \,\&\, r)$	$\Leftrightarrow (p \,\&\, (q \,\&\, r))$
	$((p \vee q) \vee r)$	$\Leftrightarrow (p \vee (q \vee r))$
Distribution (Dist)	$(p \,\&\, (q \vee r))$	$\Leftrightarrow ((p \,\&\, q) \vee (p \,\&\, r))$
	$(p \vee (q \,\&\, r))$	$\Leftrightarrow ((p \vee q) \,\&\, (p \vee r))$

Tautology (Taut) p $\Leftrightarrow (p \ \& \ p)$

                             p $\Leftrightarrow (p \lor p)$

4.9   A Second Look at the Truth Table for the Material Conditional

In this section we consider an alternative justification of the material conditional. It is just one of many ways to argue for the correctness of the truth table for the material conditional, but it has the advantage of exhibiting some of the connections between our rules of inference and the meaning of the logical connectives.

The justification of the truth table for the conditional to be presented here makes the following two basic assumptions:

1. Certain rules of inference are logically correct, and a truth table should *show* that these rules are logically correct.

2. The truth table for the conditional *is truth-functional;* that is, the truth value of any statement of the form 'if p, then q' is *uniquely determined* by the truth values of its antecedent and consequent.

With these basic assumptions in mind, let's begin. How will we fill in the following table?

p	q	$(p \rightarrow q)$
T	T	
T	F	
F	T	
F	F	

Starting with the second row, let's ask, "Why can't we put T when p is true and q is false?" The answer is quite compelling: (1) MP is a sound rule of inference. (2) If we were to put the value T in the second row of the table, it would be telling us that, with the MP form of argument, it is logically possible to have simultaneously true premises and a false conclusion. Therefore, (3) the table would be incorrect if we put T in the second row. Hence, the table must *at least* look like this:

p	q	$(p \rightarrow q)$
T	T	
T	F	F
F	T	
F	F	

Next, why must we put T in the *first* row? Our argument here is based on the assumption that there are cases in which Modus Ponens can be applied; that is, there are cases in which the two premises of Modus Ponens, p and $(p \rightarrow q)$, are both true so that a conclusion q can be correctly inferred. Given this assumption, together with the fact that the second row must be F, we see that the first row must be T. If the first and second rows were *both* F, then it would, contrary to our assumption about the real applicability of Modus Ponens, be impossible for any statements of the forms p and $(p \rightarrow q)$ to simultaneously be true.

p	q	$(p \rightarrow q)$
T	T	T
T	F	F
F	T	
F	F	

Finally, why can't we put F in the third or fourth row, or both? At least one answer is again related to Modus Ponens. In particular, consider the associated conditional for Modus Ponens:

$$[(p \rightarrow q) \& p] \rightarrow q.$$

As we know, if an argument is valid, then its corresponding conditional ought to be not merely true but a *necessary* truth (see Section 3.4). Since this is the corresponding conditional for Modus Ponens, it therefore ought to be a necessary truth—that is, true regardless of the truth values of its component statements:

$$[(p \rightarrow q) \& p] \rightarrow q$$
$$\text{T}$$
$$\text{T}$$
$$\text{T}$$
$$\text{T}$$

Now consider these facts: (1) In the third and fourth rows of the table, p takes the value F. (2) Since the antecedent of the corresponding conditional is a conjunction with p as one of the conjuncts, the antecedent takes the value F in both rows. (3) Note, too, that in the third row of the table q takes the value T and in the fourth row q takes the value F. However, (4) we see that the corresponding conditional takes the value T in both these rows. Therefore, (5) since the conditional is a truth *function* it *must* be the case that a false antecedent and true consequent takes the value T and that a false antecedent and false consequent takes the value T:

p	*q*	$(p \rightarrow q)$
T	T	T
T	F	F
F	T	T
F	F	T

The arguments just given are not the only ones logicians have offered over the years to justify the truth conditions of the material conditional. Indeed, though we have adopted this traditional interpretation of the conditional, philosophers of logic still discuss and debate its proper interpretation.[12]

---

[12]For a recent and interesting example that argues for the usual truth-functional analysis on the basis of the method of Conditional Proof together with other natural deduction rules, see William H. Hanson, "Indicative Conditionals Are Truth-Functional," *Mind* 100.397 (January 1991): 53–72.

CHAPTER FIVE

Predicate Logic I:
Syntax and Semantics

5.1 Introduction

The language *SL* developed in Chapters 2–4 is certainly useful in several ways. For one thing, it helps us make precise what might be imprecise or ambiguous if left in ordinary language. Once statements of ordinary language have been symbolized in *SL,* we have available many tests that can be used to investigate various logical properties of statements and relationships among them.

All along, however, it has been pointed out that there exist arguments, statements, and sets of statements for which the methods of truth-functional analysis are not adequate. As an example, consider the following argument originally given in Chapter 1:

> All astronomers are stargazers
> Hypatia is an astronomer
> _____
> ∴ Hypatia is a stargazer.

This argument is clearly valid: It would be impossible for the two premises to be true while, at the same time, the conclusion were false. However, it is also clear that this argument is not *truth-functionally* valid. The methods of logical analysis so far developed force us to count all three statements as logically simple. Symbolizing it in *SL* therefore produces the following argument:

$$A$$
$$B$$
$$\overline{\hspace{1.2cm}}$$
$$\therefore C$$

As a truth table for this argument reveals, it is possible for the symbolized argument to take simultaneously true premises and a false conclusion. This example illustrates the fact that we can't always use truth-functional methods as a reliable test for deductive validity.

It should not be surprising that there exist valid arguments whose validity cannot be demonstrated by truth-functional analysis. Indeed, it is arguable that there exist valid arguments whose proper analysis lies entirely beyond the scope of formal analysis. Nonetheless, it is interesting to wonder how far we might go in developing formal methods for logical analysis. We can go much further than statement logic, but exactly *how much* further is still a subject of much investigation among philosophers, logicians, and computer scientists.

In this and the next three chapters, we take a look at more powerful methods of formal analysis. The methods we are going to develop start by extending the vocabulary, syntax, and semantics of statement logic so that the logical form of statements can be brought into even clearer focus. In Chapter 6 the method of truth trees will be expanded to handle the extended language. This will provide us with a mechanical test for the consistency of sets of statements written in the extended language, which we introduce in this chapter. Since we will have a mechanical test for consistency, we will also have a test for argument validity, logical truth, and other semantic properties analogous to those discussed in connection with statement logic. In Chapter 7 additional rules will be added to our system of natural deduction in order to provide a sound and complete deduction system for the new language.

5.2 Informal Introduction to the Language of Predicate Logic

Let's call the new language that we will develop '*L*'. *L* is an *extension* of statement logic, which means that *L* includes (1) all the statements of statement logic, plus (2) new statements that can be obtained using new symbols and new rules of formation. As in the corresponding section of Chapter 2, we begin this section with an informal introduction to the new language by showing how to symbolize natural language statements in *L*. We start by considering the second premise of the argument given on the first page of this chapter:

(1) Hypatia is an astronomer.

In *SL,* we would symbolize this statement by associating with it a single statement letter, say, 'S':

(2) S.

Here we do something different. Consider the grammatical subject of statement (1)—that is, 'Hypatia'. Let us substitute for 'Hypatia' the lowercase letter 'h'. The result of this substitution is

(3) h is an astronomer.

Next, consider the grammatical predicate of (1), 'is an astronomer'. Let us replace this, too, by a symbol. In this case we use the capital letter 'A':

(4) hA.

Finally, let's switch the position of 'h' and 'A':

(5) Ah.

Expression (5) is an example of a symbolic statement of *L.* In effect, given the meanings we have associated with 'h' and 'A', (5) may be read as saying that the property expressed by 'A' belongs to the object denoted by 'h'. In this case, Hypatia is the **denotation** (i.e., person or object denoted) of 'h', and being an astronomer is the property expressed by 'A'. Yet another way to interpret 'A', which will prove quite useful to us in Section 5.4, is to take it as *denoting* the *set* (i.e., collection) of astronomers. Looked at in this way, (5) may also be read as saying, in effect, that the object denoted by 'h' is contained in the set denoted by 'A'.

The symbolic statement (5) introduces two new kinds of symbol. The first kind, of which 'A' is an example, is called a **predicate symbol.** Besides using capital letters to stand in place of English statements, we will now also use them in this way to stand in place of predicates. Next, the lowercase letter 'h', an example of an **individual constant** or **name,** is used to represent a single individual. 'A' is a **monadic** (or **one-place**) **predicate symbol** because it must be followed by a single symbol that refers to an individual. In effect, you can think of 'A' as having a single blank space next to it, 'A__', to be filled in by a single individual symbol.

Let's now combine this method with the methods of symbolization already introduced in previous chapters. Consider, for example, the following statement:

Paul is a chemist, and Beverly is a therapist.

Recall that in *SL* we would simply associate each simple statement with a statement letter, then add an appropriate connective symbol. In this case let 'P' stand for 'Paul is a chemist' and 'B' stand for 'Beverly is a therapist' and complete the *SL* symbolization by writing

P & B.

In *L*, however, we follow the same method as used to symbolize 'Hypatia is an astronomer': Let 'p' denote Paul, 'b' denote Beverly, 'C' stand for the property of being a chemist, and 'T' stand for the property of being a therapist. Pulling it all together, we write

Cp & Tb.

The characteristic difference between *SL* and *L*, we see, is that in *L* we may "dig deeper" into the grammatical structure of a statement. By writing predicate symbols followed by names, we take the symbolic statement thus formed to represent the assertion that the property represented by the predicate symbol is possessed by the object denoted by the name.

In *SL* recall that we specify the meaning of statement letters by writing a **statement key** consisting of a list of statement letters together with their associated English statements. For instance,

H: Hypatia is an astronomer

is a statement key. In *L* we write a similar kind of key:

Ax: x is an astronomer
h: Hypatia.

We call this key a **symbol key.** It is like the statement keys used for *SL*, except that now we must specify the meanings of individual constants and predicate symbols. Notice the 'x' that appears in the symbol key. The letter 'x' is an **individual variable,** or, as we usually simply say, a *variable.* The variable is used here merely as a placeholder to help us describe in English the intended meaning of the predicate symbol.

Here is how we would specify a symbol key for the statement about Paul and Beverly:

Cx: x is a chemist
Tx: x is a therapist
b: Beverly
p: Paul.

Analogously to statement keys in *SL,* symbol keys provide a method for specifying the meaning of symbols used in *L* statements. And just as we did in *SL,* we will supplement our notion of a symbol key with a more formally rigorous definition of an interpretation for a set of *L* statements.

Besides monadic predicate symbols, *L* also contains symbols standing for **polyadic predicates** (also called *n*-**adic**, *n*-**place,** or **relational predicates**). Polyadic predicates express relationships between and among individuals. The following statement provides us with an example:

Donald loves Claire.

This statement does not attribute a property to Donald or Claire but rather asserts a relationship between them. To symbolize this statement in *L,* we again use a capital Roman letter for a predicate symbol, but in this case the predicate symbol is followed by two individual symbols, one for the lover and a second for the lovee:

Ldc.

In this case, the symbol 'L' is a **two-place** predicate symbol. In our symbol key we indicate the meaning of 'L' as follows:

Lxy: x loves y.

In the symbolic expression 'Ldc', the order of constants is important, for the relationship need not go both ways. If, for example, Donald loves Claire but Claire does not love Donald, we would express this fact in *L* by the statement

Ldc & ~Lcd

while, if their love were mutual, we would write

Ldc & Lcd.

There of course exist many more than just two-place relations. For example, we might use a three-place predicate, 'Bxyz', to express the relationship of a number *x* being between numbers *y* and *z,* and so on for four-place, five-place, and, in general, *n*-place relations.

So far, *L* has not seemed especially different from *SL,* except that instead of using capital Roman letters to represent whole statements, *L* uses capital letters to represent predicates and uses lowercase letters to represent individuals. Furthermore, since *L* is an *extension* of *SL,* it is also still permissible to use capital letters to stand for simple statements. However, in the expression 'Ah', the letter 'A' cannot meaningfully be taken to stand for a simple statement. Whenever a capital letter is juxtaposed to the left of an individual constant or variable, the capital letter must be interpreted as a predicate symbol.

Now we come to the place where *L* differs quite significantly from the language *SL*. This is in its use of *quantifiers*. Consider the first premise of the "Hypatia" argument:

(1) All astronomers are stargazers.

Let's say the same thing in a slightly wordier way:

(2) For any object you please, if that object is an astronomer, then that object is a stargazer.

Now, replace the word 'object' by the individual variable 'x':

(3) For any x you please, if that x is an astronomer, then that x is a stargazer.

This can be tidied up a bit by eliminating some words that are not essential to the meaning of the statement:

(4) For any x, if x is an astronomer, then x is a stargazer.

Next let's substitute symbols to stand in place of the English predicates. Here we replace 'is an astronomer' with 'A', and we replace 'is a stargazer' with 'G':

(5) For any x, if Ax then Gx.

Since we have a symbol, '→', to represent the conditional, we now use it and add appropriate parentheses:

(6) For any x, (Ax → Gx).

Lastly, we introduce a *new* symbolic expression in place of 'for any x':

(7) ∀x(Ax → Gx).

This final string of symbols is the language *L* version of statement (1). The string of symbols '∀x' is called a **universal quantifier,** and is read 'for any x', 'for all x', or 'for every x'. The variable 'x' functions quite like the English pronoun 'it'.

With the addition of quantifiers, it becomes necessary to also expand on what needs to be included in a symbol key. Specifically, we must add a note indicating the class of objects over which we are quantifying, since there would otherwise remain an ambiguity in the meaning of the symbolic expression. For example, for the symbolization of 'All astronomers are stargazers', we introduced the symbolic expression '$\forall x(Ax \rightarrow Gx)$'. As noted, this is read 'For any x, if x is A, then x is G'. But when we say 'for *any* x', do we mean 'any x at all in the universe'? Or are we speaking just about human beings? This question is answered by adding to our symbol key an indication of the **domain** over which the quantifiers range:

> Domain: human beings
>
> Ax: x is an astronomer
>
> Gx: x is a stargazer
>
> h: Hypatia.

The domain may also be referred to as the 'universe', 'universe of discourse', or 'domain of discourse'. It is simply a nonempty set of objects. In general, to specify the meaning of a collection of *L* statements, the domain must be included.

Given the above key, we may now give a full symbolic representation of the argument at the start of this chapter:

$$\forall x(Ax \rightarrow Gx)$$
$$\underline{Ah}$$
$$\therefore Gh$$

To complete the informal presentation of the language *L,* we need to introduce one more symbol. Whereas the universal quantifier points to *all* objects of a specified domain, another quantifier, the *existential* (or *particular*) quantifier, points to only *some* objects of a specified domain. Below is a sequence of expressions, like the sequence for the universal quantifier, that starts with an English statement and ends with its transformation into a symbolic statement of *L:*

1. Some astronomers are stargazers
2. At least one astronomer is a stargazer
3. There exists at least one object such that this object is an astronomer, and this object is a stargazer
4. There exists at least one x such that x is an astronomer, and x is a stargazer
5. There exists at least one x such that Ax and Gx
6. There exists at least one x such that (Ax & Gx)
7. $\exists x(Ax \,\&\, Gx)$.

The string of symbols '∃x' is called an **existential quantifier** and is read 'there is an x such that', 'there exists at least one x such that' or 'for some x', where 'some' is used in the sense of 'at least one'.

With the symbols for existential and universal quantification, we have in essence introduced all new symbols of the language L. It remains for us to give a more precise and formal definition of the language and then to discuss techniques for symbolizing English. The formal definitions in Sections 5.3 and 5.4 may require some careful thought to fully appreciate. When the language SL was presented, we left the formal specification of the language until the end of the chapter. Here, however, a great deal depends on the use of terminology, which must be introduced in the formal description of the language, and so to this we now turn.

5.3   Syntax for *L*

The formal presentation of L is rather more involved than the formal presentation of SL. As with SL we begin the formal presentation of L with (1) a list of basic symbols of the language, (2) rules for properly forming statements of L, and (3) some descriptive terminology.

We have already remarked that we will use capital Roman letters to stand both for predicate symbols and for statement letters. In practice we can easily rely on context to determine the intended use of a letter, but for theoretical purposes this dependence on context is inconvenient. Consequently, in our "official" definition we adopt the convention of requiring that predicate symbols be capital Roman letters with a superscript indicating the number of places associated with the predicate. Thus, according to our official definition,

$$A \qquad B \qquad C_1 \qquad G_{234}$$

are statement letters, whereas

$$A^1 \qquad G^1_{12} \qquad H^1 \qquad Z^1_1$$

are one-place predicate symbols,

$$B^2 \qquad G^2_{12} \qquad H^2 \qquad V^2_{14}$$

are two-place predicate symbols, and so on for any superscript n representing a positive integer (i.e., 1, 2, 3, . . . , etc.). Although this is our *official* definition, in practice we will adopt the convention of dropping superscripts as long as no ambiguity results.

Now let's turn to our list of symbols for *L*. Notice that the first three groups of symbols are ones we have already met in *SL:*

Statement letters	An infinite supply of capital Roman letters, with or without subscripts:
	A, B, . . . , Z, A_1, B_1, . . . , Z_1, A_2, . . .
Statement connectives	~ & ∨ → ↔
Punctuation symbols	( ) [ ]
Predicate symbols	An infinite supply of capital Roman letters, with or without subscripts, and with a numerical superscript indicating the number of places for the predicate:
	$A^1, B^1, \ldots, Z^1, A_1^1, B_1^1, \ldots, Z_1^1, A_2^1, \ldots$
	$A^2, B^2, \ldots, Z^2, A_1^2, B_1^2, \ldots, Z_1^2, A_2^2, \ldots$
	$A^3, B^3, \ldots, Z^3, A_1^3, B_1^3, \ldots, Z_1^3, A_2^3, \ldots$
	. . . . . .
	. . . . . .
	. . . . . .
Individual constants	An infinite supply of lowercase Roman letters, 'a' through 't', with or without subscripts:
	a, b, . . . , t, a_1, b_1, . . . , t_1, a_2, . . .
	These will also be called **constants** or **names.**[1]
Individual variables	An infinite supply of lowercase Roman letters, 'u' through 'z', with or without subscripts:
	u, v, . . . , z, u_1, v_1, . . . , z_1, u_2, . . .
	These will also be called simply **variables.**
Quantifier symbols	∀ ∃

The connectives, punctuation symbols, and quantifiers are collectively referred to as the **logical symbols** of *L,* and the rest are the **nonlogical symbols** of *L*. Before we can formally define an '*L* Statement', we need to introduce several more

---

[1]If you are using the program Inference Engine with this text, you will notice that its version of *L* does not allow the letters 'f' through 'i' to be used as constants. They are reserved for function symbols, introduced in Chapter 8.

definitions, including the definition of an 'L formula'. The first step toward this goal is the definition of a term:

> **Definition**
>
> 1. Any individual constant or individual variable is a **term.**
>
> 2. No other symbols or strings of symbols are terms.

More informally, a term is a symbol that can be used to denote an individual. There are two kinds of terms, **constant terms** and **variable terms.** Constant terms denote particular individuals relative to interpretations. Variable terms, on the other hand, are said to 'range over objects in the domain'. Variables function like pronouns and pronominal expressions in English—like 'she', 'he', 'it', 'the first one', and 'the second one'. For the moment the only variable terms are individual variables, and the only constant terms are individual constants. We have used the word 'term' to describe these, since it will facilitate later discussion, in Chapter 8, when we introduce other kinds of terms.

When one language is used to describe or discuss a second language, the first is called the **metalanguage,** and the second is called the **object language.** Since in the present case English is used to discuss SL and $L,$ English is the metalanguage, and SL and L are the object languages. To define 'L formula', we have to make use of special variables to refer to certain types of symbols in L. These variables are not part of L but are part of the language (English) that we are using to define L. Because English is the metalanguage, we call these variables **metalinguistic variables.** We have already used such variables in our discussion of $SL,$ where the symbols 'p' and 'q' and others were used to refer to arbitrary SL statements. Lowercase italic letters, like 'p' and 'q', will be used here to range over statements and formulas of L. In addition to these, we use lowercase Greek letters such as 'α' (alpha) and 'β' (beta) to range over terms in L. With these things now explained, here is our definition of an L formula:

> **Definition**
>
> 1. All statement letters are **L formulas.**
>
> 2. Any n-place predicate symbol followed immediately by n terms is an **L formula.**
>
> 3. If p and q are any L formulas, then each of the following is an **L formula:**
>
>   a. $\sim p$
>
>   b. $(p \mathbin{\&} q)$
>
>   c. $(p \vee q)$
>
>   d. $(p \rightarrow q)$
>
>   e. $(p \leftrightarrow q)$

4. Let p be any L formula and let α be any variable. Then, the following are each **L formulas:**

   a. $\forall\alpha p$

   b. $\exists\alpha p$

The expressions '$\forall\alpha$' and '$\exists\alpha$' are called **quantifiers.** The variable α is called the **variable of quantification** or simply the **quantified variable.**

5. Nothing but what follows from (1) through (4) is an **L formula,** except that left and right brackets may be used in place of left and right parentheses, respectively.

In less constrained language, these definitions tell us (1) that all *SL* statements are *L* formulas, (2) that all *n*–place predicate symbols followed by *n* terms are *L* formulas, (3) that any truth-functional compound of *L* formulas is also an *L* formula, and finally (4) that the universal and existential quantifications of any *L* formula are also *L* formulas. As with the language *SL*, in practice we will adopt the convention that outermost parentheses may be dropped *provided that* no ambiguity or change in meaning results.

Here are some examples of *L* formulas:

F^1x

$\forall xF^2xy$

$(F^1x \ \& \ A^1y)$

$A^3bcd \vee (B^1x \rightarrow \forall yA^1y)$

$\forall x \sim\sim \exists y[A^1x \ \& \sim(B^2yy \vee S^1a)]$.

Each of these strings of symbols can be obtained by building on simpler pieces of the language in accordance with the various clauses given in the definition of an *L* formula. Since it will be clear from the context of use whether a capital letter in an *L* formula is a predicate symbol or a statement letter, the superscripts will ordinarily be suppressed (i.e., not used explicitly but understood to be present implicitly). Thus, the above formulas may equally well be written like this:

Fx

$\forall xFxy$

$(Fx \ \& \ Ay)$

$Abcd \vee (Bx \rightarrow \forall yAy)$

$\forall x \sim\sim \exists y[Ax \ \& \sim(Byy \vee Sa)]$.

By contrast, we know by clause (5) of the definition that none of the following strings is an *L* formula:

xF

(F)xF

Fz & Bac & (y∃)(Ca ∨ Bb).

Because none of these strings can be constructed according to clauses (1)–(4), they are, by clause (5), nonformulas.

Before defining '*L* statement', let's explain why not all *L* formulas are statements. The essential characteristic of a statement is that it is a sentence possessing a truth value. Relative to an interpretation, many *L* formulas will have truth values. For instance, the formula 'Fa' will be true just in case the individual denoted by 'a' has the property represented by 'F' according to the interpretation. In the *L* formula 'Fx', however, the variable 'x' does not refer to any particular individual. Consequently, the expression 'Fx' does not have a truth-value; it is somewhat like the English expression 'it is a father', without there being even a clue about to whom or to what 'it' refers. When we prefix this formula with one of the quantifiers, however, we get either '∀xFx' or '∃xFx'. Relative to an interpretation, both have truth values and, thus, both count as statements. '∀xFx' will be true just in case everything in the domain has the property assigned to 'F', and '∃xFx' will be true just in case at least one thing in the domain has this property.

What is needed for an *L* formula to be an *L* statement, then, is that the formula not contain any variables to which no quantifier has been applied. To state this requirement precisely, we will need a couple more expressions:

> **Definition** Let *p* be an *L* formula and let α be a variable that occurs in the formula *p*. If α occurs in *p* within a formula of the form ∀α*q* or ∃α*q*, then we say that any occurrences of α in those places are **bound occurrences.** Any occurrence of α in *p* that is not bound is said to be a **free occurrence** of α in *p*.

In this definition either of the formulas ∀α*q* and ∃α*q* *could* be the whole formula *p* itself or they could be smaller formulas actually contained in *p*. To illustrate the application of this definition, consider the following six *L* formulas:

(1) A ∨ Bx

(2) ∀x(A ∨ Bx)

(3) ∀xA ∨ Bx

(4) A ∨ ∀xBx

(5) ∃xFxy

(6) ∃y∃xFxy.

Let's take the formula p in the definition of 'bound occurrence' to successively be each of these six formulas as we consider them in turn.

First, suppose that p is formula (1). Notice that the variable 'x' occurs in p, but it does *not* occur in a formula either of the form ∀xq or the form ∃xq. Thus, the single occurrence of 'x' in p is a *free occurrence*.

Next, let p be formula (2). In this case, 'x' occurs in the formula p, and the form of p itself is ∀xq. (This is a case in which the remark made just after the preceding definition comes into play.) Thus, all occurrences of 'x' in (2) are *bound occurrences*.

If we take p to be formula (3), then we observe that 'x' occurs first in p in a formula of the form ∀xq,—that is, in the formula '∀xA'—and so its occurrence there is bound. However, the second occurrence of 'x', in the formula 'Bx' in p, is *not* bound since it does not occur in a formula of the form ∀αq or ∃αq. Thus, the right-hand disjunct of formula (3) contains a free occurrence of 'x'.

Letting p be formula (4), both occurrences of the variable 'x' in p are bound since both occurrences of 'x' in p are in a formula of the form ∀xq.

Finally, let's consider what happens when p is taken to be first formula (5) and then (6). If p is formula (5), notice first of all that the variable 'x' occurs in a formula of the form ∃xq, and thus 'x' occurs bound in formula (5). However, notice by contrast that the variable 'y' occurs in a formula of the form ∃xq but *not* in a formula of the form ∃yq, so the occurrence of 'y' in formula (5) is a *free* occurrence. In formula (6) both variables 'x' and 'y' are bound by quantifiers.

The definitions of 'free' and 'bound' occurrences of variables give us the final pieces we need to precisely define an L statement:

> **Definition**   An **L statement** is any L formula that contains no free occurrences of variables.

Applying this definition to the previous six formulas, we see that formulas (2), (4), and (6) are L statements since none contain free variables. However, since formulas (1), (3), and (5) each contain a free variable, they are *not* L statements.

A concept closely related to the subject of free and bound variables is that of a quantifier's scope:

> **Definition**   Let p be any L formula and let α be any variable. Then, in the following two formulas,
>
> **(1)**   ∀αp
>
> **(2)**   ∃αp
>
> we say that the formula p is the **scope** of the quantifier.

We can alternatively define the scope of a quantifier to be *the shortest string of symbols following the quantifier that is an L formula.* For instance, in the formula

$$\forall x(Px \to Qx) \;\&\; Pa$$

the scope of the quantifier is '(Px → Qx)', since, moving from left to right through '(Px → Qx)', we don't have an *L* formula until the right parenthesis has been included in the string of symbols. (Notice that our definition of the scope of a quantifier parallels the earlier definition of the scope of a negation in Section 2.4.)

We illustrate the concept of scope by referring once more to the following *L* formulas:

(1) A ∨ Bx

(2) ∀x(A ∨ Bx)

(3) ∀xA ∨ Bx

(4) A ∨ ∀xBx

(5) ∃xFxy

(6) ∃y∃xFxy.

In formula (1) there are no quantifiers, so talk of a quantifier's scope does not arise, but in formulas (2)–(4) it does. To determine the scope of a quantifier, we use the principle that the scope of a quantifier is the shortest string of symbols following that quantifier that is an *L* formula. In (2) the scope of the universal quantifier, '∀x', is the whole formula '(A∨ Bx)'. In formula (3) the scope of the quantifier is the formula 'A'. In (4) the scope of the quantifier is the formula 'Bx'. The scope of the quantifier '∃x' in (5) is 'Fxy', as it is in (6). Finally, the scope of '∃y' in (6) is the formula '∃xFxy'. Observe that any variable identical to the variable of quantification within whose scope that variable occurs is bound by that quantifier.

Two patterns of quantification that are permitted by our definitions sometimes prove confusing to beginning students. The first is called **vacuous quantification.** In general, we say that a quantifier '∀α' or '∃α' occurring anywhere in an *L* formula is **vacuous** just in case there are no free occurrences of α within the scope of that quantifier. In statements such as '∀xA' or 'B → ∃yPa', for example, the quantifier is said to be 'vacuous' since the variable of quantification is not found anywhere within the scope of the quantifier. Similarly, in formulas such as '∀x∀xAx', the outer quantifier is vacuous since all occurrences of the quantified variable within the scope of the outer quantifier are already bound: *It is the innermost quantifier that does the binding.* If a vacuous quantifier is prefixed to a statement, the meaning of the statement is not altered. In terms of truth value, '∀xA' has precisely the same value as 'A'. Similarly, the truth value of the statements '∀x∃xAx', '∃x∃xAx', and '∃x∀x∃xAx' (etc.) is the same as just '∃xAx'.

A related problem arises in connection with *L* statements like the following:

∃x(Px & ∃xQx).

The scope of the outer quantifier overlaps with the scope of the inner quantifier, where both quantifiers use the same variable of quantification. The quantifiers are said in this case to be **overlapping quantifiers.** Although a bit confusing to read, overlapping quantifiers pose no real difficulty. If a variable is within the scope of more than one quantifier of that variable, it is bound by the innermost quantifier. When a statement contains overlapping quantifiers, the occurrences of the variable inside and outside the scope of the inner quantifier should be thought of as occurrences of *different* variables, even though the same symbol is used in both occurrences. Thus, in our example above, the statement expresses the proposition that something has P and something—possibly, but also not necessarily, different from the first—has Q, not the proposition that some one thing has both P and Q. The statement can be thought of as merely a typographical variant of the statement '∃x(Px & ∃yQy)'. Since the form of this latter statement is more readily apparent, we generally prefer it in practice to the former.[2]

We have defined '*L* formula' in such a way that both vacuous quantifiers and overlapping quantifiers are allowed because it turns out that, by allowing these kinds of formulas, the definition can be put much more simply. Although no theoretical problems arise from allowing these formulas, we will in practice avoid using them in our examples and exercises, since they can be confusing.

In the next section we present the formal semantics for *L*. To this end, it will be useful to classify *L* formulas as belonging to one of the following three categories:

> *Definition:*   A **simple *L* formula** is an *L* formula that contains no quantifiers or connectives.
>
> *Definition*   A **compound *L* formula** is an *L* formula that has one of the following forms: ~p, (p & q), (p ∨ q), (p → q), or (p ↔ q).
>
> *Definition*   A **general *L* formula** is an *L* formula that is of the form ∀αp or ∃αp.

Just as in *SL,* simple formulas of *L* are sometimes called 'atomic formulas', and compound formulas of *L* are sometimes called 'molecular formulas'. Because all *L*

---

[2]The program Inference Engine, which accompanies this text, in fact prohibits *L* statements containing vacuous or overlapping quantifiers.

statements are L formulas, we may replace the word 'formula' by the word 'statement' in these three definitions to obtain definitions of **simple L statement, compound L statement,** and **general L statement,** respectively. Because our principal concern will be with statements, it is these last three expressions that we will most often employ.

Exercises for Section 5.3

Formal Aspects of L Syntax   Unless otherwise noted in the following exercises, we adopt the convention that superscripts and outermost parentheses may be dropped. Thus, for example, 'Ax ∨ Bx' counts as an L formula, even though strict adherence to the definition of L formula would require it to be written as '$(A^1x ∨ B^1x)$'.

(A) Each of the following L formulas contains quantifiers. For each formula, state the scope of all quantifiers.

♦1. ∀x(Ax ∨ B)   ♦5. ~∀x~~Ax ∨ By   9. ∃x(Ax & (C ∨ Ay)) & L

2. ~∃x(Ax ∨ ~Bx)   6. ∀x(Gx → ∃y∃zFxyz)   10. ∀xCxy & Ax

3. Ax & ∃zAx   7. ∃yMx & Ry   11. ∃x(Px & Bxa) → Pa

4. ∀xAx ∨ B   8. ∀x∃y(Axy & Px)   12. ∀zLaz & ∃yMya

(B) For each of the following L formulas, state which occurences of variables are free and which are bound.

13. ~∀xAx   16. Bx ∨ ∃xAxx   ♦19. ∀x(Lab & ∀yBx)

14. ∀x∃y(Az & Bya)   17. ∀x(Ax → (Pb ∨ Px))   20. ∃y(~By ↔ (~Axz ∨ Cy))

♦15. ∀x∀yAx & By   18. ∃zAz ∨ ∀yAy   21. ∀xAbx

(C) Return to (A) and (B). For any formula that is *not* a statement, introduce parentheses and/or quantifiers so that the formula becomes a statement.

(D) Using the *strict* definitions of L formula and L statement (i.e., *not adopting* the convention about dropping superscripts or outermost parentheses), indicate which of the following strings of symbols are L formulas, which are L statements, and which are neither.

22. $(A_2 \& B4)$ 26. ∀x(A ∨ B)

23. ∀x∃y[$(A^1x ∨ B^1y)$ & C_{22}]   ♦27. $(A^1a ∨ ∀y(A^1y → ∃zR^1z))$

24. ∀x(A^1x) 28. A^1xx

25.)x(Az^1 29. [∃xxA & ∀yyB]

30. xAx

31. x(Ax ↔ Bx)

32. & A ∨ ∀xbx

33. ∃y(A¹y → B¹y)

34. ∀xR

35. (A∀x & ∀x~Bx)

36. P³xyz

♦37. (Q²aA & B)

38. (B²ab → B)

39. (∃x)D²xa

(E) For each of the following *L* statements, indicate whether the statement is simple, compound, or general. (Our informal conventions regarding parentheses and superscripts are in use here.)

40. ∃y∀xAxy

41. A

42. ∀x(Ax & Ba)

♦43. ~∀x(Ax & Ba)

44. ∃y~[∀x(Ax & Ba) & (My ∨ Ay)]

45. Qabc

46. ∀x∃y(Lxy ∨ Lyx)

47. ∀xAxa ↔ Aaa

48. ∀x∃y(Axy & Byx) → ∃zHz

♦49. ∀x∃y[(Axy & Byx) → ∃zHz]

50. ∀yA

Statement w/ quantifier in front = gen

5.4   Formal Semantics I: Interpretations

When we presented the semantics of *SL,* we began with an informal specification of the meaning of statements—the statement key—and then augmented it by the formal definition of an *interpretation*. We proceed analogously here. We now augment our informal notion of a symbol key with the concept of an interpretation for a set of *L* statements.

An interpretation for a set of *SL* statements consists of an assignment of truth values to each of the statement letters occurring within the set. Such an assignment is sufficient to fix the truth values of every statement within the set. In specifying an interpretation for a set of *L* statements, our goal is still to fix the truth values of statements within the set. To do this, however, much more than truth value assignments to statement letters must be specified. In particular we must specify (1) a set of individuals (the domain) together with (2) the *extensions* of our *nonlogical* symbols: statement letters, predicate symbols, and constants. We consider each item in turn, starting with the domain.

In our informal discussion of interpretations (Section 5.2), it was noted that, in giving a symbol key, a domain had to be specified. The domain of an interpretation will be denoted by the symbol '$\mathcal{D}$'. What kinds of individuals can we have in domains? There is no real limit here. The individuals, or 'objects' as we will sometimes say, may be of any kind whatsoever. They may be ordinary physical objects, persons, places, or events. They may also include fictional objects, like the characters in *Hamlet,* or abstract objects, like numbers or propositions. They may even include things like colors, which we would not ordinarily think of as objects. Basically, anything that can be referred to as the subject of a sentence is a candidate for membership in a domain.

A domain is specified by indicating the set to be denoted by $\mathcal{D}$. If we choose colors as our domain, for example, we would write

$\mathcal{D}$:   colors.

It must be understood that the domain is a *set* of objects. In order to emphasize this fact, we can alternatively specify the domain of an interpretation by the use of formal set notation:

$\mathcal{D}$:   {x | x is a color}.

The expression '{x | x is a color}' is read 'the set of all x, such that x is a color'. Although commonly we take domains to be "natural" sets—that is, sets that we can specify with a simple phrase, like 'the natural numbers' or 'the set of all humans'—from a formal point of view any collection of individuals, no matter how heterogeneous, can form a domain. Thus, the following collection is a perfectly acceptable domain:

$\mathcal{D}$:   {1, Hamlet's nose, the smallest cicada in the universe, Spiderman}.

Once the domain of an interpretation has been specified for a set of statements, the nonlogical symbols in the set of statements need to be interpreted. Recall that in Chapter 3 we said that the meaning of a statement could be divided into two parts, the *intension* and the *extension*. We defined the intension of a statement to be the proposition it expresses, and its extension to be its truth value. This was all we needed to say for *SL* because the basic building blocks for all statements were statement letters. In *L,* however, our statements may have parts, and these parts have both intensions and extensions. Consider first monadic predicate symbols. We said earlier that in our symbol keys we associate monadic predicate symbols with *properties.* By a 'property' we mean some characteristic that can be attributed to individuals. For example,

$\mathcal{D}$:   animals

Px: x is a fish

a: Wanda.

Using this key, the statement 'Pa' is taken to express the proposition that Wanda has the property of being a fish or, more simply, that Wanda is a fish. The property expressed by the predicate 'P' is what we define to be the **intension of the predicate.**

Given any property, the individuals of a domain can be classified according to whether or not they have that property. For instance, suppose as above that our symbol key specifies the domain to be the set of all animals. Then, there will be some subset of the domain that is the set of all fish. This subset is what we call the **extension of the predicate.** Thus, in our example, the intension of 'P' is the property of being a fish, and the extension of 'P' is the set of all fish. Using set notation, we can give the symbol key in more overtly extensional terms:

$\mathcal{D}$:   {x | x is an animal}

P: {x | x is a fish}

a: Wanda.

Notice that in this case, in contrast to the former version of the same interpretation, the predicate symbol 'P' is not followed by the variable 'x'. In most cases, however, we *will* put variables after predicate symbols when we give an interpretation. This will both remind us that the symbols are indeed predicate symbols (i.e., as opposed to statement letters) and indicate whether the predicate is monadic or polyadic.

If a domain is finite, then we do not in principle even have to rely on the English predicate in the set expression. For example, if all the fish in the world had names, we could specify 'P' in the above interpretation by writing 'P: { Jan, Arvid, Gloria, Boyce, . . . , Betty, Clarence}' where the names occurring between the set braces taken all together named all the fish in the world. If a set is small enough, it is sometimes actually convenient to specify an interpretation in this way. For example, let $\mathcal{D} = \{1, 2, 3, 4, 5, 6\}$ and suppose we wish to interpret the predicate 'P' to mean 'is even'. Instead of writing 'P: {x | x is even}', we could simply put 'P: {2, 4, 6}'. This alternative method of specifying the extension of a predicate symbol is quite explicitly extensional.

One reason that we are careful to distinguish between the intensions and extensions of predicates is that two predicates may have identical extensions but *different* intensions. To use an ancient example, consider the property of being a human being and the property of being a featherless biped. If philosophical lore is correct, the only featherless bipeds among animals on Earth are human beings. Thus, the set of human beings and the set of featherless bipeds turn out to have the same members:

$$\{x \mid x \text{ is a featherless biped}\} = \{x \mid x \text{ is a human being}\}.$$

In this case, it is usual to say that the predicates are 'coextensive'. Even though these two sets are coextensive, we should certainly be hesitant to say that the expressions 'featherless biped' and 'human being' *mean* the same thing. We therefore say that, although these two sets have the same *extension,* they have different *intensions.*[3]

Although there are excellent reasons for distinguishing between properties and extensions, many philosophers have questioned whether such things as properties really exist. The reasons for their skepticism are quite analogous to the reasons that philosophers have expressed skepticism about the existence of propositions. (You might review our remarks on difficulties with propositions in Chapter 1.) For one thing, properties, like propositions, appear to be abstract entities. They are neither symbols nor words within a language, nor can they be thought of as mental entities or physical objects. There are also problems of vagueness; it is not always clear what individuals have a property. Consider the property of being a tree. Is there a clear and nonarbitrary line of demarcation between trees, bushes, and other plants? Probably not, and the same goes for many other properties. Finally, there is the problem of property identity. When are two properties the same? It is fairly clear, for instance, that the property of being a human being and the property of being a featherless biped are different properties, but what of the property of being water versus the property of having the chemical composition H_2O? It is not obvious whether or not these two properties are the *same* property. Attempting to answer these questions would be extremely difficult and would, in any case, take us far afield of our study.

The problems discussed above regarding intensions yield an important moral for our study of logic: In working with *L* statements, we will need to restrict our concept of a formal interpretation to the *extensional* aspects of semantics. Thus, when a predicate symbol is interpreted in the strict sense, its interpretation must be understood to be a subset of the domain. Nevertheless, it will be convenient to slip informally into "property talk" and intensional language from time to time in order to describe a particular interpretation.

Let's turn now to polyadic predicates. We call the **intension of a polyadic predicate** a **relation** (or a **relational property**). The interpretation of a polyadic

---

[3]In general, two sets are said to be identical just in case they have precisely the same elements as one another. This principle is called the 'principle of extensionality'.

predicate symbol is indicated in a way quite similar to the way the interpretations of monadic predicates are specified. Consider the two–place predicate 'P^2' as an example. To interpret this symbol we would add a line like the following to our symbol key:

P^{2}xy: x is a parent of y.

Relations are to polyadic predicates what properties are to monadic predicates. Like properties and propositions, talk of relations is often useful; however, philosophical difficulties lead some philosophers to doubt that there really are such things as relations. Although relations are not part of our formal semantics, we will speak informally of polyadic predicates as expressing relations.

Just as in the monadic case, we take the extension of a polyadic predicate symbol to be a set. But rather than a set of individuals, in the polyadic case the extension of an n-place predicate symbol will be a set of 'n-tuples' of individuals in the domain. An 'n-tuple' of objects is a sequence of n objects in a certain order, where order matters. An n-tuple with which most of us are familiar is the *ordered pair* of high school plane geometry. Every point in the Euclidean plane can be represented as a pair of numbers x and y, usually denoted '$<x, y>$'. The first member of the pair stands for the x coordinate of the point, the second for its y coordinate. In general, $<x, y> \neq <y, x>$ unless $x = y$ (or, to be more precise, $<x, y> = <u, v>$ if, and only if, $x = u$ and $y = v$). In giving the formal semantics for L, an ordered n-tuple can be represented by '$x_1, \ldots, x_n$'.

Given any n-place relation, there will be a set of n-tuples of individuals that stand in that relation to one another. We can denote this set by using formal set notation. Suppose that the intension of 'P^2' is the relation of parent to child. Taking the domain to be the set of people, this can be indicated in an interpretation as follows:

$\mathcal{D}$: $\{x \mid x$ is a person$\}$

P^{2}xy: $\{<x, y> \mid x$ is a parent of y$\}$.

Although we have used the intension of the predicate symbol to define this set, it is sometimes possible (given a domain) to write down the members of the set directly. Suppose our domain, $\mathcal{D}$, consists of Carol, Bob, Sally, John, and Paul and that Carol and Bob are parents of Sally and Sally is a parent of John and Paul. The extension of 'P^2' on this domain is then given as follows:

$\mathcal{D}$: $\{$Carol, Bob, Sally, John, Paul$\}$

P^{2}xy: $\{<$Carol, Sally$>, <$Bob, Sally$>, <$Sally, John$>,$
              $<$Sally, Paul$>\}$.

For this domain, notice that $P^2xy = \{<x, y> \mid x$ is the parent of $y\} = \{<Carol,$ Sally>, <Bob, Sally>, <Sally, John>, <Sally, Paul>$\}$. The order of the names appearing in the ordered pairs is crucial. That is, for example, <Carol, Sally> $\neq$ <Sally, Carol>: Carol is the parent of Sally, but Sally is not the parent of Carol.

These techniques for specifying two-place predicates can be extended to predicates of three or more places. For example, we could interpret a three-place predicate symbol 'S³' in the following way:

S³xyz: y is a number immediately preceded by x and immediately
           succeeded by z.

The extension of any predicate depends on the domain. If the domain is the set of natural numbers (i.e., positive integers), then the set associated with 'S³' would contain infinitely many three-tuples:

S³xyz: $\{<1, 2, 3>, <2, 3, 4>, <3, 4, 5>, \ldots\}$.

On the other hand, if the domain were the real numbers, the extension of 'S³' would have no members at all, since a real number (like .5 or $\sqrt{2}$) has no unique predecessor or successor. In this case, using either of two notations for the empty set, we would write the extension of the predicate as

S³xyz: $\{\ \}$

or

S³xyz: $\varnothing$.

The **empty set,** as the name implies, is the set containing no elements at all.

We come at last to individual constants. We take the **extension of an individual constant** to be the individual denoted by that constant. So, in our example concerning Wanda, the constant 'a' denotes the fish called 'Wanda', and Wanda (the fish, not the name) is thus the extension (or **denotation**) of 'a'. But what of intensions? Some philosophers (even among those who grant the existence of properties and propositions) have argued that constants do not have intensions at all. Constants in *L,* like proper names in English, refer directly to the bearer of the name. It is difficult to see what role an intension would have in specifying the meaning of a name.

However, a famous example strongly suggests that individual constants, too, have intensions. Gottlob Frege, who is to a great extent the founder of modern logic, noted that there are cases in which two or more names denote the same individual (i.e., have the same extension), but in which the names seem to have *different* meanings. Frege suggested, in particular, that we consider two names for the planet Venus, 'the Morning Star' and 'the Evening Star'. It turns out that at certain times during the year Venus appears as a bright star just before morning, while at other times it appears as a bright star just after dusk. It appeared self-evident to Frege that there is a difference in meaning between the following two statements:

>The Morning Star is the Morning Star
>
>The Morning Star is the Evening Star.

The first statement is a trivial and uninformative truth, whereas the second statement is neither trivial nor uninformative. Since 'the Morning Star' and 'the Evening Star' refer to the same object, there must therefore be something more than their denotation involved in an account of why the two statements have different meanings. Frege attributed the difference to what he called a difference in the *Sinn* ("sense") of the two proper names involved. It is therefore tempting to identify the intension of a name (or individual constant) with its Fregean "sense." Though this argument by no means establishes with certainty that names and constants have intensions, it does suggest that it is at least a possibility.[4]

These philosophical problems are intrinsically interesting, and they are indeed important for understanding the nature of our language and its relation to *L*. Nevertheless, as noted in the course of our discussion in this section, our formal semantics are entirely extensional. This restriction places certain limits on what arguments can be shown to be valid, since some arguments may depend on the intensional characteristics of the statements involved.

Let's now pull together the threads of our discussion and give a concise statement of the definition of an 'interpretation' for the language *L:*

> ***Definition***   An **interpretation,** $\mathcal{I}$, of *L* consists of the following:
>
> 1. A nonempty set $\mathcal{D}$ of objects, called the **domain** of the interpretation.
> 2. For every statement letter in *L,* a truth value. We say that the interpretation $\mathcal{I}$ makes a **truth value assignment** to the statement letter.

---

[4]Frege's original argument is set out with considerable clarity in his famous paper "On Sense and Denotation" ("Über Sinn und Bedeutung," 1892), which has been translated and reprinted in many anthologies of articles on philosophy of logic and philosophy of language. The most prominent critic of Frege's views on names was Bertrand Russell. Some of his best known responses to Frege on these points can be found in his article "On Denoting" (1905), which has also been reprinted in many anthologies. We should admit here that we have considerably simplified Frege's views. In particular, there is some question about how closely Frege's concept of 'Sinn' corresponds to our concept of 'intension'.

3. For every constant β, an element of $\mathcal{D}$. We say that an interpretation $\mathcal{I}$ makes a $\mathcal{D}$-**assignment** to the name β. $\mathcal{I}$ can assign more than one constant to a single element of $\mathcal{D}$, but no one constant can be assigned to more than one element in $\mathcal{D}$.

4. For every n-place predicate symbol, a set of n-tuples of objects in the domain of $\mathcal{I}$. We say that the interpretation **assigns** the set of n-tuples to the predicate symbol.

Notice that clause (4) applies to both monadic and polyadic predicates. A monadic predicate is a one-place predicate and hence, has as its extension a set of one-tuples; but a set of one-tuples of objects in the domain is, for all practical purposes, just the same as a set of objects from the domain. That is, we assume that for any objects a_1, $a_2, \ldots, a_n$, the set $\{<a_1>, <a_2>, \ldots, <a_n>\}$ is the same as the set $\{a_1, a_2, \ldots, a_n\}$.

Although interpretations will generally be given for finite sets of statements, it is important to notice that our definition is of an interpretation of L as a whole. This means that, strictly speaking, an interpretation assigns a meaning (i.e, an extension) to *every* nonlogical symbol in L. In practice, however, we only need to specify an interpretation for the symbols that occur within a particular finite set of L statements.

In general, interpretations are given to symbolize a particular set of statements from a natural language such as English. However, it also sometimes happens that we are given a set of statements in symbolic form alone, and we need to give them an interpretation. As an example, suppose we are given the following set of statements and asked to provide an interpretation for it:

{A, Bh, ∀xBx}.

To give an interpretation for this set, all we need to do is to specify a domain along with the extensions of 'A', 'B', and 'a'. We can stipulate that all other nonlogical symbols in L have an arbitrary value. For instance, all statement letters not occurring in the set could be assigned false, and all the predicate symbols not occurring in the set could be assigned the empty set. However, it is ordinarily not required that the statement of an interpretation for a set make explicit anything more than what is needed to take care of the given set itself. Thus, for the above set, we may write

$\mathcal{D}$:   {x | x is a scientist}

A: T

Bx: {x | x is an astronomer}

a: Hypatia.

Although we haven't yet given the formal definition of 'truth under an interpretation' for L, it is intuitively clear that on this interpretation 'A' is true, 'Bh' is true, and '∀xBx' ("all things in the domain are astronomers") is false.

The subject of symbolization in L will be taken up in earnest presently. We close this section, however, with one more example showing how to provide a purely formal interpretation for a given set of statements:

$$\{\forall x(Ax \rightarrow Bx),\ \sim Br,\ C,\ \exists xQrx\}.$$

First, we must stipulate a domain. This requires us to specify a set, but how do we do this? The most straightforward way is to simply list the individuals in the set in set braces. In this case, a convenient collection is the following:

$\mathcal{D}$:   {1, 2, 3, 4, 5}

We can then specify a truth value for the statement letter 'C' in the usual way:

C: T.

We may specify sets for each monadic predicate symbol quite arbitrarily, as long as the interpretation specifies subsets of the domain for each:

Ax: {1, 2}
Bx: ∅.

Notice that every element of these sets is an element of the domain, as required by the definition.[5]

For polyadic predicates, we must specify a set of n-tuples of objects in $\mathcal{D}$. For instance,

Qxy: {<1, 2>, <2, 3>, <3, 1>}.

Finally, we specify a $\mathcal{D}$-assignment for the constant 'r':

r: 1.

---

[5]It might seem odd that all elements of the empty set ∅ are elements of $\mathcal{D}$, but this is in fact the case. To see this, reflect that one way of understanding the expression 'Every element of S is an element of P' is to see it as meaning the same thing as 'There are no elements of S that are nonelements of P'. This is the usual contemporary way to interpret statements of the form 'All S are P', called the 'Boolean' interpretation of the statement form. Applying this reading to the present case, the statement 'All elements of ∅ are elements of $\mathcal{D}$' means the same as 'There are no elements of ∅ that are nonelements of $\mathcal{D}$'. Since ∅ has no elements, there are obviously no elements in ∅ that are nonelements of $\mathcal{D}$.

Are the four statements in our original set true or false in this interpretation? The first statement can be understood to assert that every individual in the extension of 'A' is in the extension of 'B'. However, according to our interpretation, the numbers 1 and 2 are in the extension of 'A', but *nothing* is in the extension of 'B'. Thus, this statement is false under this interpretation. The second statement can be understood to assert that the extension of 'r' is not in the extension of 'B'. Since 'r' denotes the number 1 and since the extension of 'B' is empty, this statement is true. The third statement is simply a statement letter, which according to our interpretation is true. The fourth statement, which asserts that the extension of 'Q' contains at least one two-tuple whose first element is 1 (the denotation of 'r'), is true since <1, 2> is an element of the extension of 'Q'.

The preceding example is rather artificial. Neither the domain nor the predicate letters have any obvious intensional characteristics. The example highlights the extensional nature of interpretations. Nonetheless, it is often practical, and sometimes essential, to specify the sets making up an interpretation using intensional language. Here is an alternative interpretation for our set of statements:

$\mathcal{D}$: $\quad$ {x | x is a mammal}

Ax: $\quad$ {x | x is a cat}

Bx: $\quad$ {x | x howls at the Moon}

Qxy: $\quad$ {<x, y> | x is a godparent of y}

r: $\quad$ Ronald Reagan

C: $\quad$ Cicero was a Roman orator.

Relative to this interpretation, the first statement in the set may now be read 'All cats howl at the Moon', '~Br' may be read 'Ronald Reagan does not howl at the Moon', and '∃xQrx' may be read as 'Ronald Reagan is some mammal's godparent'.

We would be hard pressed to list every member of the domain of this interpretation. For one thing the domain is quite large, having presumably many billions of members. For another, only a very small number of these members have names, so we would not have a way to refer to most members of the domain individually. Though only a practical difficulty for this domain, there are domains for which this limitation is more than practical because they are infinitely large. A frequently used domain, for example, is the set of natural numbers. For any infinite domain, it would be impossible to actually list each member. Some domains, typically used in mathematics, are of such a nature that their elements could not all be listed *even if we had an infinite amount of time available*. (Such domains are called 'uncountable'; an example is the set of real numbers.)

Because we cannot specify the members of a large or infinite domain by listing its members (as we say, *extensionally*), we describe the domain as the set of individuals having a certain property. We use the same strategy for specifying the sets denoted by predicate symbols. While we continue to emphasize that the domain and the extensions of predicates are *sets,* in practice set notation is not required for the specification of a domain. For instance, we can rewrite the interpretation above as

$\mathcal{D}$:   mammals

C: Cicero was a Roman orator

Ax: x is a cat

Bx: x howls at the Moon

Gxy: x is a godparent of y

r: Ronald Reagan.

Specified in this way an interpretation looks just like an informal symbol key, of the kind presented in Section 5.2. A symbol key like the one above should be understood as an *intensionally* worded specification of an interpretation. Because we so often use intensional language to specify an extensional interpretation, the distinction between a symbol key and an interpretation will sometimes be somewhat blurred. This should not cause trouble as long as you remember that, when we refer to interpretations in the definitions to come, we mean *formal extensional* interpretations.

Exercises for Section 5.4

Part I: Extension and Intension

1. Give an example of two *different* properties having the same extension.

2. Give an example of two different expressions that specify the *same* property.

3. The number denoted by 'nine' and the number denoted by the expression 'the number of planets' are identical. Thus, 'nine' and 'the number of planets' have the same extension. Now, it is necessarily true that nine is greater than seven. Does it follow that the number of planets is necessarily greater than seven? Discuss.

4. Suppose that Jim's favorite contemporary philosopher is Smith, whom Jim really likes. Suppose, too, that while driving in traffic, Jim observes the man in the car ahead of him throw some trash out of the car window. Jim is very keen on keeping his city beautiful, and despises litterers, so he is infuriated at the driver of the car ahead of him. Unknown to Jim, however, 'Smith' and 'the driver of the car ahead of Jim' are coextensive. Does Jim like, or dislike, Smith? Discuss.

5. In some cases an obvious choice of domain would be "everything." Nonetheless, logicians believe it is problematic to speak of the set of everything. Why might this be so? Discuss.

Part II: Translation into English   Below are listed two interpretations, followed by several symbolic statements. Translate the symbolic statements into clear English using $\mathcal{I}_1$, and $\mathcal{I}_2$.

$\mathcal{I}_1$	$\mathcal{D}$:	animals		$\mathcal{I}_2$	$\mathcal{D}$:	natural numbers $\{1, 2, 3, \ldots\}$
	Ax:	x is a mammal			Ax:	x is even
	Bx:	x is a ferret			Bx:	x is odd
	Cx:	x is female			Cx:	x is prime
	Mxy:	x is married to y			Mxy:	x is greater than y
	a:	Mickey Mouse			a:	2
	b:	Minnie Mouse			b:	3
	c:	Donald Duck			c:	4

6. Ca

♦7. ~Ba ∨ Ca

8. ~(Ba ∨ Ca)

9. ∀x(Bx & Ax)

10. ~(Aa → Bb)

11. ∀xBx → Ca

12. ∃x(Bx → Cx)

♦13. ∃x(Ax & Cx)

14. ~∀xCx

15. ∃x(Cx ∨ ~Cx)

16. (Ba & Bb) → ∀zBz

17. ∀x(Bx → Cx)

18. Mba & ~Mab

19. ∃xMxa

20. ~∃x∀yMxy

♦21. ∃xAx & ∃x~Ax

22. ∀x∀y(Mxy → ~Myx)

23. ∀x[(Mxa & Cx) → Bx]

For all things x and, if x is married to why

5.5   Formal Semantics II: Truth under an Interpretation

Like *SL*, *L* is an uninterpreted language. This means that statements of *L*, like the statements of *SL*, have no truth value unless they are interpreted. Thus, the truth or falsity of an *L* statement is always relative to an interpretation. Instead of saying merely that a statement 'is true' or 'is false', we say that a statement is true or false *under an interpretation*. In Chapter 3 we offered a definition of truth under an interpretation for *SL* statements. Here we extend that definition to obtain a definition that applies to all *L* statements.

Our definition is of necessity more involved than the one we needed for *SL* statements. We need three preliminary definitions:

> **Definition**   Let *p* be an *L* formula, α be a variable, and β be a constant. Then, the expression '*p*α/β' designates the formula that results from replacing all *free* occurrences of the variable α in *p* by the constant β.

> **Definition**   Given a statement ∀α*p* or ∃α*p*, the statement *p*α/β that results from deleting the quantifier and replacing all free occurrences of α by the constant β is called an **instance** of the quantified statement.

(The expression '*p*α/β' is read *pee-alpha-beta*.) Thus, if *p* is the formula 'Ax ∨ ∀xBx', α is the variable 'x', and β is the constant 's', then *p*α/β for this formula is the statement 'As ∨ ∀xBx'. The second and third occurrences of 'x' remain unchanged because they are bound, not free. Notice that 'As ∨ ∀xBx' is *not* said to be an 'instance' of the *formula* 'Ax ∨ ∀xBx'. Rather, it is an instance of the *statements* '∀y(Ay ∨ ∀xBx)' and '∃y(Ay ∨ ∀xBx)'. The final preliminary definition we need is this:

> **Definition**   Given any interpretation $\mathcal{I}$, a β-**variant** $\mathcal{I}_\beta$ of $\mathcal{I}$ is an interpretation that is identical to $\mathcal{I}$, except that $\mathcal{I}_\beta$ may assign to the constant β some object in $\mathcal{D}$ that is not assigned to β by $\mathcal{I}$.

More informally, a β-variant of an interpretation is an interpretation identical in all respects to the original interpretation *except,* possibly, that it assigns to the constant β a different object than it was assigned by $\mathcal{I}$. Notice that we do not *require* a β-variant to make a different assignment to β, which means that, strictly speaking, one β-variant of $\mathcal{I}$ is $\mathcal{I}$ itself. This fact will prove very useful presently.

To present the definition of 'truth under an interpretation', a few last bits of notation are helpful. Interpretations assign extensions to every nonlogical symbol in *L*. For any nonlogical symbol *s,* we use the notation '$\mathcal{I}(s)$' to mean 'the assignment $\mathcal{I}$ makes to *s*'. For example, $\mathcal{I}(A)$ is the truth value $\mathcal{I}$ assigns to 'A', $\mathcal{I}(P^1)$ is the set of elements of $\mathcal{D}$ that $\mathcal{I}$ assigns to 'P¹', and $\mathcal{I}(a)$ is the object $\mathcal{I}$ assigns to 'a'. Finally, we will need the symbol '∈', which is read 'is an element of'. Thus, for example, we may write '1 ∈ {1, 2, 3}' for 'the number 1 is an element of the set {1, 2, 3}' and, similarly, 'A ∈ {A, B → A, ~(A & C)}' for "A' is an element of the set {A, B → A, ~(A & C)}". Since for any individual constant—say, 'a'—of *L*, $\mathcal{I}(a)$ is an element of the domain, we will sometimes write '$\mathcal{I}(a) \in \mathcal{D}$'.

In Section 5.3 *L* statements are divided into three categories: simple, compound, and general. In saying precisely what it is for an *L* statement to be true under an interpretation, our definition stipulates truth criteria for statements of each category. The definition is recursive, like the definitions of '*SL* statement' and '*L* statement' already given. It shows us how to determine the truth or falsity of larger statements in terms of the smaller statements from which they have been built.

> **Definition**   Let *p* be any *L* statement and *q* and *r* be any *L* formulas. Let α be any variable and β any constant term. Let $\mathcal{I}$ be any interpretation. Then, the definition of **true under** $\mathcal{I}$ is as follows:

1. Simple statements

   a. If *p* is a statement letter, then *p* is true under $\mathcal{I}$ if, and only if, $\mathcal{I}(p)$ has the truth value T.

   b. If *p* is an *n*-place predicate symbol R^n followed immediately by *n* constant terms $\beta_1, \ldots, \beta_n$, then *p* is true under $\mathcal{I}$ if, and only if, $<\mathcal{I}(\beta_1), \ldots, \mathcal{I}(\beta_n)> \in \mathcal{I}(R^n)$.[6]

2. Compound statements

   a. If *p* is a negation ~*q*, then *p* is true under $\mathcal{I}$ if, and only if, *q* is not true under $\mathcal{I}$.

   b. If *p* is a conjunction (*q* & *r*), then *p* is true under $\mathcal{I}$ if, and only if, both *q* and *r* are true under $\mathcal{I}$.

   c. If *p* is a disjunction (*q* ∨ *r*), then *p* is true under $\mathcal{I}$ if, and only if, *q* is true under $\mathcal{I}$, or *r* is true under $\mathcal{I}$, or both.

   d. If *p* is a conditional (*q* → *r*), then *p* is true under $\mathcal{I}$ if, and only if, *q* is not true under $\mathcal{I}$, or *r* is true under $\mathcal{I}$, or both.

   e. If *p* is a biconditional (*q* ↔ *r*), then *p* is true under $\mathcal{I}$ if, and only if, *q* and *r* have exactly the same truth value under $\mathcal{I}$.

---

[6]In set theory notation the set of all *n*-tuples of elements of $\mathcal{D}$ is denoted '$\mathcal{D}^n$'. Thus, note that for an *n*-place predicate symbol R^n, $\mathcal{I}(R^n) \subseteq \mathcal{D}^n$. The symbol '⊆' means 'is a subset of'. One set is a subset of another if all members of the first set are members of the second. More precisely, for any sets *x* and *y*, $x \subseteq y$ if, and only if, for any *z*, if $z \in x$, then $z \in y$. You might want to try writing this definition in *L*, using 'Sxy' for '*x* is a subset of *y*' and 'Exy' for '*x* is an element of *y*'.

3. General statements

   a. If p is a universally quantified statement $\forall \alpha q$, then p is true under $\mathcal{I}$ if, and only if, for some constant β not occurring in p, the instance $q\alpha/\beta$ is true under every β-variant of $\mathcal{I}$.

   b. If p is an existentially quantified statement $\exists \alpha q$, then p is true under $\mathcal{I}$ if, and only if, for some constant β not occurring in p, the instance $q\alpha/\beta$ is true under at least one β-variant of $\mathcal{I}$.

4. Closure clause

   Any statement that is not true under $\mathcal{I}$ is said to be **false under $\mathcal{I}$.**

Though this definition is lengthy, much of it is simply a restatement of material from the definition of 'truth under an interpretation' for *SL*. There are only two new components: the part dealing with the truth of simple statements containing predicate symbols and the part dealing with general statements. We explain each in turn.

Clause (1b), concerns simple statements containing predicates. In the monadic case ($n = 1$), it says that $\mathcal{R}\beta$ is true if, and only if, the object in the domain denoted by the individual constant β is in the extension of the predicate symbol $\mathcal{R}$. As a concrete example, consider the statement 'Ab'. If the extension of 'A' is the set {Ted, Alice}, for example, and the extension of 'b' is Ted, then 'Ab' will be true under this interpretation because $\mathcal{I}(b) \in \mathcal{I}(A)$—that is, because Ted $\in$ {Ted, Alice}.

The application of (1b) is slightly more complicated in the polyadic case. As an example, let's consider a domain $\mathcal{D}$ consisting of the set {1, 2, 3, 4, 5}—that is, a domain whose elements are the first five positive integers. Define 'B^3xyz' to mean 'x is between y and z in numerical order'. Using the preceding definitions, we would put this as follows:

$$\mathcal{I}(B^3) = \{<x, y, z> \mid x \text{ is between } y \text{ and } z\}$$
$$= \{<2, 1, 3>, <2, 3, 1>, <3, 2, 4>, <3, 4, 2>,$$
$$<4, 3, 5>, <4, 5, 3>\}.$$

Next assign names as follows:

$$\mathcal{I}(a) = 1 \quad \mathcal{I}(c) = 3 \quad \mathcal{I}(e) = 5$$
$$\mathcal{I}(b) = 2 \quad \mathcal{I}(d) = 4$$

Clearly, the statement 'B^3cbd' is true under this interpretation. It is true because the statement "says" that 3 is between 2 and 4. By formal application of the definition, the statement is seen to be true because

$$<\mathcal{I}(c), \mathcal{I}(b), \mathcal{I}(d)> \in \mathcal{I}(B^3),$$

that is, because

$$<3, 2, 4> \in \{<2, 1, 3>, <2, 3, 1>, <3, 2, 4>, <3, 4, 2>, <4, 3, 5>,$$
$$<4, 5, 3>\}.$$

By contrast, the statement 'B³dab' is false under this interpretation because the number 4 is *not* between the numbers 1 and 2 in numerical order. In terms of the set theory notation, we would put it this way: 'B³dab' is false under this interpretation because

$$<\mathcal{I}(d), \mathcal{I}(a), \mathcal{I}(b)> \notin \mathcal{I}(B^3),$$

that is, because

$$<4, 1, 2> \notin \{<2, 1, 3>, <2, 3, 1>, <3, 2, 4>, <3, 4, 2>, <4, 3, 5>,$$
$$<4, 5,3 >\},$$

where the symbol '$\notin$' means 'is not an element of'.

Let's now turn to the meaning of the two clauses in our definition of 'truth under an interpretation' that concern general statements. We can understand these clauses better by considering a couple of (perhaps more intuitive) alternatives, which might have been tried, and seeing why our actual formulation is superior to them.

Consider a universally quantified statement, say,

∀xAx.

Intuitively, this statement says 'Everything is an A'. When an interpretation is given for this statement, a set is assigned to the predicate symbol 'A'. Now, it is certainly natural, in connection with this statement, to think that 'truth under an interpretation' *could* be defined quite simply as follows:

The statement '∀xAx' is true under an interpretation $\mathcal{I}$ if, and only if, every element in the domain is a member of the set $\mathcal{I}$ assigns to 'A'.

In fact, if this condition is satisfied by an interpretation $\mathcal{I}$, then that interpretation would indeed make '∀xAx' true. The problem is, however, that we would like to define 'true under an interpretation $\mathcal{I}$' so that it applies to more complicated statements, statements like the following:

∀x[(Ax ∨ Bx) → Cx].

In this case it would not do us any good to say that this statement is true under an interpretation $\mathcal{I}$ if, and only if, every element in the domain "is a member of the set $\mathcal{I}$ assigns to '[(Ax ∨ Bx) → Cx]'." Since '[(Ax ∨ Bx) → Cx]' is not a predicate symbol, $\mathcal{I}$ assigns no set to it (at least not directly). Thus, this approach would not seem to work for giving a comprehensive definition of 'true under an interpretation $\mathcal{I}$' that applies to *all* statements of the form ∀αp.

At this point, it is tempting to try another move:

A statement of the form ∀αp is true under an interpretation $\mathcal{I}$ if, and only if, pα/β comes out true for all individual constants β in the language L.

That is, according to this definition, we would say that the statement '∀x[(Ax ∨ Bx) → Cx]' is true under an interpretation $\mathcal{I}$ if, and only if, *every one* of the following were also true under $\mathcal{I}$:

(Aa ∨ Ba) → Ca
(Ab ∨ Bb) → Cb
(Ac ∨ Bc) → Cc
(Ad ∨ Bd) → Cd

.
.

Here, the list of statements is infinite—*every* instance of the statement would be included in the list, so each of the infinitely many constants in L occurs in the list at some point.[7] Again, this possible solution is partially correct. In fact, *if* the universally quantified statement in question is true under an interpretation, *then* it must follow that all its instances are true as well. The converse, however, is problematic: If every instance of the statement is true under some interpretation, it could still turn out to be rather awkward to claim that the quantified statement itself is true as well (even though it would be "true" according to the proposed definition). This is because, in our definition of an interpretation, we have not made it a requirement that *everything* in the domain be denoted by some constant in the language L. For example, we could let $\mathcal{D}$ = {0, 1, 2, 3, . . .}, let 'a' denote 1, 'b' denote 2 (etc.) so that every constant in the language denotes a number. On this interpretation, the number zero would not be denoted by *any* of the constants because of the way we assigned elements of the domain to them. We could then interpret 'Ax' to

---

[7]In fact, some logicians adopt this definition, called 'substitutional quantification'.

mean 'x is larger than zero'. On such an interpretation, *each* of the infinitely many statements, 'Aa', 'Ab' (etc.) would be *true*. However, '∀xAx' would not seem to be true intuitively, if we think of it as being the proper symbolization for 'Everything in 𝔇 is A', since we know that there is at least one thing, zero, which is *not* A— that is, which is not larger than zero.

It is of course possible to add the stipulation that *every* object in the domain must be named by a unique constant of the language. The above definition would then work as an intuitively correct way to give truth conditions for the symbolic version of 'Everything in 𝔇 is A'. However, making this stipulation would *also* have undesirable consequences later on down the line, when we come to the method of formal proof for L. One consequence, in particular, is that the system of formal proof would not be *complete;* that is, there would be valid arguments in L that could not be proved (see Section 4.4).[8] A second consequence is that some domains, called 'uncountable domains', are so large that even our infinite supply of constants would be insufficient to supply each member of the domain with a name. (One such domain is the set of real numbers.) To avoid these undesirable consequences, it turns out to be convenient to define 'truth under an interpretation', in connection with general statements, in just the way that we have.

Well, all that may be fine; however, we still have not made it clear exactly how the definition we have settled on is supposed to work. To see how it works, start with the statement '∀xAx' as an example. Under the definition of truth we have adopted, to say that the statement '∀xAx' is true under an interpretation 𝒥 means that the statement 'Ax x/β' is true under every β-variant of 𝒥. For β we can choose any constant not occurring in '∀xAx', so let's choose 'a'. 'Ax x/β' in this case is then 'Aa'. Thus, by our definition, '∀xAx' is true under 𝒥 if, and only if, the statement 'Aa' is true under every 'a'-variant of 𝒥. Remember that an 'a'-variant of 𝒥 is an interpretation like 𝒥 in all respects except possibly for its 𝔇-assignment to 'a'. Consequently, if 'Aa' is true under every 'a'-variant, then 'Aa' is true for any possible 𝔇-assignment to 'a'. This could only be the case if every object in the domain is in the set denoted by 'A'—that is, if everything "is an A". The definition says, in effect, the following: If 'Aa' comes out true *no matter what* 'a' denotes in 𝔇, then '∀xAx' must be true.

---

[8]An example is the case we just considered. Suppose we were to adopt the substitutional definition of 'true under an interpretation' for a universally quantified statement, along with the stipulation that *everything* in the domain must be denoted by some constant in L. Then, notice that if all elements of the set {Aa, Ab, Ac, . . . , Aa$_1$, Ab$_1$, . . .} were true under some interpretation, where *all* the constants in L get used up, then '∀xAx' would be true under that interpretation as well. Thus, the argument {Aa, Ab, Ac, . . . , Aa$_1$, Ab$_1$, . . .} /∴ ∀xAx would be valid. However, there could be no derivation—i.e., no formal proof in our sense—of the statement '∀xAx' from {Aa, Ab, Ac, . . . , Aa$_1$, Ab$_1$, . . .}. This is because, among other things, proofs can only be of finite length.

Applying this same approach to the statement '∀x[(Ax ∨ Bx) → Cx]', we may say that '∀x[(Ax ∨ Bx) → Cx]' is true under 𝒥 if, and only if, the statement '(Aa ∨ Ba) → Ca' is true under every possible 'a'-variant of 𝒥. This means the statement '(Aa ∨ Ba) → Ca' is true no matter what 'a' denotes in 𝒟.

Now let's apply our definition of truth under an interpretation in two specific cases. The first is for the statement '∀xAx → B'. Here is a possible interpretation:

> 𝒟: positive integers {1, 2, 3, . . .}
>
> Ax: x is positive
>
> B: F.

Note that we have specified the extension of the predicate 'A' using the phrase 'x is positive'. Formally, this should be understood as specifying that 'A' is assigned the set of positive integers. Given this interpretation we may evaluate the truth value of the statement. First, since the consequent 'B' is false under this interpretation, we see that the truth or falsity of the whole statement turns on the truth or falsity of its antecedent: If '∀xAx' is true, then the statement is false; if it is false, then the statement is true. Clearly, the antecedent is true under this interpretation: No matter what element of the domain is assigned to the constant 'a', the statement 'Aa' will be true under this interpretation. Thus, by definition, '∀xAx' is true under this interpretation; hence, the given conditional is *false* under this interpretation.

Here is another example: We are given the statement '∀x(Ex & ∃yOy) ∨ Ea'. We stipulate the following interpretation:

> 𝒟: positive integers {1, 2, 3, . . .}
>
> Ex: x is an even number
>
> Ox: x is an odd number
>
> a: 2.

Since a disjunction is true if one of its disjuncts is true and since in this case the disjunct 'Ea' *is* true, the given statement is true under this interpretation. It is instructive, however, to continue on to determine the truth value of the left-hand disjunct, '∀x(Ex & ∃yOy)'. We proceed in a step-by-step way, using the relevant clauses in the definition of truth as we go (we use 'true' instead of constantly repeating 'true under the given interpretation'; however, it should be understood that truth is *always* truth *under an interpretation*):

1. '∀x(Ex & ∃yOy)' is true if, and only if, the statement 'Ea & ∃yOy' is true *no matter what* element of 𝒟 is assigned to 'a'.

2. Now, the statement 'Ea & ∃yOy' is true no matter what element of 𝒟 is assigned to 'a' if, and only if, both 'Ea' and '∃yOy' are true no matter what element of 𝒟 is assigned to 'a'.

3. However, notice that if the number 3 were assigned to 'a', then 'Ea' would *not* be true; hence, 'Ea & ∃yOy' is not true regardless of what element of 𝒟 the interpretation assigns to 'a'; hence, the statement '∀x(Ex & ∃yOy)' is false on the given interpretation.

The last result should not be surprising, of course, if you understand the English rendering of what this statement "says" on the given interpretation. The statement '∀x(Ex & ∃yOy)' says, in effect, "All positive integers are even, and some positive integer is odd," which is false.

Our final examples involving general statements contain a two-place predicate:

∀x∃yFxy

∃x∀yFxy

∀y∃xFxy.

It will be instructive to use the following interpretation, 𝒥:

  𝒟: people

  Fxy: x is the father of y.

The first statement, '∀x∃yFxy', is true under 𝒥 if, and only if, the statement '∃yFay' is true under *every* 'a'-variant of 𝒥. Now, the statement '∃yFay' is true under one of these 'a'-variants, 𝒥ₐ, just in case 'Fab' is true under at least one 'b'-variant of 𝒥ₐ. In other words, for '∀x∃yFxy' to be true under 𝒥, it must turn out that, no matter whom we choose in 𝒟 as the denotation of 'a', there's at least one person in 𝒟, whom we can call 'b', such that a is the father of b. In still more straightforward terms: '∀x∃yFxy' is true under 𝒥 if, and only if, *everybody* is somebody's father, which is false. Thus, the statement '∀x∃yFxy' is false under 𝒥.

Cases like this one illustrate the utility of learning how to translate easily between ordinary English and the formal language *L*. Once this skill is mastered, determining the truth value of statements like these is greatly facilitated. It is then easy to avoid the explicit language of β-variants and the like, and instead to give an English paraphrase of the symbolic statement. Using this technique, the second statement, '∃x∀yFxy', may be read 'There is somebody who is the father of everyone', which is false. Similarly, the third statement, '∀y∃xFxy', may be read 'everybody has at least one father', which is true. Techniques for translating symbolic language into ordinary English, and vice versa, are discussed in the next two sections.

Exercises for Section 5.5

(A) Below are listed three interpretations, followed by several statements involving monadic predicates. Evaluate the truth values of each statement, using $\mathcal{I}_1$, $\mathcal{I}_2$, and $\mathcal{I}_3$.

$\mathcal{I}_1$ $\mathcal{D}$:   animals

	Ax:	x is a mammal
	Bx:	x is a ferret
	Cx:	x is female
	a:	Mickey Mouse
	b:	Minnie Mouse
	c:	Donald Duck

$\mathcal{I}_2$ $\mathcal{D}$:   natural numbers $\{1, 2, 3, \ldots\}$

	Ax:	x is even
	Bx:	x is odd
	Cx:	x is prime
	a:	2
	b:	3
	c:	4

$\mathcal{I}_3$ $\mathcal{D}$:   {Burt, Ernie, Elmo, Cookie Monster, Big Bird}

	Ax:	{Burt, Ernie}
	Bx:	{Burt, Elmo, Cookie Monster}
	Cx:	$\varnothing$
	a:	Big Bird
	b:	Elmo
	c:	Cookie Monster

1. Ca	6. ~∀x~Cx	11. ∀x(Bx → Cx)
2. ~(Aa → Bb)	♦7. ∃xAx & ∃x~Bx	12. ∃x(Bx → Cx)
♦3. ~(Ba ∨ Ca)	8. ∀x(Bx ↔ Ax)	♦13. ∀xBx → Ca
4. ~Ba ∨ Ca	9. ∃x(Ax & Cx)	14. (Ba & Bb) → ∀zBz
5. ∃xAx	10. ∃x(Cx ∨ ~Cx)	15. ∀x[(Ax & Bx) → ~Cx]

(B) For each of the following *L* statements involving monadic predicates, provide two interpretations: one under which the given statement is true and one under which the given statement is false.

Example: Given: $\forall x(Ax \rightarrow Bx)$

1. $\mathcal{D}$:	people		2. $\mathcal{D}$:	people
Ax:	x is a person		Ax:	x is a man
Bx:	x has a mother		Bx:	x is a father

Under interpretation 1 the statement says 'All people have mothers', which is true. Under interpretation 2 the statement says 'All men are fathers', which is false.

16. Ar

17. $\forall xAx \rightarrow \exists yBy$

18. Br & $\forall xAx$

♦19. Ar & Br

20. $\exists xAx \rightarrow \forall yBy$

21. Mg $\rightarrow$
   $\forall x(Bx \leftrightarrow Mx)$

22. Ma $\vee$ Fb

23. $\exists xAx \rightarrow \forall xAx$

24. $(\exists xAx$ & $\exists xBx)$
   $\rightarrow \forall zKz$

♦25. $\exists x(Fx \vee Mx)$

26. $\exists zFz \vee \exists yGy$

27. $\forall x(Ax \rightarrow Bx)$
   $\rightarrow \exists x\sim Cx$

28. $\exists x(Fx$ & $Mx)$

29. $\sim\exists x(Ax \vee Bx)$

30. $\forall x((Ax$ & $Bx) \leftrightarrow Cx)$

♦31. $\exists xAx \rightarrow \forall xBx$

32. $\sim\forall x(Ax \rightarrow Bx)$

33. $\forall x[Fx \rightarrow (Gx \vee Hx)]$

34. $\forall y[(Ay$ & $By)$ & $Cy]$

35. $\forall xWx \rightarrow \forall z(Vz \vee \sim Pz)$

(C) Below are listed three interpretations, followed by several statements involving polyadic predicates. Evaluate the truth values of each statement, using $\mathcal{I}_1$, $\mathcal{I}_2$, and $\mathcal{I}_3$.

$\mathcal{I}_1$	$\mathcal{D}$:	natural numbers $\{1, 2, 3, \ldots\}$
	Gxy:	x is greater than y
	Lxy:	x is less than y
	Sxyz:	the sum of x and y is z
	Pxyz:	the product of x and y is z
	Ex:	x is even
	Ox:	x is odd
	a:	1
	b:	2
	c:	3

$\mathcal{I}_2$ $\mathcal{D}$:   {Susan, Emily, Lucinda, Samantha, Kirk, Lily, Holden, James, David, Molly, Ben, Camille, Cal, Bob, Kim, Jack, Margo, Tom, Adam}

Gxy: {<Lucinda, Lily>, <Kim, Tom>, <Susan, Emily>, <Margo, Adam>}

Lxy: {<Tom, Adam>, <Bob, Tom>}

Sxyz: {<Tom, Margo, Adam>, <Margo, Tom, Adam>, <Kim, Bob, Tom>, <Bob, Kim, Tom>}

Pxyz: {<Lucinda, Samantha, Lily>, <Samantha, Lucinda, Lily>, <Lily, Lucinda, Samantha>, <Samantha, Lily, Lucinda>}

Ex: {Holden, James, David, Ben, Cal, Bob, Tom, Jack}

Ox: {Susan, Emily, Lucinda, Samantha, Lily, Molly, Camille, Kim, Margo}

a: Lucinda

b: Samantha

c: Lily

$\mathcal{I}_3$ $\mathcal{D}$:   states of the USA

Gxy: x is larger in area than y

Lxy: x is more populous than y

Sxyz: x is is between y and z (ie., east of y and west of z)

Pxyz: x is bordered by y and z

Ex: x is a coastal state

Ox: x is one of the contiguous 48 states

a: Alaska

b: Maryland

c: Illinois

36. Sabc

37. Pabb

38. Gca & Lac

♦39. Lab & ~Gac

40. ∃x(Ex & Gxb)

41. ∃x(Ox & Gxc)

42. ~∃xGxx

43. ∃xSabx

44. ∃x(Sccx & Ox)

♦45. ∀x∀y(Gxy → ~Gyx)

46. ∀x∀y(Gxy → Lyx)

47. ∀x∀y(~Gxy → Lxy)

48. ∀x∀y∃zSxyz

49. ∀x∃yGxy

50. ∃x∀yGxy

51. ∀x∀y(Gxy → ∃zSyzx)

52. ∀x∀y(Gxy → ∃zPyzx)

♦53. ∀x∀y(Lxy → ∃zSxzy)

54. ∀x∀y∀z(Pxyz → ∃uSxuz)

55. $\forall x \forall y((Ex \ \& \ Oy) \rightarrow \exists z(Sxyz \ \& \ Oz))$
56. $\forall x \forall y((Ex \ \& \ Oy) \rightarrow \exists z(Sxyz \ \& \ Ez))$
57. $\forall x \forall y((Ex \ \& \ Oy) \rightarrow \exists z(Pxyz \ \& \ Oz))$
58. $\forall x \forall y((Ex \ \& \ Oy) \rightarrow \exists z(Pxyz \ \& \ Ez))$

(D) For each of the following *L* statements involving polyadic predicates, provide two interpretations: one under which the given statement is true and one under which the given statement is false.

Example: Given: $\forall x \forall y(Axy \rightarrow Bxy)$

	1. $\mathcal{D}$:	people		2. $\mathcal{D}$:	people
	Axy:	x is a parent of y		Axy:	x is the sister of y
	Bxy:	y is a child of x		Bxy:	y is the brother of x

Under interpretation 1. the statement says 'Anybody who is the parent of another has that other as their child', which is true. Under interpretation 2. the statement says 'Anybody who is the sister of another has that other person as her brother', which is false.

59. Mab	65. $\forall x \forall y(Lxy \rightarrow Lyx)$	71. $\forall x(Pxa \rightarrow \exists yQxy)$
60. ~Mab	66. $\forall x \forall y(Lxy \rightarrow {\sim}Lyx)$	72. $\exists xAxa \lor \forall yBay$
61. Mab $\lor$ Mba	67. $\forall x \exists yAxy$	73. Rabc
62. Mab $\&$ Mba	68. $\exists x \forall yAxy$	74. $\exists xRabx$
♦63. $\forall xMax$	♦69. $\forall x \forall yAxy$	75. $\exists xRaxb$
64. $\exists xMax \ \& \ {\sim}\forall xMax$	70. $\exists x \exists yAxy \ \& \ \exists z \exists u{\sim}Azu$	76. $\exists xRxbc$

5.6 Symbolizing English I: Monadic Logic and Categorical Forms

Because *L* enables us to symbolize aspects of the logical structure of English statements that exist within atomic statements, *L* is a much more powerful tool for the analysis of arguments than is *SL*. The task of symbolizing English statements in *L* is, however, correspondingly more complex. We divide our discussion of symbolization into two sections. In this section we concentrate on monadic predicates. In Section 5.7 we turn to polyadic predicates and multiple quantifiers.

To take on the problem of symbolizing English statements in *L,* we begin by saying something more about what we understand by the terms 'predicate' in general and '*L* predicate' in particular. Predicates are, like words and sentences, linguistic expressions; in particular, predicates, like sentences, are certain strings of symbols. Thus, for instance, the two words comprising the expression 'is white' constitute a predicate in English. When we place a noun in front of this predicate, we get a statement. As suggested in Section 5.4, we need to be careful to distinguish among the predicate expression itself, the property or relation it expresses (its intension), and the set it denotes (its extension).

If *L* predicates are certain strings of symbols in *L,* our next task is to specify which strings of symbols should count as *L* predicates. We have already identified some of the predicates—namely, predicate symbols like 'A' and 'B'. However, there are other predicates besides these. To see this, consider how we might symbolize the statement 'All bachelors are unmarried'. We could start with a partial symbolization like this:

$$\forall x(x \text{ is a bachelor} \to x \text{ is unmarried}).$$

How should we complete this symbolization? One way would be to let one predicate symbol (say, 'B') stand for the property of being a bachelor, and another (say, 'U') stand for the property of being unmarried. Using this symbol key, we would get

$$\forall x(Bx \to Ux).$$

However, by symbolizing the statement in this way, we lose important information. The property of being a bachelor is a complex one. To be a bachelor (we'll suppose) *means* to be unmarried and male. We might therefore like to express the property of being a bachelor with the expression '(~Wx & Mx)', where 'W' stands for the property of being married and 'M' stands for the property of being male. Similarly, for the property of being unmarried, we can use the expression '~Wx'. We then get

$$\forall x((\sim Wx \ \& \ Mx) \to \sim Wx).$$

This example shows that properties may be expressed either by single monadic predicate symbols *or* by more complex symbolic expressions. What all these expressions have in common is that if one substitutes into the expression a constant for the individual variable, one gets a statement that attributes a property to the individual named by that constant. For instance, 'Mx' is a predicate (though not a predicate *symbol*) because 'Ma' is a statement that attributes the property represented by 'M' to the individual denoted by 'a'; '(~Wx & Mx)' is a predicate because, to put it informally, '(~Wa & Ma)' is a statement that attributes the property of "being both non-W and M" to the denotation of 'a'. Thus, a *predicate* must be distinguished from the individual *predicate symbols* themselves. In particular:

> ***Definition*** An ***n*-place *L* predicate** is an *L* formula with *n* free variables.

Monadic *L* predicates are *n*-place predicates in which *n* = 1. Our examples so far in this section have been cases of monadic predicates.

A predicate symbol followed by a string of one or more terms, at least one of which is a variable, is a **simple** (or **atomic**) predicate. All other predicates are **compound** or (**molecular**) predicates. We use script letters like '$\mathcal{A}$' and '$\mathcal{B}$' as (metalinguistic) predicate variables. These variables play a role in predicate logic similar to that of metalinguistic statement variables (like '*p*' and '*q*') in statement logic.[9]

The fact that *any* *L* formula containing free variables is a predicate greatly facilitates our discussion of the logical form of statements involving predicates—whether these predicates are simple or complex. The statements '$\forall x((\sim Wx \mathrel{\&} Mx) \rightarrow \sim Mx)$' and '$\forall x(Bx \rightarrow Ux)$' share a common logical form. Both are formed by prefixing universal quantifiers to the conditionals formed from two predicates. Using our predicate variables together with 'α' to designate an arbitrary individual variable, we can express the statement form in this way:

$$\forall\alpha(\mathcal{A}\alpha \rightarrow \mathcal{B}\alpha).$$

We now are in a position to consider more systematically the task of symbolizing English statements in *L*. Let's consider four extremely useful forms of quantified statement:

A	All $\mathcal{S}$ are $\mathcal{P}$
E	No $\mathcal{S}$ are $\mathcal{P}$
I	Some $\mathcal{S}$ are $\mathcal{P}$
O	Some $\mathcal{S}$ are not $\mathcal{P}$.

These four types of statement, named 'A', 'E', 'I', and 'O', are known as Aristotelian **categorical statements;** they are among the most common forms of quantified statement. The A and I statements are said, respectively, to express **universal affirmative** and **particular affirmative** propositions. The E and O forms are said to express **universal negative** and **particular negative** propositions. The letter names reportedly come from medieval philosophers, who took them from the vowels in the Latin 'affirmo' (I affirm) and 'nego' (I deny). These four forms are especially useful. Some English examples are

---

[9]Notice that the script used for predicate variables is the same as that used for indicating the domain of an interpretation, '$\mathcal{D}$'. This is because predicates actually designate sets of *n*-tuples, viz., the sets of *n*-tuples to which the predicates apply.

A   All surgeons are doctors

E   No crabs are crows

I   Some apples are pippins

O   Some chess pieces are not works of art.

Traditionally, the term in place of S is called the **subject term** and that in place of P is the **predicate term**. *Both* the subject term and predicate term are predicates, however, in the sense being presented here. As such, each denotes a set of objects, so we may interpret the above statements as follows:[10]

A   The set of surgeons is completely included in the set of doctors

E   The set of crabs is completely excluded from the set of crows

I   There is at least one object that is in both the set of apples and the set of pippins

O   There is at least one object that is in the set of chess pieces but is not included in the set of works of art.

Our task is to find statements of L that, relative to appropriate interpretations, symbolize the above English statements. The following L statements will do the job:

A $\forall x(Sx \rightarrow Dx)$

E $\forall x(Cx \rightarrow \sim Rx)$

I $\exists x(Ax\ \&\ Px)$

O $\exists x(Cx\ \&\ \sim Wx)$.

In each case, a predicate symbol has been chosen that is suggestive of the relevant interpretation. Note too that in the cases of the I and O forms, 'some' has been interpreted to mean 'There exists at least one'.

In the preceding examples, the subject and predicate terms were symbolized by simple L predicates. However, the pattern of symbolization given holds even if the subject and predicate of a categorical statement are expressed by compound L predicates—as we did when we symbolized 'All bachelors are unmarried'. The preceding examples illustrate a general principle for translating categorical statements into L. For any predicates, simple or compound, we have the following symbolizations:

---

[10]This is generally known as a 'Boolean' interpretation of the categorical statements.

Categorical Form		Symbolic Form
A	All S are P	$\forall\alpha(S\alpha \to P\alpha)$
E	No S are P	$\forall\alpha(S\alpha \to {\sim}P\alpha)$
I	Some S are P	$\exists\alpha(S\alpha\ \&\ P\alpha)$
O	Some S are not P	$\exists\alpha(S\alpha\ \&\ {\sim}P\alpha)$

In each symbolic form, 'S' and 'P' stand in place of the relevant L predicates. For example, if one wishes to symbolize 'Some mathematicians are women', one needs predicates expressing 'is a mathematician' and 'is a woman'—say, 'Mx' and 'Wx'—so that the result is '$\exists x(Mx\ \&\ Wx)$'. If one wishes to symbolize 'Some red-haired mathematicians are American women,' one then needs compound predicates expressing 'is a red-haired mathematician' and 'is an American woman'—say, 'Rx & Mx' and 'Ax & Wx', respectively. Plugging these predicates into the appropriate form (the I form in this case) gives

$$\exists x((Rx\ \&\ Mx)\ \&\ (Ax\ \&\ Wx)).$$

Yet again, if one wishes to symbolize a statement like 'Some red-haired mathematicians who live in mansions are American women who ride bicycles to work', even more complex L predicates would be needed.

The compound predicates just presented are conjunctions, 'Rx & Mx' and 'Ax & Wx'. The first conjunction represents the predicate 'x is a red-haired mathematician', and the second represents the predicate 'x is an American woman'. Some predicates, by contrast, *look* as if they should be represented as conjunctions when they in fact should not. For example, the predicate 'is a suspected bicycle thief' is *not* properly analyzed as a combination of being (1) suspected *and* (2) a bicycle thief. Similarly, being an imitation emerald ring is *not* the same as being both (1) imitation and (2) an emerald ring. Unlike being a red-haired mathematician, in these two cases the predicates express a property that is not a coincident occurrence of two separate properties.

Conjunctions are not always what are needed to symbolize compound predicates. An example in which the needed compound formulas are not conjunctions is the symbolization of the statement 'All North Americans and South Americans are Westerners'. In this case the property of being a Westerner is captured by a simple predicate, 'Wx'. What are we to do with 'North Americans and South Americans', however? Here we must resort to paraphrase; that is, what does the English statement express? One way to go would be to break the statement into two statements: 'All North Americans are Westerners, and all South Americans are Westerners'. We could then produce the symbolization

$$\forall x(Nx \to Wx)\ \&\ \forall x(Sx \to Wx).$$

This will certainly do; however, there is a more efficient symbolization:

$\forall x((Nx \lor Sx) \to Wx)$.

The formula '$(Nx \lor Sx)$' is a compound predicate that serves as the subject term of the categorical statement. The statement can be translated back into English as 'Anything that is either a North American or a South American is a Westerner'. One key to knowing that this second symbolic statement is a correct symbolization of the original English is recognizing that this second English paraphrase expresses the same proposition as the original English one.

The four categorical forms of statement are useful for two reasons: (1) many arguments employ statements of these forms and (2) many statements not taking one of these forms are *equivalent* to statements that *do,* as was just shown. Here is another example:

Only state residents can run for governor.

This statement can be paraphrased to match one of the categorical forms. Which one? Well, the easy part, first, is to note that we need only two predicate symbols, for 'is a state resident' and 'can run for governor'—say, 'Sx' and 'Cx', respectively. Now, this statement does *not* express the claim that *all* state residents can run for governor. Therefore, the symbolic statement '$\forall x(Sx \to Cx)$' is *not* the symbolization needed. Rather, it expresses the claim that *if* someone can run for governor, *then* that person must be a state resident. The key, in this case, is to distinguish a necessary from a sufficient condition and recall that a necessary condition becomes the *consequent* of a conditional. Thus, the correct symbolization is

$\forall x(Cx \to Sx)$,

or, in English, 'All people who can run for governor are state residents'. This illustrates the point that statements of the form

Only S are P

can be symbolized as

$\forall \alpha(P\alpha \to S\alpha)$.

Symbolizing English in *L* takes practice. Like *SL*, there is unfortunately no mechanical way to go from English into the formal language. Mastery of symbolization really turns on your mastery of the semantics of *L*. If you acquire a firm understanding of how to interpret *L* statements, then it becomes much easier to travel back and forth between *L* and English: You learn to think in what has sometimes been called 'Loglish', a hybrid language that combines some symbols of *L* with rather literal English translations from the syntax of *L*. For example, you acquire a knack for "reading" statements like 'Only state residents can run for governor' as 'Only x's that are S are x's that are C', from which it is an easy step to 'All x's that are C are x's that are S', and from this to the *L* statement '∀x(Cx → Sx)'.

Another aid to determining whether a symbolization is correct is the method of translating the symbolic statement back into English and then asking whether the translated English makes the same statement as the one we are trying to symbolize. Here is an example:

No person plays in the ocean at night.

We give an interpretation:

𝒟:	animals
Px:	x is a person
Bx:	x plays in the ocean at night.

Suppose, as a first attempt, we think the statement should be symbolized like this:

~∀x(Px → Bx).

To determine whether this symbolization is correct, translate it back into English (via Loglish):

1. It is not the case that for all x, if x is a person, then x plays in the ocean at night
2. It is not the case that all persons play in the ocean at night
3. Not everyone plays in the ocean at night

However, statement (3), 'Not everyone plays in the ocean at night', does *not* state the same thing as 'No person plays in the ocean at night'. Although (3) implies that some people do not play in the ocean at night, it leaves open the possibility that others *do*. However, the statement we are trying to symbolize does not admit this possibility. Thus, the two English statements do not say the same thing, and, since the symbolic statement '~∀x(Px → Bx)' symbolizes (3), it cannot be the right symbolization for the statement in question.

So, what is the correct symbolization? As earlier, it is helpful to determine the categorical form into which this statement fits. In this case, a correct paraphrase would be 'No persons are players in the ocean at night', the E form; hence, its symbolization is '∀x(Px → ~Bx)'.

As another example, consider the following:

Some people are mortal.

Although you have been instructed (above) that this form of statement *should* be symbolized as

(1)   ∃x(Px & Mx),

you may wonder why it could not properly be symbolized like this:

(2)   ∃x(Px → Mx).

The answer comes from the semantics for the symbols '&' and '→'. To see that statement (2) is incorrect, first reflect that statement (1) *does* give a correct symbolization. In the original English it is asserted that there is at least one person who is mortal, and, interpreting 'Px' as 'x is a person' and 'Mx' as 'x is mortal', this is just what (1) expresses. This at least shows that (1) is right, but why is (2) wrong?

Recall what is meant by the symbol '→'. A conditional statement is true when the antecedent is false or the consequent is true. Hence, a statement of the form $p \rightarrow q$ is logically equivalent to one of the form $\sim p \vee q$. This principle carries over to formulas as well, so the formula 'Px → Mx' is equivalent to '~Px ∨ Mx'. So, symbolization (2) is actually logically equivalent to

(3)   ∃x(~Px ∨ Mx),

which translated is 'There exists at least one thing which is either not a person or else is mortal'. But *this* statement would be true even if no people existed! Once this has been noticed, it is clear that (3) cannot be the proper symbolization of the English statement, since the English statement implies that people exist—*and* that at least some of them are mortal.

The preceding should be remembered as a general rule: When symbolizing English, *avoid existentially quantifying a conditional*. More than likely—at least at the beginning stages—you will be giving an incorrect symbolization. There is nothing *logically* or *syntactically* wrong with existentially quantifying a conditional statement. However, it is simply unlikely that an English statement encountered in an argument will require such a symbolization.

Now examine this statement:

If anyone loves baseball, Rachel loves baseball.

How should the word 'anyone' be handled here? It's clear that we have a conditional, and the consequent, 'Rachel loves baseball', is easily enough symbolized as 'Br' (for 'r loves baseball'). Thus, we at least know that a partial symbolization will be

Anyone loves baseball → Br.

At this point, it might seem that a universal quantifier is called for:

∀xBx → Br.

Assume that the domain $\mathcal{D}$ is the set of all people. This symbolic statement may then be read, 'If *all* people love baseball, then Rachel loves baseball'. But this does not seem to capture the sense of the original English; in fact, '∀xBx → Br' is a necessary truth—it's true under *all* possible interpretations: (1) If the consequent is true, then the conditional is true. (2) If the antecedent is false, then, again, the conditional is true. (3) If the antecedent is true under an interpretation, then 'Ba' comes out true no matter what the interpretation assigns to 'a'—even when it assigns to 'a' exactly what it assigns to 'r'. But this last observation implies that 'Br' is also true under this interpretation! Hence, this is a statement that cannot be made false.

Use of the word 'anyone' here expresses, rather, the existential quantifier. The correct symbolization is

∃xBx → Br.

In general, 'if anyone . . .' is semantically different from 'if everyone . . .'; 'if anyone' should be read as 'if someone . . .'. However, you must always look to the context in which a statement is made in order to grasp its full meaning.

Just as with *SL,* the language *L* is a formalism whose statements are given precise meanings relative to interpretations. If an English statement is ambiguous, we can use *L* to give precise expression to the various possible propositions that the English might be taken to express. Recall, for example, the discussion of 'only if' in statement logic. Although we adopted the principle that '*p* only if *q*' should be symbolized as '*p* → *q*', we did this knowing that contexts might arise in which a biconditional relationship was meant. Similarly, 'unless' might be used with one meaning rather than another, and even the word 'or', we have seen, has both an inclusive and an exclusive sense. Thus, it is up to you, as a fluent speaker of a natural language, to determine what symbolic statement appropriately represents the intended meaning. This in turn requires you to acquire a strong fluency in the symbolic language.

We close our discussion of symbolization with a technique for simplifying symbolization problems. Consider the following statement:

All humans are mortals.

Since this has the form 'All *S* are *P*', we could use the symbolic statement appropriate to this categorical form, symbolizing the statement as '$\forall x(Hx \rightarrow Mx)$', where

$\mathcal{D}$:   everything

Hx: x is human

Mx: x is mortal.

However, we can cleverly simplify the symbolization by a shrewd choice of domain. In particular, if we adopt the following interpretation, things get easier:

$\mathcal{D}$:   humans

Mx: x is mortal.

On this interpretation, the symbolization of 'All humans are mortals' becomes just '$\forall x Mx$'. This illustrates a useful method for economizing on the number of symbols needed. As an example, consider the following English argument:

All males eighteen years or older must register for the draft
Some males are eighteen years or older
∴ Some males eighteen years or older must register for the draft.

If our domain is *people,* a symbolization for the argument is

$\forall x[(Mx \,\&\, (Ex \lor Ox)) \rightarrow Rx]$
$\exists x[Mx \,\&\, (Ex \lor Ox)]$
∴ $\exists x[(Mx \,\&\, (Ex \lor Ox)) \,\&\, Rx]$

where

Mx: x is male

Ex: x is eighteen years old

Ox: x is older than eighteen years

Rx: x must register for the draft.

If, however, we change the domain from people to *males who are at least eighteen years or older,* the argument is correctly symbolized as

$\forall x Rx$
$\exists x(Mx \,\&\, (Ex \lor Ox))$
∴ $\exists x Rx$

Thus, such a maneuver can realize a helpful savings in the complexity of a symbolic statement.[11] On the other hand, notice, too, that much of the structure of the argument is lost when this is done. Especially as our language is enriched even further, losing this logical structure would prevent us from being able to fully analyze the logical properties of the argument. Learning when and when not to simplify in this way is something that requires practice.

We conclude this section with a few remarks about some important equivalences between statement forms. These equivalences show us something about the relationships between the quantifiers and the truth-functional connectives. Being aware of these equivalences will help you both in recognizing logical equivalence among specific statements and in correctly symbolizing statements and arguments.

To start, consider a statement beginning with a negated universal quantifier— that is, a statement of the form $\sim\forall\alpha p$. Taking 'p' as an L predicate, the intuitive meaning of this statement is that not everything is p. But this will be the case if, and only if, something is not p. This suggests the following equivalence schema:

$$\sim\forall\alpha p \quad \Leftrightarrow \quad \exists\alpha\sim p$$

Similarly, a statement asserting that nothing is p, $\sim\exists\alpha p$, will be true if, and only if, everything is not p:

$$\sim\exists\alpha p \quad \Leftrightarrow \quad \forall\alpha\sim p$$

In general then, we can move a negation symbol across a quantifier, by switching the quantifier from universal to existential or vice versa.

Suppose we have a statement of the form $\forall\alpha(p \,\&\, q)$. Can we move the quantifier inside the parentheses? We can, using the following pattern of equivalence:

$$\forall\alpha(p \,\&\, q) \quad \Leftrightarrow \quad (\forall\alpha p \,\&\, \forall\alpha q)$$

Intuitively, this makes sense, since if everything is both p and q, then everything must be p and everything must also be q. Notice that we cannot make the corresponding move for universally quantified *disjunctions*. Statements of the form $\forall\alpha$ $(p \lor q)$ and $(\forall\alpha p \lor \forall\alpha q)$ are *not* equivalent. The first says that everything (in the domain) is either p or q, and the second says that either everything is p or everything is q. A particular case will illustrate why these statement forms are not equivalent. Suppose that p is 'Ox' and q is 'Ex', that our domain is natural numbers, and

---

[11]In fact, since the domain must be nonempty, and since the domain consists of males eighteen years or older, in this case the second premise is, technically speaking, no longer needed since its truth is implicitly assumed by the formal requirements of the interpretation.

that 'E' and 'O' denote the sets of even and odd numbers. Under this interpretation the statement '∀x(Ex ∨ Ox)' expresses the proposition that all numbers are even or odd, which is true. On the other hand, the statement '∀xEx ∨ ∀xOx' expresses the proposition that either all numbers are even or all numbers are odd, which is false.

In the case of existential quantifiers, the opposite pattern obtains. An existentially quantified disjunction $\exists\alpha(p \vee q)$ will be true under an interpretation as long as something is p or something is q. This gives us the following correspondence:

$$\exists\alpha(p \vee q) \quad \Leftrightarrow \quad (\exists\alpha p \vee \exists\alpha q)$$

On the other hand, we cannot move the quantifier inside the parentheses in an existentially quantified conjunction. Statements of the form $\exists\alpha(p \, \& \, q)$ are *not* generally equivalent to statements of the form $(\exists\alpha p \, \& \, \exists\alpha q)$. We leave it to you to find a particular case that will illustrate this point.

We have not rigorously proved that the equivalences we have discussed are in fact correct. We could do so, of course, by appealing to our formal definition of 'truth under an interpretation'. In the next two chapters, as we extend our methods of truth trees and natural deduction, we will demonstrate, for specific instances of these statement forms, that the equivalences we have described here are in fact correct.

Exercises for Section 5.6

(A) Use the following interpretation to symbolize the given English statements.

𝒟:	cats		
Cx:	x is cute	a:	Annie
Dx:	x sleeps all day	b:	Buffer
Lx:	x has a pleasant disposition	f:	Fluffer
Px:	x prowls at night	m:	Masha
Sx:	x is smart	r:	Ratso

1. Buffer is cute.

2. Buffer is cute, but Fluffer is smart.

♦ 3. Either Ratso or Annie has a pleasant disposition.

4. Annie, but not Fluffer or Buffer, sleeps all day.

5. Masha and Ratso prowl at night.

6. Ratso prowls at night only if he has a pleasant disposition.

♦7. Some cats are cute.

8. Some cats are not cute.

9. All cats prowl at night.

10. All smart cats sleep all day.

11. All cats with pleasant dispositions are cute.

12. Some cats with pleasant dispositions do not sleep all day.

13. Some cats who do not sleep all day do not have pleasant dispositions.

14. Some cats sleep all day, but not Fluffer or Buffer.

♦15. No cat does not prowl at night.

16. There is a cat who sleeps all day, but it isn't Masha.

17. It's not true that all cats prowl at night.

18. It's not true that all smart cats have pleasant dispositions.

19. Some cats who do not sleep all day are neither smart nor cute.

20. No cat is smart, if it is cute.

21. Only cats who are smart prowl at night.

22. No cat prowls at night unless it is cute; however, all cats are cute.

(B) Use the following interpretation to symbolize the given English statements.

$\mathcal{D}$:	psychologists and psychiatrists		
Ax:	x has studied anthropology	f:	Sigmund Freud
Bx:	x emphasizes biological factors	j:	Carl Jung
Cx:	x has studied cybernetics	k:	Karen Horney
Ex:	x is an effective therapist	p:	Fritz Perls
Fx:	x is a Freudian	s:	Virginia Satir
Gx:	x practices Gestalt therapy		
Sx:	x studied Freud's work		
Vx:	x emphasizes environmental factors		

23. Although she studied Freud's work, Karen Horney is not a Freudian.

24. Neither Carl Jung nor Virginia Satir is a Freudian.

♦25. Although she is not a Freudian, Virginia Satir has studied anthropology.

26. Only Freudians are effective therapists.

27. Whereas Sigmund Freud emphasizes biological factors, Karen Horney emphasizes environmental ones.

28. Any psychologist or psychiatrist who practices Gestalt therapy is an effective therapist.

29. Only psychologists or psychiatrists who practice Gestalt therapy are effective therapists.

30. If anyone has studied cybernetics, Virginia Satir has.

♦ 31. Every Freudian has studied anthropology.

32. If a psychologist or psychiatrist has studied cybernetics, then both Freud and Jung have.

33. Carl Jung has studied anthropology if any psychologist or psychotherapist has.

34. Any Freudian who practices Gestalt therapy must have studied cybernetics and anthropology.

35. Fritz Perls is an effective therapist who is not a Freudian; Perls emphasizes environmental factors.

36. Karen Horney and Sigmund Freud are effective therapists, but all Freudians are effective therapists.

37. No Freudian who emphasizes biological factors is an effective therapist unless she or he has studied anthropology.

38. Unless Freud is an effective therapist, there are no effective therapists.

39. If either Fritz Perls or Virginia Satir emphasizes environmental factors, then at least one of them is an effective therapist.

(C) Provide symbol keys and symbolize each of the following arguments.

40. Some people are wise. All wise people like sports. Thus, some people like sports.

41. No person who likes sports is a friend of the family. Any friend of the family likes to drink Vernor's Soda. Therefore, no one who likes to drink Vernor's Soda likes sports.

42. Charlene is a mountain climber, and only mountain climbers enjoy the cold. Therefore, if anyone likes the cold, Charlene does.

43. If Jack gets a raise, then everyone he knows will be happy for him. However, Jack gets a raise only if someone he knows is not happy. Hence, Jack will not get a raise.

44. Every electrode is either positive or negative. If an electrode is negative, it emits protons; if it is positive, it emits electrons. Gary emits neither protons nor electrons, so it follows that Gary is not an electrode.

45. Only utilitarians calculate the consequences of their actions. Kantians, on the other hand, base their ethics on reason alone. John Stuart Mill calculated the consequences of his actions. Thus, Mill was a utilitarian and not a Kantian.

46. It's not the case that only utilitarians calculate the consequences of their actions. One is a utilitarian if one considers the welfare of all humans equally. Thus, although Ayn Rand calculates the consequences of her actions, she does not consider the welfare of all humans equally. Therefore, she is not a utilitarian.

47. Only declarative sentences express propositions. Any sentence that does not express a proposition is meaningless. No expression of feeling is a declarative sentence. Thus, expressions of feeling do not express propositions and are meaningless.

48. If Hegel is right, then the world is a place of order and reason. If Heraclitus is right, then the world is a place of constant flux. Now, the world is neither a place of order and reason nor is it in constant flux. But either Heraclitus or Hegel is right. If these statements are all true, then square circles exist. Hence, these statements are not all true.

(D) Provide symbol keys and symbolize each of the following statements. Take care to determine whether or not a compound predicate should be represented by a conjunction or by a single predicate symbol.

49. Fake diamonds are sold in New York.

50. Expensive diamonds are sold in Manhattan.

51. All well-known actors are television stars.

52. No famous mathematicians are nervous mathematicians.

53. Only potential winners will be notified.

54. There are black cats who are not fast eaters.

5.7 Symbolizing English II: Polyadic Logic and Nested Quantifiers

We begin this section by looking at how the categorical forms can be applied in the case of *n*-place predicates. Start with the following English statement:

Everyone whom somebody loves is happy.

This statement can be seen to have the A form of a categorical statement. A reasonable paraphrase is

All people who are loved by somebody are people who are happy.

Thus, you might think that the following symbol key will do the trick:

> $\mathcal{D}$: people
> Sx: somebody loves x
> Hx: x is happy.

Then, we might write '$\forall x(Sx \rightarrow Hx)$'. However, this symbolization misses out on two elements of the original English. First, the subject expression, 'whom somebody loves', contains an existential quantifier. Second, this expression also contains a relational predicate. Though 'x is happy' is well-enough symbolized by 'Hx', we can do better than 'Sx' for 'somebody loves x'. In particular, we can employ the relational predicate 'Lyx', interpreted to mean 'y loves x'. Given this two-place predicate symbol, the predicate 'Somebody loves x' may then be rendered as '$\exists y Lyx$', and this formula thus becomes the antecedent of the correct symbolization of the original English:

> $\forall x(\exists y Lyx \rightarrow Hx).$

As a second example, consider the following:

> Some people whom everybody in the U.S. knows are people that nobody in Paris loves.

This statement has the O categorical form and may be partially symbolized as follows:

> $\exists x[(\text{everybody in the U.S. knows } x) \ \& \ (\text{nobody in Paris loves } x)].$

Notice that the two predicates themselves have categorical form:

> All people in the U.S. are people who know x
> No people in Paris are people who love x.

The first predicate has the A form, the second the E form. Let's use the following symbol key:

> $\mathcal{D}$: people
> Ux: x is a person in the U.S.
> Px: x is a person in Paris
> Kxy: x knows y
> Lxy: x loves y.

Using this interpretation, we may symbolize the two predicates as '∀y(Ux → Kyx)' and '∀y(Py → ~Lyx)', respectively. Finally, these predicates may be put in place of the partially symbolized predicates in the O statement above to obtain the correct symbolization:

$$∃x[∀y(Ux → Kyx) \& ∀y(Py → ~Lyx)].$$

Besides understanding how to employ the categorical forms as an aid to symbolization, understanding symbolization and translation comes also from a clear understanding of how the quantifiers work. In particular, the *order* of quantification is extremely important, especially when one quantifier is "nested" in the scope of another quantifier.

To understand how order comes into play with nested quantifiers, let's examine a two-place predicate—say, 'Lxy' for 'x loves y'. Assume that $\mathcal{D}$ = the set of people. If 'x' and 'y' are replaced by names, then it is easy to understand the resulting symbolic expression. For example, using 'r' and 'm' to denote Rudi and Mary, 'Lmr' asserts that Mary loves Rudi, 'Lrm' asserts that Rudi loves Mary, and 'Lmr & Lrm' is a perfectly good way to symbolize 'Mary and Rudi love each other'. However, once quantifiers come on the scene, things require more subtle understanding. Consider the following list of statements:

(1)   ∀x∀yLxy

(2)   ∀x∃yLxy

(3)   ∃y∀xLxy

(4)   ∀y∃xLxy

(5)   ∃x∀yLxy

(6)   ∃x∃yLxy.

Statements (1) and (6) are not hard to understand. The first says that everybody loves everyone, and the sixth says that somebody loves someone. As for the statements in-between, however, it is easy to be confused about their exact meanings. Let's consider these middle statements one at a time.

Starting with statement (2), '∀x∃yLxy', a first reading is 'For every person x, there exists a person y such that x loves y'. We can paraphrase this as 'Given any person at all, there exists some person whom she or he loves'. That is, there exists someone whom Alex loves, and there exists someone whom Kay loves, and someone whom Jim loves, and someone whom Jamie loves, and so on for all people in the domain. Putting this more concisely, '∀x∃yLxy' can be read simply as 'Everybody loves somebody'.

Next on the list is statement (3), '∃y∀xLxy', which results from the former statement by switching positions of the two quantifiers. Translating it produces 'there exists at least one person y such that, for all persons x, x loves y'; that is, 'There is at least one person whom everybody loves'. It is important that you recognize the difference between this statement and the preceding one. One can sometimes become confused over the differences in meaning between potentially ambiguous English expressions, but this ambiguity is *not* present in the formalized language.

One key to understanding these statements is to think of an existentially quantified statement as a "big disjunction" and a universally quantified statement as a "big conjunction." That is to say, assuming that everything in the domain has a name, a statement like '∀xFx' means, roughly, the same as 'Fa & Fb & Fc & . . .' for all constants in the language. Similarly, a statement like '∃xFx' means, roughly the same thing as 'Fa ∨ Fb ∨ Fc ∨ . . .' for all constants in the language. This equivalence in meaning is not exact but is suggestive of how to understand statements like those under discussion. The statement '∃y∀xLxy', for example, "means"

∀xLxa ∨ ∀x Lxb ∨ ∀xLxc ∨ . . .

That is, 'Someone is loved by everyone' means "Everyone loves a, or everyone loves b, or everyone loves c, . . ." (etc.). By contrast, the statement '∀x∃yLxy' "means"

∃yLay & ∃yLby & ∃yLcy & . . .

Thus, '∀x∃yLxy' is true only if there is somebody whom a loves, and there is somebody whom b loves, and so on. However, in this case, a, b, c, and d (etc.) need not all love the *same* person.

Fourth on the list is the statement '∀y∃xLxy': 'For every person in the domain, there exists at least one person by whom she or he is loved'; that is, 'Everybody is loved by someone', though the statement does not say that everybody is loved by the *same* person. This last statement is made by statement (5), '∃x∀yLxy': 'There exists at least one person who loves everybody'.

Exercises for Section Section 5.7

(A) Use the following interpretation to symbolize the given English statements.

> 𝒟: natural numbers {1, 2, 3, . . .}
>
> Ex: x is even
>
> Ox: x is odd

Px:	x is prime
Gxy:	x is greater than y
Lxy:	x is less than y
Dxyz:	$x - y = z$
Pxyz:	$x \cdot y = z$
Sxyz:	$x + y = z$
a:	1
b:	2
c:	3
d:	4

1. Four is not odd, but 3 is. $\left(Ex \, \diagdown \, \alpha \right)$

2. Three is greater than 2 but less than 4.

♦3. One plus two equals three.

4. Two times 2 equals four.

5. One plus 2 sum to 3, but 2 and 1 have a difference of 1.

6. Some number is greater than 2 and less than 3.

7. No even prime number is greater than 2.

8. If two numbers are even, then they have a sum that is even.

♦9. If two numbers are odd, then they have a sum that is even.

10. If one number is even and another odd, then they have a sum that is odd.

11. There is a number whose product with itself and sum with itself equals 4.

12. There is no prime number less than 2.

13. A sum of any two numbers is greater than either of them.

14. A product of any two numbers is not less than their sum.

15. There is no number that is either greater than, or less than, itself.

16. If a number is prime and greater than 2, then that number is odd.

♦17. Any odd prime number between 2 and 4 is odd.

18. There is no greatest number.

19. Three is a number at least as great as 2, but not as great as 4.

20. There is no greatest prime number.

21. Any two odd numbers have a difference that is itself even.

22. The difference between any two odd numbers is itself even.

(B) Use the following interpretation to symbolize the given English statements.

$\mathcal{D}$:	soap opera characters
Bx:	x is brave
Dx:	x is devious
Gx:	x is good-hearted
Hxy:	x is the husband of y
Jxy:	x is jealous of y
Kxy:	x knows the truth about y
Lxy:	x loathes y with a burning passion
Sxy:	x secretly loves y
Wxy:	x is the wife of y
e:	Emily
h:	Holden
j:	James
l:	Lucinda
m:	Margo
s:	Susan
t:	Tom

23. Emily secretly loves Tom, even though Tom is Margo's husband.

24. James is devious, and Lucinda knows the truth about him.

♦25. Lucinda loathes both James and Emily with a burning passion.

26. Susan knows the truth about Emily, but Susan is not brave and Emily is devious.

27. Emily is jealous of Tom's wife; Holden is good-hearted, and he has a wife.

28. Even though Emily is secretly in love with Tom, Tom is married to Margo and does not secretly love Emily.

29. James is married to Lucinda, who secretly loves Holden; however, James is not jealous of Holden.

30. Emily is both brave and devious and, if she knows the truth about Lucinda, she is not good-hearted.

31. If anyone knows the truth about Lucinda, it's Emily.

32. Anyone who is a husband is brave.

♦33. Nobody who loathes somebody with a burning passion secretly loves that person.

34. Some people who loathe someone with a burning passion secretly love that person.

35. No husbands are wives, and no wives are husbands.

36. If two people know the truth about each other, then neither is jealous of the other.

37. Not everybody who is married is both brave and good-hearted.

38. Anyone who loathes somebody with a burning passion is secretly loved by somebody.

39. Anyone who loathes somebody with a burning passion is jealous of that person.

40. It's not the case that a person ever both secretly loves somebody and also loathes that person with a burning passion.

♦41. A person is both jealous of, and also has a burning loathing for, anybody about whom they know the truth.

42. Anybody who secretly loves someone and who is jealous of that person's husband or wife is not good-hearted.

43. Lucinda loathes Emily only if there is someone about whom Lucinda knows the truth whom Emily secretly loves.

5.8 Semantic Properties and Relationships for *L*

Prior to our study of deduction systems in Chapters 3 and 4, we offered a number of definitions of what we called 'semantic properties and relationships'— specifically, tautologousness, truth-functional validity, truth-functional self-contradictoriness, truth-functional contingency, truth-functional equivalence, truth-functional mutual contradictoriness, and truth-functional consistency. We then learned how to apply tests to determine whether *SL* statements have these properties or whether collections of *SL* statements stand in these relationships. In the next two chapters, we pursue the same strategy for *L*.

In Chapter 3 we offered definitions of these concepts only for *SL* statements. In this section we define analogous concepts for *L* statements. We supplement our definitions of truth-functional validity, tautologousness, truth-functional self-contradiction, truth-functional contingency, truth-functional equivalence, truth-functional contradictories, and truth-functional consistency with, respectively, *logical validity, logical truth, logical falsehood, logical contingency, logical equivalence, logical contradictories,* and *logical consistency:*

Definition   An argument in *L* is **logically valid** if, and only if, there is no interpretation under which all the argument's premises are true but its conclusion false.

Definition   An *L* statement is a **logical truth** if, and only if, it is true under every interpretation.

Definition   An *L* statement is called a **logical falsehood** if, and only if, there is no interpretation under which it is true.

Definition   An *L* statement is said to be **logically contingent** if, and only if, there is at least one interpretation under which it is true and one interpretation under which it is false.

Definition   Two *L* statements *p* and *q* are said to be **logically equivalent** if, and only if, *p* and *q* have the same truth value under every interpretation.

Definition   Two *L* statements *p* and *q* are said to be **logically contradictory** if, and only if, *p* and *q* have opposite truth values under every interpretation.

Definition   A set of *L* statements is **logically consistent** if, and only if, there is at least one interpretation under which all elements of the set are true.

The definitions of these concepts for *L* statements are parallel to the definitions we gave for the corresponding *SL* concepts in Chapter 3. The only difference is that we have replaced the word '*SL*' with '*L*'. This in turn implies that the interpretations referred to in the definitions are *L* interpretations rather than *SL* interpretations.

In Chapter 3 we made a point of emphasizing the existence of (1) valid arguments that are not truth-functionally valid and (2) necessary truths that are not tautologous. Our new definitions of logical validity and logical truth will allow us to study formally some of these arguments and statements, because these definitions are *more inclusive* than definitions of truth-functional validity and tautologousness. On the other hand, our definition of logical consistency is *less* inclusive than that of truth-functional consistency, since there are some sets of statements that are truth-functionally consistent but logically inconsistent. You may, yourself, determine whether the remaining concepts we have defined are more or less inclusive than their truth-functional counterparts.

We have formally defined these semantic concepts only for *L* statements, but we can apply them informally to statements of other languages, and in particular to statements of English. How might we use *L* to help determine whether, for example, the following statement is a logical truth?

If everything is white, then something is white.

'Logical truth' is defined only for *L*, not for English. Thus, we must symbolize the English statement in *L*, and then test the *L* statement for logical truth. The following is a correct symbolization: '∀xWx → ∃xWx'. Since it turns out that this symbolic statement *is* a logical truth, we may say that the English statement is a logical truth as well.

Though truth-functional concepts have been defined formally only for *SL* statements, we can apply them informally to *L* statements. The *L* statement '∀xPx ∨ ~∀xPx', for example, may be regarded as a tautology, since it is an instance of the tautological form *p* ∨ ~*p*. By contrast, the statement '∀xWx → ∃xWx' is a logical truth but *not* a tautology: The statement is true under all interpretations, but *not* in virtue of its truth-functional structure.

To extend the tree method and our natural deduction system for use with *L* statements, we make use of the following *L* versions of the four propositions stated and justified in Chapter 3:

> **Proposition L1**   An argument in *L* is logically valid if, and only if, its associated conditional is a logical truth.
>
> **Proposition L2**   An argument in *L* is logically valid if, and only if, the set consisting of the argument's premises and the negation of its conclusion is logically inconsistent.
>
> **Proposition L3**   An *L* statement *p* is logically true if, and only if, the set {~*p*} is logically inconsistent.
>
> **Proposition L4**   Two *L* statements *p* and *q* are logically equivalent if, and only if, *p* ↔ *q* is a logical truth.

The proofs of these propositions are exactly analogous to those given in Chapter 3 for the corresponding propositions concerning *SL*, so we will not repeat them here (see Sections 3.4–3.6).

Exercises for Section 5.8

1. The following argument is valid:

$$\frac{\forall xPx}{\therefore \exists xPx}$$

Suppose we dropped the requirement that the domain of an interpretation be nonempty. Would the argument still be valid? Justify your answer.

2. Is the concept of logical contradictoriness more or less inclusive than that of truth-functional mutual contradictoriness? Justify your answer.

♦ 3. Is the concept of logical equivalence more or less inclusive than that of truth-functional equivalence? Justify your answer.

4. Is the concept of logical contingency more or less inclusive than that of truth-functional contingency? Justify your answer.

5.9   Classifying Logical Relations

A number of types of two–place relations are of special interest to logicians, mathematicians, computer scientists, linguists, and others who study structural relationships. Several of these are summarized here:

> ***Definitions of Some Logical Relations***   A two-place relation represented by a two-place relation symbol R is
>
> **Reflexive** if, and only if, $\forall \alpha R\alpha\alpha$
>
> **Nonreflexive** if, and only if, $\exists \alpha {\sim} R\alpha\alpha$
>
> **Irreflexive** if, and only if, $\forall \alpha {\sim} R\alpha\alpha$
>
> **Symmetric** if, and only if, $\forall \alpha \forall \beta (R\alpha\beta \rightarrow R\beta\alpha)$
>
> **Nonsymmetric** if, and only if, $\exists \alpha \exists \beta (R\alpha\beta \,\&\, {\sim} R\beta\alpha)$
>
> **Asymmetric** if, and only if, $\forall \alpha \forall \beta (R\alpha\beta \rightarrow {\sim} R\beta\alpha)$
>
> **Transitive** if, and only if, $\forall \alpha \forall \beta \forall \gamma [(R\alpha\beta \,\&\, R\beta\gamma) \rightarrow R\alpha\gamma]$
>
> **Nontransitive** if, and only if, $\exists \alpha \exists \beta \exists \gamma ((R\alpha\beta \,\&\, R\beta\gamma) \,\&\, {\sim} R\alpha\gamma)$
>
> **Intransitive** if, and only if, $\forall \alpha \forall \beta \forall \gamma [(R\alpha\beta \,\&\, R\beta\gamma) \rightarrow {\sim} R\alpha\gamma]$.

> ***Definition***   A relation R is said to be an **equivalence relation** if, and only if, it is simultaneously reflexive, transitive, and symmetric.

As an example, notice that the mathematical relation 'is greater than' is a transitive, irreflexive, and asymmetric relation. Letting 'Gxy' stand for 'x is greater than y' (formally, $\{<x, y> \mid x > y\}$) and letting $\mathcal{D}$ = the natural numbers (the set $\{1, 2, 3, \ldots\}$), each of the following is true on this domain:

Transitivity	$\forall x \forall y \forall z[(Gxy \,\&\, Gyz) \to Gxz]$
Irreflexivity	$\forall x \sim Gxx$
Asymmetry	$\forall x \forall y(Gxy \to \sim Gyx).$

The classification of properties has great use in the study of mathematical theories and other formalized systems.

These types of relation can also be recognized outside the object language *L*. The identity relation of mathematics, '=', is an obvious example of an equivalence relation. We may employ these classifications to characterize, from a metalinguistic standpoint, how connectives in our object language work. Another example of an equivalence relation is expressed by our symbol '$\leftrightarrow$':

Transitivity	For all statements *p*, *q*, and *r*, if it is true that $p \leftrightarrow q$ and $q \leftrightarrow r$, then it is true that $p \leftrightarrow r$
Reflexivity	For all statements *p*, $p \leftrightarrow p$ is true
Symmetry	For all statements *p* and *q*, if $p \leftrightarrow q$, then $q \leftrightarrow p$.

A great deal can be known about a formal logical, mathematical, or linguistic system by knowing the properties its various relations possess.

Exercises for Section 5.9

(A) Several relations are defined below. In each case classify the relations according to the table of logical relations presented in this section.

Example 1: Given $\mathcal{D}$: integers; $\mathcal{I}(R)$: {<1, 1>}. This relation is nonreflexive on the given domain, since there are objects in the domain not included in $\mathcal{I}(R)$. It is also symmetric and transitive.

Example 2: Given $\mathcal{D}$: {1}, $\mathcal{I}(R)$: {<1, 1>}. This relation is reflexive, symmetric, transitive, and an equivalence relation on the given domain. Notice how the choice of domain affects the classification of the relation here, in contrast to Example (1).

♦ 1. $\mathcal{D}$: natural numbers; $\mathcal{I}(R)$: {<1, 2>, <2, 1>}

2. $\mathcal{D}$: natural numbers; $\mathcal{I}(R)$: {<1, 1>, <1, 2>, <2, 1>, <2, 2>}

3. $\mathcal{D}$: natural numbers; $\mathcal{I}(R)$: {<x, y> | x = y}

4. $\mathcal{D}$: natural numbers; $\mathcal{I}(R)$: {<x, y> | x ≠ y}

5. $\mathcal{D}$: natural numbers; $\mathcal{I}(R)$: {<x, y> | the remainder of x/3 = the remainder of y/3}

6. $\mathcal{D}$: people; $\mathcal{I}(R)$: {<x, y> | x and y are siblings}

♦7. $\mathcal{D}$: people; $\mathcal{I}(R)$: {<x, y> | x and y are married}

8. $\mathcal{D}$: people; $\mathcal{I}(R)$: {<x, y> | x and y have a common ancestor}

9. $\mathcal{D}$: people; $\mathcal{I}(R)$: {<x, y> | x reveals his/her innermost secrets to y}

10. $\mathcal{D}$: mountains; $\mathcal{I}(R)$: {<x, y> | x is higher than y}

11. $\mathcal{D}$: dish detergents; $\mathcal{I}(R)$: {<x, y> | x cleans dishes more effectively than y}

12. $\mathcal{D}$: sets of natural numbers; $\mathcal{I}(R)$: {<x, y> | x $\subseteq$ y}

(B) Answer each of the following as indicated.

13. Under what relationship classifications does the material conditional, represented by '→', fall?

14. Under what relationship classifications does the relation of logical implication, represented by '⊨', fall?

♦15. If a relation is symmetric, must it be reflexive as well? Present reasons (and, if needed, examples) to show that your answer is correct.

16. If a relation is reflexive, must it be symmetric as well? Present reasons (and, if needed, examples) to show that your answer is correct.

17. Is it possible for a relation to be both transitive and irreflexive? Present reasons (and, if needed, examples) to show that your answer is correct.

18. Is it possible for a relation to be both nonsymmetric and transitive? Present reasons (and, if needed, examples) to show that your answer is correct.

19. Consider the relation 'greater than or equal to' (≥) of mathematics. Is this relation symmetric, asymmetric, nonsymmetric, or none of these? Present reasons (and, if needed, examples) to show that your answer is correct.

20. Suppose that 'R' stands for an equivalence relation, and that there are two objects, a and b, for which 'Rab' is true. Does it follow that a and b are identical to each other—that is, must they denote one and the same object? Present reasons (and, if needed, examples) to show that your answer is correct.

CHAPTER SIX

Predicate Logic II: Semantic Methods

6.1 Introduction

The goal of this chapter is to provide a mechanical technique for determining whether or not arguments in L are valid, whether or not an L statement is a logical truth, and for answering other related questions. Our task is accomplished by expanding the method of truth trees to handle quantified predicate logic. All we require are four more truth tree rules: one for universally quantified statements, one for existentially quantified statements, and one each for the negations of these.[1]

One important feature of the extended tree method is that trees for sets of L statements can, in some cases, contain infinitely many nodes. The existence of infinite trees leads to difficulties in using the tree method as a decision procedure for logical truth in L. It turns out, as we will show at the end of this chapter, that the tree method provides an effective decision procedure for logical truth only for those L statements that do not contain any polyadic predicates.

---

[1]It is instructive to reflect on why we cannot extend the method of truth tables to predicate logic. Each row of a truth table corresponds to a possible interpretation of the statements at the top of the table. Since there are only a finite number of possible interpretations for any set of SL statements, no truth table requires more than a finite number of rows. The case is different for $L,$ since there are an infinite number of possible interpretations for any set of statements. This follows from, among other things, the fact that the domains of interpretations may be of any size.

6.2   Truth Trees for *L*

Consider the following symbolic argument, a symbolization of the "Hypatia" argument given at the start of Chapter 5:

$$\forall x(Ax \rightarrow Gx)$$
$$\underline{Ah}$$
$$\therefore Gh$$

To test an argument for validity, it is sufficient to test the set consisting of the argument's premises and the negation of its conclusion for consistency. In the case of the above argument, the list of statements in question is

$$\forall x(Ax \rightarrow Gx)$$
$$Ah$$
$$\sim Gh$$

If this set of statements is inconsistent, then the argument is valid.[2]

It is clear that the list of statements above *is* inconsistent. The first statement says that all A's are G's, the second statement asserts that h is an A, and these two clearly imply that h is a G, which is of course inconsistent with '~Gh'. To produce a method for *demonstrating* this, however, we must add rules enabling us to decompose statements in such a way that the resultant tree contains no open branches. What is needed in the case above is a rule for the decomposition of universally quantified statements:

> ***Rule U***   If a statement of the form $\forall \alpha p$ occurs as a node in a tree, add the instance $p\alpha/\beta$ at the bottom of every open branch through that node, for one or more constant terms β that appear in any statement on that branch. If no constant terms have yet appeared, choose a single new constant for β. *Do not check the original statement.*

We use the expression 'constant term' rather than 'individual constant'. Recall that the only constant terms in *L* are the individual constants (Chapter 5). In Chapter 8 we present an extension of *L* in which additional constant terms are introduced, and it is convenient to write Rule U in this way so that we won't need to modify it later.

---

[2]Because we are generally going to be using these concepts only with regard to the language *L* from this point on, 'valid' will be used in place of 'logically valid'. Similarly, from now on we will use 'consistent' and 'inconsistent' instead of 'logically consistent' and 'logically inconsistent'.

We can divide applications of Rule U into three cases: the case where no constants have yet appeared on the branch, the case where a single constant appears on the branch, and the case where multiple constants appear on the branch. The tree we are considering has a single constant 'h' in it, so it is an example of the second case. Applying our rule in this case, we substitute 'h' for 'x' in the formula '(Ax → Gx)' and add it to the bottom of the tree:

$$\forall x(Ax \rightarrow Gx)$$
$$Ah$$
$$\sim Gh$$
$$Ah \rightarrow Gh$$

Notice that the tree now contains no quantified statements to which a rule has not been applied. We may proceed with the tree simply by applying the familiar truth-functional tree rules learned earlier. In essence, the quantifier rules will help us "reduce" the problem to one of propositional logic. Let's therefore apply the rule for the conditional to the bottom statement on the tree:

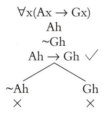

On the left, '~Ah' is inconsistent with 'Ah', and 'Gh' and '~Gh' are inconsistent on the right. Since no open branches remain, the set is inconsistent, thus proving that the original argument is valid.

Consider two more examples to illustrate the other cases in which we apply Rule U. Here is an example of a tree where we must apply Rule U, but there are no constants on the branch. Suppose we start with a single initial statement:

$$\forall x(Px \& \sim Px)$$

Since there are no constants on the branch containing this statement, we must supply a new one for Rule U:

$$\forall x(Px \& \sim Px)$$
$$Pa \& \sim Pa$$

This example shows why we must supply a new constant. Given that a domain must contain at least one object, it is evident that the statement that we started with is a logical falsehood; however, unless we could instantiate it with a constant, we would never be able to close this tree. Once the statement has been instantiated, we can apply the conjunction rule to the second statement and obtain a pair of contradictory nodes.

Lastly, consider an example where there is more than one constant on the branch. Suppose we have the following tree:

$$\forall xPx$$
$$\sim Pa$$
$$Qb$$

Rule U stipulates that when there is more than one constant on an open branch containing a universally quantified statement, you may choose to instantiate the quantified statement with one or more of those constants. For this example, this means that we can add 'Pa', 'Pb', or both to the bottom of our tree. We choose to add 'Pa' for obvious reasons:

$$\forall xPx$$
$$\sim Pa$$
$$Qb$$
$$Pa$$
$$\times$$

We could have added 'Pb' as well, but it would have served no purpose. In general, you need not instantiate *all* constants found in a branch, as long as you can make the branch close. To get a finished *open* branch, however, you must apply the rule for *all* constants.

Let's consider the justification of our Rule U. Consider the statement from our "Hypatia" argument. The universally quantified statement '$\forall x(Ax \rightarrow Gx)$' is true under an interpretation just in case all elements of the domain that are assigned to 'A' are also assigned to 'G'. Relative to the "Hypatia" interpretation, that is, the statement asserts that all astronomers are stargazers. It is an immediate consequence that if Hypatia is an astronomer, then she is a stargazer. The rule simply enables us to make this immediate inference, from universal generalization to particular instance. Though Rule U does not completely "spell out" the truth conditions for a universally quantified statement (in the way, say, that the tree rule for conjunction completely "spells out" the truth conditions for a conjunction), it *almost* does: We are allowed to add *any* arbitrarily large (though finite) number of instances. This in effect tells us that the formula 'Ax $\rightarrow$ Gx' will produce a true statement no matter what constant is substituted for 'x', which is implied by the assumption that '$\forall x(Ax \rightarrow Gx)$' is true.

A similar rule needs to be introduced for existentially quantified statements. The rule allows us to pass from a quantified statement to an instance of that statement. The rule is subject to more restrictions than Rule U, however:

> **Rule E**   If a statement of the form ∃α*p* occurs as a node on a branch,
> add the instance *p*α/β at the bottom of every open branch
> through that node, where the constant β is a *new* constant—
> that is, a constant that has not yet appeared in any statement
> on that branch. The statement ∃α*p* is then checked and can-
> not be returned to, for application of this rule.

Consider the following example:

$$\exists x(Ax \lor Bx)$$
$$\sim Aa$$

Applying Rule E we add to the tree the statement that results from '∃x(Ax ∨ Bx)'
by deleting the quantifier and substituting a constant for the variable 'x'. The constant must be *new* to the branch. Since the constant 'a' has already appeared, we
choose a new constant, say, 'b':

$$\exists x(Ax \lor Bx) \checkmark$$
$$\sim Aa$$
$$(Ab \lor Bb)$$

A check has been placed next to the statement to which Rule E has been applied,
indicating that we may not return to the statement again to apply a rule. The tree
is completed in the usual way, by applying the rule for disjunction:

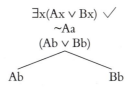

No branches close. Therefore, the set of two statements that the tree began with is
logically consistent (or simply *consistent*).

To justify Rule E, note that an existentially quantified statement, like '∃xAx', is
true under an interpretation just in case there exists at least one object in the domain
that is assigned to 'A' (i.e., that "has" the property associated with 'A'). By adding an
instance of '∃xAx', 'Ab', where 'b' is a *new* constant, the rule in effect establishes 'b' as
denoting that object in the domain that has the property A. The reason that a *new*
constant is used is that, since earlier constants already refer to objects in the domain,
it would be incorrect to assume that those constants denote objects that *also* have the
property A. For example, if 'o' were interpreted to refer to the number one and if

'Ex' meant 'x is even' and 'Ox' meant 'x is odd', then the following two statements would be true under an ordinary mathematical interpretation:

$$\exists xEx$$
$$Oo$$

Applying Rule E, we certainly would *not* want to allow the addition of

$$\exists xEx \checkmark$$
$$Oo$$
$$Eo \quad \longleftarrow \quad \textbf{\textit{Error!}}$$

Since 'o' is interpreted to be something that has the property associated with 'O', we cannot simply *assume* that it also has the property associated with 'E'; in this case, it would lead us to the inference that 1 is even, which is incorrect.

You might think that by *requiring* that we not use an old constant we would run into the opposite problem. Consider again the tree beginning with '∃xEx' and 'Oo'. The existential statement "says" that something is in the set denoted by 'E'. What if it turns out that only one individual is in that set and that individual is denoted by 'o'? Would we not somehow rule out this possibility by choosing a new constant? In fact, we have not ruled out this possibility. The reason? Nothing in our definition of an interpretation requires that different constants denote different individuals in the domain. So, when we introduce a new constant, we do not rule out the *possibility* that it refers to an individual that has already been referred to by other constants earlier in the tree.

The final two rules that we need concern statements of the forms ~∀αp and ~∃αp. The two rules are as follows:

> ***Negated Universal (NU)***   If a statement of the form ~∀αp occurs as a node on an open branch, add the statement ∃α~p at the bottom of that branch.
>
> ***Negated Existential (NE)***   If a statement of the form ~∃αp occurs as a node on an open branch, add the statement ∀α~p at the bottom of that branch.

In both cases we check off the statement to which we have applied the rule. These rules are correct because, as we argued in Section 5.6, statements of the form ~∀αp are logically equivalent to statements of the form ∃α~p and statements of the form ~∃αp are logically equivalent to statements of the form ∀α~p.

Now let's examine a tree that involves the application of all four new rules. We test the following list of *L* statements for consistency:

$$\forall x((Ax \ \& \ Bx) \to Cx)$$
$$\sim\forall x\sim(Ax \ \& \ Bx)$$
$$\sim\exists xCx$$

The first thing to do is to apply the rules NU and NE. In general, we will get a shorter tree if we apply rules for negated quantifiers before applying the quantifier rules:

$$\forall x((Ax \ \& \ Bx) \to Cx)$$
$$\sim\forall x\sim(Ax \ \& \ Bx) \ \checkmark$$
$$\sim\exists xCx \ \checkmark$$
$$\exists x\sim\sim(Ax \ \& \ Bx)$$
$$\forall x\sim Cx$$

We now have two statements to which we could apply Rule U and one to which we could apply Rule E. If we start with the universal statements, we would have to introduce a constant (since none yet occur on the branch) and then add an additional *different* constant when the existential rule is applied. In general, by applying Rule E before Rule U, we will need to use fewer constants and hence have a shorter tree. Rule E requires us to add an instance of the statement at the bottom of every open branch containing the statement, where the constant used to form the instance is a new one to that branch. Since no constants have yet appeared, we simply choose one, say, 'a':

$$\forall x((Ax \ \& \ Bx) \to Cx)$$
$$\sim\forall x\sim(Ax \ \& \ Bx) \ \checkmark$$
$$\sim\exists xCx \ \checkmark$$
$$\exists x\sim\sim(Ax \ \& \ Bx) \ \checkmark$$
$$\forall x\sim Cx$$
$$\sim\sim(Aa \ \& \ Ba)$$

Note that for double-negation rule *cannot* be used until the quantifier is gone. *Now* the double–negation rule may be applied:

$$\forall x((Ax \ \& \ Bx) \to Cx)$$
$$\sim\forall x\sim(Ax \ \& \ Bx) \ \checkmark$$
$$\sim\exists xCx \ \checkmark$$
$$\exists x\sim \sim(Ax \ \& \ Bx) \ \checkmark$$
$$\forall x\sim Cx$$
$$\sim \sim(Aa \ \& \ Ba) \ \checkmark$$
$$Aa \ \& \ Ba$$

Rather than apply the rule for conjunction to the last statement added to the tree, let's instead continue to "eliminate" quantified statements. One objective, in a sense, is to "reduce" the problem to one that can be handled by the tree rules for *SL* statements. Thus, we'll turn to the two universally quantified statements and add instances for each of these:

$$\forall x((Ax \;\&\; Bx) \to Cx)$$
$$\sim\forall x\sim(Ax \;\&\; Bx) \;\checkmark$$
$$\sim\exists xCx \;\checkmark$$
$$\exists x\sim \sim(Ax \;\&\; Bx) \;\checkmark$$
$$\forall x\sim Cx$$
$$\sim \sim(Aa \;\&\; Ba) \;\checkmark$$
$$Aa \;\&\; Ba$$
$$(Aa \;\&\; Ba) \to Ca$$
$$\sim Ca$$

Note that checks have not been placed next to the two universally quantified statements to which rules have just been applied. This is because we may return to them, if needed, to apply Rule U again. The tree is completed by applying the rule for conditionals to the next-to-last statement:

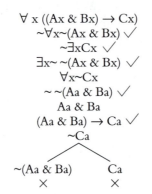

On the left, 'Aa & Ba' is inconsistent with '~(Aa & Ba)', and 'Ca' is inconsistent with '~Ca' on the right. Thus, the tree ends with no open branches, demonstrating that the initial list of statements is not logically consistent: There does not exist an interpretation under which all elements of the set are simultaneously true.

The preceding examples demonstrate the use of truth trees to test an argument of *L* for validity by means of consistency, and then simply to test sets of *L* statements for consistency. Truth trees have at least two other applications: to determine (1) whether or not a statement is a logical truth and (2) whether or not two statements are logically equivalent. We will give examples of each.

Is the following a logical truth?

$$\exists x(Fx \to \forall yFy).$$

We test an *L* statement for logical truth just as we tested an *SL* statement for tau-tologousness—that is, by determining whether there is some interpretation under which it is false. More specifically, in the case of *SL* we relied on the fact, expressed in Proposition 3 (Section 3.6), that an *SL* statement *p* is a tautology if, and only if, the set {~*p*} is truth-functionally inconsistent. To test an *SL* statement, *p*, then, we construct a tree beginning with ~*p*. If it closes, we judge that {~*p*} is inconsistent and consequently, that *p* is a tautology. Relying on the analogous Proposition L3 (Section 5.8), we know that if an *L* statement *p* is a logical truth, then the set {~*p*} is logically inconsistent. In the particular case we are considering, then, let's con-struct a tree to determine whether {~∃x(Fx → ∀yGy)} is inconsistent. We start the tree with this statement:

$$\sim \exists x (Fx \rightarrow \forall y Fy)$$

This statement is a negated existential quantification. Thus, only Rule NE can be applied at this stage. Note that we *cannot* use Rule E to produce '~(Fa → ∀yFy)': To apply Rule E, the existential quantifier must occur on the *outside* of the whole statement. Similarly, it would be *incorrect* to apply Rule U to '∀yFy' on the inside of the statement to obtain '~∃x(Fx → Fa)'. Truth tree rules apply to *whole statements* occurring as nodes on the tree, *not* to parts of statements on the tree. Thus, apply-ing NE produces

$$\sim \exists x (Fx \rightarrow \forall y Fy) \checkmark$$
$$\forall x \sim (Fx \rightarrow \forall y Fy)$$

Again, there is only one rule that can be applied at this stage: the rule for a univer-sally quantified statement. Since no constant has yet appeared, we choose a con-stant arbitrarily as we apply Rule U:

$$\sim \exists x (Fx \rightarrow \forall y Fy) \checkmark$$
$$\forall x \sim (Fx \rightarrow \forall y Fy)$$
$$\sim (Fa \rightarrow \forall y Fy)$$

Applying the rule for a negated conditional gives

$$\sim \exists x (Fx \rightarrow \forall y Fy) \checkmark$$
$$\forall x \sim (Fx \rightarrow \forall y Fy)$$
$$\sim (Fa \rightarrow \forall y Fy) \checkmark$$
$$Fa$$
$$\sim \forall y Fy$$

Applying NE to the bottom statement yields

$$\sim\exists x(Fx \rightarrow \forall yFy) \checkmark$$
$$\forall x\sim(Fx \rightarrow \forall yFy)$$
$$\sim(Fa \rightarrow \forall yFy) \checkmark$$
$$Fa$$
$$\sim\forall yFy \checkmark$$
$$\exists y\sim Fy$$

Next we apply Rule E to the bottom statement:

$$\sim\exists x(Fx \rightarrow \forall yFy) \checkmark$$
$$\forall x\sim(Fx \rightarrow \forall yFy)$$
$$\sim(Fa \rightarrow \forall yFy) \checkmark$$
$$Fa$$
$$\sim\forall yFy \checkmark$$
$$\exists y\sim Fy \checkmark$$
$$\sim Fb$$

We are not finished with the tree yet. Since no branch has closed, Rule U requires that, for any universally quantified statement on an open branch, we must add instances for *every constant that appears* on that branch. We have an instance containing 'a', but now a new constant, 'b', has appeared in a statement on the branch. Therefore, we must *return* to the second statement of the tree and apply Rule U again, this time using the constant 'b':

$$\sim\exists x(Fx \rightarrow \forall yFy) \checkmark$$
$$\forall x\sim(Fx \rightarrow \forall yFy)$$
$$\sim(Fa \rightarrow \forall yFy) \checkmark$$
$$Fa$$
$$\sim\forall yFy \checkmark$$
$$\exists y\sim Fy \checkmark$$
$$\sim Fb$$
$$\sim(Fb \rightarrow \forall yFy)$$

Applying the rule for a negated conditional to the bottom statement closes the tree:

$$\sim\exists x(Fx \rightarrow \forall yFy) \checkmark$$
$$\forall x\sim(Fx \rightarrow \forall yFy)$$
$$\sim(Fa \rightarrow \forall yFy) \checkmark$$
$$Fa$$
$$\sim\forall yFy \checkmark$$
$$\exists y\sim Fy \checkmark$$
$$\sim Fb$$
$$\sim(Fb \rightarrow \forall yFy) \checkmark$$
$$Fb$$
$$\sim\forall yFy$$
$$\times$$

Since 'Fb' and '~Fb' occur on the same branch, the branch (and therefore, in this case, the tree) closes: The statement with which the tree began is true under *no* interpretation; hence, the statement in question, '∃x(Fx → ∀yFy),' must be true under *every* interpretation—that is, it is a logical truth.

Our examples so far have involved only monadic predicates. The techniques for building trees containing polyadic predicates are exactly the same as for the monadic case. As an example of a tree with relational predicates, let's prove that the statement '∀x∀y(Rxy → Ryx)' is not a logical truth. In so doing we will (using the terminology introduced in Section 5.9) be proving that not all relations are symmetric. To test whether or not our statement is a logical truth, we begin with the negation of our statement:

$$\sim\forall x\forall y(Rxy \to Ryx)$$

To eliminate the first quantifier, we apply Rule NU, followed by rule E:

$$\sim\forall x\forall y(Rxy \to Ryx) \checkmark$$
$$\exists x\sim\forall y(Rxy \to Ryx) \checkmark$$
$$\sim\forall y(Ray \to Rya)$$

We have another negated universal statement, so we repeat our first two steps again, followed by an *SL* rule to complete the tree:

$$\sim\forall x\forall y(Rxy \to Ryx) \checkmark$$
$$\exists x\sim\forall y(Rxy \to Ryx) \checkmark$$
$$\sim\forall y(Ray \to Rya) \checkmark$$
$$\exists y\sim(Ray \to Rya) \checkmark$$
$$\sim(Rab \to Rba) \checkmark$$
$$Rab$$
$$\sim Rba$$

Since the tree is open and finished, we conclude that the statement whose negation we started with is not a logical truth.

As our last example, let's construct a tree to tell us whether the statements '∀x(Fx → A)' and '∀xFx → A' are logically equivalent. We proceed just as we did in *SL,* relying in particular on Proposition L4 (Section 5.8), which tells us that two *L* statements *p* and *q* are logically equivalent if, and only if, the statement $(p \leftrightarrow q)$ is a logical truth. In this particular case this means that we start the tree with the following statement:

$$\sim[\forall x(Fx \to A) \leftrightarrow (\forall xFx \to A)]$$

Begin by applying the rule for a negated biconditional:

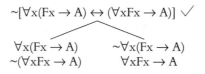

We can work on either branch. Let's work on the right, applying the rule for negated universal quantifiers:

$$\sim[\forall x(Fx \rightarrow A) \leftrightarrow (\forall xFx \rightarrow A)] \checkmark$$

$\forall x(Fx \rightarrow A)$	$\sim\forall x(Fx \rightarrow A) \checkmark$
$\sim(\forall xFx \rightarrow A)$	$\forall xFx \rightarrow A$
	$\exists x\sim(Fx \rightarrow A)$

Continuing on this branch, we will first instantiate the existentially quantified statement and then apply the appropriate *SL* rule to the resulting negated conditional:

$$\sim[\forall x(Fx \rightarrow A) \leftrightarrow (\forall xFx \rightarrow A)] \checkmark$$

$\forall x(Fx \rightarrow A)$	$\sim\forall x(Fx \rightarrow A) \checkmark$
$\sim(\forall xFx \rightarrow A)$	$\forall xFx \rightarrow A$
	$\exists x\sim(Fx \rightarrow A) \checkmark$
	$\sim(Fa \rightarrow A) \checkmark$
	Fa
	$\sim A$

Next we apply the rule for conditionals to the second statement from the top on the right-hand branch:

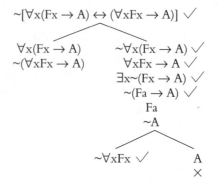

One branch closes. We complete the tree by applying Rule NU and instantiating the resulting existentially quantified statement:

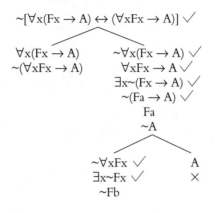

This tree is complete because we have found a finished open branch. All compound statements on the branch ending in 'Fb' have been checked, as have the existential statements. We could of course finish the other branches, but there is no need. Since the branch ending in 'Fb' is a finished open branch, it indicates that there is an interpretation under which the initial statement is true. This in turn shows that '[∀x(Fx → A) ↔ (∀xFx → A)]' is *not* a logical truth, and hence, by Proposition L4, that '∀x(Fx → A)' and '∀xFx → A' are not logically equivalent.

In completing the tree above, we referred to the notion of a 'finished open branch'. However, we have not actually stated just what a 'finished open branch' *is* in the case of a tree for a set of *L* statements. Recall that in Chapter 3 we said that a branch through an *SL* tree is 'open and finished' if, and only if, the branch is not closed and it contains no unchecked nodes except those consisting simply of statement letters or negations of statement letters. Two changes in this definition are needed to accommodate *L*. First, we now have simple statements other than statement letters—namely, statements consisting of predicate symbols followed by constant terms. These statements and their negations should be allowed in finished open branches. Second, since we can never check off universal statements, we need to specify exactly when open branches containing these statements are finished. In the following definition, when a term β occurs in place of a variable α to form an instance pα/β of a quantified statement, we will say that β is the 'instantial term' in that instance:

> ***Definition***   A branch of a tree is said to be a **finished open branch**
> if, and only if, the branch is not closed, and it contains no
> unchecked nodes except, at most,
>
> 1. Simple statements or their negations, or
> 2. Universally quantified statements, where, for each such
>   statement on the branch, (a) the branch contains at least one
>   node that is an instance of that statement, and (b) for each
>   constant term β appearing anywhere on the branch, the
>   branch includes a node that is an instance of the quantified
>   statement whose instantial term is β.

Clause (2) is cumbersome, but it merely states formally the requirement we have
made: Before we are finished with a universally quantified statement, it must be
instantiated at least once, and (if there is no way to close the branch) it must also be
instantiated for *all* constant terms on the branch(es) it is on. Once we have done
this, we can be sure that introducing additional instances of the statement would
not cause the branch(es) to close.

Exercises for Section 6.2

Part I: Consistency   Use the method of truth trees to determine whether or not
the following sets of *L* statements are logically consistent.

♦ 1. $\{\forall x(Ax \lor Bx), \forall xAx, \exists x{\sim}Bx\}$

2. $\{\forall xAx \rightarrow Ba, {\sim}(Ba \lor \exists y{\sim}Ay), \forall xAx\}$

3. $\{\exists x[Bx \lor \forall y(Ay \rightarrow {\sim} By)], Am \lor Cm, {\sim}\exists x(Bx \lor Cx)\}$

4. $\{\exists xAx, {\sim}\forall xAx\}$

5. $\{{\sim}\exists xBx, {\sim}\forall x{\sim}Bx\}$

6. $\{\forall x[Ba \rightarrow ({\sim}Kx \lor {\sim}Lx)], \exists x(Lx \lor Kx), \forall xBx \leftrightarrow Ba\}$

♦ 7. $\{{\sim}[Am \lor \forall x(Mx \mathbin{\&} {\sim}\exists y(Ay \lor Ly))], \exists z{\sim}Az\}$

8. $\{\forall x(Ax \leftrightarrow Bx), {\sim}\exists x(Ax \mathbin{\&} {\sim}Bx)\}$

9. $\{\exists x(Ax \mathbin{\&} Bx), {\sim}\forall x(Ax \rightarrow {\sim}Bx)\}$

10. $\{\forall x(Mx \rightarrow Lx), \forall x(Lx \rightarrow Nx), \forall x(Nx \rightarrow {\sim}Mx)\}$

♦ 11. $\{\exists x\exists yPxy, {\sim}\forall x\forall yPyx\}$

12. $\{\forall x\forall y({\sim}Rxy \rightarrow Ryx), {\sim}Raa\}$

13. $\{\exists xLxx \rightarrow \exists y\forall xLxy, \forall x{\sim}Lcx, Lbb\}$

Part II: Logical Truth   Use the method of truth trees to determine whether or
not the following *L* statements are logical truths.

14. $\forall x(Ax \lor \sim Ax)$

15. $\exists x(Ax \lor \sim Ax)$

16. $\exists xAx \lor \exists x \sim Ax$

♦17. $\forall xAx \lor \forall x \sim Ax$

18. $\sim Ba \rightarrow \sim \forall x \sim Bx$

19. $\forall x(Fx \rightarrow \exists yFy)$

20. $\forall x(Mx \leftrightarrow Lx) \rightarrow (\forall xMx \leftrightarrow \forall xLx)$

21. $\exists y \forall x[(Ax \& Bx) \rightarrow Cy]$

22. $[\forall xAx \& \forall y(Ay \rightarrow By)] \rightarrow \forall zBz$

♦23. $\sim \exists z(Bz \lor Lz) \rightarrow \forall x(\sim Lx \leftrightarrow \exists yBy)$

24. $\forall x \exists yLxy$

25. $\forall xAxb \lor \exists x \sim Axb$

26. $\forall x(Rax \rightarrow Rxa)$

27. $\forall x \forall y \forall z(Bxyz \rightarrow Bxzy)$

28. $\forall x \exists yRxy \rightarrow \forall x(Rxa \rightarrow \exists yRya)$

♦29. $\forall x \forall y \forall zBxyz \rightarrow \forall x \forall y \forall zBxzy$

30. $\forall x(Rxa \leftrightarrow \sim Px) \rightarrow \forall x(Px \lor \sim \exists yRxy)$

Part III: Validity   Use the method of truth trees to determine whether or not the following *L* arguments are logically valid.

31. $\forall x(Ax \lor Bx) \; / \therefore \; \forall xAx \lor \forall xBx$

32. $\forall x(Ax \leftrightarrow Bx) \; / \therefore \; \forall xAx \leftrightarrow \forall xBx$

33. $\exists x \forall y(Ax \& By) \; / \therefore \; \forall y \exists x(Ax \& By)$

34. $\forall xAx \& \forall yBy \; / \therefore \; \forall z(Az \& Bz)$

♦35. $\forall zAz \lor \forall zBz \; / \therefore \; \forall z(Az \lor Bz)$

36. $\forall x(Ax \& \sim Ax) \; / \therefore \; P \& \sim P$

37. $P \rightarrow P \; / \therefore \; \sim \forall x[(Aa \lor Bb) \rightarrow Cx] \rightarrow \sim Aa$

38. $\forall x[\forall yAy \leftrightarrow Lx] \; / \therefore \; \exists x[\exists yLy \leftrightarrow Ax]$

39. $\forall x[(Ax \lor Bx) \rightarrow \forall y(Cy \rightarrow Dy)], \; Aa \& (Cb \& \sim Db) \; / \therefore \; \forall x(Ax \& \sim Ax)$

40. $\sim \exists xAx \lor \forall yAy, \; \exists x \sim Ax, \; \forall x[Ax \rightarrow (Bx \lor Cx)] \; / \therefore \; \exists y[Ay \lor (By \lor Cy)]$

♦41. $\forall x \forall y(Axy \leftrightarrow Bxy), \; \forall x \forall yBxy \; / \therefore \; \forall x \forall yAxy$

42. $\forall x(Axa \rightarrow \forall yAxy), \; \exists x \forall y \sim Axy \; / \therefore \; \exists x \exists y \sim Axy$

43. $\forall x(Axa \lor \sim Aax), \; \forall x(Bax \lor \sim Bxa) \; / \therefore \; \forall x(Aax \leftrightarrow Bax)$

44. $\forall x(Bgx \rightarrow Cgx), \; \forall x \forall y \sim Cxy \; / \therefore \; \forall x \forall y(Bxy \rightarrow Dxy)$

45. $\forall x \forall y[Axy \rightarrow \exists zBzy], \; \forall x \forall y(Bxy \rightarrow \exists zCyz) \; / \therefore \; \exists x \exists yAxy \rightarrow \exists x \exists yCxy$

46. $\forall x \forall y \forall zKxyz, \; \exists x \exists y \exists z[Kxyz \rightarrow \forall u(Quz \rightarrow Ruy)] \; / \therefore \; \forall x \forall y(Rxy \lor \sim Qxy)$

Part IV: Logical Equivalence   Use the method of truth trees to determine whether or not the following pairs of L statements are logically equivalent.

47. $\forall x(Px \lor Qx)$ $\forall xPx \lor \forall xQx$

48. $\forall xAx$ $\sim\exists x\sim Ax$

♦49. $\forall x\exists y(Px \& Qy)$ $\exists y\forall x(Px \& Qy)$

50. $\forall x\exists y(Ax \leftrightarrow \sim Ay)$ $\exists y\forall x(Ax \leftrightarrow \sim Ay)$

51. $\forall x(S \to Px)$ $(S \to \forall xPx)$

52. $\exists x(S \to Px)$ $(S \to \exists xPx)$

53. $\forall x\exists yLxy$ $\exists x\forall yLxy$

54. $\forall x\forall y(Lxy \to A)$ $\forall y\forall x(Lxy \to A)$

6.3   Reading Interpretations from Finished Open Branches

In Chapter 3 we noted that you may use a finished open branch to "read off" an interpretation in which all the statements that you started with are true. We can extend our original method to truth trees for L. To do so it will be convenient to make use of the following definition:

> ***Definition***   A **model** of a set of L statements is an interpretation of L under which all statements in the set are true.

We now describe a procedure for using a finished open tree to construct a model for the set of statements with which that tree began.

To read a model off of a finished open branch:

1. For any constant symbol β that appears on the branch, add a distinct object o to the model's domain and let $\mathcal{I}(\beta) = o$.
2. For any statement letter p that appears as a node on the branch, assign p the truth value T. For any negated statement letter $\sim p$ that occurs as a node on the branch, assign p the truth value F.
3. For any simple statement of the form $\mathcal{A}^n\beta_1 \ldots \beta_n$ that appears as a node on the branch, add the n-tuple $<\mathcal{I}(\beta_1), \ldots, \mathcal{I}(\beta_n)>$ to the set $\mathcal{I}(\mathcal{A}^n)$.
4. For any statement letters occurring in the original set of statements that have not been assigned a truth value by clause (2), assign any value. For any predicate symbols to whose denotations have not been added any objects by clause (3), assign the empty set.

Let's apply this procedure to the last sample truth tree we completed in Section 6.2. Our task is to find a model for the set $\{\sim[\forall x(Fx \to A) \leftrightarrow (\forall xFx \to A)]\}$. Using the tree we have already completed, reading up along the one finished open branch, we get

$\mathcal{D}$: $\{1, 2\}$

a: 1

b: 2

Fx: $\{1\}$

A: F.

For our arbitrary objects in $\mathcal{D}$, we have chosen numbers. It is convenient to assign the number 1 to the first constant on the branch, the number 2 to the second, and so on; however, you can make the constants denote any distinct objects you like. You should use the definition of 'truth under an interpretation' to verify our claim that this interpretation is indeed a model for the set $\{\sim[\forall x(Fx \to A) \leftrightarrow (\forall xFx \to A)]\}$.

Our technique for finding models of statements on a tree can be put to another purpose. To say that an argument in L is invalid is just to say that there is some interpretation where all the argument's premises are true and the conclusion is false. So, if an argument is invalid, we should be able to produce such an interpretation, which we call a *counterexample*.

> **Definition**   A **counterexample** to an argument is an interpretation under which the argument's premises are all true while its conclusion is false.

A counterexample, then, is a model for the set composed of an argument's premises and the negation of its conclusion.

We illustrate the application of this definition on the following argument:

$$\forall x(Ax \to Bx)$$
$$\underline{\forall x(Ax \to \sim Cx)}$$
$$\therefore \forall x(Bx \to \sim Cx)$$

To test for validity, we test the appropriate set for consistency by constructing a truth tree:

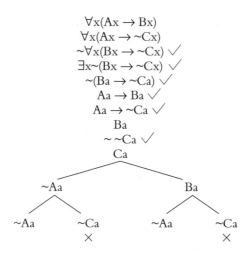

The set that started the tree is consistent, so the argument is invalid. Following the instructions in our procedure, we read the following interpretation from the tree off the open branch on the left:

$\mathcal{D}$: $\{1\}$

a: 1

Ax: $\varnothing$

Bx: $\{1\}$

Cx: $\{1\}$.

This is both a model for the set with which the tree began and a counterexample to the corresponding argument.

Our technique for finding models and counterexamples is completely formal, and it relies on the fact that interpretations are extensional. We have specified sets for the domain and for each of the predicates, and we have not specified any properties of which these sets are extensions. It is certainly possible to use intensionally defined properties to specify the same extensional interpretation. For instance, we could specify the same interpretation of the three predicate letters as follows:

Ax: x is even

Bx: x is odd

Cx: x is the lowest positive integer.

You need not use a tree to find a model or counterexample, but in cases where you cannot immediately find one, you can always rely on this technique.

As a final illustration let's work with an argument containing polyadic predicates. We test the following argument for validity:[3]

$$\frac{\exists x \exists y (Rxy \;\&\; {\sim}Ryx)}{\therefore\; \forall x \forall y (Rxy \to {\sim}Ryx)}$$

We complete an appropriate tree in the usual way:

$$\exists x \exists y (Rxy \;\&\; {\sim}Ryx) \;\checkmark$$
$${\sim}\forall x \forall y (Rxy \to {\sim}Ryx) \;\checkmark$$
$$\exists y (Ray \;\&\; {\sim}Rya) \;\checkmark$$
$$(Rab \;\&\; {\sim}Rba) \;\checkmark$$
$$Rab$$
$${\sim}Rba$$
$$\exists x {\sim} \forall y (Rxy \to {\sim}Ryx) \;\checkmark$$
$${\sim}\forall y (Rcy \to {\sim}Ryc) \;\checkmark$$
$$\exists y {\sim} (Rcy \to {\sim}Ryc) \;\checkmark$$
$${\sim}(Rcd \to {\sim}Rdc) \;\checkmark$$
$$Rcd$$
$${\sim}{\sim}Rdc \;\checkmark$$
$$Rdc$$

This tree has one open branch, from which we can read off an interpretation:

$\mathcal{D}$:	$\{1, 2, 3, 4\}$
a:	1
b:	2
c:	3
d:	4
Rxy:	$\{<1, 2>, <3, 4>, <4, 3>\}$.

Notice how the procedure has been applied in connection with the predicate 'R'. Reading up from the bottom, we first encounter 'Rdc'. By clause (1) we assign distinct objects in the domain to 'd' and to 'c—in this case, $\mathcal{I}(d) = 4$ and $\mathcal{I}(c) = 3$. By clause (3) we must interpret 'R' so that $<\mathcal{I}(d), \mathcal{I}(c)> \in \mathcal{I}(R)$—that is, so that the ordered pair $<4, 3>$ is one of the elements of the set assigned to 'R' by the interpretation. This interpretation, as in the previous example, provides both a model

---

[3]Note that, using the terminology introduced in Section 5.9, we are testing to see whether a relation R's being nonsymmetric entails that it is asymmetric.

for the set of statements that started the tree, as well as a counterexample to the argument being tested.

Note that we have included assignments to the four constants that occur in the tree above. They are not really needed for the model, however, because none of the four constants appears in the initial list of statements; that is, if we allow 'R' to be interpreted as it is but let assignments to the individual constants of L be arbitrary in this case, the resulting interpretation would still be a model of the given set of statements. To see that in this case the individual constants do not need to be explicitly interpreted, observe that the following, less formal interpretation also provides a counterexample to the argument:

$\mathcal{D}$:   persons

Rxy: x loves y.

Under this interpretation the argument's premise is true, and its conclusion is false. The premise is true because love is nonsymmetric: There are people whose love is not returned by their loved ones. The conclusion is false because love is *not* asymmetric: Not every lover is unloved by those whom he or she loves.

Exercises for Section 6.3

Part I: Consistent Sets   Each of the following sets is logically consistent. Build a finished truth tree for each one and in each case read off a model of the set from a finished open branch.

 1. {Fa & ~Ga, ~Fb & Gb, ~Fc & ~Gc}
 2. {Fa → Ga, ~Gb ↔ Hb, Fc ∨ ~Hc, Fa}
 ♦ 3. {∃xAx & ∃xBx, Aa & Bb}
 4. {∀x(Ax → Bx), ∃x(Ax & ~Cx), ∃x(Bx & ~Cx)}
 5. {∀x(Ax → (Bx ∨ Ca)), ∃xAx & ∀y~Cy, ∃xBx}
 6. {∀x(Ax ↔ (Bx & ~Ca)), ~(∃xAx ∨ ∀yCy), ∃xBx → ∀xAx}
 7. {(Lab ↔ (Ma → (Brb & Lar)), ~(Ma ∨ Brb)}
 8. {Sbbc, ~Sbcb, ∀x∀y(Sxxy → Syyx)}
 ♦ 9. {∀x∀y(Lxy → ~Lyx), Lab, ~Lba}
 10. {(~∃x∀yAxy → ∀y∃xAyx), ∀x~Axx, ∃xAxb}
 11. {∃x∃yPxy ∨ ~∀x∀yPxy, ~∃x∃y~Pxy}
 12. {∀x(Kxa → ~Kax) → ∃y∃zRayz, ∃x∃y(~Raxy & ~Rayx), ~Rcde}

Part II: Counterexamples   Each of the following arguments is logically invalid. Build a finished truth tree for each one and in each case read off a counterexample for the argument from a finished open branch.

13. ∀x(Ax → Bx), ∀x(Ax → Cx) /∴ ∀x(Bx → Cx)

14. ∀x(Ax → Bx), ∃xBx /∴ ∃xAx

♦15. ∀xAx ↔ ∀xBx /∴ ∀x(Ax ↔ Bx)

16. Fa & Gb, ∀x(Fx → Gx) /∴ Fb & Gb

17. Fa ∨ Gb, ∀x(Fx → ~Hx), ∀x(Gx → ~Kx) /∴ ∃x~(Hx ∨ Kx)

18. ∃x(Mx ∨ Nx) & ∀y(My → ~Ky), ~(Ka & La), Mb ∨ Nc
    /∴ ∀x[Mb & (~Kx → Nx)]

19. ∃x∀yAxy /∴ ∀x∃yAxy

20. ∀x∀y(Axy → ~Ayx) /∴ ∀xAxx

♦21. ∃x∃yGxy, ∀x∀y(Gxy → Hxy) /∴ ∃xHxx

22. ∀x∀y(Kxy ∨ Kyx), ∃x(Kxa & ∃y~Mxy) /∴ ∃x~Mxa

23. ∀x(∃yAyx → ∃zBzx), ∀x(∃yCyx → ∃zBzx) /∴ ∀x(∃yCyx → ∃zAzx)

24. ∀x∀y(Gxy → ~~Gxy), ∀x∀y(Gxy ↔ Lyx) /∴ ∀x∀y(~Gxy → Lyx)

6.4   The Problem of Infinite Trees

In the case of a set of *SL* statements, a truth tree always terminates at some finite point, either with all branches closed or with at least one branch remaining open. But the assumption that all trees eventually terminate does *not* hold in the case of quantified logic. For example, let's consider a truth tree for the following statement:

$$\forall x \exists y (Ax \ \& \ By)$$

Proceeding in the usual way, we first apply Rule U, picking a new constant to substitute for the variable 'x':

$$\forall x \exists y (Ax \ \& \ By)$$
$$\exists y (Aa \ \& \ By)$$

Next, again as usual, we pick a constant that has not yet been used to substitute for the variable 'y', in order to apply Rule E:

$$\forall x \exists y (Ax \ \& \ By)$$
$$\exists y (Aa \ \& \ By) \ \checkmark$$
$$Aa \ \& \ Bb$$

The tree has not closed. Notice, now, that since a new constant ('b') has appeared on the tree, we must *return* to the universally quantified statement at the top of the trunk and substitute 'b' for 'x':

$$\forall x \exists y (Ax \ \& \ By)$$
$$\exists y (Aa \ \& \ By) \ \checkmark$$
$$Aa \ \& \ Bb$$
$$\exists y (Ab \ \& \ By)$$

Then, picking yet *another* new constant for 'y' in the bottom statement yields

$$\forall x \exists y (Ax \ \& \ By)$$
$$\exists y (Aa \ \& \ By) \ \checkmark$$
$$Aa \ \& \ Bb$$
$$\exists y (Ab \ \& \ By) \ \checkmark$$
$$Ab \ \& \ Bc$$

It is apparent that this process will go on *infinitely:*

$$\forall x \exists y (Ax \ \& \ By)$$
$$\exists y (Aa \ \& \ By) \ \checkmark$$
$$Aa \ \& \ Bb$$
$$\exists y (Ab \ \& \ By) \ \checkmark$$
$$Ab \ \& \ Bc$$
$$\exists y (Ac \ \& \ By) \ \checkmark$$
$$Ac \ \& \ Bd$$
$$\cdot$$
$$\cdot$$
$$\cdot$$

The risk of an infinite tree typically arises when, as in this example, an existential quantifier occurs within the scope of a universal quantifier.[4] Our question then is

---

[4]Note that there are certain statements in which a universal quantifier falls within the scope of another universal quantifier that also give rise to infinite trees. For instance, the statement '$\forall x \sim \forall y Axy$' will generate an infinite tree because, as we apply the tree rules, the inner universal quantifier will be transformed to an existential quantifier. In general, whenever an existentially quantified statement *q* can be derived by a sequence of applications of tree rules from universally quantified statements, the branch or branches containing *q* will, if consistent, be infinite.

this: Is there any way to determine *when* we may stop—when we have gone "far enough" to know whether the initial set of statements is consistent or inconsistent? Our rules for tree construction do not yet answer this question. This means that our tree method, as we have presented it so far, does not provide an *effective decision procedure* for deciding the consistency of every given set of L statements.

Just because our current tree method is not an effective decision procedure, however, does not mean that we might not alter the procedure somehow to make it effective for deciding the consistency of sets of L statements. The answer to the question of whether we can do this depends crucially on whether or not the sets to be tested contain polyadic predicate symbols. Our truth tree method can be modified so that it is effective for all sets of L statements *not containing* polyadic predicate symbols.

Let's consider **monadic predicate logic** as a language in its own right. We call this language 'L_m'. L_m is easily defined: The statements of the language L_m are all and only those statements of L not containing polyadic predicate symbols. Though it is possible to modify our tree method to create an effective decision procedure for consistency for sets of L_m statements, there is unfortunately no possible modification that will yield an effective decision procedure for L. We now present a modification to the tree method that makes it effective for L_m, and explain why the modification does not work for *all* sets of L statements.

The required modification involves changing our rule for existentially quantified statements. We replace Rule E by Rule E★ as follows:

> **Rule E★**   To the end of each branch in which a statement $\exists \alpha p$ occurs as a node and in which also occur distinct constant terms $\beta_1, \ldots, \beta_n$, add $n + 1$ branches. The first n branches should, for each $i \leq n$, end in one of the instances $p\alpha / \beta_i$. The $n + 1$st branch should end in $p\alpha / \beta_{new}$, where the constant β_{new} is a *new* constant—that is, a constant that has not yet appeared in any statement on the branch. The statement $\exists \alpha p$ is then checkmarked and cannot be returned to for application of this rule.

As an example, we'll look at how a tree for the statement '$\forall x \exists y(Ax \ \& \ By)$' can be terminated in a finite number of steps using E★. Here are the first two nodes of the tree:

$$\forall x \exists y(Ax \ \& \ By)$$
$$\exists y(Aa \ \& \ By)$$

Instead of applying Rule E next, we use Rule E★:

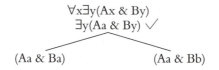

The "usual" application of Rule E would have produced only the statement entered on the right-hand branch. In applying Rule E★, however, we've also added the left-hand branch containing the constant 'a', *even though* 'a' has already appeared in the second statement of the tree. We may now proceed in the usual way, applying the conjunction rule to the left-hand branch:

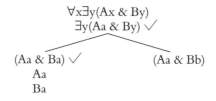

Applying our definitions, we discover that the left-hand branch is a finished open branch and that, consequently, the statement that we started with is consistent. In effect, we are extending the tree by adding a slightly more complicated implication of '∃y(Aa & By)'. The branch "says" that either a has properties A and B, or else that while a has A, something else—call it 'b'—has property B. If assuming that a has B had produced an inconsistency, then, as usual, the left-hand branch would have closed.

Since, according to our definition, a tree is complete if it has a single finished open branch, we could complete the above tree without completing the right-hand branch. That is all we need to show that the statement we started with is consistent. If we *had* been asked to do more, we would never have been able to finish our task. As we have said, the application of Rule E★ always produces one branch that corresponds to an application of the old Rule E. That branch will, as before, go on indefinitely. Fortunately, we need not follow that branch to determine the consistency of our original statement.

When you construct truth trees to check statements for consistency, you may choose to use either Rule E or Rule E★. In general, it will be much quicker to use Rule E. Sometimes, however, Rule E★ will allow you to quickly find a finished open branch. In some cases, as we have seen, the only way to complete a tree is to use Rule E★.

The statement '∀x∃y(Ax & By)', which started the tree above, is a statement of L_m. Rule E★ also allows you to complete in a finite number of steps many trees involving statements with polyadic predicate symbols. Consider the statement '∀x∃yGxy'. If we try to complete a tree using Rule E, we get an infinite tree:

∀x∃yGxy
∃yGay √
Gab
∃yGby √
Gbc
∃yGcy

.

.

.

However, using E⋆, a tree for this statement is quickly completed:

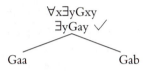

As we said above, E⋆ will produce a finished tree for *every* consistent, finite set of L_m statements. This fact has the following, somewhat surprising, consequence:

> **Proposition L_m1**   Every consistent finite set of L_m statements has a finite model.

Recall that a model for a set of statements is an interpretation under which all elements of the set are true. To say that a model or interpretation is 'finite' means that its domain has a finite number of elements. A domain consisting just of the numbers 1 through 10 is finite, whereas a domain consisting of all natural numbers is infinite. What this proposition therefore tells us is this: *If* a finite set of L_m statements has a model, then it has a model whose domain contains only finitely many individuals.

The crucial step in a proof of Proposition L_m1 is to show that it is possible to construct a finished a tree (using Rule E⋆ when necessary) for any finite, consistent set of L_m statements. A finished tree for a consistent set of statements will contain a finished open branch, and once we have a finished open branch, we can easily read an interpretation off that branch. The domain of this interpretation is always finite because a finished open branch has at most a finite number of statements containing at most a finite number of individual constants, and we add to our domain at most one individual for each constant occurring on the branch.[5]

---

[5]A full proof of Proposition L_m1 is given by George Boolos in his paper "Trees and Finite Satisfiability: Proof of a Conjecture of Burgess," *Notre Dame Journal of Formal Logic* 25, no. 3 (1984): 193–197.

Whereas every consistent finite set of L_m statements has a finite model, some consistent finite sets of L statements do not have finite models. One such set is the following:

$$\{\forall x \exists y Gyx, \ \forall x {\sim} Gxx, \ \forall x \forall y \forall z [(Gxy \ \& \ Gyz) \rightarrow Gxz]\}.$$

The existence of sets such as this has the consequence that the tree method does not provide an effective procedure for consistency in L. A tree for a consistent set of L statements is finished if, and only if, it has a finished open branch, and a tree will have a finished open branch if, and only if, the original set of statements has a finite model. So, if this set is consistent but has no finite model, a tree demonstrating its consistency cannot be completed in a finite number of steps.

To complete our remarks on Proposition $L_m 1$, we need to show first that the set above is consistent and second that every model of the set has an infinite domain. To do this we take the elements of the set one at a time, starting with

(1) $\forall x \exists y Gyx$.

Statement (1) is consistent. A model for (1) *can* contain an infinite domain, but this is not required. As demonstrated on the most recently completed truth tree, we can read the following interpretation from the left-hand branch of that tree:

$\mathcal{D}$: $\{1\}$
Gxy: $\{<1, 1>\}$.

Let's consider what happens to the domain when we look for a model for the set containing statement (1) *and* the second statement in the set:

(2) $\forall x {\sim} Gxx$.

The set $\{\forall x \exists y Gyx, \ \forall x {\sim} Gxx\}$ is consistent, but notice that '$\forall x {\sim} Gxx$' is false under the first interpretation. The consistency of the set can be seen by noting that both elements of the set are true under the following interpretation:

$\mathcal{D}$: $\{1\}$
Gxy: $\{<1, 2>, <2, 1>\}$.

Though this interpretation, too, has a finite domain, adding the third statement forces the domain of any model for the set to be infinite:

(3) $\forall x \forall y \forall z [(Gxy \ \& \ Gyz) \rightarrow Gxz]$.

The second interpretation won't do for the set {∀x∃yGyx, ∀x~Gxx, ∀x∀y∀z[(Gxy & Gyz) → Gxz]}. Notice that under this interpretation statement (3) comes out false. To prove that the set is consistent, we must provide an interpretation under which all three statements are true. One such interpretation is this:

> 𝒟: natural numbers
>
> Gxy: x is greater than y.

Each statement in the set is true under this interpretation, since (a) for every natural number, there exists some number that is greater; (b) no number is greater than itself; and (c) if one number is greater than a second and that second number is greater than a third, then the first number is greater than the third number. These are fairly obvious truths of arithmetic, which shows intuitively at least that the set in question is consistent. But this of course is a model with an infinite domain. It is left to you, in Exercise 17, to prove that *every* model of this set of statements has an infinite domain.

Exercises for Section 6.4

Infinite Trees   Using Rule E★ presented in this section, along with the other usual tree rules, test each of the following statements for consistency using a truth tree.

◆1. ∀x∃y(Ax ∨ By)

2. ∀x∃y[(Ax ∨ ~Ax) → (By & ~By)]

3. ∀y∃z[(Ay ∨ Aa) & Bz]

4. ∀x∀y∃z[Ax ∨ (Ay & Bz)]

5. ∀x[Kx & ∃y(Ay → Lx)]

6. ∀x∃y∀z[(Ax & By) → (~Bz → Ay)]

◆7. ∀x(Ax & ∃y(Bx ∨ Cy))

8. ∀x∃y∃z[(Fx ∨ Gz) & (Fy ∨ Hz)]

9. ∀x∃yLxy

10. ∀x∃yLxy & ∃x∀yLxy

11. ~∃xLxx & ∃x∀yLxy

12. ∀x(∃yGxy → ~Gxa)

Part II: Theoretical and Philosophical Problems

13. Write a non-contradictory statement of *L* that is not true in any domain containing less than two objects.

14. Write a non-contradictory statement of *L* that is not true in any domain containing less than three objects.

15. Proposition $L_m 1$ states that every finite consistent set of L_m statements has a finite model. But, as we said in our discussion, some infinite sets of L_m statements have only infinite models. Prove that this is the case by giving an example of such a set.

16. We argued informally that the set $\{\forall x \exists y Gyx, \forall x {\sim} Gxx, \forall x \forall y \forall z[(Gxy$ & $Gyz) \rightarrow Gxz]\}$ has a model with an infinite domain. Rigorously prove this by using the formal definition of 'truth under an interpretation' for L.

17. We claimed in this section that the set $\{\forall x \exists y Gyx, \forall x {\sim} Gxx, \forall x \forall y \forall z[(Gxy$ & $Gyz) \rightarrow Gxz]\}$ has no models with finite domains. Prove that this is true. (*Hint:* Assume that you have a finite domain of size n and prove that if the first two elements of the set are made true under this interpretation, then it will be impossible to make the third true under this interpretation as well.)

18. The problem of infinite trees generally arises when an existential quantifier occurs within the scope of a universal. A natural question might be the following: Why can't we simply switch positions of the universal and existential quantifiers? Isn't the result going to be logically equivalent? This certainly is not the case for polyadic predicate symbols: '$\forall x \exists y Lxy$' does not even intuitively mean the same thing as '$\exists y \forall x Lxy$'. The first can be interpreted to mean, for example, 'Every number is lower than some number', which is true, and the second would by contrast mean 'There is some number than which every number is lower', which is false. You might think, however, that the situation is different for L_m. Consider, as an example, the statement considered in this section: '$\forall x \exists y(Ax$ & $By)$'. This statement *is* logically equivalent to '$\exists y \forall x(Ax$ & $By)$', and this latter statement produces a finite tree. However, this strategy will not work in general. To prove this, give an interpretation that assigns opposite truth values to the following two statements: '$\forall x \exists y(Ax \leftrightarrow By)$' and '$\exists y \forall x(Ax \leftrightarrow By)$'.

6.5   The Adequacy of the Tree Method for L_m and L

Just as for *SL*, the semantic properties and relations for L, which we have discussed, are defined in terms of *truth under an interpretation*. These properties and relations are *not* defined in terms of truth trees. Truth trees are simply one of a number of possible methods for determining whether L statements have these various semantic properties or stand in these relations. Consequently, it is important to prove that the tree method is adequate to this task.

Let's recall some important terminology. In Section 3.11 we distinguished two aspects of the truth tree method. First, there is the deduction system T_{SL}, composed of the rules and definitions that specify when one has correctly constructed a truth tree and when a truth tree is complete. Second, there is the decision procedure TD_{SL}, which is a mechanical procedure for building truth trees to test for tautologousness. We now make the same distinction for *L*: we have a truth tree–based deduction system, T_L, and an associated decision procedure, TD_L.

The questions we ask about the adequacy of our deduction system and our decision procedure for *L* are essentially the ones we asked about in connection with *SL*. First, we would like the deduction system T_L to be both sound and complete. The system we have presented possesses both of these properties. Using the notation introduced in Chapter 3, they may be stated as follows:

> **Soundness**   For any *L* statement *p*, if $\vdash_{T_L} p$, then $\vDash p$.

That is, if *p* is a truth tree theorem, then *p* is a logical truth.

> **Completeness**   For any *L* statement *p*, if $\vDash p$, then $\vdash_{T_L} p$.

That is, if *p* is a logical truth, then *p* is a truth tree theorem. Recall that the expression '$\vDash p$' is read '*p* is true under every interpretation'. If *p* is an *SL* statement, '$\vDash p$' means that *p* is a tautology; if *p* is an *L* statement, it means that *p* is a logical truth. From the soundness and completeness of T_L, it follows immediately that the associated decision procedure TD_L is also sound and complete.

Besides soundness and completeness, we would like our decision procedure to have the additional property of effectiveness. An *effective* decision procedure is a procedure that always gives an answer within a finite amount of time. Although TD_{SL} is an effective decision procedure for tautologousness and other semantic properties in *SL*, TD_L is *not* an effective decision procedure for logical truth in *L*, for reasons having to do with the problem of infinite trees. Furthermore, there *is no way* of improving TD_L to make it effective.

The discovery that it is impossible to create an effective decision procedure for logical truth in *L* is among the most important theoretical results in logic in the twentieth century (and will be discussed in the next section). Here, let's explain briefly how it is that we know T_L is sound and complete and how we know that TD_L is non–effective. A rigorous proof is beyond the scope of our discussion, but we will make a few informal remarks in support of our assertions about T_L.[6]

First, let's consider the soundness of T_L. As we saw from our discussion of T_{SL}, the tree method is sound if, and only if, trees don't close unless they "should"—that is, unless the set of statements that they begin with are inconsistent. This guarantees that if the tree method does classify a statement as logically

---

[6]For a full proof of the adequacy and limitations of the tree method, see Richard Jeffrey's *Formal Logic* (see Appendix 1).

true, then that statement indeed *is* logically true. To obtain this guarantee, we devised our tree rules for *SL* to have the following important property, also called **soundness:**

> **Definition:** A tree rule is **sound** if, and only if, for any statement p to which the rule can be applied, if p is true under an interpretation $\mathcal{I}$, then, on at least one of the branches resulting from the application of the rule, all new statements added by the rule on that branch are true under $\mathcal{I}$ as well.

For instance, the conjunction rule is sound: If a conjunction, p & q, is true under some interpretation $\mathcal{I}$, it turns out that all the new statements added beneath it by the application of the rule (namely, p and q) must be true under $\mathcal{I}$ as well. Similarly, the rule for the conditional is sound because, if we take any conditional, $p \rightarrow q$, which is true under some interpretation $\mathcal{I}$, we find that either the statement ~p (from the left-hand branch added by the rule) or the statement q (from the right-hand branch) must be true under $\mathcal{I}$ as well.

All tree rules for *L* are sound *except* the Rules E and E★. How can we be sure that these rules don't lead to trouble? We consider just Rule E, for similar remarks apply to E★. Now, there are certainly interpretations under which an existential statement like '∃xPx' is true while 'Pa', an instance arrived at by application of Rule E, is false. This fact does not lead to trouble because, in applying Rule E, a constant that is *new* to the branch is used to instantiate the existentially quantified statement. Though 'Pa' may not be true in all interpretations where '∃xPx' is true, *if* there is *some* interpretation where '∃xPx' and all other statements on the branch containing it are true, then there *does* exist *some* interpretation under which those statements *and* 'Pa' are true as well. In other words, the application of Rule E produces an instance that is consistent with all statements on the branch containing it, as long as that branch terminates and is open. This is enough to ensure that no unwarranted inconsistencies are introduced into a branch extended by the application of Rule E. This fact, together with the soundness of the remaining tree rules as described in the preceding paragraph, is enough to ensure that our tree method is sound.

Now consider completeness. For T_L to be complete, it must turn out that every tree that begins with an inconsistent set eventually closes. This means that, as we apply the tree rules and check off statements, we must not make branches look consistent when they are not. To be more specific, suppose that a branch of a tree contains nodes $p_1, \ldots, p_n$, q and that the set $\{p_1, \ldots, p_n, q\}$ is inconsistent. We must ensure that every branch containing the set $\{p_1, \ldots, p_n\}$ plus the statements added to the tree by applying a rule to q is inconsistent as well. Aside from Rule U, each of the tree rules has a property, called **completeness:**

> **Definition:**   A tree rule is **complete** if, and only if, for any statement
> p to which the rule can be applied, if p is false under an
> interpretation $\mathcal{I}$, then, on *every* branch resulting from the
> application of the rule, at least one of the new statements
> added by the rule is false under $\mathcal{I}$ as well.

The rule for conjunction, for instance, is complete because, if we take any conjunction p & q that is false under some interpretation $\mathcal{I}$, we find that at least one of the new statements added by the rule (either p or q) must be false under $\mathcal{I}$ as well. Similarly, the rule for the conditional is complete because, if we take any conditional $p \rightarrow q$ that is false under some interpretation $\mathcal{I}$, we find that both the statement ~p (from the left-hand branch added by the rule) and the statement q (from the right branch) must be false under $\mathcal{I}$ as well. The "preservation of falsity" ensured by the completeness of the tree rules guarantees that, as we apply a rule to a statement q, "replacing" q by the statements derived from it, any inconsistency in paths containing q will be maintained.

It is easy to see, however, that U is not a complete rule: A universal statement like '∀xPx' may be false under an interpretation $\mathcal{I}$ even when a statement obtained from it by Rule U, like 'Pa', is true under $\mathcal{I}$. Even if we add more instances, we can never write down *all* the consequences of a universally quantified statement. What guarantees completeness of the tree method despite this fact are the restrictions on what counts as a finished open branch. As long as a branch containing a universally quantified statement has not closed, we must continue to write down every instance of it involving the individual constants found on the branch, until either the branch closes or all individual constants on it have been exhausted. This implies that if there *is* an inconsistency between a universally quantified statement and the remaining statements on the branch, then it is eventually going to be found; that is, if some consequence of a universally quantified statement comes into logical conflict with another statement on a branch, this conflict must be exhibited through one of its instances. If neither of the statements in conflict are themselves logical falsehoods, then they can come into conflict only if they imply two statements such that one of them is the negation of the other. If constants occur in these two statements, then the statements in question can conflict with each other only if the constants contained in the two statements are the same. Rule U, together with the remaining tree rules, implies that this conflict must eventually be in evidence on the tree, and this is what guarantees completeness.

Finally, let's turn to the question of the effectiveness of truth trees as decision procedures for L. Here we find an important difference between monadic and relational predicate logic. We have the following two theorems:

> **Theorem** TD_{L_m} is an effective decision procedure for logical truth in L_m.

> **Theorem** TD_L *is not* an effective decision procedure for logical truth in *L*.

As long as we exclude statements containing polyadic predicate symbols, truth trees will always tell us whether a statement is a logical truth. Once we allow polyadic predicates, however, the truth tree method will not always yield an answer. Let's examine what makes these two claims true.

To test a statement *p* for logical truth, construct a tree beginning with ~*p*. If the resulting tree is closed, we conclude that *p* is a logical truth; if it is open, we conclude *p* is not a logical truth. For this decision procedure to be effective, it must be possible for us to mechanically complete every such tree in a finite amount of time.

Because we always check off compound *SL* statements when we apply tree rules to them and because the rules require us to add statements that are shorter than the statements from which they are derived, it is fairly obvious that trees involving only the application of *SL* rules can be completed in a finite number of steps. The case for *L* is complicated by the fact that we can never check off a node containing a universally quantified statement. As we saw in Section 6.4, in certain circumstances this fact can lead to a tree having an infinite branch. This situation was improved somewhat by our addition of E★. As we claimed in the last section, when we use E★ rather than E, any tree consisting only of L_m statements can be completed within a finite number of steps. In specifying the decision procedure TD_{L_m}, however, we do need to be careful. In the case of *SL,* every branch can be completed, so it doesn't matter in what order you choose to apply rules to statements. For trees involving L_m statements, although we know that either the tree closes or at least one branch can be completed in a finite number of steps, it may be the case that some open branches are infinite. Our procedure must enable us to mechanically apply rules in such a way that we never get stuck on an infinite branch. Such a procedure can certainly be created.[7]

As proved at the end of the Section 6.4, the difficulty posed by polyadic predicate symbols is that some consistent statements containing polyadic predicate symbols do not have finite models. This fact entails that TD_L is not an effective decision procedure for logical truth—for, if ~*p* is a consistent statement with no finite models, it will turn out that TD_L will never halt its tree building for this statement. Since it thus never manages to complete a tree for ~*p*, TD_L can never indicate that *p* is not a logical truth.

---

[7]An example of such a procedure is that employed by the program Inference Engine, which accompanies this text.

Although the decision procedure TD_L, as we have described it, is not effective, you may rightly wonder whether we could modify it to make it effective. We have said that the only statements for which infinite trees may be produced by TD_L are *consistent*. It is thus quite reasonable to ask whether there is some mechanical way to determine whether a tree-building routine has become stuck on an infinite branch. If such a supplementary procedure could be specified, then we would indeed have an effective decision procedure for the whole of L. The suggestion seems plausible; after all, in the examples of infinite trees that we have discussed, it is fairly obvious (after looking for a bit) that the trees could be continued without end. However, it turns out that, due to a theorem known as the Church–Turing Undecidability Theorem, *no such procedure exists.*

Exercises for Section 6.5

Theoretical and Philosophical Problems

1. Suppose we were to omit the requirement on Rule E that the instantiated constant must not yet have appeared on the branch containing the existentially quantified statement. Show that our method would then be unsound, by exhibiting a tree that would incorrectly indicate that a statement is a logical truth.

2. To convert our tree method to a completely mechanical procedure (i.e., an effective decision procedure), we need to specify a procedure for choosing, at any point in the construction of the tree in which there is more than one choice, which node a rule should be applied to. Invent such a procedure L_m, making sure that it tells how to choose nodes in such a way that the procedure will always terminate in a finite amount of time. (*Note:* The rules should specify when Rule E★, rather than Rule E, is to be applied.)

3. At the end of Section 6.3, we claimed that the statement '$\forall x(Ax \rightarrow Bx)$' was true under the following interpretation:

$\mathcal{D}$: $\{1\}$

Ax: x is even

Bx: x is odd

Cx: x is the lowest positive integer.

Given this interpretation, this statement reads 'All even numbers are odd numbers'. At least intuitively, one would ordinarily be inclined to say that such a statement is *false.* Explain why the statement is nevertheless true under the given interpretation.

4. Consider the following truth tree:

$$\sim\exists x(Ax \lor \sim Ax) \checkmark$$
$$\forall x\sim(Ax \lor \sim Ax)$$
$$\sim(Aa \lor \sim Aa) \checkmark$$
$$\sim Aa$$
$$\sim\sim Aa$$
$$\times$$

According to the tree, the statement '$\exists x(Ax \lor \sim Ax)$' is logically, and hence necessarily, *true*. Whatever property or set 'A' is interpreted to be, it is interesting to observe that this necessarily true statement entails that *at least one thing exists* that either is, or is not, A. But this would seem to be an extraordinary consequence— that it is *necessarily true* that at least one thing exists! Has it or has it not been established by this tree that, necessarily, at least one thing exists? Discuss.

6.6   Generalized Soundness, Completeness, and Undecidability

We have now completed the presentation of the language L, together with the truth tree method for L. It is therefore a good time to step back and review the central theoretical properties of SL, L_m, and L and their respective deduction systems and decision procedures. In Sections 3.11 and 6.5, we discussed the soundness, completeness, and effectiveness of the tree method. In addition, if you have studied the material in Section 4.7 concerning natural deduction systems, you have also encountered a discussion of the soundness and completeness of natural deduction systems.

In those previous sections we discussed these theoretical properties in the context of the adequacy of particular deduction systems, but here we would like to talk about them on a more abstract level. Rather than talking about the soundness, completeness, and effectiveness of a particular deduction system or decision procedure, we will talk more generally about these conditions as they apply to any deduction system or decision procedure. For instance, rather than talking about the soundness of the tree method for L, we wish to talk about the soundness of a deduction system for L in general. To do this, we require a few more definitions.

First ,we must formally define the notions of soundness and completeness for an arbitrary deduction system $\mathcal{D}$ for a logical language $\mathcal{L}$ and of the soundness and completeness of a language itself:[8]

---

[8]In the context of these definitions, we take a logical truth of a language $\mathcal{L}$ to be a statement that is true under any interpretation of the nonlogical symbols of $\mathcal{L}$.

Definition A deduction system $\mathcal{D}$ for a language $\mathcal{L}$ is **sound** if, and only if, every theorem of that deduction system is a logical truth of $\mathcal{L}$.

Definition A deduction system $\mathcal{D}$ for a language $\mathcal{L}$ is **complete** if, and only if, every logical truth of $\mathcal{L}$ is a $\mathcal{D}$ theorem.

Definition A language $\mathcal{L}$ is **sound and complete** if, and only if, there exists a deduction system for $\mathcal{L}$ that is both sound and complete.[9]

Next, we have the following definitions related to an arbitrary decision procedure P and language $\mathcal{L}$:

Definition A decision procedure P for a set of statements S of language $\mathcal{L}$ is **effective** if, and only if, for any statement p of $\mathcal{L}$, P determines within a finite number of steps whether or not p is a member of S.

Definition A set of statements of language $\mathcal{L}$ is **decidable** if, and only if, there exists an effective decision procedure for that set.

Definition A language $\mathcal{L}$ is **decidable** if, and only if, the set of logical truths of $\mathcal{L}$ is a decidable set.

With these definitions in hand, we are in a position to concisely summarize the most important metatheoretical results regarding the various languages we have introduced:

LANGUAGE	SOUND AND COMPLETE	DECIDABLE
SL	Yes	Yes
L_m	Yes	Yes
L	Yes	No

The five 'yes' entries in this table summarize the positive results of our previous discussions of the adequacy of the tree method. The soundness and completeness of SL, L_m, and L follow from the existence of sound and complete deduction

---

[9]Notice that for a language $\mathcal{L}$ to be sound and complete we need to have a single deduction system that is both sound and complete. Trivially, for any language we can construct (1) a sound but incomplete deduction system where no statement is a theorem and (2) a complete but unsound deduction system where every statement is a theorem.

systems for these languages. We also have these in, respectively, T_{SL}, T_{L_m}, and T_L, as well as in the natural deduction systems presented in Chapters 4 and 7.

In the remainder of our discussion we concentrate on the negative result in the bottom right corner of our table. The undecidability of L was discovered, more or less simultaneously in the 1930s, by two eminent mathematical logicians, Alonzo Church and Alan Turing. Their result is generally referred to as the 'Church–Turing Undecidability Theorem':

> ***Theorem*** (Church–Turing) The set of logical truths of L is undecidable.

Though this theorem has been stated with respect to the concept of logical truth, it implies (via the various propositions we have discussed relating logical truth to other semantic concepts like consistency and validity) that the set of consistent sets of statements is undecidable, as is the set of valid arguments, and the like.

It was shown in Sections 6.4 and 6.5 that our best candidate for a decision procedure for L, TD_L, is not effective. But the Church–Turing Undecidability Theorem is a much stronger and more striking result. It implies the noneffectiveness of TD_L, but the noneffectiveness of TD_L (or of any other particular decision procedure) does not imply the truth of the Church–Turing Undecidability Theorem. This is because, in terms of its logical form, the Church–Turing Theorem is a universal generalization. It says something about *all possible* decision procedures. We might put the theorem in Loglish as follows:

> For all x, if x is a decision procedure, then there is some statement y whose status as a logical truth cannot be decided by x.

How could we prove this without explicitly checking all possible decision procedures, of which there must be infinitely many?

Before answering this question, we need to make the notion of a decision procedure more precise. It is in fact impossible to make a general statement about all decision procedures without such a characterization. We have sometimes said that a decision procedure must be *mechanical,* by which we mean that a computer or other machine is able to execute the procedure. But how do we spell this out more precisely?

The standard technique of spelling this out is to refer to a very simple but powerful kind of computer called a Turing machine. A Turing machine is very much like an ordinary digital computer, except that (1) the set of instructions one can use to program it are exceedingly simple and (2) it has an unlimited amount of memory. One can prove fairly easily that Turing machines can execute any program that any standard digital computer (like a Macintosh or an IBM PC) can execute. Furthermore, a variety of theoretical results shows that many mathematical functions that can be calculated by diverse methods can be calculated by a Turing machine.[10] The fact that we cannot conceive of any sort of decision procedure that cannot be implemented by a Turing machine suggests the plausibility of the following conjecture, known as Church's Thesis:

> **Church's Thesis**   Any effective decision procedure can be implemented by a Turing machine.

Because the notion of a decision procedure is vague and open-ended, Church's thesis is not susceptible to proof. Nonetheless, most philosophers, logicians, mathematicians, and computer scientists believe it to be true, at least given any reasonable definition of a decision procedure.

The vagueness of the concept of a decision procedure makes it impossible to formulate technically rigorous proofs of results that apply to every possible decision procedure. Consequently, the strategy logicians use to study decision procedures is to prove theorems about 'Turing decision procedures'—that is, decision procedures implemented by Turing machines. Logicians say that a set is Turing decidable if, and only if, membership in that set can be effectively decided by a Turing decision procedure.

Thus, a more precise formulation of the Church–Turing Theorem, which does not depend upon Church's Thesis, is this:

> **Theorem**   (Church–Turing, careful version) The set of logical truths of *L* is not Turing decidable.

If Church's thesis is correct, then every decidable set is Turing decidable, so we can replace 'Turing decidable' with 'decidable'.

Even after we have made the notion of a Turing machine precise, it is still not at all obvious how one might prove the Church–Turing Theorem. After all, there are an infinite number of programs that can be run by a Turing machine, and we cannot check each of them for effectiveness. Proving this theorem is one of the central tasks of a second course in symbolic logic. We will make only a single suggestion about how the proof goes. As noted, if a tree has an infinite branch, then the statement(s) that the tree began with are consistent. Suppose we could modify an algorithm (i.e., a complete set of instructions) for mechanical tree construction in such a way that it could detect ahead of time, for any given statement, whether

---

[10]For an excellent introduction to Turing machines, computability, and decision procedures, see George Boolos & Richard Jeffrey's *Computability and Logic* or Jeffrey's *Formal Logic* (see Appendix 1). In addition, the computer program Turing's World, by Jon Barwise and his colleagues, allows one to construct Turing machines to solve various computational problems.

a tree would go on forever along an infinite branch. We could then use the modified algorithm as a decision procedure. Any time a tree beginning with a negated statement ~*p* is determined to potentially contain such a branch, we could conclude that the original statement *p* is not a logical truth. But it can be shown that the kinds of Turing machines that could be used as decision procedures cannot decide for all possible inputs whether or not they are going to get caught in an infinite loop.[11]

Exercises for Section 6.6

Part I   Using the symbol key below, symbolize the following metatheoretical results.

$\mathcal{D}$:	statements, languages, deduction systems, and decision procedures
Sxy:	x is a statement of language y
Lxy:	x is a logical truth of language y
Txy:	x is a theorem of deduction system y
Dxy:	decision procedure y terminates in a finite time with an answer about whether statement x is a logical truth

a:	T_{SL}
b:	TD_{SL}
c:	D_{SL} (the natural deduction system for *SL*, presented in Chapter 4)
d:	T_L
e:	TD_L
f:	the tree decision procedure for *L* that uses Rule E rather than Rule E★
s:	*SL*
m:	L_m
r:	*L*
h:	second-order logic[12]

---

[11]For a proof of this theorem, see Boolos and Jeffrey, or Jeffrey (see Appendix 1).

[12]Second-order logic is an extension of *L* in which quantifiers are allowed to range over predicates as well as individuals. It is briefly discussed in Chapter 9.

1. The deduction system D_{SL} is complete (for *SL*).
2. The truth tree deduction system T_{SL} is sound (for *SL*).
♦ 3. The original tree decision procedure that does not use E⋆ is not effective for either L_m or *L*.
4. TD_L is an effective decision procedure for L_m, but not for *L*.
♦ 5. L_m is complete and decidable
6. *L* is undecidable (Church–Turing Undecidability Theorem).
7. Second-order logic is incomplete.

Part II

8. Symbolize in *L* the three definitions related to soundness and completeness that occur at the beginning of this section. Make sure to write out a complete symbol key. (*Hint:* As a first step in symbolizing the first definition, paraphrase the definition as follows: 'For all x and y, if x is a deduction system and y is a language, then . . .')
9. Symbolize in *L* the three definitions related to decision procedures and decidability that occur at the beginning of this section. Make sure to write out a complete symbol key. (*Hint:* As a first step in symbolizing the first definition, paraphrase the definition as follows: 'For all x, y, and z, if x is a decision procedure and y is a set of statements of language z, then . . .')

CHAPTER SEVEN
Predicate Logic III: Syntactic Methods

7.1   Introduction

In this chapter the system of natural deduction D_{SL} is extended to handle arguments in the language L. This extended deduction system we will call 'D_L'.[1] As with all of the items previously presented involving formal aspects of the language L, the system of proof for L is somewhat more involved than the SL case. The main additions are rules to deal with quantifiers. These rules allow one to move from quantified statements to nonquantified statements and back. In general, proof strategy involves the application of quantifier rules in order to remove quantifiers so that statements may be manipulated with the rules for statement logic. Under appropriate conditions, quantifiers may then be reintroduced.

7.2   The Rules UI, EG, and Q

We begin with the two simplest rules:

---

[1]Since we are treating D_L as a different deduction system than D_{SL}, we should, strictly speaking, offer new definitions of the terms 'D_L proof' and 'finished D_L proof'. These are obtained from our definitions in Chapter 4 by replacing all occurrences of 'SL' by 'L'.

> **Universal Instantiation (UI)** If a statement of the form $\forall \alpha p$ occurs as line n in a proof, then the instance $p\alpha/\beta$ may be added as a new line of the proof for any constant term β. As a justification for the line, put 'n UI'.
>
> **Existential Generalization (EG)** If a statement of the form $p\alpha/\beta$ occurs as line n in a proof, where β is any constant term, then the statement $\exists \alpha p$ may be added as a new line of the proof. As a justification for the line, put 'n EG'.

In schematic form:

> **Universal Instantiation (UI)** $\qquad \forall \alpha p$
> $$\therefore p\alpha/\beta$$
>
> **Existential Generalization (EG)** $\quad p\alpha/\beta$
> $$\therefore \exists \alpha p$$

The justifications of these rules are intuitively straightforward. Clearly, if a universal statement is true, then so is every substitution instance of the statement, so UI is a sound inference rule. Similarly, if a statement involving some particular named individual is true, then so must be the statement obtained by replacing that particular name with the generic "something," which is the effect of EG.

A proof for the following argument gives us an example of UI in use:

$$\forall x(Ax \rightarrow Gx)$$
$$Ah$$
$$\therefore Gh$$

As always, a proof begins by listing the premises of the argument:

1.	$\forall x(Ax \rightarrow Gx)$	PR
2.	Ah	PR

Applying UI to line 1 produces

1.	$\forall x(Ax \rightarrow Gx)$		PR
2.	Ah		PR
3.	Ah $\rightarrow$ Gh	1	UI

At this point, we simply return to the rules of natural deduction for statement logic, all of which carry over here. They may be applied to any statements in the same way they were applied in Chapter 4. Hence, we derive the desired conclusion:

1.	$\forall x(Ax \rightarrow Gx)$		PR
2.	Ah		PR
3.	Ah $\rightarrow$ Gh	1	UI
4.	Gh	2, 3	MP

Next, consider an argument that uses EG. Let's construct a proof for the following argument:

> If anyone likes baseball, Rachel does
> Angela likes baseball
> _____
> ∴ Rachel likes baseball.

Symbolizing, with an obvious interpretation, we obtain

> $\exists xLx \rightarrow Lr$
> La
> _____
> ∴ Lr

The proof starts in the usual way:

| 1. | $\exists xLx \rightarrow Lr$ | | PR |
| 2. | La | | PR |

It is surely a good inference that if Angela likes baseball, then *someone* likes baseball. It is just this inference that EG lets us make: '$p\alpha/\beta$' represents a statement containing the constant β in place of the variable α in the formula p. In other words, $p\alpha/\beta$ is an *instance* of $\exists \alpha p$. EG allows us to infer *from* the instance *back* to the existential quantification:

1.	$\exists xLx \rightarrow Lr$		PR
2.	La		PR
3.	$\exists xLx$	2	EG

The proof is completed by again drawing on our collection of *SL* rules:

1.	$\exists xLx \rightarrow Lr$		PR
2.	La		PR
3.	$\exists xLx$	2	EG
4.	Lr	1, 3	MP

The final rule introduced in this section is the Rule Q, for 'Quantifier Exchange'. It allows us to manipulate statements involving negated quantifiers.

> **Quantifier Exchange (Q)**   If a statement of any one of the following forms appears as a line in a proof, then the statement form directly across from it may be added as a new line of the proof:
>
> 1. ~∃αp   ∀α~p } "push in
> 2. ~∀αp   ∃α~p } push out
> 3. ~∃α~p   ∀αp   } Double
> 4. ~∀α~p   ∃αp   } Negation "

As an object-language example of the above forms, let '*p*' be the formula 'Ax' and let '*α*' be the variable 'x', which yields the following four pairs of exchangeable statements:

~∃xAx   ∀x~Ax
~∀xAx   ∃x~Ax
~∃x~Ax   ∀xAx
~∀x~Ax   ∃xAx.

Rule Q tells us, in effect, that the top left statement, 'There is nothing that is an A', is equivalent to the top right statement, 'Everything is a non-A'; that the next statement on the left, 'Not everything is an A', is equivalent to 'There is at least one non-A'; and so on, for the remaining statements.

The next example employs all three rules introduced in this section. A proof is given for the following argument:

~∃xAx
∀x~Bx → As
(∃xBx ∨ ∃xCx) → (Cb & ∀yRy)
∴ ∃xCx

The premises are listed first:

1.   ~∃xAx   PR
2.   ∀x~Bx → As   PR
3.   (∃xBx ∨ ∃xCx) → (Cb & ∀yRy)   PR

Applying Q to line 1 produces

4.   ∀x~Ax   1   Q

This in turn lets us apply UI to line 4, followed by MT:

5. ~As	4	UI
6. ~∀x~Bx	2, 5	MT

By Q, we derive from line 6,

7. ∃xBx	6	Q

Next, we need to derive the disjunction that is the antecedent of the third premise. To do so we use a reductio argument:

8. ~(∃xBx ∨ ∃xCx)		PA–RAA
9. ~∃xBx & ~∃xCx	8	DeM
10. ~∃xBx	9	CE
11. ∃xBx & ~∃xBx	7, 10	CI
12. ∃xBx ∨ ∃xCx	8–11	RAA

To complete the proof we use MP, CE, and EG. Here is the proof in its entirety:

1. ~∃xAx		PR
2. ∀x~Bx → As		PR
3. (∃xBx ∨ ∃xCx) → (Cb & ∀yRy)		PR
4. ∀x~Ax	1	Q
5. ~As	4	UI
6. ~∀x~Bx	2, 5	MT
7. ∃xBx	6	Q
8. ~(∃xBx ∨ ∃xCx)		PA–RAA
9. ~∃xBx & ~∃xCx	8	DeM
10. ~∃xBx	9	CE
11. ∃xBx & ~∃xBx	7, 10	CI
12. ∃xBx ∨ ∃xCx	8–11	RAA
13. Cb & ∀yRy	3, 12	MP
14. Cb	13	CE
15. ∃xCx	14	EG

Here is a final example for this section that involves polyadic predicate symbols:

∀x∀y(Rxy → Lyx)
~∃xLxa
∴ ∃x~Rxa

We use RAA:

1. ∀x∀y(Rxy → Lyx)		PR
2. ~∃xLxa		PR
3. ~∃x~Rxa		PA–RAA

Next, apply rule Q:

4.	∀x~~Rxa	3	Q
5.	∀x~Lxa	2	Q

Now, let's work with the statement on line 1. To apply UI, we must work inward from the outermost quantifier; that is, we *cannot* instantiate with respect to 'y' unless we have first instantiated with respect to 'x'. Since 'a' occurs in line 3, it is useful to instantiate with respect to 'x' using 'a':

6.	∀y(Ray → Lya)	1	UI

Let's do the same thing for 'y' and for 'x' in lines 4 and 5:

7.	Raa → Laa	6	UI
8.	~~Raa	4	UI
9.	~Laa	5	UI

By DN, MP, and CI, we derive

10.	Raa	8	DN
11.	Laa	7, 10	MP
12.	Laa & ~Laa	9, 11	CI

The proof is completed by RAA:

1.	∀x∀y(Rxy → Lyx)		PR
2.	~∃xLxa		PR
3.	~∃x~Rxa		PA-RAA
4.	∀x~~Rxa	3	Q
5.	∀x~Lxa	2	Q
6.	∀y(Ray → Lya)	1	UI
7.	Raa → Laa	6	UI
8.	~~Raa	4	UI
9.	~Laa	5	UI
10.	Raa	8	DN
11.	Laa	7, 10	MP
12.	Laa & ~Laa	9, 11	CI
13.	∃x~Rxa	3–12	RAA

Exercises for Section 7.2

Part I: Monadic Arguments   Give formal proofs in D_L for each of the following arguments, which do not include polyadic predicate symbols.

1. $\forall x Wx$ & $\forall y Yy$ /∴ $\exists x(Wx \lor Yx)$

2. $\forall x(Ax$ & $Bx)$ /∴ $\exists x Ax$ & $\exists x Bx$

♦3. $\forall x(Fx \rightarrow Gx)$, $\sim\exists x Gx$ /∴ $\sim\forall x Fx$

4. $\forall x(Ax \lor Bx)$, $\forall x(Ax \rightarrow \sim Bx)$ /∴ $\forall x(Ax \leftrightarrow \sim Bx)$

5. $Pr \rightarrow Qr$, $\forall x[\exists y Ry \rightarrow Px]$, Ra /∴ Qr

6. $\forall x(Sx \rightarrow Tx)$, $\exists x\sim Sx \rightarrow (\forall x Tx \lor Rr)$, $\sim Ta$ /∴ $\exists x Rx$

♦7. $\forall x(Fx \rightarrow Gx)$, $\forall x(Gx \rightarrow Jx)$ /∴ $\exists x(Fx \rightarrow Jx)$

8. $\exists x\sim Bx \rightarrow \exists x\sim Cx$ /∴ $\forall x Cx \rightarrow \forall x Bx$

9. $Aa \lor \sim\forall x Bx$ /∴ $Aa \lor \exists x\sim Bx$

10. $Aa \lor \sim\forall x Bx$ /∴ $\exists y\exists x(Bx \rightarrow Ay)$ $\exists y \exists x (\sim Bx \lor Ay)$

11. $\forall x\sim Bx \rightarrow \forall x\sim Ax$, $\exists x Ax$ /∴ $\exists x Bx$

12. $\forall x[(Ax \lor Bx) \rightarrow Cx]$, $\sim(Ca \lor Cb)$, $\forall x[\sim(Aa \lor Bb) \rightarrow Hx]$ /∴ Hc

♦13. $\forall x\forall y\forall z[((Px$ & $Qy)$ & $Rz) \rightarrow Sx]$, $\sim St$ /∴ $Rt \rightarrow (Qt \rightarrow \sim Pt)$

14. $\forall x(Fx \rightarrow \forall y Gy)$, $\sim\exists x\sim Fx$, $\forall x(Hx \lor \sim Gx)$ /∴ $\exists x Hx$

15. $\forall x\sim(Ax \lor Bx)$, $\sim(Aa \lor Bb) \rightarrow \forall z(Cz \rightarrow Bz)$ /∴ $\sim(Ca \lor Cb)$

Part II: Polyadic Arguments   Give formal proofs in D_L for each of the following arguments, all of which include polyadic predicate symbols.

16. $\forall x\forall y Rxy$ /∴ $\exists y\exists x Rxy$

17. $\forall x\forall y(Axy \rightarrow \sim Ayx)$ /∴ $\exists x\exists y\sim Axy$

18. Ga, $\forall y(\exists x Gx \rightarrow Hby)$ /∴ $\exists x Hxb$

19. $\forall x\forall y\forall z[(Kxy$ & $Kyz) \rightarrow Kxz]$, Kab & Kbc /∴ $\exists x(Kax$ & $Kbx)$

20. $\sim\exists x\exists y(Gxy$ & $Lxy)$, Gab /∴ $\sim Lab$

♦21. $\forall x(\exists y Fxy \rightarrow \forall z\sim Gzx)$, $\forall x Fxa$, $\forall x\forall y(Hxy \lor Gxa)$ /∴ $\exists x\exists y Hxy$

22. $\forall x\forall y[Kxy \rightarrow \forall z(Lz \leftrightarrow \exists u Mu)]$, Kab & Ma /∴ $\exists x Lx$

23. $\forall x(Axa \lor Bbx)$ /∴ $\exists x\exists y Axy \lor \exists u\exists z Buz$

24. $\sim\exists x\exists y(Axy \lor \sim Axy) \lor \forall x(\exists y Bxy \lor (Cx$ & $\sim Cx))$ /∴ $\exists y Bay$

25. $\forall x\forall y\forall z(Axy \rightarrow Bxz)$, $\forall x\forall y\forall z(Bxy \rightarrow Cxz)$ /∴ $Aab \rightarrow \exists x\exists y Cxy$

7.3   The Rules UG, R, PA-EI, and EI

The Rule UI allows us to move from universal statements to particular statements, and the Rule EG allows us to move from particular statements to existential statements. To complete our system we must now add rules that let us move from particular statements to universal statements and from existential statements to particular statements. These rules are somewhat trickier than UI and EG, because in general it is not sound to infer a general statement like '∀xPx' from a particular statement like 'Pa', nor to infer a particular statement like 'Pa' from an existential statement like '∃xPx'. Under special conditions, described below, such inferences will be warranted.

The statement of our rules requires use of the concept of a provisional assumption, which we introduced in Chapter 4. Recall that when a rule is used that introduces a provisional assumption (either PA-CP or PA-RAA), that provisional assumption must be *discharged* at some later line by a corresponding rule (either CP or RAA). In this section we introduce one additional rule that can be used to introduce a provisional assumption, PA-EI, and another rule to discharge it, EI. We first provide some helpful terminology.

If a line occurs after the introduction of a provisional assumption but before the provisional assumption has been discharged, we say that the line is *covered* by the provisional assumption. More formally,

> **Definition** A provisional assumption on a line j is said to **cover** a statement on a line *k* if, and only if (1) *k* ≥ *j* and (2) the assumption on line *j* has not been discharged at line *k* or earlier.

Pictorially, a provisional assumption is discharged by the line immediately below the partial box containing a subproof, and all lines within the box are said to be covered by the provisional assumption that is on the first line within the box. As an example,

1.	~∀xAx → G		PR
2.	(∃x~Ax → G) → H		PR
3.	∃x~Ax		PA-CP
4.	~∀xAx	3	Q
5.	G	1, 4	MP
6.	∃x~Ax → G	3–5	CP
7.	H	2, 6	MP

The provisional assumption on line 3 covers lines 3–5 and is discharged on line 6. When a provisional assumption has been discharged, it means that no statements on or after the discharge line depend logically on the provisional assumption, but depend at most only on the premises of the argument and any provisional assumptions that might still be covering them.

With this terminology in hand, the last three quantifier rules can be stated. We begin with UG:

> ***Universal Generalization (UG)***   If a statement $p\alpha/\beta$ occurs on line m of a proof, where α is a variable and β is an individual constant, then the statement $\forall\alpha p$ may be added as a new line of the proof *provided that* (1) β does not occur in $\forall\alpha p$, (2) β does not occur in any premise, and (3) β does not occur in any provisional assumption covering line m.

Schematically,

$$\frac{p\alpha/\beta}{\therefore \ \forall\alpha p}$$

In general, of course, it is *incorrect* to infer a universal generalization from a specific case, as the following example illustrates:

$$\frac{\text{Edward likes snakes}}{\therefore \ \text{Everyone likes snakes.}}$$

Nevertheless, there do exist cases in which reasoning *like* this is perfectly acceptable. In particular, if one can show that some predicate—say, P—holds for any *arbitrarily* selected individual of a certain kind—say, a—then under those circumstances it would be legitimate to infer '$\forall x Px$'. The three restrictions in the statement of Rule UG ensure that the inference from $p\alpha/\beta$ to $\forall\alpha p$ is of this kind and hence that UG is a sound rule of inference.

An informal example of such reasoning is the following. Suppose we wish to argue for this conclusion: All *SL* statements, built strictly according to the given formation rules, always contain twice as many parentheses as the number of their two-place connectives. The rigorous proof of this conclusion is somewhat more involved than the following, but it *roughly* goes like this:

1. Let p stand for any *SL* statement at all. Assume only that it has been built strictly according to the *SL* formation rules of Chapter 2.
2. If p is a statement letter, or a negated statement letter, then it contains zero two-place connectives. Hence, p contains twice as many parentheses as the number of its two-place connectives (viz., $2 \times 0 = 0$).
3. Suppose next that p is the result of putting together simpler components. We note that *each time* two *SL* statements are combined using a two-place connective, a pair of parentheses is introduced around the whole string of symbols. If two statement letters (or negated statement letters, or some combination of the two) are put together in this way, with one two-place

connective, we add two parentheses; if the resulting statement is joined with another using a two-place connective, we get two two-place connectives and *four* parentheses in all, and so on.

4. Thus, *p* will have to contain twice as many parentheses as the number of its two-place connectives.

5. Now, *p* was assumed to be just *any SL statement at all*. Thus, the result holds quite generally: All *SL* statements, built strictly according to the given formation rules, always contain twice as many parentheses as the number of their two-place connectives.

More formally, suppose 'Sx' stands for 'x is an *SL* statement built strictly according to the given formation rules' and 'Tx' stands for 'x contains twice as many parentheses as the number of two-place connectives it contains'. The reasoning above can then be given in outline as

1.	S*p*	(We assume that '*p*' names any statement at all having property S.)
	.	
	.	
	.	
4.	T*p*	(Derived based only on the assumption that *p* has property S—but *not* based on any other assumptions about *p* in particular.)
5.	∀xTx	4, UG

To illustrate, here is an argument followed by a proof of it using UG:

∀x(Ax & Bx)
―――――――――
∴ ∀xAx & ∀xBx

We list the premise, then use UI and CE:

1.	∀x(Ax & Bx)		PR
2.	Aa & Ba	1	UI
3.	Aa	2	CE
4.	Ba	2	CE

We need to derive the statements '∀xAx' and '∀xBx' from lines 3 and 4 by UG. To use UG in either of these cases, the three conditions in the rule must be met. First, 'a' must not occur in any premise. Second, 'a' must not occur in the statements resulting from the rule's application (here, '∀xAx' and '∀xBx'). Finally, the resulting statement must not be covered by any provisional assumptions containing 'a'. Since these conditions are all met, we may use UG. Here is the completed proof:

1.	$\forall$x(Ax & Bx)		PR
2.	Aa & Ba	1	UI
3.	Aa	2	CE
4.	Ba	2	CE
5.	$\forall$xAx	3	UG
6.	$\forall$xBx	4	UG
7.	$\forall$xAx & $\forall$xBx	5, 6	CI

Notice that the constant that was generalized upon was originally introduced by UI. This is entirely typical. UG stipulates that the constant to be generalized must not occur in any premise nor undischarged provisional assumption. One way that you can introduce such a constant is by UI, and since, with UI, we could have chosen any constant, we see that the choice of that constant was arbitrary, and thus that the subsequent generalization is justified. The only other way you can introduce a new constant into a proof is by introducing it in a provisional assumption. In most cases the constant in the provisional assumption will not appear in the conclusion of the line that discharges that assumption, but if it does the constant will prove to be arbitrary.

Finally, we turn to rules for making inferences from existentially quantified statements. The need for such rules is illustrated by considering the following argument:

> Some number is even
> All even numbers are divisible by two
> ---
> ∴ Some number is divisible by two.

This argument is clearly valid (and sound), but how do we prove this? Informally, we must argue something like this: "From our first premise we know that some (i.e., at least one) number is even. We don't know what number it is, but let's call it something, say, '*a*'. Now from our second premise we can infer that if *a* is even, then it is divisible by two. So, by modus ponens we may infer that *a* is divisible by two. And if *a* is divisible by two, then clearly (by existential generalization) there exists some number that is divisible by two." The key step in this proof is the temporary assignment of an arbitrary constant to an individual that we know must exist, in light of the existential first premise. As long as we assume nothing about the named individual besides what can be inferred from the existential statement, our inferences will not be unsound.

In D_L we formalize this pattern of reasoning by a proof method called *existential instantiation*. The method uses two rules, and it is very similar in structure to the methods of conditional proof and reductio ad absurdum.

Before stating this method, however, it will be especially convenient to pause and introduce a rule to the D_{SL} basis of our system:

> **Immediate Reductio (R)** p
>
> $$\frac{\sim p}{\therefore q}$$

Since the effect of this rule can already be achieved with the existing rules of D_{SL}, it is not essential to the construction of a complete deduction system for D_L.[2] However, its addition will make proofs using existential instantiation significantly less cumbersome. It may therefore be used from now on.

Here is the method:

> **Method of Existential Instantiation** Suppose the statement $\exists \alpha p$ occurs as line k of a proof. One may proceed by completing *all* the following steps:
>
> 1. $p\alpha/\beta$ may be entered as a new line of the proof—say, on line m—with the notation 'k PA-EI' for 'Provisional Assumption for Existential Instantiation of line k'. The individual constant β must be one that has appeared *in no statement before line m*, including the statement $\exists \alpha p$ itself. Line m is indented to the right to indicate the beginning of a subproof.
>
> 2. Proceed with the proof until the statement q, not containing β, occurs, say, on line n. These lines are indented to the right to the same degree as line m.
>
> 3. The statement q may then be added on line $n + 1$ with the justification 'm–n EI', meaning 'from lines m through n by Existential Instantiation'. This line should be moved back to the left so that it is indented to the same degree as the line immediately preceding line m. The provisional assumption is said to be **discharged** at line $n + 1$.
>
> 4. A partial box is placed around lines m through n, indicating that these lines are sealed off and may not be used to justify subsequent inferences in the proof.

The following illustrative schema should be familiar to you by now, reminiscent as it is of CP and RAA proofs:

---

[2]Recall from Section 4.7 that a deduction system is (weakly) complete if, and only if, every logical truth is a theorem.

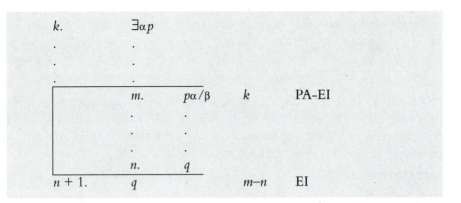

As an example of the use of this strategy, let's prove the validity of the argument we just proved informally above. Using a natural symbolization we get

$\exists x E x$
$\underline{\forall x(E x \rightarrow D x)}$
$\therefore \exists x D x$

We begin with the premises and apply PA-EI to line 1:

1.	$\exists x E x$		PR
2.	$\forall x(E x \rightarrow D x)$		PR
3.	Ea	1	PA-EI

Note that line 3 is indeed an *assumption;* it is *not* a logical consequence of line 1. However, to justify the presence of this provisional assumption, our rule requires that an existentially quantified statement appear on an earlier line. This is why we include a line number in the justification column indicating 'PA-EI'. Next, applying UI, MP, and EG,

4.	Ea $\rightarrow$ Da	2	UI
5.	Da	3, 4	MP
6.	$\exists x D x$	5	EG

The constant 'a' was new to the proof when it appeared in line 3, and on line 6 we have a statement that does not contain the constant 'a'. We may therefore discharge the assumption made on line 3:

1.	$\exists x E x$		PR
2.	$\forall x(E x \rightarrow D x)$		PR
3.	Ea	1	PA-EI
4.	Ea $\rightarrow$ Da	2	UI
5.	Da	3, 4	MP
6.	$\exists x D x$	5	EG
7.	$\exists x D x$	3–6	EI

As with the two proof methods CP and RAA in D_{SL}, the existential instantiation method requires the use of two paired rules. Here is their formal statement:

> **Provisional Assumption for Existential Instantiation (PA-EI)**   The statement $p\alpha/\beta$ may be entered on a new line m of a proof if (1) a statement $\exists\alpha p$ occurs on an earlier line k and (2) the individual constant β occurs nowhere in the proof prior to line m. Line m and the lines following it are shifted to the right, until the assumption has been discharged. As justification for line m, put 'k PA-EI'.
>
> **Existential Instantiation (EI)**   A statement q may be entered on line $n + 1$ of a proof if (1) a statement $p\alpha/\beta$ occurs on line m with the justification 'k PA-EI', (2) the statement q occurs on line n of the proof and does not contain the individual constant β, and (3) no further undischarged provisional assumptions have been introduced between m and n. Line $n + 1$ and subsequent lines are shifted to the left, and lines m through n are enclosed in a partial box. As a justification for line $n + 1$, put 'm–n EI'. Line $n + 1$ discharges the assumption on line m.

In condition (1) of the PA-EI rule, it should of course be understood that when it said that $\exists\alpha p$ must occur on an earlier line k, that occurrence is *outside* any earlier boxed subproof; that is, a provisional assumption might be covering line k, but line k must not be contained in a *finished* subproof.

This completes the rules for the deduction system D_L. The next example uses UI, EI, RAA, and R, the last of which we have not used so far. We give a proof for the following argument:

$$\frac{\exists x(Ax \vee Bx)}{\therefore \; \exists xAx \vee \exists xBx}$$

We begin a proof for this argument by making some fairly routine moves:

1.	$\exists x(Ax \vee Bx)$		PR
2.	$\sim[\exists xAx \vee \exists xBx]$		PA-RAA
3.	$\sim\exists xAx \;\&\; \sim\exists xBx$	2	DeM
4.	$\sim\exists xAx$	3	CE
5.	$\sim\exists xBx$	3	CE
6.	$\forall x\sim Ax$	4	Q
7.	$\forall x\sim Bx$	5	Q

At this stage there are a couple of good ways to go. We *could* apply UI to lines 6 and 7, and then eventually use UG on the way to obtaining the desired conclusion. Here, let's instead have another look at the EI strategy:

8.	Aa ∨ Ba	1	PA-EI
9.	~Aa	6	UI
10.	~Ba	7	UI

Notice that, if we had *first* used UI, we would have had to choose a new constant for the EI provisional assumption. Then, to use UI, we would have had to go back to lines 6 and 7 and instantiate with the new constant. Making the EI assumption first saves us two steps. Continuing on,

11.	~Aa & ~Ba	9, 10	CI
12.	~(Aa ∨ Ba)	11	DeM

Now, you may think that here we should simply put lines 8 and 12 in conjunction, for then we would have a contradiction. Well, yes, we would; however, the contradiction would *still* be covered by the EI assumption on line 8. So, we would not be able to discharge the assumption to set the contradiction on its own, since the constant 'a' appears in it. This is where our rule R comes in handy. From any statements *p* and *~p*, we may derive *anything we please* as a new line:

13.	P & ~P	8, 12	R

On line 8 is our *p*, on line 12 is *~p*, and on line 13 is our new line *q*. This "logician's trick" allows us to avoid the problem just described.[3] Pulling the whole proof together, here is what we have so far:

1.	∃x(Ax ∨ Bx)			PR
2.	~[∃xAx ∨ ∃xBx]			PA-RAA
3.	~∃xAx & ~∃xBx		2	DeM
4.	~∃xAx		3	CE
5.	~∃xBx		3	CE
6.	∀x~Ax		4	Q
7.	∀x~Bx		5	Q
8.		Aa ∨ Ba	1	PA-EI
9.		~Aa	6	UI
10.		~Ba	7	UI
11.		~Aa & ~Ba	9, 10	CI
12.		~(Aa ∨ Ba)	11	DeM
13.		P & ~P	8, 12	R

---

[3]Actually, of course, it's not a trick at all, just a nice convenience. We could do without Rule R and proceed to derive 'P & ~P' in a few extra steps if we had to.

Since 'a' does not occur in line 13, we may now discharge the EI assumption so that we create a situation in which 'P & ~P' depends on the provisional assumption for RAA:

1.	∃x(Ax ∨ Bx)		PR
2.	~[∃xAx ∨ ∃xBx]		PA-RAA
3.	~∃xAx & ~∃xBx	2	DeM
4.	~∃xAx	3	CE
5.	~∃xBx	3	CE
6.	∀x~Ax	4	Q
7.	∀x~Bx	5	Q
8.	Aa ∨ Ba	1	PA-EI
9.	~Aa	6	UI
10.	~Ba	7	UI
11.	~Aa & ~Ba	9, 10	CI
12.	~(Aa ∨ Ba)	11	DeM
13.	P & ~P	8, 12	R
14.	P & ~P	8–13	EI

The proof is then completed by discharging the RAA assumption:

1.	∃x(Ax ∨ Bx)		PR
2.	~[∃xAx ∨ ∃xBx]		PA-RAA
3.	~∃xAx & ~∃xBx	2	DeM
4.	~∃xAx	3	CE
5.	~∃xBx	3	CE
6.	∀x~Ax	4	Q
7.	∀x~Bx	5	Q
8.	Aa ∨ Ba	1	PA-EI
9.	~Aa	6	UI
10.	~Ba	7	UI
11.	~Aa & ~Ba	9, 10	CI
12.	~(Aa ∨ Ba)	11	DeM
13.	P & ~P	8, 12	R
14.	P & ~P	8–13	EI
15.	∃xAx ∨ ∃xBx	2–14	RAA

For your study, here is the same argument proved with the use of UG instead of EI:

1.	∃x(Ax ∨ Bx)		PR
2.	~[∃xAx ∨ ∃xBx]		PA-RAA
3.	~∃xAx & ~∃xBx	2	DeM
4.	~∃xAx	3	CE
5.	~∃xBx	3	CE
6.	∀x~Ax	4	Q
7.	∀x~Bx	5	Q
8.	Aa	6	UI
9.	~Ba	7	UI
10.	~Aa & ~Ba	8, 9	CI
11.	~(Aa ∨ Ba)	10	DeM
12.	∀x~(Ax ∨ Bx)	11	UG
13.	~∃x(Ax ∨ Bx)	12	Q
14.	P & ~P	1, 13	R
15.	∃xAx ∨ ∃xBx	2–14	RAA

You should inspect the proof carefully to see that the proper UG restrictions were met, ensuring the correctness of line 12.

Next is an example of a proof involving polyadic predicates:

∃x(Ax & ∀yBxy)
∴ ∃x∃yBxy

We will use the EI method for this proof:

1.	∃x(Ax & ∀yBxy)		PR
2.	Aa & ∀yBay	1	PA-EI
3.	∀yBay	2	CE
4.	Baa	3	UI
5.	∃yBay	4	EG
6.	∃x∃yBxy	5	EG
7.	∃x∃yBxy	2–6	EI

A couple of observations in connection with this proof should be made. First, notice the order in which Rule EG was applied: The inner quantifier, '∃y', was added *before* the outer quantifier, '∃x'. Rule EG allows us to infer a statement of the form ∃αp from the statement pα/β, where pα/β is the whole statement occupying the line on which it occurs. We are *not* allowed to move from ∃αp to ∃α∃γp. Similar remarks apply to Rule UG.

Second, notice that on line 4 we instantiated the universal quantification of line 3 by using the constant 'a'. We *could* have used 'b', to infer 'Bab' on line 4. If we had done this, the proof could still have been finished just as it has been above.

However, the following sequence of generalizations would *not* be permitted if we were using UG; that is, the following sequence of steps is *not* allowed:

n.	Baa		
n + 1.	∀yBay	*n*	UG
n + 2.	∀x∀yBxy	*n* + 1	UG

Recall that the first condition for the application of UG is that, in moving from *p*α/β to ∀α*p*, the individual constant β *must not occur* in ∀α*p*. Thus, if the use of UG were permitted on line *n* + 1, all occurrences of 'a' would have to be replaced by a variable, so the result would be, for example, '∀xBxx'.

To complete this section, we should point out that, just as in system D_{SL}, logical truths can be proved as theorems in system D_L. In D_{SL} the only logical truths that are provable are tautologies. Here, any *L* statement that is true under all interpretations—that is, any logical truth—is derivable from the empty set. As in system D_{SL}, proof of a logical truth requires that no premises appear in the proof, and so a proof begins with only one or more provisional assumptions. When a statement *p* is derived from the empty set in this way, we say that the statement *p* is a D_L **theorem**, denoted '⊢$_{D_L}$ *p*'. As a final example of a formal proof in system D_L, we prove the theorem '∀x(Ax → Bx) → (∀xAx → ∀xBx)':

1.	∀x(Ax → Bx)		PA-CP
2.	∀xAx		PA-CP
3.	Aa → Ba	1	UI
4.	Aa	2	UI
5.	Ba	3, 4	MP
6.	∀xBx	5	UG
7.	∀xAx → ∀xBx	2–6	CP
8.	∀x(Ax → Bx) → (∀xAx → ∀xBx)	1–7	CP

As you can see, just as with proofs of validity, the main difference between a proof of a D_{SL} theorem and a proof of a D_L theorem is in the use of additional rules for handling quantified statements. Note that for all statements *p*, if ⊢$_{D_{SL}}$ *p*, then ⊢$_{D_L}$ *p*.

Exercises for Section 7.3

Part I: Monadic Arguments   Give formal proofs in D_L for the following arguments, none of which contain polyadic predicate symbols. UG or EI will be needed to complete these proofs.

1. ∀x(Ax → Bx), ∀xAx /∴ ∀xBx
2. ∀x(Bx → Ax), ∃x(Bx & ~Cx) /∴ ∃x(Ax & ~Cx)
◆3. ∀x(Ax → ~Bx), ∀x(Cx → Ax) /∴ ∀x(Cx → ~Bx)

4. $\exists x(Ax \mathbin{\&} Bx), \exists x(Bx \mathbin{\&} Cx) \mathbin{/}\therefore \forall xAx \to \exists x(Ax \mathbin{\&} Cx)$

5. $\forall x(Ax \lor Bx), \forall x(Ax \to Cx), {\sim}\exists xCx \mathbin{/}\therefore \forall xBx$

6. $\forall x(S \to Bx) \mathbin{/}\therefore S \to \forall xBx$

7. $\exists x(Ax \to S) \mathbin{/}\therefore \forall xAx \to S$

8. $\forall x(Ax \to S) \mathbin{/}\therefore \exists xAx \to S$

9. $\exists x(S \to Ax) \mathbin{/}\therefore S \to \exists xAx$

10. $\forall xAx \mathbin{\&} \forall xBx \mathbin{/}\therefore \forall x(Ax \mathbin{\&} Bx)$

11. $\exists xFx \lor \exists xGx \mathbin{/}\therefore \exists x(Fx \lor Gx)$

12. $\forall x(Ax \to Bx), \forall x(Bx \to Cx) \mathbin{/}\therefore \forall x(Ax \to Cx)$

♦13. $\forall x(Fx \to Gx), \exists x{\sim}Gx \mathbin{/}\therefore \exists x{\sim}Fx$

14. $\forall x\exists y(Fx \mathbin{\&} Gy) \mathbin{/}\therefore \exists y\forall x(Fx \mathbin{\&} Gy)$

15. $\forall x\forall y(Fx \to Gy) \mathbin{/}\therefore \exists xFx \to \exists yGy$ $\sim ExFx \lor \exists y\,by$

16. $\forall x\forall y(Fx \to Gy) \mathbin{/}\therefore \forall y(\exists xFx \to Gy)$

17. $\forall x[(Ax \mathbin{\&} \forall yGy) \to \forall zRz] \mathbin{/}\therefore \exists y[(\exists xAx \mathbin{\&} Gy) \to \forall zRz]$

Part II: Polyadic Arguments   Give formal proofs in D_L for the following arguments, all of which contain polyadic predicate symbols. UG or EI will be needed to complete these proofs.

18. $\forall x[Px \leftrightarrow \exists y(Fxy \lor Mxy)], \exists xFax \mathbin{/}\therefore Pa$

19. $\forall x\forall y(Axy \to Axy) \to \forall x\forall yBxy \mathbin{/}\therefore \exists x\exists yBxy$

20. $\forall x\forall y(Axy \to Bxy), \exists x\exists y{\sim}Bxy \mathbin{/}\therefore \exists x\exists y{\sim}Axy$

21. $\forall x\forall y(Axy \to Bxy), \forall x\forall y{\sim}Bxy \mathbin{/}\therefore {\sim}\exists x\exists yBxy$

22. $Ba, {\sim}\forall x(Fxa \to \exists yBy) \lor \forall xFbx \mathbin{/}\therefore Ba \mathbin{\&} Fba$

23. $\exists x\exists y\exists z({\sim}Pxy \lor Qyz) \mathbin{/}\therefore \exists y(\exists x{\sim}Pxy \lor \exists zQyz)$

24. $\exists x\exists y(Axy \mathbin{\&} {\sim}Ayx), \forall x\forall y[(Axy \mathbin{\&} {\sim}Ayx) \to \exists zBxyz],$
    $\forall x\forall y\forall z(Cxy \leftrightarrow {\sim}Bxyz) \mathbin{/}\therefore {\sim}\forall x\forall yCxy$

♦25. $\exists x(\forall yAxy \mathbin{\&} (Bx \mathbin{\&} Cx)), \exists x\exists y(Axy \mathbin{\&} Cx) \to \forall x(Dx \leftrightarrow Cx)$
    $\mathbin{/}\therefore \exists x(Dx \mathbin{\&} Cx)$

26. $\forall x\forall y\forall z[(Ax \mathbin{\&} (Pyx \mathbin{\&} Czx)) \to (Vx \leftrightarrow {\sim}\exists u(Iu \mathbin{\&} (Tyu \mathbin{\&} {\sim}Tzu)))],$
    $Aa \mathbin{\&} \exists u[Iu \mathbin{\&} (Tbu \mathbin{\&} {\sim}Tcu)] \mathbin{/}\therefore (Pba \mathbin{\&} Cca) \to {\sim}Va$

27. $\forall x(Lcx \to {\sim}Lxx), \forall x[Lxx \to (Tx \lor Vx)], \forall x(Vx \to {\sim}Lcx)$
    $\mathbin{/}\therefore \forall x[(Vx \lor Lxx) \to ({\sim}Tx \to {\sim}Lcx)]$

Part III: Monadic Theorems   Give proofs in D_L for the following D_L theorems, none of which contain polyadic predicate symbols.

28. $\forall x(Ax \to Ax)$

29. $\forall x(Ax \lor \sim Ax)$

30. $\sim\exists x(Fx \;\&\; \sim Fx)$

31. $\exists x(\forall yFy \to Fx)$

32. $\forall x\exists y(Fy \to Fx)$

♦ 33. $\forall xFx \to \forall yFy$

34. $\sim\exists xBx \to \forall x(Bx \to Ax)$

35. $\forall x(Px \lor Qx) \lor \exists y(\sim Py \;\&\; Qy)$

36. $\exists x(Hx \;\&\; \sim Jx) \to \sim\forall x(Hx \to Jx)$

37. $[\forall x(Gx \to Hx) \;\&\; \forall x\sim Hx] \to \sim\exists zGz$

38. $[\exists xNx \;\&\; \exists xMx] \to [\forall xNx \to \exists x(Nx \;\&\; Mx)]$

♦ 39. $\forall x\exists y\forall z[(Ry \;\&\; \sim Ux) \to \sim Vz] \to [\exists zVz \to (\forall yRy \to \forall xUx)]$

40. $\forall x\exists y\forall z[Vz \to (Ry \to Ux)] \to [(\forall yRy \;\&\; \exists x\sim Ux) \to \forall z\sim Vz]$

41. $[\exists zVz \;\&\; (\forall yRy \;\&\; \exists x\sim Ux)] \to \exists x\forall y\exists z[Vz \;\&\; (Ry \;\&\; \sim Ux)]$

Part IV: Polyadic Theorems   Give proofs in D_L for the following D_L theorems, all of which contain polyadic predicate symbols.

42. $\sim\exists x\forall y(Axy \;\&\; \sim Axx)$

43. $\forall x\forall y\sim Hxy \lor \exists x\exists yHxy$

44. $\forall x\forall y\sim(Axy \to Ayx) \to \forall x\exists y\sim Axy$

♦ 45. $\forall x\forall y(\sim Axy \to Ayx) \to \forall xAxx$

46. $\forall x\forall y(Ay \to Bxy) \to \forall x(Ax \to \forall yByx)$

47. $\forall x\forall y(Axy \to \sim Ayx) \to \forall x\sim Axx$

48. $\forall x(\exists yAxy \to P) \to \forall y(\exists xAxy \to P)$

49. $(\forall x\sim\exists yHxy \;\&\; \forall y\sim\exists xHxy) \to \sim\exists x\exists yHxy$

50. $\exists x\exists y\exists z\exists u(Azy \to Bxu) \to (\forall z\forall yAzy \to \exists x\exists uBxu)$

51. $\forall x\forall y(Axy \to Bxy) \to [\exists xAax \to \exists z\exists u(Azu \;\&\; Bzu)]$

7.4   The Adequacy of D_L

As in Chapter 4, our emphasis in introducing a system of natural deduction is on proving the validity of arguments. But our system D_L, as with D_{SL}, can be used to prove that statements or sets of statements have additional semantic properties and relationships. We simply substitute the logical properties and relationships defined in Section 5.8 for the truth-functional properties and relationships defined in Sections 3.4 and 3.6.

In this context the same question arises for D_L as arose for D_{SL}—namely, whether D_L is adequate for proving claims about these properties and relationships. The basic requirements for adequacy are these:

Soundness   For any L statement p, if $\vdash_{D_L} p$, then $\vDash p$.

Completeness   For any L statement p, if $\vDash p$, then $\vdash_{D_L} p$.

That is, all D_L theorems are logical truths (soundness), and all logical truths of L are D_L theorems. D_L has both of these properties, which together imply that an L statement is a theorem if, and only if, it is derivable from the empty set of premises. Related results hold for other semantic properties and relationships. Just as with D_{SL}, system D_L also possesses the "strong" versions of the above properties as well:

Strong Soundness   For any set S of L statements and for any L statement p, if $S \vdash_{D_L} p$, then $S \vDash p$.

Strong Completeness   For any set S of L statements and for any L statement p, if $S \vDash p$, then $S \vdash_{D_L} p$.

Furthermore, both of these can be used to prove that every set of L statements has a theoretically interesting property called **compactness:**

Definition   A set S of L statements, possibly infinitely large, is **compact** if, and only if, if S is logically inconsistent, then there exists some *finite* subset of S that is logically inconsistent.[4]

Proving that every set of L statements is compact is left as an exercise for you at the end of the chapter.[5]

It was noted in Section 4.7 that the set of inference rules for system D_{SL} is not a primitive set; that is, the set contains rules that could be eliminated from the system without a loss of completeness. Our additional set of rules for D_L also

---

[4]A set T is a subset of a set S if, and only if, every element of T is an element of S. Note that, according to this definition, S is a subset of itself.

[5]You can find proofs of these theorems in more advanced texts, such as Bergmann, Moor, and Nelson's *The Logic Book* and Benson Mates's *Elementary Logic* (see Appendix 1). The proof of the completeness of a deduction system for L is non-trivial and was first proven by the logician Kurt Gödel in 1930.

contains derived rules. For example, both EG and EI can be eliminated without a loss of completeness. To see this, it must be shown that any logical consequence that can be arrived at with the help of these rules can also be derived without them. Let's see how this is done, starting with EG.

Suppose that the rules EG and EI were dropped from D_L. Call the resulting system D_L*. We could still derive in D_L* without the use of EG anything we could get with its use in D_L by inserting the following sequence of steps:

$n.$	$p\alpha/\beta$		
$n+1.$	$\sim\exists\alpha p$		PA-RAA
$n+2.$	$\forall\alpha\sim p$	$n+1$	Q
$n+3.$	$\sim p\alpha/\beta$	$n+2$	UI
$n+4.$	$p\alpha/\beta\ \&\ \sim p\alpha/\beta$	$n, n+3$	CI
$n+5.$ $\quad\exists\alpha p$		$(n+1)-(n+4)$	RAA

Thus, if $p\alpha/\beta$ occurs as a line in a proof, we can still derive its existential generalization without the use of EG. This proves that EG is a derived rule. Since EI was also not used, the above pattern does not depend on the presence of EI in the system, either.

To see that EI is also a derived rule, let's now observe that anything that can be derived with its use in D_L could still be derived without it in D_L*:

$n.$	$\exists\alpha p$		
$n+1.$	$\sim q$		PA-RAA
$n+2.$	$p\alpha/\beta$		PA-RAA
	$.$		
	$.$		
	$.$		
$n+k.$	q		
$n+k+1.$	$q\ \&\ \sim q$	$n+1, n+k$	CI
$n+k+2.$	$\sim p\alpha/\beta$	$(n+2)-(n+k+1)$	RAA
$n+k+3.$	$\forall\alpha\sim p$	$n+k+2$	UG
$n+k+4.$	$\sim\exists\alpha p$	$n+k+3$	Q
$n+k+5.$	$\exists\alpha p\ \&\ \exists\alpha\sim p$	$n, n+k+4$	CI
$n+k+6.$ $\quad q$		$(n+1)-(n+k+5)$	RAA

Notice that the use of UG on line $(n+k+3)$ is justified just in case (1) β does not occur in any premise, (2) β does not occur in any provisional assumption covering line $(n+k+3)$, and (3) β does not appear in the statement $\forall\alpha\sim p$ itself. But these are precisely the same conditions that must obtain if we are to apply Rule EI to a statement q in system D_L.[6] Thus, anything we can derive with the use of EI we

---

[6]Well, as we've stated the conditions, they're not *precisely* the same. But with a little work we could show that the conditions amount to the same thing. Trust us!

could equally well derive without it. However, the inclusion of EI (and EG) is of great utility in proof construction.

In closing this chapter, we remark on some limitations of D_L and other systems of natural deduction. We have emphasized at earlier points in this text that natural deduction systems do not provide an effective decision procedure for determining the validity of an argument; indeed, the method of natural deduction as we have presented it is not a decision procedure at all.

A related limitation of D_L is that, though we can use D_L to demonstrate the validity of an argument in L, we cannot use it to demonstrate the *invalidity* of an argument. To show that an argument of L is invalid by the methods of natural deduction, we would have to show that there is *no* proof of the conclusion from the premises. But the mere fact that we are unable to find a proof for an argument does not show that no such proof exists. It may only be that we haven't yet discovered what it is. If we had a way of looking through all of the infinitely many derivations of conclusions from a set of premises and if *none* of these were a proof of some specific statement of interest, we would know (in virtue of completeness) that the argument is invalid. In principle it is possible to show how to mechanically construct a list of proofs (i.e., a list such that every possible proof in system D_L from a given set of premises eventually occurs on the list), but there is no way to run through the infinitely long list in any finite amount of time. Similar remarks can be made about other semantic properties and relationships. For instance, it is possible to use D_L to prove that a set of statements is inconsistent, but not to prove that a set is consistent.

The limitations we mention are limitations of D_L, and the mere fact that D_L has a certain limitation does not imply that there are no proof methods for L that avoid that limitation. In the case of SL, for instance, we found that, although the natural deduction system D_{SL} does not provide an effective decision procedure for determining the validity of an argument in SL, the method of truth trees does. The situation in the case of L is different, however. It turns out out that there is *no possible* effective decision procedure for validity in L. The method of truth trees, discussed in Chapter 6, provides an effective decision procedure for arguments involving only monadic predicates, but neither it *nor any other* procedure is effective for all L arguments. This result, known as the Church–Turing undecidability theorem, is discussed in Section 6.6.

Exercises for Section 7.4

1. Suppose we were to drop the restriction in Rule UG that the generalized constant not occur in a premise of a proof. Would the resulting system be sound? Would it be complete? If the modified system would be unsound, give an example of an invalid argument that would be provable in it. If it would be incomplete, give an example of a valid argument that would not be provable in it.

2. Show how Rule R can be derived from other rules of D_{SL}.

3. Use the fact that D_L is both strongly sound and strongly complete to show that the following is true:

> If the statement 'P & ~P' can be derived from a set $\mathcal{A}$ of L statements, then there is no interpretation under which all elements of $\mathcal{A}$ are simultaneously true.

4. Use the fact that D_L is both sound and complete to show that the following is true:

> Every set $\mathcal{S}$ of L statements is compact.

CHAPTER EIGHT

Extensions to L:
Identity and Functions

8.1 Introduction

In this chapter we introduce two important extensions to the language of predicate logic: the sign of identity and function symbols. These extensions considerably enhance the expressive power and applicability of *L*.

In order to add identity, we add the symbol '=' to the other symbols of *L*. We call the new language '$L_=$', which is a formal extension of *L*. This means that all statements of *L* are statements of $L_=$, but not all statements of $L_=$ are statements of *L*. With the addition of the identity sign, the formal syntax and semantics of *L* must be augmented slightly to produce the full syntax and semantics for $L_=$. We then consider the new challenges and opportunities for symbolization. Finally, we make adjustments to the truth tree method and to our system of natural deduction.

After presenting $L_=$ we turn to function symbols. The language $L_=$ will be extended to a language we call 'L^*'. As with $L_=$, the presentation of L^* requires the addition of new symbols, plus some modifications of the formal syntax and semantics to accommodate the extended language. Symbolization techniques will be discussed, as will the truth tree method and natural deduction system. The system L^* is the most powerful system of predicate logic that is developed in detail in this book.

8.2   Syntax and Semantics for $L_=$

The extension from L to $L_=$ is made by adding the symbol '=' of identity to the language L. The definition of an **$L_=$ formula** is identical to that of an L formula stated in Section 5.3, except that we add the following clause:[1]

> 2a.   If β_1 and β_2 are terms, then $\beta_1 = \beta_2$ is an **$L_=$ formula.**

We do not put parentheses around identity formulas $\beta_1 = \beta_2$, and such formulas count as simple. Although we do not include it in our formal definition, in practice we allow you to abbreviate statements of the form $\sim\beta_1 = \beta_2$ with the expression $\beta_1 \neq \beta_2$.[2] As before, we do not have a *statement* unless the formula contains no free variables. Thus, 'x = y' is not a statement, whereas 'a = b' and '$\forall x \forall y x = y$' are.

The symbol '=' has its usual mathematical meaning, namely, identity. We thus must extend the formal semantics for L to accommodate this meaning. To do this we need to add a clause to the definition of 'truth under an interpretation' presented in Section 5.5:

> 1c.   For any constant terms β_1 and β_2, the expression $\beta_1 = \beta_2$ is true under an interpretation $\mathcal{I}$ if, and only if, $\mathcal{I}(\beta_1) = \mathcal{I}(\beta_2)$.

In other words, an identity between two constant terms is true under an interpretation if, and only if, the two terms are assigned the same element of the domain by that interpretation. To illustrate, consider the following symbol key:

---

[1] If we were being formally fastidious, we would have to revise *all* our definitions in Chapter 5, replacing occurrences of the language name 'L' with the new language name '$L_=$'. This would lengthen the text and would obstruct its pedagogical goals. We therefore just "fudge" these definitions, proving that, at least by the standards of most philosophers and logicians, we are not victims of any obsessional disorder.

[2] Note well that in any expression of the form $\sim\beta_1 = \beta_2$, the negation sign '$\sim$' applies to the *identity, not* to the *individual symbol β_1!* Since β_1 is a constant term, "negating" it would not make syntactic or semantic sense.

$\mathcal{D}$:   numbers

a: 1

b: 1

c: 2.

Under this interpretation, the statement 'a = b' is true, because the object $\mathcal{I}$(a) is identical to the object $\mathcal{I}$(b). By contrast, the statement 'a = c' is false under this interpretation, since the object $\mathcal{I}$(a) is different than $\mathcal{I}$(c). The statement '~a = c' is true under this interpretation. Additionally, notice that the statement '~∃xx = a' ("There is nothing identical to 1") is false, and '∃x∃yx = y' ("Something is identical to something") is true.

Exercises for Section 8.2

Determine the truth values of each $L_=$ statement in Parts I and II under the following interpretation:

$\mathcal{D}$:	natural numbers {1, 2, 3, . . .}		
Ex:	x is even	a:	1
Ox:	x is odd	b:	1
Lxy:	x is less than y	c:	2
Gxy:	x is greater than y	d:	2
Sxyz:	x + y = 2	e:	3
Pxyz:	x × y = 2	f:	4

Part I: Monadic $L_=$

1. a = b
2. ∃xx = a
♦3. ∃xx ≠ b
    4. ∀x(x = a → Ox)
    5. ∀x(x = b → Eb)
    6. ∀x(x = a → x = b)
♦7. ∀x(x = d → ~x = e)
    8. ∃x(Ox & x = c)
    9. ∃x(Ex & x = f)
10. ∃x[(Ex ∨ Ox) & (x = a ∨ x = b)]   12. ∀x[(x ≠ a → Ex) & (x ≠ c → Ox)]
♦11. ∀x[(x = c & x = e) → (Ex & Ox)]

Part II: Polyadic $L_=$

13. (Saac & Sbbd) & c = d
14. ∃x[(Sccx & Pddx) & x = f]
♦15. ∀x(Gxa ∨ x = a)
    16. ∀x[∀y(Gyx ∨ y = x) → x = a]
    17. ∀x∃y[(Lxy ∨ x = y) ↔ x = a]
    18. ∀x[(Ex & Sxxf) → x = d]

8.3   Symbolization in *L*_ I: 'At Least', 'At Most', and 'Exactly'

Our discussion of symbolization begins with some remarks about how simple identity statements are expressed in English. Identity is usually expressed by the word 'is', as in the statement

Karol Wojtyla is Pope John Paul II.

Here the word 'is' stands between two names. We symbolize such a statement by placing the identity symbol between two constant symbols:

a = b.

On the other hand, there are many cases in English where the word 'is' does *not* represent the identity relation, as in the following example:

Karol Wojtyla is Polish.

We have seen many statements of this kind. We symbolize them using a constant and a predicate symbol, say, 'Pa'. Philosophers refer to these two different uses of 'is' as the **'is' of identity** and the **'is' of predication.** Failure to distinguish between these two uses can sometimes cause confusion or result in mistaken inferences.

It is in general easy to distinguish the identity 'is' from the predication 'is'. When used to express identity, the word 'is' stands between names, typically proper nouns. When it is used to express predication, 'is' stands between a name and a predicate expression. Some cases, however are not clear. Consider the following statement:

Karol Wojtyla is pope.

Should we symbolize this as an identity statement or as a statement asserting that a named individual has a property? The statement is ambiguous. Probably the most natural reading is to take it as asserting that Karol Wojtyla is *the* pope. In this case, the phrase 'the pope' functions like a name, so we might render the whole statement as 'a = b'. On the other hand, if what is meant is that Karol Wojtyla is *a* pope, we would be asserting that Karol Wojtyla has the property of being the pope, expressed by a statement such as 'Pa'.

The phrase 'the pope' is an example of a *definite description*. A **definite description** is a descriptive phrase that denotes a single object or individual. Definite descriptions are indicated by the presence of the definite article 'the'. For some purposes it is adequate to treat definite descriptions as names and symbolize them by constants in $L_=$. However, in other cases this symbolization can lead to mistaken inferences; consequently, a more complex symbolization is required. More is said about definite descriptions in Section 9.2.

Adding identity to our formal language enables us to symbolize statements that are beyond the expressive power of the language L. In L, the question of 'how many?' was in general answered by 'some' or 'all'. With the addition of identity, however, we can easily specify quantities precisely. To start, consider the following English statement:

(1)   At least two people attended Burton's party.

Using tools from the language L, it is possible to say 'Somebody attended Burton's party': Assume the domain $\mathcal{D}$ is the set of people. A symbolization for 'Somebody attended Burton's party' is then

∃xAx.

Here, 'Ax' stands for 'x attended Burton's party'. However, in L it is *not* possible for us to say in an intuitively straightforward way what statement (1) says. For one thing, the statement

∃x∃y(Ax & Ay),

which might be suggested as a symbolization for (1), is in fact *logically equivalent* to '∃xAx', and therefore says no more than '∃xAx' does (you may wish to verify the equivalence on a truth tree or by a formal proof). Confining ourselves to the tools of the language L, we *may* use a "trick" like the following: Introduce some arbitrary predicate symbol—say 'B'—as follows:

(2)   ∃x∃y[(Bx & ~By) & (Ax & Ay)].

Since according to (2) there is at least one object to which B applies and at least one object to which B does not apply, it must be the case that the object having B is different than the object lacking it. Thus, this last statement is true under an interpretation only if there exist at least *two* things that have A—that is, that attended Burton's party.

Though the above "trick" works, using this strategy in general is somewhat awkward and requires us to introduce an arbitrary predicate symbol merely for the sake of distinguishing between two objects in the domain. Further, if we are interested in *more* than at least two things, such a strategy becomes unacceptably unwieldy. Instead, the new *identity* sign may be used as follows:

(3) $\exists x \exists y [x \neq y \; \& \; (Ax \; \& \; Ay)]$.

This statement asserts that there exist at least two *distinct* (i.e., *non-identical*) objects, each of which has the property A—in this case, at least two people attended Burton's party.

You may take statement (3) as giving a template for symbolizing any statement of the form 'At least *n* objects are P': First construct a formula with *n* conjuncts of the form $P\alpha_i$ for each of the *n* variables α_i, plus enough conjuncts of the form $\alpha_i \neq \alpha_j$ between variables to guarantee that there must be *n distinct* objects referred to by the symbolic expression. Next, the formula is prefixed with an appropriate string of *n* existential quantifiers. Schematically, the identity formulas are

At least one object is P	$\exists \alpha \, P\alpha$
At least two objects are P	$\exists \alpha_i \exists \alpha_j (\alpha_i \neq \alpha_j \; \& \; (P\alpha_i \; \& \; P\alpha_j))$
At least three objects are P	$\exists \alpha_i \exists \alpha_j \exists \alpha_k [((\alpha_i \neq \alpha_j \; \& \; \alpha_i \neq \alpha_k) \; \& \; \alpha_j \neq \alpha_k)$ $\& \; (P\alpha_i \; \& \; (P\alpha_j \; \& \; P\alpha_k))]$

and so on. After three objects, formulas become rather unwieldy—but *not* as unwieldy as trying to do *without* identity! The principle is clear: We may write a statement that specifies *precisely* how many objects *at least* must be contained in a domain in order for the statement to be true under an interpretation.

Besides writing statements that require the existence of *at least* some specific number of objects in a domain, we may also use identity to write statements that can be satisfied only in domains containing *at most* a certain number. For example, consider a slight modification of the statement we examined above:

At most one person attended Burton's party.

Using identity we obtain the following:

(4) $\forall x \forall y [(Ax \; \& \; Ay) \rightarrow x = y]$.

That is, any "two" things that have A are really just *one* thing: At most, one object has A—that is, at most one person attended Burton's party. (Note that (4) does *not* imply '$\exists x Ax$'; that is, it does not imply that somebody attended the party.) The statement 'At most two people attended Burton's party' may be symbolized as

(5) $\forall x \forall y \forall z [(((Ax \; \& \; Ay) \; \& \; Az) \; \& \; x \neq y) \rightarrow (z = x \lor z = y)]$.

That is, if any "three" things have A, then the "third" of them is really just one of two: At most, two objects have A—that is, at most, two people attended Burton's party.

By pulling (1) and (5) together, we obtain a symbolization for our third notion, that of 'exactly':

(6) $\exists x \exists y(x \neq y \,\&\, (Ax \,\&\, Ay)) \,\&\, \forall x \forall y \forall z[(((Ax \,\&\, Ay) \,\&\, Az) \,\&\, x \neq y) \rightarrow (z = x \vee z = y)]$.

This says, 'At least two people attended Burton's party, and at most two people attended Burton's party,' that is, '*Exactly* two people attended Burton's party.' This statement can be put into a more concise logically equivalent form:

(7) $\exists x \exists y[x \neq y \,\&\, \forall z(Az \leftrightarrow (z = x \vee z = y))]$.

Statement (7) employs a particularly convenient equivalent form. In the case of specifying a unique object (i.e., 'exactly one') having a property P, you may write $\exists \alpha_i \forall \alpha_j (P\alpha_j \leftrightarrow \alpha_j = \alpha_i)$ in place of the more cumbersome expression $\exists \alpha_i [P\alpha_i \,\&\, \forall \alpha_j (P\alpha_j \rightarrow \alpha_j = \alpha_i)]$.

Consider some further examples. Given a statement of the form 'Every S except β is P', we find a possible source of ambiguity. On the one hand, we may use the symbolic form

$S\beta \,\&\, \forall \alpha[(S\alpha \,\&\, \alpha \neq \beta) \rightarrow P\alpha]$.

Using this form the statement 'Every prime number except 2 is odd' becomes

Pt $\&\, \forall x[(Px \,\&\, x \neq t) \rightarrow Ox]$,

where 'Px' is 'x is prime', 'Ox' is 'x is odd', 't' stands for the number 2, and $\mathcal{D}$ is the set of numbers. The ambiguity, however, is whether in asserting 'Every S except β is P', one means to include as part of the assertion the claim that β is S *and* not P. In the case of 'Every prime number except 2 is odd', it would certainly be correct to understand this as asserting 'Two is a prime number, and 2 is not odd, and all *other* prime numbers are odd'. For this statement, the correct symbolization would be

(Pt $\&$ ~Ot) $\&\, \forall x[(Px \,\&\, x \neq t) \rightarrow Ox]$.

This observation underscores the importance of being clear about just what it is that you mean to assert when giving a symbolization. In addition, note that the symbolic statement '(Pt $\&$ ~Ot) $\&\, \forall x[(Px \,\&\, x \neq t) \rightarrow Ox]$' is logically equivalent to the statement '$\forall x[(Px \,\&\, \text{~}Ox) \leftrightarrow x = t]$'; that is, 'Two is the only non-odd prime number'. This last point illustrates the fact that once a statement has been symbolized, your knowledge of logical equivalences can actually help obtain a more concise or lucid version of the original English. In the context of argument analysis, the process of going from given English statements into symbols can often reveal hidden ambiguities of the English premises and conclusion. It may well be that the validity of a piece of reasoning turns on how such ambiguities are resolved.

Similar considerations about meaning arise in connection with each of the following English statements and suggested symbolic counterparts:

No S except β is P $S\beta$ & $\forall\alpha[(S\alpha \ \& \ \alpha \neq \beta) \rightarrow \sim\!P\alpha]$

Some S other than β is P $S\beta$ & $\exists\alpha[(S\alpha \ \& \ \alpha \neq \beta) \ \& \ P\alpha]$

Some S other than β is not P $S\beta$ & $\exists\alpha[(S\alpha \ \& \ \alpha \neq \beta) \ \& \ \sim\!P\alpha]$

In analogy to the form 'Every S except β is P', the form 'No S except β is P' could alternatively be cast as '$(S\beta \ \& \ P\beta)$ & $\forall\alpha[(S\alpha \ \& \ \alpha \neq \beta) \rightarrow \sim\!P\alpha]$'. Indeed, this would ordinarily be the correct symbolization. For the next two statements, if 'other than' were intended to mean 'in addition to', we would have

Some S in addition to β is P $(S\beta \ \& \ P\beta)$ & $\exists\alpha[(S\alpha \ \& \ \alpha \neq \beta) \ \& \ P\alpha]$

Some S in addition to β is not P $(S\beta \ \& \ \sim\!P\beta)$ & $\exists\alpha[(S\alpha \ \& \ \alpha \neq \beta) \ \& \ \sim\!P\alpha]$

There is thus a kind of interplay between English and the symbolic language, mediated by your own reflection on language, meaning, and the symbolic idiom. Through reflection on the meaning of the original English and on the truth conditions for possible symbolic representations of that English, you will gain skill at more quickly seeing logical possibilities and problems in cases of everyday argument analysis.

Use of the identity sign also allows us to make assertions about the existence of objects, independently of what properties these objects might have or lack. For example, we introduced the sign '=' by showing how to symbolize statements such as 'Exactly two people attended Burton's party', but we may also symbolize statements about "how many things exist," like 'Exactly one thing exists':

$\exists x \forall y \, x = y.$

We may also express general principles of identity, such as 'Any two things identical to a third are identical to each other':

$\forall x \forall y \forall z[(x = z \ \& \ y = z) \rightarrow x = y].$

The first statement will be true in any domain containing exactly one object and will be false under any interpretation whose domain includes more than one object. The second statement, by contrast, will be true under all interpretations since it is a logical truth. One thing that *cannot* be done in monadic logic, L_m, however, is to write out a single statement that will be true only under interpretations having an infinite domain; that is, we cannot write out a consistent statement of *L* that has *no* finite models. Neither can we do this with $L_=$ restricted to monadic predicates.

Exercises for Section 8.3

Provide symbolizations in $L_=$ for each of the following English statements. Be sure to include a symbol key in each case.

   1. Sylvia and Sophia are the same person.
   2. If Sylvia is Sophia and Sylvia went ice fishing, then Sophia went ice fishing.
 ♦ 3. At least one person other than Charlie has taken a course in woodworking.
   4. For every pair of distinct cities, there is at least one highway that connects them.
   5. Nobody is not self-identical.
   6. Everybody is self-identical.
 ♦ 7. If one thing is identical to a second, and that second thing is identical to a third, then the first thing is identical to the third.
   8. If one thing is identical to another, and if that second thing is not identical to a third, then neither is the first thing identical to that third.
   9. At least two numbers are greater than 0.
  10. At least two fish swim in the sea.
  11. There is a fish who swims in the sea, and there is a fish who jumps through the waves, but these fish are actually one in the same.
  12. At least three numbers between 1 and 10 are even.
 ♦ 13. At least three fish who swim in the sea are green.
  14. At most, two numbers are greater than 0.
  15. At most, two fish swim in the sea.
  16. There are at most three people in the elevator.
  17. There is exactly one bright blue fish in the sea.
  18. There is exactly one even prime number.
 ♦ 19. If there is at least one even prime number, then there is at most one even prime number.
  20. There is exactly one even prime number, and this number is 2.
  21. There is exactly one fish who swims in the sea, his name is Charles, and he lives in the coastal waters of Bermuda.
  22. Exactly one person baked a cake, and it was either Davis or Hawthorne.

23. If one number is identical to a second, then that second number is identical to the first.

24. If Tully and Cicero are identical, and if Tully crossed the Rubicon, then so did Cicero.

♦ 25. If one thing is conceivable as lacking extension but another is not, then the two things are not identical.

26. If a mind can be imagined to lack extension but a body cannot be imagined to lack extension, then that mind and body are distinct.

27. If I think, then there exists something which I am. ("If I think, then I exist.")

8.4 Symbolization in *L* = II: Identity and Polyadic Predicates

In our discussion of symbolization in Section 8.3, we confined ourselves to monadic predicates. We now examine the symbolization of statements involving both identity and polyadic predicates. Combining these two elements gives us a language of remarkable power, though symbolization becomes correspondingly complex. The complexity of these problems tells us something interesting about ordinary English statements. Often their logical structure is more complicated than we at first realize. Learning to correctly symbolize these statements will give you considerable insight into the logical structure of English statements and arguments.

To symbolize the statements discussed in this section, we do not need any radically new techniques. It is simply a matter of breaking complex statements into simpler parts and then applying the methods you have learned earlier. Let's begin by trying to symbolize the statement 'No woman loves a man who loves only himself'. We use the following symbol key:

$\mathcal{D}$:   people

Mx: x is a man

Wx: x is a woman

Lxy: x loves y.

There are a couple of ways (at least) to proceed. One way is to notice that the statement has roughly the form of an E statement No *S* are *P*—that is, 'No women are lovers of men who love only themselves'. The '*S*' part is of course easy: 'Wx'. This gives the partial symbolization

∀x[Wx → ~(x loves a man who loves only himself)].

To symbolize the expression 'x loves a man who loves only himself', call on our knowledge of identity: ∃y[My & (Lxy & ∀z(Lyz → z = y))]; that is, 'There exists a y such that y is a man whom x loves, and everyone whom y loves is y'. Hence, the whole symbolization is

∀x[Wx → ~ ∃y(My & (Lxy & ∀z(Lyz → z = y)))].

The combination of relational predicates and identity symbols is especially helpful in symbolizing mathematical statements. As an example, consider the statement 'There is a smallest positive integer'. This statement is evidently an existential claim:

∃x(x is the smallest positive integer).

In somewhat more refined terms, but still in a hybrid form, this becomes

∃x(x is a positive integer and x is smaller than any other positive integer).

Even more refinement, plus the predicate 'I', gives us

∃x(Ix & for any y, if Iy and y ≠ x, then x is less than y).

The complete symbolization is thus apparent:

∃x[Ix & ∀y((Iy & y ≠ x) → Lxy)].

If we let 𝒟 be the set of positive integers, the symbolization becomes just '∃x∀y (y ≠ x → Lxy)'.

Now consider the statement 'Every person has exactly one father and one mother'. In hybrid form, this is

∀x[x is a person → (x has exactly one father & x has exactly one mother)].

Let's introduce 'Px' for 'x is a person' and use the existential quantifier:

∀x[Px → (∃y(y is the only father of x) & ∃y(y is the only mother of x)].

We know that 'Fxy' and 'Mxy' can be used to express fatherhood and motherhood, but the symbolization also needs to indicate that the father and mother of an individual are *unique*. This can be accomplished by taking the parts one at a time. First, how do we completely symbolize '∃y(y is the only father of x)'? As earlier, we simply need to say that (1) x has *at least* one father and (2) x has *at most* one father: ∃y[Fyx & ∀z(Fzx → z = y)]. This last can be shortened to just '∃y∀z(Fzx ↔ z = y)'. Similarly, '∃y(y is the only mother of x)' becomes '∃y∀z(Mzx ↔ z = y)'. Thus, the symbolization of the whole statement is

$$\forall x[Px \to (\exists y \forall z(Fzx \leftrightarrow z = y) \ \& \ \exists y \forall z(Mzx \leftrightarrow z = y))].$$

Eliminating 'P' by letting $\mathcal{D}$ = the set of people yields

$$\forall x(\exists y \forall z(Fzx \leftrightarrow z = y) \ \& \ \exists y \forall z(Mzx \leftrightarrow z = y)).$$

In considering the preceding examples, note the utility of (1) using hybrid forms that mix both English and symbols as a tool to arrive at the final symbolization and (2) breaking the statement to be symbolized into its component clauses. Also extremely important is (3) your knowledge of logical equivalences.

Here are some further examples for you to study:

1. Nobody is everyone's parent:

   ~∃x∀yPxy

2. Any prime number greater than 2 is odd:

   ∀x[(Px & Gxt) → Ox]

3. Jung is the only psychiatrist who treated Freud:

   (Pj & Tjf) & ∀x[(Px & Txf) → x = j]

4. Every even number greater than 2 is equal to the sum of two primes:

   ∀x[(Ex & Gxt) → ∃y∃z((Py & Pz) & Syzx)]

5. Any two distinct points determine a unique line:

   ∀x∀y[((Px & Py) & x ≠ y) →
   ∃z((Lz & Dxyz) & ∀w((Lw & Dxyw) → w = z))]

6. Alvah is a grandfather (using 'Mxy' for 'x is mother of y' and 'Fxy' for 'x is father of y'):

   ∃x[Fax & ∃y(Fxy ∨ Mxy)]

7. Any grandmother is the mother of somebody who is either a father or mother:[3]

   With $\mathcal{D}$ = people: ∀x[Gx → ∃y(M^2xy & (Fy ∨ My))]

---

[3]Notice that using the superscript here allows us to use 'F' and 'M', which suggest the predicates for which they stand.

8. No two people share all the same properties:

$\forall x \forall y[((Px \ \& \ Py) \ \& \ x \neq y) \rightarrow \sim\forall z(Rz \rightarrow (Hxz \leftrightarrow Hyz))]$

Exercises for Section 8.4

Part I: Symbolization

(A) Using the interpretation provided, symbolize the English statements in $L_=$. (*Note:* Not *all* statements require use of '='.)

$\mathcal{D}$:	people		
Cx:	x is an eclectic	a:	Jolanda Jacobi
Fx:	x is a Freudian	f:	Sigmund Freud
Jx:	x is a Jungian	j:	Carl Jung
Px:	x is a psychologist	s:	Virginia Satir
Sx:	x is a psychiatrist		
Rx:	x is a Rogerian		
Exy:	x is a more effective therapist than y		
Mxy:	x earns more money than y		
Txy:	x was a teacher of y		

1. Freud had at least two students.
2. There are at least two students of Satir who are not Rogerians.
◆ 3. Although Jung was a student of Freud, Virginia Satir was not.
4. Any psychiatrist who was taught by Freud is better than any who was not.
5. At most, two non-Jungians are psychiatrists.
6. Jung is the only student of Freud's who is a more effective therapist than Freud.
7. Some psychiatrist other than Freud was a teacher of Virginia Satir.
8. No psychiatrist earns less than any psychologist.
◆ 9. All teachers earn more money than their students.
10. There is a student of Freud's who is identical to Jacobi's only student.
11. Only students of Jung are Jungians, although none are more effective therapists than Jung.
12. There are at most two eclectic psychologists who are more effective therapists than any Freudian.
13. All psychiatrists, other than Freud, earn less than their students, but no pyschologists, other than Satir, earn more than their students.

14. Sigmund Freud earns at least as much money as Virginia Satir, but not as much as Carl Jung.

♦ 15. While all psychiatrists are taught by Freudians, psychologists are taught by either Rogerians, Jungians, or eclectics.

16. Anyone who is both a psychologist and a psychiatrist is a more effective therapist than anybody who is one or the other but not both.

17. No Rogerian, except a psychiatrist who studied with either Freud or Jung, is a more effective therapist than somebody who is both an eclectic and less effective at therapy than Jolanda Jacobi.

18. At least one psychiatrist, other than Freud or Jung, is a psychologist who is a more effective therapist than Jolanda Jacobi.

19. Exactly two Freudians were taught by Rogerians, but neither of them earns more money than any non-Freudian Rogerian.

20. Any psychiatrist earns more than her or his teachers, but less than her or his students.

(B) Using the interpretation provided, symbolize the following English statements in $L_=$.[4] (*Note:* Not *all* statements require use of '='.)

$\mathcal{D}$:	philosophers		
Ex:	x wrote mainly on ethical doctrines	a:	Aesara
Mx:	x wrote on metaphysical doctrines	g:	Pythagoras
Px:	x is a Platonist	h:	Hypatia
Wx:	x is a woman	l:	Plato
Yx:	x was a Pythagorean	m:	Themistoclea
Kxy:	x is more well known than y	n:	Phyntis of Sparta
Lxy:	x lived before y	p:	Perictione
Sxy:	x was a student of y	r:	Aristotle
		s:	Socrates
		t:	Theano

21. Plato and Socrates are not two different people.

22. Hypatia lived later than Themistoclea, Theano, and Aesara.

---

[4]These exercises are not all intended to be historically accurate. The reader interested in learning more about the history of women philosophers may wish to consult the recent four-volume series, *A History of Women Philosophers*, edited by Mary Ellen Waithe (Dordecht: Kluwer, 1987–1995). The women philosophers whose names are used in this exercise are discussed in volume 1 of the series, *600BC–500AD*.

♦ 23. Neither Theano nor Themistoclea was a student of Plato or Socrates.

24. There is at least one woman philosopher not identical to some Platonist.

25. Hypatia, who lived after both Plato and Aristotle, wrote on metaphysical doctrines.

26. Theano was not the only woman student of Pythagoras.

27. At least two women philosophers were students of Aristotle.

28. Some students of Phyntis were not students of Perictione.

♦ 29. There are women who were Socrates' teachers.

30. Aesara, Theano, and Perictione are three distinct Pythagoreans.

31. Some Pythagoreans who were students of Theano wrote metaphysical doctrines.

32. Themistoclea was the only woman student of Pythagoras to teach Theano.

33. Perictione is not the same person as Aesara unless Plato is Aristotle.

34. Some women Platonists were also Pythagoreans.

♦ 35. Unless a woman studied with Themistoclea, she is not as well known as Themistoclea.

36. If Themistoclea and Phyntis of Sparta are the same person, then one of them wrote on metaphysical doctrines just in case the other did.

37. Any woman who was a student of Socrates wrote on ethical doctrines.

38. Exactly one woman philosopher is more well known than Plato or Aristotle, and that woman philosopher is Hypatia.

39. Some women philosophers who wrote mainly on ethical doctrines are more well known than some who wrote on metaphysical doctrines.

40. If any philosopher who wrote on metaphysical doctrines is a different person than any who wrote mainly on ethical doctrines, then Theano isn't identical to herself.

(C) Using the interpretation provided, symbolize the following English statements in $L_=$. (*Note:* Not *all* statements require use of '='.)

$\mathcal{D}$:	numbers		
Ex:	x is an even number	a_1:	1
Mx:	x is prime	a_2:	2
Nx:	x is a natural number	a_3:	3
Ox:	x is an odd number	a_4:	4
Qx:	x is a rational number	a_5:	5
Rx:	x is a real number		
Gxy:	x is greater than y		

Lxy: x is less than y

Bxyz: x is between y and z

Sxyz: $x + y = z$

♦41. There is no least real number.

42. There is no greatest prime number.

43. There are exactly two odd numbers between 1 and 5.

44. There are exactly two prime numbers between 1 and 5.

45. The sum of 2 and 2 is equal to the sum of 1 and 3.

46. There is exactly one even prime number.

47. The only natural number between 3 and 5 is 4.

48. There are numbers between 3 and 5, but not natural numbers.

♦49. No odd prime is less than any even prime.

50. The sum of any two numbers is a unique number.

51. The sum of two distinct odd numbers is always even.

52. Although all rationals are real, not all reals are rational.

53. Every even number greater than 2 is equal to the sum of two primes.

54. The sum of 2 and 3 is identical to a number larger than either of them.

55. Two numbers are greater than or equal to each other only if they are identical.

56. No numbers are greater than one another.

♦57. The sum of two distinct numbers is less than the sum of one of them added to twice the other.

58. There is exactly one natural number that is less than all the rest.

59. The sum of 1 and 1 added to the sum of 2 and 2 is greater than or equal to the only natural number that is between 5 and the sum of 5 and 2.

60. The sum of 4 and 1 is between 4 and the sum of 5 and 1 and is distinct from the sum of 4 and 3.

Part II: Theoretical Problems

61. Recall that in Section 5.9 we introduced a list of types of logical relations that are of theoretical importance. With the addition of identity, we can add two new types to this list:

    A relation R is **antisymmetric** if, and only if, $\forall x \forall y[(Rxy \ \& \ Ryz) \rightarrow x = y]$

    A relation R is **connex** if, and only if, $\forall x \forall y[x \neq y \rightarrow (Rxy \lor Ryx)]$.

A relation is said to induce a **partial ordering** on a domain if that relation is antisymmetric and transitive on that domain. A relation is said to induce a **total ordering** on a domain if that relation is antisymmetric, transitive, and connex. Give examples of a relation that (a) induces a partial but not total ordering on a domain, as well as one that (b) induces a total ordering.

8.5   Truth Trees for $L_=$

Expanding on the method of truth trees to accommodate the extended language $L_=$ requires us to add a new rule to those given in Chapter 6. In addition, we need to change our rules for closing branches and for deciding when an open branch is finished. The rule for identity is based on a well-known and intuitively obvious principle about identity statements, which we can call 'the substitution principle for identity': If one individual has two (or more) names, then we may substitute one name for the other in any statement without changing the truth value of that statement.

Consider, for instance, the following valid (and sound) argument:

> Karol Wojtyla is Polish
> Karol Wojtyla is Pope John Paul II
> ∴ Pope John Paul II is Polish.

Symbolically in $L_=$:

> Pa
> a = b
> ∴ Pb

This argument is certainly valid. Under any interpretation $\mathcal{I}$, notice that if both premises are true, then the following hold:

> $\mathcal{I}(a) \in \mathcal{I}(P)$
> $\mathcal{I}(a) = \mathcal{I}(b)$.

Thus, it must be the case that under $\mathcal{I}$, $\mathcal{I}(b) \in \mathcal{I}(P)$—that is, that 'Pb' is true under $\mathcal{I}$ as well. Since the names 'a' and 'b' denote precisely the same object, any $L_=$ statement containing 'a' will retain its truth value (whether true or false) if the name 'b' is put in its place, and vice versa.

Our rule for identity statements formalizes this substitution principle:

> **Rule I**   If a statement of the form $\beta_1 = \beta_2$ occurs as a node on an open branch, where β_1 and β_2 are any constant terms, and if the statement p containing occurrences of β_1 (or β_2) is another node on that branch, then one or more statements $p*$ may be added to the bottom of the branch, where $p*$ is obtained from p by replacement of some or all occurrences of β_1 by β_2 (or, respectively, β_2 by β_1). *The identity statement $\beta_1 = \beta_2$ is not checked off after a substitution is made.*

Let's apply this principle by testing the argument above for validity on a truth tree:

$$Pa$$
$$a = b$$
$$\sim Pb$$

Rule I states that we may extend the tree by substituting 'b' for 'a' in the statement 'Pa':

$$Pa$$
$$a = b$$
$$\sim Pb$$
$$Pb$$
$$\times$$

This closes the tree, showing that the argument is valid. Notice that we could also have used Rule I to obtain the statement '~Pa' from '~Pb'. This choice, too, would have closed the tree.

The fact that our symbolic languages are extensional becomes especially clear now that we have added the identity sign and admitted a substitution rule. Although our substitution principle holds for all $L_=$ statements, it does *not* always hold for ordinary English. Here is an invalid argument in English that fallaciously makes use of the substitution principle:

Masha believes that Karol Wojtyla is Polish
Karol Wojtyla is Pope John Paul II
———————————————————————
∴ Masha believes that Pope John Paul II is Polish.

Masha might well believe that Karol Wojtyla is Polish *without* believing that Pope John Paul II is Polish, since she might not believe that Karol Wojtyla is Pope John Paul II. The reason that we cannot make this inference has to do with the fact that 'Masha believes that . . .' is not a truth-functional connective. As discussed briefly in Section 1.4, expressions like 'believes that' create a context that is 'opaque' to substitution, so that the truth value of a statement of the form 'b believes that *p*' does *not* depend logically on the truth value of the statement *p*. When we say that our symbolic languages are *extensional* in nature, what is meant in part is that codenoting (or 'coextensive') names may be substituted one for the other in a statement without altering the truth value of that statement. Thus, when symbolizing an argument like the one above in *L* or *L=*, we may not allow any names or variables to occur within the scope of 'believes that'. In other words, the partial symbol key

> Bx: x believes that Karol Wojtyla is Polish

is allowed, but *neither* of the following is allowed:

> Bx: Masha believes that x is Polish
> B^2xy: x believes that y is Polish.

The reason that neither of these latter two is allowed is that, in our symbolic languages, substitution of codenoting terms *must* preserve the truth value of the original statement. Since allowing these to count as legitimate symbolizations would contradict this requirement, we must disallow them as correct symbolizations.[5]

Returning to our use of tree rules, let's look at a more complicated argument, which we symbolize and test for validity with a truth tree:

> Robert is the only person who had the appetizer recipe
> The appetizer was made by somebody who had the recipe
> ∴ Robert made the appetizer.

In symbols,

> Ar & $\forall$x(Ax → x = r)
> $\exists$x(Mx & Ax)
> ∴ Mr

---

[5]More is said about opaque and intensional contexts in Section 9.9.

We begin with the appropriate trunk:

$$Ar \& \forall x(Ax \rightarrow x = r)$$
$$\exists x(Mx \& Ax)$$
$$\sim Mr$$

Apply the conjunction rule to the top statement and then introduce an unused constant in place of 'x' for the existentially quantified statement:

$$Ar \& \forall x(Ax \rightarrow x = r) \checkmark$$
$$\exists x(Mx \& Ax) \checkmark$$
$$\sim Mr$$
$$Ar$$
$$\forall x(Ax \rightarrow x = r)$$
$$Ma \& Aa$$

Now apply the conjunction rule to the bottom statement:

$$Ar \& \forall x(Ax \rightarrow x = r) \checkmark$$
$$\exists x(Mx \& Ax) \checkmark$$
$$\sim Mr$$
$$Ar$$
$$\forall x(Ax \rightarrow x = r)$$
$$Ma \& Aa \checkmark$$
$$Ma$$
$$Aa$$

To complete the application of quantifier rules, substitute 'r' and 'a', respectively, for 'x' in the universally quantified statement:

$$Ar \& \forall x(Ax \rightarrow x = r) \checkmark$$
$$\exists x(Mx \& Ax) \checkmark$$
$$\sim Mr$$
$$Ar$$
$$\forall x(Ax \rightarrow x = r)$$
$$Ma \& Aa \checkmark$$
$$Ma$$
$$Aa$$
$$Ar \rightarrow r = r$$
$$Aa \rightarrow a = r$$

Applying the conditional rule produces

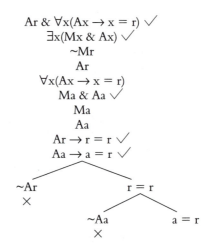

Only the right-most branch remains open. At this point we must apply Rule I. Notice that both '~Mr' and 'Ma' occur higher up on the branch and that 'a = r' appears as the bottom statement. Applying Rule I—that is, adding either '~Ma' or 'Mr' to the bottom of the branch—closes the tree:

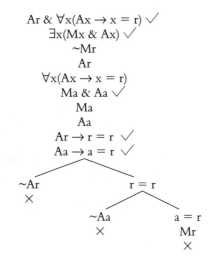

All branches close, so the initial list is inconsistent: The argument in question is valid.

To accommodate the introduction of '=' and Rule I to truth trees, we must amend our definitions of a 'closed branch' and of an 'finished open branch'. Here is the first definition:

> ***Definition***   A **branch** through a tree is said to be **closed** if, and only if, either it contains a node *p* together with a node ~*p*, or it contains a node of the form ~β = β.

The final clause of this rule employs the obvious fact that it is logically impossible for something not to be self-identical. To illustrate, note that the statement

$$\forall xx = x$$

is a logical truth, as is shown by the following tree:

$$\sim\forall xx = x \checkmark$$
$$\exists x\sim x = x \checkmark$$
$$\sim a = a$$
$$\times$$

The tree shows that $\sim\forall xx = x \vDash \sim a = a$. Since '$\sim a = a$' is false under every interpretation, we know that $\vDash\forall xx = x$.

As for finished open branches, you may have noticed that our rule for identity statements is in some respects like our rule for universally quantified statements. In both cases we may return as needed to reapply the respective rule. Therefore, we don't check off either universally quantified statements or identity statements. In view of this we need to amend the definition of a 'finished open branch' to tell us when we have added "enough" statements by the use of the identity rule. 'Enough' in this case means enough to guarantee that the branch won't close and, consequently, that the set of statements on the branch is consistent. Our rule is contained in the following definition, the first two clauses of which are identical to those given in Section 6.2:[6]

> ***Definition*** A branch through a tree is said to be a **finished open branch** if, and only if, the branch is not closed, and it contains no unchecked nodes except, at most,
>
> 1. Simple statements or their negations, or
>
> 2. Universally quantified statements, where, for each statement on the branch, (a) the branch contains at least one node that is an instance of that statement and (b) for each constant term β appearing anywhere on the branch, the branch includes a node that is an instance of the quantified statement whose instantial term is β, or

---

[6]Recall from Section 6.2 that when a term β is substituted in place of a variable α to form an instance $pα/β$ of a quantified statement, β is the 'instantial term' in that instance.

3. Identity statements $\beta_1 = \beta_2$, where (a) every statement that can be formed by substituting some or all occurrences of β_1 for β_2 in any unchecked statement on the branch also occurs on the branch, and (b) every statement that can be formed by substituting some or all occurrences of β_2 for β_1 in any unchecked statement on the branch also occurs on the branch.

Before we are done with an identity statement then, we must have added to a tree *every* possible statement that can be derived by substituting into unchecked statements on the tree one of the terms in the identity for the other. In practice this can mean adding *many* statements. Here is one example:

$$\sim Pb$$
$$Ra \lor (Qa \to Sb)$$
$$a = b$$

We demonstrate this set's consistency by constructing a finished tree for it. We begin by applying our rule for disjunction:

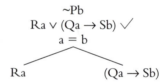

The tree is finished by adding the only two substitutions possible for *unchecked* statements on the left-hand branch:

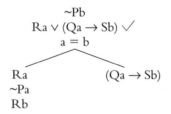

Notice that we achieve considerable economy in our tree by putting off substitutions until after we have decomposed as many statements as we possibly can. The statement 'Ra ∨ (Qa → Sb)' generates seven additional statements by the use of Rule I, each of which would lead to three branches! By waiting to apply the identity rule until this statement is checked, we avoid adding these statements. In general, if a statement has a total of n occurrences of either of the terms in an identity statement, there will be $2^n - 1$ additional statements that will need to be added.

Even if you wait until the last possible moment to perform identity substitutions, our current definition of a finished open branch may sometimes require you to build very long trees, especially when those trees contain statements with universal quantifiers. Since universally quantified statements are not checked off, if such statements contain a number of constants, you will have to make many substitutions. Consider the following:

$$\forall x((Rxa \ \& \ Rab) \ \& \ Rxc)$$
$$a = b$$
$$a = c$$

Given clause (3) of the definition of a 'finished open branch', you would have to add *eight* new universally quantified statements using Rule I and then decompose each of these, before you would have completed the tree. It is possible, however, to reformulate the definition of a finished open branch in a way that affords more economy in tree construction. If a tree can be made to close by substituting into complex statements like the quantified statement at the top of be trunk above, then it can also be closed by substituting only into the negated simple statements derived from those complex statements. In particular we can substitute for our clause (3) of the definition a new clause, (3'):

> 3'. Identity statements $\beta_1 = \beta_2$, where (a) every statement that can be formed by substituting some or all occurrences of β_1 for β_2 in any negated simple statement on the branch also occurs on the branch, and (b) every statement that can be formed by substituting some or all occurrences of β_2 for β_1 in any negated simple statement on the branch also occurs on the branch.

What we have done is to take clause (3) and substitute 'negated simple statement' for 'unchecked statement'. Recall from Chapter 5 that a simple statement is any statement that contains no quantifiers or connectives. These include statement letters, n-place predicates followed by n constant terms, or identity statements. Since statement letters do not contain any constant terms, the only negated simple statements that concern us are negated identities or negated predicate symbols followed by constant terms.

Using this revised definition of a complete open branch, we can complete the above tree:

$$\forall x((Rxa \ \& \ Rab) \ \& \ Rxc)$$
$$a = b$$
$$a = c$$

(Raa & Rab) & Rac $\checkmark$
(Rba & Rab) & Rbc $\checkmark$
(Rca & Rab) & Rcc $\checkmark$
Raa & Rab $\checkmark$
Rac
Raa
Rab
Rba & Rab $\checkmark$
Rbc
Rba
Rab
Rca & Rab $\checkmark$
Rcc
Rca
Rab

Although this tree is long, it is much shorter than would have resulted from adhering to the original clause (3). Notice that *we didn't even have to use the identity rule,* since there are no negated simple statements on the tree.

Why, you might wonder, do we only have to substitute into negated simple statements to complete a tree? Why do we get to omit non-negated simple statements? The reason is this: We want to use the identity rule, if possible, to obtain statements of the form p and $\sim p$ on a particular branch. Suppose that p is a simple statement and that $\sim p$ occurs as a node on a branch and that substituting one term of an identity for another transforms a statement q into the statement p. Notice that making a similar appropriate substitution into the statement $\sim p$ would transform $\sim p$ into $\sim q$. Thus, only negated simple statements need be considered with respect to substitution.[7]

The important metatheoretic facts about the tree method for $L_=$ are as follows. Regardless of whether (3) or (3') is used in the definition of 'finished open branch', the tree method for $L_=$ is both sound and complete. Since the tree method does not provide a decision procedure for L (see Section 6.5), it follows immediately that it doesn't provide an effective decision procedure for logical truth in $L_=$, either. If, however, we restrict ourselves to statements involving only monadic predicates and identity, the tree method presented here *does* provide an effective decision procedure for logical truth.

---

[7]The modified definition of a finished open branch is the one used by the program Inference Engine, which accompanies this text. Its increased efficiency reduces computing time.

Exercises for Section 8.5

Part I: Monadic L= Logical Truth Construct truth trees to determine whether the following statements are logical truths, logical contradictions, or neither.

1. ∀xx = x
2. ∀x∀y∀z[(x = z & y = z) → x = y]
♦3. ∀x∀y∀z(x = y ∨ y = z)
4. ∀x∀y∀z[(x ≠ z & y ≠ z) → x ≠ y]
5. ∀x∃yx = y
6. ~∃xx = x ∨ ∀yy = a
7. a = b ↔ b = a

8. (Pa → ∀xx = a) ∨ (∀xx = a → Pa)
♦9. ∀xx = a ↔ P
10. [Pa & ∀x(Px → x = a)] →
    ∀x (Px ↔ x = a)
11. ∀xx = a ↔ (P & ~P)
12. ∀x∀y[(Ax ↔ Ay) ↔ x = y]

Part II: Polyadic L= Logical Truth Construct truth trees to determine whether the following statements are logical truths, logical contradictions, or neither.

13. ∀xx = a ↔ (P ∨ ~ P)
14. ∀x∀y[((Px & Py) & x ≠ y) →
    ∃z(Lz & Dxyz)]
15. (Sac & Sad) → c = d
16. ∀x∀y[Rxy ∨ ∃z(y = z & ~Rxz)]
♦17. ∃x(Rxa ↔ x = a)

18. ∀x∀y(Rxy ↔ x ≠ y) → ∀x∃yRxy
19. ∀x(Rxa ↔ x = a)
20. ∀x∀y[(Rxy → x = y) →
    (x = y → Rxy)]
21. ∀x[(x = x → Rxa) → Rxa]
22. ∃x∀y(Say ↔ y = x) →
    [(Sac & Sad) → c = d]

Part III: Arguments in Monadic L= Construct truth trees to determine whether the following arguments are valid or invalid. Indicate any tree that does not terminate.

♦23. a = b, b ≠ c /∴ a ≠ c
24. a ≠ b, b ≠ c /∴ a ≠ c
25. ∀x[∃yx = y → Pa] /∴ Pa
26. ∀x∃yx = y /∴ ∃y∀xx = y
27. ∀x[(x = x → Pa) ∨ ~ Pa], ~Pa & a = b /∴ Pb
28. ∃x∃y(Bx & ~By) /∴ ∃x∃yx ≠ y
♦29. ∀x(Ax → Bx), ∀x(Bx → ~x ≠ x) /∴ ∀x~Ax
30. ∀x(Ax → x = a) ∨ ∀x(Bx → x = b) /∴ ∀x(x = a ∨ x = b)
31. ∀x[a = x → (Px ∨ Gx)], ∀x~Gx, ∃xx = a /∴ ∃xPx

32. $\forall x(Ax \leftrightarrow Bx)$, $\exists x[Ax \mathbin{\&} \forall y(Ay \rightarrow y = x)]$ /∴ $\exists x[Bx \mathbin{\&} \forall y(By \rightarrow y = x)]$

Part IV: Arguments in Polyadic L₌   Construct truth trees to determine whether the following arguments are valid or invalid. Indicate any tree that does not terminate.

33. $\exists x \exists y Axy$ /∴ $\exists x \exists y x \neq y$

34. $\forall x \forall y Axy$ /∴ $\exists x \exists y (Axy \mathbin{\&} x \neq y)$

♦35. $\exists x \exists y x \neq y$, $\forall x \forall y Axy$ /∴ $\exists x \exists y (Axy \mathbin{\&} x \neq y)$

36. $\forall x \exists y (Ay \mathbin{\&} Byx)$, $\sim Aa$ /∴ $\exists x (Ax \mathbin{\&} x \neq a)$

37. $\forall x[Abcx \mathbin{\&} \forall y(Abcy \rightarrow y = x)]$ /∴ $\sim\exists z Abcz \vee \exists x \exists y (Abcx \mathbin{\&} Abcy)$

38. $\forall x \forall y (Axy \rightarrow \sim Axy)$ /∴ $\forall x \forall y (Axy \rightarrow x \neq y)$

39. $\forall x \forall y (Axy \rightarrow \sim Axy)$, $\exists x \exists y Axy$ /∴ $\exists x \exists y x \neq y$

40. $\forall x (Axa \rightarrow \forall y Axy)$, $\exists x \forall y \sim Axy$ /∴ $\forall x \forall y \sim Axy$

41. $\forall x \forall y \forall z[(Axy \vee Byz) \rightarrow \exists u(Cu \mathbin{\&} y = u)]$, $\forall z(z = z \leftrightarrow Bzz)$ /∴ $\exists x Cx$

Part V: Theoretical Problems

42. Rule I depends on the principle that if two terms denote the same individual, then in any statement, any occurrence of one term may be replaced by the other term without altering the truth value of the original statement. This principle always works in $L_=$, but it does not always work in English. Give an example of two English statements where the second statement can be obtained from the first by substitution of codenoting terms, where the first statement is true and where the second statement is false.

43. Rule I follows from a principle known as Leibniz's law:

Two things are identical if, and only if, they have all of the same properties.

Explain why this law cannot be properly expressed in $L_=$.

44. The following proposition, known as the 'Löwenheim–Skolem Theorem', holds for the language L:

If a set P of L statements has a model, then it has a model whose domain is the set of all natural numbers $\{1, 2, 3, \ldots\}$.

Does this theorem also hold for all sets of $L_=$ statements? Why, or why not (give an example if needed)?

8.6   Natural Deduction in $L_=$

We add two rules to those already presented for L in order to ensure a sound and complete system for $L_=$. The resulting system will be an extension of the deduction system D_L, which we call $D_{L_=}$. The first new rule concerns substitution:

> ***Identity (I)***   If the statement q is just like the statement p, except that q contains occurrences of the constant term β_2 at one or more places where p contains β_1, then q may be added as a new line to a proof, provided that both p and $\beta_1 = \beta_2$ occur as whole statements on earlier lines m and n, respectively. As a justification for the line, put '$m, n,$ I'.

Here is an example of the rule's application:

1.	Aa & Ba		PR
2.	a = b		PR
3.	Aa & Bb	1, 2	I

The second rule is called *Identity Introduction:*

> ***Identity Introduction (I Int)***   The statement $\beta = \beta$ may be entered as a new line in a proof at any point, for any constant term β. As a justification for the line, put 'I Int'.

We illustrate the use of this rule by using it to prove that '$\forall x x = x$' is a $D_{L_=}$ theorem:

1.	~$\forall x x = x$		PA-RAA
2.	$\exists x x \neq x$	1	Q
3.	$a \neq a$	2	PA-EI
4.	$a = a$		I Int
5.	P & ~P	3, 4	R
6.	P & ~P	3–5	EI
7.	$\forall x x = x$	1–6	RAA

In fact, I Int can be used to give an even shorter and easier proof of this theorem:

1.	a = a		I Int
2.	$\forall x x = x$	1	UG

This is a perfectly good proof of the theorem. Because 'a' does not occur in line 2 and does not occur in any premise or provisional assumption covering line 2 (since there are no premises or provisional assumptions!), the use of UG is correct.

The next sample proof involves a more interesting use of Rule I. It is a derivation verifying a claim made earlier, when the sign '=' was first introduced as part of the formal language. It was stated in Section 8.3 that in order for the statement '∃x∃y[(Bx & ~By) & (Ax & Ay)]' to be true under a given interpretation, there have to exist at least two distinct objects in the domain of that interpretation. Let's therefore prove that, from this statement as a premise, it follows that there exist at least two distinct things—that is, '∃x∃yx ≠ y' is true:

1.	∃x∃y[(Bx & ~By) & (Ax & Ay)]			PR
	2.	~∃x∃yx ≠ y		PA-RAA
		3.	∃y[(Ba & ~By) & (Aa & Ay)]	1	PA-EI
			4.	(Ba & ~Bb) & (Aa & Ab)	3	PA-EI
			5.	∀x~∃yx ≠ y	2	Q
			6.	~∃ya ≠ y	5	UI
			7.	∀y~a ≠ y	6	Q
			8.	~a ≠ b	7	UI
			9.	a = b	8	DN
			10.	(Ba & ~Bb)	4	CE
			11.	Ba	10	CE
			12.	~Bb	10	CE
			13.	~Ba	9, 12	I
			14.	P & ~P	11, 13	R
		15.	P & ~P		4–14	EI
	16.	P & ~P		3–15	EI
17.	∃x∃yx ≠ y			2–16	RAA

Among other things, note the importance of introducing *distinct* names for the nested existential quantifiers in the EI method. Note, too, why 'P & ~P' had to be introduced—that is, why using 'Ba & ~Ba' as our reductio conclusion would have run into trouble when we tried to apply the rule EI.

As a final example, we present a proof for the following argument:

$$∃x∀y(Fy ↔ y = x), ∀x(Fx ↔ Gx) /∴ ∃x∀y(Gy ↔ y = x)$$

There are of course innumerably many different ways to give a correct proof for this argument. No claim is made about economy here—indeed, the proof could be done more quickly. However, a long proof provides you with an opportunity to examine several steps and to reflect on possible alternate (shorter) strategies:

1.	∃x∀y(Fy ↔ y = x)		PR
2.	∀x(Fx ↔ Gx)		PR
3.	∀y(Fy ↔ y = a)	1	PA-EI
4.	Gb		PA-CP
5.	Fb ↔ Gb	2	UI
6.	(Fb → Gb) & (Gb → Fb)	5	Equiv
7.	Gb → Fb	6	CE
8.	Fb	4, 8	MP
9.	Fb ↔ b = a	3	UI
10.	(Fb → b = a) & (b = a → Fb)	9	Equiv
11.	Fb → b = a	10	CE
12.	b = a	8, 11	MP
13.	Gb → b = a	4–12	CP
14.	b = a		PA-CP
15.	Fb ↔ b = a	3	UI
16.	(Fb → b = a) & (b = a → Fb)	15	Equiv
17.	b = a → Fb	16	CE
18.	Fb	14, 17	MP
19.	Fb ↔ Gb	2	UI
20.	(Fb → Gb) & (Gb → Fb)	19	Equiv
21.	Fb → Gb	20	CE
22.	Gb	18, 21	MP
23.	b = a → Gb	14–22	CP
24.	(Gb → b = a) & (b = a → Gb)	13–23	CI
25.	Gb ↔ b = a	24	Equiv
26.	∀y(Gy ↔ y = a)	25	UG
27.	∃x∀y(Gy ↔ y = x)	26	EG
28.	∃x∀y(Gy ↔ y = x)	3–27	EI

As an exercise, try to discover a shorter proof for this argument.

Exercises for Section 8.6

Part I (A): Arguments in Monadic L₌   Give formal proofs for each of the following arguments.

1. a = b /∴ b = a

2. ∀xx = a, ∃xPx /∴ Pa

♦ 3. ∀x(x = a ∨ x = b), Ga ↔ ~Gb /∴ ∃xx ≠ b

4. ∃x∀y(Ay ↔ y = x) /∴ Aa → ∀y(Ay → y = a)

5. Ac, ~Aa, ∀x[(Ax ∨ Bx) → (x = a ∨ x = b)] /∴ Bc → c = b

6. $\forall y(Ay \leftrightarrow y = m)$ /$\therefore$ Am

7. Am, $\forall x(Ax \rightarrow x = m)$ /$\therefore$ $\forall y(Ay \leftrightarrow y = m)$

8. $\forall x(Rx \rightarrow x \neq m)$, $\forall x(Dx \rightarrow x = m)$, Dn /$\therefore$ Dn & ~Rn

♦9. Ac, $\forall xx = c$, $\forall x(Bx \leftrightarrow \sim Ax)$ /$\therefore$ $\sim\exists xBx$

10. $\forall x\forall y\forall z[(Rx \leftrightarrow y = x) \rightarrow (Az \rightarrow Bz)]$, Aa $\rightarrow$ (~Bc & Ac), Ra
   /$\therefore$ $\sim\forall x\forall y(Ax \& My)$

Part I (B): Arguments in Polyadic L$_=$ Give formal proofs for each of the following arguments.

11. $\forall x\forall y(Pxy \rightarrow \sim Pyx)$ /$\therefore$ $\forall x\forall y(Pxy \rightarrow x \neq y)$

12. $\forall x\forall y(\sim Pxy \rightarrow x \neq y)$ /$\therefore$ $\exists x\exists yPxy$

13. $\forall x(Gax \& x = b)$ /$\therefore$ $\forall x(Gxb \& a = x)$

14. $\forall x\forall y[x \neq y \rightarrow (Qxy \& \sim Qyx)]$ /$\therefore$ $\forall x\forall y[(Qxy \rightarrow Qyx) \rightarrow x = y]$

♦15. $\forall y(Ay \leftrightarrow y = a)$, $\forall x(Bxc \leftrightarrow Ax)$ /$\therefore$ $\forall x(Bxc \rightarrow x = a)$

16. $\forall x\forall y\forall z[Sxyz \rightarrow (Gzx \& Gzy)]$, $\forall x\forall y(Gxy \rightarrow \sim Gyx)$
   /$\therefore$ $\forall x\forall y\forall z(Sxyz \rightarrow x \neq z)$

17. $\forall x\forall y\forall z[(Rxy \& Ryz) \rightarrow Rxz]$, $\forall x\sim Rxx$, $\forall x\exists yRxy$ /$\therefore$ $\forall x\exists yx \neq y$

18. $\exists x\sim Rxx \rightarrow \sim a = a)$, $\forall xRxx \rightarrow \exists x\forall y(By \leftrightarrow y = x)$
   /$\therefore$ $\forall x\forall y[(Bx \& By) \rightarrow x = y]$

19. $\forall x\forall y\forall z\forall u[(Sxyz \& Sxyu) \rightarrow z = u]$ /$\therefore$ $\forall x\forall y(Sxya \leftrightarrow \sim Sxyb) \rightarrow a \neq b$

20. $\forall x(Gax \rightarrow Gxa)$, Gac & (Gca $\rightarrow$ $\forall xGxb$), $\exists xGxa \rightarrow a = b$ /$\therefore$ $\forall xGxa$

Part II (A): Monadic L$_=$ **Theorems**   Give formal proofs for each of the following theorems.

♦21. $a = b \rightarrow (Fa \leftrightarrow Fb)$

22. $\exists x\forall yx \neq y \rightarrow P$

23. $\exists xx = a \lor \forall yy \neq a$

24. $\forall x(Fx \leftrightarrow x = a) \rightarrow Fa$

25. $\forall x\forall y[(x = a \& y = a) \rightarrow x = y]$

26. $\forall x\forall y[(Ax \& \sim Ay) \rightarrow x \neq y]$

♦27. $\exists y\forall xx = y \rightarrow \forall x\exists yx = y$

28. $\sim\exists x[x = a \& \exists y(y = x \& (Ha \& \sim Hy))]$

29. $\forall x\forall y\forall z[(x = y \lor x = z) \rightarrow (Gx \rightarrow (Gy \lor Gz))]$

30. $\forall x\forall y\forall z[(Fx \leftrightarrow (\sim Fy \lor \sim Fz)) \rightarrow (x \neq y \lor x \neq z)]$

31. $\forall xx = a \rightarrow \forall x\forall yy = x$

Part II (B): Polyadic L= Theorems   Give formal proofs for each of the following theorems.

32. $\forall x \forall y[(x = a \& y = a) \rightarrow (Rab \leftrightarrow (Rxb \& Ryb))]$
33. $\forall x \forall y(Rxy \rightarrow x = y) \rightarrow \forall x \forall y(Rxy \leftrightarrow Ryx)$
34. $\forall x \forall y[x = y \rightarrow \forall z((Gxy \& Gyz) \rightarrow Gxz)]$
35. $(Pa \& Pb) \leftrightarrow \exists x \exists y[(Px \& Py) \& (x = a \& y = b)]$
36. $\forall x x = a \rightarrow [\exists x Pxa \rightarrow \forall x \forall y Pxy]$
♦37. $\forall x \forall y[Rxy \leftrightarrow x = y] \rightarrow \forall x \forall y \forall z[(Rxy \& Ryz) \rightarrow Rxz]$
38. $\forall x \forall y \forall z[Cxyz \leftrightarrow (Rxy \& y = z)] \rightarrow [a = b \rightarrow (Rab \leftrightarrow Cabb)]$
39. $\forall x \forall y \forall z[Bxyz \leftrightarrow (x = y \vee z = y)] \rightarrow [(Babc \& b \neq c) \rightarrow a = b]$
40. $\forall x \forall y[((Py \& Ey) \rightarrow y = x) \& Lxa] \rightarrow \forall x \forall y[(Py \& Ey) \rightarrow (Lxa \rightarrow Lya)]$

Part III: Theoretical Problems[8]

41. Rule I depends upon the principle that if two terms denote the same individual, then in any statement, any occurrence of one term may be replaced by the other term without altering the truth value of the original statement. This principle always works in $L_=$, but it does not always work in English. Give an example of two English statements where the second statement can be obtained from the first by substitution of codenoting terms, where the first statement is true and where the second statement is false.

42. Rule I follows from a principle known as Leibniz's law:

    Two things are identical if, and only if, they have all of the same properties.

    Explain why this law cannot be properly stated in $L_=$.

43. The following proposition, known as the 'Löwenheim–Skolem Theorem', holds for the language L:

    If a set P of L statements has a model, then it has a model whose domain is the set of all natural numbers $\{1, 2, 3, \ldots\}$.

    Does this theorem also hold for all sets of $L_=$ statements? Why, or why not (give an example if needed)?

---

[8]These problems duplicate the theoretical problems from the previous section. They are repeated here as a convenience for those who have not studied Section 8.5.

8.7   Functions

In this section we present our second extension to L, the introduction of function symbols. Though it is possible to consider a language that contains function symbols but no identity symbol, the most interesting and important applications of functions involve identity, so we treat the addition of function symbols as an extension of our language $L_=$ rather than of L. We call this extension 'L^*'.

You were probably first exposed to functions in high school algebra. For instance, here is an equation for a parabola written in functional form:

$$f(x) = x^2 + 2.$$

This is sometimes written simply as '$y = x^2 + 2$', but the notation '$f(x)$' reminds us that "y is a function of x." To say that y is a function of x is simply to say that a given value of x determines a *unique* value for y. We can think of a function as a rule for determining a single "output" on the basis of one or more "inputs." The inputs are generally referred to as 'arguments'.

In the above equation, we *cannot* say that x is a function of y, because, if we solve the equation for x we get

$$x = \pm\sqrt{y - 2}.$$

For any value of $y > 2$, there are actually *two* values of x. Consequently, y does not determine a *unique* value for x. In mathematics the above equation is said to express a 'relation', but it does not give x as a function of y.

The function given by the equation '$f(x) = x^2 + 2$' is a *one-place function*, or a function of one argument. We can also define functions with more than one argument. Addition is an example of a *two-place function*. Using the same style of notation as above, we can express the addition function:

$$f(x, y) = x + y.$$

This is a function because for any "input" choice of x and y there is a unique "output" value $x + y$.

Although functions defined on the real numbers are perhaps the most familiar of functions, many functions take non-numerical arguments (inputs) and have non-numerical values (outputs). One class of functions that we have already discussed is the class of truth functions. Recall that the reason we call the *SL* connectives 'truth-functional' is that the truth values of the constituent statements (the arguments, in the present terminology) determine a unique truth value.[9]

A formal interpretation gives us yet another example of a function. In introducing the formal semantics of *L*, we noted that an interpretation assigns a unique extension to every non-logical symbol in the language being interpreted. We used the functional notation '$\mathcal{I}(s)$' to denote that assignment, indicating that each possible interpretation is a function *from* symbols *to* their extensions.

Since not all functions involve numbers, it is important to specify the kinds of values a function can take as arguments, and what kinds of values it gives as results. For example, the function $f(x) = x^2$ is well defined for all real numbers as arguments, and to these arguments the function assigns real numbers as results. In this case, we say that it is a function 'from the real numbers to the real numbers'.[10] There are other possibilities that it would not make sense to consider as arguments. What, for instance, would be the value of f(Andrew)? Similarly, interpretations of *L* are functions from symbols of *L* to extensions of those symbols, and it would not make much sense to ask for the value of, say, $\mathcal{I}(24)$, since 24 is not a symbol of *L*. The set of all "input" values on which a function is defined is called the **domain** of the function. The set of all "output" values is called the **range** of the function. Thus, in the case of $f(x) = x^2$, the domain of the function is the set of real numbers, and the range is also the set of real numbers. In the case of an interpretation, the domain of the function $\mathcal{I}$ is the set of all non-logical constants of the formal language being interpreted, and the range is a collection of sets including the domain $\mathcal{D}$ plus various sets of *n*-tuples of elements of $\mathcal{D}$.

Let's begin our discussion of *L** by considering how to symbolize the following statement:

Anna's father is in the army.

Using the following interpretation,

$\mathcal{D}$:   people

Ax: x is in the army

d: Anna's father.

---

[9]See Section 2.2. Thinking of truth functions as analogous to algebraic functions leads to a type of mathematical system called *Boolean algebra* (named after George Boole, an important nineteenth-century mathematician and logician). Boolean algebra is like algebra, except that the variables range over truth-values rather than over numerical values.

[10]A standard mathematical way of indicating this "from–to" aspect of a function is by use of the notation '$\rightarrow$' to indicate direction. Letting '$\mathbb{R}$' denote the set of real numbers, we can indicate that the function $f(x) = x^2$ goes "from the reals to the reals" by writing '$f: \mathbb{R} \rightarrow \mathbb{R}$'.

we can symbolize this statement simply as

Ad.

This symbolization loses important information because it does not exhibit the fact that the individual denoted by 'd' is Anna's father. We *could* solve this by introducing a relation symbol 'Fxy' to represent the relation of father to child and a constant 'a' to denote Anna. We might then symbolize the English as

∃x(Fxa & Ax).

This is better but still not perfect, for it fails to express the fact that Anna has *only one* father. We can remedy this by turning to $L_=$ as follows:

∃x((Fxa & ∀y(Fya → y = x)) & Ax)

Though this does the trick, we can symbolize our statement in a more compact and intuitive way by introducing a function symbol. Every person has a unique (biological) father, so fatherhood is a function from persons to persons. Let's use the symbol 'f^1' to represent this function. The superscript '1' indicates that the function takes one argument. We now specify its interpretation:

f^1x: the father of x.

The original statement can now be symbolized quite concisely as

Af^1a.

What is the domain and range of the function denoted by 'f^1'? Since every person has a father, its domain is the same as the domain of the interpretation. On the other hand, since not every person *is* a father, the range of the function is some subset of the domain. For L^* we require that all functions be defined for every object in the domain of interpretation and that the set of values of the function (its range) will be some subset of the domain.

8.8   Syntax and Semantics for L^*

The first step in extending $L_=$ to L^* is the introduction of new symbols that represent functions. For this purpose we use selected lowercase letters with numerical superscripts. The value of the superscript specifies the number of argument places for the function. Formally, we add to the list of symbols presented in Section 5.3 the following:

> ***Function symbols***[11]   An infinite supply of lowercase Roman letters 'a' through 't', with or without numerical subscripts, and a numerical superscript n, $n \geq 1$:
>
> $$a^1, b^1, \ldots, t^1, a^1_1, b^1_1, \ldots, t^1_1, a^1_2, \ldots$$
> $$a^2, b^2, \ldots, t^2, a^2_1, b^2_1, \ldots, t^2_1, a^2_2, \ldots$$
> $$a^3, b^3, \ldots, t^3, a^3_1, b^3_1, \ldots, t^3_1, a^3_2, \ldots$$
>
> .
>
> .
>
> .

Note the similarities between our treatment of predicate symbols and our treatment of function symbols. Actually, an n-place predicate symbol denotes (relative to an interpretation) an n-place function from n-tuples of elements of the domain to the set of truth values as its range. Similarly, an n-place function symbol denotes (relative to an interpretation) an n-place function from n-tuples of elements of the domain to a subset of the domain as its range. Notice as well that we may think of individual constants as "zero-place" functions, just as we may think of statement letters as zero-place relation symbols.

To complete the presentation of syntax for function symbols, we need to specify formation rules for *L**. We do not need to modify the definition of $L_=$ formula at all. Instead, we modify the definition of an '$L_=$ term'. Informally, a term is any expression that denotes an individual (i.e., an element of $\mathcal{D}$). Until now, the only terms we have dealt with have been variables and individual constants. When a function symbol is followed by terms, the result is an expression that can be used to pick out individual objects in the domain, so it too is a term. Here is the revised formal definition of a term:

> ***Definition***   1.   Any individual constant or individual variable is an *L** **term.**
>
> 2.   Any n-place function symbol followed by n terms is an *L** **term.**
>
> 3.   No other symbols or strings of symbols are *L** terms.

---

[11]Some texts use the term 'functor' or 'operator' or 'operation symbol'. We include among function symbols only 'a' through 't' with superscripts to maintain the parallel to individual constants.

Aside from the replacement of '$L_=$' by '$L*$', clause (2) is the new item in the definition. Clause (2) makes this definition recursive, since it allows that more complex terms may be formed from simpler ones. Unlike the language of mathematics, we do not place commas between the arguments of a function, nor do we mark the arguments off by parentheses. That is, we will write 'f^1a' instead of '$f^1(a)$', 'f^2ab' instead of '$f^2(a, b)$', and so on. Here are some more examples of terms:

$$f^1c \qquad g^2xb \qquad f^1f^1f^1f^1f^1f^1y \qquad g^2h^1f^1f^1ab$$

For some of the longer examples, it may take a bit of thought to see why an expression is a term. Consider our last example: 'g^2' is a two–place function symbol. Thus, for the whole string to count as a properly formed term, we must find two terms following it. The first complete term following 'g^2' is the string '$h^1f^1f^1a$', so we take it as the first argument. Immediately following '$h^1f^1f^1a$' we find 'b', which is also a term. Since 'g^2' is followed by two terms, the entire expression is itself a term. Granted, this is a case in which parentheses and brackets would assist us in easier reading (giving '$g^2[h^1(f^1(f^1(a))), b]$'), we will nevertheless omit such grouping symbols from functional notation in $L*$.

By contrast, here are some examples of non–terms:

$$f^1(a) \qquad g^2xbb \qquad f^1f^1f^1f^1f^1f^2y \qquad g^2h^1f^1f^1a$$

We leave it to you to discover why each of these expressions is not a term.[12] From here on, we will also adopt the simplifying convention of dropping superscripts from function symbols when the context clearly implies how many argument places a function symbol has.

As with L and $L_=$, terms are divided into constant terms and variable terms. A term containing one or more variables is a **variable term;** otherwise, it is a **constant term.** Thus, 'f^1a' and '$g^2h^1f^1f^1ab$' are constant terms, whereas 'g^2xb' and '$f^1f^1f^1f^1f^1f^1y$' are variable terms.

Having now finished with the additional formal syntax, we turn to the semantics for function symbols in $L*$. This involves adding two clauses to the defini-

---

[12]The notation we use here, where the function symbol precedes its arguments, is called **prefix notation.** It contrasts with the notation we are familiar with in mathematics for the standard arithmetic functions like addition and multiplication. For those functions, the function symbol (e.g., '$\times$' or '$+$') stands *between* the arguments. This kind of notation, called **infix notation,** does not work for functions of more than two arguments, and it also requires parentheses.

tion of an interpretation. Since the definition of 'truth under an interpretation' already refers to terms, no further changes are needed there.

Let's call any variable term that contains at least one function symbol a **functional expression**. A **simple functional expression** is a functional expression containing only a single function symbol, such as 'm¹x' and 'g³xyz'. A **compound functional expression** is a functional expression containing multiple function symbols, such as 'm¹m¹x'. There are many cases in which there is no need to employ a distinct simple function symbol for each function. For instance, if the symbol 'm¹' is interpreted as 'is the mother of', we may express the function 'is the maternal grandmother of' as 'm¹m¹'.

It is not obvious what we should take to be the *intension* of a functional expression. We might call it simply 'a function', but we would still have not specified just what a function *is*. One way to solve this problem is to say that a function is a *rule* for associating arguments (the inputs) with values (the outputs). The way that we have informally specified interpretations is consistent with this, for we have always written down some expression that allows us to find or calculate the value of the function for a given argument. Of course, in saying that a function is a 'rule', we have not advanced our understanding of the intension of a function unless the meaning of 'rule' can be made precise. Whereas talk of the 'intension' of a functional expression may be obscure, the *extension* of a functional expression is easily made precise.

We define the extension of an *n*-place function symbol to be a set of $(n + 1)$-tuples of individuals from the domain of interpretation. The first *n* individuals in the $(n + 1)$-tuple are arguments for the function, and the $n + 1$st individual is the result of applying the function to those arguments. As an example, let's consider the "successor function" (i.e., the "add 1" function) of arithmetic. In an interpretation we might specify this function informally and intensionally as follows:

$$s^1x: \qquad x + 1.$$

Since this function has one argument, its extension is a set of 2-tuples—that is, $(1 + 1)$-tuples. The first member of each pair is an element of the domain as an argument of the function, and the second member of each pair is the value of the function for that argument. If $\mathcal{D}$ is the set of natural numbers, then the set of ordered pairs assigned to 's¹', is infinite:

$$\mathcal{I}(s^1) = \{<1, 2>, <2, 3>, <3, 4>, <4, 5>, \ldots\}.$$

To accommodate this change we add another clause to our definition of an interpretation given in Section 5.4:

5. For every n-place function symbol, there is a set of $(n + 1)$-tuples
    of objects in the domain of $\mathcal{I}$. The set must contain *exactly* one
    $(n + 1)$-tuple for each possible sequence of n objects in the domain.
    We say that the interpretation **assigns** a set of $(n + 1)$-tuples to the
    function symbol.

The second sentence in clause (5) requires an explanation. A function expressed in
L^* must be defined for every combination of arguments from the domain. In the
case of a one-place function symbol, this means that the associated function must
have a value for each object in the domain. For a two-place function symbol, the
associated function must have a value for each ordered pair of individuals in the
domain, and so on for $n > 2$. Furthermore, for any possible combinations of n arguments, there must be *at most* one $(n + 1)$-tuple. This guarantees that the function
will have a *unique* value for each n-tuple of arguments.

Clause (4) of the definition of an interpretation tells us what objects in the
domain are denoted by individual constants, but we also need to know what objects are denoted by constant terms in which function symbols occur. We thus add
a final clause to the definition:

6. If t is a constant term of the form $\theta^n \beta_1, \ldots, \beta_n,$ then there is a unique
    $(n + 1)$-tuple $<\mathcal{I}(\beta_1), \ldots, \mathcal{I}(\beta_n), \delta> \in \mathcal{I}(\theta^n)$, where δ is some ob-
    ject in the domain and $\mathcal{I}$ assigns δ to t.

The easiest way to understand what this means is to consider an example. Suppose
we have the following interpretation:

$\mathcal{D}$:   natural numbers $\{1, 2, 3, \ldots\}$

a: 1

b: 2

fxy: $x + y$.

What is the object that $\mathcal{I}$ assigns to 'fab'? The denotation of the function symbol
'f' is an infinite set of three-tuples:

$$\mathcal{I}(f) = \{<x, y, z> \mid z = x + y\}.$$

We can list some of the members of the set like this:

$$\mathcal{I}(f) = \{<1, 1, 2>, <1, 2, 3>, <2, 1, 3>, <2, 2, 4>, <2, 3, 5>,$$
$$<3, 2, 5>, \ldots\}.$$

According to the interpretation, $\mathcal{I}(a) = 1$ and $\mathcal{I}(b) = 2$. Observe that there exists a 3-tuple in $\mathcal{I}(f)$ having 1 and 2 as its first two members, respectively: <1, 2, 3>. By clause (6) then, $\mathcal{I}(fab) = 3$. Notice how important it is that there is exactly one 3-tuple with the numbers 1 and 2 as its first two members. This is what ensures that $\mathcal{I}(fab)$ has a definite value.

Exercises for Section 8.8

Part I: Functions   Indicate which of the following expressions are functions. For those that not, indicate why they are not.

1. 'mother of x'; $\mathcal{D}$: human beings
2. 'daughter of x'; $\mathcal{D}$: human beings
♦3. 'senator of x'; $\mathcal{D}$: U.S. citizens
4. 'congressional representative of x'; $\mathcal{D}$: U.S. citizens
5. 'lesser of x and y'; $\mathcal{D}$: natural numbers
6. 'successor of x'; $\mathcal{D}$: natural numbers
♦7. 'predecessor of x'; $\mathcal{D}$: natural numbers
8. 'number between x and y'; $\mathcal{D}$: natural numbers
9. 'negation of x'; $\mathcal{D}$: formulas of *L**
10. 'conjunction of x and y'; $\mathcal{D}$: formulas of *L**

*Part II: Formal Syntax of L**   Indicate whether each of the following expressions is a constant term, a variable term, or neither. If it is not a term, indicate why it is not.

11. f^1a	16. a^2xa
12. f^1g^1	♦17. $g^2g^2abg^2cd$
♦13. $g^2(a, b)$	18. $f^1g^1m^2px$
14. $f^1a = b$	19. r^3abf^1a
15. a^2x	20. $g^2g^2g^2aaaa$

*Part III: Formal Semantics of L**   Use the interpretation below to determine the truth values of the statements that follow.

$\mathcal{D}$:	people
Fx:	x is female
Mx:	x is male

Axy: x is a biological aunt of y

Bxy: x is a biological brother of y

Sxy: x is a biological sister of y

Uxy: x is a biological uncle of y

fx: the biological father of x

gx: the biological mother of x

♦21. $\forall x \exists y fx = y$ 26. $\forall x \forall y [Axy \to \exists z (Sxz \ \& \ (gy = z \lor fy = z))]$

22. $\forall x Mfx$ 27. $\exists x Fgx \to \exists x Fx$

23. $\exists x fx = gx$ 28. $\exists x \exists y (fx = y \ \& \ {\sim} \exists z Bxz)$

24. $\forall x \forall y (Uxy \to \exists z fxz)$ 29. $\exists x \exists y fgfx = fgfy$

♦25. $\forall x (\exists y ggy = x \to \exists y gy = x)$ 30. $\forall x \forall y [(Sxy \lor Bxy) \to (fx = fy \lor gx = gy)]$

8.9   Symbolization in L*

As a first symbolization problem, let's consider an application from mathematics. Consider the following distributive law from arithmetic:

$$x \cdot (y + z) = (x \cdot y + x \cdot z).$$

We can easily symbolize this mathematical statement in L*, using function symbols:

$\mathcal{D}$:   natural numbers

axy: $x + y$

mxy: $x \cdot y.$

The distributive law is a universal statement that holds for all natural numbers, so we symbolize it as follows:

$\forall x \forall y \forall z mxayz = amxymxz.$

The next example arises from a common mathematical principle used for proving that all natural numbers have some property. This is the *principle of (weak) mathematical induction*:

> **Mathematical Induction**   To prove that all natural numbers *n* have the property *P*, prove that both of the following statements are true:
>
> 1. The number 1 has the property *P*.
> 2. For any natural number *n*, if *n* has the property *P*, then *n* + 1 has the property *P*.

For any property *P* we choose, we can express the principle of mathematical induction in *L**. Let's begin with a paraphrase in English:

> If the natural number 1 is *P*, and if any natural number is *P* only if its immediate successor is *P*, then all natural numbers are *P*.

Let's use the one-place function symbol 'sx' to represent the function 'the immediate successor of x' and 'a' to denote the number 1. We can then symbolize the statement 'Any natural number is *P* only if its immediate successor is *P*' as follows:

$$\forall x(Px \rightarrow Psx).$$

The desired symbolization is thus

$$(Pa \,\&\, \forall x(Px \rightarrow Psx)) \rightarrow \forall x Px.$$

This statement form is a very important one for formalized theories of arithmetic, a subject briefly introduced in Chapter 9.[13]

Function symbols generally make symbolization tasks easier than they would otherwise be. Nonetheless, the symbolization process can be complicated when compound functional expressions are involved. For the the next few examples, we make use of the following interpretation:

---

[13]Notice that what we have produced is a statement *form*, not a statement. The metalinguistic variable '*P*' ranges over all possible one-place predicate expressions of *L**. Relative to our interpretation of 'a' and 'sx', the principle of mathematical induction implies that every statement of this form is true. To fully capture the mathematical induction principle in symbolic form, however, we must be able to symbolize this: 'For any property *P*, if the natural number 1 is *P*, and if any natural number is *P* only if its immediate successor is *P*, then all natural numbers are *P*'. This statement includes a quantifier that ranges not over individuals, but over *properties* of individuals. To symbolize this statement in a formal language, we need what is called 'second-order logic' (see Section 9.6).

$\mathcal{D}$:   people

Gx: x is male

Hx: x is happy

Mxy: x is married to y

fx: the father of x

mx: the mother of x

a: Anna

g: Gretel.

Use the following as a start:

Anna's grandfather is happy.

When you attempt to symbolize this, you will notice an ambiguity: People have *two* grandfathers. Presumably, in the context where a statement like this one is expressed, it would be clear which grandfather is being mentioned. If the intended person is the maternal grandfather, then we symbolize the statement as follows:

Hfma.

That is, "Happiness applies to the father of the mother of Anna." If the person is the paternal grandfather, we instead use

Hffa.

That is, "Happiness applies to the father of the father of Anna." Notice that we can have no *function* 'the grandfather of x', since a function must specify a unique value for its argument. However, we can have functions 'the paternal grandfather of x' or 'the maternal grandfather of x', since every person has a unique maternal and paternal grandfather.

How should we symbolize the following?

Anna's maternal grandparents are not married.

We can use the expression 'mma' to refer to Anna's maternal grandmother and the expression 'fma' to refer to her maternal grandfather. So, we simply say

~Mmmafma.

Let's also consider a case involving quantifiers:

Some father has no father.

This is an O-type statement. We know how to symbolize it, as long as we can find predicate expressions for 'x is a father' and 'x has a father' using our function 'the father of x'. The expression '∃yx = fy' is an *L** predicate (i.e., a formula containing a free variable) that will be true of x just in case x is a father. Similarly, the expression '∃zz = fx' is a predicate that will be true of x just in case x has a father. Putting these together in the O form, we get

$$\exists x(\exists yx = fy \;\&\; {\sim}\exists zz = fx).$$

Notice that the above *L** statement is a logical contradiction. This is because, given our specification that every function must take a value for *every* object in the domain, the second conjunct can never be true for any value of 'x' whatsoever. Logical falsehoods of this sort raise an interesting puzzle. In our discussions of symbolization, we have generally viewed symbolizations that are logically equivalent to our preferred symbolization as correct. For instance, the statement

$$\exists x(\exists yfy = x \;\&\; \forall z{\sim}z = fx)$$

is logically equivalent to the symbolic statement that precedes it, and it is an equally good way to express the original English statement in *L**. However, if we allow *every* logically equivalent statement to be correct, we would also have to say that

A & ~A

is a correct symbolization of 'Some father has no father'. This is an undesirable consequence. It seems, rather, that some logically equivalent statements are better than others for rendering a given proposition into symbolic form. Unfortunately, no one has yet devised a principled way to decide which of infinitely many logically equivalent statements would best express the proposition we mean to express on any given occasion. This example well illustrates the problem of propositional identity that we described in Section 1.3.

As a final example, consider the symbolization of the statement

Gretel's brother is unmarried.

We use only the symbols given in the interpretation on page 370. The first step is to express the relation 'x is the brother of y' with only our function symbols 'f' and 'm'. We need a formula with 'x' and 'y' as free variables that represents this relation. For simplicity, we assume that siblings must share both a father and a mother:

$((fx = fy \ \& \ mx = my) \ \& \ x \neq y)$.

Further, we want to say that x is a *brother* of y, so we must add a formula expressing the fact that x is male. The following gives us 'x is the brother of y':

$(Gx \ \& \ ((fx = fy \ \& \ mx = my) \ \& \ x \neq y))$.

Let's abbreviate this expression as '$\mathcal{B}xy$'. Next we need to find an expression that represents "being unmarried." We have a predicate symbol representing the relation of being married, so we can express the property of not being married as

$\sim\exists y Mxy$.

Let's abbreviate this symbolic expression as '$\mathcal{M}x$'. The expression 'Gretel's brother' denotes a unique individual, indicating that Gretel has only one brother. We thus need to say that there is somebody who has the property of being Gretel's brother, that this brother is unique, and that he is unmarried. Our first approach is the following:

There exists somebody who is the brother of Gretel, and who is unmarried, and nobody else is the brother of Gretel.

Using our temporary abbreviations we can write this as

$\exists x[(\mathcal{B}xg \ \& \ \mathcal{M}x) \ \& \ \forall y(\mathcal{B}yg \rightarrow x = y)]$.

Now all that we have to do is substitute the respective L^* formulas for $\mathcal{B}$ and $\mathcal{M}$:

$\exists x[((Gx \ \& \ ((fx = fg \ \& \ mx = mg) \ \& \ x \neq g)) \ \& \ \sim\exists y Mxy)$
$\ \ \ \& \ \forall y((Gy \ \& \ ((fy = fg \ \& \ my = mg) \ \& \ y \neq g)) \rightarrow x = y)]$.

To conclude our discussion of symbolization, we should mention that from a purely formal standpoint, function symbols are unnecessary. This is because, given any *n*-place function, we can represent the function using an (*n* + 1)-place relation. We already saw that this was the case in the example concerning Anna's father that concluded Section 8.7. We saw that the relationship between father and child could be represented either by a one-place function symbol 'fx' (father of x) or a two-place relation symbol 'Fxy' (x is father of y).

To stipulate that a function symbol and a relation symbol represent the same relationship, we may write a statement that serves as a kind of "definition" of one expression in terms of the other. Here is such a statement for the function symbol 'f' and relation symbol 'F':

$$\forall x \forall y (y = fx \leftrightarrow Fyx)$$

Relative to this biconditional, we may write equivalent statements using either the function or relation symbol. Recalling our earlier example, we wrote (1) 'Afa' to symbolize 'Anna's father is in the army'. We can symbolize this same statement using a relation symbol by writing (2) '∃y(Fya & Ay)'. Of course, (1) and (2) are not logically equivalent, but, when we conditionalize on the biconditional definition, we find

$$\forall x \forall y (y = fx \leftrightarrow Fyx) \rightarrow [Afa \leftrightarrow \exists y(Fya \ \& \ Ay)]$$

is logical truth.

To use relation symbols *alone* to express function relationships, we need some way to guarantee that the relation associates a single object (the function value) with each object (argument) in the domain. Once again using the relation symbol 'F' to illustrate, the following statement does the trick:

$$\forall x \exists y \forall z (z = y \leftrightarrow Fzx)$$

In any interpretation under which this statement is true, the relation denoted by 'F' will be functional. We leave it to you to check that this statement entails both '∀x∃yFyx', which asserts that the function has a value for every object in the domain, and '∀x∀y∀z((Fyx & Fzx) → y = z)', which asserts that the value is unique. Using this second quantified biconditional, we can find an alternative symbolization for 'Anna's father is in the Army'. We simply conjoin the biconditional to statement (2) above to get

$$\forall x \exists y \forall z (z = y \leftrightarrow Fzx) \ \& \ \exists y(Fya \ \& \ Ay)$$

These examples suggest how we can get along without function symbols, if need be. Their practical convenience is considerable, however, as can be seen by considering how much more complicated the symbolic statement abbreviated as '∃x[(ℬxg & 𝓜x) & ∀y(ℬyg → x = y)]' would become *without* the use of function symbols.

Exercises for Section 8.9

Part I: Symbolization

(A) Using the interpretation provided, symbolize the following English statements in *L**.

$\mathcal{D}$:	persons
Fx:	x is a woman
Hx:	x is humble
Lxy:	x loves y
Mxy:	x is married to y
fx:	the father of x
mx:	the mother of x
a:	Alonzo
c:	Carlos
d:	Damita
e:	Eldora

♦ 1. All mothers are women, but some women are not mothers.

2. No father is a mother.

3. Carlos and Alonzo's mother is Eldora.

4. Carlos and Alonzo are siblings.

5. Damita has a half brother.

6. Alonzo's parents love each other.

♦ 7. Some parents are not married (to each other).

8. Some fathers are paternal grandfathers.

9. Damita and Carlos are not married, but they have two children.

10. Damita is an only child (no siblings or half siblings).

11. Every person has exactly one father.

(B)   Using the interpretation provided, symbolize the following English statements in L*.

$\mathcal{D}$:	everything
Sx:	x is a set
Ix:	x is an individual (object)
Px:	x is a predicate
Cx:	x is a constant
Exy:	x is a member of y
Txy:	the statement formed by concatenating predicate x and constant y is true

ex: the extension of x

ix: the intension of x

12. The extension of a predicate is a set.

♦13. The extension of a constant is an individual.

14. If two predicates have a common intension, then they have a common extension.

15. Some constants may have the same extension but different intensions.

16. If two sets have the same members, then they are the same set.

♦17. No set is a member of itself.

18. The extensions of some predicates are empty (are sets that have no members).

19. A statement formed by concatenating a predicate and a constant together is true if, and only if, the extension of the constant is an element of the extension of the predicate.

Part II: Theoretical Problems

(A) For each of the following statements, give two *L** symbolizations: (1) one containing function symbols and (2) an equivalent statement containing no function symbols.

20. The mother of Samantha is a biologist.

♦21. The successor of 3 is even.

22. Ten is the sum of 6 and 4.

23. Six is the product of 2 and 3.

24. The successor of 3 is the predecessor of 5.

(B)

25. In Exercise 11 the correct symbolization of the English statement 'Every person has exactly one father' is a logical truth of *L**. Nonetheless, it seems like it is at least *logically possible* that a person should have no father. In fact, if we symbolize the statement 'Some person has no father' without function symbols as

$\exists x \exists y (Fxy \ \& \ \sim\exists z Fzx)$,

where 'Fxy' means 'x is the father of y', the result is an *L** statement that is consistent. Is the statement 'Every person has exactly one father' a logical truth? Why, or why not?

8.10   Truth Trees in L^*

The introduction of function symbols does not require us to change any of our truth tree rules or definitions. Whereas in L the only constant terms were individual constants, in L^* there are also constant terms involving function symbols. A number of truth tree rules and definitions make reference to constant terms. All we have to do now is to apply these rules and definitions, keeping in mind that we now have more constant terms than we had before.

We consider universally quantified statements first. Suppose we have the following trunk of a tree:

$$Pf^1a$$
$$\forall xQx$$
$$Qa$$

Is this tree finished? The first and third statements are simple, so the only question is whether we are done with the universally quantified statement. Our definition states that for an open branch to be complete, every universally quantified statement must be instantiated for every constant term on the branch. The statement '$\forall xQx$' is instantiated for the constant term 'a', but it is not instantiated for the other constant term, 'f^1a'. To finish the tree, we must add one more line:

$$Pf^1a$$
$$\forall xQx$$
$$Qa$$
$$Qf^1a$$

From a semantic point of view, if '$\forall xQx$' is true under an interpretation, every individual in the domain must be in the set denoted by 'Q'. It follows that this set must include not only the individual denoted by 'a' but also the (possibly different) individual denoted by 'f^1a'.

Our next example presents a slightly more difficult tree involving a universally quantified statement. We start with a single statement:

$$\forall xCf^1x$$

The single branch of this tree contains no constant terms, so to complete it we must instantiate the quantifier with a new constant term, say, 'a':

$$\forall xCf^1x$$
$$Cf^1a$$

By instantiating the quantifier, we have managed to introduce the *new* constant term 'f^{1}a'. We must thus instantiate the quantifier with this term as well:

$$\forall x Cf^1x$$
$$Cf^1a$$
$$Cf^1f^1a$$

Clearly, this tree is infinite. Every time we instantiate the universal statement, we create a new constant term:

$$\forall x Cf^1x$$
$$Cf^1a$$
$$Cf^1f^1a$$
$$Cf^1f^1f^1a$$
$$Cf^1f^1f^1f^1a$$
$$Cf^1f^1f^1f^1f^1a$$
$$\cdot$$
$$\cdot$$
$$\cdot$$

This tree shows immediately that our truth tree method does not provide an effective decision procedure for *L**. This holds true even if, as in the tree above, we exclude statements involving polyadic predicates. Before we added function symbols, the only statements in *L* that could generate infinite trees were statements containing an existential quantifier within the scope of a universal quantifier. Using the rule E* we amended our procedure to solve this problem for all sets of statements not involving polyadic predicates, as well as for many sets of statements including polyadic predicates. With the introduction of function symbols, however, the problem arises in statements containing no existential quantifiers at all, so it provides no help with the difficulty.[14]

Next consider how function symbols affect our application of the tree rules for identity statements. If we have an identity statement involving constant terms, our rules for identity allow us to substitute one term for the other in statements on the branch. Consider a branch containing the following two statements:

$$Qa \rightarrow Qfa$$
$$a = fa$$

---

[14]The fact that our existing tree rules do not allow us to complete this tree does not show that we couldn't somehow amend our tree rules so that it would. In fact, the statement '$\forall x Cf^1x$' has a model with only a single individual in the domain. We know, however, via the Church–Turing Undecidability Theorem, that it is impossible to amend the tree rules to make the tree method an effective decision procedure for consistency in *L**.

Let's decompose the conditional first:

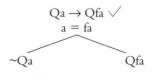

According to our final definition of a finished open branch (see Section 8.5), the right-hand branch is already complete. It is complete because it contains no negated simple statements; hence, no substitutions from the identity statement are required. It is fortunate that we can complete the tree in this way, since the other branch turns out to be infinite. We first substitute 'fa' for 'a' in '~Qa', giving us '~Qfa'. To finish the newly extended branch, we must now substitute 'fa' for 'a' in '~Qfa', and so on. In attempting to complete this branch, we obtain a similar pattern to the one we found in the tree beginning with a universal quantifier:

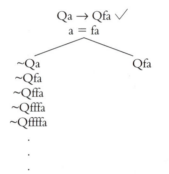

    We have emphasized the fact that there are no effective decision procedures for L or L*. In previous discussion we also pointed out that there is no way to effectively determine whether a truth tree is potentially infinite. How, then, to proceed? How do you know *when* you've worked "long enough" on a problem? The answer: Sometimes you can see and even explain how you know that a tree can be continued indefinitely; other times, you just can't tell at all—and that, unfortunately, is the best that you can do! Disconcerting as this may be, it is the predicament of mechanical methods applied to these formal languages.

Exercises for Section 8.10

Part I: Arguments   Build truth trees for each of the following to determine whether or not the arguments are valid. Indicate any infinite trees.

♦1. $\forall x fx = x / \therefore \forall x \forall y yx = y$

2. $fa = b \;\&\; {\sim}fb = a \;/ \therefore\; {\sim}\forall x \forall y yx = y$

3. $a = b \;/ \therefore\; Fa \leftrightarrow Fb$

4. $Fa \leftrightarrow Fb / \therefore\; a = b$

5. $Pa, \forall x(Px \to Pfx) \;/ \therefore\; \forall x Px$

6. $\forall x \forall y hxy = hyx, Phab \;/ \therefore\; Phba$

♦7. $\forall x \exists y y = fx \;/ \;\therefore\; \forall y \exists x y = fx$

8. $\forall x(Rax \to Rafx), Rab \;/ \therefore\; Raffb$

9. $\exists y Py \;/ \therefore\; \exists y Pfy$

10. $\forall x \forall y(y = fx \lor x = fy) \;/ \therefore\; {\sim}\exists x \exists y \exists z(x \neq y \;\&\; (x \neq z \;\&\; y \neq z))$

Part II: Logical Truths Construct truth trees to determine whether the following statements of *L** are logical truths, again indicating any trees that are infinite.

11. $\forall x x = fx$

12. $\forall x \exists y fx = y$

♦13. $\forall x(fx = ffx \to x = fx)$

14. $\exists x \forall y yx = fy \;\&\; \forall x {\sim}x = fx$

15. $\forall x \forall y(h^2 xy = a \to h^2 fxfy = fa)$

16. $\forall x \forall y(x = y \leftrightarrow gx = gy)$

Part III: Theoretical Problems

17. A method was given in Section 6.3 for reading interpretations off a finished open branch of a truth tree for *L*. Extend this method by explaining how to read an interpretation off a finished open branch for a set of *L** statements.

8.11   Natural Deduction in *L**

Nothing needs to be added to the system $D_{L_=}$ of natural deduction in order to use it to produce proofs in the language *L**. Nonetheless, we do need to emphasize a couple of points about the inference rules of $D_{L_=}$ that become significant now only because the set of constant terms has been expanded to include terms involving function symbols.

To begin, recall that in the statement of the rules UG, PA-EI, and EI in Chapter 7, β is referred to as an 'individual constant'. In the statement of rules UI and EG, however, we use the expression 'constant term'. This difference is critical here. If this distinction were not maintained, trouble would ensue regarding the soundness of our deductive system. We illustrate the use of each of these quantifier rules in connection with function symbols.

Let's give an example of the use of rules UG and UI to show that the statement '∀xFfx' is a logical consequence of '∀xFx':

1.	∀xFx		PR
2.	Ffa	1	UI
3.	∀xFfx	2	UG

It is important to notice that UG permits you (under appropriate restrictions) to generalize on *any* individual constant, even if that individual constant is contained within a constant term. However, you may *not* apply UG to the whole constant term 'fa'. In the above context, such a move might "do no harm," but allowing it generally would. We illustrate the problem such a use would entail with the following incorrect proof:

1.	∀xAfx		PR	
2.	Afa	1	UI	
3.	∀xAx	2	UG	←——————— ***Wrong!***

The constant term 'fa' does not occur in line 1, the premise, and so you might think that UG can be employed at this stage. However, if $\mathcal{D}$ is the set {0, 1, 2, 3, . . .}, $\mathcal{I}$(A) = {1, 2, 3, . . .}, and $\mathcal{I}$(f) = the successor function, then line 1 is true and line 3 is false! To avoid such an error in reasoning, the statement of rule UG requires that the term that is generalized on must be an individual constant, *not* just any constant term. As noted, this restriction does *not* apply in the case of UI or EG.

Here is another example illustrating the use of UI with function symbols to prove that '∀xAfx → ∃xAx' is a theorem:

1.	∀xAfx		PA-CP
2.	~∃xAx		PA-RAA
3.	∀x~Ax	2	Q
4.	~Afa	3	UI
5.	Afa	1	UI
6.	Afa & ~Afa	4, 5	CI
7.	∃xAx	2–6	RAA
8.	∀xAfx → ∃xAx	1–7	CP

Compare and contrast the use of rule UI on lines 4 and 5: On line 4 UI was employed to substitute the whole constant term 'fa' for 'x', whereas on line 5 UI was used to insert only the individual constant 'a' in place of 'x'.

The next two examples involve identity. First, we prove that the statement '$\forall x \forall y (x = y \rightarrow fx = fy)$' is a theorem:

1.	$a = b$		PA–CP
2.	$fa = fa$		I Int
3.	$fa = fb$	1, 2	I
4.	$a = b \rightarrow fa = fb$	1–3	CP
5.	$\forall y (a = y \rightarrow fa = fy)$	4	UG
6.	$\forall x \forall y (x = y \rightarrow fx = fy)$	5	UG

Here is a second example that makes use of identity:

1.	$\forall x s^2 x a = x$		PR
2.	$\forall x \forall y s^2 x s^1 y = s^1 s^2 x y$		PR
3.	$\forall y s^2 s^1 a s^1 y = s^1 s^2 s^1 a y$	2	UI
4.	$s^2 s^1 a s^1 a = s^1 s^2 s^1 a a$	3	UI
5.	$s^2 s^1 a a = s^1 a$	1	UI
6.	$s^2 s^1 a s^1 a = s^1 s^1 a$	4, 5	I

Assuming that 'a' denotes the number 0, 's^1' is the successor function, and 's^2' is the summation function, what is the conclusion proved on line 6?

The next sequence of lines show the different ways that EG may be used:

1.	$\forall x Fx$		PR
2.	$Ff^3 abc$	1	UI
3.	$\exists x Fx$	2	EG
4.	$\exists x Ff^3 axc$	2	EG
5.	$Ff^1 g^3 abc$	1	UI
6.	$\exists x Ff^1 x$	5	EG

As you can see, this isn't so much a serious proof as it is a sequence of applications of EG and UI for the purpose of illustration. Observe that we may generalize on the entire constant term 'fabc' (line 3), or on just one individual constant in the 3-tuple in the constant term (line 4), or on an entire constant term that occurs within another constant term (line 6).

As a final example, let's see what can go wrong when the rule EI is misapplied:

1.	$\exists x Ax$		PR	
2.	$\forall x (Ax \rightarrow Bx)$		PR	
3.	Afa	1	PA–EI	*Incorrect!*
4.	$Afa \rightarrow Bfa$	2	UI	
5.	Bfa	3, 4	MP	
6.	$\exists x Bfx$	5	EG	
7.	$\exists x Bfx$	3–6	EI	

The rule PA-EI has been misapplied: We did not introduce an individual constant on line 3 but a constant term 'fa'. It is also apparent that the application of EI on line 7 is problematic, since in the formulation of the rule it is said that 'the individual constant β does not occur in q', where in this case q is the statement '∃x Bfx'. However, the expression 'the individual constant β' would ordinarily have taken the place of 'fa' in line 3. To see that the given premises do not logically imply the statement on line 7, consider the following interpretation:

$\mathcal{D}$:   people

Ax: x is a woman

Bx: x is a daughter

fx: the father of x.

Under this interpretation, the premises are 'There are women' and 'All women are daughters'; line 7 says 'Some father is a daughter'. Thus, as with the use of rule UG, you have to be very careful to attend to the restrictions on the use of EI.

Exercises for Section 8.11

Part I: Arguments   Construct formal proofs for each of the following arguments in $L*$.

1. fa = fb /∴ Ffa ↔ Ffb   4. ∀xfx = a, Pfa & ~Pfb /∴ Q & ~Q

2. ∀xx = fx, Pc /∴ Pffc   5. ∀x∀yhxy = hyx /∴ Shac → Shca

◆3. ∀xfx = gx, Rfa /∴ Rga

6. ∀x∀y(fx = fy ↔ Rxy), ∃x∃yRxy /∴ ∃x∃yfx = fy

Part II: Theorems   Construct formal proofs for each of the following theorems in $L*$.

7. ∀xAfx → ∀xAffx

8. ∀x∃yy = fx

9. ∃x∃yfx ≠ fy → ∃x∃yx ≠ y

10. ∀x∀y∀z((y = fx & z = fy) → z = ffx)

◆11. ∀x∀y(x = fy → y = fx) → ∀xffx = x

12. ∀x∀y(x = fy → x = ffy) → ∀x∀y (x = fy → x = fffy)

13. ∀x∀y((y = fx & y = ffx) → fx = ffx)

14. ∃x(Px & ~Pfx) → ~∀xx = x

CHAPTER NINE
Some Applications, Limitations, and Extensions of L*

9.1 Introduction

We have devoted considerable time to developing the languages of statement and predicate logic and to developing systems of deduction and decision procedures for these languages. Aside from the interest these systems have from a purely mathematical perspective, they are also of interest because of their promise for solving a variety of mathematical, philosophical, and scientific problems. Up until now the chief application we have considered has been the formalization and assessment of arguments in natural language. We begin this chapter by taking the process further. We introduce a number of applications of predicate logic. The language L* will figure prominently in our discussion, since most of these applications require L*.

Although our survey of some applications of L* will show that it is a useful and powerful language for philosophical, mathematical, and scientific purposes, we have seen already (for instance, in our discussion of the material conditional) that certain kinds of problems and theories cannot be adequately represented in L*. These limitations have led some philosophers to construct alternative systems of logic. Many, but not all, of these alternative systems are extensions of L*, in the sense that the statements and theorems of L* are contained in them as parts.

Most of these alternative systems are constructed to aid in the study of philosophical problems, including traditional questions in metaphysics (the study of the ultimate nature of reality), epistemology (the study of the nature and limits of knowledge), and moral theory. Some philosophers doubt that any of these alternative systems of logic are really part of logic at all, but these formal systems have nevertheless proved fruitful in furthering our understanding of philosophical issues. In Sections 9.6–9.12, we offer a brief synopsis of a few of these other types of logic.[1]

9.2 Definite Descriptions and Ontological Commitment

One especially important application of symbolic logic is the philosophical analysis of meaning in natural language. An example of this kind of application is the following. In a famous paper of 1905, the philosopher Bertrand Russell posed a puzzle. Consider the statement

(1) The present king of France is bald.

Is this statement true? The grammatical form of this statement is that of a subject, 'the present king of France', followed by a predicate, 'is bald'. We might symbolize (1) as 'Bk'. According to our semantics this statement will be true under an interpretation just in case the extension of the predicate 'is bald' ('P') contains the present king of France. If our domain is the set of all presently living persons, then 'Bk' comes out false on this interpretation, and on similar but less formal grounds we are entitled to conclude that (1) is false. It would seem then that we should also conclude that the *negation* of this statement,

(2) The present king of France is not bald.

(symbolized as '~Bk') is true. But, if we examine the extension of the predicate 'is not bald', this set does not contain the king of France either! The reason for this, as you have probably noticed, is that there is no present king of France. This shows that there is something mistaken about our symbolizations of (1) and (2) as 'Bk' and '~Bk', since obviously they cannot *both* be false. Our investigation so far shows that we may have missed something important about the logical structure of each English statement when we put them into symbols. How, then, should we symbolize a statement of this kind?

The phrase 'the present king of France' is an instance of a class of expressions called **definite descriptions.** The basic logical form of such expressions is 'the *P*',

---

[1] A much more extensive but still fairly elementary introduction to some of these alternative systems can be found in John Nolt's *Logics* (Belmont, CA: Wadsworth Publishing Co., 1997).

where P is some predicate expression (the descriptive phrase). Russell argued convincingly that when one uses a definite description, one is implicitly asserting that there is *exactly* one individual that satisfies the description. Consequently, when we make an assertion of the form 'The P is Q', we are implicitly asserting the *conjunction* of three things:

(a)   There is at least one thing that is P

(b)   There is at most one thing that is P

(c)   The existent and unique thing that is P is Q.

So, in Russell's example, when we assert that the present king of France is bald, we are actually asserting that (a) there is a present king of France, (b) there is at most one present king of France, and (c) this individual is bald. This would explain the falsity of statement (1): It is false because, properly understood as the conjunction of the above three statements, we know that the first of these conjuncts is false.

Given our experience in Chapter 8 with symbolizing statements involving 'at least' and 'at most', the symbolization of a statement of the form 'The P is Q' is straightforward:

(3) $\exists\alpha[(P\alpha \mathbin{\&} \forall\gamma(P\gamma \to \alpha = \gamma)) \mathbin{\&} Q\alpha]$.

Thus, using the predicate 'B' to express baldness and the predicate 'K' to express the property of being the present king of France, we may symbolize (1) as

(4) $\exists x[(Kx \mathbin{\&} \forall y(Ky \to x = y)) \mathbin{\&} Bx]$.

There are of course other logically equivalent symbolizations, such as '$\exists x \forall y[(Kx \leftrightarrow x = y) \mathbin{\&} Bx]$'.

How should we symbolize statement (2)? Russell's analysis suggests that there is actually an ambiguity in this English sentence. On the one hand, we might symbolize this statement simply by negating statement (4):

(5) $\sim\exists x[(Kx \mathbin{\&} \forall y(Ky \to x = y)) \mathbin{\&} Bx]$.

However, there is a plausible alternative symbolization:

(6) $\exists x[(Kx \mathbin{\&} \forall y(Ky \to x = y)) \mathbin{\&} \sim Bx]$.

The difference, as you can see, is that in (5) we have negated the entire statement (4), whereas in (6) we have negated only 'Bx'. Statement (6) is an instance of the statement form (3) in which Q is taken to be '~B'. When a statement of the form 'The P is not Q' is symbolized as in (5), we say that the negation has been interpreted to have **broad scope;** when it is symbolized as in (6), we say that the negation has been interpreted to have **narrow scope.** Statements (5) and (6) are not logically equivalent. If there is no present king of France, statement (5) is true and statement (6) is false. Which of these two is the correct symbolization of statement (2)? Outside the context in which the statement is made, there really is no uniquely correct answer. Ordinarily, however, statements like (2) are not made unless the subject under discussion actually exists, in which case (6) would be the preferred symbolization.

Let's consider a second problem, similar in many respects to the first. What is the truth-value of the following statement?

(7)   Heracles has brawny biceps.

If we look at the set of real people having brawny biceps, we will find Arnold Schwarzenegger, Hulk Hogan, and others, but we will not find Heracles. On the other hand, if we look at the set of individuals not having brawny biceps, we'll find many persons, but we won't find Heracles here either. The problem of course is that there is not (and presumably never was) such a person as Heracles, the legendary demigod of ancient Greek mythology.

But that's not the end of the story. The semantics of $L*$ is defined in such a way that, under any interpretation, *every* individual constant must refer to some individual in the domain. Taking $\mathcal{D}$ to be people and using the constant 'h' as Heracles' name, it turns out that the $L*$ statement '$\exists x x = h$', which we might naturally take to symbolize the statement 'Heracles exists', is a *logical truth*. Surely, however, it seems that the statement 'Heracles exists' *ought* to be contingently false! Has something gone wrong with our symbolization or with the formal semantics?

Our difficulty with symbolizing statements like 'Heracles exists' derives from the fact that our own language allows for the meaningful use of non-referring names, but our semantics for $L*$ does not. It might be possible to alter our semantics to allow for this possibility, but, if we did so, we would almost inevitably have to adopt a view, like Frege's, that names have intensions. After all, even if 'Heracles' does not refer to any real individual, we would say that 'Heracles' does have some definite meaning.[2]

Russell took an alternative approach to non-referring names. He argued that most of the expressions of English that we call 'proper names' are in fact disguised definite descriptions. For instance, 'Heracles', though grammatically a name, can

---

[2]See the discussion of intension in Section 5.4 and the remarks on free logic in Section 9.11.

be thought of as a kind of abbreviation for a description. A descriptive phrase, as we have seen, is represented in L^* by a one-place L^* predicate (i.e., a formula with one free variable). We might use the following predicate for Heracles:

> x is the son of Zeus and Alcmene, and x was hated by Hera, and x was ordered to perform twelve impossible labors by Eurystheus.

We could symbolize this in L^* by a complex predicate P. We could express the claim that Heracles exists in L^*, by saying that some individual satisfies the description P—that is, as

$$\exists x P x.$$

Perhaps better, we might take the statement 'Heracles exists' to imply that exactly one individual meeting Heracles' description exists, in which case we would symbolize the statement as

$$\exists x[P x \ \& \ \forall y(P y \to x = y)].$$

Using the principles we discussed above, we could render any sort of statement involving 'Heracles' by a statement involving the associated definite description.

In cases where descriptive phrases are complex, writing out statements involving definite descriptions can be cumbersome. Philosophers thus often use a **definite description operator,** '$\imath$', to simplify them. For any one-place L^* predicate P and one-place predicate symbol Q, we may symbolize statements of the form 'The P is Q' as

$$Q \imath \alpha P \alpha.$$

Since '$\imath$' is not a symbol of L^*, symbolic expressions using the definite description operator are not statements of L^*. Expressions in which the operator occurs should be taken as *abbreviations* for L^* statements. In particular, any expression of the form $Q \imath \alpha P \alpha$ is to be understood as an abbreviation for an L^* statement of the form

$$\exists \alpha[(P \alpha \ \& \ \forall \gamma(P \gamma \to \alpha = \gamma)) \ \& \ Q \alpha],$$

which is just the statement form (3) introduced earlier.

Here are two examples of the use of the definite description operator. First, we symbolize 'The girl who played on the swing set this morning while eating ice cream went to the movies in the afternoon', using 'Px' for 'x played on the swing set this morning, 'Ex' for 'x ate ice cream this morning', and 'Mx' for 'x went to the movies this afternoon'. Using the definite description operator, we then get

M⌉x(Px & Ex)

which is understood as an abbreviation for

$\exists x[((Px \& Ex) \& \forall y((Py \& Ey) \to x = y)) \& Mx]$.

We have defined the definite description operator only for cases where Q is a one-place predicate symbol. Suppose, however, that we wish Q to be a compound predicate. For example, let our statement be 'The girl who played on the swing set this morning while eating ice cream went to the movies and ate popcorn in the afternoon'. If we add to our previous symbol key 'Cx' for 'x ate popcorn in the afternoon', we have the compound formula 'Mx & Cx' for Q. To symbolize the whole statement, we must actually use *two* occurrences of the description operator:

M⌉x(Px & Ex) & C⌉x(Px & Ex).

This in turn is an abbreviation for

$\exists x[((Px \& Ex) \& \forall y((Py \& Ey) \to x = y)) \& Mx]$
  $\& \exists x[((Px \& Ex) \& \forall y((Py \& Ey) \to x = y)) \& Cx]$.

Using inference rules it can be shown that this long conjunction is logically equivalent to

$\exists x[((Px \& Ex) \& \forall y((Py \& Ey) \to x = y)) \& (Mx \& Cx)]$,

which again has the form of statement (3) given previously.

One last point about the definite description operator concerns the scope of negations. How should we understand a statement of the form $\sim Q\!\urcorner\alpha P\alpha$? For consistency with the syntactic conventions of L^*, it is perhaps easiest to stipulate that this statement form is simply the negation of the statement form that $Q\!\urcorner\alpha P\alpha$ abbreviates. Thus, $\sim Q\!\urcorner\alpha P\alpha$ is just an abbreviation for

$\sim\exists \alpha[(P\alpha \& \forall \gamma(P\gamma \to \alpha = \gamma)) \& Q\alpha]$

which means that the negation has broad scope. If the appropriate symbolization of a statement requires a narrow-scope negation, however, you cannot use the definite description operator.

There are a number of problems both with Russell's analysis of statements involving definite descriptions and with his treatment of proper names. We discuss a few of them briefly. First, some philosophers (notably P. F. Strawson) have argued that it is a mistake to suppose that statements involving nonreferring (or multiply-referring) definite descriptions are false. According to Strawson the use of a definite description *presupposes* that the description denotes a unique object rather than asserts it. Consequently, when that presupposition is mistaken, it is best to say that the statement does not have a truth value at all. If Strawson is right about this, it implies that predicate logic (in which every statement has a definite truth value relative to an interpretation) is ill suited to symbolizing claims involving definite descriptions.[3]

Russell's analysis of proper names as definite descriptions has even more serious difficulties. Perhaps the most obvious one is this: If a name is an abbreviation for a definite description, what definite description does a name stand for? Consider the description of Heracles stated earlier. Where does it come from? One possibility is that it represents a particular person's (say, Stuart Glennan's) idea of Heracles. But what if Stuart Glennan's description of Heracles differs from Joe Bessie's? Would this mean that when Stuart Glennan says 'Heracles does not exist' and Joe Bessie says 'Heracles does not exist' they are saying different things? This is surely a counterintuitive consequence of taking descriptions to be psychological objects.

Furthermore, what should we say if part of a person's description of something was incorrect? Suppose, for instance, that Stuart Glennan, who mistakenly believes that Ronald Reagan was the thirty-ninth president of the United States (he was the fortieth president), asserts that Ronald Reagan was governor of California (which is true). If part of Stuart Glennan's description includes 'was the thirty-ninth president of the United States', then his assertion that Ronald Reagan was once governor of California would, according to Russell's analysis, be false. That is, there would be nobody fitting Stuart Glennan's description of Ronald Reagan, hence no one of that description who was once governor of California. But this is a controversial consequence, because we would ordinarily be inclined to say something like, "Stuart is right that Reagan was once governor of California, but he is incorrect in thinking that Reagan was the thirty-ninth president." These problems, and others like them, suggest that a descriptive phrase associated with a proper name cannot be identified with an individual's beliefs about the bearer of that name, but by something less individualistic and subjective. But if this is so, it is unclear what could be the correct descriptive phrase or if there really is one.[4]

Whatever the difficulties with Russell's theory of descriptions and its application to the problem of proper names, Russell's analysis is extraordinarily important in the history of philosophy because of the approach it suggests we should take to solving philosophical problems. Russell originally proposed his theory of descriptions to

---

[3]Strawson's critique of Russell as well as Russell's response are reprinted in Robert R. Ammerman's (ed.) *Classics of Analytic Philosophy* (Indianapolis: Hackett, 1990).

[4]The subject of proper names and their relation to definite descriptions is a complex and widely debated issue in the philosophy of language. For a useful collection of views on the subject, see A. P. Martinich's (ed.) *Philosophy of Language,* 2nd ed. (New York: Oxford University Press, 1990).

solve a problem about the nature of existence. He was concerned with criticizing a theory that he attributed to another English philosopher, Meinong. Here is Russell's description of Meinong's theory:

> [Meinong's] theory regards any grammatically correct denoting phrase as standing for an object. Thus 'the present King of France', 'the round square', etc., are supposed to be genuine objects. It is admitted that such objects do not subsist, but nevertheless they are supposed to be objects.[5]

Meinong's view is puzzling, for it seems to imply that there is more than one kind of existence. Everything exists in some sense, but only some of these existent things 'subsist' (have substantial reality). Russell notes also that such a theory could easily lead to contradictions, for it would seem to imply, for instance, that a round square (1) is an object that exists, in some sense of 'exists', and (2) is both round and not round.

According to Russell, Meinong's mistake was to take too seriously what seems to be implied by the grammar of our language. Definite descriptions function grammatically like proper nouns, and our use of proper nouns presupposes the existence of a referent for them. If we take our grammar at face value, it seems to imply that all grammatically proper names, and all phrases that can function as proper nouns, must refer to actual individuals. Taking our grammar too seriously or too literally, then, can result in an unwarranted philosophical conclusion.

Russell's suggestion is that the "surface" structure of language can be misleading and that a difference exists between its surface grammatical structure and its underlying logical structure. Russell believed that many philosophical problems arise from failing to recognize the underlying logical structure of principles and arguments. The task of discovering this structure is what Russell called 'analysis'. Logic is an essential tool for analysis, because in a language like L*, unlike English, the logical structure of any statement (and therefore its logical consequences) is entirely clear. In light of Russell's views, we can understand our task in looking for the appropriate symbolization of various English statements as the task of finding an appropriate analysis of those statements.

Exercises for Section 9.2

Part I   Give symbolizations for each of the following statements. Use definite descriptions where appropriate. Do *not* use the definite description operator.

♦ 1. The woman in the blue car is Rebecca.

2. Helen's first child and Jonathan are one and the same person.

---

[5]Bertrand Russell, "On Denoting" *Mind* 14 (1905): 483.

3. Shlomo placed his cloak on the armchair in the living room.

4. The man who wore a loud tie yesterday is handsomely dressed today.

5. The child who dressed as a Roman senator is different than the child who dressed as a Viking.

6. Arvid's second son and Helen's first son are both named 'Jonathan', but the two are not the same person.

7. The child who scored the lowest on the first algebra test ended up getting a better grade than anybody else in the algebra class.

8. The customer who waited in line for thirty minutes is not happy. (Use (1) narrow scope and (2) broad scope for the negation.)

♦9. The person who donated $100,000 is not the woman who owns the big hotel. (Use (1) narrow scope and (2) broad scope for the negation.)

10. The man who worked late last night and the woman who came in early this morning are the only two people who will get raises this year.

Part II   Rework Exercises 1–10, this time using the definite description operator in place of the more lengthy style of definite description.

9.3   Axiom Systems for Arithmetic

Modern ideas about mathematical proofs have their origins in the work of the ancient Greek geometer Euclid. In his famous work, *The Elements,* Euclid set out five axioms (i.e., basic assumptions) for geometry. These axioms were taken to describe basic properties of points, lines, and planes. In his book, Euclid used these axioms as the starting point for proving all of his theorems of geometry. Quite likely, your own first exposure to mathematical proofs came in a high school geometry course. The systems of proof presented in those courses closely resemble the system originally proposed by Euclid.

We have discussed two sorts of proofs in this text: truth tree proofs and natural deduction proofs. Natural deduction proofs in particular bear a strong resemblance to proofs that you may have seen in high school geometry, but both truth tree proofs and natural deduction proofs differ in two important respects from geometric proofs. First, all natural deduction and truth tree theorems of L^* are (in virtue of soundness) logical truths. As such, they are true under every interpretation of the symbols of L^*. In contrast, geometrical theorems are true under interpretations in which predicates and constants refer to a domain containing the standard geometric objects and properties, but not in some other domains.[6] The second major difference is that in neither of our systems of proof do we have axioms. These two differences are related, since, assuming that we add axioms that are not logical truths, any axioms we added would be false in some interpretations.

Now, it is possible to construct deduction systems for *L** that use *logical axioms*. A logical axiom is an axiom that is a logical truth. Axiomatic deduction systems are like natural deduction systems, except that most of the rules of inference are eliminated and replaced by axioms.[7] And, although it is true that contemporary logic texts tend to use natural deduction systems, axiomatic deduction systems have been of great significance historically.

Even though we have not developed our logical systems from an axiomatic standpoint, axioms are still especially useful and important. In particular, we come now to the idea of a 'formal theory'. In broad outline a **formal theory** consists of four things: (1) a formal language with suitable expressive power for the theory in question, (2) a sufficiently strong deductive system for the language (i.e., one that is both sound and complete), (3) a set of non-logical axioms (i.e., a set of basic premises embodying the basic assumptions of the theory), and (4) an intended interpretation (i.e., an interpretation that attaches "appropriate meanings" to the non-logical symbols contained in the non-logical axioms). Using *L**, it is possible to give formal axiom systems for a wide variety of different mathematical and scientific theories. Geometry is one example, as are axiom systems for set theory and arithmetic. In the natural sciences, axiom systems have been developed for various areas of physics and even for evolutionary theory.

To give you a sense of how formal axiom systems can be used, we consider one axiom system for arithmetic known as Robinson Arithmetic, which we will refer to as '*QA*'.[8] We start by listing the symbols that will be needed to express these axioms. In addition to our logical symbols, our axioms will require three function symbols and a constant:

$$s^1 \qquad m^2 \qquad p^2 \qquad a$$

---

[6]When an alternative way of interpreting the usual arithmetic or geometric symbols is given, one is said to have a **non-standard interpretation.)**

[7]Actually, there's not exactly a one-to-one replacement of rules by axioms. More would need to be explained than would be appropriate in this text, however. For an advanced introduction to symbolic logic from an axiomatic basis, see Mendelson (Appendix 1).

[8]Robinson's system has been adapted somewhat for expression in our system. For a fuller discussion of Robinson Arithmetic, see Boolos and Jeffrey (Appendix 1) or, at a more advanced level, Mendelson (Appendix 1).

Our intended interpretation of these symbols, which we will call the "standard model" ℕ of arithmetic, is as follows:

$\mathcal{D}$:   natural numbers and 0 {0, 1, 2, . . .}

s^1x: $x + 1$ (the successor of x)

m^2xy: $x \cdot y$ (the product of x and y)

p^2xy: $x + y$ (the sum of x and y)

a: 0.

Let's call the subset of the language L^* containing only the four symbols above plus logical symbols the language 'LA' (for 'the language of arithmetic'). The statements of LA are just those statements of L^* that contain no non–logical symbols other than variables and the constant and function symbols listed above.

One of the things that might strike you about LA is that there are no symbols for any numbers other than 0. Using the successor function, we can, however, write a constant term to denote any number we wish. For example, the term 's^1a' denotes the number 1, and the term '$s^1s^1s^1s^1s^1a$' denotes the number 5. In general, we can denote the number n by a term consisting of a sequence of n instances of 's^1' followed by 'a'. Here are some samples of statements of LA:

$$p^2s^1s^1as^1s^1a = s^1s^1s^1s^1a$$
$$\forall x \forall y p^2xy = p^2yx.$$

The first statement says '2 + 2 = 4', and the second expresses the commutative law for addition (viz., for any numbers x and y, $x + y = y + x$). Although we have used only standard function symbols from L^*, we could have used alternative function symbols. We could then write the above functions as follows:

$$+s^1s^1as^1s^1a = s^1s^1s^1s^1a$$
$$\forall x \forall y +xy = +yx.$$

This is still somewhat odd looking because, in arithmetic, we are used to having our function symbols occur between the arguments rather than in front of them ('infix notation' rather than 'prefix notation'). If we let function symbols stand between their arguments, we would state the above as

$$s^1s^1a + s^1s^1a = s^1s^1s^1s^1a$$
$$\forall x \forall y (x + y = y + x).$$

Continuing along these lines we could introduce the numerals '0', '1', '2' (etc.), as new individual constants of $LA;$ the eventual result would be a language of formal arithmetic that closely resembles the familiar one. To introduce all these symbols here, however, would require us to change our syntax, semantics, and proof systems. Still, you can make these changes informally to help you see the meaning of *LA* statements.

Here now is the set of axioms for Robinson Arithmetic:

A1: $\forall x \forall y (s^1x = s^1y \to x = y)$

A2: $\forall x a \neq s^1x$

A3: $\forall x(x \neq a \to \exists y x = s^1y)$

A4: $\forall x p^2xa = x$

A5: $\forall x \forall y p^2xs^1y = s^1p^2xy$

A6: $\forall x m^2xa = a$

A7: $\forall x \forall y m^2xs^1y = p^2m^2xyx$

We will use the name '*QA*' to refer collectively to this set of axioms, the language *LA*, and its rules of inference. Using standard arithmetic notation, Axiom 2 can be translated as 'For any value of x, $0 \neq x + 1$', and Axiom 6 can be put 'For any value of x at all, $x \cdot 0 = 0$'. As you translate each axiom, you will find that they all express true statements of arithmetic.

These axioms can be used to prove theorems of arithmetic. In what follows we drop the superscript 1 from the function 's' in order to keep our lines a bit shorter. We begin with an example using truth trees and then turn to an example using natural deduction. For our truth tree example, let's prove that 1 plus 1 equals 2. We express this statement in *QA* as follows:

$p^2sasa = ssa$

This statement is a logical consequence of the axioms, hence a theorem of *QA*. Theoremhood in *QA* can be expressed by means of our symbol for syntactic consequence: $\vdash_{QA} p^2sasa = ssa$.

To start our tree, we actually only need Axioms 4 and 5, to which we add the denial of the statement we wish to prove. We've added line numbers to make it clearer how the tree rules have been applied:

1.	$\forall x p^2xa = x$		Axiom 4
2.	$\forall x \forall y p^2xsy = sp^2xy$		Axiom 5
3.	$\sim p^2sasa = ssa$		Denial of conclusion
4.	$\forall y p^2sasy = sp^2say$	2	Rule U
5.	$p^2sasa = sp^2saa$	4	Rule U
6.	$p^2saa = sa$	1	Rule U
7.	$p^2sasa = ssa$	5, 6	Rule I

$\times$

Because the tree closes, 'p²sasa = ssa' is a logical consequence of the *QA* axioms and therefore a *QA* theorem.

We now show how a theorem may be proved by means of natural deduction rules. We demonstrate that $\vdash_{QA}$ m²ssasa = ssa—that is, 2 • 1 = 2. Begin with the required axioms as premises:

1. ∀xp²xa = x   PR
2. ∀xm²xa = a   PR
3. ∀x∀ym²xsy = p²m²xyx   PR
4. ∀x∀yp²xsy = sp²xy   PR

Next we instantiate the third premise with 'ssa' (i.e., 2) for 'x' and 'a' (i.e., 0) for y:

5. ∀ym²ssasy = p²m²ssayssa   3   UI
6. m²ssasa = p²m²ssaassa   5   UI

Line 6 states that 2 • 1 = (2 • 0) + 2. We use the axiom from line 2 to simplify this to 2 • 1 = 0 + 2:

7. m²ssaa = a   2   UI
8. m²ssasa = p²assa   6, 7   I

Now we use the axioms from lines 1 and 4 to simplify the right-hand term to '2', completing the proof. To assist in understanding the meaning of lines 10 through 16, the expressions to the right of these lines give translations of corresponding statements into standard algebraic notation ('s' is still used to denote the successor function):

9. ∀yp²asy = sp²ay   4   UI
10. p²assa = sp²asa   9   UI   0 + 2 = s(0 + 1)
12. p²asa = sp²aa   9   UI   0 + 1 = s(0 + 0)
13 m²ssasa = sp²asa   8, 10   I   2 • 1 = s(0 + 1)
14. m²ssasa = ssp²aa   12,13   I   2 • 1 = ss(0 + 0)
15. p²aa = a   1   UI   0 + 0 = 0
16. m²ssasa = ssa   14, 15   I   2 • 1 = 2

At this stage you may well wonder what the benefit of formalizing arithmetic in this way might be. Why should we need to go through all of that trouble to prove that 2 times 1 equals 2? After all, plowing through proofs of elementary arithmetic truths by means of *L** appears, perhaps, to be an unnecessarily complicated way of demonstrating what is more easily shown by more ordinary means. As we will see in the next section, however, there are dramatic discoveries about the nature of mathematical systems, as well as about computing systems and related subjects, that have been made by the application of these formal methods.

Exercises for Section 9.3

Part I: Symbolization   Symbolize the following arithmetic expressions, using the language of Robinson Arithmetic.

♦ 1. $1 + 2 = 3$

2. $2 \cdot 6 = 12$

3. $3 + 3 = 2 \cdot 3$

4. $(1 + 2) \cdot (2 + 2) = (2 \cdot 3) + (4 + 2)$

Part II: Formal Proof   (1) Symbolize each of the following statements. Then construct either (2) natural deduction proofs or (3) truth trees to demonstrate that they are theorems of *QA*.

♦ 5. One plus two equals three.

6. Three times two equals six.

7. The successor of one is the sum of one and one.

8. The product of zero and one is not equal to the sum of zero and one.

Part III: Additional Problems

9. In our discussion above, English translations were provided for Axioms 2 and 6 of QA. Write English translations of the other five axioms.

10. Using the language of *QA*, write a two-place predicate expression (i.e., an *L** formula with two free variables) that expresses the relation 'x is divisible by y'.

11. We can, if we wish, extend *QA* by adding predicates to express various arithmetic properties and relations. Suppose we add a one-place predicate symbol 'Px' whose intended interpretation is 'x is prime'. Write an axiom that expresses the fact that a number is prime if, and only if, it is divisible only by 1 and itself.

9.4   The Incompleteness of Arithmetic

Many true statements of arithmetic (i.e., statements that are true under $\mathbb{N}$) can be proved to be true given the axioms of Robinson Arithmetic. There are, however, many true statements of arithmetic that are not logical consequences of the axioms. For instance, the statement '$\forall x \forall y p^2 xy = p^2 yx$' (i.e., $x \cdot y = y \cdot x$) is not a theorem of *QA*. Because not all arithmetic truths are consequences of the *QA* axioms, we say that *QA* is not a complete theory. This fact alone is unsurprising, since there is no reason to believe that *QA* contains all the axioms needed for proving all the true statements of arithmetic.

What *is* surprising, however, is that we *cannot* remedy this situation by adding more axioms to *QA*. By adding more axioms we can add more *QA* theorems. One might think that we could eventually find the right set of axioms so that all arithmetic truths would become theorems. It turns out that this is impossible to do. This result is known as Gödel's Incompleteness Theorem and is one of the most significant results in the history of logic. To state the theorem correctly, we need four definitions:

Definition A formal theory is **theory complete** (or just **complete**) if, and only if, for any statement *p* in the language of the theory, either *p* or ~*p* is provable from the theory's axioms.

Definition A formal theory is said to be **axiomatizable** if, and only if, the set of axioms for the theory is decidable.[9]

Definition A formal theory *𝒥** containing the same symbols as a theory *𝒥* is said to be an **extension of** *𝒥* if, and only if, every theorem of *𝒥* is a theorem of *𝒥**.

Definition A formal theory *𝒥* is **consistent** if, and only if, there is no statement *p* such that both *p* and ~*p* are theorems of *𝒥*.

Note that 'theory complete' means something different than 'complete' in the sense of 'complete for logical consequence', which is the sense in which we have employed the word up to now. *QA is* complete in this latter sense—that is, if a statement *p* of *QA* is a logical consequence of the *QA* axioms, then $\vdash_{QA} p$. However, as Gödel proved, it is not theory complete:

---

[9]On 'decidability', see the discussion in Section 6.6.

> **Theorem**   Every consistent, axiomatizable extension of QA is in-
> complete.[10]

Put less formally, this theorem says that no matter what axioms we add to the set of axioms of QA, there will *always* be true statements of arithmetic that *cannot* be derived from those axioms in the system L*.

Notice that Gödel's theorem does not say that *no extension* of QA is complete. Only consistent and axiomatizable extensions are incomplete. If a set of axioms is inconsistent, it is easy to see that *every* statement of QA will be a theorem—not something we would want! What about the requirement that the set of axioms be decidable? Recall (from Chapter 6) that a set of statements is decidable if, and only if, there is a mechanical procedure for determining whether or not a particular statement is a member of that set. We *could* simply take the axioms of arithmetic to be *all* the true statements of arithmetic. Trivially, this set of axioms would be complete (since every truth in the language of arithmetic would be a theorem), but we couldn't use this axiom system in proofs: We could not decide what the axioms were unless we *already* knew which statements of arithmetic were true.

Gödel's incompleteness theorem, like the Church–Turing Undecidability Theorem, is difficult to prove. The difficulty has a good deal to do with the fact that Gödel's theorem, at least as it is stated here, has the logical form of a negative existential statement.[11] Proving the theorem would seem to require that you must go through every possible extension (of which there are an infinite number) and show that each extension leaves some statement and its negation unproved. This strategy clearly cannot succeed. Gödel came up with an ingenious alternative.

---

[10]The original theorem was proved by Gödel in 1931. In the original the consistency condition was slightly more complicated. Here we have stated Gödel's theorem in connection with the theory QA. However, the system QA is significantly weaker than the arithmetic theories for which Gödel's theorem is usually proved. Proofs of the theorem can be found, for example, in Boolos and Jeffrey (Appendix 1) and Mendelson (Appendix 1). The above theorem is sometimes also referred to as the 'Gödel–Rosser Theorem', due to a significant simplification by J. Rosser in 1936 that enabled the straightforward statement given here. For a collection of original fundamental papers on mathematical logic (including Gödel's proof on incompleteness), see Jean Van Heijenoort (ed.), *From Frege to Gödel: A Source Book in Mathematical Logic 1879–1931* (Cambridge, MA: Harvard University Press, 1967).

[11]Another, equivalent formulation of the theorem is put as a universal quantification of an existential: For any consistent formal theory containing a certain amount of arithmetic, there exists a statement p in the language of the theory such that neither p nor $\sim p$ is a theorem of that theory. The 'certain amount of arithmetic' would need to be specified, but to do so here would be beyond the scope of this text. In the course of the proof, it is actually shown how to construct a statement p such that neither it nor its negation is derivable from the theory's axioms. A proof of the theorem in this form is given in Mendelson (Appendix 1), and a proof of the theorem in the form given here can be found in Boolos and Jeffrey (Appendix 1).

The details of Gödel's proof are quite complicated, but a rough picture of how the argument goes can be sketched as follows. Suppose we could write a statement in the language of QA that meant the following:

This statement is true if, and only if, it is not provable in QA.

Assuming it is not possible to prove anything in QA that is false (under $\mathbb{N}$), this statement *must* be true (i.e., if it were false, then the statement would be provable in QA, so QA would allow the proof of a falsehood). We of course don't have the pronoun 'this' in QA, but Gödel discovered a way to steer around this particular difficulty:

G: $p \leftrightarrow p$ is not provable from the axioms of QA.

Gödel showed how this type of statement can be "encoded" as a statement of arithmetic, as can the statements p and 'p is not provable from the axioms of QA'. Suppose, then, that G (in its encoded form) is a theorem of QA. We can then show that neither p nor $\sim p$ is a theorem of QA, *if QA is consistent*. Suppose (1) that p is a theorem of QA. Then, since G is also a theorem, it follows that the statement 'p is not provable from the axioms of QA' is itself a theorem. As it turns out, however, from the way statements are encoded, we would then be able to derive $\sim p$ from 'p is not provable from the axioms of QA', in which case we would have both $\vdash_{QA} p$ and $\vdash_{QA} \sim p$ so that QA would be *inconsistent,* contrary to our earlier assumption. On the other hand, suppose (2) $\sim p$ is a theorem of QA. Then, this together with G implies that 'p is provable in QA' must be a theorem, in which case, by the encoding methods alluded to, p is also a theorem. In this case QA would again be inconsistent. Thus, it must be the case that neither p nor $\sim p$ is a theorem of QA, if QA is consistent. Such a statement is called an **undecidable statement.** Since p and $\sim p$ are both statements of arithmetic, exactly one of which is true, it follows that there exists a true sentence of arithmetic that cannot be derived from the QA axioms.

You might wonder whether we hadn't actually proved p to be true after all. Since neither p nor its negation is a theorem of QA and since the statement G holds just in case p and 'p is not provable from the axioms of QA' necessarily have the same truth value, it would seem to follow that p must be true. What else is there to prove? There is something correct in this objection. We have indeed shown that p must be true. However, our proof is not a proof *in* the object language QA but a proof in the metalanguage English. We *could* now add p to our set of axioms for QA, calling the new system 'QA*'. But the purport of the theorem is that there will then be another true but unprovable statement for QA*, and so on for all extensions of QA.

Gödel originally proved his theorem using a language and axiom system like QA that was intended to describe arithmetic. However, Gödel's result has much broader implications. What he has shown is that we *cannot* equate truth with provability: The semantic concepts of truth cannot be completely captured by syntactic methods. This, along with the Church–Turing theorem, places important limitations on what we can express and prove using the apparatus of *L**. But one example of such limitations is the following: The question "Could we ever construct a digital computer and write an appropriate program for it so that the program could correctly solve every problem of arithmetic given to it?" is answered 'no'. Assuming the truth of Church's Thesis, the hope of inventing *any* effective method at all to decide mechanically whether any given piece of reasoning is logically correct—even if appropriately expressed in first-order logic—is doomed to failure.

9.5 Applications of Axiomatic Theories to the Philosophy of Science

There are many applications of logic to the philosophy of science in this century. The most remarkable applications have come from the school of thought known as 'logical positivism' (or 'logical empiricism'). Beginning in the 1920s in Vienna, a group of scientists and scientifically minded philosophers began a project aimed at making philosophy "more scientific." The development of this project involved the application of the methods of formal logic to scientific theories. In particular it was believed that theories of the natural sciences could be successfully axiomatized.

Axiomatized theories could in principle be used for a number of purposes. For one thing, axioms expressing laws governing a physical system could be combined with additional statements representing the initial state of a physical system. For instance, axioms describing Newton's laws of motion and the law of universal gravitation could be combined with statements describing the position and momentum of the planets at a particular time. From these statements it should be possible to prove as theorems statements predicting the position and momentum of the planets at subsequent times. These predictions could then be used to test the correctness of a law or scientific theory.

The pursuit of this logical project has produced much work on the analysis of just what it means to say that something is a 'law of nature' and on what it takes to confirm, or disconfirm, such a law. The tools of symbolic logic have enabled philosophers to hone and precisely state various theoretical and methodological problems in science. One of these has been the idea that a law of nature is some kind of universal truth of the form $\forall \alpha(S\alpha \rightarrow P\alpha)$, such as 'All metals expand when heated'. However, it is obvious that not *every* statement of this form, even if true, counts as a law of nature. In consequence of this observation, philosophers have exerted much effort in an attempt to say just what it is that entitles us to confer the qualification 'It is a law of nature that . . .' on a universal truth. Some philosophers have thought that something about the logical form of a statement would be enough to make this determination, but many more doubt that such a criterion will work.

Although developed for the analysis of deductive relationships, formal methods in the philosophy of science have helped us deepen our understanding of issues that arise in inductive contexts. One such case is this: Suppose we have the following list of observations in support of a generalization:

$$Aa_1 \ \& \ Ra_1$$
$$Aa_2 \ \& \ Ra_2$$

.

.

.

$$\frac{Aa_n \ \& \ Ra_n}{\therefore \ \forall x(Ax \rightarrow Rx)}$$

Suppose that 'Ax' means 'x is an apple', 'Rx' means 'x is red', and $a_1, a_2, \ldots, a_n$ denote objects that have been examined, one after the other. In an ordinary way of thinking, we would usually say that the probability that '$\forall x(Ax \rightarrow Rx)$' is true gets higher as *n* gets larger, assuming no negative pieces of evidence arise. Another way of putting it is to say that the increasing evidence in favor of the conclusion tends to confirm it. Of course, we can never run through the infinitely many possibilities covered by the universal statement, and so we speak of 'probability'. Notice now that the conclusion is logically equivalent to '$\forall x(\sim Rx \rightarrow \sim Ax)$'—that is, "If something's not red, then it's not an apple." Imagine that we collect the following evidence for this conclusion:

$$\sim Ra_1 \ \& \ \sim Aa_1$$
$$\sim Ra_2 \ \& \ \sim Aa_2$$

.

.

.

$$\frac{\sim Ra_n \ \& \ \sim Aa_n}{\therefore \ \forall x(\sim Rx \rightarrow \sim Ax)}$$

Presumably, this collection of evidence supports its conclusion as much as the previous evidence supported the previous conclusion. Yet the two conclusions are *logically equivalent,* and it seems that we *ought* to say that if a set of evidence confirms one conclusion, it must confirm another to which it is logically equivalent as well. But in cases like this one such a claim sounds very strange: How can a collection, no matter how large, of non-red non-apples tend to confirm the claim that all apples are red? Such apparent paradoxes as this have been the focus of much work in the philosophy of science.

Besides prediction and theory testing, axiomatic approaches to scientific theories have been used to develop philosophical models of scientific explanation (see Section 1.1). A particularly influential model, developed by the logical empiricist Carl Hempel, is called the 'deductive nomological' model of explanation. According to this view, scientific explanations should ultimately be able to be formalized as deductively valid arguments in L^*. The conclusion of the argument is a statement expressing the fact to be explained. This statement is called the **explanandum.** The premises of the argument state general laws together with particular conditions, collectively called the **explanans,** which entail the explanandum. The explanation of why a particular sample of metal expands under certain conditions, for example, might consist of an explanandum asserting that the metal expands, derived from an explanans stating (1) the general law that all metals expand when heated and (2) that the particular sample in question was heated under certain conditions.

A further application of axiomatic approaches to scientific theories that was particularly important to the logical empiricists is called 'theoretical reduction'. Philosophers generally understand empiricism to be the epistemological thesis that all knowledge of the physical world is ultimately derived from sensory experience. Logical empiricists, who were committed to this thesis, had to find a way to reconcile empiricism with the increasing use by natural scientists of theories that refer to "unobservables" like electrons, magnetic fields, and quarks. Their solution was to say that a scientific theory must include special axioms called 'bridge laws' that relate theoretical terms to "observables," like the position of a needle on a meter in a laboratory. Such laws were generally thought to have the form of a universal biconditional; for instance,

$$\forall\alpha(\alpha \text{ is an electron} \leftrightarrow P\alpha),$$

where $P\alpha$ is a complicated formula in which all the predicate symbols refer to observables. These bridge laws provide a certain kind of definition of theoretical language in terms of observation terms. If one had a complete set of bridge laws, one should be able to test theories referring to unobservables by measuring the related observables. Such a theory is said to be 'reduced to' a theory of observables. The project of reducing scientific theories to an observable basis is widely acknowledged to have been unsuccessful (and impossible to complete), but there is still considerable debate about whether or not scientific theories of one type might be reduced to more fundamental theories. For instance, some philosophers believe that psychological theories should be reducible to neurobiological theories and that an important task of psychology and biology is to find the appropriate bridge laws.

All these applications of formal logic in the philosophy of science have met with considerable technical and philosophical difficulties, but the attempts that have been made have undoubtedly led to an increased understanding of the nature of science. Moreover, even if the grander projects of their "formalizing science" have failed, it is often very useful in the analysis of a scientific theory to formalize a part of the theory that is of special interest. This is especially true in connection with philosophical questions concerning, for example, to what sorts of objects' existence a theory is committed, or in deciding whether a physical theory is "deterministic" or "indeterministic."[12]

9.6   Higher-Order Logic

The systems of logic that we have concerned ourselves with are collectively referred to as 'first-order logic'. There are, it turns out, higher-order logics as well. A *higher-order logic,* in general, is a system of formal logic in which quantifiers are added to range not only over individuals but also over other kinds of object. For example, we could develop a new theory of statement logic by adding 'propositional variables' to *SL,* along with universal and existential quantifiers that are taken to quantify over propositions. Of course, this would involve some complications in the semantics for the theory. However, it has at times seemed to philosophers and logicians that such a formal theory would be desirable. For example, a possible theorem of 'quantified propositional logic' would be the statement '$\forall p(p \lor \sim p)$'; that is, "Every proposition is either so or not so."

Other higher-order logics are extensions of some form of predicate logic. For example, we might add new symbols—say, 'Ψ_i' (with or without the subscript i, for all natural numbers i)—as *predicate variables* and allow quantification over predicates. This is usually referred to as *second-order logic.* Using second-order logic, we can express interesting philosophical principles such as the following:

$$\forall x \forall y [\forall \Psi (\Psi x \leftrightarrow \Psi y) \rightarrow x = y]$$
$$\forall x \forall y [x = y \rightarrow \forall \Psi (\Psi x \leftrightarrow \Psi y)].$$

The first principle, the *identity of indiscernibles,* says that any objects that are indiscernible (i.e., share precisely the same properties) are identical. The second principle, the *indiscernibility of identicals,* asserts that any identical objects share all the same

---

[12]For an example of the analysis of determinism in physical theories using formal logic, see, for example, "Deterministic Theories" by Richard Montague in *Formal Philosophy: Selected Papers of Richard Montague,* Richmond Thomason, ed. (New Haven and London: Yale University Press, 1974). For a detailed exposition of the history of the program of logical positivism and its use of logic, see especially the introduction to *The Structure of Scientific Theories,* 2nd ed., Fred Suppe, ed. (Urbana: University of Illinois Press, 1977).

properties. Besides philosophical applications, second-order logic has many interesting applications in the philosophy of logic and the philosophy of mathematics.

The following is an example of a proof of the Identity of Indiscernibles principle in second-order logic:

1.	$\forall\Psi(\Psi a \leftrightarrow \Psi b)$		PA-CP
3.	$a = a \leftrightarrow a = b$	1	UI
4.	$(a = a \rightarrow a = b) \,\&\, (a = b \rightarrow a = a)$	3	Equiv
5.	$a = a \rightarrow a = b$	4	CE
6.	$a = a$		I Int
7.	$a = b$	5, 6	MP
8.	$\forall\Psi(\Psi a \leftrightarrow \Psi b) \rightarrow a = b$	1–7	CP
9.	$\forall y[\forall\Psi(\Psi a \leftrightarrow \Psi y) \rightarrow a = y]$	8	UG
10.	$\forall x \forall y[\forall\Psi(\Psi x \leftrightarrow \Psi y) \rightarrow x = y]$	9	UG

Notice the use of 'a =' as a one-place predicate in the derivation of a UI instance on line 1. Whether or not this is a correct application of UI in second-order logic is a matter of philosophical controversy.

Higher-order logics are interesting not only because of what they can be used to accomplish, but also because of what they *cannot* accomplish. For example, we have seen many times over that it is highly desirable for a system of formal proof to be logically complete (i.e., be such that all logical truths are theorems). In second-order logic, however, completeness in this sense cannot be achieved. That is, no matter what system of inference rules is created for second-order logic along the lines discussed in connection with *L**, there will always exist a statement of second-order logic that cannot be derived as a theorem in that system; a gain in expressive power comes at the expense of what can be proved within the system.[13]

Exercises for Section 9.6

◆ 1. Show that the indiscernibility of identicals principle is a theorem of second-order logic.

2. Symbolize the following: 'There exists an object that has a property possessed by no other object'.

3. Symbolize the following: 'There exists an object that possesses no properties'. Give a formal proof showing that this statement is a second-order logical falsehood.

4. In Section 8.9 we remarked that the principle of mathematical induction could not be adequately formulated in first-order logic. After reviewing the

---

[13]For more on higher-order logics, see the article by Johan van Benthem and Kees Doets, "Higher-Order Logic," in vol. 1 of Gabbay and Guenthner (Appendix 1).

material in this section, symbolize the principle as a statement of second-order logic. (Be sure to specify an interpretation for the statement.)

5. Symbolize the following: 'There is no property possessed only by those things that are not identical to themselves'. Next show that the symbolic statement is a theorem of second-order logic. (*Hint:* Use reductio ad absurdum. Note that an appropriate application of UI to an expression of the form $\forall\Psi\Psi a$ is '~b = a', where 'Ψ' has been replaced by '~b ='.)

9.7   Modal Logic

Modal logic concerns the systems of logic that result from elementary symbolic logic when "modalities" are added. In years past logicians recognized several distinct modalities, but contemporary logicians generally have in mind *possibility* and *necessity*. As we have already seen (Section 3.5), some statements are said to be 'possibly true' and 'possibly false', like the statement 'Hillary Rodham Clinton is an attorney'. Other statements are said to be true (or false) 'necessarily', like the statement 'Hypatia was an ancient astronomer, or she wasn't'. Contemporary modal logic seeks to precisely define these modalities and to explore the ways in which these concepts operate in connection with truth, falsity, and logical inference.[14]

The first step in developing a logic of modality is the introduction of new symbols to represent possibility ('◇') and necessity ('□'). These two symbols are referred to as **modal operators.** For example, the definitions of '*SL* statement' and '*L** statement' can be modified, respectively, by the inclusion of one clause:

If p is an **SL statement,** then so are $\Diamond p$ and $\Box p$

If p is an **L* formula,** then so are $\Diamond p$ and $\Box p$.

'$\Diamond p$' may be read 'It is possibly true that p', and '$\Box p$' is 'It is necessarily true that p.' If we desire, the statement $\Box p$ can be introduced by definition, as equivalent to $\sim\Diamond\sim p$—that is, as 'p is not possibly not true'. Similarly, $\Diamond p$ can be defined as $\sim\Box\sim p$—that is, as 'p is not necessarily not true'.

Note that the clause that introduces modal operators into L^* mentions formulas, not statements. Putting the definition in this way allows us to put quantifiers on

---

[14]For a starting point in the study of modal logic, see Hughes and Cresswell (Appendix 1).

the *outside* formulas governed by modalities. We may then contrast statements like '∃x□Ax' with '□∃xAx'. The first statement asserts that something exists that necessarily has the property expressed by 'A', and the second asserts that it is necessarily the case that something exists having the property expressed by 'A'. It is an interesting semantic and philosophical question whether the location of a modal operator inside, versus outside, the scope of a quantifier affects the meaning or truth value of a statement. Some of these questions can be answered by stipulating a formal semantics for modal logic.

There are in fact several versions of semantics for modal logic. Here we present one of the simplest. We remarked earlier in passing in the text that interpretations for *SL, L,* and *L** can be understood as representing "possible realities" or "possible worlds." We make use of that way of looking at interpretations here:

> **Defintion**   An **interpretation for modal L*** is a set of possible worlds $\mathcal{W}$, where each possible world $w \in \mathcal{W}$ is an *L**interpretation. One of these worlds, w_a, is the *actual world*. When a statement is true under an interpretation $w \in \mathcal{W}$, we say that that statement is **true at world w**.

In each of these worlds w, we will assume that all individual constants have the same extensions. We will also assume that predicate symbols have the same *intensions* across worlds, but that their *extensions* at a world (i.e., under an interpretation) may differ. These assumptions bring with them philosophical difficulties that are beyond the scope of our discussion.

The above definition is not completely rigorous, but it will do for our purposes here. As an example of an interpretation for modal *L**, let's take the symbol 'Wx' to express the English predicate 'x wins the 2000 World Series'. Here are two possible worlds:

w_1 $\mathcal{D}$:   major league baseball teams

      a: Atlanta Braves

      b: Baltimore Orioles

      c: Chicago Cubs

      .

      .

      .

    W: {Orioles}

w_2 $\mathcal{D}$:   major league baseball teams

a: Atlanta Braves

b: Baltimore Orioles

c: Chicago Cubs

.

.

.

W: {Cubs}.

To fill out the full set of worlds, we would have to add interpretations in which each major league team wins the World Series, the entire collection of interpretations being the set $\mathcal{W}$. How would we evaluate the truth of the following statements under $\mathcal{W}$?

(1)   Wb

(2)   Wc

(3)   ◇Wc

(4)   □Wb.

Translating these into English, they express, respectively,

(1a)   The Orioles win the 2000 World Series.

(2a)   The Cubs win the the 2000 World Series.

(3a)   It's possible that the Cubs win the 2000 World Series.

(4a)   It's necessarily the case that the Orioles win the 2000 World Series.

Assume that w_1 is the actual world in $\mathcal{W}$. Statement (1) is true at w_1 and hence true under $\mathcal{W}$. Statement (2) is false at w_1 and hence false under $\mathcal{W}$. But how do we evaluate statements (3) and (4)? Informally, we can think of the modal operators as *quantifiers over possible worlds*. We may say that a statement of the form $□p$ is true under $\mathcal{W}$ just in case it is true at *every* world in $\mathcal{W}$. A statement of the form $◇p$ is true under $\mathcal{W}$ just in case it is true at *some* world in $\mathcal{W}$. Since the Cubs win at w_2, '◇Wc' is true under $\mathcal{W}$; since the Orioles don't win at any world except w_1, '□Wb' is false under $\mathcal{W}$.

This approach to the semantics of modal logic is intuitively appealing, but it leaves many questions unanswered. For one thing, what worlds should be included in the set $\mathcal{W}$? One answer is '*all* possible worlds', by which is meant all possible L^* interpretations. This answer has a number of difficulties, however. First, we don't have a way to identify or enumerate all these possibilities. Moreover, some intuitively possible worlds are *not* possible according to the formal definition of an interpretation. Consider, as an example, the statement 'It's possible that nothing exists'. This is certainly an intuitively plausible possibility; indeed, a traditional philosophical question has been, 'Why is there something, rather than nothing?' But a world in W corresponding to this possibility would be an interpretation in which the domain is empty; thus, such a possibility is ruled out by our definition of an interpretation. There are ways to address this difficulty (see Section 9.11), but new problems are thereby introduced.

Perhaps the most serious objection to our modal semantics is that we have not yet distinguished between the different varieties of possibility and necessity. It is common to distinguish between, among other things, logical possibility, physical possibility, technological possibility, metaphysical possibility, epistemic possibility, and moral possibility. In this book our main concern has been with logical possibility. We say that an L^* statement is 'logically possible' if, and only if, there is some interpretation under which it is true. If we take as our set W of worlds the set of all possible L^* interpretations, the necessity and possibility operators can be thought of as expressing logical necessity and possibility. However, much of the interest of modal logic arises from its ability to represent other, more restrictive varieties of possibility and necessity. They are more restrictive in the sense that many statements that are logically possible, for example, may not be physically or metaphysically possible: Although it is *logically* possible to travel faster than light, it is (if current physics is correct) *physically* impossible to do so.

To model other forms of possibility and necessity, we limit the set of worlds that are treated as possibilities. Returning to our previous example, philosophically minded Cubs fans have speculated that it is metaphysically impossible for the Cubs to win the World Series. If this is correct and if our set of worlds W is taken to be the collection of all metaphysically possible outcomes of the World Series, w_2 would be removed from W.

According to our definitions, the truth of $\Box p$ and $\Diamond p$ does not depend on the world at which they are evaluated. The statement $\Box p$ is true at w just in case p is true at every world in W, and the statement $\Diamond p$ is true at w just in case p is true at some world in W. But a simple example suggests that, for some forms of possibility (and necessity) at least, the truth of such statements *should* depend upon the world at which they are evaluated. Suppose that 'P' is the statement 'Joe Bessie builds a time machine'. Joe has not, in this world, built a time machine, so P is false. But is $\Diamond P$ true or false? If logical possibility is at issue, the answer would seem to be 'true'. But what if, in this case, we take '$\Diamond$' to stand for physical possibility? Whether '$\Diamond P$' is true or false would depend, among other things, on whether or not time travel is physically possible. 'Physical possibility' must be defined in terms of the laws of physics: Something is possible relative to the laws of physics if is not inconsistent with those laws. Suppose the laws of physics in the actual world are such that time travel is *not* possible. Then it follows that, in this world, Joe could not possibly build a time machine, and hence that '◇P' is false in the actual world. But consider a possible world *w*' in which Joe exists and has not built a time machine, but where the laws of physics do permit time travel. 'P'would be false at *w*', but '◇P' would be true.

The idea suggested by this example is that a proposition *p* may be possible (or necessary) when evaluated at one possible world, while being impossible (or not necessary) relative to another possible world. This idea can be incorporated into the formal semantics for modal logic by adding to the set of worlds W an **accessibility relation,** R. 'Rxy' is read 'y is accessible to x' or 'y is possible relative to x'. In our time-machine example, the reason it is not physically possible for Joe Bessie to build a time machine in the actual world is that all the *logically* possible worlds in which Joe Bessie *does* build a time machine are not accessible from this world; that is, they are not *physically* possible relative to the laws of the actual world. By placing restrictions on the nature of the accessibility relation (e.g., by requiring that it be symmetric, transitive, or both), alternative systems of modal logic may be constructed. Much philosophical discussion has been devoted to investigating which varieties of modal semantics are appropriate for representing different types of possibility and necessity.

Once a semantics for modal logic has been specified, the methods of formal proof can be extended to allow proofs of valid arguments in the modal language. Ideally, we would create a sound and complete deduction system. Since we have not fully specified a semantics, and since, as we have said, there are a number of alternative systems of modal logic with different semantics, we will not attempt to present a complete deduction system here. But to give you a sense of how such an extension would proceed, we'll provide a few additional inference rules that can be added to our systems of natural deduction and show how these can be used to prove some simple theorems of modal logic.

As an example of the simplest additions we might make, consider adding the following three rules to our system D_{SL} to handle the addition of modal operators to *SL:*

> ***Necessity Introduction (NI)*** If *p* has been derived as a theorem at line *m* of a formal proof, the statement □*p* may be added to the proof as a new line. As justification for the new line, write '*m* NI'.
>
> ***Necessity Elimination (NE)*** If the statement □*p* occurs as a line *m* in a formal proof, then the statement *p* may be added to the proof as a new line. As justification for the new line, write '*m* NE'.

> ***Necessity Implication (N Imp)*** If a statement of the form $\Box p$ occurs as
> a line *m* in a formal proof and a statement of the form
> $\Box(p \to q)$ occurs as a separate line *n* of that proof, then
> the statement $\Box q$ may be added to the proof as a new
> line. As justification for the new line, write '*m, n* N Imp'.

We would also need some replacement rules establishing the equivalence of various
modal forms. These include

Modal Replacement (MR)	$\sim\Box\sim p$	$\Leftrightarrow$	$\Diamond p$
	$\sim\Box p$	$\Leftrightarrow$	$\Diamond\sim p$
	$\sim\Diamond p$	$\Leftrightarrow$	$\Box\sim p$
	$\sim\Diamond\sim p$	$\Leftrightarrow$	$\Box p$

The resulting system of modal logic is sometimes referred to as '*T*' (also as '*M*'). It
is generally considered to be among the weakest systems of modal logic. ('Weak' in
this case means that there are other systems of modal logic in which all *T* theorems
are theorems, but the theorems of those other systems are not all *T* theorems.)

As an example of a formal proof in the system *T,* let's show that '$\Diamond$A' is a logical consequence of 'A':

1.	A		PR
2.	$\sim\Diamond$A		PA-RAA
3.	$\Box\sim$A	2	MR
5.	$\sim$A	3	NE
6.	A & $\sim$A	1, 5	CI
7.	$\Diamond$A	2–6	RAA

Notice that, if we had put 'PA-CP' in place of 'PR' on line (1), then the proof
could have been extended to line (8) with 'A $\to$ $\Diamond$A' as a theorem and thus, on
line (9), '$\Box$(A $\to$ $\Diamond$A)' by NI.

In the next two proofs, we illustrate the use of all the modal inference rules
presented here by proving the theorems '$\Box[\Box(A \to B) \to (\Box A \to \Box B)]$' and
'$\Diamond P \to \Diamond(P \lor Q)$'.

1.	$\Box(A \to B)$		PA-CP
2.	$\Box$A		PA-CP
3.	$\Box$B		1, 2 N Imp
4.	$\Box$A $\to$ $\Box$B	2–3	CP
5.	$\Box(A \to B) \to (\Box A \to \Box B)$	1–4	CP
6.	$\Box[\Box(A \to B) \to (\Box A \to \Box B)]$	5	N Int

1.	P		PA–CP
2.	P ∨ Q	1	DA
3.	P → (P ∨ Q)	1–2	CP
4.	~(P ∨ Q) → ~P	3	Trans
5.	□[~(P ∨ Q) → ~P]	4	N Int
6.	□~(P ∨ Q)		PA–CP
7.	□~P	5, 6	N Imp
8.	□~(P ∨ Q) → □~P	6–7	CP
9.	~□~P → ~□~(P ∨ Q)	8	Trans
10.	◊P → ~□~(P ∨ Q)	9	MR
11.	◊P → ◊(P ∨ Q)	10	MR

Systems of modal logic have been and continue to be used to explore logical relationships and philosophical questions ranging from issues in the philosophy of religion (e.g., the ontological argument for the existance of God with which we began Chapter 3) all the way through questions about "physical possibility" or "natural necessity" in such areas of contemporary physics as quantum mechanics (e.g., the "many worlds" interpretation of quantum theory) and the analysis of cause–effect relations in nature. Modal logic has also proved fruitful in analyzing conditional statements. In the next section we sketch a modal analysis of conditionals.

Exercises for Section 9.7

Part I Symbolize each of the following statements in modal *SL*.

1. It's possible that snow is not white.
2. It's not possible that snow is both white and not white.
♦ 3. It's possible that snow is white and possible that snow is not white.
4. It's not possible that snow is white and not possible that snow is not white.
5. If snow is white, then, necessarily, it's not nonwhite.
6. It's necessarily the case that, if snow is possibly not white, then it is not white.
♦ 7. If it's possibly not the case that snow is white, then it's not necessarily the case that snow is white.
8. If Newtonian physics is true only if indeterminism is impossible, then Newtonian physics is impossible.
9. Quantum mechanics and Newtonian physics cannot possibly both be true; however, if one of them is, this means that the other necessarily is not.
10. If God's existence is possible and if it is necessarily true that if God exists, then God's existence is necessary, then God exists.

Part II   Symbolize each of the following in modal *L**.

11. Two is necessarily less than five.

12. If Pippi is taller than Tanya, then, necessarily, they are not the same height.

♦13. If Sonya is a chemist, then it is possible that chemists exist.

14. There is a number that is necessarily greater than all other numbers.

15. It is necessary that there exists a number greater than all others.

16. It's not possible that there exists a greatest number.

♦17. There exists a number that cannot possibly be the greatest number.

18. It's not possible for one thing to be in more than one place at one time.

19. No two things can possibly occupy the same place at the same time.

20 An argument is valid if, and only if, it is not possible for the argument to have all true premises but a false conclusion.

Part III   Give formal proofs for each of the following *T* theorems.

21. $\sim\lozenge P \rightarrow \square\sim P$

22. $\square A \rightarrow \lozenge A$

♦23. $\square\sim B \rightarrow \square\sim(A \mathbin{\&} B)$

24. $\square(P \rightarrow Q) \rightarrow (\sim\square Q \rightarrow \lozenge\sim P)$

♦25. $\square(J \rightarrow K) \rightarrow [\square(K \rightarrow L) \rightarrow \square(J \rightarrow L)]$

26. $\square(R \mathbin{\&} S) \rightarrow (\square R \mathbin{\&} \square S)$

27. $\square(F \vee G) \rightarrow (\lozenge\sim F \rightarrow \lozenge G)$

28. $[\square(A \vee B) \mathbin{\&} \square\sim A] \rightarrow \square B$

♦29. $\lozenge G \rightarrow \lozenge[(G \rightarrow H) \rightarrow H]$

30. $[\square(P \leftrightarrow Q) \mathbin{\&} \square P] \rightarrow \square Q$

9.8   Strict and Counterfactual Conditionals

In our discussion of the material conditional in Chapters 2–4, it was emphasized that the material conditional is not a fully adequate rendering of many ordinary-language conditionals. The main reason for this is that many English language conditionals are not truth-functional. Since in modal logic the truth-value of a statement at a given world depends on more than the truth values of its constituents at that world, modal logic provides a promising resource for a more adequate rendering of these conditionals. In this section we discuss two kinds of conditionals that appear in modal logic: strict conditionals and counterfactual conditionals.

Strict implication and the strict conditional were briefly discussed in Chapter 2. The modal semantics presented in Section 9.7 enables us to examine this conditional a bit more carefully. The symbol for the strict conditional is the fishhook, '$\dashv$'. A strict conditional, $p \dashv q$, is true if, and only if, there is no possible world in which p is true and q is false;[15] any statement of the form $p \dashv q$ is logically equivalent to $\Box(p \to q)$.

The nature of the relationship expressed by the strict conditional depends on what type of possibility is expressed by the basic modal operators. We noted in Chapter 2, for example, that the relationship between the premises and the conclusion of a valid argument is a relation of strict implication. This is so, as long as the modal operators express *logical* possibility and necessity. When we turn to other kinds of necessity, however, we find that relatively few conditionals are strict conditionals. For example, if the kind of necessity at issue is physical necessity, then a physical conditional might well be true (i.e., there might be no *physically* possible world in which its antecedent is true but its consequent false), even though there are *logically* possible worlds in which the statement has a true antecedent and false consequent.

Although the strict conditional is useful for rendering certain English conditionals, the kind of conditional to which philosophers have devoted the most discussion are counterfactual conditionals. Recall that a counterfactual conditional, in English, is a statement in which the antecedent is false (or is assumed to be false by the person making the statement). Two examples are

(1) If Clinton had not won the 1996 presidential election, Dole would have won

(2) If Clinton had not won the 1996 presidential election, Bob Dylan would have won.

To symbolize these statements, we use the symbol '$\Box\!\!\to$' to represent the counterfactual conditional. We can read $p \Box\!\!\to q$ as, 'If it were the case that p, then it would be the case that q'. This symbol was introduced by the philosopher David Lewis,

---

[15]If we add the complication of the accessibility relation, the truth condition becomes this: $p \dashv q$ is true at w if, and only if, there is no possible world accessible from w at which p is true and q is false.

who developed a system of semantics for these conditionals. The formal apparatus required for this semantics is quite formidable.[16] Still, the idea behind Lewis's semantics can be seen relatively easily by consideration of the examples above.

Using the new symbol, the two statements above may be symbolized thus:

(1a) $\sim$C $\Box\!\!\rightarrow$ D

(2a) $\sim$C $\Box\!\!\rightarrow$ B.

The antecedent of each statement is false. However, unlike the case of the material conditional, these two statements have different truth values. It seems reasonable to say that the first of the English conditionals above is true and the second is false. What accounts for the difference? The difference cannot be that Dole wins the election in all the possible worlds that Clinton doesn't, while Dylan wins in none of them. There are some possible worlds in which neither Clinton nor Dole wins. For example, Clinton and Dole might both have dropped out of the race prior to the election. There are also possible worlds in which Clinton lost but Bob Dylan won: Dylan might suddenly have become persuaded of the virtues of the Republican party, won against Dole in the primaries, and defeated Clinton in the general election. The difference rather seems to be one of how likely the alternative possibilities are. Although there are possible circumstances in which Dylan could have defeated Clinton in the 1996 election, these circumstances are remote at best. A world in which Dylan won the election would be much more different from the actual world than a world in which Dole won.

These observations suggest the following approach to counterfactual conditionals. We start by assuming that we can meaningfully talk of the degree of similarity or difference between alternative worlds. Specifically, we will suppose that there is some function, $s(w_i, w_j)$, that specifies a "distance" between worlds w_i and w_j. Using this function to define which worlds are closer to which, we can give the following truth condition for a counterfactual conditional:

> **Definition** $p \Box\!\!\rightarrow q$ is **true at world** w, if, and only if, in the closest world to w in which p is true, q is true as well.

Hence, our first counterfactual is true, because in the world closest (i.e., most like) our world in which Clinton didn't win the election, Dole did. The second counterfactual is false because, in the world closest to our world in which Clinton didn't win the election, Dylan wasn't the winner either. How we are supposed to make the determination of the value of $s(w_i, w_j)$, however, is a matter of significant difficulty.

---

[16]See David Lewis, *Counterfactuals,* (Cambridge, MA: Harvard University Press, 1973).

9.9 General Intensional Logic

We have noted that certain forms of expression cannot be correctly symbolized in the language L^*. These are cases that are nonextensional in nature. For example, consider the statement

(1) Stuart knows, merely by thinking about it, that Sally is Sally.

Many difficulties arise in trying to find an adequate symbolization for this statement. 'Sally is Sally' can of course be symbolized as '$s = s$'; but what about 'Stuart knows, merely by thinking about it, that . . .'? The clause 'Sally is Sally' occurs within the scope of the word 'knows', which, as we noted earlier in our text, introduces an opaque context—that is, a context within which substitution of co-denoting terms is not generally permitted. In the present case, for example, suppose that, unknown to Stuart, Sally = the superhero who single-handedly saved Earth from invasion by the subterranean spider-people. Making the substitution would produce

(2) Stuart knows, merely by thinking about it, that Sally is the super-hero who single-handedly saved Earth from invasion by the subterranean spider-people

which (we would presume) is false. How can formal methods be employed in the logical analysis of such cases?

One move is to add 'epistemic operators' and propositional variables to the formal language. Epistemic operators concern such locutions as 'knows that' and 'believes that', and propositional variables range over propositions. The formalized syntax for such an extension of L^* would admit such statements, for example, as '$K(x, p)$' for 'x knows that p' and '$B(x, p)$' for 'x believes that p'. As usual the semantics and syntax would have to be spelled out in sufficient detail for the resulting formal systems to capture the notions we are trying to analyze.

To address the problem exemplified above, we would have to place restrictions on what kinds of substitutions would be allowed in such a system. Such stipulations are a matter of some difficulty and discussion philosophically. Nevertheless, the prospect of providing us with a rich and interesting logical analysis of the epistemic concepts involved has made the subject a very important one.

Within such a system, such interesting propositions as '$\forall x \forall p(K(x, p) \rightarrow B(x, p)$' ("If a person knows that p, then that person believes that p") and '$\forall x(K(x, p) \rightarrow p)$' ("If anybody knows that p, then p is so") might be theorems. Indeed, the combination of the epistemic, propositional, and modal symbols discussed here and the previous two sections help us prove extremely interesting philosophical statements.

Here is an interesting philosophical example involving epistemic logic. In what follows, 'K(p)' (i.e., "Proposition p is known") is used in place of 'K(x, p)'. While more correct, use of the latter expression would make the example some-what more complicated than needed to present the philosophical point at issue. Consider, then, the following three statements:[17]

   1. $\forall p \forall q[\Box(K(p) \to \sim K(q)) \to \sim \Diamond K(p \,\&\, q)]$.

That is, if p being known entails that q is not known, then it's not possible to know both p and q simultaneously.

   2. $\forall p \Box(p \to \sim K(\sim p))$.

That is, necessarily, if p is true, then it is not known that not p.

   3. $\exists p(p \,\&\, \sim K(p))$.

That is, there exists at least one proposition that holds, but it is not *known* to hold. These three statements are quite plausible; indeed, the first two might arguably hold necessarily. However, from these three premises it may easily be proved that '$\exists p(p \,\&\, \sim \Diamond K(p))$'; that is, there exists a true proposition that cannot possibly be known to be true. This conclusion, if accepted, flies in the face of any philosoph-ical doctrine holding that the concept of truth entails the *possibility of knowing* the truth.

Exercise for Section 9.9

Give a formal proof of the statement '$\exists p(p \,\&\, \sim \Diamond K(p))$' from the three premises given in this section. Note that a correct application of UI in this system allows the instantiation of p with a statement of such forms as 'K($p \,\&\, q$)', '$\sim$K(p)', and 'K($\sim p$)', for example.

---

[17]These premises are based on work by the philosopher Frederic Fitch in "A Logical Analysis of Some Value Concepts," *Journal of Symbolic Logic* 28 (1963): 135–142. The presentation given here is based on a discussion of Fitch's work by the philosopher and logician C. Anthony Anderson in "To-ward a Logic of A Priori Knowledge," *Philosophical Topics* 21 (1995): 1–10. Further information about intensional logic can be found in Anderson's article "General Intensional Logic" in vol. 2 of Gabbay and Guenthner (Appendix 1).

9.10 Deontic Logic

Deontic logic concerns the logic of moral obligation. Whereas in modal logic symbols representing possibility ('◊') and necessity ('□') are introduced, deontic logic involves the use of symbols representing moral permissibility and moral obligation. For example, let's take the expression 'Axy' to mean 'Person x performs action y'. As well, we can introduce a new class of variables and constants that range only over actions. Thus, in the expression 'Axy', the position of the 'y' variable would have to be restricted to admit only terms denoting *actions* that a person might perform. Now, for example, we might introduce the operators '**O**' ('It is morally obligatory that') and '**P**' ('It is morally permissible that'). Proceeding in this fashion we can then attempt to formalize some of the precepts of a possible moral theory:

(1) $\forall x \forall y (\sim\!\mathbf{O}Axy \rightarrow \mathbf{P}\!\sim\!Axy)$

(2) $\forall x \forall y (\mathbf{O}Axy \rightarrow \Diamond Axy)$

(3) $\forall x \forall y \sim\!\Box(Axy \rightarrow \mathbf{O}Axy)$.

Precept (1) says that if a person is not morally obligated to perform an action, then she or he is morally permitted to refrain from that action; (2) asserts that if a person is morally obligated to perform an action, then it must be possible for her or him to do it (i.e., 'ought' implies 'can'); (3) says that it's not necessarily the case that just because somebody *does* do something, that they *ought* to do it (i.e., "you can't get an 'ought' from an 'is'"). These suggest only the beginning of how one might proceed in the formal analysis of the logic of moral concepts.

Exercises for Section 9.10

Using '**P**' for 'It is permissible that' and '**O**' for 'It is morally obligatory that', symbolize each of the following English statements.

♦ 1. Some morally permissible actions are not morally obligatory.

2. It is not permissible to avoid performing actions that are morally obligatory.

3. Lying is permissible in a situation only if lying in that situation produces more good than bad.

4. A person is morally obligated to perform only those actions that maximize the net utility.

5. If one action produces more good than another, then the one that produces less happiness is morally prohibited.

6. There are actions that are morally obligatory, even though they do not produce as much good as other actions.

♦7. An action is charitable if, and only if, it produces good consequences but one is not morally obligated to perform it.

8. There are actions that are morally permissible in one culture but morally impermissible in another.

9. There are actions that are morally obligatory but that nobody performs.

10. If everything were morally permissible, then nothing would be morally obligatory.

11. Any action that a person must necessarily perform is morally obligatory.

12. It's not the case that an action can be both impossible to perform and morally obligatory.

9.11   Free Logic

In an exercise at the end of Chapter 6, it was pointed out that it seems to be a necessary truth, according to quantified logic, that at least one thing exists. For example, the statement '$\exists x x = x$' is a theorem of $L_=$ and of any of its extensions. We remarked that this seemed to be philosophically problematic: How could it turn out to be a truth of *pure logic* that something exists? This kind of question, along with others having to do with the use of names and their referents, has led to the exploration of logics with semantics different than that given in this text. One such alternative is 'free logic', which involves allowing the introduction of names (like 'a') that stand for non–existent objects.

The formulation of a free logic system requires a new symbol, revised quantifier rules for natural deduction, and a revised system for formal semantics for the modified language.[18] The easiest of these three items is the introduction of the symbol 'E!', called 'E shriek', which is defined as follows:

For any constant term β, E!β is equivalent to $\exists x x = \beta$.

---

[18]The presentation of free logics here is based largely on the article by Ermanno Bencivenga, "Free Logics" in vol. 3 of Gabbay and Guenthner (Appendix 1).

The symbol 'E!' works, in effect, as an "existence predicate." Thus, 'E!a' may be read as asserting 'a exists'.

In the systems of quantified logic so far studied, the inference from 'Fa' to '∃xFx' has been allowed. However, systems of free logic allow that a name, such as 'a', may occur in a statement even if 'a' does not denote an existing object. This semantic change requires the revision of quantifier rules for natural deduction. Although a full system of natural deduction in free logic will not be presented here, it is instructive to examine a couple of quantifier rules for free logic:

> ***Free Existential Generalization (FEG)*** If a statement of the form $p\alpha/\beta$ occurs as line *m* in a proof and the statement E!β occurs as another line *n*, where β is any constant term, then the statement $\exists\alpha p$ may be added as a new line of the proof. As a justification for the line, put '*m,n* FEG'.

Unlike the standard EG rule, you can't *assume* the existence of an object merely because a name is used in an expression. Because the statement E!β is not a necessary truth in free logic, it must occur as an earlier line in the proof in order for one to generalize from $p\alpha/\beta$ to $\exists\alpha p$.

As a second example, consider the alterations that must be made to the rule UG. Recall that UG allows one to infer $\forall\alpha p$ from $p\alpha/\beta$, as long as β does not occur in any premise or provisional assumption or in $\forall\alpha p$ itself. The idea was this: If one can prove that a predicate P applies to an object denoted by β without making any assumptions about which object β denotes, then one is entitled to infer that P applies to every object in the domain. Notice that in making this argument, though we don't make any assumptions about *which* object β denotes, we do assume that β denotes *something*. In *L* this assumption is built into the semantics, but in free logic, where not all names denote objects in the domain, we must explicitly make this provisional assumption. Hence, we have the following two-step method:

> ***Provisional Assumption for Free Universal Generalization (PA-FUG)***
> The statement E!β may be entered on a new line *k* of a proof if the individual constant β occurs nowhere in the proof prior to line *k*. Line *k* and the lines following it are shifted to the right until the assumption has been discharged. As justification for line *k*, put 'PA-FUG'.

> ***Free Universal Generalization (FUG)*** A statement $\forall \alpha p$ may be entered on line $m + 1$ of a proof if (1) a statement E!β occurs on line k with the justification 'PA-FUG'; (2) the statement $p\alpha/\beta$ occurs on line m of the proof, and (3) no further undischarged provisional assumptions have been introduced between k and m. Line $m + 1$ and subsequent lines are shifted to the left, and lines m through n are enclosed in a partial box. As a justification for line $m + 1$, put '$k–m$ FUG'. Line $m + 1$ discharges the assumption on line k.

Perhaps the most difficult problem for systems of free logic is the formulation of a semantic system. So far, however, there has been no general agreement about the best way to do this. To give you an idea of how one might proceed, however, here is one approach that is already somewhat familiar. In essence, the domain $\mathcal{D}$ of a standard interpretation for L^* is supplemented by an additional, nonoverlapping domain $\mathcal{D}'$, containing "nonexistent" objects. The interpretation $\mathcal{I}$ then assigns all constants and predicates of the formal language in the usual way to elements (or sets of n-tuples of elements) of $\mathcal{D}$ and $\mathcal{D}'$. The set $\mathcal{D}$ containing existing objects is referred to as the **inner domain,** and the set $\mathcal{D}'$ of "nonexistent" objects is referred to as the **outer domain.** The whole structure composed of $\mathcal{D}$, $\mathcal{D}'$, and $\mathcal{I}$ is referred to as a **Leblanc–Thomason structure** (or 'LT structure'). If the inner domain is empty, then the structure is said to be a **null LT structure;** otherwise, it is **nonnull.**

A structure that employs inner and outer domains is fairly straightforward, in that 'truth under an interpretation' can be defined in the usual way. What needs to be decided is which objects go in the outer domain and how sentences containing references to these objects *should* be evaluated. For example, the denotation of the name 'Supergirl', the fictional superheroine, would presumably be a member of the outer domain. Yet, one would still have to decide how a statement such as 'Supergirl fights crime' ought to be evaluated. The semantic system does not settle this question for us.

Free logics allow us to study logical relationships among statements free of the requirement of a nonempty domain. Free logics have been studied for some time now, but they have not been as extensively investigated as systems such as modal logic. It is still even debated, for example, whether free logics constitute a restriction on, or rather a generalization of, classical quantified logic. If free logics are to prove widely useful, a host of philosophical questions having to do with existence, language, and meaning must first be confronted and resolved in a generally acceptable way.

9.12   Many-Valued Logic

The systems of logic presented up to this point have been built on the assumption that all statements are either true or false. However, we have seen many examples of sentences that do not easily fit this assumption. One example is the case of fictional sentences (e.g., 'Snow White married a prince'). Although these have the form of assertions, they also seem problematic in terms of truth value. Another example involves statements about the future: If the future is not presently determined, then predictions—like 'A meteor will collide with the Moon at 12:00 AM Eastern Standard Time on June 14 in the year 2043'—might be said to be neither true nor false at present. And there are many other examples as well, some of which arise even in science and mathematics.

Because of cases like these, it is interesting to wonder whether logic might be adapted or modified to take into consideration sentences that are neither true nor false or that have some third "intermediate" truth value. Indeed, one might well wonder whether there aren't a number of possible "truth values" that different classes of sentences might have. Such possibilities bring us into the realm of **many-valued logic**—that is, systems of logic built on the assumption that more than two possible truth values exist.

Many-valued logic is a generalization of the familiar bivalent (two-valued) logic of truth functions. In bivalent logic, statement letters are interpreted to be either true or false; in (finite) many-valued logic, statement letters are assigned values from a set $\{0, 1, \ldots, n\}$ for some natural number n. As in standard bivalent logic, functions are given from k-tuples of values into single values. In bivalent logic, for example, we define the conjunction function, represented by the symbol '&'. Written in explicitly functional notation, we have

$$\&(p, q) \quad = \quad \begin{cases} \text{T} & \text{if } p = q = \text{T} \\ \\ \text{F} & \text{otherwise.} \end{cases}$$

In many-valued logic we similarly define k-place functions from k-tuples of elements of $\{0, 1, \ldots, n\}$ into $\{0, 1, \ldots, n\}$. For example, we can define a three-place function represented by '*' for a three-valued logic:

$$*(p, q, r) \quad = \quad \begin{cases} 1 & \text{if } p = q = r = 2 \\ \\ 0 & \text{otherwise.} \end{cases}$$

In a more familiar format, we may tabulate values for a statement in the language of our theory in terms of all possible interpretations:

A	B	C	*(A, B, C)
0	0	0	0
0	0	1	0
0	0	2	0
0	1	0	0
0	1	1	0
.	.	.	.
.	.	.	.
.	.	.	.
2	2	0	0
2	2	1	0
2	2	2	1

For a k-place connective, there are $(n + 1)^k$ possible combinations of associated values and $(n + 1)$ possible ways of assigning a value to each of these possibilities. Thus, for a given k-place connective, there are

$$(n + 1)^{(n + 1)^k}$$

possible $(n + 1)^k$-tuples of values that can be assigned as the "truth table" for the given connective. In constructing a theory of many-valued logic, we select just one of these and designate it the *basic many-valued truth table* for the connective. Just as in bivalent logic, we compute the possible combinations of values for a statement containing k distinct statement letters by raising the number of values for the logic to the nth power, where n is the number of distinct statement letters in the statement in question.

Corresponding to the concepts 'tautology', 'soundness', and 'completeness' of bivalent logic, we have analogous concepts in many-valued logic. Each assignment of values to the letters in a statement counts as an interpretation, just as in bivalent logic. Then, many-valued "tautologousness" may be defined as follows:

> ***Definition***   Pick natural numbers m and n such that $0 \le m < n$. We define the numbers $0, \ldots, m$ to be the **designated values.**
>
> ***Definition***   A statement that takes designated values under every interpretation is called **exceptional.**

In bivalent logic there is just one designated value: T. The exceptional statements of bivalent logic are the tautologies. In the three-valued logic given above, we could take as designated values 0 and 1. Then, any statement whose main connective is '*' would be exceptional, since its associated many-valued truth function never takes the value 2.[19]

Soundness and completeness may be combined as one concept for many-valued logic:

> **Definition**   A system is **suitable** for a many-valued logic when its theorems are exactly the statements whose associated many-valued truth functions are exceptional.

To speak, then, of a 'many-valued logic' is to speak of a semantical system with its associated syntactic system. A particular many-valued logic is determined by fixing the numbers m and n and then setting out a list of basic truth functions.

As an example of a system of many-valued logic, we consider Hans Reichenbach's three-valued logic for quantum mechanics.[20] One of the peculiar features of quantum mechanics is that, according to the standard interpretation of that theory, there exist statements about quantum mechanical systems that do not always have definite truth values. Reichenbach attempted to represent this feature with a many-valued logic by positing three truth values: true, false, and indeterminate. The following tables specify the truth functions associated with the connectives used in Reichenbach's system:

A	Cyclical Negation ~A	Diametrical Negation −A	Complete Negation $\overline{A}$
T	I	F	I
I	F	T	T
F	T	T	T

---

[19]Observe that, from a purely formal standpoint, two-valued logic does not *require* us to adopt the truth functions we in fact have adopted; theoretically, many other functions may be associated with the usual truth-functional symbols '&', '∨', '~', etc.

[20]This system is presented by Hans Reichenbach, *Philosophic Foundations of Quantum Mechanics* (Berkeley and Los Angeles: University of California Press, 1944).

	Disjunc- tion	Conjunc- tion	Standard implica- tion	Alternative implica- tion	Quasi- implica- tion	Standard equiva- lence	Alterna- tive Equiva- lence
A B	A ∨ B	A · B	A ⊃ B	A → B	A ⇒ B	A = B	A ≡ B
T T	T	T	T	T	T	T	T
T I	T	I	I	F	I	I	F
T F	T	F	F	F	F	F	F
I T	T	I	T	T	I	I	F
I I	I	I	T	T	I	T	T
I F	I	F	I	T	I	I	F
F T	T	F	T	T	I	F	F
F I	I	F	T	T	I	I	F
F F	F	F	T	T	I	T	T

Exercises for Section 9.12

Part I   Using the definition of the connective '*' given in this section, complete many-valued truth tables for the following statements.

♦1. *(A, A, A)
  2. *(A, A, B)
  3. *(A, B, B)
  4. *(A, B, A)
♦5. *(*(A, A, B), *(B, B, A), *(A, A, A))
  6. *(*(A, A, A), *(B, B, B), *(A, B, A))

Part II   Using Reichenbach's many-valued logic, compute many-valued truth tables for the following statements (note that the symbols defined for L* and other systems in our book have different meaning in Reichenbach's system):

  7. A → (A ⇒ B)
  8. (A → A) ⇒ B

♦9. (A ⊃ B) ⊃ (A → B)

10. (A → B) ⊃ (A ⊃ B)

11. (A ⊃ B) ⊃ (A ⇒ B)

12. (A ⇒ B) ⊃ (A ⊃ B)

♦13. (A = B) ⊃ (A ≡ B)

14. (A ≡ B) ⊃ (A = B)

15. [A → (B → C)] → [(A → B) → (A → C)]

16. ~(A ⇒ A)

17. A & ~A

18. A & –A

19. A & A̅

Part III   Invent natural deduction rules for each of the following connectives. In each case specify (1) a sound whole-line inference rule and (2) a sound replacement rule. For a rule in many-valued logic to be sound, it must be the case that, if all statements occurring on lines justifying the inferred line take designated values under an interpretation $\mathcal{I}$, then the inferred line takes a designated value under $\mathcal{I}$ as well. The only designated value for Reichenbach's logic is T.

20. ~

21. –

22. →

♦23. ⇒

24. ≡

25. •

Appendix I: Additional Reading in Logic

The following is a (non-exhaustive) list of several texts we consider excellent resources for further study of logic.

K. Jon Barwise and H. Jerome Keisler. *Handbook of Mathematical Logic.* Amsterdam; New York: North-Holland Pub. Co., 1977. An excellent reference work on technical subjects in symbolic logic.

Merrie Bergmann, James Moor, and Jack Nelson. *The Logic Book.* 3d ed. New York: McGraw-Hill, 1997. An excellent general introduction to statement and predicate logic. The text is notable for its detailed and mathematically rigorous demonstrations of central metatheoretical results.

Daniel Bonevac. *Deduction.* Palo Alto, CA: Mayfield Publishing Co., 1987. Covers the material presented in this book, including a careful discussion of symbolization. The text also includes introductions to modal logic, the logic of counterfactual statements, free logic, and deontic logic. The book is very well written and covers in more detail some subjects we only touch on in this text.

George Boolos and Richard C. Jeffrey. *Computability and Logic.* 3d ed. New York: Cambridge University Press, 1989. This text has become a modern classic. It contains a wealth of material on the nature of logical systems, the relationship between logical systems and computability, Turing machines, the foundations of mathematics, modal and higher-order logic, and other topics in logic of technical and philosophical interest.

Martin Davis. *Computability and Unsolvability.* New York: McGraw-Hill, 1973. A text similar in some ways to that of Boolos and Jeffrey. Like that text, this one includes a wealth of material, especially of technical interest.

Heinz-Dieter Ebbinghaus, Jörg Flum, and Wolfgang Thomas. *Mathematical Logic.* 2d ed. New York: Springer-Verlag, 1994. An advanced introduction to logic for students comfortable with abstract mathematics and set theory. The text covers first-order logic and intermediate metatheory, higher-order logics, computability, logic programming, and an introduction to the algebraic treatment of logic.

Graeme Forbes. *Modern Logic.* New York: Oxford University Press, 1994. This text covers much of the material considered in this text, plus an introduction to alternative systems of logic, including modal logic, intuitionistic logic, and an area of growing current interest called 'fuzzy logic'.

Dov Gabbay and Franz Guenthner, eds. *Handbook of Philosophical Logic.* Dordrecht; Boston: Kulwer Academic Publishers, 1994. A four-volume collection of articles covering a wide range of topics in philosophical logic. The volumes are: v. 1, *Elements of Classical Logic;* v. 2, *Extensions of Classical Logic;* v. 3, *Alternatives to Classical Logic;* v. 4, *Topics in the Philosophy of Language.*

Ronald N. Giere. *Understanding Scientific Reasoning.* 4th ed. Fort Worth: Harcourt, Brace, Jovanovich, 1997. This popular text is an excellent introduction to inductive and scientific reasoning.

Susan Haack. *Philosophy of Logics.* Cambridge; London: Cambridge University Press, 1985. A good introductory text that covers a wide range of topics in the philosophy of logic. It includes many references for further detailed study.

Richard Hodel. *An Introduction to Mathematical Logic.* Boston: PWS Publishing Co., 1995. An advanced introduction to logic aimed primarily at mathematics students. The text covers first-order logic and metatheory, with an emphasis on algorithms. Formal theories of arithmetic are discussed, as well as undecidability, recursive function theory, and computability theory.

George E. Hughes and Max J. Cresswell. *An Introduction to Modal Logic.* London: Methuen, 1968. This is one of the few fairly comprehensive introductions to the subject of modal logic. The approach to natural deduction is somewhat different than that presented here (it is an *axiomatic* system, which has been discussed, though not developed, in this text).

Richard C. Jeffrey. *Formal Logic: Its Scope and Limits.* 3d ed. New York: McGraw-Hill, 1990. This is a concise volume filled with information relevant to logic and mechanical decision procedures.

Howard Kahane and Nancy Cavender. *Logic and Contemporary Rhetoric: The Use of Reason in Everyday Life.* 8th ed. Belmont, CA: Wadsworth Pub. Co., 1997. This well-known text is an excellent introduction to applied critical thinking skills, particularly in those areas not easily amenable to formal methods.

Howard Kahane and Paul Tidman. *Logic and Philosophy: A Modern Introduction.* 8th ed. Belmont, CA: Wadsworth Pub. Co., 1999. In addition to its treatment of elementary logic, this text also includes introductory sections on modal, deontic, and epistemic logic, as well as chapters on inductive logic, probability, and axiom systems.

William Kneale and Martha Kneale. *The Development of Logic.* Oxford: Clarendon Press, 1962. This lengthy text provides a comprehensive history of logic, from the ancient Greeks up through the fundamental developments in the 20th century.

Hughes Leblanc and William A. Wisdom. *Deductive Logic.* 3d ed. Englewood Cliffs, N.J.: Prentice Hall, 1993. A solid text filled with material for an advanced introduction to logic and its further study.

Benson Mates. *Elementary Logic.* 2d ed. New York: Oxford University Press, 1972. This text is generally considered to be a contemporary classic. Mates's text is known for its elegance and economy of style and for the articulate precision with which its material is presented. The text includes several concise discussions of problems concerning technical and philosophical issues.

Robert P. McArthur. *From Logic to Computing.* Belmont, CA: Wadsworth, 1991. Besides the material covered in the present text, the book includes chapters on Boolean logic and Boolean algebra, numerical systems, logic circuits, computing, and computability.

Elliott Mendelson. *Introduction to Mathematical Logic.* 4th ed. London: Chapman & Hall, 1997. This is a fine advanced introduction to logic, especially appropriate for those interested in logic from a mathematical perspective. It includes sections on set theory and computability, as well as on logical theory and number theory.

W. V. Quine. *Methods of Logic.* 4th ed. Cambridge, Mass.: Harvard University Press, 1982. A contemporary classic by one of the most influential philosophers of this century. The text covers numerous subtleties and discusses several techniques for the application of logical tools. Quine is noted for his precision, elegant style, and articulate exposition.

W. V. Quine. *Philosophy of Logic.* 2d ed. Cambridge, Mass.: Harvard University Press, 1986. An introduction to philosophical issues in logic, by one of this century's most influential philosophers.

Wesley C. Salmon. *The Foundations of Scientific Inference.* Pittsburgh: University of Pittsburgh Press, 1967. This is a classic introduction to some of the main difficulties facing inductive reasoning, written by a well-known and influential philosopher of science.

Joseph Shoenfield. *Mathematical Logic.* Reading, Mass.: Addison-Wesley Pub. Co., 1967. Like the text by Mendelson, this will be most interesting perhaps to those who approach logic from a mathematical perspective. This is a well-known advanced introduction to the subject and requires some sophistication on the part of the reader.

Brian Skyrms. *Choice and Chance.* 4th ed. Belmont, CA: Wadsworth Pub. Co., 1999. A classic introduction to probability and inductive reasoning by a well-known philosopher of science.

APPENDIX TWO
Solutions to Selected Exercises

Chapter 1

Section 1.1

1.   Earth and this bowling ball are both massive objects.

      There is a relation of attraction between any two massive objects.

      Earth and the bowling ball exert attractive forces on one another.

∴ When the bowling ball is held suspended in the air and then released, it falls.

   Comment: First, notice that this passage is best interpreted as an explanation, since we already know that bowling balls fall when dropped when released in the air! Second, notice that the original passage contains the qualification, 'according to Newton'. This qualification might be interpreted in two different ways: (1) It may be interpreted merely as a way of emphasizing that what is being asserted is true and thus is not really part of the statement being made (this is how the qualification has been interpreted here). (2) It might be seen as part of the argument, in which case the conclusion would more properly be put as 'according to Newton, when the bowling ball is held suspended in the air and then released, it falls'.

9.   Course grades represent a specific level of mastery of the material covered during the semester.

      If grades were given on a curve, they would be relative to the achievement of students enrolled in a given semester.

∴ Grading for this course is not given on a curve.

   Comment: The examples contained in the original passage help clarify but do not add to the passage. Like Exercise 1, this, too, is best interpreted as an explanation, not an argument.

13. This passage reports historical information and employs an example to illustrate the point being made. Note that the example given in the passage itself supports, although very weakly, the general point that human intellectual history is filled with cases where an idea that had no application at the time of its discovery bore fruit later. If more examples were included, it might be plausible to interpret the passage as an argument. As the passage stands, however, use of a single illustration, together with the expression 'for example', indicate that the passage is best interpreted as a nonargument.

19. This passage reports historical information but does not present an argument.

Section 1.2

1.   Harry likes to eat tofu.

     Tofu is healthy.
     _____

     ∴ There is at least one healthy food that Harry likes to eat.

     This argument is deductively valid. Notice that in the original the premises are connected by the word 'and'. Although we have separated them here, it would also be acceptable to give the argument as having the single premise 'Harry likes tofu and tofu is healthy'.

5.   If ESP really occurred, it is highly probable that more people would know about it than presently say that they do.
     _____

     ∴ ESP does not really occur.

     This is an inductively strong argument.

9.   Some fish have tails.

     Some fish have scales.
     _____

     ∴ Some fish have both tails and scales.

     This is neither deductively valid nor inductively strong.

13. If there is plant life on Earth, then there is oxygen on Earth.

     There is plant life on Earth.
     _____

     ∴ There is oxygen on Earth.

17. All lawyers are professors.

     Some dogs can speak French.
     _____

     ∴ Some cars use natural gas for fuel.

Section 1.3

1. Statement

7. It is not clear how to classify this sentence, because exclamation marks are used in various ways. On the one hand, they may be used to make a statement emphatically—in

this case to state emphatically that logic is a difficult subject. On the other hand, sentences with exclamation points may merely be *expressions* of feelings, in which case saying "Logic is hard" is similar to saying "Logic—UGH". Since this latter expression is, as an expression of one's frustrations, neither true nor false, it is not a statement.

13. Statement

17. Statement. However, the meaning of this sentence requires paraphrase, such as 'The physical appearance of a person whom people find attractive is not indicative of his or her inner moral character'.

23. Ordinarily, for somebody to "be president," he or she must be president *of something*. As long as the people involved in conversation know that 'is president' *means* 'is president of the United States', we can say that the two sentences express the same proposition. In any context in which this meaning is not understood, however, the sentence 'Bill Clinton is president' is simply ambiguous. Hence, it would not carry the same meaning as 'Bill Clinton is president of the United States' in that context.

Section 1.4

3. Not everybody is named 'Anna Livia Plurabelle'.

7. In the United States, the expression 'the United States' stands for the United States.

11. While the letter 'x' is standardly used as a letter of the alphabet, 'x' is also employed in mathematics, as when one writes an algebraic expression such as '$x + 3 = 6$'.

15. The wife of President Bill Clinton is a highly successful attorney.

Chapter 2

Section 2.1

3. Case (a) (true): Let p be the statement 'Earth orbits the Sun' and let q be the statement 'Mars orbits the Sun'. Case (b) (false): Let p be the statement 'The United States Declaration of Independence was made in 1900' and let q be the statement 'The Sun orbits Earth'.

9. Case (a) (true): Let p be the statement 'The Sun orbits Earth' and let q be the statement 'The Sun orbits Mars'. Case (b) (false): Let p be the statement 'Earth orbits the Sun' and let q be the statement 'Mars orbits the Sun'.

Section 2.2

3. Compound. The statement can be rephrased as 'It's not the case that all that glitters is gold'. Note that the meaning of the given statement is *different* than the meaning of 'All that glitters is nongold', which is a simple statement.

9. Simple. *Comment:* You might think that this is a compound whose two components are (a) 'The information about a physical system is complete' and (b) 'Quantum mechanics says that predictions about the behavior of a physical system give only probabilities at best.' It might then be thought that the statement could be paraphrased as 'If the information about a physical system is complete, then quantum mechanics says that predictions about the behavior of a physical system give only probabilities at best'. The difficulty with this is that there is no way to simultaneously indicate (1) that the physical system referred to in the antecedent is the *same* physical system referred to in the consequent and (2) that the statement holds for *any* such physical system at all. Thus, we cannot treat this statement as a compound of two simple statements.

13. Simple. *Comment:* It is also possible to treat this as the negation of the statement 'We have something to fear besides fear'.

19. Simple

Section 2.3

3. A: Arnold has had a bath in the last ten years. ~A

9. A: Alex has a spouse; B: Betsy has a spouse. (B & A)

19. G: You go to work; C: You call in sick. (G ∨ C)

25. L: Lenny gets into the show; P: Lenny produces a ticket. (L → P)

31. M: The mice will play; C: The cat is away. (M ↔ C)

Section 2.4

1. A: Andy will stay at the party; L: Luc will stay at the party. (~(A & L) & (A ∨ L))

5. C: The concept of an electromagnetic field should be introduced in physics; P: The problems of wave-particle duality can be satisfactorily resolved. (C → ~P)

11. S: These two people can stay together; C: These two people constantly fight; R: The relationship is a good one; B: These two people should split up.

   (S → C) → (~R & B)

15. W: War will occur; N: There are nuclear weapons. Both of the following symbolizations are correct: (~W ↔ N) and ~(W ↔ N)

19. W: Luc wants to stay at the party; L: Luc will stay at the party; S: Sam will stay at the party G: Sylvia will have a good time.

   ~W

   L → S
   _____

   ∴ ((G → L) → (~S → ~G))

23. E: Everyone will be allowed to go; L Lisa will go.

   (E ∨ ~E)

   ((E → L) & (~E → ~L))

   E
   _____

   ∴ L

Comment: Notice that 'Someone will not be allowed to go' is equivalent to 'Not everyone will be allowed to go'. Thus, no new statement letter is needed to symbolize this statement. Notice too how we have interpreted 'Lisa will stay here' as meaning 'Lisa will not be allowed to go'. If you do not think that these statements mean the same thing, then a new symbol should be used for 'Lisa will stay here', say, 'S'. Then, in the symbolization, 'S' would be put in place of '~L'.

29. A: Annie swats Ratso; C: Ratso appears to cower; W: Sylvia worries that Ratso is being psychologically stunted; R: Ratso realizes he's a third larger than Annie; K: Ratso cowers.

   A → C

   W → C

   R → ~(K ∨ C)

   ~(K ∨ C) → ~A
   _____

   ∴ R → ~W

Comment: In the original English it is fairly clear that Ratso's no longer cowering or appearing to cower, Annie's not swatting Ratso, and Sylvia's not worrying about Ratso are all asserted to flow from Ratso realizing that he's a third larger than Annie. For this reason we have interpreted the conclusion to be a conditional. A more literal reading would take the conclusion simply to be '~W'.

Section 2.5

3. (a) and (c) cannot be obtained from $(\sim p \to q)$.

7. Not a statement. A two-place connective is required between '~A' and 'C'.

13. Not a statement. Parentheses are required around either 'A ∨ M' or 'M ↔ L'.

19. Not a statement. The symbol ';' is *not* an *SL* connective.

Chapter 3

Section 3.2

3.

P	Q	P → ~Q
T	T	T F FT
T	F	T T TF
F	T	F T FT
F	F	F T TF

7.

A	B	~A & B
T	T	FT F T
T	F	FT F F
F	T	TF T T
F	F	TF F F

15.

F	G	~(F ∨ G)
T	T	F T T T
T	F	F T T F
F	T	F F T T
F	F	T F F F

17.

R	S	~R ↔ S
T	T	FT F T
T	F	FT T F
F	T	TF T T
F	F	TF F F

Section 3.3

In the following, $\mathcal{I}_T$ is an interpretation under which the statement is true, and $\mathcal{I}_F$ is an interpretation under which the statement is false.

1. A ∨ B $\mathcal{I}_T = \langle A{:}T, B{:}T \rangle$, $\mathcal{I}_F = \langle A{:}F, B{:}F \rangle$

7. ~(A & B) $\mathcal{I}_T = \langle A{:}F, B{:}F \rangle$, $\mathcal{I}_F = \langle A{:}T, B{:}T \rangle$

15. ~(~A → B) $\mathcal{I}_T = \langle A{:}F, B{:}F \rangle$, $\mathcal{I}_F = \langle A{:}T, B{:}T \rangle$

23. A → (B → C) $\mathcal{I}_T = \langle A{:}T, B{:}T, C{:}T \rangle$, $\mathcal{I}_F = \langle A{:}T, B{:}T, C{:}F \rangle$

Section 3.4

3. The statement is a tautology.

A	~ (A & ~A)
T	T T F -F T
F	T F F TF

11. The statement is a tautology.

P	Q	(P → Q) ∨ (P → ~Q)
T	T	T T T T T F FT
T	F	T F F T T T TF
F	T	F T T T F T FT
F	F	F T F T F T TF

19. The statement is not a tautology.

A	B	C	[~A & (~B & ~C)] ∨ (A & B)
T	T	T	FT F FT F FT T TT T
T	T	F	FT F FT F TF T TT T
T	F	T	FT F TF F FT F TF F
T	F	F	FT F TF T TF F TF F
F	T	T	TF F FT F FT F FF T
F	T	F	TF F FT F TF F FF T
F	F	T	TF F TF F FT F FF F
F	F	F	TF T TF T TF T FF F

23. Row 7 shows that the argument is not valid.

E	F	G	~(E & G)	E ∨ F
T	T	T	FT T T	T T T
T	T	F	TT F F	T T T
T	F	T	FT T T	T T F
T	F	F	TT F F	T T F
F	T	T	TF F T	F T T
F	T	F	TF F F	F T T
F	F	T	TF F T	F F F
F	F	F	TF F F	F F F

31. The argument is valid.

F	G	F → G	~F → G	G
T	T	T T T	FT T T	T
T	F	T F F	FT T F	F
F	T	F T T	TF T T	T
F	F	F T F	TF F F	F

39. Row 8 shows that the argument is not valid.

P	Q	R	~P ∨ Q	~Q ∨ R	~R	P
T	T	T	FT T T	FT T T	FT	T
T	T	F	FT T T	FT F F	TF	T
T	F	T	FT F F	TF T T	FT	T
T	F	F	FT F F	TF T F	TF	T
F	T	T	TF T T	FT T T	FT	F
F	T	F	TF T T	FT F F	TF	F
F	F	T	TF T F	TF T T	FT	F
F	F	F	TF T F	TF T F	TF	F

47. Row 2 shows that the argument is not valid.

H K M	~[H → (K → M)]	K & ~M	H → (K → M)
T T T	F T T T T T	T F FT	T T T T T
T T F	T T F T F F	T T TF	T F T F F
T F T	F T T F T T	F F FT	T T F T T
T F F	F T T F T F	F F TF	T T F T F
F T T	F F T T T T	T F FT	F T T T T
F T F	F F T T F F	T T TF	F T T F F
F F T	F F T F T T	F F FT	F T F T T
F F F	F F T F T F	F F TF	F T F T F

53. E: Animals speak English; T: Animals think.

   E→T
   ~(T → E)
   ∴ T

E T	E → T	~ (T → E)	T
T T	T T T	F T T T	T
T F	T F F	F F T T	F
F T	F T T	T T F F	T
F F	F T F	F F T F	F

The *SL* argument is valid.

Comment: Intuitively, the English argument we have symbolized is *not* valid. In particular, the meaning of the second premise is not completely captured using the material conditional.

59. A: Alice received a passing grade; B: Bob received a passing grade; C: Cal received a passing grade.

   (((A & B) ∨ (B & C)) ∨ (A & C)) & ~((A & B) & C)
   C
   ───
   ∴ A → ~B

A B C	(((A & B) v (B & C)) v (A & C)) & ~((A & B) & C)	C	A → ~B
T T T	T T T T T T T T T T T F F T T T T T	T	T F F T
T T F	T T T T T F F T T F F T T T T T F F	F	T F F T
T F T	T F F F F F T T T T T T T T F F F T	T	T T T F
T F F	T F F F F F F F T F F F T T F F F F	F	T T T F
F T T	F F T T T T T T F F T T T F F T F T	T	F T F T
F T F	F F T F T F F F F F F F T F F T F F	F	F T F T
F F T	F F F F F F T F F F T F T F F F F T	T	F T T F
F F F	F F F F F F F F F F F F T F F F F F	F	F T T F

The argument is valid.

63. I: Interstellar space travel is possible; Y: It will take years to get from one solar system to another; L: Light speed is attained; P: Modern physics is right.

$$I \rightarrow (Y \vee L)$$
$$(P \rightarrow \sim L) \ \& \ P$$
$$\therefore I \rightarrow Y$$

I L P Y	I → (Y v L)	(P → ~L) & P	I → Y
T T T T	T T T T T	T F F T F T	T T T
T T T F	T T F T T	T F F T F T	T F F
T T F T	T T T T T	F T F T F F	T T T
T T F F	T T F T T	F T F T F F	T F F
T F T T	T T T T F	T T T F T T	T F F
T F T F	T F F F F	T T T F T T	T F F
T F F T	T T T T F	F T T F F F	T T T
T F F F	T F F F F	F T T F F F	T F F
F T T T	F T T T T	T F F T F T	F T T
F T T F	F T F T T	T F F T F T	F T F
F T F T	F T T T T	F T F T F F	F T T
F T F F	F T F T T	F T F T F F	F T F
F F T T	F T T T F	T T T F T T	F T T
F F T F	F T F F F	T T T F T T	F T F
F F F T	F T T T F	F T T F F F	F T T
F F F F	F T F F F	F T T F F F	F T F

The argument is valid.

67. Any statement of the form $p \ \& \sim p$ is false under every interpretation. Thus, if an argument contains such a statement as a premise, there is no interpretation under which all of its premises are true; hence, there is no interpretation under which all of its premises are true while its conclusion is false; hence, the argument must be valid.

Section 3.5

1. The statement is truth-functionally contingent.

G	G → ~G
T	T F F T
F	F T T F

9. The statement is a truth-functional self-contradiction.

F G	F & ~(G → F)
T T	T F F T T T
T F	T F F F T T
F T	F F T T F F
F F	F F F F T F

17. The statement is a tautology.

L M	(L & ~M) → ~(L → M)
T T	T F F T T F T T T
T F	T T T F T T T F F
F T	F F F T T F F T T
F F	F F T F T F F T F

19. The statements are neither equivalent nor contradictory.

L M	~(M ∨ L)	~M ∨ ~L
T T	F T T T	F T F F T
T F	F F T T	T F T F T
F T	F T T F	F T T T F
F F	T F F F	T F T T F

27. The statements are truth-functionally equivalent.

P Q R	P → (Q → R)	(P & Q) → R
T T T	T T T T T	T T T T T
T T F	T F T F F	T T T F F
T F T	T T F T T	T F F T T
T F F	T T F T F	T F F T F
F T T	F T T T T	F F T T T
F T F	F T T F F	F F T T F
F F T	F T F T T	F F F T T
F F F	F T F T F	F F F T F

35. The statements are truth-functionally equivalent.

G H	G ↔ H	~H ↔ ~G
T T	T T T	F T T F T
T F	T F F	T F F F T
F T	F F T	F T F T F
F F	F T F	T F T T F

43. 'A & B' is equivalent to '~(~A ∨ ~B)'. 'A → B' is equivalent to '~A ∨ B'.

47. No, *q* need not be truth-functionally equivalent to *s*. *Proof:* Let *p* and *r* each be the statement 'A & ~A', and let *q* be 'A' and *s* be 'B'. Then *p* & *q* is equivalent to *r* & *s*, *p* is equivalent to *r*, but *q* is not equivalent to *s*.

Section 3.6

3. The set of statements is truth-functionally inconsistent.

A B	A ∨ B	A ∨ ~B	~A
T T	T T T	T T FT	F T
T F	T T F	T T TF	F T
F T	F T T	F F FT	T F
F F	F F F	F T TF	T F

13. The set of statements is truth-functionally consistent.

M N O	M → (N & O)	O & ~N	M ↔ N
T T T	T T T T T	T F FT	T T T
T T F	T F T F F	F F FT	T T T
T F T	T F F F T	T T TF	T F F
T F F	T F F F F	F F TF	T′F F
F T T	F T T T T	T F FT	F F T
F T F	F T T F F	F F FT	F F T
F F T	F T F F T	T T TF	F T F
F F F	F T F F F	F F TF	F T F

Section 3.8

5. The statement is a tautology.

```
     (F ∨ ~F) & ~(G & ~G)
×     T        F F T T  TT
×  F F  FT  F
```

Comment: Notice that the case in which both conjuncts are assigned F has already been accounted for by the cases considered.

13. The statement is a tautology.

```
    ~ [ ~ (K ∨ ~ L)   &   (~ K → ~ L)]
 ✗  F  T F F  FT    T   TF T FT
```

23. The argument is not valid.

```
~(E & G)   //   E ∨ F
TF F  F         F F F
```

31. The argument is valid.

```
     F → G    /     ~F → G     //     G
 ✗   F T F         TF T  F            F
```

41. The argument is not valid.

```
 X & ~Y    /      ~Y ∨ ~Z     //       X & ~Z
 T T TF          TF T  FT              T F  FT
```

51. To determine whether or not *p* is a self-contradiction, construct a brief truth table for ~*p*. If ~*p* is a tautology, then *p* is a self-contradiction.

57. Since the negation of '(F & (F ↔ ~G))' is not a tautology, '(F & (F ↔ ~G))' is not a self-contradiction.

```
~(F & (F ↔ ~G))
 F T T  T T  TF
```

Section 3.9

3. The set is truth-functionally inconsistent.

9. The set is truth-functionally consistent. $\mathcal{I} = \langle H{:}F, L{:}T \rangle$

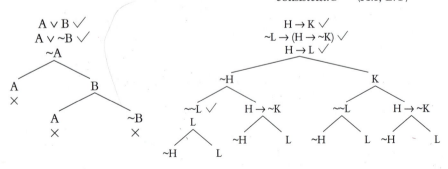

13. The set is truth-functionally consistent.
$\mathcal{I} = \langle \text{N:F, M:F, O:T} \rangle$

17. The set is truth-functionally consistent. $\mathcal{I} = \langle \text{A:F, C:F, B:F, D:T} \rangle$

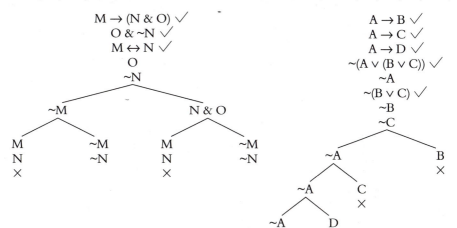

Section 3.10

3. The statement is a tautology.

11. The statement is a tautology.

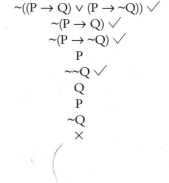

17. The statement is a tautology.

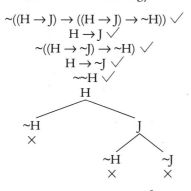

21. The argument is valid.

22. 29. The argument is valid.

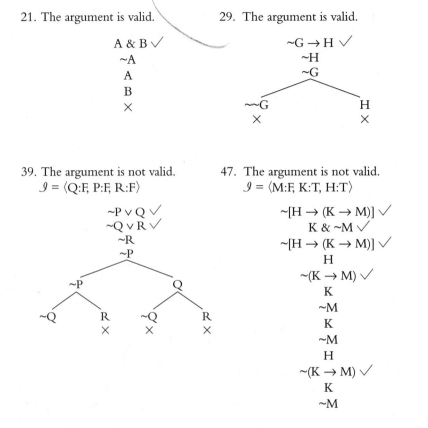

39. The argument is not valid.
$\mathcal{I} = \langle Q{:}F,\ P{:}F,\ R{:}F \rangle$

47. The argument is not valid.
$\mathcal{I} = \langle M{:}F,\ K{:}T,\ H{:}T \rangle$

55. The statements are not equivalent. $\mathcal{I} = \langle R{:}F,\ S{:}T \rangle$

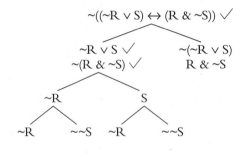

63. The statements are not equivalent. $\mathcal{I} = \langle$D:T, B:F$\rangle$

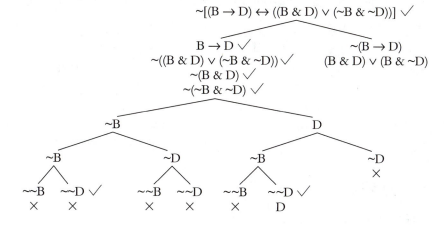

71. The statements are not equivalent. $\mathcal{I} = \langle$A:F$\rangle$

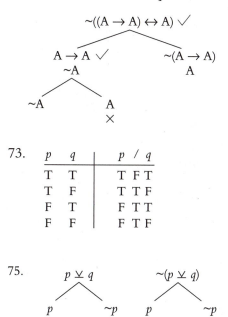

73.

p	q	p / q
T	T	T F T
T	F	T T F
F	T	F T T
F	F	F T F

75.

$p \veebar q$

p $\sim p$
$\sim q$ q

$\sim(p \veebar q)$

p $\sim p$
q $\sim q$

77. There are many correct answers to this problem. The answers given here are shown with intermediary transformations that show why the statements are equivalent.

~A	⟺	~A ∨ ~A		⟺	A/A
A ∨ B	⟺	~(~A ∨ ~A) ∨ ~(~B ∨ ~B)		⟺	(A/A)/(B/B)
A & B	⟺	~(A/B)		⟺	(A/B) / (A/B)
A → B	⟺	~(A & ~B) ⟺ ~~(A/~B)		⟺	A/(B/B)

79. False. Consider a finished tree beginning with the statement 'A ∨ A'. This statement will have two open branches but will be true only under a single interpretation.

Section 3.11

3. This implies that TD_{SL} is sound.

Chapter 4

Section 4.2

1. Lines 2 and 3 are incorrect. Any line to which CE is applied must be a conjunction, and MT requires that one of the lines be a conditional.

7. Line 2 is incorrect. To obtain 'C', you must use CE twice.

11. Line 2 is incorrect. MT requires a second premise.

13.
1.	A & B		PR
2.	A → C		PR
3.	A	1	CE
4.	C	2, 3	MP
5.	B	1	CE
6.	C & B	4, 5	CI

17.
1.	A → B		PR
2.	~A → C		PR
3.	~B & D		PR
4.	~B	3	CE
5.	~A	1, 4	MT
6.	C	2, 5	MP
7.	D	3	CE
8.	C & D	6, 7	CI

21. 1. (A → B) → ~(C & ~D)   PR
    2. E → (A → B)   PR
    3. ~~(C & ~ D)   PR
    4. ~(A → B)   1, 3   MT
    5. ~E   2, 4   MT

Section 4.3

1. Line 2 is incorrect. The disjunction should be a conjunction.

5. Lines 2, 5, and 6 are incorrect.

11. 1. ~F → G   PR
    2. F → ~~G   1   DN
    3. ~F → ~~G   2   Impl

15. 1. ~[A & (B & C)]   PR
    2. ~A ∨ ~(B & C)   1   DeM
    3. ~A ∨ (~B ∨ ~C) 2   DeM
    4. A → (~B ∨ ~C)   3   Impl
    5. A → (B → ~C)   4   Impl

19. 1. ~(P ↔ Q)   PR
    2. ~((P → Q) & (Q → P))   1   Equiv
    3. ~(P → Q) ∨ ~(Q → P)   2   DeM
    4. ~(~P ∨ Q) ∨ ~(Q → P)   3   Impl
    5. ~(~P ∨ Q) ∨ ~(~Q ∨ P)   4   Impl
    6. (~~P & ~Q) ∨ ~(~Q ∨ P)   5   DeM
    7. (~~P & ~Q) ∨ (~~Q & ~P)   6   DeM
    8. (P & ~Q) ∨ (~~Q & ~P)   7   DN
    9. (P & ~Q) ∨ (Q & ~P)   8   DN

23. 1. A ↔ (B ↔ C)   PR
     2. [A → (B ↔ C)] & [(B ↔ C) → A]   1   Equiv
     3. [~A ∨ (B ↔ C)] & [(B ↔ C) → A]   2   Impl
     4. [~A ∨ (B ↔ C)] & [~(B ↔ C) ∨ A]   3   Impl
     5. [~A ∨ (B ↔ C)] & [~((B → C) & (C → B)) ∨ A]   4   Equiv
     6. [~A ∨ (B ↔ C)] & [(~(B → C) ∨ ~(C → B)) ∨ A] 5   DeM
     7. [~A ∨ ((B → C) & (C → B))] &
         [(~(B → C) ∨ ~(C → B)) ∨ A]   6   Equiv
     8. [~A ∨ ~~((B → C) & (C → B))] &
         [(~(B → C) ∨ ~(C → B)) ∨ A]   7   DN
     9. [~A ∨ ~(~(B → C) ∨ ~(C → B))] &
         [(~(B → C) ∨ ~(C → B)) ∨ A]   8   DeM
    10. [~A ∨ ~(~(~B ∨ C) ∨ ~(C → B))] &
         [(~(B → C) ∨ ~(C → B)) ∨ A]   9   Impl
    11. [~A ∨ ~(~(~B ∨ C) ∨ ~(~C ∨ B))] &
         [(~(B → C) ∨ ~(C → B)) ∨ A]   10   Impl
    12. [~A ∨ ~((~~B & ~C) ∨ ~(~C ∨ B))] &
         [(~(B → C) ∨ ~(C → B)) ∨ A]   11   DeM
    13. [~A ∨ ~((~~B & ~C) ∨ (~~C & ~B))] &
         [(~(B → C) ∨ ~(C → B)) ∨ A]   12   DeM
    14. [~A ∨ ~((~~B & ~C) ∨ (C & ~B))] &
         [(~(B → C) ∨ ~(C → B)) ∨ A]   13   DN
    15. [~A ∨ ~((B & ~C) ∨ (C & ~B))] &
         [(~(B → C) ∨ ~(C → B)) ∨ A]   14   DN

27. 1. ~(P & ~ Q)   PR
     2. P   PR
     3. ~P ∨ ~~Q   1   DeM
     4. ~P ∨ Q   3   DN
     5. P → Q   4   Impl
     6. Q   2, 5   MP

33. 1. (P ∨ H) → (J & K)   PR
     2. J → ~K   PR
     3. ~J ∨ ~K   2   Impl
     4. ~(J & K)   3   DeM
     5. ~(P ∨ H)   1, 4   MT
     6. ~P & ~H   5   DeM

39. 1. ~[A ∨ (B → C)]   PR
    2. (~A → D) & (~C → E)   PR
    3. ~A & ~(B → C)   1   DeM
    4. ~(B → C)   3   CE
    5. ~(~B ∨ C)   4   Impl
    6. ~~B & ~C   5   DeM
    7. ~~B   6   CE
    8. B   7   DN
    9. ~C → E   2   CE
    10. ~C   6   CE
    11. E   9, 10   MP
    12. B & E   8, 11   CI

45. 1. (A & B) → C   PR
    2. (C & D) → E   PR
    3. ~E & D   PR
    4. ~E   3   CE
    5. ~(C & D)   2, 4   MT
    6. ~C ∨ ~D   5   DeM
    7. C → ~D   6   Impl
    8. D   3   CE
    9. ~~D   8   DN
    10. ~C   7, 9   MT
    11. ~(A & B)   1, 10   MT
    12. ~A ∨ ~B   11   DeM
    13. A → ~B   12   Impl

Section 4.4

1. 1. A ∨ ~B   PR
   2. ~~A ∨ ~B   1   DN
   3. ~A → ~B   2   Impl

   > 4. B   PA-CP
   > 5. ~~B   4   DN
   > 6. ~~A   3, 5   MT
   > 7. A   6   DN

   8. B → A   4–7   CP

7. 1. A   PR

   > 2. B   PA-CP

   3. B → B   2–2   CP

17. 1. T ∨ T   PR
    2. T → S   PR

    ┌─────────────────────────────────
    │   3. ~T   PA-RAA
    │   4. ~~T ∨ T   1   DN
    │   5. ~T → T   4   Impl
    │   6. T   3, 5   MP
    │   7. T & ~T   3, 6   CI
    └─────────────────────────────────
    8. T   3–7   RAA
    9. S   2, 8   MP

25. 1. R → S   PR
    2. R → T   PR

    ┌─────────────────────────────────
    │   3. R   PA–CP
    │   4. S   1, 3   MP
    │   5. T   2, 3   MP
    │   6. S & T   4, 5   CI
    └─────────────────────────────────
    7. R → (S & T)   3–6   CP

29. 1. ~(J → K) → (G & F)   PR
    2. G → (F → ~F)   PR
    3. (J → J) → J   PR

    ┌─────────────────────────────────
    │   4. J   PA–CP
    └─────────────────────────────────
    5. J → J   4–4   CP
    6. J   3, 5   MP

    ┌─────────────────────────────────
    │   7.   ~K   PA-RAA
    │   8.   J & ~K   6, 7   CI
    │   9.   ~~(J & ~K)   8   DN
    │   10. ~(~J ∨ ~~K)   9   DeM
    │   11. ~(J → ~~K)   10   Impl
    │   12. ~(J → K)   11   DN
    │   13. G & F   1, 12   MP
    │   14. G   13   CE
    │   15. F → ~F   2, 14   MP
    │   16. F   13   CE
    │   17. ~F   15, 16   MP
    │   18. F & ~F   16, 17   CI
    └─────────────────────────────────
    19. K   7–18   RAA

Section 4.5

3. 1.	M ∨ L		PR
2.	~M ∨ ~L		PR
3.	~~(M ↔ L)		PA-RAA
4.	M ↔ L	3	DN
5.	(M → L) & (L → M)	4	Equiv
6.	M → L	5	CE
7.	M → ~L	2	Impl
8.	~~M		PA-RAA
9.	M	8	DN
10.	L	6, 9	MP
11.	~L	7, 9	MP
12.	L & ~L	10, 11	CI
13.	~M	8–12	RAA
14.	~~M ∨ L	1	DN
15.	~M → L	14	Impl
16.	L	13, 15	MP
17.	L → M	5	CE
18.	M	16, 17	MP
19.	M & ~M	13, 18	CI
20.	~(M ↔ L)	3–19	RAA

7. 1.	P → (R → S)		PR
2.	[(P → R) → (P → S)] → (R & ~S)		PR
3.	~~P		PA-RAA
4.	P	3	DN
5.	R → S	1, 4	MP
6.	~~(R → S)	5	DN
7.	~~(~R ∨ S)	6	Impl
8.	~(~~R & ~S)	7	DeM
9.	~(R & ~S)	8	DN
10.	~[(P → R) → (P → S)]	2, 9	MT
11.	~[~(P →R) ∨ (P → S)]	10	Impl
12.	~~(P → R) & ~(P → S)	11	DeM
13.	~(P → S)	12	CE
14.	~(~P ∨ S)	13	Impl
15.	~~P & ~S	14	DeM
16.	~S	15	CE
17.	~R	5, 16	MT
18.	~~(P → R)	12	CE
19.	P → R	18	DN
20.	~P	17, 19	MT
21.	P & ~P	4, 20	CI
22.	~P	3–21	RAA

Section 4.6

3.

1. G		PA-CP
2. ~~G	1	DN
3. G → ~~G	1–2	CP

11.

1. ~(H ∨ (G → ~H))		PA-RAA
2. ~H & ~(G → ~H)	1	DeM
3. ~H	2	CE
4. ~(G → ~H)	2	CE
5. ~(~G ∨ ~H)	4	Impl
6. ~~G & ~~H	5	DeM
7. ~~H	6	CE
8. ~H & ~~H	3, 7	CI
9. H ∨ (G → ~H)	1–8	RAA

19.

1. ~[(A ∨ B) ∨ (~A ∨ ~B)]		PA-RAA
2. ~(A ∨ B) & ~(~A ∨ ~B)	1	DeM
3. ~(A ∨ B)	2	CE
4. ~A & ~B	3	DeM
5. ~(~A ∨ ~B)	2	CE
6. ~~A & ~~B	5	DeM
7. ~A	4	CE
8. ~~A	6	CE
9. ~A & ~~A	7, 8	CI
10. (A ∨ B) ∨ (~A ∨ ~B)	1–9	RAA

25.

1. (R → S) & (R → T)		PA-CP
2. R → S	1	CE
3. R → T	1	CE
4. R		PA-CP
5. ~(S → T)		PA-RAA
6. ~(~S ∨ T)	5	Impl
7. ~~S & ~T)	6	DeM
8. ~T	7	CE
9. T	3, 4	MP
10. T & ~T	8, 9	CI
11. S → T	5–10	RAA
12. ~(T → S)		PA-RAA
13. ~(~T ∨ S)	12	Impl
14. ~~T & ~S	13	DeM
15. ~S	14	CE
16. S	2, 4	MP
17. S & ~S	15, 16	CI
18. T → S	12–17	RAA
19. (S → T) & (T → S)	11, 18	CI
20. S ↔ T	19	Equiv
21. R → (S ↔ T)	4–20	CP
22. [(R → S) & (R → T)] → [R → (S ↔ T)]	1–21	CP

Section 4.7

7. Whole-line rule:
$$\frac{(p \downarrow q)}{\therefore \, \sim p} \quad \text{and} \quad \frac{(p \downarrow q)}{\therefore \, \sim q}$$

Replacement rule: $(p \downarrow q) \quad \Leftrightarrow \quad \sim(p \vee q)$

Chapter 5

Section 5.3

1. (Ax ∨ B)

5. ~~Ax

15. All occurrences of 'x' are bound. The first (left-most) occurrence of 'y' is bound, but the second is free.

19. All occurrences of 'x' and 'y' are bound.

27. *L* statement

37. Neither an *L* statement nor an *L* formula

43. Compound

49. General

Section 5.4

7. ($\mathcal{I}_1$) Either Mickey Mouse is not a ferret or Mickey Mouse is female.

($\mathcal{I}_2$) Either 2 is not odd or 2 is prime.

13. ($\mathcal{I}_1$) Some animal is a female mammal.

($\mathcal{I}_2$) There is at least one even prime natural number.

21. ($\mathcal{I}_1$) Some animal is a mammal, and some animal is not a mammal.

($\mathcal{I}_2$) At least one natural number is even, and at least one natural number is not even.

Section 5.5

3. ($\mathcal{I}_1$) true; ($\mathcal{I}_2$) false ($\mathcal{I}_3$); true

7. ($\mathcal{I}_1$) true; ($\mathcal{I}_2$) true; ($\mathcal{I}_3$) true

13. ($\mathcal{I}_1$) true; ($\mathcal{I}_2$) true; ($\mathcal{I}_3$) true.

19. True:

	$\mathcal{D}$:	$\{2\}$	False:	$\mathcal{D}$:	$\{1, 2\}$
	Ax:	$\{2\}$		Ax:	$\{1\}$
	Bx:	$\{2\}$		Bx:	$\{1\}$
	r:	2		r:	2

25. True:

	$\mathcal{D}$:	people	False:	$\mathcal{D}$:	people
	Fx:	x is female		Fx:	x can lift ten tons bare-handed
	Mx:	x is male		Mx:	x can levitate a house by mere thought

31. True:

	$\mathcal{D}$:	animals	False:	$\mathcal{D}$:	animals
	Ax:	x is a tree		Ax:	x is a goat
	Bx:	x is a bear		Bx:	x is a bear

39. ($\mathcal{I}_1$) true; ($\mathcal{I}_2$) false; ($\mathcal{I}_3$) false

45. ($\mathcal{I}_1$) true; ($\mathcal{I}_2$) true; ($\mathcal{I}_3$) true

53. ($\mathcal{I}_1$) true; ($\mathcal{I}_2$) true; ($\mathcal{I}_3$) false

63. True:

	$\mathcal{D}$:	$\{Alan\}$	False:	$\mathcal{D}$:	people
	Mxy:	$\{<Alan, Alan>\}$		Mxy:	x is a child of y
	a:	Alan		a:	Alexis

69. True: 𝒟: {Alan}   False: 𝒟: people

   Axy: {<Alan, Alan>}   Axy: x is a child of y

Section 5.6

3. La ∨ Lr

7. ∃xCx

15. ~∃x~Px or ∀xPx

25. ~Fs & As

31. ∀x(Fx → Ax)

Section 5.7

3. Sabc

9. ∀x∀y[(Ox & Oy) → ∃z(Sxyz & Ez)]

17. ∀x[(Px & (Gxb & Lxd)) → Ox]

25. Llj & Lle

33. ∀x∀y(Lxy → ~Sxy)

41. ∀x∀y[Kxy → (Jxy & Lxy)]

Section 5.8

3. The concept of logical equivalence is more inclusive than that of truth-functional equivalence. This is because every pair of truth-functionally equivalent statements are logically equivalent as well, but some logically equivalent statements are not truth-functionally equivalent. For example, the statements 'Some people are not parents' and 'It's not the case that all people are parents' are logically, but not truth-functionally, equivalent.

Section 5.9

1. Nonreflexive, irreflexive, symmetric, nontransitive, intransitive

7. Nonreflexive, irreflexive, symmetric, nontransitive, intransitive

15. No. An example is the relation 'x is a sibling of y'.

Chapter 6

Section 6.2

1. The set is consistent.

$\forall x(Ax \lor Bx)$
$\forall xAx$
$\exists x\sim Bx \checkmark$
$\sim Ba$
$Aa \lor Ba \checkmark$

```
          Aa        Ba
                     ×
```

7. The set is consistent.

$\sim[Am \lor \forall x(Mx \& \sim\exists y(Ay \lor Ly))] \checkmark$
$\exists z\sim Az \checkmark$
$\sim Aa$
$\sim Am$
$\sim\forall x(Mx \& \sim\exists y(Ay \lor Ly)) \checkmark$
$\exists x\sim(Mx \& \sim\exists y(Ay \lor Ly)) \checkmark$
$\sim(Mb \& \sim\exists y(Ay \lor Ly)) \checkmark$

```
        ~Mb          ~~∃y(Ay ∨ Ly)
```

11. The set is consistent.

$\exists x\exists yPxy \checkmark$
$\sim\forall x\forall yPyx \checkmark$
$\exists x\sim\forall yPyx \checkmark$
$\sim\forall yPya \checkmark$
$\exists y\sim Pya \checkmark$
$\sim Pba$
$\exists yPcy \checkmark$
Pcd

17. The statement is not a logical truth.

$\sim(\forall xAx \lor \forall x\sim Ax) \checkmark$
$\sim\forall xAx \checkmark$
$\sim\forall x\sim Ax \checkmark$
$\exists x\sim\sim Ax \checkmark$
$\sim\sim Aa \checkmark$
Aa
$\exists x\sim Ax \checkmark$
$\sim Ab$

23. The statement is not a logical truth.

$\sim[\sim\exists z(Bz \lor Lz) \to \forall x(\sim Lx \leftrightarrow \exists yBy)] \checkmark$
$\sim\exists z(Bz \lor Lz) \checkmark$
$\sim\forall x(\sim Lx \leftrightarrow \exists yBy) \checkmark$
$\exists x\sim(\sim Lx \leftrightarrow \exists yBy) \checkmark$
$\sim(\sim La \leftrightarrow \exists yBy) \checkmark$
$\forall z\sim(Bz \lor Lz)$

```
      ~La                    ~~La
   ~∃yBy ✓                   ∃yBy
   ∀y~By
  ~(Ba ∨ La) ✓
     ~Ba
     ~La
```

29. The statement is a logical truth.

$\sim[\forall x\forall y\forall zBxyz \to \forall x\forall y\forall zBxzy] \checkmark$
$\forall x\forall y\forall zBxyz$
$\sim\forall x\forall y\forall zBxzy \checkmark$
$\exists x\sim\forall y\forall zBxzy \checkmark$
$\sim\forall y\forall zBazy \checkmark$
$\exists y\sim\forall zBazy \checkmark$
$\sim\forall zBazb \checkmark$
$\exists z\sim Bazb \checkmark$
$\sim Bacb$
$\forall y\forall zBayz$
$\forall zBacz$
$Bacb$
$\times$

35. The argument is valid.

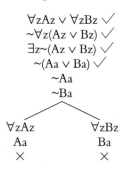

∀zAz ∨ ∀zBz ✓
~∀z(Az ∨ Bz) ✓
∃z~(Az ∨ Bz) ✓
~(Aa ∨ Ba) ✓
~Aa
~Ba

∀zAz   ∀zBz
Aa   Ba
×   ×

41. The argument is valid.

∀x∀y(Axy ↔ Bxy)
∀x∀yBxy
~∀x∀yAxy ✓
∃x~∀yAxy ✓
~∀yAay ✓
∃y~Aay ✓
~Aab
∀y(Aay ↔ Bay)
Aab ↔ Bab ✓

Aab   ~Aab
Bab   ~Bab
×   ∀yBay
    Bab
    ×

49. The statements are equivalent.

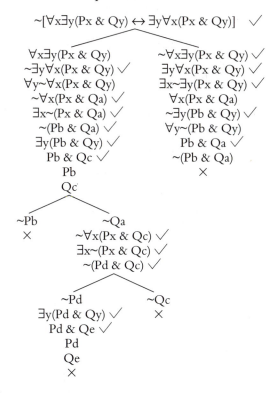

~[∀x∃y(Px & Qy) ↔ ∃y∀x(Px & Qy)] ✓

∀x∃y(Px & Qy)   ~∀x∃y(Px & Qy) ✓
~∃y∀x(Px & Qy) ✓ ∃y∀x(Px & Qy) ✓
∀y~∀x(Px & Qy)   ∃x~∃y(Px & Qy) ✓
~∀x(Px & Qa) ✓   ∀x(Px & Qa)
∃x~(Px & Qa) ✓   ~∃y(Pb & Qy) ✓
~(Pb & Qa) ✓   ∀y~(Pb & Qy)
∃y(Pb & Qy) ✓   Pb & Qa ✓
Pb & Qc ✓   ~(Pb & Qa)
Pb   ×
Qc

~Pb   ~Qa
× ~∀x(Px & Qc) ✓
   ∃x~(Px & Qc) ✓
   ~(Pd & Qc) ✓

~Pd   ~Qc
∃y(Pd & Qy) ✓ ×
Pd & Qe ✓
Pd
Qe
×

Section 6.3

3. 𝒟: {1, 2, 3, 4}   ∃xAx & ∃xBx ✓
    a: 1   Aa & Bb ✓
    b: 2   Aa
    c: 3   Bb
    d: 4   ∃xAx ✓
    Ax: {1, 4}   ∃xBx ✓
    Bx: {2, 3}   Bc
                                 Ad

9. 𝒟: {1, 2}   ∀x∀y(Lxy → ~Lxy)
    a: 1   Lab
                                 ~Lba
    b: 2   ∀y(Lay → ~Lya)
    Lxy: {<1, 2>}   ∀y(Lby → ~Lyb)
                                 Laa → ~Laa ✓

```
                    ~Laa ✓                    ~Laa
                 Lab → ~Lba              Lab → Lba

            ~Lab          ~Lba
             ×         Lba → ~Lab ✓

                   ~Lba              ~Lab
              Lbb → ~Lbb ✓            ×

            ~Lbb              ~Lbb
```

15. 𝒟: {1, 2, 3}   ∀xAx ↔ ∀xBx ✓
    a: 1   ~∀x(Ax ↔ Bx) ✓
                                 ∃x~(Ax ↔ Bx) ✓
    b: 2   ~(Aa ↔ Ba) ✓
    c: 3
    Ax: {1}
    Bx: { }

```
           ∀xAx                              ~∀xAx ✓
           ∀xBx                              ~∀xBx ✓

      Aa          ~Aa              Aa              ~Aa
     ~Ba          Ba              ~Ba              Ba
      Ba          Aa          ∃x~Bx ✓          ∃x~Bx
      ×           ×              ~Bb            ∃x~Ax
                            ∃x~Ax ✓
                               ~Ac
```

21. $\mathcal{D}$: {1, 2}

Gxy: {<1, 2>}

Hxy: {<1, 2>}

a: 1

b: 2

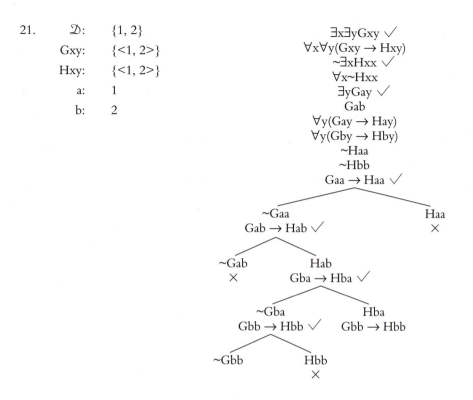

$\exists x \exists y Gxy$ ✓
$\forall x \forall y (Gxy \rightarrow Hxy)$
$\sim\exists x Hxx$ ✓
$\forall x \sim Hxx$
$\exists y Gay$ ✓
Gab
$\forall y (Gay \rightarrow Hay)$
$\forall y (Gby \rightarrow Hby)$
$\sim Haa$
$\sim Hbb$
$Gaa \rightarrow Haa$ ✓

Section 6.4

1. The set is consistent.

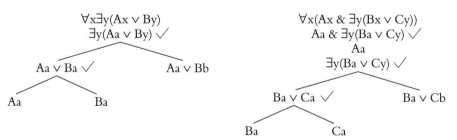

$\forall x \exists y (Ax \vee By)$
$\exists y (Aa \vee By)$ ✓

$Aa \vee Ba$ ✓ $Aa \vee Bb$

Aa Ba

7. The set is consistent.

$\forall x (Ax \,\&\, \exists y (Bx \vee Cy))$
$Aa \,\&\, \exists y (Ba \vee Cy)$ ✓
Aa
$\exists y (Ba \vee Cy)$ ✓

$Ba \vee Ca$ ✓ $Ba \vee Cb$

Ba Ca

Section 6.6

3. $\exists x (Sxm \,\&\, \sim Dfx) \,\&\, \exists x (Sxr \,\&\, \sim Dfx)$

5. $\exists x \forall y (Sym \rightarrow (Lym \rightarrow Tyx)) \,\&\, \exists x \forall y (Sym \rightarrow Dxy)$

Chapter 7

Section 7.2

3. 1. $\forall x(Fx \rightarrow Gx)$ PR
    2. $\sim\exists xGx$ PR
    3. $\forall x\sim Gx$ 2   Q
    4. $Fa \rightarrow Ga$ 1   UI
    5. $\sim Ga$ 3   UI
    6. $\sim Fa$ 4, 5   MT
    7. $\exists x\sim Fx$ 6   EG
    8. $\sim\forall xFx$ 7   Q

7. 1. $\forall x(Fx \rightarrow Gx)$ PR
    2. $\forall x(Gx \rightarrow Jx)$ PR
    3. $Fa \rightarrow Ga$ 1   UI
    4. $Ga \rightarrow Ja$ 2   UI
    > 5.   Fa   PA–CP
    > 6.   Ga   3, 5   MP
    > 7.   Ja   4, 6   MP
    8. $Fa \rightarrow Ja$ 5–7   CP
    9. $\exists x(Fx \rightarrow Jx)$ 8   EG

13. 1. $\forall x\forall y\forall z[((Px \ \& \ Qy) \ \& \ Rz) \rightarrow Sx]$ PR
    2. $\sim St$ PR
    3. $\forall y\forall z[((Pt \ \& \ Qy) \ \& \ Rz) \rightarrow St]$ 1   UI
    4. $\forall z[((Pt \ \& \ Qt) \ \& \ Rz) \rightarrow St]$ 3   UI
    5. $((Pt \ \& \ Qt) \ \& \ Rt) \rightarrow St$ 4   UI
    6. $\sim((Pt \ \& \ Qt) \ \& \ Rt)$ 2, 5   MT
    7. $\sim(Pt \ \& \ Qt) \vee \sim Rt$ 6   DeM
    > 8.   Rt   PA–CP
    > > 9.   Qt   PA–CP
    > > > 10. $\sim\sim Pt$ PA–RAA
    > > > 11.   Pt   10   DN
    > > > 12. $Pt \ \& \ Qt$ 9, 11   CI
    > > > 13. $(Pt \ \& \ Qt) \rightarrow \sim Rt$ 7   Impl
    > > > 14. $\sim Rt$ 12, 13   MP
    > > > 15. $Rt \ \& \ \sim Rt$ 8, 14   CI
    > > 16. $\sim Pt$ 10–15   RAA
    > 17. $Qt \rightarrow \sim Pt$ 9–16   CP
    18. $Rt \rightarrow (Qt \rightarrow \sim Pt)$ 8–17   CP

21. 1. ∀x(∃yFxy → ∀z~Gzx)   PR
    2. ∀xFxa   PR
    3. ∀x∀y(Hxy ∨ Gxa)   PR
    4. ∃yFay → ∀z~Gza   1   UI
    5. Faa   2   UI
    6. ∃yFay   5   EG
    7. ∀z~Gza   4, 6   MP
    8. ∀y(Hay ∨ Gaa)   3   UI
    9. Haa ∨ Gaa   8   UI
    10. ~Gaa   7   UI
    11. ~~Haa ∨ Gaa   9   DN
    12. ~Haa → Gaa   11   Impl
    13. ~~Haa   10, 12   MT
    14. Haa   13   DN
    15. ∃yHay   14   EG
    16. ∃x∃yHxy   15   EG

Section 7.3

3. 1. ∀x(Ax → ~Bx)   PR
   2. ∀x(Cx → Ax)   PR
   3. Aa → ~Ba   1   UI
   4. Ca → Aa   2   UI
   | 5. Ca   PA-CP
   | 6. Aa   4, 5   MP
   | 7. ~Ba   3, 6   MP
   8. Ca → ~Ba   5–7   CP
   9. ∀x(Cx → ~Bx)   8   UG

13. 1. ∀x(Fx → Gx)   PR
    2. ∃x~Gx   PR
    | 3. ~Ga   2   PA-EI
    | 4. Fa → Ga   1   UI
    | 5. ~Fa   3, 4   MT
    | 6. ∃x~Fx   5   EG
    7. ∃x~Fx   3–6   EI

25. 1. ∃x(∀yAxy & (Bx & Cx))   PR
    2. ∃x∃y(Axy & Cx) → ∀x(Dx ↔ Cx)   PR

3. ∀yAay & (Ba & Ca)	1	PA–EI
4. ∀yAay	3	CE
5. Aaa	4	UI
6. Ba & Ca	3	CE
7. Ca	6	CE
8. Aaa & Ca	5, 7	CI
9. ∃y(Aay & Ca)	8	EG
10. ∃x∃y(Axy & Cx)	9	EG

    11. ∃x∃y(Axy & Cx)   3–10   EI
    12. ∀x(Dx ↔ Cx)   2, 11   MP

13. ∃y(Aby & Cb)	11	PA–EI
14. Abc & Cb	13	PA–EI
15. Cb	14	CE
16. ∃xCx	15	EG
17. ∃xCx	14–16	EI

    18. ∃xCx   13–17   EI

19. Cd	18	PA–EI
20. Dd ↔ Cd	12	UI
21. (Dd → Cd) & (Cd → Dd)	20	Equiv
22. Cd → Dd	21	CE
23. Dd	19, 22	MP
24. Dd & Cd	19, 23	CI
25. ∃x(Dx & Cx)	24	EG

    26. ∃x(Dx & Cx)   19–25   EI

33.

1. ∀xFx		PA–CP
2. Fa	1	UI
3. ∀yFy	2	UG

    4. ∀xFx → ∀yFy   1–3   CP

39.

1. $\forall x \exists y \forall z[(Ry \;\&\; {\sim}Ux) \to {\sim}Vz]$		PA-CP
2. $\exists z Vz$		PA-CP
3. $\forall y Ry$		PA-CP
4. ${\sim}\forall x Ux$		PA-RAA
5. $\exists x {\sim}Ux$	4	Q
6. ${\sim}Ua$	5	PA-EI
7. $\exists y \forall z[(Ry \;\&\; {\sim}Ua) \to {\sim}Vz]$	1	UI
8. $\forall z[(Rb \;\&\; {\sim}Ua) \to {\sim}Vz]$	7	PA-EI
9. Vc	2	PA-EI
10. $(Rb \;\&\; {\sim}Ua) \to {\sim}Vc$	8	UI
11. Rb	3	UI
12. $Rb \;\&\; {\sim}Ua$	6, 11	CI
13. ${\sim}Vc$	10, 12	MP
14. $P \;\&\; {\sim}P$	9, 13	R
15. $P \;\&\; {\sim}P$	9–14	EI
16. $P \;\&\; {\sim}P$	8–15	EI
17. $P \;\&\; {\sim}P$	6–16	EI
18. $\forall x Ux$	4–17	RAA
19. $\forall y Ry \to \forall x Ux$	3–18	CP
20. $\exists z Vz \to (\forall y Ry \to \forall x Ux)$	2–19	CP
21. $\forall x \exists x \forall y[(Ry \;\&\; {\sim}Ux) \to {\sim}Vz] \to$ $[\exists z Vz \to (\forall y Ry \to \forall x Ux)]$	1–20	CP

45.

1. $\forall x \forall y({\sim}Axy \to Ayx)$		PA-CP
2. $\forall y({\sim}Aay \to Aya)$	1	UI
3. ${\sim}Aaa \to Aaa$	2	UI
4. ${\sim}Aaa$		PA-RAA
5. ${\sim}{\sim}Aaa$	3, 4	MT
6. ${\sim}Aaa \;\&\; {\sim}{\sim}Aaa$	4, 5	CI
7. Aaa	4–6	RAA
8. $\forall x Axx$	7	UG
9. $\forall x \forall y({\sim}Axy \to Ayx) \to \forall x Axx$	1–8	CP

Chapter 8

Section 8.2

3. True

7. True

11. True

15. True

Section 8.3

3. $\mathcal{D}$: people; Wx: x has taken a course in woodworking; C: Charlie
   Wc & $\exists x(Wx \& x \neq c)$

7. $\forall x \forall y \forall z[(x=y \& y=z) \rightarrow x=z]$

13. $\mathcal{D}$: fish; Sx: x swims in the sea; Gx: x is green
   $\exists x \exists y \exists z([(x \neq y \& y \neq z) \& x \neq z] \& [((Sx \& Gx) \& (Sy \& Gy)) \& (Sz \& Gz)])$

19. $\mathcal{D}$: natural numbers; Ex: x is even; Px: x is prime
   $\exists x(Ex \& Px) \rightarrow \forall x \forall y[((Ex \& Px) \& (Ey \& Py)) \rightarrow x = y]$

25. $\mathcal{D}$: objects; Lx: x is conceivable as lacking extension
   $\forall x \forall y((Lx \& {\sim}Ly) \rightarrow x \neq y)$

Section 8.4

3. Tfj & ~Tfs

9. $\forall x \forall y(Txy \rightarrow Mxy)$

15. $\forall x[Sx \rightarrow \exists y(Fy \& Tyx)] \& \forall x[Px \rightarrow \exists y(((Rx \vee Jx) \vee Cx) \& Txy)]$

23. ~[(Stl $\vee$ Sts) $\vee$ (Sml $\vee$ Sms)]

29. $\exists x(Wx \& Ssx)$

35. $\forall x[Wx \rightarrow (Sxm \vee Kmx)]$

41. $\forall x[Rx \rightarrow \exists y(Ry \& Lyx)]$

49. ~$\exists x[(Ox \& Px) \& \exists y((Ey \& Py) \& Lxy)]$ *or*
   $\forall x[(Ox \& Px) \rightarrow {\sim}\exists y((Ey \& Py) \& Lxy)]$ *or*
   $\forall x \forall y[((Ox \& Px) \& (Ey \& Py)) \rightarrow {\sim}Lxy]$

57. $\forall x \forall y \forall z \forall v \forall w[(((x \neq y \& Sxyz) \& Sxxw) \& Sywv) \rightarrow Lzv]$

Section 8.5

3. The statement is not a logical truth.

$$\sim\forall x\forall y\forall z(x = y \lor y = z) \checkmark$$
$$\exists x\sim\forall y\forall z(x = y \lor y = z) \checkmark$$
$$\sim\forall y\forall z(a = y \lor y = z) \checkmark$$
$$\exists y\sim\forall z(a = y \lor y = z) \checkmark$$
$$\sim\forall z(a = b \lor b = z) \checkmark$$
$$\exists z\sim(a = b \lor b = z) \checkmark$$
$$\sim(a = b \lor b = c) \checkmark$$
$$\sim a = b$$
$$\sim b = c$$

9. The statement is not a logical truth.

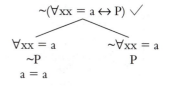

$$\sim(\forall xx = a \leftrightarrow P) \checkmark$$

$\forall xx = a$	$\sim\forall xx = a$
$\sim P$	P
$a = a$	

17. The statement is not a logical truth.

$$\sim\exists x(Rxa \leftrightarrow x = a) \checkmark$$
$$\forall x\sim(Rxa \leftrightarrow x = a)$$
$$\sim(Raa \leftrightarrow a = a) \checkmark$$

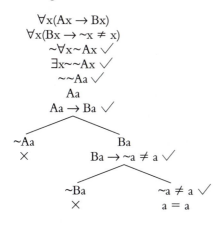

Raa	~Raa
~a = a	a = a
X	

23. The argument is valid.

$$a = b$$
$$b \neq c$$
$$\sim a \neq c \checkmark$$
$$a = c$$
$$a \neq c$$
$$\times$$

29. The argument is invalid.

$$\forall x(Ax \to Bx)$$
$$\forall x(Bx \to \sim x \neq x)$$
$$\sim\forall x\sim Ax \checkmark$$
$$\exists x\sim\sim Ax \checkmark$$
$$\sim\sim Aa \checkmark$$
$$Aa$$
$$Aa \to Ba \checkmark$$

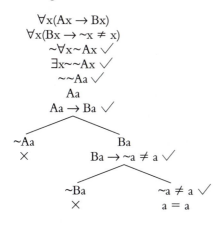

~Aa   Ba
X   Ba → ~a ≠ a ✓

    ~Ba   ~a ≠ a ✓
    X   a = a

35. The argument is valid.

$$\exists x\exists yx = y \checkmark$$
$$\forall x\forall yAxy$$
$$\sim\exists x\exists y(Axy \& x \, p \, y) \checkmark$$
$$\exists ya \, p \, y \checkmark$$
$$a \, p \, b$$
$$\forall x\sim\exists y(Axy \& x \, p \, y)$$
$$\sim\exists y(Aay \& a \, p \, y) \checkmark$$
$$\forall y\sim(Aay \& a \, p \, y)$$
$$\sim(Aab \& a \, p \, b) \checkmark$$

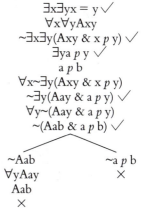

~Aab	~a p b
∀yAay	X
Aab	
X	

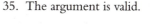

Section 8.6

3. 1. ∀x(x = a ∨ x = b)   PR
   2. Ga ↔ ~Gb   PR

3. ~∃x~x = b	PA-RAA
4. ∀xx = b	3	Q
5. a = b	4	UI
6. (Ga → ~Gb) & (~Gb → Ga)	2	Equiv
7. Ga → ~Gb	6	CE
8. ~~Gb		PA-RAA
9. ~Ga	7, 8	MT
10. ~Gb	5, 9	I
11. ~Gb & ~~Gb	8, 10	CI
12. ~Gb	8–11	RAA
13. ~Gb → Ga	6	CE
14. Ga	12, 13	MP
15. Gb	5, 14	I
16. Gb & ~Gb	12, 15	CI

   17. ∃x~x = b   2–16   RAA

9. 1. Ac   PR
   2. ∀xx = c   PR
   3. ∀x(Bx ↔ ~Ax)   PR
   4. Bc ↔ ~Ac   3   UI
   5. (Bc → ~Ac) & (~Ac → Bc)   4   Equiv
   6. Bc → ~Ac   5   CE
   7. ~~Ac   1   DN
   8. ~Bc   6, 7   MT

9. ~~∃xBx		PA-RAA
10. ∃xBx	9	DN
11. Ba	10	PA-EI
12. a = c	2	UI
13. Bc	11, 12	I
14. Bc & ~Bc	8, 13	CI
15. Bc & ~Bc	11–14	EI

   16. ~∃xBx   9–15   RAA

15. 1. ∀y(Ay ↔ y = a)   PR
    2. ∀x(Bxc ↔ Ax)   PR

3. Bdc		PA–CP
4. Bdc ↔ Ad	2	UI
5. (Bdc → Ad) & (Ad → Bdc)	4	Equiv
6. Bdc → Ad	5	CE
7. Ad	3, 6	MP
8. Ad ↔ d = a	1	UI
9. (Ad → d = a) & (d = a → Ad)	8	Equiv
10. Ad → d = a	9	CE
11. d = a	7, 10	MP

    12. Bdc → d = a   3–11   CP
    13. ∀x(Bxc → x = a)   12   UG

21.
1. a = b		PA–CP
2. Fa		PA–CP
3. Fb	1, 2	I
4. Fa → Fb	2, 3	CP
5. Fb		PA–CP
6. Fa	1, 5	I
7. Fb → Fa	5, 6	CP
8. (Fa → Fb) & (Fb → Fa)	4, 7	CI
9. Fa ↔ Fb	8	Equiv
10. a = b → (Fa ↔ Fb)	1–9	CP

27.
1. ∃y∀xx = y		PA–CP
2. ∀xx = a	1	PA–EI
3. b = a	2	UI
4. ∃yb = y	3	EG
5. ∀x∃yx = y	4	UG
6. ∀x∃yx = y	2–5	EI
7. ∃y∀xx = y → ∀x∃yx = y	1–6	CP

37.

1. $\forall x \forall y(Rxy \leftrightarrow x = y)$		PA-CP
2. Rab & Rbc		PA-CP
3. $\forall y(Ray \leftrightarrow a = y)$	1	UI
4. $Rab \leftrightarrow a = b$	3	UI
5. $(Rab \rightarrow a = b)$ & $(a = b \rightarrow Rab)$	4	Equiv
6. $Rab \rightarrow a = b$	5	CE
7. Rab	2	CE
8. $a = b$	6, 7	MP
9. Rbc	2	CE
10. Rac	8, 9	I
11. $(Rab \& Rbc) \rightarrow Rac$	2–10	CP
12. $\forall z[(Rab \& Rbz) \rightarrow Raz]$	11	UG
13. $\forall y \forall z[(Ray \& Ryz) \rightarrow Raz]$	12	UG
14. $\forall x \forall y \forall z[(Rxy \& Ryz) \rightarrow Rxz]$	13	UG
15. $\forall x \forall y(Rxy \leftrightarrow x = y) \rightarrow$ $\forall x \forall y \forall z[(Rxy \& Ryz) \rightarrow Rxz]$	1–14	CP

Section 8.8

3. 'Senator of x' does not denote a function, since each U.S. citizen has two senators.

7. 'Predecessor of x' does not denote a function on the natural numbers, since the number 1 does not have a predecessor that is a natural number.

13. '$g^2(a, b)$' is not a term. It would be a term if the parentheses and comma were omitted.

17. '$g^2g^2abg^2cd$' is a constant term.

21. The statement is true under the interpretation and is in fact a logical truth.

25. This statement, which is a symbolization of 'All maternal grandmothers are mothers', is true under this interpretation and is in fact a logical truth.

Section 8.9

1. $\forall x(\exists ymy = x \rightarrow Fx) \& \exists x(Fx \& \sim\exists ymy = x)$

7. $\exists x \exists y(\exists z(fz = x \& mz = y) \& \sim Mxy)$

13. $\forall x(Cx \rightarrow \forall y(y = ex \rightarrow Iy))$

17. $\sim\exists x(Sx \& Exx)$

21. $\mathcal{D}$: natural numbers; Ex: x is even; Sxy: x is a successor of y; sx: the successor of x; a: 3. Then we have (1) 'Esa and' (2) '$\sim\exists x((Sxa \& \forall y(Sya \rightarrow y = x)) \& Ex)$'.

Section 8.10

1. The argument is invalid. Note that the following tree is not complete and is in fact infinite. To continue, for instance, add '~ffa = b' from 'fa = a' and '~fa = b'.

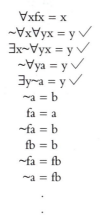

$$\forall x f x = x$$
$$\sim\forall x \forall y x = y \checkmark$$
$$\exists x \sim\forall y x = y \checkmark$$
$$\sim\forall y a = y \checkmark$$
$$\exists y \sim a = y \checkmark$$
$$\sim a = b$$
$$fa = a$$
$$\sim fa = b$$
$$fb = b$$
$$\sim fa = fb$$
$$\sim a = fb$$
.
.
.

7. The argument is invalid. Here again is an initial segment of an infinite tree that was the Rule E★.

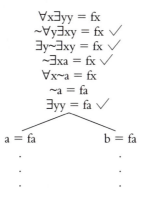

$$\forall x \exists y y = fx$$
$$\sim\forall y \exists x y = fx \checkmark$$
$$\exists y \sim\exists x y = fx \checkmark$$
$$\sim\exists x a = fx \checkmark$$
$$\forall x \sim a = fx$$
$$\sim a = fa$$
$$\exists y y = fa \checkmark$$

a = fa   b = fa
.   .
.   .
.   .

Notice that the premise of this argument is a logical truth and the statements derived from this one generate the infinite tree. Since the premise is a logical truth, the argument will be valid if, and only if, the conclusion is a logical truth. One can construct a finished open tree to show that the conclusion is in fact *not* a logical truth.

13. The statement is not a logical truth. The tree generated from the statement's negation is infinite. Below is an initial segment.

$$\sim\forall x(fx = ffx \rightarrow x = fx) \checkmark$$
$$\exists x\sim(fx = ffx \rightarrow x = fx) \checkmark$$
$$\sim(fa = ffa \rightarrow a = fa) \checkmark$$
$$fa = ffa$$
$$\sim a = fa$$
$$\sim a = ffa$$
$$\cdot$$
$$\cdot$$
$$\cdot$$

Section 8.11

3. 1. $\forall x fx = gx$ PR
   2. Rfa   PR
   3. fa = ga   1   UI
   4. Rga   2, 3   I

11.

1. $\forall x \forall y(x = fy \rightarrow y = fx)$		PA-CP
2. $\forall y(fa = fy \rightarrow y = ffa)$	1	UI
3. $fa = fa \rightarrow a = ffa$	2	UI
4. $fa = fa$		I Int
5. $a = ffa$	3, 4	MP
6. $ffa = ffa$		I Int
7. $ffa = a$	5, 6	I
8. $\forall x ffx = x$	7	UG

9. $\forall x \forall y(x = fy \rightarrow y = fx) \rightarrow \forall x ffx = x$ 1–8   CP

Chapter 9

Section 9.2

Part I

1. $\mathcal{D}$: people; Wx: x is a woman; Bx: x is in a blue car; r: Rebecca.
   $\forall x[(Wx \& Bx) \leftrightarrow x = r]$

9. This is a difficult problem; notice that the sentence contains *three* descriptions: 'the person who donated $100,000', 'the woman who owns the big hotel', and 'the big hotel'. We let $\mathcal{D}$ = everything, and introduce appropriate predicates:

Px: x is a person

Dx: x donated $100,000

Wx: x is a woman

Hx: x is a big hotel

Oxy: x owns y

(1) $\exists x[\forall y((Py \ \& \ Dy) \leftrightarrow y = x) \ \& \ \exists z[\forall u(Hu \leftrightarrow u = z) \ \& $
$\exists v(\forall w((Ww \ \& \ Owz) \leftrightarrow w = v) \ \& \ v \neq x)]]$

(2) $\sim\exists x[\forall y((Py \ \& \ Dy) \leftrightarrow y = x) \ \& \ \exists z[\forall u(Hu \leftrightarrow u=z) \ \& $
$\exists v(\forall w((Ww \ \& \ Owz) \leftrightarrow w = v) \ \& \ v = x)]]$

Part II

1. $r = 1x(Wx \ \& \ Bx)$

9. Note that the broad scope/narrow scope distinction cannot be made with the definite description operator. We are stuck with the broad scope reading:

$1x(Px \ \& \ Dx) \neq 1x(Wx \ \& \ Ox1yHy)$

Section 9.3

1. $p^2sassa = sssa$

5. (1) As in Exercise 1, above.

   (2) By formal proof:

1.	$\forall x p^2 xa = x$		Axiom 4
2.	$\forall x \forall y p^2 xsy = sp^2 xy$		Axiom 5
3.	$\forall y p^2 sasy = sp^2 say$	2	UI
4.	$p^2 sasa = sp^2 saa$	3	UI
5.	$p^2 saa = sa$	1	UI
6.	$p^2 sasa = ssa$	4, 5	I
7.	$\forall y p^2 sasy = sp^2 say$	2	UI
8.	$p^2 sassa = sp^2 sasa$	7	UI
9.	$p^2 sassa = sssa$	6, 8	I

(3) By truth tree:

1.	$\forall x p^2 xa = x$		Axiom 4
2.	$\forall x \forall y p^2 xsy = sp^2 xy$		Axiom 5
3.	$\sim p^2 sassa = sssa$		Denial of conclusion
4.	$\forall y p^2 sasy = sp^2 say$	2	Rule U
5.	$p^2 sasa = sp^2 saa$	4	Rule U
6.	$p^2 saa = sa$	1	Rule U
7.	$p^2 sasa = ssa$	5, 6	Rule I
8.	$\forall y p^2 sasy = sp^2 say$	2	Rule U
9.	$p^2 sassa = sp^2 sasa$	8	Rule U
10.	$p^2 sassa = sssa$	7, 9	Rule I
	$\times$		

Section 9.6

1.

1. $a = b$		PA-CP
2. $\exists \Psi \sim (\Psi a \leftrightarrow \Psi b)$		PA-RAA
3. $\sim (Pa \leftrightarrow Pb)$	2	PA-EI
4. $\sim (Pa \leftrightarrow Pa)$	1, 3	I
5. Pa		PA-CP
6. $Pa \rightarrow Pa$	5–5	CP
7. $(Pa \rightarrow Pa) \ \& \ (Pa \rightarrow Pa)$	6, 6	CI
8. $(Pa \leftrightarrow Pa)$	7	Equiv
9. $P \ \& \sim P$	4, 8	R
10. $P \ \& \sim P$	3–9	EI
11. $\sim \exists \Psi \sim (\Psi a \leftrightarrow \Psi b)$	2–10	RAA
12. $\forall \Psi (\Psi a \leftrightarrow \Psi b)$	11	Q
13. $a = b \rightarrow \forall \Psi (\Psi a \leftrightarrow \Psi b)$	1–12	CP
14. $\forall y[a = y \rightarrow \forall \Psi (\Psi a \leftrightarrow \Psi y)]$	13	UG
15. $\forall x \forall y[x = y \rightarrow \forall \Psi (\Psi x \leftrightarrow \Psi y)]$	14	UG

Section 9.7

3. S: Snow is white. $\Diamond S \ \& \ \Diamond \sim S$

7. S: Snow is white. $\Diamond \sim S \rightarrow \sim \Box S$

13. $\mathcal{D}$: people; Cx: x is a chemist; s: Sonya. $Cs \rightarrow \Diamond \exists x Cx$

17. $\mathcal{D}$: everything; Nx: x is a number; Gxy: x > y. $\exists x[Nx \ \& \sim \Diamond \forall y(Ny \rightarrow Gxy)]$

23.

1. A & B		PA-CP
2. B	1	CE

3. (A & B) → B	1–2	CP
4. ~B → ~(A & B)	3	Trans
5. □[~B → ~(A & B)]	4	NI

6. □~B		PA-CP
7. □~(A & B)	5, 6	N Imp

8. □~B → □~(A & B)	6–7	CP

25.

1. □(J → L)		PA-CP
2. ~[□(K → L) → □(J → L)]		PA-RAA
3. □(K → L) & ~□(J → L)	2	NC
4. ~□(J → L)	3	CE
5. □(J → L) & ~□(J → L)	1, 4	CI
6. [□(K → L) → □(J → L)]	2–5	RAA
7. □(J → L) → [□(K → L) → □(J → L)]	1–7	CP

29.

1. ~[(G → H) → H]		PA-CP
2. ~[~(G → H) ∨ H]	1	Impl
3. ~~(G → H) & ~H	2	DeM
4. ~~(G → H)	3	CE
5. G → H	4	DN
6. ~H	3	CE
7. ~G	5, 6	MT
8. ~[(G → H) → H] → ~G	1–8	CP
9. □[~[(G → H) → H] → ~G]	8	NI
10. □~[(G → H) → H]		PA-CP
11. □~G	9, 10	N Imp
12. □~[(G → H) → H] → □~G	10–11	CP
13. ~□~G → ~□~[(G → H) → H]	12	Trans
14. ◇G → ~□~[(G → H) → H]	13	MR
15. ◇G → ◇[(G → H) → H]	14	MR

Section 9.10

1. ∃x∀y(*P*Ayx & ~*O*Ayx)

7. ∀x[Cx ↔ (Gx & ~∃y*O*Ayx)]

Section 9.12

1.

A	*(A, A, A)
0	0
1	0
2	1

5.

A B	* (* (A, A, B),	* (B, B, A),	* (A, A, A))
0 0	0 0 0 0 0	0 0 0 0	0 0 0 0
0 1	0 0 0 0 1	0 1 1 0	0 0 0 0
0 2	0 0 0 0 2	0 2 2 0	0 0 0 0
1 0	0 0 1 1 0	0 0 0 1	0 1 1 1
1 1	0 0 1 1 1	0 1 1 1	0 1 1 1
1 2	0 0 1 1 2	0 2 2 1	0 1 1 1
2 0	0 0 2 2 0	0 0 0 2	1 2 2 2
2 1	0 0 2 2 1	0 1 1 2	1 2 2 2
2 2	0 1 2 2 2	1 2 2 2	1 2 2 2

9.

A B	(A ⊃ B) ⊃ (A → B)
T T	T T T T T T T
T I	T I I I T F I
T F	T F F T T F F
I T	I T T T I T T
I I	I T I T I T I
I F	I I F T I T F
F T	F T T T F T T
F I	F T I T F T I
F F	F T F T F T F

13.

A B	(A = B) ⊃ (A ≡ B)
T T	T T T T T T T
T I	T I I I T F I
T F	T F F T T F F
I T	I I T I I F T
I I	I T I T I T I
I F	I I F I I F F
F T	F F T T F F T
F I	F I I I F F I
F F	F T F T F T F

23. (1) $p \Rightarrow q$ (2) $\sim(p \Rightarrow p) \Leftrightarrow \sim p$

$$\underline{p}$$

$$\therefore q$$

Index

Additional Natural Deduction Rules for L and L=

Universal Instantiation (UI)

$$\forall\alpha p$$
$$\therefore\ p\alpha/\beta$$

Existential Generalization (EG)

$$p\alpha/\beta$$
$$\therefore\ \exists\alpha p$$

Quantifier Exchange (Q) If a statement of any one of the following forms appears as a line in a proof, then the statement form directly across from it may be added as a new line of the proof:

$\sim\exists\alpha p$	$\forall\alpha\sim p$
$\sim\forall\alpha p$	$\exists\alpha\sim p$
$\sim\exists\alpha\sim p$	$\forall\alpha p$
$\sim\forall\alpha\sim p$	$\exists\alpha p$

Universal Generalization (UG)

$$p\alpha/\beta$$
$$\therefore\ \forall\alpha p$$

β must not occur in $\forall\alpha p$, nor in any premise or provisional assumption covering $p\alpha/\beta$.

Existential Instantiation (EI)

k. $\exists\alpha p$

β must not occur on any line prior to m nor in q.

m. $p\alpha/\beta$ k PA-EI

n. q

n + 1. q m–n EI

Immediate Reductio (R)

$$p$$
$$\sim p$$
$$\therefore\ q$$

Identity (I)

$$p\alpha/\beta_1 \quad (or\ p\alpha/\beta_2)$$
$$\beta_1 = \beta_2$$
$$\therefore\ q$$

q is a statement obtained from $p\alpha/\beta_1$ (or $p\alpha/\beta_2$) by substituting β_2 (or β_1) for one or more occurrences of β_1 (or β_2)

Identity Introduction (I Int)

$$\beta = \beta$$